Series: Of Islands and Women
Number 4

C000183669

Malta

Also by Susanna Hoe

Lady in the Chamber (Collins 1971)

God Save the Tsar (Michael Joseph/St Martin's Press 1978)

The Man Who Gave His Company Away: A Biography of Ernest Bader, Founder of the Scott Bader Commonwealth (Heinemann 1978)

The Private Life of Old Hong Kong: Western Women in the British Colony 1841–1941 (Oxford University Press 1991)

Chinese Footprints: Exploring Women's History in China, Hong Kong and Macau (Roundhouse Publications Asia 1996)

Stories for Eva: A Reader for Chinese Women Learning English (Hong Kong Language Fund 1997)

The Taking of Hong Kong: Charles and Clara Elliot in China Waters (with Derek Roebuck) (Curzon Press 1999; Hong Kong University Press 2009)

Women at the Siege, Peking 1900 (HOLO Books 2000)

At Home in Paradise: A House and Garden in Papua New Guinea (HOLO Books 2003)

Madeira: Women, History, Books and Places (HOLO Books 2004)

Crete: Women, History, Books and Places (HOLO Books 2005)

Watching the Flag Come Down: An Englishwoman in Hong Kong 1987–97 (HOLO Books 2007)

Tasmania: Women, History, Books and Places (HOLO Books 2010)

Travels in Tandem: The Writing of Women and Men Who Travelled Together (HOLO Books 2012)

Malta

Women, History, Books and Places

Susanna Hoe

For Margaret
Another Island, far
from Papua New Guinea
Love
Susanna
4/1/23

HOLO BOOKS
THE WOMEN'S HISTORY PRESS
OXFORD

Published in 2015 by The Women's History Press
A division of HOLO Books
Clarendon House
52 Cornmarket, Oxford OX1 3HJ
www.holobooks.co.uk

www.centralbooks.com

British Library Cataloguing in Publication Data
A catalogue record for this book is available from the British Library

ISBN 978-0-9572153-5-1 paperback
ISBN 978-0-9572153-7-5 e-book
ISBN 978-0-9572153-6-8 kindle

This book is printed on paper suitable for recycling and made from fully managed
and sustained forest sources. Logging, pulping and manufacturing processes are
expected to conform to the environmental regulations of the country of origin.

10 9 8 7 6 5 4 3 2 1

Produced and typeset for HOLO Books by
Stanford DTP Services, Northampton, England
Printed in the European Union

For the artist Anna Grima

My first Maltese woman contact for this book, and all those other generous women she represents.

Contents

List of Illustrations

Preface

We had spent the previous night in Wadi Halfa, the Viking aircraft flying from Nairobi to England having developed engine trouble high above rolling sand dunes. I remember only sunset on the Nile from a dhow. I remember being sick at Khartoum aerodrome the following day but of the newly built Phoenicia in Malta, where we spent the second night of the journey, I remember nothing. Lunch the following day was at Nice, where I was made to leave my cherries because the flight was about to take off. I have a very clear impression of that! I was just seven years old; it was May 1952.

I do have a vague memory of Malta on the return journey six weeks later, staying once again at the Phoenicia. We were to accompany Carolinda, the daughter of friends, back to Kenya, and to pick her up from her grandmother. I see a courtyard full of greenery bright with flowers and being given a little basket full of things to keep me amused on the flight home. Both Carolinda and I were sick coming in to land at Khartoum.

I didn't visit Malta again until the late 1960s when my parents had taken a flat there for a few months, with a view to living on Gozo. I suspect it was somewhere near Sliema. A few years later I did some research into 1919 Russian refugees, staying at a modern hotel, goodness knows where – again my memories are vague, though I can see myself on the restaurant dance floor after dinner.

When my husband, Derek Roebuck, and I visited Malta in March 2013, it was not with the intention of writing this book, even though I'd already published three in my series 'Of Islands and Women': it was meant to be a holiday without Derek being dragged round cemeteries. But the islands beguiled and demanded to be written about. I discovered it was not all about Knights and brave people during the Second World War. The story started, instead, with the women who arrived from Sicily 7,000 years ago.

We returned to further my research in September that year, and in September 2014, so that I could fill in last-minute gaps. This is the result.

There are, not surprisingly, differences between recreating women's history and the traditional history that was mostly about men. For the latter, you need to be judicious about what you leave in and what you take out, so as not to overload the narrative. With women, details are often so scarce that you need to include all the often tiny nuggets found in many different places, and even then the narrative can seem a bit bony. This occurred to me particularly when writing in Chapter 3 about Imperia Gatto Inguanez whose name, the Maltese-born Australian writer Rosanne Dingli told me, 'resonates down through history'. I find myself in those circumstances, where the flesh around a woman's life is lacking, unable to resist asking questions, some of which may be anachronistic, and sieved through the twenty-first-century sensibility of a stranger.

Perhaps the question that most requires an answer is brought to light by looking at two portraits: one is of Margarita d'Aragona (?1336–1418) in Chapter 3; the other is of Flaminia Valenti in Chapter 6 who entered a nunnery in 1636. The two appear to be portraits of the same woman, and yet the legend under each clearly reads that one is Margarita, and the other Flaminia. The conundrum arises too late in the publication process for me to resolve it.

Although I have used as many sources as possible by Maltese writers, I am conscious of only being able to access those in English, and those available in the public domain, in print or on the internet. A Maltese woman historian would have written a different history of her islands. But I have been much helped by Maltese scholars and others knowledgeable about their country, women, and men. I thank them in the acknowledgements. I am also only too conscious that the title of the book is simply 'Malta'. I can only hope that Gozitan people will understand that Gozo, though its own island, is very much included; Comino, so far as I am aware, lacks written women's history, at least in English.

I have ended the history section, to all intents and purposes, with women's suffrage in 1947, and the possibility then of women standing for election. It has to be said, though, that on reading a draft of that chapter, a Maltese woman scholar and activist took the trouble to suggest:

> I believe that you could have included a paragraph or two about women and politics after independence in 1964. As you can well understand, independence (together with the accession to the EU in 2004) was a very important and challenging stage in the history of Malta. ... I believe that attaining the right to vote and run for elections – on its own – does not automatically bring about gender equality. This right has to be followed up by holistic planning and programmes in all areas.

By chance, I received that email just as I was updating this preface and had written, as if in reply to her: I have ended where I have because, as far as possible, I have tried to steer clear of the complicated politics of Malta – even those of women's rights – which only an insider would attempt, or have the right, to unravel. But, following her email, I did add a paragraph, drawing on it, which I hope goes some way to bringing the story more up to date.

The 'Of Islands and Women' series

This is the fourth in my series 'Of Islands and Women', following *Madeira*, *Crete* and *Tasmania*. I devised the term 'livret' for these volumes, envisaging little books that would go in a pocket or bag so as easily to accompany the visitor to a particular place. Because of the richness of the available research into Malta's history and, indeed, the complexity of the islands' past, this book has outgrown that concept, and that shape and size. But it still consists of part women's history, part women's places (itineraries), and still seeks to explore and marry those elements of the subtitle, Women, History, Books and Places.

Oxford
July 2015

Acknowledgements

When I started my research, I knew no one in Malta. I have dedicated the book to Anna Grima, the first Maltese woman to give me her time and her confidence in my project, as well as a gift of her work to be seen on the back cover. I wonder if Christine Muscat knew what she was agreeing to when, sitting together outside the Archaeological Museum, I asked if she would read the manuscript. Nor did I realise how knowledgeable and meticulous she was. I cannot thank her enough, though any remaining errors are mine. Also long-suffering has been Caroline Bayly Scallon, former resident of Malta and now regular visitor. When I was unable to visit some places, she did so for me, detailed how to get there, and took wonderful photographs, three of which I have used. Denizen of Birgu Colin Westmarland devoted a morning to showing me round; without him that itinerary would be much the poorer.

Nicholas de Piro has been more than generous with his time, spending several hours exchanging ideas and discussing images; Joe Vella helped with those. Muffy, Baroness of Tabria, and Justine Pergola were very kind at the Palazzo Parisio, and Penelope Sheppard tactfully supervised the follow-up. Jasper de Trafford took time out from his busy running of Villa Bologna to show me round and discuss the Strickland family, particularly his grandmother Cecilia. Interviewing Antony Debono not only gave me information about his mother, Josephine, but also enabled me to make an essential link with other members of the extended Agius family. I would particularly like to thank members of the Trapani Galea Feriol family for the trouble they took to ensure that the portrait of Elisabetta (Bettina) Moscati Dorell could be included.

Giovanni Bonello has answered endless questions, read relevant chapters and supplied me with two invaluable images. Several others have read chapters for which I drew on their work (sometimes supplying that as well), improved where necessary, and given me permission to quote, for which I thank them: Robert Attard, George Azzopardi, Jennifer Blue, Anna Borg, Hillary Briffa, Angela Callus, Neville Cardona, Carmel Cassar, Anthony de Trafford, Patricia Duncker (*James Miranda Barry*, Bloomsbury Publishing Plc, 2000), Stanley Fiorini, Henry Frendo, George Galdies, Frederick Galea, Paul Knepper, Ilona Strachwitz La Rosée, Celia Lee, Lorraine Portelli, Edward Said, Lillian Sceberras, James Selby Bennett, David Vassallo, Yosanne Vella, David Vernon, Paul Xuereb for the late Godfrey Wettinger.

Others have trustingly given me permission to quote, taken trouble to answer questions, or helped in some other way; I thank them warmly: Alison Alexander, Eric Avebury, Godfrey Baldacchino, Lisa Baldacchino, Richard Bauckham, Anthony Bonanno, Daniel Borg, Joseph Buhagiar, Mario Buhagiar, Father Daniel Cardona, Stefan Caruana, Matthew Cassar, Simon Cauchi, JosAnn Cutajar, Marcelle d'Argy Smith, Rosanne Dingli, Carol Drinkwater, Kirsten Ellis, Joseph Eynaud, Vicki Farrar Hockley, Cristina

Feier, Alastair Gordon-Cumming, Julia Grech, Isabelle Vella Gregory, Jos Gregson, James Holland, Igor Judge, Ross Kraemer, Anne Leaver, Victor Mallia-Milanes, Deborah Manley, Christopher New, John Parascandola, Helen Rappaport, Juliet Rix, Claudia Sagona, Caroline Said Lawrence, Charles Said-Vassallo, Charles Savona-Ventura, John Scerri, Stephen Sedley, Jane Taylor, Joanna Trollope, Meme Cortis Turner, Peter Vassallo. I have made every endeavour to secure permissions.

Permission for the use of images is noted formally attached to them; but those who supplied them from various libraries and institutions were endlessly helpful and I would like to thank them, too, together with others in such places who gave more than mere service: Frederica Agius (Wignacourt Museum), Anonymous at the Carmelite Priory, Mdina, Mgr John Azzopardi (Wignacourt Museum), Nils Bhinda, Julie Cochrane (National Maritime Museum, Greenwich), Nicola Cook (Wellcome Library), Rosalind Esche (Reference Department, Cambridge University), David Johnson (verger, St Paul's church, Valletta), Lloyd Langley (Wallington Museum, Northumberland), Nicholas McBurney (Quaritch), Peter Moore, Rebecca Russell (Woodson Research Center, Rice University), Adrienne Sharpe (Beinecke Rare Books and Manuscripts Library, Yale University), Maria Singer (Yale Centre for British Art), Staff at the British Library, Staff at the National Library of Malta, Staff at Rhodes House, Oxford, Elizabeth Taylor (National Portrait Gallery), Anna Towlson (London School of Economics, Archives and Special Collections), Judith Valletta (Wignacourt Museum), Sarah Walpole (Royal Anthropological Institute), Jenny Wedgbury (UCL Art Museum), Sarah Welcome (Yale Center for British Art), Bridget Whittle (William Ready Division of Archives and Research Collections, McMaster University Library), Gemma Wild (ATG Media).

After 15 years, HOLO Books has had to face the retirement of Ray Addicott who has seen the books of both my husband, Derek Roebuck, and me through the publication process with such care, flair and patience. We will never be able to thank him sufficiently. For this book I have relied heavily and happily on Susan Faircloth, who was first my editor at Oxford University Press in Hong Kong in 1990/91, and Dave Stanford, who has always typeset us but now managed the production process as well. I also thank Bob McIntyre who has helped so much with the images.

Derek has always read and improved my manuscripts, but this time he has not only contributed substantially to a chapter but also read three versions of the book and, in the second reading, at least, improved it out of all recognition. Without his support in every other way, he knows that life, let alone work, would not be the same.

Author's Note

Women's names are in bold in the text where their fullest details occur, or where they are just mentioned once, including in quotations. As usual in my writing, I tend to be familiar and use first names for historical characters after they are first introduced. I am more formal with contemporaries, who are not in bold. The substantial mention is bold in the index; women mentioned only once may not be there.

The Maltese and British have different ways of showing a married woman's name as it was before marriage. Many Maltese women historically often have simply their unmarried name with an indication to follow of their husband's name. Where both names are given I believe I may have sometimes inadvertently caused confusion by putting the first name, followed by the unmarried name, followed by the married name, when it should be the other way round. For British women I have put née in front of their maiden name in brackets; sometimes I have done that for Maltese women too.

It is impossible to be consistent in the spelling of names and places: sometimes they are Maltese, sometimes Italian, sometimes Anglicised; to a large extent it depends on sources, as well as period. The same applies to street names.

There are two Rabats, one on Malta, the other on Gozo, where it is more formally the later Victoria. But since on Gozo 'Rabat' is used more often than 'Victoria', where necessary I indicate which Rabat it is. A similar confusion could prevail concerning the word 'convent'. In English English this a place for nuns; in Roman Catholic countries it more often applies historically to one for monks. I have, therefore called women's convents 'nunneries' to make the distinction clear; and the men's 'monasteries'.

In previous titles in my series 'Of Islands and Women', cross-references between history and places (itineraries) have been indicated by page numbers in brackets. This does not work for an e-book, which does not have page numbers. Cross-referencing in this book, therefore, is by chapter number, and the index will help. To facilitate the use of the itineraries, each can be downloaded separately from www.holobooks.co.uk: click on updates/ in progress. Any update will also be put there. To get the best out of the itineraries, you need to read the history section. I hope there will also be Kindle and e-book editions of this paperback.

The bibliography is extensive and may seem, at first sight, unduly complicated. It is split into several sections. If the title you seek is not immediately obvious, persevere. I have drawn on books of appeal to the general reader and books and articles by scholars indiscriminately in the text. To aid accessibility, I have omitted footnotes or endnotes, but for ease of identification, and for those who know more than I do, I have, where practical, made it clear in the text where quotations and information come from.

This is not a guide book and, therefore, the two maps – of Malta, Gozo and Comino; and that showing Malta's place in the Mediterranean – are simple guidance to the places most mentioned.

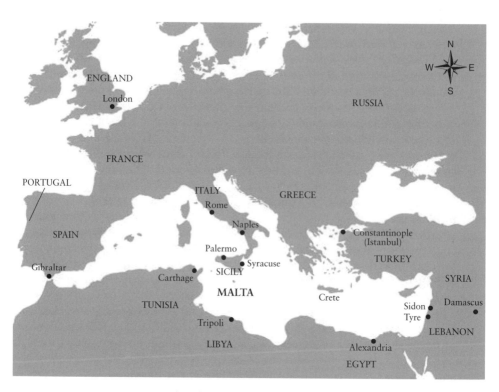

Map of Malta's place in the Mediterranean

Map of Malta, Gozo and Comino

Women's History

Introduction

Of the eight planets in the Solar System, Mercury is the smallest and closest to the sun. You can sometimes see it in the morning sky, or in the evening, though not at night. But what you cannot see with the naked eye are its craters. One of them is named after Maria de Dominici (1645–1703), the earliest known Maltese woman artist. Her existence is little spoken of, certainly outside Malta, though her family name is familiar in artistic circles because two brothers were painters, and a nephew the historian of painters.

In spite of Maria's obscurity, her paintings and sculptures are dotted about, usually rather inaccessibly, in Maltese churches; the best known is probably the sculpture of the Virgin Mary in the Church of the Immaculate Conception in Cospicua, one of the Three Cities that pre-date today's Maltese capital, Valletta. Details of the churches containing her work, including that as assistant to Mattia Preti in St John's Cathedral, feature in Women's Places (Itineraries).

But how did a crater on Mercury come to be named Dominici in 2010, following the second fly-by of the NASA-MESSENGER spacecraft? The internet gives a list of 10 other artists, composers and writers after whom Mercury craters were named that year, including Aaron Copland, the Persian poet Firdousi, Picasso and one other woman.

I wrote to the International Astronomical Union to find out, and was eventually put in touch with Jennifer Blue of the US Geological Survey, Astrogeology Science Center. She contacted the member of the MESSENGER team responsible for proposing the crater names who explained that she had lettered the craters alphabetically in order of targeting. One of the team members then looked in the Mercury name bank, which included names from the *Dictionary of Women Artists* (ed. Delia Glaze, 1997), and selected those that began with the same letters as the targeted craters. The name selected for the crater lettered 'D' was Dominici, for Maria de Dominici. Simple as that. Jennifer was sorry that it was neither exciting nor inspiring.

Exciting or not as an explanation, the thought of a crater on Mercury named after a neglected Maltese woman artist is delightful, inspiring even, particularly when you come across Maria's crater on the internet, a lovely sight! And look out for Mercury in the early morning sky.

The naming of those craters high above on Mercury is so modern compared with the history of humans on Malta still being revealed and discussed by archaeologists. New Stone Age farmers arrived from Sicily as long ago as 5200 BC. But the remains of dwarf animals such as elephants and hippopotamuses, found in the Għar Dalam cave by early archaeologists, are older, probably 250,000 years.

This discovery of insular dwarfism in fauna fossils, as well as that of later human occupation in Għar Dalam, and the determination of Malta's geological status, have taken place over time. That allows me to venture not just on an exploration of the history of Maltese women, through those who

3

1.   Gertrude Caton-Thompson, courtesy of the Royal
Anthropological Institute (Rai360, Ramsey & Muspratt)

have written memoirs, histories, articles, travel accounts, novels and poems, but also on an investigation of the women who found their remains.

Fauna fossil documenting had already begun as early as 1865 when the archaeologist **Gertrude Caton-Thompson** (1888–1985) arrived in Malta in 1922 in a party of other women archaeologists. She had recently started out on her career and had studied palaeontology under Dorothea Bate at the Natural History Museum in London. She came to excavate in Għar Dalam again in 1924 and wrote 60 years later in *Mixed Memoirs* (*c*.1983):

On May 24th I had finished the cave and returned home … The dig had not been rewarding. There was no further trace of Pleistocene or other occupation apart from animals, and the elephant and hippopotamus bones were friable and incomplete. The Valletta Museum took what they wanted and the remainder went to the Natural History Museum in South Kensington.

Dorothea Bate (1878–1951) was not to visit Malta, and Għar Dalam, until 1934 but, as recounted in *Discovering Dorothea: The Life of the Pioneering Fossil-Hunter Dorothea Bate* (Karolyn Shindler, 2005), she worked on the animal deposits from Għar Dalam from receiving the first batch in 1915, when she identified a dwarf elephant, and on a stream of material in the years thereafter. Devastating for Dorothea at the time, but interesting for today's reconstruction of the history of Maltese archaeology, she later learnt that many fossils she had been told were from Għar Dalam came, in fact, from elsewhere on the island. The discovery of two Neanderthal teeth in the same layer as the fauna fossils has since been discredited.

It is with the early Neolithic people that the history of women in Malta begins, as far as possible drawing on the work of women archaeologists. They were initially foreigners and, although Maltese men were early involved, it is comparatively recently that Maltese women archaeologists such as Isabelle Vella Gregory have begun to make their mark. And, happily too, women historians such as Yosanne Vella and Christine Muscat have joined the Maltese men who have started uncovering the later history of women in the archipelago.

1 – The Women from Sicily
5000 BC–800 BC

The Earliest Neolithic Settlers

Malta is only 60 miles (96 km) due south of Sicily – on a clear day you can see the one from the other. But it is still striking to think of boatloads of Sicilian farming people crossing the Mediterranean Sea over 7,000 years ago, for it was not a coast-hugging journey. They were the first human inhabitants of Malta; there is no evidence, as there is in Sicily, of earlier hunter gatherers. They went to settle, leaving Sicily probably because of communal tensions caused by increasing pressure on resources and exhaustion of fertile land, as well as rising sea levels. And, given their long-term intention, they would increasingly have gone as families – women and children as well as men. Scouts must have earlier ascertained the lie of the land and noted that the quite short crossing between the islands, known today as the Malta Channel, was more daunting than benign. And although the main island of Malta is small to us – only 17 miles (27 km) long, 9 miles (14.5 km) wide – it was big enough to people then looking for a place to settle. And when they got there, bringing with them domesticated plants and animals, it cannot have been easy to establish the first settlements on a rocky island.

The earliest were in the area of today's Birżebbuġa on the south-east coast, in an almost direct line from the south-east coast of Sicily, and with a good harbour in what is now Marsaxlokk Bay. In the nearby Għar Dalam (Cave of Darkness) the earliest remains of pottery, dating from 5200–4500 BC, have been excavated; thus the Għar Dalam Phase – the first archaeological phase in Malta's prehistory. The greyish or brownish potsherds were found in levels above the fossils of the pigmy fauna, long extinct, though wild boar still roamed the island. Their similarity to the Stentinello pottery found in Sicily, some incised, some with simple finger-pinching marks known as impressed ware, has determined the provenance of the settlers. The heads of two small clay animals – sheep or cattle – have also been unearthed in the Għar Dalam cave, one of them seemingly the handle of a jug, as well as a goat skull and cattle bones (see Chapter 21 itinerary).

Slightly later pottery remains, from the phases known as Grey Skorba (4400–4300 BC) and Red Skorba (4400–4100 BC) named also for their colour (using red ochre), came from Skorba and Mġarr just inland from the north-west coast. In Mġarr complete vessels have survived and part of a figurine, very obviously female. Polished as well as chipped stone implements were used, some made from obsidian from the islands to the north of Sicily. It is clear that there was continuing trade between Malta and Sicily, as well as family ties. The earliest settlers lived in caves.

From the Żebbuġ Phase (4100–3800 BC) comes a carved stone, apparently representing a human head, excavated near the entrance to – perhaps

6

guarding – a rock-cut chamber tomb at Ta' Trapna, suggesting more formal burial customs. The Żebbuġ Phase is said to mark the arrival of a new wave of immigrants; were they from Sicily, or perhaps from Southern France or Sardinia?

From the Mġarr Phase (3800–3600 BC) evidence has been unearthed at the Skorba site of a Neolithic village, including an oval wattle and daub hut. In it, fragments of small clay and stone figurines, recognisably female, have been found and connected to fertility. From a little later, another hut was found and the remains of a brick wall. That dwelling is known as 'the Hut of Querns'.

The part women played in that early period – the division of labour between the sexes – has to be pieced together. Were women involved in pottery making; in the growing on small plots of crops – wheat, barley and legumes such as lentils (determined from carbonised grains found in the Għar Dalam cave and Skorba); foraging for edible and medicinal plants in the surrounding area; tending the animals they brought with them – sheep, goats, pigs and cattle – and processing their meat and milk; spinning and weaving wool or plant fibres to produce textiles for clothing, or curing animal hides and making garments from them?

John Evans, one of the mid-twentieth-century doyens of Maltese archaeology, writes in *Malta* (1959) of 'days before pottery became an industrial product, when it was home-made, generally by the women of the community for local use …'.

In *The Goddess of Malta* (1992), Dutch cultural anthropologist and art historian Veronica Veen writes of pottery, 'It was not only the most important Neolithic means of expression, but it was also – not without reason – assigned to women.' Elaborating on her title, she sets out at length, and with feeling, to prove that claim, as well as her more general interpretation – further discussion of which will appear in the the Megalithic Period that follows in this chapter. She later suggests that 'wherever the pottery wheel began its march, nearly all over the world, the women were kicked out of the job'. In Malta the wheel was to arrive with the Phoenicians.

J. Busuttil writes in his article 'The Maltese Textile Industry in Antiquity' (1966):

It is not known when this industry was first introduced in Malta. Apparently it had already been in existence in prehistoric times … Sir T. Zammit in his work Prehistoric Malta relates how incinerated specimens of calcined textile going back to prehistoric times were obtained from debris. These specimens were examined in a laboratory and it has been established that the material is most likely flax or fibre of that type.

Evidence from elsewhere, and common sense, suggest that women were involved in any number of those activities. I wrote in *Crete: Women, History, Books and Places*, of Neolithic women there (7000–3000 BC):

There is some evidence that women were not only weavers, but also potters, the latter craft being connected with both food and medicinal plants and their potency. It is fair to assume that they were also involved in agriculture. We should think, too, of the place of domestic water in all societies where it is not on tap, and women's role in its collection.

It should be said, though, that there has, as yet, been no unearthing in Malta of clay spindle whorls from this early period such as those found in Crete. But then the early archaeology of Malta was somewhat haphazard and findings from storage are still being examined, as well as excavation continued. Isabelle Vella Gregory, in *The Human Form in Neolithic Malta* (2008), with the wonderful photographs by Daniel Cilia, usefully provides a history of the archaeology, dating back to 1826, under the sub-heading 'The Context of Statuary'. As she says, 'no statue has been found in a domestic context.'

Margaret Ehrenberg, archaeologist and anthropologist in women's studies programmes, writes in *Women in Prehistory* (1995):

> The discovery of farming techniques is usually assumed to have been made by men, but it is in fact very much more likely to have been made by women. On the basis of anthropological evidence for societies still living foraging life-styles and those living by simple, non-mechanised farming, taken in conjunction with direct archaeological evidence, it seems probable that it was women who made the first observations of plant behaviour, and worked out, presumably by long trial and error, how to grow and tend crops.

Giulia Battiti Sorlini, an Italian specialising in archaeomythology, in 'The Megalithic Temples of Malta' (1986), felt that prehistoric women gatherers

> might have noticed certain peculiarities and recurrences about certain grasses that could not only be gathered, but also stored and pounded to provide staple food on a yearly basis. This discovery might have brought about the so called agricultural revolution and one of the most radical changes in the way of life of our forebears.

Kathryn Rountree, feminist professor of anthropology in New Zealand, in an article about Neolithic goddesses in Malta, showed that by 2003 the claim of women as 'inventors' of agriculture had common currency when she used this quotation from a film: 'Seven thousand years ago, the first raising of crops was done by hand tools, probably by women, for we know that women developed agriculture and the domestication of animals.'

Some of the reconstruction of Neolithic women's roles may be speculative, but it does allow us to begin to picture the life of those very early Maltese women in a possibly egalitarian and ritually satisfying society. And the fact that no weapons have been found suggests that it was a peaceful one – peace in which women may well have played a part. If we accept that women were the primary potters, it is pleasing to note that it is these remains that determine the chronology of Malta's prehistory.

The Megalithic Period

About 1,600 years after their arrival in Malta, the successors of those immigrants began developing a culture which led, from about 3600 BC, to the building of stone structures, described as stupendous megalithic temples, now known to be older than, for example, that at Stonehenge. They were unique to Malta, owing nothing to Sicily or elsewhere. And by that time there were also settlements on the island of Gozo, 5 miles (8 km) to the north-east of Malta; indeed, there is some evidence that immigrants of the Għar Dalam Phase settled in sites such as Il Mixta cave, just north of Santa Lucija, but few sherds have been found and archaeology has been difficult owing to structural problems caused by nearby quarrying; as a result, it is little written about, but it is fair to assume that the women who settled there led a life similar to those at Għar Dalam.

Gozo is half the size of Malta, being 9 miles (14.5 km) long and 4.5 miles (7 km) wide but is as rich in archaeological interest, and from there comes the phase known as Ġgantija (3600-3300 BC), after the temples of that name found near what is more recently known as Xagħra Circle (originally the Brochtorff Circle), north of Rabat (Victoria), with a burial cave, or hypogeum, containing fragmentary remains of 822 individuals buried together, and a similar stone carved face as that at Żebbuġ. Burials continued to take place there for centuries thereafter (see Chapter 23 itinerary).

The Saflieni Phase (3300–3000 BC) is named not for a temple but for the Hypogeum not far from Valletta, made up of underground passages and rooms on successive floors. There 6,000 skeletal remains have been found. There was also fine pottery, figurines, decorated friezes, charms and carved objects (see Chapter 21 itinerary).

The last temple phase is the Tarxien (3000–2500 BC). From that period come three temples at Tarxien – not far, when planning an itinerary, from the Hypogeum; the temple complex on the south-east coast of Ħagar Qim and Mnajdra; and the finds at Tas-Silġ. This last is perhaps the most intriguing because of the layers above the Neolithic, with their ritual traces of the peoples who followed: Phoenicians, Romans, Christians (see itineraries).

What has been discovered about the Neolithic women who lived in these places over a thousand or so years BC? I'll try and tease out some reality, but this is where the most recent archaeological interpretations start to get complicated, based particularly on work at the Xagħra Circle, Gozo – where archaeological finds have been excavated recently in their proper context – for they question those of the past.

Many obviously female figures have been found in archaeological sites, including the dozens of temples scattered around the two islands. The most famous of these are traditionally known as 'the Sleeping Lady', from the

Hypogeum; the 'Venus of Malta' and the 'Fat Lady' series from Ħagar Qim. Other sources talk of the 'Great Sansuna Mother' or the 'Great Goddess Sansuna'; and myth suggests that part of the Ġgantija temple complex was built by Sansuna, a superwoman or giantess. That myth still exists in folk lore. She lived on broad beans and honey and bore a child with a human man. With the child clinging around her neck, she shifted the giant stones. Some of these limestone blocks weighed as much as 20 tons.

The female figurines have been interpreted as goddesses of fertility or love. From this interpretation and, for example, those found on Crete, there has grown up what is known as the 'Goddess Movement'; and there are Goddess tour operators who take you to the relevant archaeological sites. Malta has come to epitomise worship of the great 'Mother Goddess'.

Kathryn Rountree wrote at least two papers on the subject following several trips to Malta between 1998 and 2002. In 'Goddess Pilgrims as Tourists' (2002), she added to their purpose: 'Contemporary "local culture" and the pleasures of local landscapes are also relished: elements of ethnic tourism, environmental tourism and historical tourism are integral to these pilgrimages.' Later in her paper she added:

> Answering the accusation that they could be seen as appropriating other cultures' religious traditions and sacred sites, even as perpetuating a colonialist or imperialist impulse, women have stressed that they treat sacred sites with reverence and indigenous societies with respect, and are deeply concerned about the sites' preservation, indeed sometimes more concerned than the host communities themselves.

A year later she added, in 'The Case of the Missing Goddess' (2003),

> The foreign Goddess pilgrims who visit the temples and Malta's National Museum of Archaeology, where the Neolithic artefacts are displayed, often enthuse about their experiences, relating deeply emotional, inspirational, or epiphanic moments and a sense of "coming home" to spiritual roots.

Archaeologist Caroline Malone, with her husband Simon Stoddart, led a team from the universities of Cambridge and Malta, working for some years in the Xagħra Stone Circle. In 'God or Goddess: The Temple Art of Ancient Malta' (1998); 'Introduction: The "Goddess" problem in Prehistory', she explains:

> ... the very existence of a 'Mother Goddess' in ancient Malta is still hotly debated. Temples, tombs, art and remarkable anthropomorphic figurines are evidence in abundance, but their relationship and their individual functions may be rather more complex than the simple interpretation of a fertility deity.

In the introduction to *Ancient Goddesses* (1998), in which that chapter appears, the editors, Lucy Goodison and Caroline Morris, elaborate:

> Recent decades have seen the emergence of a new movement which claims that human society and religion began with the worship of a Goddess in a peace-loving, egalitarian, matriarchal society, and that female divinities everywhere represent survivals of this early mode of religious expression. A stream of books by non-specialists, artists, psychotherapists, feminists and amateur historians has drawn attention to powerful and often neglected ancient images of the female. These many voices have together been termed the 'Goddess movement'.
>
> Some Goddess movement writers accuse the academics – archaeologists and ancient historians – of wilfully ignoring the evidence for female power in pre-history. Some have fulminated against the prejudice of conventional scholars for keeping the 'real history' of women in the dark. Contemporary academics on the other hand have, with a few notable exceptions, either remained silent, ignoring the claims, or have tended to dismiss the Goddess story as an invention of polemic and hysteria.
>
> Is one side reinventing the past? What can or cannot be proved by the evidence from prehistory? Can we debate competing reconstructions of the past in a way which is both respectful and flexible?

However carefully that sort of questioning is couched, exponents of the supremacy of the goddess and matriarchal society in the prehistory of Malta mount a strong defence. Veronica Veen wrote, following extensive fieldwork, that she felt

> ... obliged to write this book because of the total lack of willingness, showed by the local archaeologists to cover this subject. In the few cases they touched on it, they tended to ridicule or distort matters. As a feminist, I could hardly endure it any longer, that such an inspiring part of women's history and culture was ignored and abused. The peak so far was the attempt by two leading Malta-archaeologists to picture the Fat Lady statuettes as male!

Veronica Veen's work was summed up rather pithily, and it has to be said accurately, in the *Times of Malta*: 'There was hardly a sherd of pottery that wasn't covered in vulvas, breasts, or buttocks.' And the same could be said of her reading of the shape of the temples. And the red ochre, liberally applied, is menstrual blood.

Caroline Malone takes up Veronica Veen's challenge:

> ... the traditional 'Fat Lady' or goddess figurine, that is, the classic image of prehistoric Malta, is in fact no more female than it is male. The excessive obesity (especially buttocks and thighs) has been used as the principal

identifier for female gender, in spite of the missing detail of genitalia or breasts which would normally be depicted, or the other ignored fact that Mediterranean males are frequently as obese as females!

Cristina Biaggi, an American sculptor focussing on The Great Goddess and early pre-history, had already suggested an answer, drawing on the work of other scholars, in 'The Significance of the Nudity, Obesity and Sexuality of the Maltese Goddess Figures' (1986). Noting the usual roll of fat on the chest of these figurines, she continues,

> The fact that there is no central division within this mass of fat to separate the breasts in a naturalistic fashion has caused scholars to claim that the figures represent males. However, if one examines the seated or standing figures from the back, one will notice that the furrow of the buttocks is not delineated – in fact the buttocks appear as a continuous surface. This stylized departure from realism was obviously adopted in the depiction of the breasts. Furthermore, the vulvas of the figures are not visible in the seated or standing figures because they are obfuscated by the fat.

But if the figurines are female, did they signify fertility? Anthony Bonanno, a colleague of Caroline Malone's working on the Xagħra Circle, notes in 'Women and Society in Prehistoric and Ancient Gozo' (2010):

> Although 'fertility' or 'fecundity' is traditionally said to be the manifest meaning of these figures, I am informed by … medical colleagues that this type of obesity is far from being conducive to fertility; on the contrary, it actually hinders fertility.

Anthony Bonanno also discusses the piece of sculpture from the Xagħra Hypogeum that shows two fat figures seated side by side on a couch, one holding what could be a child. Assuming that one is female, the other male, he writes, 'I am more inclined to accept the portrayal of a male and a female in complementary opposition.' If one is 'mother goddess', the other is 'a father god'. No one, he adds, has ever suggested that. Might they not simply be 'ancestors or rulers, whether male or female, rather than divinities?'

When it comes down to it, I rather like the earlier summing up by medical historian and ethnographer of Malta, Paul Cassar, in 'Women of Malta: An Historical Vignette' (1975–77):

> It is not clear what is the significance of these fat women and various suggestions have been put forwards with regard to their purpose and to the message which the stone-age carver meant to convey. It has been surmised that they are:
>
> (a) goddesses or divinities or perhaps priestesses; or

(b) symbols of maternity or fertility used in connection with some form of religious or magical ceremonial intended to promote the birth-rate of the community or of agricultural and animal produce; or
(c) Neolithic man's ideal of feminine beauty and sexual attraction; or
(d) pointers to the existence of matriarchal society in our Islands; or
(e) pathological specimens of a disordered fat metabolism caused by a leisurely life in an affluent society. If this last surmise is correct then we can say with reasonable probability that even in those far off days, the Maltese were already suffering from such illnesses as diabetes and high blood pressure since we know that obesity is very often an indirect index of the existence of such conditions which reduce the opportunities for a long and healthy life.

David Trump, another member of the Xagħra Circle team, and one time director of the National Museum of Archaeology, suggests, in *Malta: An Archaeological Guide* (2000), that the bones from there show people enjoyed at least average health. As Paul Cassar also points out, there are similar representations of Neolithic people in other countries, and there are also more obvious representations of Neolithic women among the figurines in Malta. It is worth noting that no obese figurines have been found before the Temple Phase. If you want to see images of the full range of these corpulent figures, you will find them in Isabelle Vella Gregory's *The Human Form in Neolithic Malta*.

In May 2013, the *Times of Malta* reported a wonderful breakthrough in how real Maltese Neolithic women looked. It reported on the work of Professor Caroline Wilkinson, chief facial anthropologist at the University of Dundee. Commissioned by Heritage Malta, she had taken the prehistoric skull of a woman excavated from the Xagħra Stone Circle, Gozo, dating back roughly 5,600 years, and reconstructed her head and face. The woman, known by the research team as 'The Malteser' was estimated to have been between 25 and 40 years old and thought to have died of natural causes. The 3D result, not so different from a Maltese woman today, can be seen at the Ġgantija visitors' centre, less than a kilometre away from where the skull was found, or on the internet.

One other woman comes to life from the Xagħra Hypogeum. Anthony Bonanno writes of

… the articulated skeleton of an elderly lady … discovered lying directly on the ground underneath layers of other loosely scattered human bones. The lady was laid to rest with a unique headdress of 30 cowry shells. Both the headdress and the intact primary deposition of the skeleton suggest a special status enjoyed by this woman in her lifetime and at the point of death. In life, she could have enjoyed a leading position in her society accruing from her longevity, her wisdom, or simply from her self-assertion. At death, she is likely to have remained in the collective memory as an ancestor to be remembered and revered.

Elsewhere in the hypogeum were male skeletons and one of a mature male lying in a similar position, suggesting a similar status. Anthony Bonanno concludes:

> This balance between the two genders apparent in the identifiable patterning of funerary deposition goes some way to confirming the view, that is derived from a similar balance in the artistic iconography, that the social structure of the Temple Culture was characterized by a precocious equality of sexes based on the complementary role of the two sexes.

Another newspaper piece found on the internet about 'The Malteser' incorporates ideas from the very large, scholarly tome *Mortuary Customs in Prehistoric Malta: Excavations at the Brochtorff Circle at Xaghra (1987–94)* (2009), of which both Caroline Malone and Anthony Bonanno were editors. There the archaeologists go a little further than the dry bones they found to suggest aspects of the funeral rites that help bring the scene to life: 'the buzzing of flies and the smell of rotting flesh'. *An Archaeology of the Senses: Prehistoric Malta* (Robin Skeates, 2010) allows a little respite: 'the pleasing aroma of burnt substances in the temples' offered in contrast to the 'threatening odour of putrefaction in the rock-cut tombs and hypogea'. And a more general sensory view of Neolithic life: 'The barking dogs, the bleating sheep and goats, buzzing flies, scratching hoes, crackling hearths, the slap of daubed clay.'

Of all the articles and chapters that I have trawled to get to the bottom of the figurines, the one I found most satisfying, because it explores real women in some detail, was by Sara A Rich who spent from 2006 to 2008 doing anthropological fieldwork on Gozo: 'Midwifery and Neolithic Malta: Interpreting and Contextualizing Two Terracotta Figures' (2008). She has the advantage of being able to make use of most of the interpretations that have gone before. She explains that two figurines 'sit somewhere in the margins outside the corpus of Malta's Neolithic sculptures'. One was found (in 1915) in a rubbish dump outside the Tarxien temples complex; 'it was fired with bits of shell and bone wedged into the wet clay'. The other was found (in 1910) in a pit at the Mnajdra temple site. 'Both sculptures have well-articulated breasts, vagina and spinal column, despite having been formed in a "crude" fashion.' (There are several full-page, and detailed, colour photographs of these obviously pregnant women in Isabelle Vella Gregory's book.) While most scholars have seen these figures as evidence of a predominant fertility cult associated with the worship of a Great Mother Goddess, Sara Rich ends her introduction: 'This paper proposes that the creators of the figurines may have been midwives making offerings on behalf of their female clients.' Some points in her paper stand out:

Because pregnancy is a physical process that is experienced exclusively by women, it is possible that these sculptures were votives offered by women for the purpose of adjuring the assistance of a supernatural force to ensure healthy offspring. The creators of the figurines may perhaps have been the pregnant women depicting themselves in a terracotta self-portrait to be offered at the temple. They also could have been created and/or dedicated by the male partners of the expecting women. However, it is also possible that the midwives would have created small votive sculptures on behalf of their clients to ward off dangerous forces. The midwives might have an additional function; and here Sara Rich drew on the more general study of midwives in history and society of Jean Toweler and Joan Bramall:

> During this period of increasing social organization, elderly women, at first from within the family and then from within the community, replaced men as attendants at birth. These 'experienced women' came to fulfil the role of midwife. Once they assumed the right to this office, they retained it, to the exclusion of men, for at least the next 10,000 years … [It] is conceivable that the 'experienced woman' would come to care professionally for other women in disease and sickness as well as in childbirth.

And, from ethnographer Barbara Tedlock, who writes about women, religion and magic, Sara Rich further develops the idea:

> Besides the nurturing and supportive role they take with pregnant women, midwives regularly administer treatments for sterility, give massages and sweat baths, and provide herbal remedies and advice on nutrition and childcare. They know how to concoct herbal aphrodisiacs and abortives, and how to treat female ailments and children's illnesses.

One of the more important points Sara Rich makes is to suggest that 'The relationship between healer, diviner and midwife exemplifies the presence of women in the public domain of the community. Ethnographically these women hold relatively high social statuses.' This may be a little removed from the interpretations of Mother Goddess, priestesses and matriarchal society, but it is about women whom we can easily picture.

Somehow, to link the Neolithic past to the present is the most appealing part of Sara Rich's paper. After talking to an 84-year-old retired Gozitan midwife who had started practising in 1948, she notes:

> According to Gozitan folklore, pregnant women, especially from the village of Xaghra, would sit upon the dolmen of Sansuna to ensure a safe delivery. This is because of a popular legend that tells of a giantess who, while carrying her baby on her back, carried the lintel stone on her head and the two posts stones in either hand.

Just to confuse the issue, Margaret Murray, archaeologist in Malta between 1920 and 1929 (whom we shall meet in the section below on the Bronze Age), writes in the 1923 introduction to the three-volume study of her work, transposing the story from Gozo to Malta,

The only tradition I could find which refers to these Neolithic buildings, is that the whole of Hagiar Kim was built by women. This is remarkable as Hagiar Kim is not only the largest in area of all the Neolithic structures, but also contains the largest blocks of stone.

Sara Rich's midwives are not necessarily connected with temple culture. But then, having questioned the sex and function of figurines, this may, I suggest, be the appropriate place to question the function of the 'temple' – *pace* explorers of Malta's Neolithic past such as Veronica Venn with her minute detailing of the Goddess presence in the shape of 'temples', and all the artefacts found therein. I note that in the 1923 quotation from Margaret Murray above, she does not use the word. In *Pagan Britain* (2013), questioning that of henges, such as Stonehenge, Ronald Hutton remarks that 'it is impossible to determine with any precision the nature of the religious beliefs and rites of the prehistoric British'. He goes on to suggest that it is hard to distinguish ritual from practical behaviour and asks if henges served a secular or religious purpose, or if the distinction itself is a modern invention. Certainly there is evidence of the grinding of corn in the Maltese 'temples'. May there have been other more secular community functions, such as redistribution of commodities and dispute resolution? Women may well have been involved. There is also evidence, as in similar structures throughout the world, of account having been taken in their positioning of the seasonal equinoxes; this is usually assumed to have had a religious function, but where was the distinction between religion and science? Whatever their function, or functions, the tombs, at least, had an obvious purpose.

At the Tarxien Temple complex one statue stands out – the remains of a 2-metre high figure in a skirt; a reconstruction of what the original may have looked like is in the Archaeological Museum in Valletta (see Chapter 21 itinerary). Does it represent a female or a male? Caroline Malone, in her original chapter, suggests it could have been a 'priest'.

Also from Tarxien comes a sculpture of three phalluses, joined together and standing on a triangular base, and similar phalluses, in pairs or singly, proliferated elsewhere, including from earlier phases. These at least can be positively ascribed as male, but what was their significance? Isabelle Vella Gregory, whose book illustrates many phalluses, tells us 'No statue exhibiting definitely male characteristics has been found to date.' Caroline Malone, in her drawing of the Tarxien phallus sculpture, uses the word 'shrine'. From the Hagar Qim Temple of the same period comes the naked, standing 'Venus of Malta'; no figure could be more obviously a woman.

Before leaving the fraught subject of female or male, matriarchy or patriarchy, Goddess or not, it is worth taking in Isabelle Vella Gregory's three-page 'The Archaeology of Gender', of which this is a flavour:

Among the subject's concerns are the correction of male bias and a general critique thereof in academia and a reassessment of existing interpretations of past societies ... it was only in the 1970s that archaeological discourse showed an explicit concern with gender issues. The continuing debate has not only challenged traditional assumptions, but also offered a variety of perspectives on the past.

If you wanted just one book about Maltese Neolithic archaeology, it would be that of Isabelle Vella Gregory but, be warned, it comes in a large format, is heavy and rather expensive, as you would expect of such a beautifully illustrated and scholarly, though accessible, work. The 'Sleeping Lady' found in the Saflieni Hypogeum, for example, is photographed from every angle, as well as close up as modern photography allows – there are six large colour images – a seventh is of the underside of her bed, or couch, hinting at lengths of wood supporting the base and perhaps suggesting domestic furniture of the period. And her significance is meticulously discussed: is she connected with death? Is she engaged in sleeping or dreaming rituals connected with the spirit world? Whatever the truth, she is a lovely work of art. And the author ends by suggesting that 'The Sleeping Lady may have provided a physical, material link between the worlds of the living and the dead.' You will not see her so well in the Museum of Archaeology, though she is nicely displayed there.

The evidence suggests that the people of the Tarxien Temple period were both technologically and artistically advanced. The graffiti incised on the megaliths were among the last of their work to be noted and interpreted. While there are no remains found of the craft that brought Sicilian migrant farmers to Malta, nor those used for trade thereafter, in 1957, **Diana Woolner** (1908–1999), whose naval commander husband was stationed in Malta for three years, not only found graffiti of incised boats but also recorded them, and wrote up her finds in 'Graffiti of Ships at Tarxien, Malta' (1957). This was just as well, because those who took an interest in them thereafter, in 1970, 1988 and 1999, found that they had deteriorated, to the extent that when they were finally taken inside for conservation in 2006, little remained, and interpretation, such as dating, has been thwarted. But Joseph Muscat, in 'The Tarxien Ship Graffiti Revisited' (2000), writes, 'One is tempted to treat the two stone slabs as if they were notice boards or votive stele, specifically erected for the benefit of those ancient mariners to incise on them either as an expression of gratitude or an insurance against the perils at sea.'

Even from Diana Woolner's sketches, it is difficult to describe them, but they seem pretty rudimentary open, canoe-like, high-ended, vessels with banks of oars either side, or are those seats across the body of the vessel? And were these boats the first inscribed communication in Malta? Diana Woolner may have been an archaeological amateur, but her mother, **Winifred Hansard**, was an archaeological artist, and her father was the well-known Egyptologist Cecil Firth.

The last, and perhaps greatest mystery of the Temple Period is the noticeable and abrupt end to the culture in 2500 BC, leading to the inevitable conclusion that the people disappeared with it. It has only been possible to speculate about the causes: extreme deforestation leading to soil erosion as a result of an increase in population – by this time it was probably between 6,000 and 7,000; social disruption caused by oppression by a ruling caste; foreign invasion; pestilence, drought. Whatever the causes, the effect on women and their children can be imagined from the images we see daily in our own news media.

The Bronze Age

Those people originally from Sicily whose culture had developed from 5200 or so BC may have chosen to desert the islands, or they may have been forced out. Certainly those who replaced them in what is known not only as the Bronze Age but also as the Tarxien Cemetery Phase (*c.*2500–1500 BC) were of a different stamp. They inserted a cemetery in the ruins of what had been the Tarxien Temple, and there they cremated their dead. Ash remains have been found in rows of open cinerary urns, and in pots nearby remains of beads, fabrics and seeds. Not only had metal arrived, but weaponry, including bronze axes, flat dagger blades and obsidian-tipped arrows.

The clay used is much coarser than previously, and less well baked; the vessels are differently shaped. From this period, at least, spindle whorls have been found, mostly of clay, but sometimes stone and, as John Evans notes, 'There is direct evidence of weaving in the form of actual fragments of dyed cloth, made apparently of flax or some similar fibre.'

The religious life of the Tarxien cemetery people is suggested by a series of stylised clay figures; two of them seated are recognisably female. One has an elaborate headdress which can be appreciated in Anthony Bonanno's finely illustrated *Malta: An Archaeological Paradise* (9th edition, 2003). These bear some affinity to the Mycenean figures from the eastern Mediterranean.

The only structures to be found from this rather mysterious period are *dolmens* – three-sided, single-room structures topped by a stone slab – a score or more are scattered around the islands with an apparent funerary purpose.

Although archaeologists such as John Evans suggest that these new people may have come from the tip of Italy's heel, the strong evidence of eastern Mediterranean influence is given credence by the work of the physical anthropologist Leonard Dudley Buxton and his team of young women colleagues from Oxford University who did fieldwork in Malta from late 1920 to 1921 written up in 'The Ethnology of Malta and Gozo' (1922).

Leonard Buxton was to make his name as a physical anthropologist, but he was only 30 in 1920, and not yet appointed a lecturer at the University, when he arrived in Malta with Mrs Jenkinson, Miss Moss and Miss Russell. The expedition was funded by the Mary Ewart Trust and Sir Alfred Mond; Miss Mond was an associate of Buxton's. **Constance Jenkinson** had been admitted as a diploma student to the department in 1915 on the strength of her modern languages; she was to die while preparing for a postgraduate BSc in Magic and Medicine; **Rosalind Moss** (1890–1990) arrived in Oxford a year later (enrolling in the Society of Oxford Home Students, later St Anne's

College), also proficient in European languages, and was to become well known as an Egyptologist and bibliographer; and **Isabel Russell** had seen service in the First World War before being admitted as a student in 1920 and gaining her diploma the following year.

The four set off for Malta in December 1920. Their purpose was to take measurements from four different periods of Maltese history: bones from the Saflieni Hypogeum ('Malta Local Neolithic'); miscellaneous ancient skeletons, chiefly Romano-Maltese; specimens from the Chapel of Bones (Late Medieval); and modern bones. From these measurements, they drew conclusions about the provenance of Malta's population over time.

In Gozo, Constance Jenkinson and Rosalind Moss took the cranial measurements of 100 women and men; Isabel Russell measured long bones and about half the children. Then Constance and Rosalind worked out a number of indices on the living, and Isabel helped in the tabulation. Back in Oxford, much the best-known physical anthropologist of them all, **Beatrice Blackwood** (1889–1975), an undergraduate at Somerville 1908–12, prepared Buxton's paper for publication during his absence. The paper ends with the following conclusion, usefully leading Malta's history from the Sicilian Neolithic farmers to the Bronze Age peoples and beyond:

> Summarizing our general conclusions, the race in Malta which is associated with the period of great megalithic buildings – a cultural stage we have termed 'Malta Local Neolithic' – appears to be closely akin to the Mediterranean race. This is our 'Malta first race.' At a later date, possibly towards the end of the Bronze Age, but more probably during the Early Iron Age, Malta was peopled by a race with different characteristics, our 'Malta second race.' These people are of Armenoid type, but probably have an admixture of Mediterranean blood. Their origin appears to be the Eastern Mediterranean. They may have come to Malta either directly or by way of Carthage. They may have destroyed the previous inhabitants, or they may merely have pursued methods of peaceful penetration. This race has firmly established itself in Malta, and all subsequent introduction of foreign blood has failed to raise the variation.

The only thing I do not understand is why that party of physical anthropologists, most of them women, doing fieldwork in Malta do not appear, according to memoirs and biographies, to have met up with the party of women archaeologists also doing fieldwork in Malta in 1921. So they will meet here!

The London University archaeologist **Margaret Murray** (1863–1963) and her team introduce us to the next Bronze Age phase, the Borġ in-Nadur (1500–800 BC). This appears to find new people in Malta, with a new culture best appreciated at the Borġ in-Nadur site between Għar Dalam and today's Birżebbuġa. These people are said to have overwhelmed the Tarxien Cemetery ones. They lived in warlike times, in fortified villages of oval huts usually sited on flat-topped hills, the fortifications being similar to those built by the Myceneans. It is not known if they were protecting themselves from other invaders, or from competing villages, although the wall at Borġ in-Nadur – 12 to 14 ft high and 4–5 ft wide – is on the landward side of the promontory. Because of the unsettled conditions, agriculture suffered, and more reliance was placed on livestock which could be brought within the village walls. Once again, findings suggest the weaving of textiles which may have been used to trade for metals. There is evidence, such as painted pottery and construction techniques, of contact between the Maltese islands and Minoan Crete and Mycenean Greece, as well as confirmation of that with Sicily and southern Italy. Similar villages have been identified elsewhere on Malta and Gozo. At fortified Borġ in-Nadur, where the village was built around an earlier temple, there was much pottery previously unknown in Malta but with a parallel in Sicily.

If one is following the chronology of the Mother Goddess and matriarchy theory, the Bronze Age would be when the change set in. The lives of the women of these new people, in this new unsettled and warlike culture, can only be surmised. But it is easy to suspect that, if there was fighting, their status in the society would be diminished. Would they, for example, have been as safe to cultivate their plots outside the village as earlier Neolithic women did? Would they have become more sedentary? What were the health implications of a diet richer in animal protein, less in vegetables and carbohydrates? There was still cultivation of grain, however, because John Evans describes how, within the precincts of the earlier temple at Borġ in-Nadur, 'the women ground flour and cooked, as shown by numerous hand-mills, mortars and traces of fire found by the excavators'. There are also the remains of shallow, bottle-shaped pits in the ground which probably stored grain or water. If the livestock were brought within the walls, families would have been living on top of them, which would not have been healthy. At what stage in Malta's history, or pre-history, did what was to become known as Malta Fever, later as Brucellosis, from drinking raw goats' milk, manifest itself? (see Chapter 12).

There is a curious, ambiguous and out-of-character parenthesis in Margaret Murray's autobiography about women, one of the surprisingly few mentions of them in any of her writing:

> The whole of the male population in the Bronze Age did not spend their entire time throughout their lives in the production of tools and other concrete objects (the women, otherwise useless, produced only babies). The people of the Bronze Age were human with all the human emotions, including gratitude to the Unseen Power which had brought them out of danger into safety.

I can find no evidence for that suggestion that women produced only babies. One of my hopes and guesses is that if there was hostility between villages, and they feared for the safety of their children, they may still have had influence through involvement in efforts to secure peace, as is often the case in today's developing societies.

Margaret Murray spent five summers in Malta, four of them excavating, one in the Museum, starting in 1920 when she was 57. She was 4 ft 10 inches (147 cm), with bright blue eyes which flashed when she was roused, and she was a strong character, making her way in the hitherto entirely male world of professional Egyptologists. Like her mother, she sought to improve the condition of women: she was a member of the Pankhursts' Women's Social and Political Union, and took part in the Mud March in 1907. In her many years at University College, London, she was unfailing in her support of female colleagues and students. She had entered the department there in 1894 under the Egyptologist Flinders Petrie, and most of her teaching, fieldwork and writing concerned Egypt. But, because she was over-loaded with teaching, she tended to jump at any chance of fieldwork – which is how she came to excavate in Malta between 1920 and 1927. The initial plan was that she should go out there and excavate some small megalithic sites which were urgently required for the new airport.

2.   Margaret Murray, courtesy of UCL Art Museum,
University College London

With Margaret was **Dr Edith Guest** (b.1873), a colleague and friend at the University. Edith Guest, after practising medicine during the First World War, including in Malta (see Chapter 13), had become Margaret Murray's student in Egyptology in 1920, and she was to be appointed Honorary Assistant in Egyptology in 1924; later still, as a physiologist, she was to teach 'Bones for the Archaeologist'. Gertrude Caton-Thompson has already appeared in the Introduction, excavating mostly at Għar Dalam. She was, though, part of Margaret Murray's team for two months in 1922 and 1924. Not only had she become a student in the archaeology department in 1921, aged 31, but they were friends, including being Suffragettes together. In Malta, Margaret trained both Edith and Gertrude in field archaeology methods.

Less easy to place as part of the 1922 team was a **Miss Hughes**. Margaret Murray wrote in one of her acknowledgements that she 'not only helped in the drawing of pots and in the excavations but also undertook the endless and wearisome task of housekeeping for which the grateful thanks of the whole party are given to her'. This member of the team does not appear in memoirs and, without a first name, she has proved elusive.

In the Museum in her final spell in Malta, Margaret Murray made a more general study of its prehistoric pottery, what was to be written up as *The Corpus of Bronze-Age Pottery of Malta* (1934). Through this, she was able to show, based on pottery from Tarxien, the division between the Neolithic and Bronze Ages. In this work, she was helped by **Teresa Strickland** (1903–1955), granddaughter of English Walter Strickland, founder member of the Society of Archaeology (set up in 1865), and Maltese aristocrat **Donna Luisa Strickland** (née Scebberas Bologna, *c.*1833–1907), an avid collector of antiquities who had helped the German archaeologist Albert Mayr with his fieldwork in Malta, mostly at Mnajdra. Teresa, known as Terry, was then yet to meet her future husband, American Harris Dunscombe Colt, who was also helping Margaret Murray. Terry will appear later fundraising in the United States on Malta's behalf in the Second World War (see Chapter 15).

Margaret Murray was to write up her archaeological findings in Malta in three slender volumes – *Excavations in Malta* (1923–1929), with two chapters by Gertrude Caton-Thompson on Għar Dalam, and thanks to Dorothea Bate 'for her report on the vertebrate remains found in Ghar Dalam', and to Miss KA Burke for her analyses of the soil. But easier to find is Margaret's autobiography, *My First Hundred Years* (1963). And there is now a well-deserved biography, *The Life of Margaret Alice Murray: A Woman's Work in Archaeology* (Kathleen L Sheppard, 2013), as well as a chapter in *Breaking Ground: Pioneering Women Archaeologists* (Martha Joukowsky and Getzel Cohen, 2004). In her autobiography she wrote, perhaps inadvertently questioning the role of women and textiles in the Bronze Age:

Some of the objects found in the temple of Borg-en-Nadur suggest that fishing was one of the main industries. A large number of holed stones, usually regarded as spindle-whorls, are too heavy for spinning the thread for even the coarsest type of cloth-weaving, the thread would break with the weight, though they might be used for the coarse heavy thread necessary for sail-canvas. Those of medium weight would be for the heavy twists required for nets for all kinds of cordage and ropes. The heaviest of all were probably net-sinkers.

It should be added that in 1927, in a letter to colleagues in Cambridge, she wrote, 'And there is a pottery object, perhaps a loom-weight, from my own dig at Borg-en-Nadur.' Her biographer, who quotes that letter, sums up her legacy in Malta: 'In Maltese archaeology today Murray is still recognised as an important pioneer in the field.' And Caroline Malone and her colleagues remark that her reports, while not aiding in sequence dating or many other cultural conclusions, do offer archaeologists a broad assembly of systematic samples of material culture, thus making hers the most easily quantifiable prehistoric excavations to date from the Maltese islands.

As Egyptologists Margaret Murray and Rosalind Moss finally come together in two articles: 'Egyptian Objects Found in Malta' (1928) and 'An Egyptian Statuette in Malta' (1949), but Egyptian involvement in Malta has been questioned to destruction by later scholarship. The finds were, it is concluded, imported at a later date.

The last Bronze Age phase is the Bahrija (900–700 BC). The people involved – a small number – were also new, probably from southern Italy, and they settled on the naturally defended Qlejgha promontory on the east coast of Malta. That is their only known site, though their pottery has been found at Għar Dalam, Borġ in-Nadur and Tas-Silġ. There is no evidence of hostility between them and the Borġ in-Nadur people with whom they coincided.

The Mythology of the Later Bronze Age

Greek and Roman writers have a lot to answer for! Homer's *Odyssey* is set, it is said, between 1250 and 1100 BC, and there is archaeological evidence of Troy around which the Trojan War swirled. Whether or not there was such a person as Odysseus who wandered for years thereafter on his way home to Penelope; whether or not there was a nymph called Calypso who inveigled him spend seven years with her in a cave on the island of Ogygia; whether or not that island was Gozo, and that cave on its north coast, are not of great import. The Gozitans and the Maltese accept it is so, and if you visit Gozo you will be taken there, and much will you enjoy the view (see Chapter 23 for Gozo itinerary).

Then there is Ovid and his story of Anna Perenna, apparently the younger sister of Queen Dido of Carthage. Following Aeneas's departure from Carthage and Dido's death, Anna was forced to take refuge with the rich and hospitable King Battus who ruled in Melite, or Malta. There she stayed for two years. According to the story, he may have been a Phoenician. But he may also have been the king of elsewhere. There has been no evidence found to support King Battus of Malta, but the story hangs around waiting for it to emerge.

Lastly there is the pervasive influence of Greek culture in the Mediterranean from the Borġ in-Nadur Phase to the coming of the Phoenicians, and a rather touching eighteenth-century article by the Reverend John Swinton, 'Some Observations Upon an Inedited Greek Coin of Philistis, Queen of Syracuse, Malta, and Gozo, Who Has Been Passed Over in Silence by All the Ancient Writers' (1770). John Swinton describes a coin owned for several years by a Fellow of Balliol College, Oxford: 'It exhibits on one side the same veiled head of a woman that occurs on a coin of Gozo, by me heretofore described'. It resembles other coins of Philistis,

> and this princess was Queen of Malta and Gozo when those islands were under the domination of the Greeks, and occupied by them and the Phoenicians ... . Though the time when she swayed the sceptre there cannot, for want of sufficient light from ancient history, with any precision, be so easily ascertained.

There is evidence for Hellenistic influence in Malta during this in-between period but not for Hellenistic rule, though there were Greek colonies in the central and western Mediterranean, particularly the east of Sicily and southern Italy. The Greeks and the Phoenicians vied with each other throughout the region. Perhaps, therefore, Philistis was, as the title of the paper suggests, Queen of Syracuse in Sicily. The connection with Malta and Gozo is unclear but, whatever it was, Philistis will lead the women of those islands nicely into that period when the trading Phoenicians found the islands increasingly interesting.

2 – Women from the Wider Mediterranean 800 BC–AD 1091

The Phoenicians (800 BC–480 BC)

From their base in today's Lebanon, from towns such as Tyre, the Phoenicians pushed their trading interests increasingly westwards from at least the ninth century BC. They traded in luxury goods: glassware, metals, papyrus, spices and purple dye. The significance of their presence in Malta is that they were literate, with a written language based on an alphabet. They mark the beginning of history.

The Phoenicians are notable for their practice of open sea navigation, so it is not surprising that adventurous merchants based in the east, moving westwards, found Malta conveniently and strategically placed in the Mediterranean, and with safe harbours such as that close to Borġ in-Nadur and Tas-Silġ where they could beach their oared galleys (quinqueremes) (see Chapter 21 itinerary). Indeed, they called Malta *Malet*, meaning shelter or haven; (though it should be added that Malta may have come from the Greek *melite*, or the Latin *melita*, meaning honey).

At Tas-Silġ, there are Phoenician remains not only in the layer above those of the Borġ in-Nadur Phase, but also in some cases pottery styles seem to be intermingled. The only structure from the Phoenician mercantile phase is a sanctuary dedicated to their fertility goddess Astarte, also divine protector of mariners, incorporated into the earlier megalithic temple. Excavation was carried out there between 1963 and 1970, and resumed in 1997, by an Italian team from the University of Rome which included archaeologist and pottery specialist Antonia Ciasca (1930–2001), and continued by a University of Malta team, including Claudia Sagona (based at the University of Melbourne), between 1996 and 2005.

Because my concern is always with real people, especially women and their activities, I was delighted to come across Claudia Sagona's detailed paper 'Silo or Vat? Observations on the Ancient Textile Industry in Malta and Early Phoenician Interests in the Island' (1999). Her larger work on Malta and the Phoenicians and Carthaginians is in my bibliography, but for an introduction more geared towards the general reader, and more obtainable, you cannot do better than Anthony Bonanno's *Malta: Phoenician, Punic and Roman* (2005) with its fine illustrations by the photographer Daniel Cilia. In placing the Phoenicians – what the Greeks called them – it helps to know that they were the Bible's Canaanites – what they called themselves. Anthony Bonanno also makes it clear how complicated it is to establish facts and chronology because of later contradictory written sources, and to disentangle Phoenician artefacts found in Malta from the Greek. It is good, therefore, to have Claudia Sagona's concentration on textiles because they have been mentioned, in connection with women, several times in Malta's prehistory.

Claudia Sagona suggests that the cluster of pits at Borġ in-Nadur and its seashore, what she calls silos, mentioned in the last chapter as seemingly used for storage of grain or water by the Bronze Age people, were, in fact,

> steeping vats for the dying of fabric, as part of a large dye works based on the exploitation of the marine shells *Murex brandaris* and *Murex trunculus* that were used to produce the highly sought after and profitable commodity of purple cloth.

Members of the University of Malta team in a short article about their work at Tas-Silġ (1996) mention finding murex shells, used primarily for their purple dye, but also edible, and explain that 'the purple is produced via a yellow fluid which the murex exudes, and which when left in the sunlight turns purple.' Not only were the Phoenicians known for their extraction of this dye, but the Greek name for them comes from *phoenix*, meaning purple-red.

Only 26 of the pits survive on the foreshore at Birżebbuġa. Claudia Sagona explains that the disappearance of the others is caused by modern building activities and, of those that remain, many have been 'plugged with cement, or are currently filled with seaweed and other debris'. Bottle-shaped pits were also found at Borġ in-Nadur archaeological site itself, which is hard by the town. One pit, located at the fortification wall, 'has two channels running into its mouth'. This, too, she suggests, could have been another dye vat. As for the murex shells found at Tas-Silġ, she notes that the inmates, 'though they can be eaten, their toxic properties suggest that their presence at the sites was not for their food value'.

Claudia Sagona explores other possible sites for textile dyeing, such as that at Mtarfa Ridge near today's Mdina and Rabat. She explains the ten-day process of extraction of the purple from the murex shell, and notes that the heating of the murex pulp 'may account for the discolouration of the rock from the natural yellow to red, around the mouth of the interior walls of some of the vats at St George's Bay [Birżebbuġa]'. And she notes, too, the work of another scholar:

> Barber summarizes the equipment and installations used in the process of producing dyes and colouring fabrics, vats, tanks, channels, loom weights, containers of ashy material and pierced stones have been found at various dye works.

Ash is one of the aids to absorption and fixing of dye. Other dyes are discussed, particularly their sources in the Maltese archipelago. Red ochre, probably imported, was used early on, but Malta Fungus (*cynomorium coccineum*), producing a red dye, is also found in a few rocky places there. It was later also highly valued as a medical plant – and may have been then. And Tyrian purple can be obtained from the *orchilla* weed. (This is presumed to be the lichen 'Archil' or *orseille de mer*.)

The collection of plants for the production of dye leads me to the question of women and their part in the Maltese textile industry. And, are we talking about the local women from Borġ in-Nadur, for example? Writing of this earlier, probably mercantile, phase, Anthony Bonanno asks, in *Malta: An Archaeological Paradise*, 'Did they establish a small emporium on the islands with only a few Phoenician families looking after the needs of the calling Phoenician ships, a sort of shipping agency?'

Looking back to earlier, Neolithic, times, I have itemised the possible tasks that women undertook, all of which seemed feasible and for which there was some evidence. Then there was the Bronze Age, when women's tasks may have been curtailed, their status diminished. But they still probably cultivated and collected plants for food and medicinal purposes, and spun, wove and potted. There is evidence from Phoenician times, as Thomas Ashby writes in 1915 of the excavation at Għar Dalam, 'of a Punic wheel-made amphora'. How early in Phoenician times did women's hand-made pots begin to be replaced by wheel-made ones, and who used the wheel?

Surely there would have been many parts of the production of textiles that by then seems to have become big business in Malta that belonged to women. It is not clear if the fibres that were dyed came from Malta, or if they were part of the trade of the Phoenicians. But women would surely have been involved in the production of the dye from the murex shells, in the spinning of the fibre and making the skeins to be dyed in the vats, in the weaving of cloth.

The Phoenicians appear to have used Malta as a base, a trading post, from about 800 BC until about 480 BC. The politics of the Mediterranean – Phoenician, Hellenistic, Egyptian – then found their centre of activity removed from Lebanon to Carthage on the North African coast, in today's Tunisia. Carthage is said to have been founded under the leadership of Queen Elissa, better known as Dido. By the time of the Maltese connection, the Carthaginians had established settlements throughout the Mediterranean, and now it was the turn of Malta to be colonised. This period in Malta, until the second Punic War against the Romans (218–201 BC), which the Romans won, is therefore deemed Carthaginian, or Punic.

The Carthaginians (480 BC–218 BC)

It is not always easy to differentiate between the trading Phoenicians and the colonial Carthaginians who are to all intents and purposes the same people some centuries on, but arriving from a different place, with a permanent, rather than a transitory, inclination. Gradually, or suddenly, Malta became determinedly Punic, a term given to the Phoenicians from Carthage by the Romans (from the Latin *puniceus* – purple). Increasingly, Malta was to be caught up in the international rivalries of the Mediterranean – a world full of hostilities never benefiting women and their children. And who would the women have been? Were they mainly colonised Borġ in-Nadur Phase inhabitants, or had there been an influx of colonising Carthaginians? And what was the relationship between them? At the same time, was the introduction of pottery made on a wheel doing women out of one of their creative tasks? I can find no evidence to provide answers.

During this Punic period, the temple at Tas-Silġ, devoted to the Goddess Astarte, was further developed, evidence for which is provided by the hundreds of inscriptions there of her name found on pottery, mostly offertory bowls, but also cooking pots, dated in the 1960s by Maria Giulia Amadasi Guzzo to the second century BC. Pottery excavated in the 1990s inscribed with Astarte's name is given an earlier date. Interpreting inscriptions and other remains is an evolving process.

On a promontory on the west coast of Gozo – at the end of today's road from Santa Lucija or Kerċem – was the sanctuary of Ras il-Wardija; it may well have been devoted to the Punic goddess Tanit, the chief goddess of Carthage. There is some argument over whether or not the graffito cut out and stolen from the sanctuary in 1988, and found again 20 years later, is the symbol of Tanit, or a later Christian one. To my untutored eye, reproductions of the image on the recovered masonry (now in the Gozo Archaeological Museum in Victoria, see Chapter 23 itinerary) and the symbol for Tanit from Carthage look the same. Tanit was certainly worshipped in Malta in Punic times. And the Cathedral museum at Mdina holds a gold and a bronze coin with her head (or is it that of Persephone?) on one side. (Carthaginian coins are the first known to be introduced into Malta.)

Bizarrely, Tanit is said to have been a heavenly goddess of war, a mother goddess (though unmarried and virginal), a nurse and a symbol of fertility. And, equally bizarrely, an Italian scholar (P. Mingazzini, 1976) has suggested that Ras il-Wardija was a centre for sacred prostitution; I have only seen reference to the article so cannot provide the supporting evidence. Whoever its goddess, whatever its function, Ras il-Wadija is in a spectacular position which, if you cannot get there, can be appreciated by watching an amateur, but atmospheric and comprehensive, video on YouTube.

Punic burials in Malta were in rock tombs, and several have been discovered near Rabat. In one was found an Egyptian-style bronze pendant with a cavity containing a minute piece of papyrus. On it was incised a prayer, superimposed on the figure of the Egyptian goddess Isis, soliciting protection from evil. Egyptian influence, indeed, predominates among the artefacts found from this period.

At some time during Anetto Antonio Caruana's 1890 exploration of the 35 tombs at Ghajn Klieb in the same area, he was accompanied by the wife of General Sir Henry Smyth, governor of Malta between 1890 and 1893. This was the early days of archaeology in Malta; it was not the usual province of governor's wives, so why was **Helen Smyth** (née Greaves, 1845–1912, m. 1874) with Caruana? Roger Ellul-Micallef's *Zammit of Malta* (2013) reveals that the Smyths were friends of the Egyptologist William Flinders Petrie; indeed, Henry Smyth's brother had inspired Petrie's first visit to Egypt.

I like to think that Lady Smyth was there when Caruana discovered a set of seventh-century hollow gold beads, probably part of a necklace, fragments of gold foil, a plain gold ring and a silver bracelet covered with gold foil. George A Said-Zammit in 'The Phoenician and Punic Necropoleis of Rabat, Malta' (2001) concludes that in the Punic period this was 'apparently the most inhabited region of the Maltese Islands'.

In his paper 'Women and Society in Prehistoric and Ancient Gozo', Anthony Bonanno regrets that the sex of the skeletons found in rock tombs in Gozo has never been identified, so that it is not known if the jewellery found with them was worn by women, or men, or both. As he suggests, if it had been it 'would have enabled us, possibly, to extract some inferences on the status of women among the inhabitants of the island in this period, and on their customs'. The Egyptian amulets reputedly from tombs near Xewkija are 'usually found in women's and children's tombs, and in votive deposits in temples of goddesses'. Among the amulets some are inscribed 'Bastet, the Mistress of Bubastis'. Bastet was a warrior goddess from the Nile area whose cult town was known in Greek as Boubastis.

It is interesting to note the number of goddesses from this period of whom worship is accepted, whereas there is argument concerning goddesses in Neolithic times. That is because of the inscriptions found both in Malta and elsewhere connected with the Carthaginians. There were, of course, also male gods whom I have omitted to mention, and there is no suggestion that the worship of goddesses went hand in hand with the elevated status of women, however high the status of goddesses such as Astarte.

Probably also under the Carthaginians, cultivation of olives and the production of olive oil were introduced on the lands of country villas, the remains of one of which have been found at San Pawl Milqi, on the north-east coast, near St Paul's Bay. In Crete, even today, women take part in the beating of olive trees and collection of the fruit that falls – but I have been unable to establish if the women of Malta were similarly involved. Certainly they would have used the oil in the preparation of food. Vineyards also became a feature, and it is hard to imagine that women would not be involved in cultivation of the vines. Would there not also be a difference in class: women inhabitants of the villa, women workers in the olive groves and vineyards? There are tombs with Punic inscriptions close to the San Pawl Milqi villa which, according to Antonia Ciasca, suggest a private cemetery.

An inscribed shard found in a country house near Żejtun may introduce the composite goddess Anat-Astarte; its significance is domestic, rather than sacred. Heads on early coins also suggest the merging of Astarte with the Egyptian goddess Isis. Astarte is also merged with the Roman Juno and the Greek Hera.

That the Carthaginians in Malta had to have one eye on defence is suggested by the remains of a small square Punic structure in a private garden at Żurrieq. And there are some round towers in the countryside which may have formed part of a defence system, together with a garrison of some 2,000 men. This is hardly surprising, as the Romans were coming.

The Romans (218 BC–AD 395)

The rivalry in the Mediterranean had introduced a new player. Rome had extended its control over the whole of the Italian peninsula. In 264 BC it turned its attention to taking Sicily from the Carthaginians. This led to the First Punic War (264–241 BC). Punic Malta was temporarily occupied, plundered and devastated, some time in 257 or 256 BC. Malta remained Carthaginian, however, until the Second Punic War (218–201 BC) when, apparently without a struggle, the islands fell to Rome and were incorporated into the Roman province of Sicily, but Carthaginian culture and language continued their hold for years to come, suggesting that Punic inhabitants also remained, and do not seem to have been regarded as conquered people. (The Second Punic War – between Carthage and Rome – was fought elsewhere than Malta.)

Malta was to be Roman for nearly seven centuries. In 27 BC Rome itself changed from republican to imperial. There is little in Latin literature of Malta's history, or the social changes that took place, so that much relies on interpretation of archaeological finds.

The villas that appeared in Punic times continued to flourish, some possibly still lived in by Carthaginians, some by Romans. That at San Pawl Milqi was typical and not only continued to produce olive oil, but on a grand scale. The residential part suggests sumptuousness, and the industrial part reveals evidence of extraction and large vats. These estates also produced grain, grapes, fruit and vegetables. The site is closed except for one annual open day, usually in February. As at Tas-Silġ, there is an early-modern Christian church hard by the archaeological site. Nearby was a Roman bath complex of which two sets of rooms can be identified, one probably for women, the other for men; each had a *tepidarium* and *caldarium*.

A two-storey villa excavated in 1915 near Borġ in-Nadur by Thomas Ashby is of interest because he notes in his paper 'Roman Malta' (1915) that 'Mrs A.W. van Buren (Miss E.M. Douglas), a student of the British School [at Rome] was present during the whole of the excavation, and undertook the sorting and description of the pottery.' He also says that she helped fund the excavation.

London-born **Elizabeth Douglas** (1881–1961) had studied art history and archaeology and went to Rome to research. There, she met and married Albert van Buren of the American School of Classical Studies. They stayed based in Rome as archaeologists and, indeed, they both died there. She met Ashby at the British School of which he was the head. He had already excavated in Malta in most years between 1905 and 1911. His deputy at the school, **Eugenie Strong** (1860–1943), helped him with the Malta photographs. Elizabeth Douglas van Buren is the earliest woman archaeologist in Malta that I have found.

The villa site had been used even before the Carthaginians and Romans. An earlier bell-shaped cistern was incorporated into the later house; in it were found the bones of goats and pigs, as well as a perfect Roman amphora. A larger and later cistern with channels leading to the house was excavated further away. Parts of the building were decorated with painted plaster and coloured marble, all of which suggests a comfortable lifestyle. Ashby does not give this villa a name, only a location, but I understand it is the one known as Ta' Kaccatura. It is not open to the public but you can visit it rather satisfactorily on YouTube.

The images on YouTube are of the archaeological remains but, in Anthony Bonanno's *Malta: Phoenician, Punic and Roman*, there is a watercolour reconstruction of a Roman villa in Ramla Bay, Gozo, that really nudges the imagination about how rich people lived. Excavated in 1910/11, actually on the beach, the villa of 19 rooms, including some six baths, and mosaic floors and mural decorations, was covered up to preserve it.

Did the inhabitants of Ta' Kaccatura worship at nearby Tas-Silġ? The dedication of the temple there changed from that to the Phoenician and Carthaginian goddess Astarte to Rome's supreme female deity, Juno, the wife of Jupiter, Queen of the Heavens. She protected everything to do with women, from birth to death. On their birthday, women offered sacrifices to Juno Natalis. She was concerned with the ability of women to bear children, so devoted her attention to them in all that followed from menstruation to marriage. On Gozo (Roman *Gaulos*), the remains of another temple dedicated to Juno were unearthed during the laying of the foundation stones of the Cathedral (see Chapter 23 itinerary).

The worship of Juno at Tas-Silġ has a connection with Malta coming under the jurisdiction of the governor of the Roman province of Sicily. Between 73 BC and 70 BC the governor was the Roman Caius Verres. He was not only generally corrupt – he is said to have obtained the governorship through bribes – but, according to the charges levelled at him by the Roman advocate, orator and politician Marcus Tullius Cicero when he prosecuted him before the Senate, he was particularly so in respect of Malta.

Verres had raided and stolen treasures from the temple of Juno, which some writers assume was that at Tas-Silġ, others near today's Fort S Angelo, Valletta (see Chapter 17 itinerary). He also turned the city of Melita into a textile factory to produce women's clothing for his own purposes. (Melita is the Latin name of both the island and the city.) A relevant part of Cicero's *Verrines* reads,

The island of Melita, gentlemen, is separated from Sicily by a rather wide and dangerous stretch of sea. In it there is a town, also called Melita, which Verres never visited, but which none the less he turned for three years into a factory for the weaving of women's dresses. On a headland not far from the town stands an ancient temple of Juno which has ever been held in such reverence that its sanctity has not once been violated not only in the old days of the Punic Wars, the naval operations of which took place in and around this region, but even by the pirate hordes of our own days. … The representatives of the people of Melita state officially that the temple of Juno has been robbed, that Verres has left nothing in that most holy sanctuary.

Another important Roman goddess whose worship flourished in Malta was Proserpina (or Proserpine). She was the daughter of Ceres (Demeter), goddess of agriculture and crops, and Jupiter. In 1613, at Mtarfa where the Phoenician silos have already been mentioned, engraved marble was found crediting the site to the Temple of Proserpine.

But how quickly, in any numbers, did Roman women who would have worshipped these goddesses come to Malta? Although it appears to have had its own senate and people's assembly – according to an inscription found in Rome in the sixteenth century – suggesting that Rome left the islands substantially alone, a flourishing economy must have encouraged Roman families to settle there. The agricultural villas suggest that. Further evidence comes from the Roman town house, known today as the Roman *Domus*, excavated in Rabat, alongside the Roman city Melita (Mdina), though the extent of the city itself has not left enough evidence to determine. Several fine mosaics found remain in situ, including one of a satyr being attacked by two women or nymphs, one holding his hair, the other his beard and brandishing shears. The mosaics and other finds indicate that the house belonged to a rich dignitary. It is said to have been constructed between the first half of the first century BC to the middle of the first century AD (see Chapter 20 itinerary).

Among the finds here and in other nearby houses were ivory or bone bobbins and needles, together with loom weights, proof of the intensive weaving in Melita, perhaps connected with the Verres project. A woman's head on display in the *Domus* is said to be that of the Emperor Claudius's mother, known as **Antonia the Younger** (36 BC–AD 37). There is also the headless statue of a woman. If the two pieces belong together, they may be (**Claudia**) **Antonia** (*c.* AD 30–66), his daughter by his second wife. Appropriately, also unearthed in the *Domus*, were two anthropomorphic bone hairpins, and others more plain, commonly used to hold the elaborate hairstyles of Roman women in place. Two torsos of Amazons, carved in Malta stone, may have been domestic or garden ornaments. One was found in the *Domus* itself, the other nearby. Their significance does not seem to have been explored.

Statues and inscriptions connected with imperial Roman women were not uncommon. In Gozo, indeed, an inscription shows there to have been the cult of **Julia Augusta**, depicting her as the goddess Ceres, with her own priestess, **Lutatia**. The Empress is better known to modern readers as Livia (58 BC–AD 29), wife of Augustus, mother of Tiberius and Nero – a larger than life figure in accessible depictions of Roman history. Livia Drusilla was married and pregnant in 39 BC when Octavian (the Emperor Augustus) divorced his first wife (the day she gave birth to a daughter), forced (or persuaded) Livia's husband to divorce her, and married her almost immediately. Thereafter Livia became a respectable empress, a role model for Roman households. She even handled her own finances and had her own circle of protégés for public office at a time of a firmly patriarchal Roman society.

Evidence from the literature of the period confirms the generally low status of women; and, indeed, under Roman law, while women counted as citizens, they were barred from all civil and public duties. However, in *Women in Antiquity* (1956), Charles Seltman notes that election posters painted on the walls of Pompeian houses are evidence that women proposed and supported candidates for municipal elections at Pompeii. And, certainly, the prohibition on participation could be overcome by the status and personality of a particular woman.

Livia's high status and influence are not questioned and, unsavoury rumour aside, she impeccably filled the roles in her life of consort, mother, widow and dowager. When Augustus died in AD 14, his will allowed her to retain her imperial status in the name Julia Augusta, under her son by her first husband as the Emperor Tiberius. Julia Augusta died in AD 29 (aged 85) and was deified in AD 42 (at the instigation of the Emperor Claudius). Since the cult to her on Gozo does not call her *diva*, it is assumed, by Joseph Busuttil's 'The Ceres Inscription' (1972), that Lutatia's offering to her is dated some time between her becoming Julia Augusta in AD 14, and her death. In 1787, the statue stood in a niche outside the gate of the Gozo citadel though, as with Melita (Mdina), the extent of the Roman city of Gaulos is unclear.

Julia Augusta was venerated elsewhere in the Roman empire, and it may be that a similar, though less obvious, inscription found by the Italian archaeologists on Malta itself, though Busuttil does not say where, shows that Livia (not as Julia Augusta) was also venerated there.

As for Lutatia as priestess, no other named, or unnamed, priestess has been found on Malta, though on the island of Samos, Livia had a temple and a priestess. Priestesses in the Roman Empire were not commonplace, and they tended not only to come from powerful families, but also to exercise both influence and power. Indeed, Eumachia, public priestess of Venus in Pompeii during the middle of the first century, wealthy in her own right, and achieving high social status through marriage, is viewed as a model for the increasing involvement of women in politics, using the power of a public priestess for social mobility. It is against that background that the inscription placed beneath the headless statue of Julia Augusta in the Gozo Archaeological Museum should be viewed (see Chapter 23 itinerary). Spelling out Lutatia's father, husband, his father and tribe, it reads:

To Ceres Julia Augusta (wife) of the Divine Augustus, mother of Tiberius Caesar Augustus, Lutatia, daughter of Caius (and) priestess of Augusta, (wife) of the *imperator perpetua*, wife of Marcus Livius Optatus, son of Marcus, of the Quirine Tribe (and) Flamen of Gaulos; to Julia, (wife) of Augustus, *imperator perpetuus*, has consecrated together with her five children at her own expense.

The inscription was not part of the everyday duties of tending the cult, but is more likely to have been on the specific occasion of a statue or altar, and it would have been approved of by the Gozitan community.

Identifying Julia Augusta with Ceres suggests that Gozo then was primarily agricultural. Lutatia's husband, Optatus, was a *flamen*, a priest, responsible for the worship of Augustus himself on the island which suggests either that Romans had settled there, or that it was a *municipium*, a self-governing community. It was not unusual for a wife and husband to share the title of priestess and priest of the imperial cult, but the fact that Optatus, though high-powered in his own right, is mentioned here as an adjunct to his wife could be interpreted as meaning that a particular woman, not just a member of the imperial family, could make her mark, even in Gozo. Lutatia had paid for the monument herself, so that she, as well as Julia Augusta, is honoured by it and the inscription. While this inscription is in Latin (and Busuttil also gives the Latin), an inscription concerning Augustus on Malta was in Greek.

Julia Augusta is not the only Roman empress to be commemorated on Gozo. A later inscription, unfortunately now missing, is dedicated to **Julia Domna** (AD 170–217); she too was deified after her death. It is said that the *municipium* of Gozo erected a monument, possibly a statue, in her honour in AD 195, but only the inscription remained. I have a theory about why she might have been honoured.

Julia Domna was born in Syria, probably of Arab descent, in today's Homs, daughter of a high-priest. Her family was rich and promoted to Roman senatorial aristocracy. Before her marriage, she inherited the estate of her paternal great-uncle who had been a leading centurion. In the late 180s, she became the second wife of the future Emperor Lucius Septimius Severus, considered to have been of Punic origin, and mother of two emperors. When her husband became emperor in AD 193, he had to contend with a civil war and Julia, against all Roman tradition, accompanied him on his campaigns in the east. Coins were minted with her portrait and the title *mater castrorum* (mother of the military camp), and that is how she is referred to on the inscription found on Gozo. Is it too fanciful to suggest that the campaigns in the east took the imperial party via Gozo?

Julia Domna was well read and interested in philosophy; indeed, she protected philosophers and helped the discipline to flourish in Rome where it was not always approved of. She also had her own political opinions and, like Livia, exercised power behind the Roman imperial throne. Her husband not only loved but admired her.

Severus died in York in 211, and it is probably from their time in Britain that another inscription dates. It was found on the line of the Roman wall at the camp of Magna (Caervoran) and an 1898 scholar, Thomas Hodgkin, convincingly suggests that the Syrian Goddess hymned is Julia Domna. Following her husband's death, Julia had to mediate between their two warring sons who were supposed to rule as joint emperor. One of them murdered the other and, trying to put that aside, Julia went on a campaign with the survivor who was assassinated during the course of it. She is said to have committed suicide, but there is also the suggestion that she died of breast cancer.

3.   Julia Domna, from the internet

In following the thread of two Roman empresses, I have jumped ahead chronologically almost a couple of centuries. In AD 60, between Julia Augusta and Julia Domna, an event is said to have occurred which was to leave a much more lasting mark on the islands, and it is only tangentially connected with women. That is, the apparent shipwreck in what is now called St Paul's Bay of the Apostle Paul and his comrade the Syrian physician Luke, who recorded the event in the Acts of the Apostles, on their way to be tried in Rome. The main reason for mentioning what is assumed to have taken place on that shore of Malta – though there are those who question it – is that Paul's name (often the Maltese Pawl) is attached to so many Maltese places, and the islands were not only to become Christian, but very much remain so to this day. However, the suggestion that Christianity was implanted by Paul himself is now generally accepted as an earlier, probably ideological, assumption. But there are a couple of other factors connected with his visit.

Paul and his companions were rescued in St Paul's Bay by local people – barbarians, they were described as, that is, people not speaking Latin or Greek – and then taken care of for three days by Publius, often said to be the Roman governor of Malta. But Richard Bauckham, in 'The Estate of Publius (Acts 28:7)' (2006) disputes that interpretation of 'first man of the island' (Bauckham's use or, as the King James Bible has it, 'chief man'). Instead, he writes, 'Probably ... Publius belonged to the indigenous (Punic) population of Malta,' and was, therefore, a leader within his society, probably granted

Roman citizenship as a reward for services in his political office. (It was not until AD 212 that full Roman citizenship was extended to all free-born inhabitants of the Roman empire, in Malta's case still under the jurisdiction of the provincial governor based in Sicily). Anthony Bonanno explains that this Publius was unlikely to be the St Publius to whom many Christian churches in Malta were later dedicated as one of the patron saints of Malta.

Richard Bauckham explores the possibilities of the exact location of the villa where Publius sheltered Paul and Luke; one of them being San Pawl Milqi, and he uses another scholar's description of the inhabitants' lifestyle there:

> The family which at first occupied the house, apparently had Punic char-
> acteristics, as indicated by utensils and some writing and incisions. In fact,
> the family's manner of living and acting seems to have been influenced by
> African habits. This conforms with other evidence that among the natives,
> Punic traditions, customs, etc., prevailed until the II century.

There is one problem: that villa burnt down, probably before Paul arrived. (It was later rebuilt.) But there were other villas in the area, one of them with the remains of an apiary; Malta was famous for its honey, which was a major export. Wherever Publius lived, who lived with him? We know that his father was with him at the time, suffering from a fever, probably dysentery, because Paul is said to have healed him, though surely it is more likely to have been the physician Luke. (The main hospital in Valletta is, to this day, called St Luke's.) So was Publius's mother there too? And his wife? History does not relate – but it should!

One other unanswered question remains concerning the women of Publius's household: at a time when slaves were common in the Roman Empire, were they in Malta? Would Publius's mother and wife have been waited on by female slaves? No evidence has been found, no slave quarters.

In relation to Paul and Luke's time in Malta, you might be intrigued to read *According to Luke* (2012), a novel, a sophisticated thriller, by Malta-born-and-raised, Australian Rosanne Dingli. To divulge the nub of the plot – which scampers from Venice, to Malta, to Damascus – would be to inflict a spoiler. But it is relevant to my theme.

Those who visit St Paul's Catacombs in Rabat, where Paul is said to have stayed for three months in a grotto, healing the sick and, no doubt, preaching, should not ignore the St Agatha Catacombs, Church and Museum which feature in the Chapter 20 itinerary. Indeed, for our purposes, they must be given priority.

Agatha (*c.*234–*c.*253) was born in Catania, Sicily into a rich and noble family. Other details of her life are arguable but the following is the gist. By the age of 15, she had already dedicated herself to God when she took the fancy of the low-born Roman prefect Quintanus. She rejected his advances and he then started to persecute her for her Christian faith, Christianity then being a new sect. She and some friends fled to Malta in AD 249 and took refuge there. The length of her stay is uncertain but she spent her time in a rock-hewn crypt in Rabat, praying and teaching the Christian faith to the local children. Returning to Sicily, she was arrested and brought before Quintanus who ordered her imprisonment and torture – a torture that included having one, or both, of her breasts cut off. Thus, more recently, she has become venerated as the patron saint of breast cancer patients. (She was already that for wet nurses, fire, earthquakes, and the eruptions of Mount Etna.) She probably died in prison or under torture in AD 253. She is buried at the Badia di Sant'Agata, Catania. She will appear again in 1551, after which she became the second patron saint of Malta. (She was also the patron saint of several other places.) As Agatha, too, spoke of Christ during her time in Malta, it is just as likely that the seeds of Christianity were sown by her as by the Apostle Paul.

Early Christianity, Judaism and Byzantine Malta

The end of the Roman Empire in Malta can be dated to about AD 395, but the islands did not become part of the Byzantine empire until AD 535. The last Roman emperor was deposed in 476 by the Germanic Goths but, before that, the empire had been split into East and West and, while the western empire had declined, the eastern one prospered, ruled by the Emperor Constantine from what became Constantinople and the heart of the Byzantine Empire in 328.

In 313, Constantine had legalised Christianity throughout the Roman empire. Whatever its earlier status, Christianity must have become widespread in Malta in the fourth century, thus the catacombs of St Paul and St Agatha, with their evidence of Christian and Jewish burials, had expanded from the earlier grottos of Paul (AD 60) and Agatha (AD 251), and, in 400, a Christian church was built on top of the temple of Juno/Hera at Tas-Silġ. The whole archaeological site, though not open to the public as I write, is predicted to become so, and features in the Chapter 21 itinerary.

What was the position of women at that time? There is no evidence regarding Christian women, but there is regarding Jewish, and that evidence comes from the St Agatha Catacomb. Thanks to the discoveries by Antonio Ferrua, and Ross S Kraemer's article 'A New Inscription from Malta and the Question of Women Elders in the Diaspora Jewish Communities' (1985), we know about **Eulogia** who lived in Malta in the fourth or fifth century. What is more, although Eulogia was married, she was an elder, an official, of the synagogue in her own right. Ross Kraemer goes through all the arguments for and against this interpretation of the inscription, incised with a stylus in Greek and filled in with red, found in the catacomb, and presents a convincing case in favour. She writes in part, drawing on her wide research on women and the religions of the Greco-Roman Mediterranean:

> The more plausible explanation for Eulogia's title is that it reflects some role which she herself played in the synagogue. That her husband was

himself a *gerousiarch* need not be viewed as evidence that her title of *presbytera* reflected only her position as his wife. Rather we suggest that it reflects a marriage in which both husband and wife were active in the synagogue on Malta. ... It is not inconceivable that Eulogia achieved her role as *presbytera* because her husband was a powerful figure in the synagogue. But to say that a woman gained a position of governance and authority in antiquity by virtue of her family position is in no way to negate the fact that she attained that position. Men in antiquity attained positions of power and influence by virtue of their family connections all the time; ...

Eulogia was not the only Jewish woman buried in this hypogeum of mixed faiths: the name of **Dionisia** (also called Irene – peace) is also inscribed there, together with a seven-branched menorah, but their presence is the earliest evidence of a Hellenised Jewish colony in Malta. In his article 'The Jewish Catacombs of Roman Melite' (2011), Mario Buhagiar calculates that the population of Malta at that time was probably no more than 10,000, of which at least 300, according to the burials, was Jewish. He had earlier, in 2007, suggested that Christianity in Malta arrived from Sicily post-Constantine and went on to speculate that it 'made its first converts from the Jewish community of Melite and that the location of the hypogea is a possible indication of a Jewish community gradually adopting Christianity'. But in 2011 he added, 'The *gerousiarch* inscription points, on the other hand, to a community committed to Judaic orthodoxy. The phenomenon remains, as a result, the most intriguing feature of the Jewish hypogea of Roman Melite.' The frescoes of St Agatha – thirteen of them – St Lucy and St Barbara date from medieval times.

During the period that followed the Christianisation of Malta, and before the islands became part of the Byzantine empire, the Germanic Vandals had a powerful navy in the Mediterranean; they sacked Rome in 455. It is assumed that they would have used Malta, with its strategic position, particularly as they invaded nearby Sicily; but there is no archaeological evidence of their stay. The Ostrogoths, too, may have spent time in Malta. They seem to have been uncertain times, however, and the women of the islands must have lived in constant fear.

Byzantium under the Emperor Justinian defeated the Vandals in 533–34, the naval force 'touching' Malta on its way to North Africa; and it reasserted control over Italy and Spain. Malta was part of the Byzantine empire by 535, and had a Christian Bishop of Malta in 592. But were the islands any more than a Byzantine naval base? Were they even that? There is little evidence except some pottery and fine table ware imported from various parts of the Mediterranean. It may well have been a time of relative peace but, again, the lives of women can only be imagined until more archaeological work is undertaken.

In the second half of the seventh century, Muslim raiders increasingly operated in the Mediterranean, though there is no record of attacks on Malta before the ninth century. The islands fell to the Arabs in 871, probably from North Africa, though they had already taken Sicily so, presumably, if they had wished to attack and take Malta before then, they could have done so.

Malta under Arab Rule (870–1090)

Malta under Arab rule is more open to discussion than any other period of the islands' history. Much interpretation is seen through the prism of later struggles between Christian Malta under the Knights of St John and the Muslim Ottoman Empire. In 'The Arabs in Malta' (1986), Godfrey Wettinger, perhaps the foremost scholar on the subject in Malta, uses the word 'fraught' in relation to the psychology. Was there a time when Malta was virtually deserted? Wettinger writes,

> Much disruption of normal life must have occurred, but it is impossible to judge its extent. Undoubtedly, Maltese Christians must have joined the multitude of refugees fleeing from Sicily before the Arab advance to safer places like Calabria on the mainland [of Italy] …
> … In Malta and Gozo, no archaeological evidence of the practice of Christianity has been found for centuries after the Muslim invasion – no churches, paintings or statues belong to this period, and there are no known Christian graves either.

One of the problems about recreating this period is the lack of Arabic archaeological remains; there is, for example, no evidence of mosques. Might they have been destroyed later? There may have been a precedent: as Godfrey Wettinger suggests, '… archaeological sites in Malta at San Pawl Milqi and at Tas-Silġ have both shown signs of destruction at levels corresponding to the arrival of the Arabs'. But in the Norman architecture that was to follow there are numerous Islamic touches, and evidence of Moorish style. There are also numerous Arabic names for places and topological features, and the Maltese language itself owes more to Arabic than to any of the other languages that have influenced it.

Perhaps for a hundred or so years Malta was deserted or sparsely populated. In a 2011 interview with the novelist and historian Adel S Bishtawi, Godfrey Wettinger speculated 'that Muslims alone came for brief visits for a long period: small groups, families perhaps, people catching fish or whatever and going away again'. Eventually, in about 1050, the islands had Arabic settlements; the city of Melita/Melite became Mdina (the Fortress). Godfrey Wettinger notes, from an Arabic source, that in the Muslim year 440 (AD 1048–49) 'Malta was attacked by the Byzantines, who demanded the women and possessions of the inhabitants.' The story goes that the Arabs made a pact with the Maltese slaves, who outnumbered them, that if they united against the Byzantines, the slaves would gain their freedom. These slaves are sometimes interpreted as Christian but, as Wettinger argues, they would be unlikely to side with their Muslim masters against their Christian deliverers.

He goes on to suggest that the whole population, whatever their origin, was by then Muslim. When the Normans under Count Roger I of Sicily invaded, they made no mention of Christian Maltese inhabitants; what there were, though, were Christian captives, taken by corsairs. Indeed, Charles Dalli, in 'Satellite, Sentinel, Stepping Stone: Medieval Malta in Sicily's Orbit' (2008), notes that when Roger offered the freed captives a home in Sicily, they declined, 'preferring instead to take his concession of a free passage to their various homelands'. How many of these freed captives were women is not noted.

What was life like for Arab women threatened by Byzantine attack? They may or may not have been veiled. Veiled women preceded Islam, and under Islam country women were not necessarily veiled. While women in some parts of the newly Islamic world were being prescribed restricted lives, in other parts this was less so. The diet of the women would have differed from previously on Malta. Although so many Maltese place names have their origin in the Arabic for olive, the growing of olive trees and production of olive oil apparently died out. Citrus fruit were introduced, and the delicacies of sorbet and candied peel; bees were kept and honey collected. Wine was prohibited. Sugar cane and cotton were grown. Were country women involved in their cultivation? Were the town women sedentary and did they eat too many sweet things? Were they waited upon by enslaved Christian women?

What does seem clear is that for quite some time after the Normans took Malta from the Arabs, Muslim inhabitants remained and went about their daily lives openly; later Muslim graves have been found; indeed, it was not until Roger II reconquered Malta in 1127 that there was any move to re-Christianise Malta.

One Muslim woman has left her name from the later period. In the year of the Prophet 569 (AD 1173/74) **Majmuna** (pronounced Maimuna) died on Gozo; a translation of her gravestone, engraved in Kufic Arabic, with its quotations from the Quran, reads as follows:

In the name of Allah, the most merciful and compassionate. May Allah shower his favours on the Prophet Mohammed and his followers and grant them eternal salvation.

To God belong infinity and immortality, and He has destined that what He created should perish. Of this the prophet of Allah bears witness.

Here lies the burial of Majmuna, daughter of Hassan, son of Ali al-Hudali, called Iben as-Susi. She died – may the mercy of Allah rest upon her – on Thursday, the sixteenth day of the month of Saban of the year 569, bearing testimony that there is only one God, without equal.

Behold with your own eyes: is anything on earth everlasting? Does anything ward off death or cast spells on it? Death seized me from a palace, and alas, no barriers or latches could save me. My deeds are my evidence, and they shall be counted. Only what I have abandoned behind, remains.

O you who look upon this sepulchre, know that I am already wasted inside it. Dust weights my sight and my eyelids. On this couch, in my abode of misfortune, there are only tears. But this my admonition to you in the presence of my Creator. O my brother, fill your spirit with wisdom and repentance.

The marble funerary slab, a recycling of its Roman use, is said to have been found near Xewkija, and passed through various hands thereafter. Its provenance – whether or not it was unearthed on Gozo – has been much debated, as detailed in Mario Buhagiar's 'Gozo in late Roman Byzantine and Muslim Times' (1997) and in Giovanni Bonello's 'New Light on Majmuna's Tombstone' (2000). But the Gozo Archaeological Museum is satisfied enough with its authenticity to display it in its first room. Even if it were not found on Gozo or Malta at all, it may well give an insight into the life and death of a Muslim female at that time.

Was Majmuna a girl or a woman? If a girl, or when she was a girl, perhaps the following poem in Classical Arabic was written about her by a Maltese poet in the first half of the twelfth century. It was found in Sicily in an anthology of Arabic poetry (and is quoted, and the Maltese translation into English polished, by Godfrey Wettinger):

The girl throws the ball:
Through her the hearts are gladdened,
As if he who made her had already risen to heaven,
And had examined the celestial spheres for the
secret of the zodiac and the ecliptic.

How did the practice of Islam in Malta come to an end? In his interview, Godfrey Wettinger suggests, 'The last native Muslims in Malta probably died around 1300 and had been forced to practise Christianity for the last 50 years of their lives, so from about 1249–1250 or thereabouts you had native Islam no longer being practised.'

3 – Women's Inheritance of Wealth and Position 1091–1530

During the centuries that followed Arab control of Malta, it passed from one European royal or imperial house controlling Sicily to another – from the Normans (French 1091–1194), to the Swabians (German 1194–1266), to the Angevins (French 1266–83), to the Aragonese (Spanish 1283–1412) and, finally, to the Castilians (Spanish 1412–1530). What seems like a game of pass the parcel was caused by European strife, not excluding bloodshed, or marriage and inheritance, and came to an end when the Holy Roman Emperor Charles V enabled the Knights of St John, by donation deed, to move in.

During those years of Sicilian rule of Malta what is noticeable, in the upper echelons of society, is the part played by the inheritance of wealth and position by and through women; that includes the royal women of Sicily. Marriage and legitimacy were not always the criteria for inheritance. How much influence, let alone power, the women had is not so clear as, for Malta at least, material about them is so sparse and unrevealing.

I would have liked to present a rounded story of the flesh and blood lives of the named notable women that follow; instead, in being able only to unearth odd facts and vague impressions from a variety of sometimes contradictory sources, I may only have created a superficially confusing narrative. But by trying to put myself in their place in order to raise questions, I hope I have been able to give some idea of the particular experiences of women such as Lukina, Margarita d'Aragona, Constanza Monroy and Imperia Gatto Inguanez and, taken together, their significance in Malta's history. Some of these questions may be anachronistic, asked through the twenty-first-century sensibility of a stranger. Chapter 4, 'The Legal Position of Medieval Women', may throw more general light on the activities of the women of inherited wealth and position, as well as across class.

It took from 1060 to 1090 for the Normans to wrest Sicily from the Arabs. Count Roger of Sicily established Norman rule over Malta in 1091 as additional protection from Arab raids from the south. But for years to come, many Muslim inhabitants – such as Majmuna – continued to practise their Islamic faith. An 1175 observer described Malta as 'an island inhabited by Saracens, it is under the dominion of the King of Sicily'.

In 1240, leading up to their expulsion from the islands in 1248, there were still 800 Muslim families living there. According to the same record compiled by a contemporary administrator, there were also 250 Christian and 33 Jewish families. In a detailed interpretation of these figures, Charles Dalli, in *Malta: The Medieval Millennium* (2006), sees them not as total populations, but as crown serfs paying poll tax, and the 'Christians' as converts from Islam. The 'free' population included at least the 220-strong garrison of the three castles (fortresses), 70 of whose members had wives, and presumably children, as well as 60 slaves, female and male.

Following the Muslim expulsion, as Brian Blouet suggests in *The Story of Malta* (2007), the opening up of lands took place, settlers arriving from Sicily, southern Italy and other Mediterranean places. Whenever one talks of lands and landholdings, the size of both Malta and Gozo needs to be borne in mind.

Malta was then under Frederick II of the Holy Roman Empire who had inherited it, as well as the throne of Sicily, from his mother, **Queen Constance of Sicily** (1154–1198), posthumous daughter of Roger II of Sicily. As her son was only three when he was crowned in 1198, it was Constance who ruled until her death later that year, just as Roger's mother, **Adelaide** (*c.*1075–1118), had acted during his minority as Count of Sicily; (he became King of Sicily in 1130). Although Constance's rule was so short, she did issue a diploma (charter) in 1198 to both the Christians and Saracens of Malta and Gozo stating that the islands would never be separated from the royal demesne. Unfortunately, it soon counted for little, though it would be reissued by future overlords of Sicily.

Under Roger II (1127–1154), who seems to have had to reassert Norman rule over Malta, the islands became drawn more thoroughly into Sicily's orbit, and that of Christian Europe, though Arabic continued as the language of ordinary people. From 1190 the islands became essentially a fiefdom under the sovereignty of Sicily. The various royal or imperial overlords gave or 'rented' the islands to particular notables, the feudal Counts of Malta (*Comtes de Malte*), the first of whom was created in 1194, with their surname becoming 'de Malta'.

The Counts of Malta were as various as the sovereigns and the lands they ruled. They might come from anywhere, for it depended on who was then in overall power; at one time Counts of Malta were appointed simultaneously and independently by Aragon and Anjou. The scope for the creation of unhelpful factions is obvious, particularly as the background of a count was not always salubrious.

There is little sign of ordinary women in the history of those early medieval days, though with the proliferation of villages with the word for garden in their name, women may have been involved in agriculture, tending flocks and beehives. Would they have been if the country people were mainly Muslims? How confined would Muslim women have been in that period? And when the Muslims were deported, we need to imagine what it was like for the women to be thus uprooted, to have to live elsewhere as refugees, to have to build new homes and provide new stability for their children, or to stay as 'converts' and perhaps practise their faith in secret, fearfully. At least they could still freely speak Arabic, before later generations spoke Maltese, the language evolved from it, comfortable by then with Christianity.

Because of the expulsion of the Muslims, there is something particularly unpleasant and ironic about the exiling of a population in the opposite direction. In 1223, the Christians of Celano in the Abruzzi region of Italy were exiled to Malta (and elsewhere) for taking the wrong side in a royal dispute. Frederick II laid siege and laid waste to the town; then, according to some sources, only the male population was exiled, according to others the whole. From Paul Cassar's 'Vignette' it would appear to be the latter because in the endless discussion among historians about the origins of Maltese women's most distinctive garment, the *faldetta* or *għonnella* – the mantle which later gained a stiffened headpiece, – '... when the inhabitants of that city were deported ... it is said that these exiled women started wearing a black mantle over their head as a sign of mourning and that the custom was later followed by the women of Malta'. He puts this forward in answer to 'It has been suggested that this headgear draws its origin from the oriental veil'. At least some of the exiles were allowed to return home in 1227 but others remained; one man, at least, died in prison in chains after many long years. And in 2005 a party from Celano went looking for their roots in Malta; roots would surely only exist if there had been births there.

It was not always easy for upper class women. There are at least two examples of those who suffered because of whom they married. In 1277, Angevin King Charles received the appeal of widowed **Ricca Cafor**. Her late husband, Robert Cafor (also Cafuro, de Caforio or Gayforio) was, as Charles Dalli explains, 'a high-profile serf of the royal *curia* in Malta.' Some time before 1270, he was appointed jointly to manage the royal farms in Malta. He even had to secure leopards from North Africa for the king's menagerie. By 1274, he was royal procurator (*Secreto* – royal revenue administrator), as well as joint captain at arms for the defence of the islands (*Castellan*). The word 'serf' to describe him may be misleading because Henri Bresc, in 'The "Secrezia" and the Royal Patrimony in Malta 1240–1450' (1975), suggests:

> The *secreto* of Malta normally belonged to the richest and most influential class of civic nobility which resided in Mdina and possessed interests in Malta and in Sicily ... This was already the case in the Angevin period, when the office of *procurator* or *camerarius* was held by the Maltese Robertus Caferi; he was in some way proprietor of his office and had to furnish a list of guarantors. Their names indicate his connections with the mercantile society of Southern Italy ...

When Robert died, some time before September 1275, the Crown ordered the confiscation of his considerable possessions – a confiscation carried out by two knights related through marriage to the Count of Malta, which hints rather at politics than malfeasance. Ricca and her children – **Simona, Gallura** and Catello – were incarcerated in the *Castrum Maris* (Fort of the Sea, later S Angelo), Birgu. They were still there in November 1276.

A notary public (three of whom were appointed for the first time in 1270) drew up the act of appeal, subscribed to by four citizens of Mdina, and 38 others stood bail. In November 1277 the *Castellan* (commander of the Birgu fort or all three forts) was ordered to release the family but 'all their assets remained frozen until sufficient surety was given for Robert's administration of royal finances up to his death, furthermore, the crown demanded information on dowries stipulated for Simona and Gallura by their late father'. By December it would appear that Robert's successor had been instructed to return the seized assets. Nothing is revealed about the family thereafter, though their descendants live on in Malta (the name became Gafar, then Gafa). We want to know, surely, how Donna Ricca managed during the family's captivity? It would seem – given talk of dowries – that her two daughters were at least teenagers. She must have felt constant anxiety, in a fortress garrisoned by foreign (probably Provençal) soldiery, concerning their safety from sexual molestation.

And what was the Cafor family's position when, in 1283, French Angevin rule of that part of the Mediterranean gave way militarily to Spanish Aragonese, and Malta was involved? Then, the harbour before the *Castrum Maris*, where they had so recently been imprisoned, was full of corpses as opposing fleets fought it out, and Mdina faced attack before the townspeople came out and pledged loyalty to King Peter of Aragon. Gozo, too, was attacked.

An apparently more fortunate woman, and the first to illustrate the ambiguity of inherited position in Malta, is sometimes called **Lukina** (d.1347?), sometimes Lucina Pistore, or donna Lucina de Candia Pistore, or Lucina Pistoia. She became Countess of Malta and Lady of Candia (she was descended from Enrico de Candia – 'King' of Crete, Count of Malta, as well as a corsair). What the dates 1285–1296 and 1296–1300 refer to in two sources about Lukina is unclear, but she was the only child of **Clara de Rocka** and Guglielmo de Malta, said by Charles Dalli to be Captain and Procurator and, therefore, right-hand man of his uncle the Count of Malta to whom he was also heir apparent. On Guglielmo's death in 1299 in the Gozo *castrum*, his will, drawn up on his deathbed, named Clara as his universal heir, and required that she remain at the castle for the foreseeable future. Lukina, with a substantial dowry, inherited, through her father, rights to the County of Malta which were hers between 1300 and 1320. She is said to have held on to the rights, but had no power. And other sources suggest that the title of Count was in abeyance between 1300 and 1320.

By 1308 Lukina had married the Catalan nobleman Guglielmo Raimondo Moncada, who shared her title, or took it. He had substantial interests in Tunis where he was commander of the Christian militia, and Frederick III gave Moncada the town of Augusta and other revenues in Sicily in exchange for his wife's County of Malta. Nevertheless, as Charles Dalli explains, Lukina retained her 'rights' in the Maltese islands which she passed on to her niece **Lukinella** in 1347, presumably on her death. What is not clear is why they were not inherited by either of her two sons, one of them Guglielmo Raimondo Moncada II, nor her daughter Clara, named after her mother. There are several contradictory sources for the Lukina story, and I have had to make the best of it. I have found no other mention than Dalli's of Lukinella. He tells us that Lukina's descendants 'were still maintaining these undefined rights in the early fifteenth century'.

In 1357, a Donna Sibilla founded the Church of the Annunciation at Tas-Saqqajja, Rabat, Gozo. In 'Sibilla d'Aragona and the Foundation of the Saqqajja Benifice on Gozo' (1999), Stanley Fiorini explores the identity of Sibilla, and notes the confusion caused by earlier historians who associated her with Sibilla d'Aragona, a sister of Margarita d'Aragona (whom we shall meet next), both apparently daughters of Frederick IV's natural son Guglielmo; instead, he plumps for her being **Sibilla Solmella** (Sormella), lover of Frederick III. But he suggests that the love affair pre-dated the King's marriage, that they were both young – Sibilla 15 or 16 – and that only one daughter, **Ysabella**, was born of the relationship. But Frederick's Wikipedia entry lists five named children – including Ysabella – with Sibilla, which suggests long-term relations continuing after his 1302 marriage to Eleanor of Anjou. (He certainly had affairs after his marriage.)

Stanley Fiorini decides that on Frederick's marriage, he packed his lover off to Malta, out of the way, in the care of a high-powered relative of hers, Arnald de Solimella, Frederick's man in Malta 1316–1320, whom Charles Dalli weaves neatly into his more comprehensive history of the period. Sibilla's eldest son by Frederick, Alfonso Fadrique, was to continue an illegitimate Maltese royal branch. Having served in high positions outside the islands and marrying well in Verona, he was 'compensated' for being recalled in 1330 with the Counties of Malta and Gozo. He probably held the position until his death in 1349. It was during the time of his son as Count of Malta that, in 1357, **Queen Jeanne of Naples** appointed a rival Count, as part of a bid for an Angevin revival.

We know more about **Margarita d'Aragona** (?1336–1418) than other women of the period, partly because of her husband, and her influence on his behalf, and partly because of the survival of her will which shows the extent of her wealth and her philanthropy. Her parentage is, however, somewhat mysterious. The earliest historical records show her as daughter of Guglielmo, appointed Count of Malta. But who was he? Was he Guglielmo the son of Frederick III (also known as Frederick II) and his queen, **Eleanor of Anjou** (1289–1341), or the natural son of Frederick and a Maltese woman? As we have seen, Frederick had five children, though not apparently a Guglielmo, by Sybil Sormella; and a Guglielmo d'Aragona, said to be Frederick's natural son, was appointed Count of Malta in 1377. Trying to disentangle her parentage is certainly enough to make one giddy. Suffice it to say that she was of royal blood, probably partly Maltese. John Cilia La Corte, in his online 'Margarita d'Aragona', is satisfied that she was the daughter of Guglielmo (son of Eleanor) and a Maltese woman.

Margarita had married the privateer from Messina Giacomo de Pellegrino by 1365 when he was made *Hakem* of Malta, the first of them, a title also known as *Capitano della Verga* – Captain (of Malta). To be a *hakem*, certainly later, a stranger had to be domiciled for five years and married to a Maltese woman. He was also *Castellan* of the fortresses and various other appointments. Pellegrino, married to the king's kinswoman, was riding high and for 15 years he obtained lands hand over fist and threw his weight about, with little accountability to the Crown or the Counts of the time, one of whom was a descendant of Sibilla and Frederick. Indeed, Frederick IV and his family were financially thwarted by Pellegrino.

Pellegrino pushed his luck too far, and he was banished following an uprising led by him after Frederick, at the head of a Genoese squadron, sailed to Malta and, supported by the people, put it down. The exploration of Margarita's life by Albert Griscti-Soler continues:

In 1372, Margarita d'Aragona appealed to Federico for clemency towards her husband. In his decree of November 1372, the king ignored her pleas. It was too soon after the conflict for the king to contemplate modifying his sentence on Giacomo but he ordered the Secreto to give Margarita, *consanguineam fidelem nostram* [our faithful kinswoman] an annual grant of 50 uncie in order to enable her to maintain the position expected of her rank.

In 1373, Margarita made a further plea for clemency. This time her appeal met with greater success. The king's decree issued in Messina on 11 October 1373 stated that '... following the renewed humble supplications to our Excellency by Our faithful kinswoman and friend, the noble Margarita d'Aragona, consort of Giacomo de Peregrino [*sic*], *Milite*, We graciously grant the same noble lady that the said Giacomo, her husband (having first settled his debt to the Magnifico Doge and Commune of Genoa) may, freely and without fear of reprisal, come to the noble city of Messina. ...'

Margarita also succeeded in recovering two-thirds of her husband's estates, and eventually the remaining third. In April 1375, the Crown acknowledged that Margarita and her three daughters should have two-thirds of the couple's goods and, on Pellegrino's death in September that year, she inherited the last third, as was the custom on a spouse's death. She continued living in Malta until her own death in 1418, when her will shows how she bequeathed her wealth. One daughter was to marry Ludovico Plozasco, another Johannese de Carretto, two of six knightly landowners listed in 1408. You have to wonder how far Margarita had been aware of her husband's activities.

The appointment of Guglielmo d'Aragona, probably Margarita's father, Count of Malta in 1377, did little to calm things down and armed rebellion followed, supported by notable families. Bad harvests and plague did not help.

Stanley Fiorini provides a good example of the complications of this period, and the difficulties of trying to disentangle anything coherent about women's history at the top of the social ladder, in 'The De Malta Genoese Counts of Malta: c1192–1320' (1999):

Manfredi Chiaramonte's will of 1390 provided his daughter Elizabetta with the County of Malta but Martin Duke of Montblanch, having re-established his hold on Sicily, sought to procure local support by

4.   Margarita d'Aragona, courtesy of Carmelite Priory, Mdina

granting out these islands to various magnates, starting with Giovanna d'Aragona in 1391. A year later, Guglielmo Raimondo Moncada [Lukina's great grandson?] was offered the Marquisate of Malta and Gozo, which he turned down and which was granted in turn, as a County to Artale and Beatrice Alagona in 1393. Following their rebellion soon afterwards, the Marquisate was re-confirmed to Guglielmo Raimondo Moncada in 1396, which he now lost due to his rebellion against the King during which he also lost his life.

Manfredi Chiaramonte had headed a powerful faction in Sicily, and was 'enfeoffed' with the County of Malta in 1366 – that is, became the Count of Malta with the land and feudal rights attached to the title. **Giovanna** d'Aragona seems to have been a widow; one source suggests she may have been the natural daughter of Peter II of Sicily, or she may have been married to his natural son; more than one other source claims that she was the daughter of the natural son of Frederick II and, therefore, sister of Margarita d'Aragona, and heir to the throne after the legitimate Maria. Guglielmo Raimondo Moncada III was the great grandson of Lukina (Guglielmo Raimondo Moncada II was her son). **Beatrice** and Artale **Alagona** were cousins; she was married to Guglielmo Raimondo Moncada III. Moncada and Artale Alagona were rivals, which led to violence in Malta and the suffering of its people. The 'fief' had been elevated to a marquisate. The Wikipedia entry 'Count of Malta' suggests that although **Elizabetta Peralta Chiaramonte** inherited the title, 'actual management of the territories was probably undertaken by her brother Andrea Chiaramonte'. Can we be sure? And why not her husband Niccolo Peralta? It may, nevertheless, be so, as her holding of the title seems to have lasted from 1391 to 1392 and Andrea – who was, in fact, Chiaramonte's natural son – was 'executed in 1392 after he had been accused as a major conspirator in the anti-Aragonese unrest during the early reign of Maria of Sicily'. In 1392, the Chiaramonte possessions of Malta were seized and given to the Count of Augusta, a direct descendant of Lukina.

Aragonese **Maria** (1363–1401), daughter of Frederick IV, became **Queen of Sicily** from 1377 aged only 14, and was placed under the tutelage of Artale Alagona. What is more, in 1379, she was kidnapped by Guglielmo Raimondo Moncada to prevent her marriage. Happily Queen Maria did eventually emerge from her ordeal, though married to a different man from her original intended. On her death, first her husband (Martin I), then his father (Martin II), succeeded her. **Blanche of Navarre** (1387–1441), Martin I's widow, was then regent for two years. Her regency was followed in 1412 by a Castilian monarch, Ferdinando.

Margarita d'Aragona does not appear again in the story until her will upon her death in 1418; it can be found on the internet in Latin. The internet translation of it is somewhat haphazard, but Albert Griscti-Soler's piece lists the properties she owned which I make 26, mostly all over Malta and Gozo, but also in Sicily; his account of her life ends:

> Margarita possessed a generous but also strong will personality. She left several valuable legacies of money and land to her servants and innumerable gifts and endowments to the church.
>
> On the other hand she revoked the donation of Marnisi and Bahria she had made previously by public deed in the City of Agrigento [Sicily] in favour of her grandchildren ... sons of her daughter Leonora on the grounds that the donation had been made by coercion and against her will while she was lying ill in her daughter's house. She did however make some concessions, allowing Leonora to keep a proportion of her estate given to her as a dowry ...

Margarita, in accordance with her wish, was buried in the Cathedral of Mdina though no trace of her monument remains as the old Cathedral was destroyed in the earthquake of 1693. But the greatest monument to Margarita is the Lunziata Church near Rabat which she rebuilt and bequeathed together with other endowments to the Carmelites in her will and, for that reason, was instrumental in founding the first Carmelite community in Malta. The church, although altered over the years, still stands and is used to this day as a place of worship and retreat.

One of the other endowments was a house in Mdina which the Carmelite friars used on visits there, the remnants of which still exist at No. 3 Triq San Pietru (see Mdina itinerary in Chapter 20). Is it fair to ask if Margarita's deathbed philanthropy was, in part at least, to compensate for her husband's misdeeds?

Philanthropy through bequests in a will by notable women seems to have been common practice. Both Margarita and a Sibilla, whichever of the possible Sibillas she was, are good examples. What is more, it is useful, through Sibilla, to be able to distinguish the Lunziata (Annunciation) Church, Rabat, Gozo, from the Lunziata Church, Rabat, Malta funded under Margarita d'Aragona's will. The date of the establishment of the Gozo church, 1357, is provided by a website of Rabat churches; Stanley Fiorini suggests an earlier, unspecified, date. Margarita's country estate at San Leonardo near Rabat and attached to the Lunziata church, became, under the terms of her will, a Carmelite monastery *c*.1440 (see Chapter 20 itinerary).

In 1410 (or 1417) St Agatha's Chapel, Mdina (see Chapter 20 itinerary), was built by **Paola Castelli** (1375–?), heiress to the Barony of Buqana, which she had inherited from her mother, **Marguarita Murina** (*c*.1350–?), and Francesco Gatto, 3rd Baron di Djar il Bniet. They had married in 1397 and he was also 3rd Baron Buqana by right of his wife. He accumulated various posts under the Crown, including *Capitano* and *Castellan*, partly as a result of helping to put down an insurrection in Mdina the year after their marriage, and one on Gozo in 1410.

Were Margarita and Paola rivals? Or did they inspire each other towards church building in Rabat and Mdina? Both women belonged to exceptionally influential families; indeed Henry Bresc describes Francesco Gatto as leading a family that, with the Vaccaros, dominated public life at the turn of the century and the Gattos' daughter, their only child, Imperia, was to inherit both titles when Francesco died in 1442, by which time she had already married her father's ward Antonio Inguanez, a marriage that involved her in Malta's fortunes for years to come. The chapel built by her parents was badly damaged in the same earthquake of 1693 that damaged Mdina's cathedral and many other buildings, and rebuilt the following year.

What Albert Griscti-Soler does not mention, but other sources, such as Paul Cassar's *Medical History of Malta* (1965), do is that Margarita d'Aragona also left a bequest for the foundation of a hospital in Mdina, though what became of that is uncertain. It is sometimes suggested that the

St Peter's Nunnery took the place of St Peter's Hospital for Women in 1418, but Mario Buhagiar and Stanley Fiorini clarify the situation in *Mdina: The Cathedral City of Malta* (vol. 1, 1996):

> An indirect pointer to the fact that the hospital did not cease to function in 1418 is a document dated 1433 that talks about hospitals (in the plural) … Although the hospitals are not mentioned by name there, it is hardly likely that there existed more than two hospitals in Mdina and Rabat in that year.

For details of the Mdina nunneries, St Peter's and Scholastica, and, indeed, the difference between them, this large format, illustrated volume, one of two, is indispensable. They discuss their finances via donations and bequests, artworks, celebrations of festivals, their relations with the male church hierarchy, the health of the nuns, many of whom are named, and how they were cared for, their problems, their activities (limited), their falls from grace.

The arrival of the Benedictines had a history of its own, for some years earlier, in 1363, **Isolda de Landolina**, widow of Lancia Carobene of Noto (Sicily) and a landholder in her own right, including lands in Malta, bequeathed several of the latter to the Benedictine House in Catania (Sicily), on condition that they establish a House in Malta – a monastery of six monks to pray for her soul and that of her family, to be attached to the chapel that already existed on her lands. In the bequest, the earliest known endowment in Malta, was a townhouse and three shops in Mdina and an estate near Ħagar Qim. The monastery did not get established, however, because the Benedictines claimed, among other reservations, that the legacy was insufficient to meet the costs. But the Order held on to the legacy and tried to do so without ever setting foot in Malta. Whether or not the issues were ever resolved, and St Peter's Nunnery was the result, the sources fail to vouchsafe. Isolda's name was not, however, attached to it, as Margarita d'Aragona's was to the Carmelites.

And although the Hospital for Women seems to have continued, details, so far as I can determine, are lost in the mists of time. The *Santo Spirito*, Rabat, already functioning in 1372 under a Franciscan community, probably looked after maternity cases and foundlings and, from the fifteenth century, for those too poor or too old to care for themselves. On Gozo, the first hospital, St Julian, was established in 1454. It catered for destitute, sick women but treatment over the years was patchy. There is no evidence of women nursing, nuns or otherwise, at this time; indeed, 1599 is the first date on which they are mentioned. The Benedictines were, and still are, a closed order.

Another layer of privilege had arrived with the creation of the *Università*, a local government, based at Mdina and Rabat, Gozo, elected by local notables to safeguard their rights in the islands and maintain day-to-day management. From 1398 to 1420 control of the islands was in the hands of

the *Università*. Although this institution was supposed to be representative
of the people, and some ordinary citizens were members, it was a bastion
of a few noble families – usually of Sicilian extraction – who had power,
both political and in trade between Malta and Sicily – mainly grain from
Sicily and cotton from Malta. Margarita d'Aragona's husband had owned a
flourishing cotton warehouse, and possibly also manufactured. Famine was
a constant threat, and bread an increasingly important part of the Maltese
diet. Baking tended to run in families, including the women. And women's
involvement in what must have been the intensive cultivation of cotton is
suggested by an interchange in a trial recorded in Godfrey Wettinger's 'Wife
versus Concubine in Gozo in 1486' (2010): 'She promised to help me tend
the cotton plants and did not turn up.' The export may have been of the raw
material, but if of thread or cloth, women's role is shown earlier in the same
interchange: 'She happened to be spinning (wool or cotton) before her door
in the courtyard of her house …'.

The notables, arming galleys and investing considerable sums, also
engaged in pirating against Venetian and Arab vessels, securing both slaves
and wealth. Margarita d'Aragona's husband was a known corsair, and that
may have contributed to Frederick IV's removal of him, as suggested in Mark
A Aloisio's 'The Maltese Corso in the Fifteenth Century' (2003). He explains
that 'Corsairing was a legalized form of piracy, undertaken with the official
or implicit sanction of the authorities in return for a share of the spoils.' It
was also used as an instrument of war, and the overlord expected to have
control over all aspects. Their power is illustrated by Anthony Luttrell in
'Christian Slaves at Malta: 1271' (1987). He tells how

> In 1270 Guido De *Mohac* or Modica in Southern Sicily complained that
> he and his sons, daughters and *familia* had been imprisoned after leaving
> Siracusa and being wrecked by a storm on the islet of Comino between
> Malta and Gozo, and on 18 December 1270 the King of Sicily ordered the
> Castellan of Malta and Gozo to release them.

But he then adds details of 4 March 1271 when a 'Guido de *Moghio* freed
a Christian woman named Margarita and her three daughters, Thomasina,
Jacobina and Jannicta …'. He hypothesises that this is the same man that,
a year after his own release, was 'manumitting members of his *familia* who
had been imprisoned with him'.

Usually it was the Maltese people, as opposed to the rich corsairs, or the
powerful, who suffered from this scourge of the Mediterranean, but there
were exceptions: in Wettinger's (2001) article about Donna Simona Baldes,
which I draw on later in the next chapter, she is said to have had to sell
her dowry and personal property to ransom her once very rich husband
who, having equipped his vessel for corsairing, was captured with his ship in
Barbary. And the nefarious activity encouraged a vicious circle of violence,
enslavement, robbery and fear throughout the islands and beyond.

In his historical 'Vignette', Paul Cassar elaborates on the implications of enslavement at sea of men by corsairs for the women left behind; it was not just a question of losing the breadwinner:

This meant that a married woman whose husband had disappeared at sea could not marry again until she could prove that he had died. As there was no regular and reliable means of communication with Moslem countries, this proof could only be obtained with extreme difficulty if ever; so that a wife had either to spend the rest of her life in the hope of being re-united with her lost husband or else co-habit with a man with consequent social and ecclesiastical ostracism.

I have found no evidence for women being members of the *Università*, nor of them taking part in piracy, though it was not unknown in Elizabethan England. The purchase of slaves was also commonplace, while the manumission of one as a reward for years of service was also an act of charity, as suggested by the transcription of a copy of her master's 1324 will ordered by freed Greek domestic slave **Caterina**.

The threat and, indeed, the reality of raids, particularly following the rising power of the Ottoman state from 1300, led naturally to the need for more defensive measures which led, in turn, to the need for more money. The Crown's pressing need generally, added to that for defence spending, were the two main factors behind the 'pawning' (*impignoratio*) of Malta to the Castilian knight Gonsalvo de Monroy – a common means of raising money at the time. By 1421, the Viceroy of Sicily, Antonio de Cardona, covertly acting on behalf of Monroy, had forwarded 30,000 florins to the Crown, in return for the Lordship of Malta and Gozo. This meant that Monroy now had possession of the 'contents' of Malta, as well as civil and criminal jurisdiction over the whole population. The Maltese assumed that Viceroy Cardona was their Lord – with the obligations that went with it under the Crown – until it was too late. The definitive account of this transfer, based on newly discovered documents (following earlier less-informed attempts) is most helpfully provided by Godfrey Wettinger in 'The Pawning of Malta to Monroy' (1978).

Although Monroy's rule itself is little documented, he is said to have been selfish, greedy and cruel. In 1423, there was a Muslim raid on Malta and many of its inhabitants were carried off into slavery. Because of frequent raids, people tended to gravitate away from coastal areas and move close to the fortified towns – Mdina on Malta, Rabat on Gozo. Those who lived on farms with no walled protection were often attacked; cultivation of crops became close to impossible. Food shortage followed. What with the raids, the heavy taxes imposed by Monroy and a shortage of food, in 1425 Gozitans had had enough and rose in revolt. Malta followed in 1426. Monroy dug in his heels; after all, he had paid good money for the islands. As a result, not only were his men blockaded in the *Castrum Maris*, Birgu, but so was his wife **Donna Constanza Monroy**. It appears from George A

Said-Zammit's *The Architectural Heritage of the Maltese Islands* (2008) that the fortress could have been the Monroys' residence, so she may have been under a form of house arrest, though another source talks of the Monroys' house in Mdina being pillaged.

Constanza's background and dates have, unfortunately, eluded me. All Charles Dalli tells us, in his usually comprehensive history of the period, is that she was Gonsalvo Monroy's second wife. His family were originally from Spain but he had sought and found his fortune in the Sicilian realm under the Aragonese Crown. It is not clear, either, how long Constanza was held, and under exactly what conditions. Presumably she had women companions with her, but it would have been a frightening, uncomfortable – probably cold and damp – and uncertain captivity, though easier than it would have been for Ricca Cafor more than a century earlier. Would either of them have had access to the Chapel of St Anne (there from at least 1274)? It still forms part of the castle complex. It is also likely that the soldiers of the blockaded garrison had their dependants with them.

Meanwhile, the Sicilian Crown took Monroy's side, and the Maltese *Università* started to plead and negotiate. In the end, on 30 December 1427, it was agreed that they would raise the 30,000 florins to redeem their islands. 15,000 florins worth of assets had already been seized in Sicily; and 'the two representatives also pledged to do their utmost to convince the Maltese University to pay 5,000 florins to Constance Monroy in 30 days'. Charles Dalli does not elaborate on the significance of Constanza in this, so presumably his source does not either. Was it, perhaps to effect her release? Every effort was made to raise the money. Much involved were Imperia Gatto Inguanez's father Francesco and husband Antonio whose interests as members of the *Università* were threatened by Monroy; indeed, it seems that two of Imperia's children were at one stage offered as hostages, Antonio being one of the two envoys involved in the negotiations. But there was still a shortfall of 10,000 florins when Monroy was on his deathbed in April 1429. He therefore released the people of their obligations.

Henry Bresc's article (1975) provides an interesting tailpiece to the saga in the form of an appendix in Sicilian/Maltese(?) called 'Inventory of the contents of the Castle of Malta formally transferred to *Misser* Gutierre de Nava [*Castellan*] by the Lady Constanza, wife of the late *Misser* Gonsalvo di Monroy', and dated 30 April 1429. It consists of a list of items ranging from armaments to rope to wheat, and their value. This means that, following Gonsalvo's death earlier that month, Constanza was considered the person responsible for the contents of the fortress to which she had been confined.

There was another positive outcome for the people of Malta: Monroy was the last Count of Malta. The islands were apparently secure again under the Crown of Sicily, and Mdina was rewarded with the title *Citta Notabile*. But what happened to the new widow, Constanza? Was she confined until April 1429, while her husband was safely in Sicily? How well had she survived her ordeal? Before her imprisonment, how much did Monroy's behaviour towards the people of Malta affect her? Was she complicit? Was he also selfish and cruel to her? She is simply dumped by history. Her story, and the gaps in it, are behind the inspiration for this book.

The Maltese were not able to breathe freely for long. In 1429, a Tunisian force invaded and besieged Mdina. The city, lacking provisions and with no help arriving from Sicily, was about to surrender when the Tunisians left, taking with them, however, several thousand captives. Some were ransomed and returned; most, certainly the poorer villagers, never did. Godfrey Wettinger calculates that there were about 10,000 inhabitants in 1419, and only 8,098 in 1436. As the raiders passed through, settlements were left in ruins, fields uncultivated. Imports of wheat from Sicily were increased, and tax free. Ensuring that the wheat was distributed was one of the major functions of the *Università*. No doubt the villagers who were left were the last to receive supplies, so that women had difficulty feeding their families.

The hint of a woman involved in the trade of wheat comes in 1447/48 when Maltese officials, according to Henri Bresc, seized ships carrying grain from Sicily to Africa. One of those belonged to **Maria da Avula** and her sons; 190 *salme* were unloaded at Gozo. It is worth noting that de Avola was a Gozitan name, though what is to be made of that fact is for the more knowledgeable to determine.

For the better off, the second half of the fifteenth century saw an improvement, in spite of drought, periods of hunger and plague; indeed, drought was so bad in the three years leading up to 1469 that many fled with their families to Sicily and the '*gente inutili*' (the useless ones) – women, children and old men – were actually sent there. The *Università*, which was responsible for dealing with such visitations under a 1428 renewal of the royal charter, was also strong enough to prevent another nobleman from imitating Monroy, though there was no lack of the upper classes exercising their power of all kinds.

One of those families was that of **Imperia Gatto Inguanez** (*c*.1402–*c*.1457). Her husband Antonio Inguanez (sometimes Desguanes, from de Isguanes), whom she probably married in about 1421 (their first child was born in 1422), not only inherited her parents' titles on her father's death, as she did, but also Francesco Gatto's position as Captain. Antonio himself was closely related to the royal Aragona family of Sicily, and was rewarded for his part in the Monroy affair. Descendants of the house of Inguanez became virtually hereditary Captains until the late eighteenth century. The Inguanez coat-of-arms was placed on the inner side of Mdina's main gate, beneath the royal arms, as you will see in the Mdina itinerary (Chapter 20), and the united arms of Inguanez and Gatto were placed over the Castle of S Angelo, Birgu.

There is a historical controversy beyond my scope over Maltese, as opposed to Sicilian, titles of nobility of this period, perhaps most usefully discussed in Anthony Luttrell's *The Making of Christian Malta* (2002); he gets round the problem by using the term 'notable', instead of noble, which I have adopted where it seemed appropriate.

Imperia and Antonio's joint landholdings, apart from those in Sicily and Spain, and their palace in Mdina, included, in Rabat and Mdina, a pharmacy, five taverns, four shops (one with a mill), and the chapel of St Agatha that her parents had built. That was quite apart from the six fiefs and royal grants of land and 15 extensive rural holdings. Together they founded a dynasty (they had five daughters and six sons) which would include not only Maltese, Sicilian, Roman and Neapolitan nobility, but also twentieth-century European royalty. The Inguanez and Gatto-Murina palaces are in the Mdina itinerary (Chapter 20). King Alfonso V of Aragon (the First of Sicily) stayed at the Inguanez palace for three months in 1432, while his fleet was revictualled, with Imperia as his hostess. It was to him that two of her children had been offered as hostages five years earlier; had it been with her agreement?

How happy was Imperia with all those children, that wealth, that position? Antonio appears to have had more than one mistress: he had a daughter by the wealthy widow **Violante de Luna**, and fathered two other children. Perhaps giving birth to 11 children left Imperia philosophical; marriage was often more for property than love among the elite, and having concubines was not uncommon: her father had a daughter, **Paula Gatto**, by his slave mistress **Meymuna**.

Adultery was not the only proclivity of the males of the family. Imperia's eldest son, Francesco Gatt Desguanes, *Università* jurat (municipal magistrate), was one of the two ambassadors sent to Sicily to negotiate wheat contracts in 1468. He made good use of his time there to fiddle his expenses, as detailed in 'The Three-year Famine and the *Ambaxata Di Malta*: 1468–69' (2010). Stanley Fiorini adds, 'One cannot help remarking on the excellent quality of his fare – two square meals of meat and wine every day – when his fellow countrymen were dying of starvation.' On his return home, he not only attempted to set up a commercial company for the importation of wheat but, having made a good impression on Sicily's viceroy, he was made Captain of Malta, and given rights over land adjoining his on Gozo. But his expenses were questioned, and the case went to arbitration. Happily, Imperia was no longer alive to see this staining of the family name.

Whether or not Imperia managed her own property finds a possible answer in Chapter 4. The only sign I can find of her involvement on any level comes from Charles Galea Scannura's 'The Office of the Secrezia of Malta Previous to the Coming of the Knights of Malta' (1973):

In 1441, [the fief of] Tabara was inherited by Imperia, the wife of Antonio Inguanez, and Giovanni Landolina presented complaints against her with the result that she lost the fief, which was then handed to this Giovanni.

Antonio died in 1457; Imperia must have pre-deceased him, if only by a short time: the only apparently available source for her dates suggests that it was a year after him, but another source says that after her (undated) death he altered his will to take account of his natural children.

4 – The Legal Position of Medieval Women 1486–1545

I have hinted that from the earliest, Neolithic, times women may have been involved in the settling of disputes. Thanks to the work of anthropologists and non-governmental organisations in traditional societies, and historians of early literate ones, we now know of the naturalness of this. But I omitted to suggest that they might also be parties to a dispute – disputes, after all, have existed for as long as human society. Now we have evidence of what went on in Malta, at least in the second half of the fifteenth century.

Malta was served then by a notary from Gozo, Giacomo Zabbara, whose surviving records tell of women's lives in this respect in both islands. They also throw light on the lives of women more generally. The records, covering the years 1486–88, and 1494–97, are published in three volumes of the series *Documentary Sources of Maltese History*, in Part I nos 1, 2 and 3, edited by Stanley Fiorini (1996–), and combed, translated from the Latin (and a sprinkling of Sicilian), and written up for me by my husband, historian of dispute resolution, Derek Roebuck. I have interspersed material from other sources where it adds to or conflicts with his interpretation.

In the 972 documents, no fewer than 449 women appear by name, of every level of society from slaves to the upper classes, a useful foil to my enforced concentration on elite women of the earlier period. However, among the names that follow are (C) Habica, Guevara (Guyvara), Mazara, and Vaccaro, all of whom were of the major land-owning and office-holding families. And Charles Dalli notes that 'many of these families intermarried amongst themselves, created alliances, and competed for the island's limited resources'. After 1460, the Guevaras, for example, controlled the *Secrezia* and, as Mark Aloisio writes, they were part of the 'military aristocracy' – corsairs and galley captains. A similar situation prevailed on Gozo where prominent names were Naso and Vagnolo. Spellings vary in sources. While Jewish women also appear, it needs to be noted that Jews were expelled from Malta in 1492, as they were from elsewhere in Europe, with all the same implications for women as for the Muslims expelled two centuries earlier. Until then, it was commonplace for Jewish vendors to go from settlement to settlement carrying baskets of their wares for sale to women in their homes. Jews and Christians lived in harmony. Among the Jews of note was the medical expert Raphael Ketib; a woman with the same name is the first mentioned below.

Single, married or widowed, the women buy, sell and lease land, play their different roles in marriage settlements, and trade in everything from cloth to horses to slaves, all in their own right. The documents are in common notarial forms, inherited from late Roman law, similar to contemporary practice in western Europe, but with Maltese idiosyncrasies which tell us a lot about the status of women.

Usually, though by no means always, when something as fundamental as the sale of land was involved, the woman was accompanied by a man, often called her *mundualdus*. It is usual to translate that as 'guardian' but it is perhaps better to spell it out as 'the man under whose protection the woman lives'. The term comes from the quite different culture of Lombard law. In Zabbara's records it never meant that the woman was not carrying out the legal act in her own right. Stefan Cachia has his own interpretation in 'Husband-Wife Relations in Late Medieval Malta 1486–1488' (2001): 'The *Mundualdo* apart from being a legal reality was symbolic of that male dominant society.' Derek Roebuck always looks at the reality, the practice, behind the law, and Stefan Cachia himself gives examples that support that view.

In Maltese culture, most women needed practically to be under some man's protection. The documents usually declare that the woman had taken the advice of her *mundualdus*. In this respect Jews and Christians were no different. But that took away no legal rights:

> Sappora, widow of the Jew Rubin Ketib, with the advice and approval of David Inglish, ... in her own right and name, for herself, her heirs and successors for ever, has sold... an enclosure of arable land... at Gudja... to her brother-in-law.

It was the woman who effected the legal transfer. There are scores of records of women buying, selling and leasing land, sometimes jointly with their husbands but often on their own, like **Magnifica Donna Clara de Stunica**, according to Maltese custom with no man mentioned. Stefan Cachia, having suggested that women might manage the family estate when their husband was away, using Donna Clara as an example, then notes of **Donna Chicca de Burdino**, 'Notwithstanding the fact that her husband was in Malta, indeed present in the same contract of sales, it was the wife not the husband who bought two horses and bales of cotton [from Johannes de Guyvara]'. Even a nun could buy and sell land, as **Sister Pina de Gaglano**, abbess of the Benedictine nunnery of St Peter, Mdina, did on 19 April 1486.

Women could sue and be sued in their own names, like **Donna Jacoba de Vaccaro** in an inheritance dispute and **Donna Mansa de Manuele** on appeal in the Royal Court. They could appoint an attorney, *procurator*, to represent them in litigation. **Ysolda** of Tarxien, widow of Zaccarius **Bonnici**, herself settled her dispute after litigation about ownership of land. **Garita**, wife of Frankinus **Mullica**, and her daughters **Catherina** and **Jacoba** entered into mediation and settled their dispute with Fridericus, granting him land in exchange for barley and cotton. Women regularly made wills and gifts in contemplation of death, *donationes mortis causa*.

A woman might provide her own dowry, *sponsa seipsum dotanda*, as **Zuna**, daughter of **Imperia** and Corsu **Vella** did according to Maltese custom, *iuxta usum Melite*. A woman might be married, as was **Jacuba** of Naxxar, daughter of Zullus **Calleja**, expressly according to the custom of Maltese farmers, *iuxta usum agricolarum dicte insole*. When Marcus **Jurubutino** wanted to sell the palace in Gozo town which had come to him as the dowry of his wife **Maria**, he needed her consent, otherwise his acceptance of the price would not be enough to transfer legal ownership.

Nesa, a Jewish woman guaranteeing her son Haym **Gibli**'s debt, was allowed to take her oath *ad legem Moysi more Judaeorum*, on the law of Moses according to Jewish custom.

Donna Betta de Habica (sometimes written Chabica) of Mdina, having been in partnership with the commoner Bertus Mintoff of Gozo, settled its dissolution entirely independently of her husband, according to Gozitan custom. **Ysabella** paid off the debts of her husband Salvus **Micallef**, with his 'advice' of course. The noble Donna Chicca's IOU with her husband promised to pay when she received her first salary from the royal *Secrezia*. Widow **Donna Margarita de Habica** herself stood surety for a man's debts and was called on to pay them. **Chianchia de Arteda** of Rabat even agreed to go to gaol as personal guarantor if the debt was not repaid on time which she and her husband had incurred on the purchase of a donkey.

Many women had female slaves, whose names are known, and sometimes manumitted them or their daughters, as **Donna Dulcia** of Żebbuġ, widow of Nardus **Axiaq**, did to **Ventura**, infant daughter of her slave **Elena**. **Donna Granata**, widow of Johannes de **Falsono** was not above claiming to have been married according to Roman custom, *secundum usum Romanorum*, when that would have given her ownership of the slave in dispute.

Men might be called on to act for their wives when the Church had a say. Sisters **Donna Amata**, **Donna Ylagia** and **Donna Chusa**, daughters of Bartholomeus **de Bernardo**, inherited the right to appoint a priest to a benefice on Gozo but had to exercise it through a male administrator.

It might be thought that where the parties to a mediated settlement were male members of the family, that was evidence that women were in some way legally disabled. On 14 January 1488 Don Petrus de **Vacaro** settled a dispute with the Venerable Don Amator **Zammit**. Petrus's wife **Francia** was Amator's sister. Amator was acting for another sister, **Catherina**, and **Imperia** and **Ysabella**, the daughters of his brother Johannes. Land in various parts of the island of Malta had been in dispute in the Captain's Court, judgment had been pronounced and now an appeal was pending before the Maltese court of first appeal:

> Bearing in mind the close blood relationship and affinity between them, by the mediation of friends and relatives of both sides, they came unanimously to the following contract and settlement, *transaccionem et concordiam*.

Amator 'so far as he could and had power and authority' to do so, made concessions and Petrus, 'in the name of his wife' did the same. Could evidence be more express that the legal actors in substance were the women?

In that same year, 1488, the peace more generally was disturbed when an Ottoman squadron attacked and sacked Birgu.

There are strange stories of how women had to survive in this period. How much can be read into the deed by which Michael **Farrugia** of Zurriek (Żurrieq) pardoned his wife **Antona** and her wealthy lover, Magnifico Peri Johannes de Mazara, of their adultery. Did money change hands? None is mentioned. The forgiveness is said to spring from Michael's wish to benefit from having followed the Bible's 'forgive our debts as we forgive our debtors'. He agreed to take Antona back 'into matrimonial affection' as it was before the adultery.

Peri Johannes, of a major land-owning and office-holding family, and married since 1434 into a noble family of Palermo, had not been content with Antona. **Laurencia** had once been his concubine. Nevertheless, against his wishes, she had married Stephanus Seychel. While her husband was away at sea, Laurencia went back to Peri Johannes. He wanted to save her from an immoral life, like a prostitute or kept woman; (the word used, as has been agreed by Giovanni Bonello and Derek Roebuck, is *convestuaria* which suggests the fascinating *mélange* of language used at the time in Malta because it is not found in any dictionary but could mean, literally, 'clothed in return for horizontal services').

When Stephanus returned after some years, he was happy to take Laurencia back 'into matrimonial affection' and pardoned them both by a deed dated 27 June 1487, just as Michael had Antona. Again there was no mention of anything as sordid as money. But it did not end there; by a deed of 11 September of the same year, Stephanus related that he had been encouraged by others to start an action in the Captain's Court because Laurencia had gone back to Peri Johannes, taking with her a dress, *robichella*. Again there was no reference to any money changing hands or any consideration for Stephanus's forbearance. By 4 March 1488 Stephanus was giving Peri Johannes an IOU for a multi-coloured cloak or cape.

Both Godfrey Wettinger, in 'Honour and Shame in Late Fifteenth Century Malta' (1980), and Stefan Cachia have their own interpretation of the documents that relate this saga. Stefan Cachia writes from his perspective of husband and wife relations:

> It is evident that there was no love in the marriage between Stephanus Seykel and his wife Laurencza alias Cueyna. The marriage itself had been contracted on the invitation of Johannes de Guyvara, to whom Laurencza had been a concubine. Not only [that] but while Stephanus was away from Malta, she went back to her lover. Eventually, the same Laurencza was guilty of adultery with Petrucius de Mazara.

While Godfrey Wettinger, who has spent years studying such documents, writes and, in doing so, adds in a footnote that the Mazara and Guevara families were closely and repeatedly allied by marriage to each other as well as to the Desguanes (Inguanez) family:

Taken together the two documents seem to indicate that Peri Johannes de Mazara was preparing his spiritual accounts preparatory to meeting his creator, as he would seem to have died not long after. Michael Farruge could only have been a peasant from Zurrieq, while Stephanus Seykel was certainly only a sailor for a part of his life, neither of them able to stand up normally to the magnifico who had dishonoured them. It is in fact remarkable that, as the second contract states, Seykel had been able to marry Peri Johannes's concubine against the latter's own wishes. Inevitably one thinks that Mazara might have had something to do with his enrolment on Guyvara's galley: perhaps he had arranged it all; perhaps, as frequently happened, Seykel had been tricked into enrolling to get him out of the way. However that may be, the effect was the same. Mazara was able to take his former concubine back – to prevent her from leading a dissolute life in the absence of her husband.

Godfrey Wettinger adds further on, following the theme of his article:

In fact, though thoughts of impending death might have impelled Peri Johannes de Mazara in 1487 to make his peace with the two husbands he had cuckolded, fears of the peasants' vendetta might also have had something to do with it.

And it is certainly true that peasant reaction concerning honour and shame could be vengeful, for Godfrey Wettinger also tells the story of Nicolaus, of the well-known Mdina family of Caxaru, who met a sticky end when he called on married **Catherina** of Siġġiewi late at night with dishonourable intentions. Accusations of adultery were sometimes brought, and often not. In 'Wife versus Concubine in Gozo in 1486', Godfrey Wettinger recounts how **Donna Chanchia**, together with her father Andrea **de Bisconis**, took **Francza de Gurabe** before the Court of the Vicar-General for committing adultery with Chanchia's husband, Andriocta **Benjamin**, as well as attempting to break up their marriage by the use of sorcery. Francza defended herself with vigour and was eventually freed.

It was common for the Latin documents to be explained to the parties in Maltese, *in lingua vulgari* (e.g. to the honourable Peri Caruana), or *in materna lingua* (as to young **Zuna**, daughter of Margarita de Habica), but not all women were uneducated. At least one understood the Latin. A deed of 22 January 1495 records the sale to **Magnifica Donna Peruna de Mazara** of half of what is now Manoel Island. A marginal note records that **Magnifica Donna Margarita**, joining in the sale with her husband, Magnifico Johannes de Guyvara, declared that she understood the Latin text: *contractu … per eamdem dominam Margaritam bene intellecto in lingua latina, ut dixit.*

This is almost the first evidence that there were educated, literate, women in Malta. I cannot find details of education in the islands at this time, nor a record of Margarita's background, but her husband belonged to one of the top Maltese families so she probably did too, and may have been brought up in an educated family in Sicily. What is more, with the printing of the Bible by Johannes Gutenberg in 1445, books became increasingly available. Since we know that Margarita's husband had a concubine, as was commonplace, is it fanciful to suggest that scholarly pursuits were something of a solace?

Not all legal cases came from the Notary Zabbara, and widowhood presented problems of its own. At some time about 1460, young **Lisa** (or Aloysia) de **Vagnolu** married old Antoni de li Nasi, retired mayor of Gozo. When he died in 1465, she quickly married again. Too quickly for her reputation with some neighbours.

She was herself a woman of property and Antoni had left a considerable estate – both came from elite Gozo families. She had agreed with his nephews, who also expected to inherit under his will, that she should have 141 florins, representing the dower she had been promised on her marriage. They went back on that agreement and litigation followed. The dispute had many facets, including the value of a house in Malta and their failure to provide the black material for Lisa's mourning. They did agree to Lisa having the Gozo town house. The conveyance, though, was of a kind peculiar to Malta then. Property was transferred for a sum of money, the price, with the condition that the sellers could buy it back at the same price at any time within a fixed term. That was a kind of mortgage and a device by which Maltese moneylenders secured their loans and avoided the usury laws. The nephews promised to pay Lisa each year two *salmas* of wheat and two of barley and had eight years in which to redeem.

The evidence is preserved in the documents on which Godfrey Wettinger based his article: 'The Young Widow on Gozo Who Remarried Too Soon, 1465–68' (1997), which Derek Roebuck has reduced to the essentials for me. Much of the evidence is as colourful as it was irrelevant. A priest said that the minimum customary mourning period was 40 days. Others said Lisa had remarried just within that time, feasting in her dead husband's home, and with a band playing. She had not provided the customary silk coverlet for the grave, nor the silver goblet to stand on it. And the agreement was usurious.

On the other side, Fridericus de Pontremoli, Lisa's former guardian, said that he was there when Antoni on his deathbed called Lisa to him as he dictated his will and told her: 'See how I am about to die. Do not remain a widow. Take a husband immediately... on the third day take a husband.'

Character evidence was given for Lisa: she was a gentle lady, of distinguished families on both sides, quite unused to the ways of the world, and a good Christian who understood nothing of usury. Her new husband, Chanchius de Platamone, does not seem to have had anything to say.

On 17 May 1470 the Bishop's Court in Malta pronounced judgment: the transfer of the property was unlawful. Lisa must repay all the wheat and barley she had received from the nephews. She could keep the price she had received for the town house.

The case of Donna Lisa is slightly ambiguous: sometimes it suited a woman to be unwise in the ways of the world, and the law. In 'Donna

Simona Caruana Alias de Baldes, Twice Married and Twice Widowed'
(2001), Godfrey Wettinger sets out a legal case, based on documents in the
Cathedral Museum, Mdina, that explores the reality of women and the law;
indeed, he starts the article:

> During the fifteenth century it was not usual in Malta or Gozo for women
> to come to the front either in public or even in private and personal matters.
> Consequently, it is very difficult to determine their precise participation
> in the affairs of the time. Fortunately, in 1499 the strength of the case
> brought by Donna Simona Caruana's lawyers against the Falca brothers
> and their legal representatives turned precisely on this point.

In 1448, Donna **Simona**, daughter of the notary Carrao de **Alaymo**, married
the Catalan nobleman Petrus **de Baldes**. He died in 1480 and she remained a
widow until about 1490 when she married the Maltese businessman Jakino
Caruana. He, in turn, died in 1498. The following year,

> Her representatives alleged in the island's ecclesiastic court that she had
> been deceived into selling at a cheap price the field Taflija at Ghajn Qasab
> in Malta to the Augustinian Friary at Rabat back in 1457. It had since
> been claimed and taken by the Falca brothers on the grounds of right of
> pre-emption owing to the contiguity of their lands.

The saga is so long and complicated, including the relevance of the increase
in the value of the land since then, that I shall stick to the bare essentials.
Donna Simona's side had to show that she had been deceived by the Friary;
those acting for the Falca brothers that she had been totally in charge of the
sale of the land that formed part of her dowry. Back and forth the case went,
with each side, through numerous witnesses, peddling their relevant line.

Petrucius de Alaymo, obviously a paternal relative, acting for Donna
Simona, insisted that both her husbands

> were Maltese citizens living according to Maltese custom and usages. In
> the town and island of Malta people lived, ever since time immemorial,
> according to the customs of the city of Messina [Sicily] that the wife who
> had a husband alive had no *capud [caput] standi in iudicio active neque
> passive et precipue volendo agere* (legal standing to appear in judicial
> proceedings as defendant and especially as plaintiff).

Manfridus de la Chabica, acting for the Falca brothers, claimed the opposite:

> In Malta married women did normally resort to law personally or by
> means of their lawyers and representatives both in civil and criminal
> proceedings actively as well as passively without interference from their
> husbands. Even if the custom [i.e. Messina] existed in Malta, it was only
> exercised where the husband was a capable administrator not where he

was a spendthrift and improvident as, with due respect, was the late Petrus Baldes, her first husband.

…When Simona saw the way things were going owing to his dissolute way of life, she immediately took charge of the house, ruling herself and her husband and the whole family. She rented out the land to the tenants, bought and sold property according to the family needs and behaved as if she were the head of the family in everything important and unimportant, and all this with her husband's consent, also receiving rent-money and the price of the property that was sold. She not only sold off the field in question, called Tafalia, but also another called tal Gar in the district of Gikimeni to the late Dancio Frendu. Simona could, therefore, not say that she was under her husband's subjection and that she could not appear in legal proceedings concerning the revocation of the original contract of sale made by herself.

And many witnesses came forward to say how Donna Simona had been in charge of the couple's affairs, while her representative explained that she merely acted as his interpreter and go-between because he did not understand the Maltese language. Godfrey Wettinger paraphrases de la Chabica's summing up:

Thus it was insisted on again that Petrus de Baldes was a spendthrift, that married women could take over the administration of their goods if their husband was incapable of administering them himself, and not only on those that did not belong to their dowries. It was again claimed that it had not been proved that Malta followed the custom of Messina, namely that married women had no *capud standi* in litigation, and that it could not rightly be said that donna Simona from the mere fact of being a woman could not understand law, on the principle that *de jure in muliere non cadit ignorancia juris*. It was contended that donna Simona had always been a well-informed, wise and clever woman in mundane affairs, brought up by her father, the late notary and lawyer Corradu de Alaymo, a woman who had been for all her life considered wise and prudent in all her affairs and business undertakings, dealing and speaking with everyone and treated as such by one and all.

Frustratingly, the outcome of the case is unknown! But it is clear that women could have legal standing, if they chose to do so, whether or not they were educated, as Donna Simona's background suggests that she was. And however exaggerated the evidence put forward to prove that Donna Simona was fully in charge, that she had intentionally sold the land at issue, the question implicit in Godfrey Wettinger's first paragraph, about whether or not it was usual for women to 'come to the front', is answered; indeed, one notary who appeared as a witness stated that he had seen divers married women appearing in court personally either with their lawyers or without to press their case against others in their husband's absence. The implication is that Donna Simona might well have appeared but at the time she was ill.

Donna Simona was said to be suffering from the 'French illness' (*bruguli seu ampulli*), that is syphilis, which accords with the evidence that her first husband led a 'dissolute life'. This raises the question of how prevalent sexually transmitted diseases were, and how far the wives of the upper classes were affected, remembering that Peri Johannes de Mazara and Johannes de Guyvara shared the favours of the courtesan Laurencia. May it also have affected Imperia Gatto Inguanez and her mother Paula Castelli Gatto? Laurencia's status is ambiguous – an ambiguity explained by Godfrey Wettinger in 'Aspects of Daily Life in Late-Medieval Malta and Gozo' (1989): 'Real prostitutes as distinct from concubines were very much a part of daily life in Gozo as in Malta, but sometimes the distinction was not at all clear.'

More positively, Donna Simona's recourse to the law over her land, and the evidence given by witnesses about her competence, may also have something to say about Imperia's management of her own family landholdings.

The Zabbara records, Donna Simona's case, and Derek Roebuck's interpretation, suggest that women were in some control of their lives through the law, and had the status that went with that. Godfrey Wettinger's article 'Concubinage Among the Clergy of Malta and Gozo ca. 1420–1550' (1977) gives a different slant to women's lives. Priests could not marry and, indeed, were required to practise celibacy. Concubinage was sometimes an accepted alternative, however much frowned upon, and sometimes acted against by the Church. Using material from Church records, Godfrey Wettinger provides a list of priests – from different levels of the Church hierarchy – and their offspring, naming 46 fathers of children between 1420 and 1554. Of their children, 31 were daughters. Don Laurencius de Caxaro unashamedly fathered six daughters.

Don Brandano de Caxar(i)o, presumably a close relative in what is a somewhat prolific family, had eight sons by concubine **Catherine Aczuppardo** (daughter of **Inguterra Aczuppardo of Tarxien**). They appear to have lived together for 20 years. As Godfrey Wettinger says, 'He could live a tranquil life almost until old age, earning his living mainly by his work as a notary, accompanied and surrounded by his "wife" and family as any other married man on the island.' He was, indeed, one of those who publicly declared that priests should be allowed to marry.

Given that they were not, what was the status, legal or otherwise, of the concubines whom Godfrey Wettinger also calls common-law wives? He suggests that it was 'far from ephemeral or unstable'. Readers are, however, left drawing their own conclusions, given the position of the priest and his family origins and the original status of the women, as well as the uncertain economic conditions of the times.

The article also has three lists, 'Concubinate Clergy of Malta 1543', of 1545, and Gozo 1545. There the names of the priests are allied to those of their concubines. Of the 44 women listed, six are ex-slaves of named men (not the priest to whom they were a concubine, though Don Francisco de

Vetero made a concubine of his own slave, **Zaida**) and, as Godfrey Wettinger notes from the names, 'most of the women who were prepared to accept the status of a priest's concubine in Malta seemed to have belonged to the island's peasantry', or families owning a few fields.

What is more, from time to time the Church did come down on such liaisons, and the lists were those where priests were ordered to terminate them. A penalty could be attached to that requirement which, in at least one case, was shaming physical punishment for the woman concerned – **Paula,** daughter of **Agata Kibeylet:**

> On 5 December 1545 Don Johannes Dimech was found guilty of keeping a woman named Paula as his concubine. He was therefore sentenced to be deprived of his dignity of treasurer of the cathedral and fined the sum of twenty-five uncie, while Paula herself was sentenced to be led on an ass through the public thoroughfares of Mdina and Rabat, with bare shoulders and wearing a mitre on her head, and to be whipped and fined ten uncie.

Would Paula have been as severely punished if Dimech had not already died on 8 November, and in Sicily, rather than Malta? And how relevant was it that Paula herself was illegitimate?

The offspring of these liaisons do not, however, seem, on the whole, to have been penalised; on the contrary. Of Catherina Aczuppardo's eight sons by Don Brandano Caxar(i)o two became notaries (like their father), one a lawyer, one a Friar Minor, while the one who was apparently the eldest, 'is commonly referred to in the records as "Magnificus" a title usually reserved to the leading citizens of Mdina'. Presumably when Don Brandano died in 1565, Catherina was cared for by her sons and would have felt that it had all been worth it.

Female offspring could make advantageous marriages. **Guaglarda,** daughter of **Agatha** and Archdeacon of the Cathedral of Mdina Lancia Desguanese (Inguanez), tenth child of Imperia and Antonio Inguanez, married Manfridus Caxaro (Don Brandano's uncle), and another daughter, **Violante,** still a minor on her father's death, married Nicolaus Saguna 'a prominent man-about-town of the 1490s'. Of Don Laurencius de Caxaro's six daughters, information is only available for **Vincensica** who became the nun **Sister Francesca.**

What is ironic, given how the scions of upper class and influential families were able to behave in the Middle Ages, is how different their importance was to become after 1530, with the arrival of the Knights of St John. Behaviour of men of the cloth was not, however, to be so very different.

What was to join the Knights to Malta's past even more firmly was the continuation of incursions from south and east that had been gathering strength in the previous centuries. Of all those early raids, the one that left the greatest mark – in literature, ballad and novels, in music, both opera and instrumental, and dance – is that of 1526. By chance, the law features but it offered no protection to **Marianna Cumbo**. She was the daughter of the renowned legal practitioner Dr Giulio Cumbo, one of the four jurats of the Mdina *Università*; her mother's name does not seem to have been recorded.

On the morning in question, Marianna was in the Cumbo Tower, stronghold of the village of Mosta, about to marry Toni, scion of the Mdina Manduca family, when Muley, a one-time slave of the Cumbos, enabled corsairs, under their leader Rajes Sinen, to enter and carry her off, together with 400 assembled guests. As a result, there came into being the legend of The Bride of Mosta (*L-Gharusa tal-Mosta*). Marianna's kidnap may be legend but, certainly, there was a raid on Mosta in 1526 and hundreds of its inhabitants were carried off. While her mother and aunt, in turn, failed to ransom her, brave Toni set out to rescue her from the Sultan of Tripoli. A version of the story is told in *The Bride of Mosta: A Ballad* (2005), by Francis Berry (see Chapter 20 itinerary).

Just to confuse, there is a second version of the story which concerns **Lucia**, the only daughter of Baron Bernardo **Zammit** who disappeared from her bedroom in the Castello Zammitello, between Mġarr and Gnejna Bay, on the morning of her wedding to a rich Sicilian count. But Lucia had not been kidnapped by corsairs, as her father believed, she had run away to become a nun (see Chapter 21 itinerary).

Less well known is the reason for the construction of what is known as the Gauci Tower just outside Naxxar, at San Pawl tat-Targa (see Chapter 19 itinerary). That was built, and attached to the family home, by Francesco Gauci to protect the rest of his family after his wife (without a name) was taken during a pirate attack. The date is uncertain but it was before the arrival of the Knights because there was an attempt by them to take it from the Gaucis to house the Naxxar militia. But Gauci won his appeal and the nearby Captain's Tower was built instead. In the days before the Knights, foreign soldiers deployed in Malta's defence were billeted with private households – what kind of household is not clear. That would have its advantages and disadvantages for the women of the house: they might have felt more secure against pirate raids, but there would have been inconvenience, too, and the necessity of keeping an eye on their daughters' well-being.

The question of whether or not Marianna Cumbo's kidnap itself is a legend is perhaps answered by a dance forming part of the carnival that takes place at the beginning of Lent. In St George's Square, in front of the palace where the Grand Masters of the Knights used to live, where the British Governor was housed when in Valletta, and where the President of today's independent Malta has her office, a group of revellers perform the *Parata* dance which takes its symbolism from the capture of a Maltese bride by a Muslim corsair.

But the raid by Sinen in 1526 was as nothing to what lay in store from Ottoman forces for Malta under the Knights.

5 – Women, Knights and Turks 1530–1645

The Knights Arrive

'It was not until the coming of the Knights Hospitallers that Malta acquired an important place on the map of Europe,' writes Elizabeth Schermerhorn in *Malta of the Knights* (1929). 'This order was composed of representatives of the noblest European families pledged to the defence of Christianity against the aggressions of Ottoman power.'

But when a delegation from the Order of St John, as it became known, arrived to reconnoitre Malta in 1524, before the Order settled there in 1530, they were not impressed by the 'barren rock' with little water. It was nothing like the island of Rhodes from where Ottoman forces had dispatched them in 1523. There they had been comfortably settled for two hundred years, after being forced to leave Acre in the Holy Land in 1291. It was in Rhodes that they had divided themselves into seven *Langues* – language colleges – under a Grand Master, and gained wealth, prestige and an assumed moral superiority manifested by celibacy and philanthropy. Elizabeth Schermerhorn describes the Order as a religious and military organisation, a masculine community founded on the exclusive ideals of war and prayer. Her book, though written before recent scholarship and interpretation, is a colourful and lively account.

A French visitor to Malta in 1536 noted that apart from Mdina and 'some houses in the suburb' the Maltese otherwise lived in make-shift houses 'which one would take for African huts'. Malta and Gozo were predominantly rural – the people living in *casals* (villages). But it was the lack of fortification that was the main problem; security against Ottoman forces was the Knights' priority. In the end it was a case of needs must; they had nowhere else to go to continue their calling, since about 1070, of tending the sick and wounded, protecting the poor and Christian pilgrims, and fighting. They therefore accepted the offer made by Charles V, Holy Roman Emperor, and his mother, the so-called mad **Queen Joanna** (1479–1555). In the early days they still dreamed of returning to Rhodes.

They were to remain in Malta, however, until Napoleon ordered them to leave in 1798, and within a short time, from their initial capital, what started as the village of Birgu, they had marginalised the *Università* in Mdina. Diminishing the role of the Maltese ruling class – the Inguanez, the Murinas, the Gattos – and ignoring the ancient privileges and liberty of the islanders – 17,000 or so of them – granted by their overlords, they had soon taken control of the islands, including the imposition of taxes, and creation of laws. In his *A Concise History of Malta* (2002), Carmel Cassar succinctly notes that, between 1530 and 1798, 'The tiny archipelago of Malta was *de jure* under Spain, as part of the Kingdom of Sicily, but *de facto* under the rule of the crusading Hospitaller Order of St John'.

So dismissive was the Order of the local notables, that it would not even allow their sons, however well-bred, rich or talented, to join it; it was not unknown, therefore, for an upper-class, Maltese, expectant mother to travel to Sicily to give birth to enable her son to enter the Order.

Mdina became something of a backwater; activity centred on burgeoning and increasingly fortified Birgu. What is now the city of Valletta, redolent still architecturally of the Knights' domination, was for 35 or so years just a bare hill on Peninsula Sceberras across from their sheltered anchorage. A fortress, St Elmo, was to be built on its north-eastern tip in 1552, and another fortress, St Michael, on the Isola peninsula next to Birgu, and this led to the creation of the town of Senglea between 1553 and 1557.

In Birgu, the Knights built fine mansions – *Auberges* – for each *Langue*, which still exist. At times, there were between 400 and 600 Knights in Malta, together with servants, soldiers, attendants and slaves. The English *Langue*, the mansion of which had been bought from **Catherine Abela**, was dissolved in April 1540, and its entire property confiscated, during the time of Henry VIII's Dissolution of the Monasteries. The irony would not have been lost that the prompt for this was Henry's wish to marry Anne Boleyn. In order to do so, he had to divorce Catherine of Aragon, daughter of Charles V who had given Malta, by feudal donation, to the Knights. Ambassadors were sent to Malta to negotiate the revival of the English *Langue*, and the restitution of its property, when Catholic **Mary Tudor** (1516–1558) came to the throne in 1552, but such hope was dashed with the accession in 1558 of her Protestant half-sister **Elizabeth I** (1533–1603).

The population of Birgu grew steadily, augmented by the 500 or more Greeks who had followed the Knights from Rhodes, not wishing to live under the Turks. The 17,000 in the islands when the Order reconnoitred in 1524 had, according to the historian of the Order, Giacomo Bosio, jumped to 25,000 by October 1530. Typical of the Greeks may have been Isabella and Demetrio Petras, whose daughter Caterina Vitale was to play a prominent role later in the sixteenth century and into the seventeenth.

The next chapter touches on the everyday life of Birgu during this period, and the move to Valletta, including Caterina Vitale's relations with the Knights, and that of other women; this one concentrates on Turkish raids and sieges and what women went through and contributed, for the Knights' residence in Malta was not to be easy during the first hundred years; the Ottoman sultans were determined once again to dislodge them.

1533

The Knights had only been three years on the islands when the first recorded raid by Turkish corsairs occurred, and that seems to have been only to steal dozens of sheep and goats and capture a few slaves on Gozo. Indeed, we might not know about it if Godfrey Wettinger had not unearthed a court case, and written about it in 'Corsairs in Gozo in 1533' (2005).

The case centred on the claim that the animals that Micheli Danfasino had been looking after for his neighbours, with his own, and which he claimed had been stolen by the Turks, had in fact been sold by him 'in order to obtain money to ransom his son and daughter-in-law who had been captured on the same occasion'. Micheli had delayed the call to hurry into the Gozo fortress, as was the law when danger threatened, so no one could be sure what he had got up to. Although his daughter-in-law, **Dianora**, and son had been taken, there is some ambiguity about whether or not his unmarried daughter and wife had too, and what other women were involved.

The delight of the court record is the detail – conflicting, of course, as is the way with disputes – of a Turkish raid, and how it affected ordinary people. For our purposes, our thoughts are with those captured women, as they were grabbed, as they were transported to the waiting galleys, and how they would have been transported. And then their fear on the galley, awaiting their uncertain but terrible fate. It is not surprising that Micheli used subterfuge, if indeed he did, to retrieve his family. The outcome of the court case – which lasted four years – is unknown as the relevant court papers were lost. There were eight similar landings, mostly on Gozo and led by the Turkish commander Dragut Rais, between the 1530 arrival of the Knights on Malta and 1551.

1551

The Turkish assault of 1551 was rather more serious. This time the Turkish General Sinan Pasha under orders from Sultan Suleiman I, the Magnificent, intended to strike at the Knights themselves, not just because of the clash of religion and culture, but because the Knights were disrupting commerce in the Mediterranean through attacks on Turkish shipping by ships flying their flag.

In July 1551 an Ottoman force of 10,000 landed on Malta at Marsamxett intending to attack Birgu and Fort S Angelo. Realising the Knights' stronghold was too well defended to take easily, they turned inland instead, towards Mdina, looting and burning villages on the way. The few Knights in Mdina prevailed upon the nearby Maltese who had sought refuge there to help in the defence. When the Ottoman force arrived outside the walls, they were disconcerted to see how well it was defended.

Legend has it that the martyred St Agatha appeared to a Benedictine nun and directed that a procession should carry her image and display it on the bastion walls. Thus cowed, the besiegers departed. Thereafter, St Agatha became one of the two patron saints of Malta and, a hundred years later, in 1649, Grand Master Lascaris commissioned what was called St Agatha's Tower, also known as the Red Tower, built on the crest of the Marfa ridge, one of the defensive structures at the north-west end of Malta (see Chapter 20 itinerary). Not to be done out of a successful incursion, the Turks then sailed for Gozo, starting their attack on the citadel where the inhabitants had taken refuge on 24 July.

Not much is written about 1551 – it became so over-shadowed by the Great Siege of 1565 – so it was with pleasure that I came across Dorothy Dunnett's fat novel, *The Disorderly Knights* (1966) – third in the Lymond Saga. She obviously did impressive background research in libraries as well as on location, enabling her to spin a compelling yarn – splendid holiday reading. So successful was she at drawing me into her saga that I proceeded to read the two fat Lymond novels that follow this, both of them containing snippets about Malta.

What is factual is that before the Ottoman force landed on Malta, the fleet was spotted coming towards the islands, then veering off towards Sicily where it landed and harried the local population. But the sight of it on the horizon of Gozo had raised fears of an imminent attack, so much so that boatloads of Gozitans sought refuge at Birgu. Only Dorothy Dunnett (1923–2001) brings this bald fact to life, together with the outcome:

The fleet of Suleiman the Magnificent, rank upon rank of silken sails flashing with gold, the crescent banners like cirrus against the blue sky, was still there, far in the distance beyond the sentinel hill. But it had not swung in the wide, so-familiar arc across the blue sea to Gozo. Instead, it was moving, bright scimitar of the prophet, to the distant, rich, Viceregal shores of Sicily. ...

... The oars moved then, raggedly, to backwater, and the small lamps on the quay, in the gathering dusk, glimmered on the rowers, their brown faces upturned to the fort: on black, shawled heads and strong, knotted brown arms; on rolls and parcels and baskets and bundles which were silent and others which moved strongly and cried. It shone on a bent wicker cage in which a linnet lay dying; on a snoring child, clutching a doll sodden with tears; on the upturned eyes and untutored throats of the women and children of Gozo, who had rowed through the straits of Comino, past Mellieha Bay, past the bay where, 15 centuries before, St Paul had been wrecked and had come, like St Paul, to seek sanctuary.

'... They have come all the way from Gozo,' said Gabriel, sharpness audible even in that unshaken voice. 'If as you say the Turks have gone. ...'

'Then they have no right to encumber us here. And if the Turks have *not* gone, as you are so fond of reiterating,' said Juan de Homedès with devastating precision, 'then what are these but useless mouths obstructing the garrison?'

'And if Gozo is attacked, and not Malta?' asked Gabriel bluntly.

The Grandmaster turned away, his velvet cloak pressed peevishly against his thin flesh, the eight-pointed cross glimmering in the scented dark. 'Exactly my point, Brother,' he said. 'How do you suppose these poor men of Gozo will fight if we withdraw the very thing they want most to save? Send these people back.'

The Turks did return to the Maltese islands and Dorothy Dunnett's story moves within the walls of Mdina:

Behind the flaking walls a ditch was dug, and in the rear of this a second wall was raised: a wall of earth and crumbling stone, a heap of friable rubbish ravished in this land of naked soil from the homes which stood that morning on this site. Craftsman, artisan, nobleman, judge – each family in that fated quarter of Mdina wrecked its house, and the dark, stocky women of Malta, the veiling stuck with sweat to their cheeks, carried the precious rubble cradled in their white skirts to the new wall. And as each section of entrenchment was finished, planks were dragged in for platforms and epaulments on which artillery could rest and arquebuses fire over the ditch.

The St Agatha-led procession does not feature here, but the tactics of experienced soldiers:

'We are ten knights, but the Turk will only count crosses. Dress every man, woman and child as a warrior. Helm the grandmothers; silver-paint muslin if you have no armour. Let's have sticks for arquebuses, rods for crossbows. ...'
... Then all that could be done for Mdina had been done. Silent under the sun, knights, soldiers, servants, men and women of Mdina and the casals about – even, here and there, the best blood of Malta, the Lord of Gatto-Murino, the Inguanez whose crest for a hundred years had been wrought in Mdina's great gates – persuaded at last by Gabriel's lucid power to help the hated, usurping knights, lay at their posts.

On Gozo, our hero Frances Crawford of Lymond's former love, Oonagh O'Dwyer, was now concubine of the Governor, the Knight Galatian de Césal for, as the next chapter will show, the Knights' vow of celibacy was often something of a charade. As the Ottoman force besieges Mdina, Dorothy Dunnett sets the scene for what will follow:

High on its acropolis above the capital Rabat, the Gran' Castello, her lover's citadel, guarded the centre of Gozo, a three-mile span of sharp hills and patchwork plains, of carob trees and low, square houses and stone terraces with the fishing nets drying and the gourds seated, green and yellow and fat as aldermen on their walls.

Gozo falls, de Césal giving in far too easily. He and Oonagh and thousands of other Gozitans are transported three days' sailing away, to Tripoli, which Charles V had inveigled the Order into taking when he gave them Malta. And so the novel moves there – and to its fall to the Turks – taking all its characters. As she looks on Gozo for the last time, ironically what comes to Oonagh's mind are the words from the Quran on Majmuna's tombstone.

Finally we are told about those Gozitans who escaped the fall of their citadel, those who died and those who were captured: 'Three hundred lived by escaping to il-Harrax [a village to the north]. A thousand died. And six thousand three hundred men, women and children of Gozo were put aboard the Ottoman fleet, to be sold, at best, to slavery.'

The Disorderly Knights is the fictional version of 1551 – and none the worse for that. Equally interesting in its own way is Stanley Fiorini's long, detailed and scholarly article, 'The Resettlement of Gozo after 1551' (1986). He starts with the account of a near-contemporary chronicler who details 5,500 Gozitans taken, 700 of them men, and 40 old men spared. An undefined number of 'able-bodied men' managed to escape. That leaves a large number of women and children captured.

What Stanley Fiorini does not mention, though, is the number of citizens killed during the attack. We know the identity of one family; indeed their name is immortalised in a Citadel street name. As the Turks attacked the Citadel and fighting spread, Don Bernardo de Opuo began to suspect that any defence was in vain. He was not prepared, though, for his wife and daughters to fall into the hands of the Turks. He ran home and, having killed them, was felled in the fighting. Nowhere is Bernardo's wife named; and you have to wonder if he consulted her and their daughters before he dispatched them. The house on the site of that in which the family lived is opposite the Folklore Museum in Triq Bernardo de Opuo, and there is a plaque too; they will feature in the Gozo itinerary (Chapter 23).

The re-settling of Gozo after 1551 is too complicated to explore here, except to say that the population was not back to normal for 150 or so years. But what Stanley Fiorini provides is names of women, those who were ransomed, those who were not, and in a couple of cases more than names. Godfrey Wettinger, who has also written on the subject, and upon whom Stanley Fiorini draws, found a source recounting how Tripolitanian tradition

> would have it that a large section of these wretched Gozitans were interned by their captors in Tarhuna (a conglomeration 40 miles from Tripoli) where in the course of time, they became absorbed into the indigenous population while preserving uses, customs and expressions testifying to their partly Christian origin. In their quarrels, Arabs revile them with the words 'Iiddkom Malti' your ancestor was Maltese.

But captives were also taken to Constantinople and Stanley Fiorini, who found evidence of individuals in several places, tells, for example, of the 'Magnificent **Donna Damma**, widow of the late Magnificent Antoni **Rapa** of the place and island of Gozo of the diocese of Malta, formerly captive of the infidels but now free and liberated of her captivity living in this city of Constantinople'. She had been freed within four years of captivity. Why didn't she go back to Gozo? The genealogy of the Gozo Rapa family does not mention her but does record that a Don Antonio Rapa died in 1551. Perhaps he was killed during the Turkish attack. Perhaps she remarried in Constantinople.

The will of Petrus **Salibe** tells of his daughter: 'the said testator, wishing to rescue and free from captivity one of his daughters a slave ... from the Saracens or infidels from the Catholic faith, and in particular **Angela** his daughter who was discovered to be slave in the city of Constantinople'. This reads rather oddly: why didn't he pay the ransom before his will was drawn up which, presumably, provided funds only after his death? Perhaps he had only just discovered Angela's whereabouts and was on his deathbed. This seems possible as his son Paulus soon thereafter sold his lands in Gozo (inherited from his father?) to another Gozitan.

Then there were the women or girls initially unredeemed, and I include here those that Stanley Fiorini names (from Godfrey Wettinger's list) because they deserve it – Maltese women are often identified by the name of their husband:

Paula, wife of Andreas **Chappara**, **Paulina** wife of Dominicus **Gambino**, **Antonia** wife of Mathias **de Manuele**, **Ysabella de Manuele**, **Ioanna** wife of Fidericus **Mongebino**, **Scani** wife of Ioannes **Nicolachi**, **Decia** wife of Matheus **Saliba** ...

I note that that list includes another Gozitan **Saliba** woman, **Decia**, perhaps the aunt of Angela daughter of Petrus. Some were later redeemed but money-raising was slow and several years later the following women were still unredeemed:

... **Angela Bajada, Malgarita de Federico, Peruna** the wife of Andriotta **Gambino, Ioannella** the widow of Andriotta **Gambino, Dionora de Manuele** and her daughters **Ysabella** and **Beatrice, Malgarita** the widow of Antonio **Merchic, Paulina** the wife of Gregorio **Merchic, Ioannella** the wife of Leonardo **Rappa, Margarita Rogiles**.

Angela Bajada was obviously a relative of Father Paulo Bajada who spent more than 14 years in captivity, and then was only redeemed through the efforts of merchants who expected to be paid back. His parents were unredeemed, so Angela must have been his mother as Antonio Bajada also remained unredeemed. Were they enslaved together, or apart thereafter? If the latter, did they know where the other was? How was there a wife and a widow of Andriotto Gambino? Is it a mistake in the records, or were there two men with the same name, or was one a discarded wife? When you start to think of names on a dry list in archives as individuals they do enhance the picture of their life after 1551.

Some Gozitan women had already taken refuge on Malta: **Antonella Amfasino** at Birgu (perhaps a relative of the family involved in the sheep and goat court case of 1533), **Geronima Consura** at Qormi and **Vintura Hordob** at Birgu.

Of particular interest to us are the Gozitan women who, in the years that followed, acted as agents for enslaved relatives: 'The noble **Margarita**, widow of Gozitan Albani **Cassar**, relative of Dianore ... of Beatrice and Ysabelle Manuele captives; **Agnes**, wife of Jacop **Laurentio** of Verona and the sister of **Antonella**, wife of Antoni **Damano**, slave.'

So, Margarita was acting for the three Manuele enslaved women, and Agnes for her sister Antonella. Acting in what way is not clear, presumably attempting to free them, perhaps also looking after their property. But then Stanley Fiorini claims that a Maltese (as opposed to Gozitan) woman, **Agnes Calleya**, was climbing 'on a Gozitan band-wagon', and even more flesh is put on the skeleton of history.

Stanley Fiorini concludes

That an appreciable number of Gozitans, predominantly male and certainly more than hitherto claimed, managed to escape the tragic depopulation of Gozo in 1551. Others, in their majority the better off, arranged to get themselves redeemed and found their way back to these islands. Most of these Gozitans went back to their lands on Gozo, but a sizeable minority took refuge, even permanently, either in Sicily or in Malta, mostly in the Cities.

1565

'Its story has been related so many times, and in all ages and in all tongues, that it seems presumptuous to attempt it here again,' wrote Elizabeth Schermerhorn of the 1565 siege of Malta. And she added, since she was writing in 1929, only 11 years after the end of the First World War, 'above all for a generation for whom recitals of carnage and battle horrors have lost their attraction'. She shows by that remark how sensitive the recreation of history is to time and place.

She had started by quoting Voltaire (in French): 'Nothing is better known than the Siege of Malta'. He was writing before the French Revolution of 1789 and its aftermath. But **Catherine de Medici** (1519–1579), a contemporary of the siege, asked,

'Was it really the greatest siege' after listening with the boy king at Plessis, to the Order's Ambassador, Fra Commander de la Roche, while he described the incredible pluck and persistence with which Grand Master de Valette and his little force of Knights and Maltese had held out all summer until the tardy help from Sicily came.

Whether or not it was the greatest siege, its importance was appreciated by Queen Elizabeth I of England, another contemporary, who declared, 'If the Turks should prevail, it is uncertain what further peril might follow to the rest of Christendom.'

But of the Maltese mentioned in the report to Catherine, what part was played by women? So much has been written about this siege, the to and fro of battle, the death and destruction, the cruelty and valour, that the ground does not need to be re-trodden here. The brief, sober facts are these, as set out by Paul Cassar in the introduction to his paper, 'Psychological and Medical Aspects of the Siege of 1565' (1954):

> The siege of 1565 lasted four months, from the 18th May to the 8th of September. The main fighting took place in three areas – round the fort of St. Elmo (23rd May to 23rd June) at Senglea and Birgu (6th July to 8th September). It has been estimated that the number of fighting men involved in the siege operations was 90,000 on the Turkish side and 9,100 men under arms on the Order's side together with the civilian population which must have numbered well over 22,000.

I intend to concentrate on the women, all of them Maltese civilians. How many were left in Malta and Gozo at the time of the siege is uncertain. Following the Turkish attack on Gozo in 1551, and the enslavement of its population, a thousand women, children and the old left Malta for Sicily in 1552. Giovanni Bonello used an additional source in *Versions and Diversions* (2002) which includes in those dispatched the '*donne di malafare*' (women no better than they should be – prostitutes, foreign or native). Then anxiety diminished. But it rose again after marauders on their way to Sicily landed on Gozo in 1560 and in 1565, when it was clear that a major invasion was imminent, between 16 April and 13 May, as Paul Cassar explains,

> 'a great number of people', among whom there were many of the principal families of the Island, sailed to Sicily to be out of reach of the dangers of war. A further batch of refugees had already embarked on four galleys and were waiting for the opportune moment to sail when the Turkish fleet unexpectedly appeared off the Island and the voyage had to be put off.

Elizabeth Schermerhorn describes that moment in the present historic, making it particularly vivid, almost in the style of a novel:

> It is the 18th of May, and at the back of the armadillo's neck, where Melléha Bay and the Saline Marshes make deep cuts, the Turkish galleys are swarming like black flies, with a guard of great round-bottomed ships behind them; and two long lines of Spahis and Janissaries are running down among the humps and scales of his great sides, while the inhabitants of the little *casals* are frantically gathering in their crops and driving their animals into the Borgo for protection.

But there is also a first-hand account of the siege: Francisco Balbi Correggio, already 60 when he fought as an arquebusier in the Spanish Corps during the siege. He published his account, *The Siege of Malta: 1565*, two years later, and added to it in 1568. His quotations are taken from the English translation of the Spanish by Ernle Bradford of that second version (1965).

Correggio writes of what was going on in the countryside during the siege, giving an idea of the brutality practised by both sides:

When the armada descended on Malta, sixty Maltese men and women of varying rank had fled from their village and taken refuge in a cave near the sea, where they had been living for the past month. Among the women there was a very beautiful young girl, and when the refugees were discovered by the Turks as they overran the island, they reported the discovery of these people to a sanjak-bey [military commander]. They did not, incidentally, in any way molest these Maltese, but the sanjak-bey, as we learned, went to their cave, bought [?] the young woman, and took her away while the other Turks were holding the Maltese in conversation.

Our cavalry captain learned about this, and one day rode down to the cave from Mdina. The Turks sallied out and a fight took place, in the course of which our men killed thirty out of the sixty Turks. The remainder, together with the sanjak-bey, seeing that they were defeated, took to their heels carrying off the young woman with them. Our cavalry charged after them, and the sanjak-bey, seeing that there was no chance of escape, cut off the maiden's head with one blow of his sword. Our men attacked him, and he was finally shot dead by an arquebusier. The rest of the Maltese were rescued and taken back to Mdina. I was told this story by Miguel Cali, a Greek who lived in Mdina and who took part in the rescue.

When we read of the part the Maltese played in the siege – inhabitants of Birgu and Senglea, refugees from the countryside and Mdina, male citizens drafted in as militia, as well as Muslim slaves – it is worth being reminded of relations between the Maltese and the Knights, as Paul Cassar does in his 1952 article:

It must be remembered that the Knights, with their encroachments on the political rights and privileges of the Maltese in previous years, had provoked in the people an undercurrent of resentment and hostility against the Order. The treatment of the Maltese by the Order has been described as having been that of a 'crowd of Christian slaves bound to obey all the whimsical laws of the Knights under the usual penalties of the birch, the oar and the gallows'. The Maltese and the Knights thus formed two separate communities with little or no cohesive bonds between them. It is remarkable that even during the siege the Knights maintained their aristocratic outlook – they and their soldiers were 'i nostri' while the Maltese civilians were 'la bassa plebe' or 'il popolo minuto'. Religion formed the only ground on which the people and their rulers could meet on an equal footing. The Turks by threatening this common faith of the Maltese and the Knights strengthened the religious bond between the two communities and thus caused the people to forget their grievances for the time being and to rally unhesitatingly around the Grand-master and his Knights.

There is a touch of the *de haut en bas* in some of Correggio's description but his diary entries are also useful in showing the progress of the siege and women's involvement. It is worth noting, too, the attitude to slaves – one that reflects badly on all strata of society, as perceived, once again, through twenty-first-century sensibility. There is no evidence that some of the slaves described on 5 July were not women.

[20 May] During the day the Grand Master gave orders for the houses which stood near the walls of the Post of Castile to be demolished, in order to clear the ground before fighting began. Soldiers, women, children, and animals were engaged in carrying earth from outside the walls into Birgu. This was piled in heaps, to serve for repairing the fortifications where and when required.

[25 May] La Valette now gave orders that all the women, children, and old people who had taken shelter in the ditch around St Elmo, should be sent over to Birgu. Only men who were fit to fight or work were to be kept there.

[21 June] The feast of Corpus Christi. All day the Turks kept up their usual bombardment, as well as getting ready new siege devices for the reduction of St Elmo. We, for our part, did not fail to honour this great and noble day as best and devoutly as we could. ... All the knights, commanders, and soldiers, excepting those on guard duty, took part in the procession, together with the women and children, and begged Our Lord to deliver us.

[5 July] Having added a further twelve guns to their batteries, the Turks kept up a ceaseless bombardment by night and day. Again they concentrated on the houses, and killed many women and children who were in the streets, or working on the defences. When he saw this, La Valette refused to allow Christians to be exposed to such a danger. He gave orders that slaves should do the work on exposed positions, and they were chained together in pairs. The Grand Master hoped, that when the Turks saw who they were, they would hold their fire. But he was quite wrong, for the slaves were shot down by the score. During the whole siege over five hundred slaves were killed like this. These poor creatures grew so exhausted from their incessant labours that they could hardly stand from fatigue, and preferred to have their ears cut off, or even be killed, rather than work any more.

[28 July] The night was fraught with suspense. The never-ending bombardment of Castile and the houses near by continued. We suffered great casualties among the people working on the defences, and a great many women and children were also killed in the houses.

Before the end of Correggio's account, Ernle Bradford adds a comment of his own:

> It is also on record that when it was suggested to La Valette that he abandon Birgu he said that he would never leave the faithful Maltese men and women to the mercy of the Turk, and that it would be better no one was left alive than that anyone should be saved under such disgraceful conditions.

None of Correggio's entries gives credit to the part women played, they are more victims than participants in the defence. But Paul Cassar, drawing on several sources for his historical 'Vignette' of women, makes clear their true role:

> Other women sought safety within the fortifications of Birgu and Senglea. These women soon found themselves in the battle areas as the Turks succeeded in advancing quite close to the bastions. These women and children joined fearlessly in the fight. In fact it has been recorded that 'wives and children fought with an intrepidity that equalled in some measure the resolute bravery of the Knights. ... and there was no lack of heroic women who ran to the assistance of their fathers, their brothers and their husbands and who generously exposed themselves to the greatest danger'. Women also worked in the arsenal, helped in the repair of the fortifications and in clearing the debris from the ruined bastions. The women's contribution to the defence of the Island was acknowledged by no less a man than Grand Master Jean de la Vallette himself who did not hesitate to declare that without their help Malta might have been lost.

In his concise history, Carmel Cassar (2002) also highlights their essential contribution:

> During those five days [in August], men, women and children, worked side by side, repairing breaches, rebuilding barriers in the streets, preparing incendiaries and mending guns and weapons damaged by the bombardment.
> ... In his last communication the Viceroy [of Sicily] had declared that his troops would arrive in August. As the weeks slipped by the besieged began to fear that they would have to continue defending Malta on their own. The Christians were, on their part, in a desperate condition. Bodies of knights, men, women and children lay unburied in the streets. The wounded in the hospital would have been left to fend for themselves, had not the women of the fortified enclave taken over the duties of nurses to the sick and cooks to the garrison. The women even carried ammunition and helped repair the fortifications.

Although general provisions had been stored in advance, and a spring was discovered in one of the Birgu houses easing the shortage of water, as well as those duties described, the women would have had to provide food for their families and care for their children, well, sick, injured or dying. As for their nursing in the hospital, this short-lived involvement is the earliest account I have found of women nursing; all this while full of fear and exhausted through lack of sleep and unusual hard physical labour. Not all of them were in their own homes, and some of them who did have homes there experienced their destruction.

It is worth pausing to ask, who were the women doing the nursing? At other times, the Knights themselves nursed; indeed, hospital service was compulsory once a week, in line with the Knights' original function. The most obvious replacement was nuns, but was it? Carmel Cassar has an interesting account of the activity of at least one nun during the siege in his more woman-centred *Daughters of Eve: Women, Gender Roles, and the Impact of the Council of Trent in Catholic Malta* (2002). For their safety, the 20 or so nuns from the two Benedictine convents in Mdina, St Peter and St Scholastica, had been transferred, some time before or during the siege, to the house of Don Gioseppe Bellie within the walls of Birgu. There sister **Catherina Casha** started complaining of 'abdominal pains' which, in a deposition nearly 10 years later, two other nuns suspected was due to pregnancy.

Sister Catherina took several medicines and herbs at the time, prepared for her by a slave of the household. In due course however, Catherina, seated on a birthing stool and screaming in pain, gave birth to a stillborn baby with the aid of her sibling **Sister Cilia**. The corpse was wrapped in rags by Cilia, put in a sack, and sent to her brother-in-law in Qormi where the child was buried in the grounds of the local church of the family which seems to have been of some standing there. Carmel Cassar ends the story,

> The abbess, who was sister Catherina's aunt, was particularly concerned about this event and blamed the Reverend Master of the Augustinian friary Marco Gandolfo who had been frequenting sister Catherina for over a year. Indeed several nuns recalled that Fra Gandolfo was often seen conversing intimately with sister Catherina at the convent's chapel and they often supped privately together.

In *Mdina*, Mario Buhagiar and Stanley Fiorini give a useful table of 'The Reverend Abbesses of St Peter's' from which it is possible to name Catherina's aunt as **Lucretia Cassia**, Abbess 1542–73. Lucretia's long reign suggests that she had the ability to survive scandal.

Carmel Cassar has the capacity to dig up lovely asides during his research into the bigger picture of women's lives in the sixteenth and seventeenth centuries. One, which he describes in a footnote to *Witchcraft, Sorcery and the Inquisition* (1996), concerns the rich **Ginaina** from Żebbuġ who had earned her money from producing large amounts of linen, helped by 'a group of fati'. Whether this was a group of fates (masculine) or a group of fairies (fem. *fate*, fairies) I question. Do fates come in groups? Does it seem more likely that she put her success down to luck or to help from the fairies? What she did next may be the answer: so attached was she to her wealth that, during the siege, she left the safety of Birgu to 'recover her goods' at Żebbuġ, was caught by the Turks, and never heard of again.

That the more positive part played by women has been long remembered in some quarters, even if often skated over in descriptions of the siege, is clear from the touching tribute by Desmond Zammit Marmarà in his article, '1565 Malta celebrates the historically important victory of the Great Siege' in *The Times of Malta* (2009):

> Then, of course, there were the thousands of nameless women who are sometimes forgotten heroes of the Great Siege. Through their daily efforts they provided support for the men on the ramparts so that these could conserve their strength for the fighting proper.
>
> The concept of women's emancipation was unheard of at the time of the Great Siege but these Maltese women of 1565 provided an early example of burden-sharing between the different sexes. Credit for the Great Siege victory belongs to the women as much as it belongs to the men.

As for how the siege came to an end, in her inimitable style, Elizabeth Schermerhorn shows that it was not the suffering, bravery and hard work of the Knights or the Maltese, or the final arrival of the Sicilian relief force that caused the Turks to abandon the siege: on the Feast day of the Nativity of the Blessed Virgin, 8 September, still Victory Day in Malta:

> Not, according to Maltese tradition, because they [the Turks] were running short of provisions and ammunition and soldiers, nor because the *Gran' Soccorso* had arrived, nor yet because the season of fierce storms and tempestuous seas was at hand; but because they had seen an awful vision in the clouds – Our Lady with St John, attended by a dazzling white female figure with a shield and buckler, closely resembling the allegorical figure of the 'Religion' as Mattia Preti later represented her in the frescoes of St John's Church in Valletta; so that the besiegers were suddenly convinced of the hopelessness of fighting longer against an organisation so augustly protected.

There is no certainty over the casualties of the siege. Elizabeth Schermerhorn suggests that 9,000 Maltese were killed, 240 Knights, and 30,000 Turks. In a footnote, she gives other figures: 200 Knights, 2,500 soldiers, 7,000 Maltese, 30,000 Turks. Brian Blouet, in *The Story of Malta* (2007) suggests the figures given for the deaths of Maltese are too high; indeed, he takes great pains with the population in general of Malta over time.

Parts of Malta – urban and countryside – were left devastated, but the people, Maltese and Knights, were more united than previously, and the position of the Order as the power in the land was more firmly established than ever.

1644-1645

That was not the end of discord between the Knights of Malta and the Ottoman Empire, but an incident of 1644, almost a century after the Great Siege, was to give an ironic twist to the story.

The Ottoman navy was much depleted after the battle of Lepanto in 1571 when a coalition fleet of the European Catholic maritime states defeated it after five hours of combat off western Greece. But ships were easy enough to rebuild, even if it took longer to train experienced seamen. Knightly corsairs continued to harass Turkish shipping.

Thomas Freller's 'The Capture of the *Gran Galeone* by the Knights of Malta (28th September 1644) – *Casus Belli?*' (2005) tells the story, and the various versions of it, in minute detail, and he may well dispute that which is best known. Captain General Gabriel de Chambres Boisbaudrant had received orders to take his galley and five others of the Order to the waters of the Levant, to wait for prizes sailing along the important route between Constantinople and Alexandria. The season had come to an end when on 28 September, the Order's fleet spotted 10 Turkish vessels on the horizon, one of them a *Gran Galeone*.

The galleon was called *Gran Sultana* and was defended by 600 soldiers. Eventually, after hours of bloody battle in which Boisbaudrant and eight other Knights were killed, some of the Turkish fleet fled, some were sunk and the *Sultana* was overcome. Captives were taken, among them 30 women and 20 pages, and much booty – jewellery, Persian carpets, porcelain, precious fabrics and garments, furs, gold and silver.

When the women arrived in Malta, it was clear from the way that one of them was treated by the others, and by the richness of her possessions, that she was someone of high rank. She is said to have been 19-year-old **Sultana Basseba** (sometimes Zafira) (*c*.1625–*c*.1644), a Circassian beauty, one of the favourites in the harem of mad Sultan Ibrahim I whose all-powerful mother, **Mah-Peyker Kosem Valide Sultan** (*c*.1590–1651), ruled the empire for him. With Basseba was her two-year-old son Osmal, who received even more attention from the captured Turks.

When it was realised that Basseba and her son were out of the ordinary, they were transferred to the palace in the Strada Reale (later 249–250 Kingsway) of the rich, Turkish-speaking merchant Ignazio Ribera (see Chapter 17 itinerary). It is fair to assume that if Ribera did not have a wife, he at least had a mother or sister or other female relative living there too, but I can find no evidence of Ribera women. Ribera's brief was to find out what was what. In spite of any care taken of her, Basseba died quite soon after her arrival in Malta. Elizabeth Schermerhorn suggests that she did so with terrible convulsions 'due, we are told, to a slow poison administered by a rival'. Osmal, however, thrived, grew up and was carefully educated and received into the Roman Catholic church. He subsequently joined the

Dominican order under the name of Fra Ottoman, travelled in Europe, and was a great favourite with women wherever he went.

Godfrey Wettinger explains, in *Slavery in the Islands of Malta and Gozo ca. 1000–1812* (2002), that, while Basseba and her son would be kept, 27 other women remained available for ransom. One of them asked for permission to go to Constantinople to obtain 'their combined ransom from the Sultan's mother and other females at the Court'. This all took a long time to negotiate on both sides; in the meantime, the women were placed in the homes of 'honourable families'; three of them, for example, lived in the house of Ignazio Ribera between at least 1650 and 1655. In 1654, the group was still in Malta. Eventually, the women were ransomed.

Sultan Ibrahim, however, was incensed by what had happened to his galleys, his favourite, and his son. The Knights expected a retaliatory attack on Malta. Preparations were hastily made to repel it, including an attempt by Grand Master Lascaris to have the bronze cannons from Mdina moved to the now-established city of Valletta, and replaced with iron ones, on the grounds that Mdina was anyway untenable in the event of a siege. Paul Cassar tells in his 'Vignette' how

When his soldiers went to remove the guns from the fortifications, the women of Mdina attacked them furiously. Many of them were arrested, tried and imprisoned. It has been said that the resentment of women against the Grand Master was so great that the term *Wicc Laskri* (the face of Lascaris) became with them an expression of the utmost contempt.

But here is the twist in the story: the Order's galleys, on their return from the attack on the Turkish fleet, had tried to put in at Crete to replenish supplies. Crete was then in the hands of the Venetians, and had been since 1204. They were not pleased at the Knights' attacks made on Mediterranean shipping, including their own, and sought always to keep in with the Ottoman Empire. Thus, they turned the Maltese galleys away.

Sultan Ibrahim ignored that – as far as he was concerned, Venetian Crete had harboured the Knights' galleys. He therefore initiated an attack on Crete in 1645, instead of Malta. Rethymnon fell fairly quickly, but the besieged in Candia (today's Herakleion) held out for over twenty years. Crete then became part of the Ottoman Empire from 1669 to 1898. The fall of Crete, rather than Malta, was not the only irony, as I recount in *Crete: Women, History, Books and Places*; as a result of it,

Ten of the most beautiful women and girls who were taken to Istanbul were presented to the Sultan for his harem at Topkapi. Among them was three-year-old **Evmenia Vergitzi** (or **Vorias**) (1643–1715), daughter of the village priest of the village of Kamariotis (south-west of Candia). At the age of four or five, she was married to Mehmet IV who had then just come to the throne and was much the same age. She was his first, and favourite, wife, known as JJ Mah-para Ummatallah Rabia Gul Nuz

(Spring Rose-water) and mother of two future Sultans (Mustapha II and Ahmet II). She is buried in the Imperial Ottoman mausoleum in Istanbul.

Malta remained safe enough after 1645. In 1699, the Treaty of Karlowitz brought to an end the general hostilities between Christians and Muslims and was, indeed, the beginning of a decline in the power of the Ottoman Empire.

6 – Women, Knights, Morality and Religion 1530–1700

Contradictions

The status and treatment of women was not only to be affected by the arrival of the Knights in 1530, but also by the deliberations of the Council of Trent. Between 1545 and 1563 this sought, through the Catholic Church, to counter the Protestant Reformation, the liberalising of religion and culture, taking place in northern Europe. For Malta it meant an increase in the part piety and family were meant to play, and emphasised the confinement of women to their homes nominally under patriarchal control but, in reality, husbands were marginalised there and the wife's mother dominated. Even more constrained was the seemingly pious life of the nun. The effect of the Knights' command of the islands, on the other hand, particularly the charade of their celibacy, was the opposite.

The contradictory result of these two forces is most usefully seen through the cases that came before the Inquisition (Holy Office) which acquired formality in Malta in 1575 and lasted until the arrival of French Revolutionary forces in 1798. And, as Carmel Cassar says of the attempt to constrain women in *Daughters of Eve*, 'In many instances … women overcame such bounds or quite specifically ignored them'. Typical of this was the 1645 protest of the women of Mdina, mentioned in the last chapter, when Grand Master Lascaris tried to remove their protective cannon. A year earlier, Gozitan women had joined the men protesting against an increase in taxation.

This chapter, therefore, havers between the virtuous women and those buffeted by the exigencies, moral and economic, of the times. The contradictions and the overcoming of the bounds are clearly manifest in the person of the Greek Maltese Catherine Vitale with her use of her sexuality, her relationship with the Knights, the Church, the law and money, and her fall into the brutality commonplace then. And the contradictions emerge more generally in the sending of prostitutes (*peccatriche* or *meretriche*) – of which there were many – to the nunnery.

After the Great Siege of 1565 described in the last chapter, Grand Master Jean de Valette hastily set in motion the building of a new, heavily fortified city on the Sceberras Peninsula opposite the Knights' initial settlement of Birgu, a city to be named after him. Birgu was dubbed Vittoriosa, in honour of the part it played in the Siege but then, and even now, more commonly known as Birgu.

In Valletta, fine new *Auberges* for the various *Langues* of the Knights were thrown up – most of which, if not destroyed during the Second World War, survive, often used now as ministries of the Government. One of my favourite views of women, in Paul Cassar's 'Vignette', concerns their part in the construction of Valletta; they certainly seem to have thumbed their noses at the Council of Trent. He writes:

> In the sixteenth century women joined the male labour force engaged in the building trade. We have evidence that a number of them from Luqa travelled to Valletta to work in the construction of houses at the time of the erection of the new city. This activity was frowned upon and earned the censure of the Parish Priest of Zurrieq who, in a sermon delivered at Luqa, denounced these women workers as being of a low order (*baxxi*) and those that were organising them 'even worse'.
>
> A job connected with the building industry that, in the past, was practically monopolised by women was that of roof-beater (*ballata*) when roofs were covered with *puzzolana* [a friable mineral a bit like pumice].

More common work for women outside the home was an extension of their traditional work in it. Carmel Cassar lists washing, laundering and scrubbing as 'women's work and, as such poorly paid and marginal'. He adds that 'women sold their labour in the market, cooked, cleaned, sewed, worked in textiles. They also tended and catered for the sick and members of their family.'

Almost as common was prostitution which, as Carmel Cassar suggests, provided them 'with financial gain and autonomy often far superior to the subsistence-level existence offered by work in the textile industry or in domestic service'. But you did not have to be poorly paid or to sell your body – where there was always a risk either of sexually transmitted diseases such as the *mal francese* (syphilis) or of being taken off the street to be reformed (*convertite*) in the special *repetente* nunneries.

I like the images conjured up by Thomas Freller in his chapter in Nicholas de Piro and Vicki Ann Cremona's *Costume in Malta* (1998). He tells the story of the Swabian merchant Samuel Kiechel who came to Malta in 1587 and stayed in a hostelry in Birgu run by a Moorish woman he called **Louise**. The use of his word '*Moehrin*' then denoted a non-Christian woman of dark colouring. Louise always dressed beautifully in silk or cotton and wore gold rings. She was affianced to a rich, well-dressed Maltese merchant. But by the time Kiechel returned in 1598, Louise had married a rich French captain.

Malta, with its population of about 30,000 in 1590, was nothing if not a melting pot, for Thomas Freller continues that paragraph with a 1614 account by the Spaniard Pedro Orgonez de Cevallas who ran into a noble woman from Seville roaming the streets of Valletta in male attire. 'She had come to Malta after she had killed her noble husband.'

There were women travellers in Malta as early, at least, as 1573, and they were almost as lively as the noblewoman from Seville, but there are apparently no accounts of their travels written by them until that of two Englishwomen in the seventeenth century, and of an Italian in 1752. What a group of German women saw of Maltese women did not resemble Louise of Birgu; nor was their own forwardness appreciated. The traveller Bartolomeo de Pozzo, whose account appears in Giovanni Bonello's *Figments and Fragments* (2001), wrote:

> The appearance of some German ladies who arrived on an armed frigate together with their husbands, who served as officers of the said armies, proved to be a curious novelty. The style of their garments and their openness in conversation were looked upon with wonder by the Maltese, especially by the women, who are reserved by nature and who shy away from any public business and from appearing without veils outside their homes; while these (German women) with masculine spirit and clothes did not hesitate to follow their husbands in wars and distant countries.

The German women came, of course, from that part of Europe where the Protestant Reformation had first taken root, and they arrived in Malta where the Council of Trent was beginning to have some effect. As Giovanni Bonello's chapter 'Law v Fashion' also tells us, Maltese women's clothing and, indeed, that of the men, was influenced by sumptuary laws, restrictions on clothing, usually of excess, that was a nice money-earner, as well as a means of social control. Paul Cassar, in his 'Vignette', helpfully elaborates:

> In 1555 women were prohibited by Grand Master Claude de la Sengle from wearing dismal mourning dresses that trailed to the ground for more than three days after the death of a relative. In 1558 Grand Master Jean de la Vallette issued a decree against what he called 'the vain and dishonest pomp of dressing' and against the use of embroidered stockings by women. … A similar decree was published in 1640 by Grand Master Jean Lascaris to curb the 'temerary insolence and presumption of many women' and to ban the manufacture and wearing of gloves and bonnets ornamented with gold and silver braid, pearls and precious stones. In 1658 Grand Master Martino De Redin in an effort to limit the spending of money on clothing of luxury, prohibited the ornamentation of mantles with lace and other accessories. … Similar decrees were issued in 1697, 1724 and 1741.

If a woman disobeyed the laws, it was her husband who paid the penalty, though it would be subtracted from her dowry. An unmarried woman, or a loose one, was fined and might be publicly whipped.

A century later, the traveller Sieur Jean du Mont gives an account of women's dress that hints at the contradictions inherent in a society torn between the dictates of the Council of Trent, the sumptuary laws and the lifestyle of the Knights:

> The habit of the women in this place is as melancholic and dismal when they go abroad as it is wanton and lascivious when they are at home. In the streets you see nothing but a long black veil instead of a woman, which covers them entirely from Head to Foot, that such a sight would cost a low Briton [Catholic Frenchwoman from Brittany?] at least twenty

Signs of the Cross; for the women in this city look just like so many ghosts wrapt in shrouds, stalking about the streets.

But if they are ghosts in the streets, they are Angels at home; for though the peasants are tawny, the women who live in the City have the fairest complexions in the world.

I can only give you an account of their Summer Dress since I never had occasion to see 'em in the Winter. They wear a fine white smock, plaited at the neck like a man's shirt, but the opening is so wide that it leaves their shoulders and Breasts entirely exposed to the view of the Ravished Beholder; the sleeves are very large and tucked up to the neckband of the Smock to which they are fastened with a Pin, so that one may see their whole Arms.

This smock is almost the entire Habit, for they wear nothing above it but a very little Pair of Boddice about their waist under their Breasts, which being not above a span long serves only to set off the fineness of their Shape and rather exposes than conceals those alluring charms that strike the eyes and the hearts of the Spectator with a sweet but irresistible violence.

That passage ends rather tellingly, 'The men's habit is not very different from ours.'

But best of all the stories, and leaving way behind any talk of appearance, or contradictions of behaviour, is that of **Donna Eleonora Spadafora Sambuca**. If there was ever a woman of the period who took on the powers that be, and won, it was she.

Donna Eleonora was the daughter of Count Federico Spadafora of Spadafora-di-Biscotto, Messina, Sicily, and **Giulia Alliata** who, her name suggests, was not a noblewoman. When Eleanora was born is not clear, but it is crucial.

Count Federico had various dealings with the Knights of Malta, as detailed in Giovanni Bonello's *Closures and Disclosures* (2006), the main one of which concerned his monopoly on the collection of taxes on biscuits, lard, salt and stays (ropes for keeping ships' masts in place). In 1585, the Order of St John and all its Maltese subjects were exempted from paying this tax. To show their gratitude, the Order bound itself to nominate Count Federico's firstborn, 'and then each firstborn successor in perpetuity, Knights of Devotion of the Order'. The contract was drawn up between the Knights and the Count on 4 February the same year. Count Federico died in 1598.

Four years after her father's death, in 1602, Countess Eleonora, who had inherited his feudal rights, also claimed the title promised by the Order. And after a lot of toing and froing concerning the validity of the contract, the Knights were obliged to give in and create the first woman Knight of Devotion of their Order.

You have to wonder about how careless the Knights were in 1585. When I first read Giovanni Bonello's intriguing account in 'Some Rare Examples of Women Knights of Malta', I assumed that no children had yet been born in 1585 when the contract was signed, which would explain how the Knights were caught out. He says that Eleonora applied to become a Knight 17 years after 1585, which would suggest that she was born after that date, or the Knights, alert to the fact that she was the firstborn would surely have had a clause debarring females – unless the idea was so preposterous that it did not cross their minds. But would a 16- or 17-year-old girl at that time enter into that legal minefield? It seemed unlikely. There had to be another explanation.

Persevering on the internet finally gave me the chronological list of the Spadaforas' children: there were seven, six of them girls – Eleonora the first – and one boy, Giovanni, born second. The only birth date noted is that of the fifth child, Countess Alfonsina, a crucial one – 1582: she was born three years before the contract. So Eleonora was born well before 1585 and, therefore, well over 20 when she approached the Knights. Giovanni's date of birth is unknown, but his date of death was *c*.1586. The Knights in 1585 may have known of his birth, discounted, or not known about, his older sister, and not known of his death a year later. They would certainly never have expected his sister to claim her rights as the firstborn.

The final irony came when it was time to sign the papers. Eleonora had, in the meantime, married the Marquis Vincenzo Mastrantonio of Mastrantonio-e-Beccadelli-di-Bologna-della-Sambuca. Giovanni Bonello notes,

> As the new title-holder (*arrendatrice*) of the tax-collecting rights, she formally re-confirmed the exemption granted by her father. Acknowledging that the validity of an undertaking made by a married woman without the 'consent and assistance' of her husband then ranked low indeed, she obtained its ratification by her spouse the Marquis della Sambuca too. The Council, grudgingly, I guess, complied with her request, and the Marchesa Sambuca joined the Order of Malta to become a Knight of Devotion, entitled to wear the habit and the hallowed eight-pointed cross.

If only the evidence existed to tell us what else Eleonora did with her life! What use did she make of her Knightly title and status? Did she even visit Malta? Did she herself handle the feudal rights inherited from her father, and the administration of the Maltese tax exemption? I have learnt that her mother, following her husband's death in 1598, entered the nunnery of San Gregorio, dying there in 1629, and that two of her daughters, Maria and Bernardina, became Abbess of it. The other two daughters married, Alfonsina in 1597 when she was only 15. Why was her birth date noted, and none of the other children's?

Nuns, Courtesans and Prostitutes

It sounds rather grand and successful that two Spadafora daughters became Abbess, but Giovanni Bonello notes, paraphrasing what Henry Wotton, English ambassador at Venice, wrote in 1608, 'To save on dowries, noble parents forced three out of five daughters to take the veil. The convent was invariably the cheaper option. It operated as an institutionalised savings scheme.' Women, sometimes little more than girls, forced into this confined life were not necessarily happy and fulfilled, however high their status.

Wotton was talking about nunneries in Italy, and Giovanni Bonello develops his remark in connection with his own chapter 'Murder in a Hospitaller Monastery' (2006), a murder that took place in 1583 in a nunnery attached to the Order of St John in Florence, but it applied equally to Malta and, indeed, the nun murderer, **Maria Gratia Grisoni**, was tried in Malta, the headquarters of the Order. She was found guilty and ordered to be disrobed, expelled and condemned to spend the rest of her life in solitary confinement; it would have been with a barred window out of reach and a small slit in the solid masonry at floor level for food to be pushed in and body waste out.

Nuns attached to the Order – with a status rather different from that of Eleonora Spadafora Sambuca – did not arrive in Malta until 1582, brought by Grand Master Verdalle to look after poor orphan girls in order to safeguard their virginity. The Ursuline nunnery was established first in the Grand Master's palace in Birgu, after he had moved to his new one in Valletta (what is now the President's office, see Chapter 17 itinerary). In 1595, the Ursulines were also moved to Valletta (see Chapter 17 itinerary); the Knights' hospital in Birgu was given over to the Benedictine nuns of Santa Scholastica from Mdina (see Chapter 18 itinerary). Carmel Cassar notes that a visitor to Santa Scholastica in Mdina in 1575 found that the nuns could not read, though a boarding school for girls existed there before the Great Siege. Clearly, literacy was not the foremost talent deemed suitable for girls.

In 1575, the new nunnery of St Catherine's had been founded in the Strada Reale – now Republic Street – also to protect orphan girls from the perils of the world. Today it treasures a sculpture of the Virgin Mary by Maria de Dominici but, unfortunately, it affiliated with the Augustinians in 1851 and thus became a closed order. You can, however, ask for special permission to see it (see Chapter 17 itinerary).

The newly established Ursulines attached to the Order were known as *sorores*, if they came from noble families, and as *donatae* otherwise, and were to enjoy the same status as the conventual friars of the Order; they could wear the half-cross on their habit, while the prioress had the right to wear the full cross. In *Malta of the Knights* Elizabeth Schermerhorn gives a useful account of the background to their introduction to Malta:

And [Grand Master Verdalle] continued his predecessor's pious solicitude for the welfare of women, establishing the Ursuline Convent in Valletta, under the protection of the Hospitallers. This was not an innovation; there had always been a place for women in the traditions of Orders of Chivalry. The convent of the Blessed Gérard at Jerusalem had maintained a hospital for women as well as for men, and an affiliated Order of nuns, wearing the eight-pointed cross, took the vows of Obedience to the Master of the Hospital, as he was first called, and nursed the sick pilgrims and the wounded. ... When the wanderings of the Knights began, as the Turks pushed them steadily west, the women left Jerusalem and attached themselves to some of the European Priories of the Order, but not until Verdalle's time were there any nuns in the Convent at Valletta. ... They were cloistered, and Verdalle built them a convent on Strada St Ursola, endowing them with manors and rich revenues. The Treasury of the Religion provided them with corn, oil and wine and with medical and spiritual attendance and they were allotted a portion of booty captured by the galleys.

A history of the Ursulines, found on the internet, explains that two Poor Clare nuns came over from Sicily to set up the nunnery: **Sister Clara Febo** as prioress and **Sister Elisabetta Humano**, as her deputy; they were expected to be there for life. Sister Elisabetta died in 1610, but Sister Clara lived on and kept her post despite age and ill health. After 28 years, in 1612, the Grand Master relieved her, while allowing her to keep the privileges of the prioress. The nunnery started off with 15 sisters who were kept separate from the girls in their care. The girls were there either until they, in their turn, entered the nunnery or were married.

Elizabeth Schermerhorn's account suggests that the nuns were able to live a well-cushioned and cosy life, but how did they feel a hundred years later? She continues with her account:

But the Convent of St Ursola waxed fat, and in Grand Master Carafa's day [1680–1690] the ladies grew tired of watching, from the screened roof of their convent, the Knights go forth in their proud galleys to earn their way to Heaven by glorious adventure, while the sisters did nothing to save the Faith except to make lovely wreaths of silk flowers for the novices to wear at their reception; and they raised a mild feminist revolt. They requested the privilege of supplementing their Faith with Works, of reviving the ancient traditions of the first Sisters of the Order and participating in the nursing activities of the Knights. It became necessary to remind them that their work was to fight with their prayers for the Faith while the Knights fought with their weapons. ... and the nuns accepted their fate with pious resignation and submitted to remain definitely cloistered, and to receive only their nearest relatives on visiting days, 'seated modestly on a bench, without gesticulation or laughter or gossip or any action that does not breathe the odour of virtue and perfect,' exactly as the revised rule of Grand Master Carafa directed that they should.

While the Ursulines had been established to look after 'poor orphans', they were also expected to take in girls who had been led astray, to which they protested. Therefore another nunnery, run by the Franciscan Poor Clares, was set up for unmarried mothers and reformed prostitutes and dedicated to St Mary Magdalen of the Penitents (also known as the Maddalena) because Mary Magdalene was assumed to have been a prostitute. It was ready by

1598, and was also in Strada San Ursola; in 1609 it moved to larger premises near Fort S Elmo (see Chapter 17 itinerary). We know, particularly from Christine Muscat's *Magdalene Nuns and Penitent Prostitutes* (2013), that initially the Maddalena was poorly funded and that the inmates lived in freezing conditions. Christine Muscat usefully sets the nunnery in the context of Maddalenas with the same purpose in other parts of Europe. Enlarging on the scope of the nunnery in Malta, she writes:

This was a very special Hospitaller cloister, a philanthropic institution with the very specific mission of offering local prostitutes a refuge, and a contemplative orientation leading to a full spiritual recovery. In practice however, the spectrum of ladies accommodated in the cloister was much wider, embracing social cases from all walks of life. It received single mothers, widows, witches, and homeless women, poor women, and pregnant women, women rejected by their families, prisoners and very young girls. Moreover, rather surreptitiously, the monastery also harboured 'choice subjects' as mistresses of the Grand Master ... The Repentite were indeed a broad-based group of nuns.

Victor F Denaro, in 'House in Merchants Street Valletta' (1958) notes how the Maddalena was eventually funded:

... the Treasury sanctioned an annual grant of Sc 200. In 1612 the proceeds of a duty of four tari on every cask of imported wine was also allotted to the convent of the Maddalena. These revenues were further augmented by the bequeathing of the fifth part of the estates of all prostitutes, whose wills were made illegal and invalid unless they contained that contribution towards the nunnery.

When the property of a certain Girolama Ciantar, yielding a yearly rental of Sc 500 was incorporated to the foundation, the revenue from all sources amounted to Sc. 2,000 by which 66 nuns under the habit and rule of St Claire were maintained.

That mention of Girolama is almost in passing, but the story was much more complicated, and is disentangled by Christine Muscat under the heading 'The Ciantar Foundation' which was set up in 1620. Though the money eventually went to the Maddalena, the Ursulines were determined that it should go to them. The dispute went to litigation which lasted 25 years.

According to Victor Denaro, **Girolama Ciantar**, wife of Martino Vella, lived at what is now 77 Old Theatre Street, opposite the Manoel Theatre. The Maddalena was not the only institution that she contributed towards: in 1616, at a time of severe drought, she provided funds for Our Lady of Carmel at Fawwara (see Chapter 22 itinerary).

Gradually, the Maddalena accrued funds and property. Christine Muscat observes, 'The Magdalenes owned properties all over Malta and Gozo. They had sixty five houses in Valletta and several small properties in the maritime cities.' The list is, as she says, not exhaustive, but it is long. Her large format, fully illustrated book is a wonderful example of accessible scholarship. She sums up an impression that her detailed study leaves with the reader – a useful leaven to other accounts of nuns in Malta:

> Santa Maria Maddalena presents clear evidence that the potential of nunneries and nuns in the seventeenth and eighteenth centuries went beyond that of being simply religious philanthropic centres. Access to wealth offered opportunities for development that the Magdalene nuns in Malta skilfully exploited in spite of adversity. The economic benefits they secured led to significant autonomy. The nuns challenged the imposition of their superiors and struggled to secure the right to steer their own destiny. They had successes and failures but they never lost their motivation. In a male-dominated society, rife with prejudice against women, the *repentite* went on to become a pioneer group of resourceful females.

And there certainly was another side to the story of nuns in Malta. As the Grand Master was not a clergyman, the Ursulines came under the jurisdiction of the Grand Prior of the Conventual Church, and he could only enter the nunnery with a few attendants in order to avoid a scandal. And there were scandals to be avoided; one example was detailed in the last chapter when the nuns from two houses in Mdina moved for safety to Birgu at the beginning of the Great Siege.

In his exploration of the lives of nuns in Italy and Malta, Giovanni Bonello writes, drawing on the detailed research of Mario Buhagiar and Stanley Fiorini,

> In Mdina, religious life was lax and any rule of silence non-existent. Each nun took her meals on her own. The Inquisition called **Suor Paola de Saura** to account for her suspicious friendship with Pedro de Nava, and **Suor Clementina Muscat** found the nunnery just right when she felt in the mood for making love. They attracted attention by amity as much as by its absence *semper rixant* – they always brawl. ...
> ... The Council set up a commission of enquiry to investigate the kidnapping of a young girl (*puellam virginem*) from the monastery of St Peter called the *abazia vecchia* in Mdina. The fact that the Council of the Order took cognisance of the matter proves that the suspect or suspects were knights.

This was a snapshot of one period – regimes in nunneries changed – and nuns were by no means the only objects of the Knights' inability to keep their vows of celibacy. Chapter 3 makes clear, too, that it was not only Knights who slipped, but also members of the clergy before the Knights moved to Malta. There were also cases in that chapter of the Mdina ruling class with their concubines, sometimes not always distinguishable from prostitutes. With the coming of the Knights, maritime trade picked up and, with it, the arrival of increasing numbers of seafarers. This led, in its turn, to an increase in prostitution, as well as an influx of foreign women, some of whom joined the trade. The traveller Nicolai, who spent two days in Malta in 1551 and recorded his impressions in *Navigations et Peregrinations en Turquie* (1568), described not only the fine churches, houses, and Knights' and merchants' palaces in Birgu but especially the many 'Courtesans – Greek, Italian, Spanish, Moorish and Maltese'.

Paul Casssar recounts in his 'Vignette' how,

> With the building of Valletta after 1566, the courtesans moved to the new city so much so that in 1581 Grand Master Jean l'Eveque Cassière issued an edict banishing all street women from Valletta but allowed the concubines of his friends and of the more powerful dignitaries of the Order of St John to remain in town, a measure which was so much resented by the youthful members of the fraternity that they provoked his deposition from office.

Cassière was carted off, temporarily as it turned out, to Fort S Angelo and jeered on his way by prostitutes lining the route.

Paul Cassar adds, too, to the implication of why the nuns had been brought to Malta and why they had their work cut out in protecting girls and young women:

> Closely linked with the issue of sexual promiscuity was the existence of the illegitimate baby. Historical records show that the incidence of illegitimacy had assumed enough importance as to induce the authorities to make provision for the protection of unwanted babies. By 1575 these infants – known as foundlings – were being received in Santo Spirito Hospital but there is evidence that this arrangement had been in operation many years before as in 1575 the practice of receiving illegitimate or unwanted offspring in this hospital is referred to as an 'old' one.

The *Santo Spirito* was in Rabat, and grew out of a hospital founded in 1372. In 1574, the Order founded the *Sacra Infermeria* in Valletta which also cared for foundlings, and for male patients, but not female. In 'Female Employees in the Medical Services of the Order of St John in Malta' (1978), Paul Cassar details the various hospitals and posts within them, and who was attached to those posts over the centuries. The *Ospedaliera* (Hospitaller), for example, 'had the duty of caring for the foundlings as soon as they were deposited inside the infirmary and removed from the revolving cot or *ruota*'. These babies were eventually 'farmed out' to foster-mothers.

The post, for the best part of the seventeenth century was recruited from members of the same family. **Clemenza Borg** served 'all her life'. She contracted the plague during the epidemic of 1675–76 while caring for patients, but recovered. She was succeeded by **Domenica Muscat** whose son had married Clemenza's daughter Anna. When Domenica retired in 1696,

Anna Borg Muscat was appointed; she was deemed familiar with the duties of the post, having spent a good deal of time in the Infirmary.

George Sandys, who published his account of a visit to Malta in 1637, is quoted by Giovanni Bonello as pithily dismissing the three nunneries of Valletta as 'One for virgins, one for the penitent whores (of impenitent there are plenty) and the third for their bastards.'

The Two Catherines

The *Casetta delle Donne* – Hospital for Incurable Women – was specifically for women, the first, and founded by a woman, the Sienese **Caterina Scappi** (Sarpi, Scarpi) (d.1643) – known as *la Senese*. Although the *Casetta* was set up in its first location in 1625, it was formalised by an act on 20 June 1643. The discrepancy in dates is, as Paul Cassar explains in *Medical History of Malta*, because, initially, Caterina's hospital was in a small house – Santa Maria della Scala – later expanded along the corner of Old Bakery (Forni) and Archbishop Streets (see Chapter 17 itinerary). Caterina bought the house at 144 Archbishop Street from **Cecilia Xiblia** from Syracuse, and 53 Archbishop Street (on the corner of Old Mint Street) was bequeathed to the *Casetta* by **Maria Cajetano**. Later still it transferred to larger premises in Merchant Street.

5. Caterina Scappi, courtesy of Heritage Malta
and the *Times of Malta*

Caterina's provenance appears to be unknown, except that she came from Siena; and I cannot find her birth date. How she came to be inspired is also unclear; as far as we are aware, she was simply a good woman aspiring to do good, probably motivated by her faith. Nor is it known how she came by the money to fund the *Casetta* – did she inherit from a rich family, or was she a rich widow? Had her father been a medical man, or her late husband? But we do know that she was meticulous about how she intended to protect her project; Paul Cassar writes,

In order to ensure that [no one] would, after her death, dare to frustrate her aims or interfere with the permanence of the institution founded by her, she stipulated by means of a legal instrument that the house was to serve no other purpose but the reception and care of needy infirm women. She also laid down that should the building, for some reason or other, fall into the possession of someone else, all her wealth and property were to be employed in the acquisition of other premises for the establishment of a hospital for the treatment of incurable women. She bequeathed her fortune to the institution by a deed of the 20th June 1643 and nominated as executors of her will two knights from Siena. On the demise of these two knights the reigning Grandmaster was enjoined to appoint another two Siennese Knights as protectors and governors of the institution.

It was clear from the start that Caterina also took an active part in the management of the hospital. But the first 'governess' or matron – the person immediately responsible for the running of it – appears to have been **Prudentia**, wife of Pasquale **Grima** who, after serving in that capacity for 40 years, was succeeded by her daughter-in-law, **Diana Grima**, wife of Francesco, on 13 November 1674. There was also a midwife on hand, and a *bassa chirurgica* who performed 'blood-letting, the application of leeches, cataplasms, vessicants and cupping'. *Donne della mancia* served the food. The earliest known *serva* (servant or maid-nurse) employed to look after the patients was **Ortensia Grima** in 1655. In later years it was a woman, known as a *spalmante* or *spalmiatora* who was responsible for mercurial anointing to treat syphilis – that post too was kept within the family. The treatment also required a steam bath attendant, a *stufarola*. Thirty-nine slaves were employed for menial tasks in the *Sacra Infermeria* and the *Casetta* in 1648, but it is not clear if they were female or male.

By 1641, funds were not sufficient for the running of the hospital so the Order supplemented them. When Caterina died in 1643, the Order intervened again and, after internal Order squabbles, closed the hospital down. Paul Cassar recounts the consequences:

One class of patients who had benefited from the care afforded by the hospital were the public women who availed themselves of the mercurial treatment provided for the cure of syphilis. In this manner a certain measure of control over the propagation of syphilis had become indirectly established, but with the suppression of the hospital all opportunities of checking the spread of venereal disease were lost. Infected women were no longer in a position to obtain treatment when they desired it, while some of those who were provided with the required medicaments for domiciliary treatment refrained from using them, with the intention of deliberately prolonging the duration of their illness in order to continue receiving the 'pittance' – which was a special free allowance of food – issued to sick needy women by the Order. Those public women, moreover, who were willing to undergo the prescribed treatment were unable to do so for want of the necessary facilities for mercurial inunctions. The consequence was that they 'infected the whole Island with the French disease'.

Paul Cassar's use of that word 'pittance' is useful because Roger Ellul-Micallef, in 'The Development of Malta's Medical Services during the time of the Order' (2000), in elaborating on the system, leaves untranslated that word obviously connected with the original – one not to be found in an Italian dictionary or on the internet though, helpfully, *The Dictionary of Medieval Latin: from British sources* (2007) provides *pitanceria* and the meaning:

The *Pittanziere*, who were perhaps Malta's first social workers, used this hospital as a base from where initially they issued up to 160 loaves every day to destitute women living in Valletta. By 1771 no less than 880 loaves were being distributed daily to needy women. The *Pittanziere*, also provided house-bound women with medicines, items of bedding and some financial relief.

Paul Cassar, in his article, under the heading 'District Medical Service', describes the first social workers:

The *pitanziere* (alms-givers) were four elderly women employed to succour the indigent women who lay sick in their own homes. They visited the patients daily and brought them the medicaments and food ordered by the doctor, financial relief and items of bedding. They were assigned one each to Valletta, Senglea, Bormla and Birgu. They were helped by four female 'assistants' who carried the bread.

The *pitanziere* also distributed money to poor 'decrepit' and physically disabled handicapped women.

In his history, Paul Cassar takes further the story of the *Casetta* from the time of its closing, adding to the influence of the Church on Maltese life:

Another embarrassing circumstance arose from the fact that while, previously, moribund prostitutes received their last sacraments in the decent atmosphere of the hospital now the 'scandalous' position had arisen in which the Blessed Sacrament had to be carried into the houses of women of ill fame and even in places where 'the donkey and the pig were kept'. When representations on these happenings were made to the Grandmaster, Martin de Redin, he was so impressed that he decided to reopen the women's hospital; but this was not an easy task and when he finally succeeded in re-establishing it in April 1659 he did so only after accepting the condition, imposed by the French Langue, that the Grand Hospitaller or his Lieutenant, the Infirmarian and all the administrative officers of the Holy Infirmary could visit the '*casetta*' whenever they thought fit to do so in order to ascertain in what manner the medicaments and provisions were being consumed.

The story continues with a renewed connection between Knights and their concubines. When in 1717 the *Casetta* needed added funds for an extension, it was helped with a bequest from **Flaminia Valenti**. This must have been left in a form of trust for the *Casetta*, as she would then have been dead for some years.

Flaminia had been the mistress of Grand Master Antoine de Paule; indeed, he installed her in a villa in Attard next to his own, accessed through a small door in the boundary wall. It still stands in Anthony Street (Triq Sant' Antnin), next door to the back entrance of what was to become the Grand

6.   Flaminia Valenti, San Anton, Attard

Masters' retreat, then the British Governors' country residence and now that of the President (see Chapter 20 itinerary). The year after de Paule's death in 1636, Flaminia retired to the nunnery of the *Repentite*.

Christine Muscat tells her story best, how Flaminia, now Sister Dorothea, donated 18,000 scudi 'dishonestly acquired' to the nunnery as part of her dowry for entry, entitling her to special privileges. These included giving birth to her daughter Anna in the cloister, though by this time the Maddalena did not accept pregnant girls and those becoming pregnant while there were expelled. From the age of three, Anna was expected to take the veil on reaching adolescence, but later acquired dispensation from her religious vows. She was registered as **Anna Pittard** and had a son, Domenico Pittard. Flaminia also seems to have had a daughter, **Margherita Valenti Pittardi**, who died.

Flaminia was not the first or last woman to become philanthropical on her death bed. And de Paule was by no means the only Grand Master to keep a mistress: even the revered de Valette had a daughter called **Isabella Guasconi** whom he held at her baptism and looked after all his life. As Giovanni Bonello tells it, de Valette arranged her marriage when she was very young to the Florentine Stefano Buonaccorsi and even stood at her side at her wedding in the Church of St Lawrence, Birgu (see Chapter 18 itinerary). But the marriage unravelled and, in July 1568, believing her to be untrue, Buonaccorsi murdered her. He then fled from Malta with her jewels, and was searched for high and low by the Order. De Vallete, consumed with grief, died soon thereafter. He also had a son by **Catherine Grecque** who was legitimised by the King of France.

By 1759, as Paul Cassar recounts, the *Casetta*

had grown into a large building enclosing a central courtyard with its main entrance in Merchants Street. The ground floor, besides administrative office and the kitchen, had three large wards surrounding three of the sides of a quadrangular courtyard – the Old Ward, the Ward for Mercurial Inunctions and the Surgical Ward.

The first floor was mainly taken up by the New Ward, the largest on this floor, the Small Ward and the Great Ward which communicated directly with the chapel dedicated to St Catherine of Siena, who had been adopted as the patron saint of the hospital as a sign of respect towards the foundress.

Caterina Scappi was buried, in 1643, in the Carmelite Church, in what is now Old Theatre Street, Valletta and in 1791 a large marble plaque was erected to her there (see Chapter 17 itinerary). But the *Casetta* and the 1642 chapel which were opposite the *Sacra Infermeria* were destroyed by enemy bombing during the Second World War; only a few stones remain (see itinerary).

By a nice coincidence, also in 1791 a similar plaque was erected above the burial place of **Caterina Vitale** (1566–1619) about whom we know rather more and whose life appears to have been rather more colourful. In one woman, indeed, is contained many of the possibilities for a man of sixteenth- and seventeenth-century Malta.

She appears in some detail in Carmel Cassar's *Daughters of Eve* under the heading 'Caterina Vitale: Widow, Whore, Witch', and he has written a rather more technical article, 'The World of Caterina Vitale: A Sixteenth Century Lady of Greek Parentage in Malta' (2009); Giovanni Bonello's 'But Who Was Caterina Vitale?' appears in his *Reflections and Rejections* (2004), with its acknowledgements to Carmel Cassar's earlier work. Then there are several internet sources.

I speculated at the beginning of the last chapter that Caterina's parents, Isabella and Demetrio Patras, came over to Malta from Rhodes following the Knights' arrival. Caterina was probably born the year after the Great Siege, and grew up as Valletta was being built, so benefited from a time of relative peace and prosperity. She seems to have had a sister, **Cassandra**, but we know more about a niece, **Annica** (Anna) **Faenza** (d.1660). There is some dispute about Caterina's age, particularly how old she was when she married. Her birth date is deduced from the fact that in 1608, appearing before the Inquisition, she said she was 42; she also claimed to have been married at 12, that is, in 1578. That age was not extraordinary for the times.

Carmel Cassar, in his long article, notes, however, that her marriage certificate of 1575 gives her age as 16. Her husband was the Neapolitan Ettore Vitale, chief pharmacist to the Order of St John, and she was married in Vittoriosa 'according to the rites of the Holy Mother Church' and it would appear that she brought a handsome dowry, including a house and a shop, to a man appreciably older than her. He, too, was a person of substance, but he may have been committing bigamy; that, anyway, was the case that came before the newly established Inquisition in 1579 – his other wives being a woman in Malta and another in Naples. However, Vitale was well-protected by influential members of the Order; he appears, therefore, simply to have been rapped on the knuckles and fined. He did admit to two natural children.

Ettore Vitale died in about 1590, an internet source suggesting that it was as the result of a bomb, but Giovanni Bonello starts his chapter by claiming that the bomb went off outside the house of the widow Caterina Vitale in 1593; that might have been one of the houses she owned in Archbishop Street – numbers 135 and 138 (see Chapter 17 itinerary). She was then said to be 27 years old and had, in the meantime, managed to regain possession of her dowry and ownership of her late husband's property through the *Castellania* (the Grand Master's law courts), with the help of her lawyer, and taken over the running of Ettore's pharmacy, providing medicines to the *Sacra Infermeria*. She saw off a man claiming to be Ettore's son. As Carmel Cassar says in his article, financially independent widows 'might inherit their husbands' lands, property and sometimes his profession, craft or trade'. An eighteenth-century historian refers to Caterina as probably the first female chemist on record in Malta, and there is no reason why she should not have learnt what she needed to know from Ettore. There is a contract between her and the Order as early as 1591, and she was known as *la Speziala* (the she-chemist).

Giovanni Bonello's account continues with the information that the Council of Knights, quite exceptionally, appointed three commissioners to look into who was responsible for the attempted assassination of the rich and powerful widow, 'the inescapable inference points to one or more knights being prime suspects'. One theory has it that Caterina, who was to be accused of being a witch and a whore, had served as courtesan to one or more Knights and attempted to blackmail them. Perhaps more likely is that she was rather litigious where Knights were concerned, to do with money and business rather than sex. She and Ettore engaged in buying and selling property and stocks of medicines and, like many of her contemporaries, Caterina 'made good money' by dealing in slaves.

Giovanni Bonello writes of her career at this stage: 'It seems obvious to me that Caterina Vitale played the part of a consummate entrepreneur, perhaps the earliest female recorded in the chronicles of Malta with a personality wholly and outstandingly autonomous.' While Carmel Cassar concludes that Caterina 'found it intolerable and unrealistic to follow the precepts laid down for widows by the Catholic Church'. That may, of course, have had something to do with the fact that she was Greek, and may have been more in sympathy with Greek Orthodoxy and its precepts, and with Greek culture. Archbishop Street, where Caterina had two houses, was called Strada del Popolo under the Knights, but also known as Strada dei Greci, not necessarily because of the connection with Caterina but between 1576 and 1587, the Greek Orthodox Church, Our Lady of Damascus, was under construction. (The significance of that Church and its icon will emerge in the Chapter 17 itinerary.)

So far, there is something almost admirable about Caterina and it is fair to suggest that some of the mud thrown at her – of prostitution and witchcraft – came as a result of attempts to tarnish the name of an uppity woman. But the case against her of abusing her Muslim and black slaves – some of whom came as part of her dowry – is harder to put aside, and her behaviour towards her only child, **Isabella Vitale** (b.1598) who seems to have been adopted eight years after Ettore's death, was, at best, strange, though somewhat reminiscent of Margarita d'Aragona's two centuries earlier. Money was, and still is, often used as a means of controlling ungrateful children.

Certainly towards the end of her life Caterina's generous philanthropical bequests can be seen as acts of atonement, though she had already, in the 1580s, as Giovanni Bonello describes, established 'a pious foundation for prayers for her soul, in the monastery of St John the Evangelist, *Isola di Patmos*, one of the Dodecanese Greek islands.' And in 1583 she set up a foundation in the Carmelite Church, Valletta, dedicated to the soul of her mother, herself and her descendants – presumably still hoping to have a child of her own with Ettore. She also gave the friars a house in Senglea and jewellery, gold and silver that had belonged to her late mother – not surprising, therefore, that she came later to be buried in the Church.

Caterina's alleged brutal ill-treatment of her slaves was described by them when their case came before the Inquisition in 1608. Details of it – outside the bounds of anything we might imagine today, even though we know that torture continues – are detailed gruesomely both by Carmel Cassar in *Daughters of Eve* and by Giovanni Bonello. Her slaves, such as **Vincentia** and her sibling **Perna,** and **Madelana,** had finally rebelled against her savagery, presumably advised and helped to bring their case by those who wished Caterina ill. They also accused her of witchcraft, in which she was assisted by her long-standing slave **Selima** (Silima), and sexual incontinence; her 'carnal friends' being Knights easily identified because they arrived and departed in their tunics with the eight-pointed cross.

Caterina was, as one might expect, robust in her own defence: she had many enemies, she said; the split bean, which had formed part of the evidence concerning her witchcraft, she used only for the healing of migraine, and then because it was suggested by her physician; her slaves were, themselves, the wrong-doers, thieves who tried to abscond and even planned to murder her.

There certainly seems to have been another side to the behaviour of slaves (though not an excuse for their ill-treatment): in *Slavery in the Islands of Malta and Gozo ca. 1000–1812,* Godfrey Wettinger relates how

In the middle of the seventeenth century, Inquisitor Cardinal Federico Borromeo said that his tribunal in Malta was much preoccupied with the Muslim slaves who were spreading superstitions, incantations, love-philtres, and other 'similar vanities' among the women and the simple-minded while they went about the town 'selling their wretched goods, such as befitted their condition'.

Carmel Cassar has developed this theme in 'The Jewesses of Malta: Slaves and Pedlars, Healers and Diviners' (2013). Such slaves were often Arab-speaking Muslims able, therefore, to communicate easily with Maltese speakers; less often they were Jewesses, but no distinction was made between them. 'On a popular level Jews and Muslims seem to have been attributed with special powers making them sought after for supernatural intervention.' Caterina's slave Selima, who was said to help her in her witchcraft, was probably Muslim. Whereas Maltese women practising witchcraft were insiders 'who broke the code of eithics', Muslims and Jews were outsiders to be mistrusted and legislated against, ineffectually in practice.

The Inquisitor was not impressed by Caterina's defence. He castigated her for her passion for engaging in commerce and condemned her to house arrest under a penalty of forfeiting 300 scudi to the Inquisition if she defaulted. How long the house arrest was to last is not clear, but she was certainly free by 1610 because she was then involved in more damage to her reputation.

How long Isabella lived with Caterina as her daughter is uncertain; and it is unknown if Isabella had been encouraged to plan a future in the nunnery before her adoption. As Christine Muscat tells us, there were child nuns, seven- and eight-year-olds. Or perhaps life with Caterina was generally intolerable, or there had been too much unpleasantness when the Frenchman Villamonte asked for Isabella's hand and Caterina refused. It is certainly true that during her trial of 1608 Caterina named him as one of her enemies. Whatever the reason, when she was barely 12, Isabella entered the Maddalena, taking the name Sister Cherubina.

It was not what her rich and upwardly mobile mother had in mind for her. Isabella was 'a sinless virgin who should not spend her time doing penance' and, as Carmel Cassar explains, 'The convent was essentially an institution of penitence where fallen girls or prostitutes who wished to extricate themselves from their trade could join.' Carmel Cassar even suggests that Caterina herself had spent some time at the Maddalena in her youth, as a result of her mother's later life. There is a clause in her will, as you will see, that lends some credence to rumours of both Caterina and her mother's sometime lifestyle.

On several occasions Caterina visited the nunnery and exhorted her daughter to leave. The young teenager Sister Cherubina refused to listen, demanding to make her own decisions and lead her own life – attitudes she had perhaps learnt from Caterina. The Inquisition tribunal issued an order against her visiting her daughter which was later revoked.

On a particular day in 1610, Caterina, accompanied by her niece Annica and an elderly Greek woman, **Constanza Smeraldo**, visited the nunnery again. The Abbess, **Sister Clara** (perhaps not the Sister Clara, prioress of the Ursulines, though it was not unknown for a prioress to switch nunneries, and switch back) tried to intervene; Caterina reacted. Sister Clara 'even reported that Catherina had declared that she wanted to see the nunnery ruined ...'. When the case came before the Inquisition, witnesses were brought, among them **Sister Gratia Maria**, the sacristan of the *convertite* nunnery chapel, and **Sister Anna Maria Zara** to confirm Caterina's insults. She had called Sister Anna Maria 'a vile prostitute and witch'. This seems to have been a common insult, as it was levelled at Caterina by a witness during her 1608 trial. As far as Caterina was concerned, they were just after her wealth, through Isabella's dowry.

In the end, Caterina won. She had even appealed to the Pope, alleging that Isabella had been abducted and taken to the nunnery, through the Order, the complications of which are explained in Carmel Cassar's long article. The Pope issued an Apostolic Brief on 12 December 1610 allowing Sister Cherubina to leave the nunnery, though she does not appear to have finally done so until 1615, when, as Isabella Vitale, she married Signor Centorio Cagnolo.

Further complications ensued, best described in Giovanni Bonello's chapter, because Caterina refused to help the young couple financially, including Isabella's dowry, and initially refused to compensate the nunnery for Isabella's departure and arrears of maintenance. Her daughter and son-in-law's case went to the *Castellania* (see Chapter 17 itinerary) and then to arbitration; the nunnery was paid over time. Caterina's 1616 will, described most succinctly by Carmel Cassar in his long article, is full of ironies that turn her past life upside down.

Part of the arbitration agreement over Isabella's dowry gave the young couple a house in Strada San Georgio (today's Republic Street) and the will stipulated

> that if Isabella died without heirs the house would then be inherited by the Holy Infirmary. Caterina left her daughter a good quantity of jewels, silver, objects d'art and trousseau. Caterina also agreed to continue to pay the sum agreed upon by the Holy Congregation of the Holy Office for allowing Isabella to leave the *Repentite* convent.
>
> Caterina also left sums of money, clothing, and other items to her servants **Victoria** and **Marietta**. Her slaves Victorio and Victoria [daughter of Vicencia] had to be freed on her death. Victoria was to benefit from a dowry of 300 scudi together with a trousseau consisting of a completely equipped bed. At the same time Victorio was to receive some land in Valletta. She also assigned 50 scudi a year for the dowry of the marriage of a young girl of first marriage on the day of the Presentation of the Virgin. Victoria was to benefit from this scheme on her marriage. Furthermore her daughter Isabella was bound to free the 15 year-old slave Francisco.
>
> Caterina left one-fifth of her goods to the nunnery of the *repentite* as decreed by the Apostolic letter for ex-prostitutes. ... A small sum of money was assigned for the maintenance of prisoners at the Grand Masters' prison. ...
>
> Caterina left sums of money to several churches – particularly to the Carmelite friary and church in Valletta where both her husband, Ettore Vitale, and her parents, Isabella and Demetrio Petras, had been buried. ...
>
> She stipulated that her house bordering with the Church of Our Lady of Damascus should go to Annica Faienza who should continue to make use of it until her death. The house was then to be turned into a monastery of Greek monks of Stranfadia who would serve the church of Our Lady of Damascus. Annica was also assigned a sum of 40 scudi a year.
>
> She further left a sum of 100 scudi to the *Monte di Pietà* and her land property to the *Monte di Redenzione degli Schiavi* which was appointed her universal heir. She further stipulated that any of her mobile goods that were not assigned to anyone should be sold and the revenue passed on to the *Monte di Redenzione*.

It is the clause naming her universal heir for which Caterina is best remembered. In Malta in 1607, a Capuchin friar put forward a proposal for the establishment of an institution that would pay ransoms to obtain the release of Christians enslaved by Muslim corsairs and raiders, as detailed in the last chapter. The idea of a *Monte di Redenzione degli Schiavi* (Foundation for the Redemption of Slaves) was taken up by the Grand Master and money started to be collected. But it was never enough, so that Caterina's bequest and the wealth that it provided – particularly from vast tracts of land and

7.   Caterina Vitale, Ransom Chapel, Selmun,
by Antoine Favray

buildings round the Castle of Selmun (see Chapter 22 itinerary) – was of great benefit to the fund, so much so that it is sometimes suggested that she was responsible for the fund itself.

Isabella and her husband had assumed that the castle would be theirs, and Giovanni Bonello deduces that leaving it instead, as Caterina did, 'appears as a mean posthumous vendetta against her daughter and other relatives'. I am not so sure that was the only reason: it may have been more both an act of atonement and to enhance her posthumous reputation. In the latter she certainly succeeded.

Caterina had left for Syracuse, probably in an effort to regain her health. There she altered her will by way of a codicil. In it she remembered the de Xibilia (Xiblia, Sibilla) family of Syracuse with whom, I deduce, she was staying, probably the same family from whom Caterina Scappi was later to buy a house in Archbishop Street where Caterina Vitale herself had two houses. In particular, the codicil benefited 'the virgin' **Girolama Xibilia**, and she did now, too, leave her granddaughter, the toddler **Maddalena Cagnolo**, a piece of jewellery.

Caterina died in Syracuse in 1619 two days after that codicil, aged only 53, but she had made it clear that she was to be buried finally in Malta, in the Carmelite Church with her parents and husband, and so she was. The 1791 marble plaque was put up by the controllers of the Monte di Redenzione; in the 1950s, during renovation work, Caterina's coffin appears to have been found in a burial chamber beneath.

Giovanni Bonello, who clearly does not care for Caterina, particularly because of her cruelty to her slaves, nevertheless ends his chapter on a light note:

A lovely, but imaginary portrait of her, painted *c.*1760 by Antoine Favray for the main altar of the church of Selmun, shows her presumably discussing the pros and cons of chastity with the Virgin Mary, in the presence of a bored Melita, who seems to have already made up her mind.

Greeks, Witches, Slaves and Quakers

The next strange link is that between Caterina Vitale's niece, Annica's friend who lived near the Carmelite church, the 54-year-old Greek prostitute **Violante Vergotti** (b. *c.*1563), Violante's friend and neighbour **Sulpitia de Lango** (b. *c.*1563), also a 54-year-old Greek, and a former prostitute, and Sulpitia's 28-year-old daughter **Sperantia de Lango** (b. *c.*1589). Sperantia, according to Giovanni Bonello, was part-time mistress to a Knight, nephew of the Pope. It concerns the 1617 appearance of all four women before the Inquisition, Annica as a witness.

That institution, the Roman version, rather than the harsher Spanish one, was set up to counter the effects of the Protestant Reformation. Its brief was to prosecute those accused of any crime related to heresy, including sorcery, blasphemy, Judaising, and witchcraft; it also acted as a censor of printed literature. One of the heresies most relevant to women, and most prevalent, was the practice of witchcraft.

Giovanni Bonello mentions the case only in passing because these women, too, were Greek, following a particular occupation – sex work – because they were being accused of witchcraft, and because they were friends of Annica. But the full story is told in Carmel Cassar's *Sex, Magic and the Periwinkle: A Trial at the Malta Inquisition Tribunal 1617* (2000). The periwinkle plant in question belonged to Violante and, because she was too ill to do it herself, her friend Sulpitia – already known in her locality as a notorious witch – had been seen in the Grand Masters' crypt in the Church of St John preparing a magic love potion. This was so as to beguile her daughter's Knight who was showing signs of straying.

Even Sperantia's 18-year-old Muslim slave, **Selima** (b. *c.*1599) – who had been with her mistress for 10 years – was brought before the Inquisition as a witness. You realise when you read of her age that that she had been a working slave since the age of eight; and you learn, too, that Sperantia had 15 other slaves, female and male, and that Selima was terrified of having to give evidence against her mistress because of the retribution that would follow. The next witness was **Sileicha**, Sperantia's chambermaid. Annica Faenza was later called to give evidence regarding the sale by Violante Vergotti of packets of love potions which had helped to redeem Violante from debt, though Annica's evidence appeared to be secondhand and contradicted that of another witness.

Carmel Cassar's meticulous account is short – only 33 pages before several appendices – and provides lurid insight into the life of a certain class of women of the time: how they somehow had to gain some control over their lives; how they often lived outside the law, sometimes fearfully, and, indeed, their relations with the Church and the Knights. Sperantia, for example, became a courtesan after her husband, having committed murder, absconded to Sicily. And she had her supporters before the Inquisition:

Jannulla Barbiana explained how Sperantia was terrified when she learned how her mother had been caught preparing the concoction. She blamed her mother and wept bitterly out of fear of the repercussions of the event. Jannulla described Sperantia as a charitable person who paid for the celebration of three Masses a week and, although she was a notorious whore, she often gave donations to churches. She had recently donated 25 scudi to embellish the reliquary of St Placidus in silver and gold at the Carmelite Church. Janulla described Sperantia as a devout woman who had the misfortune of owning two female slaves who hated her because she often hit them owing to their untamed and disrespectful character.

It is interesting to imagine how much the Muslim slaves, inculcated by their original family in the piety of women, would have despised these loose-living Greek women, and found it difficult to disguise it. Not only that, they would hardly have relished being ill-treated slaves far from home, presumably with no hope of being ransomed. Mild rebellion was, perhaps, their only way of establishing an identity, even a form of light relief. There was another side to their behaviour, as I have already quoted from Godfrey Wettinger, and some resorted to prostitution to obtain their ransom.

The keeping of slaves was commonplace. Godfrey Wettinger tells how in 1634 large numbers of black slaves, female and male, were captured by the Order's galleys. Within eight months, 45 females and 36 males had been sold 'on credit terms at an average price of 115 scudi to knights and employees of the Order, and to laymen as well'. These were recorded because they involved credit facilities; scores will have gone unrecorded. The Knights were forbidden to keep women slaves younger than 50 years old in an attempt to keep them celibate, or at least to minimise illegitimate offspring.

It was not the first time that Sperantia's mother, Sulpitia, had been before the Tribunal, and she had ended up then, having failed to keep to her sentence of house arrest, in the Holy Office's prison for four months, commuted to house arrest, once again, on appeal. And both mother and daughter had been accused of practising love magic in 1605.

The initiator of the 1617 incident, Violante, was so unconvincing before the Tribunal that she was subjected to the *strappado*, a form of torture for which Carmel Cassar provides an all-too-graphic illustration. During it, Violante continued to declare herself innocent 'in the name of Christ' and St Catherine. Sperantia was then tortured and she, too, declared her belief in God.

After all that, and deliberation of some time, the accused 'were given an identical spiritual penance' but, whereas Sperantia's sentence, as an accomplice, was read out in private, those for Violante and Sulpitia were read in public in the Annunciation Church 'where they had to abjure in front of a large congregation'. That seemed the most severe punishment, yet Violante was also publicly whipped through the streets of Vittoriosa – where the Inquisition was based – and wretched Sulpitia, already found guilty twice before, was not only publicly flogged but, aged 54, sentenced to eight years in the Inquisitor's prison. That, happily for her, was not the end of it:

> Later Sulpitia appealed that she could not stand incarceration and she was released after two years' imprisonment and, since the tribunal reported that she had behaved like a 'good Catholic', she was allowed to return home. Thanks to a petition of 1620, she was allowed to move about within Valletta. In another petition, dated May 1623, Sulpitia de Lango was allowed to travel all over the island in order to visit several churches and spend her old age in prayer.

The Inquisition records provide a rich harvest of detail about women's life on the margins in Malta. And Carmel Cassar writes up another case in his article 'Magic, Heresy and the Broom Riding Midwife Witch – the Inquisition Trial of Isabetta Caruana' (2003).

Midwives, usually illiterate, were regarded, as he says, 'as some sort of medical specialists who learned their profession after long years of experience in the field with the aid of empirical means'. Late in life they were seen as wise women and, in many societies, such women were equated with witchcraft – as so much could go wrong during pregnancy and labour. Carmel Cassar does stress, however, that 'it is wrong to assume that midwives were accused *en masse* of witchcraft'.

Isabetta Caruana (née Cafor), widow of Joanello Caruana, was an inhabitant of Rabat, Gozo, and she appeared before the Holy Office in 1599 where she was denounced by the **Magnifica Victoria Formosa** of Gozo Castle. She had been 'teaching' young girls since before the Great Siege and it was she who provided details of what went on during her time – starting at the age of 10 – at the Benedictine nunnery of St Scholastica, Mdina (see Chapter 20 itinerary). She had not visited the nunnery since she left, but it was there that she had picked up the rudiments of Christianity which she taught the girls and which she was accused of distorting – that is, heresy.

She was also accused of being a procuress, but that seems to have been less important, which is surprising, or things changed as, in *Knights Hospitaller: Medicine of Malta* (2004), Charles Savona-Ventura quotes a German visitor to Malta in 1663 with a different impression:

> If a female pimp in Malta prostitutes and sells girls or is discovered in her business, she is put on a donkey. Her hands are chained in front while her feet are chained under her. Her back is bare and she has to ride through the streets of the city. She is followed by a man with a trumpet. Whenever this man blows the trumpet, she is flogged by a hangman with a whip. Then she is made to embark on a ship and perpetually exiled from the island.

Did the Baron see such a punishment, or was he spinning a yarn?

Isabetta's daughter **Romana**, widow of Andrea **de Manueli**, was also called before the Tribunal. She lived by fattening pigs, weaving and prostitution. Both mother and daughter were subjected to the *strappado*. The accusations had piled up against Isabetta, as Carmel Cassar describes:

> [She] was furthermore accused that seven years before she was seen alone dressed up as a male, more specifically with a turban on her head. In other words Isabetta was not just accused of having dressed like a male – in itself a very serious accusation because it meant the reversal of social order, but rather as a Muslim man, or the antithesis of anything Christian.

After all that, Isabetta's punishment was a ream of spiritual penances. Carmel Cassar ends with the wider conclusions to be drawn from her trial:

> The picture that emerges from the trial is that of a husbandless woman who was constrained to make a living and thus violate the norm of the caring, submissive female since she led an independent life making her particularly susceptible to witchcraft accusations. Furthermore the trial gives the impression that aggression and competitiveness by women were primarily expressed in relation to other women; direct quarrels between men and women were rather less common. In our case the man who accused Isabetta of witchcraft, Valerio Cauchi, had his own axe to grind since he strongly suspected her of dishonouring his stepdaughter. However although men may have, at times, called women 'witches', witchcraft depositions suggest that it was other women who very often made such charges.

During the time of the Inquisitor Antonio Pignatelli (1646–49), Paul Cassar notes in his 'Vignette', there were 209 denunciations of supposed witches. Such cases are an example of Carmel Cassar's suggestion in 'The Jewesses of Malta' that 'the formal Catholic doctrine (based on the rigid principles of the Council of Trent) and the religious beliefs (based on their daily needs and preoccupations) ran on parallel lines [that] hardly ever meet'.

Betta Caloiro (1519–1608) was, she said, 80 when she appeared before the Inquisitor in 1599. She had been widowed for the previous 16 years and was accused, as recounted by Carmel Cassar in *Witchcraft, Sorcery and the Inquisition*, of consorting with the devil (*farfarello*) – the standard explanation being women's 'insatiable lust'. She had first met him at the age of six, and had had an intimate relationship with him since she was twelve. Carmel Cassar sees this as a sexual metaphor concerning problems in relations between women and men, and was the fruit of 'delusion, hysteria and melancholy'. But, given Betta's age when she first confessed to meeting the devil, it seems more useful and less euphemistic to suggest that it concerns masturbation.

Betta was typical of women of her age and occupation. In 'Concepts of health and illness in early modern Malta' (2002), Charles Cassar writes that 'Domestic medicine continued to be a predominantly female field, in part because poor, elderly women were frequently driven to the margins of society and thus depended on their knowledge for their livelihood'. During Betta's tribunal hearing, she explained how from childhood she had spent 25 years seeking a remedy for a 'distorted nose'. In the end, she was cured by a Sicilian physician using a mixture containing lead 'which she then used to cure others'.

Things did not end happily for Betta, as Carmel Cassar relates:

> She was condemned to eight years imprisonment and ordered to confess once a month and recite the rosary every Saturday for the following two years. Yet she continued to invoke her friend *farfarello* even some years later, while held in the Inquisitor's prison.

Betta died in 1608, aged nearly 90, still in prison. Although life in the Inquisitor's prison was not as desperate as that in most civil prisons, it was still pretty grim and a prison warden in 1705 was found guilty of having sexual relations with a woman prisoner. Of course, she may have been seeking some advantage, but it is as likely that it was not consensual. Betta's end there, particularly at her age, hardly bears thinking about. Her death was looked into and that forms an appendix to Carmel Cassar's article. She was buried at the Palace of the Holy Office (see Chapter 18 itinerary).

A lighter note is struck by the indomitable English Quaker missionaries 50-year-old **Sarah Cheevers** (née Shenel, *c.*1608–?1664) and widowed, 40-year-old **Katherine Evans** (née Canual or Canval, 1618–1692). The two were among the first Quakers following and proselytising a dissenting Christianity and known as 'the valiant sixty'; many of those taking a lead, unlike in other faiths, were women. Katherine had already caused trouble in the Isle of Man from where she was banished, been incarcerated for four days in Ireland and, back in England, been publicly whipped in the market square of Salisbury.

In 1658, during the short-lived 'reign' in England of Oliver Cromwell's son and heir Richard, the two decided to take their Quaker message to

Alexandria. They reached Malta on the way on 21 December and, having landed, distributed a few pamphlets in Latin in Valletta. Almost immediately, they decided they would do better in Malta than Alexandria and were taken in by John Jacob Watts, the Anglo-Belgian consul. He made the mistake of taking them to visit his sister in one of the nunneries and there, too, they delivered pamphlets. I surmise this was the Maddalena because almost immediately a Franciscan friar denounced them to the Inquisition and Watts was interrogated. The Inquisition authorities then interrogated the women at his house about the reason for their presence in Malta. On 27 December, Watts was ordered to keep them in his custody and not to permit them to speak to anyone, so they shouted prophecies from the windows to passers-by. At the beginning of April 1659, they were arrested and taken to the Inquisitor's prison; they were to stay there until the summer of 1662. They blamed their host for their arrest, calling him Judas. John Jacob Watts was certainly anxious about his guests' behaviour, and how it might affect not only his own position but also that of the English community in Malta.

It is not surprising that he had ambivalent feelings towards Sarah and Katherine. Although he was the English consul, he also acted for Belgium; what is more, he was not appointed by London but, as trade between England and the Knights increased, by the Grand Master, as had been an earlier William Watts and then, in 1610, a John Watts, presumably his grandfather and father. There were, therefore, Watts women in the household over time, but I can find no trace of them – and hope that it might be possible to do so in the future, as they must have been very early English women in the islands. I owe this brief sighting of Watts men in Malta to Victor Mallia-Milanes's 'English Merchants' Initial Contacts with Malta: A Reconsideration' (1975). So much was John Jacob the Grand Master's man that when his successor, Alphonse Desclaus, was appointed, London, noting the continuing benefits of the trade, took no notice of him, and appointed their own man.

Useful introductions to the two Quaker women are contained in their entries in the *Oxford Dictionary of National Biography (ODNB)*, and their own version of what followed, based on their writings, was published as *This is a Short Relation of Some of the Cruel Sufferings of Katherine Evans and Sarah Che[e]vers, in the Inquisition of the Isle of Malta* (1662). A feminist critique of their writing is contained in Catie Gill's 'Evans and Cheevers's *A Short Relation* in Context: Flesh, Spirit, and Authority in Quaker Prison Writings, 1650–1662' (2009). Sarah and Katherine's own writing, while historically interesting, full of character and their beliefs, is not as accessible as CV (Veronica) Wedgwood's 'The Conversion of Malta' contained in her little book of essays *Velvet Studies* (1946). It adds the colour of an experienced historian who has had access to the primary source and I particularly like her description of the two:

> Women of character and courage, versed in the Scriptures and in little else, Katherine had the readier and sharper tongue, Sarah had the louder voice for preaching and the greater persistence in what she undertook. Both,

like many Englishwomen before and since, were indifferent to ridicule. They would do as they thought right, whether they be mocked by rude boys or burnt alive.

What followed their arrest was an extraordinary game of cat and mouse which lasted for over three years, as the Holy Office, via English friars, attempted to convert the two to Roman Catholicism, while they strongly resisted and, in their turn, promoted the tenets of their belief. The imprisonment, quite apart from the gruelling intellectual challenge, was not easy. They were first shut in a small inner room with 'two holes in it for light and air', and they had no means of washing, their hair began to drop out, and their skin to grow as rough as 'sheep's leather'. Soon their bibles were taken from them – though, happily, they knew them by heart. Katherine wrote to the Inquisitor, so pen and ink were removed, though later they were able to write home (see Chapter 18 itinerary).

Some months later, the two were separated. Sarah's new room gave on to an alley leading to a church; from there she would exhort – in English – the worshippers to repent. When soldiers and sailors gathered to pray for victory before a foray against the Turks, she shouted, 'Go not forth to murder, nor to kill one another.'

They were threatened with torture, to be tied with chains, and with burning, but it did not deter them; suffering was to be embraced rather than feared. Catie Gill in her exploration writes,

> Evans and Cheevers aspired to spiritual authority … the official ruling on [them] was that they were mad, a position implying their diminished responsibility. Women were also believed to be more susceptible to the devil, owing to their weakness, and according to the text of A Short Relation, this was a view held by the Catholic friars: Sarah Cheevers was told that she was led by an 'evil spirit', and that many like her were 'burnt' as witches. The women, by contrast, had no institutional authority to back up their judgments, except the doctrines of the Quaker faith; but by positioning themselves as prophets, they could proclaim the judgment, as they saw it, of their God.

Catie Gill also suggests that 'Evans and Cheevers's circumstances … brought a greater likelihood of martyrdom than almost any other Quaker case of the period'.

The new Anglo-Belgian consul in 1660, Alphonse Desclaus, sought to help them, but they were not open to negotiation. Eventually the outside world, particularly the Quakers, took action: the Pope must be approached. In July 1662, the Vatican gave orders for the unconditional release of the two prisoners. They did not immediately respond; as Veronica Wedgwood recounts, they 'distinguished clearly between the will of Christ's vicar ("so-called") and the will of Christ'. They awaited the 'inner light'. When it came, they packed their trunks and stepped out, 'not forgetting to kneel down once more on the prison threshold and implore the mercy of Heaven on their persecutors'.

It was another three months before a suitable vessel was available; these they spent with Alphonse Desclaus 'whose wife and servants, they sadly noted, became less and less civil daily', for they continued to cause trouble. On the ship home, their companions were 24 Knights, one of whom, the Inquisitor's brother, sought Katherine out. She dealt with him. Back in England at the beginning of 1663, they continued to proselytise, and pay for it. They went to Scotland and Ireland; while travelling back from Ireland in May 1664, they were arrested and kept in prison for a few months in Somerset. Sarah died shortly after her release. Katherine continued her missionary work, being constantly arrested, until she died in 1692, aged 74.

The Philanthropists

Not all women of strong will and determination caused trouble. The name of noblewoman **Cosmana** (sometimes Gusmana or Cusmana) **Navarra** (*c*.1600–1687) is even better remembered in Malta than that of Caterina Vitale, if only because a restaurant bears her name in Rabat (Malta) (see Chapter 20 itinerary). Although her maiden name was Cumbo, and, aged 25, she married Jurat and *Capitano della Verga* Lorenzo Cassar, historical records give her the maiden name of her mother **Cornelia Navarra**, who married Mdina lawyer Giovanni Cumbo in 1597. Her mother appears to have died when Cosmana was 13 years old or younger, because her father married again in 1613, which may account for her using Cornelia's name in remembrance.

Either Cosmana inherited money from her own family, or her husband was rich – or, perhaps, both – because in 1653 she resolved to build a parish church in Rabat above the grotto of St Paul and dedicated to him. She financed it herself and, during the 30 years it took to construct, she watched it take shape from her windows opposite. It was not completed until four years before her death at the age of 87 when she was buried in a side chapel of the church with her coat of arms above her tombstone.

Cosmana's philanthropy stretched far and wide: not only was she also responsible for the 'Zuntier', the passageway alongside St Paul's and the 1679 statue of St Paul, but Mario Buhagiar and Stanley Fiorini note in *Mdina* how she thought ahead beyond her death concerning the Benedictine nuns of St Peter's. After describing doctors in attendance on the nuns as late as 1781, they write,

It is of interest that payment of such medications came from a legacy left for this purpose by the noble benefactress Gusmana Navarra. Thus Michele Alfard, probably an *aromatario*, was paid from these funds for all the medicines administered to each of **Sor Celestina Mamo, Benedetta Zammit, Laurica Grima** and **Clementia Busittil** in 1713.

8.   Cosmana Navarra, courtesy of the Wignacourt Museum,
Rabat, Malta

Cosmana also donated 100 scudi to the Carmelite friars to help them build
their new church and monastery in Mdina in 1660 when, for their health
and 'the benefit of the faithful', they moved from San Leonardo. The chapel
and lands there had been bequeathed to them by Margarita d'Aragona in
1418, and they continued to draw rents from there. The friars also bought
a house from **Ursula Habela** for 400 uncie to form part of the new Mdina
monastery; this shows that women continued to deal in property on their
own account. It suggests, too, how women philanthropists might come by
their wealth.

Women also engaged in other financial dealings. There is a hint of their
involvement in the grain trade in Chapter 3, with Maria da Avula and her
ship in 1447/48. But such involvement was still going strong between 1583
and 1602. *In Society, Culture and Identity in Early Modern Malta* (2000),
Carmel Cassar describes investors in grain which included women such as
the Benedictine nuns of St Scholastica and 'prosperous ladies' who 'often
invested money through the intervention of their husbands, as is the case of
Joanne Xara's wife'. Other women preferred to invest in grain with the help
of a notary. Rich **Caterina Habela**, a widow, owned the grain vessel *Santa*

Crucis which took an active part in the grain trade. But even women of the lower classes invested, often between four and 15 scudi each.

Rich women also financed embellishments to churches, as did **Marietta Bonello** who, in 1605 or 1606, married the lawyer Dr Antonio Cassar from an earlier generation of the Cassar family than Cosmana's husband, and had two children. In about 1644, she provided a new altar for the Rabat Church of the Annunciation, Ta' Duna (or Ta' Doni), a mile or so away from what would become Cosmana's St Paul's, and also referred to in the Rabat itinerary (Chapter 20). **Margaret Tabone** provided a new altar piece for the Assumption ta' Cwerra in Siġġiewi in 1621; and in 1645 **Teodora Testaferrata de Robertis** (née Bonici) and her husband Giacomo funded the building of Our Lady of Trapani at Siġġiewi.

Maria de Dominici

More is known about one who had her own way of embellishing Malta's churches, the painter and sculptor **Maria de Dominici** (1645–1703) whose relevance to our own time opens this book. Details of her life are best revealed in Franca Trinchieri Camiz's chapter '"*Virgo-non Sterilis* ...": Nuns as Artists in Seventeenth Century Rome' in *Picturing Women in Renaissance and Baroque Italy*, edited by Geraldine A Johnson and Sara F Matthews Grieco (1997). It includes illustrations of Maria's known, or assumed, works in Malta, indispensable when trying to track them down in their various locations. The same author is responsible for Maria's entry in *The Dictionary of Women Artists*, and thus for the naming of the crater on Mercury. Nicholas de Piro's 'Mattia Preti and the Young Maltese Artist Nun' in the gloriously illustrated *The Temple of the Knights of Malta* (1999) usefully fills in the gaps, drawing on, among others, Giovannantonio Ciantar's *Malta Illustrata* (1772).

Maria is often known as Suor Maria because she was a Carmelite tertiary nun – one who professed vows of chastity and obedience, but not of poverty and who could live in the community and outside family ties. She also had the advantage of being born into a family of artists based in Birgu (Vittoriosa): her father Onofrio de Dominici was a goldsmith and official appraiser of valuables for the Order; two of her brothers, Raimondo and Francesco, were painters, and her nephew Bernardo was to write biographies of seventeenth- and eighteenth-century Neapolitan artists, in which he paid tribute to his aunt. He was also the author of a 'Life' of Mattia Preti, the important church artist in Malta who was so crucial to Maria's artistic development.

Maria knew what she wanted to do from an early age. Giovannantonio Ciantar notes that she showed a certain

> repugnance to apply her energies to female duties and was thus often rebuked by her parents ... She would do nothing other than draw figures and other things according to her whim and natural talents. At last her

parents, seeing her so inclined and disposed to painting, provided an art master to teach her design.

It is worth noting that use of the word 'parents' because it includes her mother who, it takes perseverance to discover, was **Genevra Rofelli**. Is it fanciful to suggest that Orofio and Genevra's children's artistic talent was fostered by their mother? Might she, herself, have been artistic?

Mattia Preti arrived in Malta in 1659, aged 46, already a much sought after artist, and remained there for the rest of his long life. He and his work are very well known in Malta; his pupil Maria de Dominici is not. But while engaged on his best known work, a series of paintings depicting the life and martyrdom of St John the Baptist to decorate the vault of St John's Church,Valletta, which took him from 1661 to 1666, he was assisted by Maria (see Chapter 17 itinerary).

Giovannantonio Ciantar adds, 'under his direction she worked well and as he was painting the ceiling of the Church of St John he allowed her to paint some of the female figures; in doing this she succeeded almost more felicitously than the master.' Giuseppe Maria de Piro goes further in *Squarci di Storia* (1839): '[She] superseded any other of his pupils, so much so that the celebrated master chose her to collaborate with him in painting the great vault of the church of St John, in which the female figures were, to a great extent, executed by her.' This would suggest that Maria was up on the scaffolding with Preti and any male assistants. Mattia Preti also established a workshop in which Maria participated.

It may be that Maria 'mothered' Preti, as well as being his assistant. He tended to give what he earned away, and over-worked to do so. She is quoted as exhorting him, 'For the love of God, stop working.' To which he replied, 'You are right but these poor people are hungry.'

Nicholas de Piro goes so far as to suggest that there are visual clues to hint that Maria may also have had a hand in 'The Martyrdom of St Sebastian' in the chapel of the Auvergne *Langue* in St John's, and I understand that there is a drawing by her depicting the Annunciation in the Cathedral Museum which I have not seen; but attribution of her work in various churches in Malta is still uncertain.

It is not always easy, either, to find Maria's work, even armed with images of the churches and illustrations of the paintings, and, should one do so, it is often difficult to see them. The paintings themselves tend to be dark, perhaps uncleaned, they are often hung very high with little light coming in, as in the sacristy of Żebbuġ Parish Church; or elusive, as was the second one in the same church; or with the light shining in the wrong place, as in the Carmelite Church, Valletta; or inaccessible, as in the chapel of Our Lady of Mercy (Madonna ta-Hniena), Qrendi which seemed rather closed (see itineraries, Chapters 17 and 22).

Of Maria's sculptures, to view that of the Virgin Mary in St Catherine's Nunnery, Valletta, requires special permission from the Abbess (see Chapter 17 itinerary). Only the wooden statue of the Virgin in the Church of the

Immaculate Conception, Cospicua – probably sculpted about 1680 – is accessible, and on 8 December each year it forms part of an important religious procession (see Chapter 18 itinerary).

Franca Camiz tells us that Maria left Malta in 1682, probably in the entourage of the Grand Master's nephew, and his wife **Isabella d'Avalos d'Aquino d'Aragona** who, along with Mattia Preti, encouraged her to spread her wings in Rome. Drawing on Bartolomeo dal Pozzo, Nicholas de Piro names the wife of Don Carlo Carafa Prince of Rocella and Botera, Princess Teresa of Avalos; genealogical sources give the name Isabella; perhaps she had both forenames. The couple arrived in Malta on 25 February that year and, as relatives of the Grand Master, they were royally received: 'A thirty-gun salvo welcome was fired, the Order's galleys were decorated overall with lanterns, and the flag flew for the royal salute.' They stayed at the palace and 'they dined with the Grand Master in public. It was while on tour of the principal attractions of the city that they got to know the work of the nun.' Again, I am going to suggest that it was the woman, the princess, who took the initiative to support Maria. On 17 March, 'accompanied by a great procession and much solemnity, together with Suor Maria they set sail for Naples'.

Maria stayed with her patrons for a while and began to study the works of antiquity and the sculpture of the great Bernini who had only recently died. In due course, she had her own studio in Rome and, having brought with her letters of introduction from the Grand Master, began to obtain commissions, both sculpture and painting; from 1690 she lived with a woman companion. Her will names as her executor the Order's ambassador to Rome who was also her benefactor, and for whose family she painted several portraits.

Maria's will shows her to have been a woman of some spirit, determined to protect the financial value of her artworks which she listed, as well as noting who still owed her money. She died in Rome aged 58 and was buried there. Franca Camiz notes that 'In a competitive market that distinguished then, as it still does today, between "major" and "minor" works of art, Maria de Dominici's artistic identity became obscured.'

Disasters

One more church with a woman connection needs to be mentioned, perhaps one of the most touching: it is that of San Roque built in the centre of Żebbuġ by **Katerina Vassallo** and her husband Tommaso during the plague of 1592, in the hopes that the saint would save the village from the dread infection. We don't even know if Katerina survived (see Chapter 22 itinerary).

That devastating epidemic coincided in Malta with a time of famine. Elizabeth Schermerhorn describes how 'The emaciated peasants crawled about the streets of Valletta covered with sores, begging for food and alms.' And how families were quarantined in their homes and all the washing places were disinfected. The expert put in charge ordered that 'by an excess of precaution, the streets, which were strewn with rags and refuse, were swept and the rubbish burned'. Nine hundred suspected cases were confined to a hastily constructed Lazaretto where, thereafter, all visiting travellers were to be quarantined. Three thousand died during the plague, including 40 of the 800 Knights.

Plague struck again in 1676, also at a time of drought and bad harvests. Birgu suffered worst: as Brian Blouet suggests, its population of 3,000 was reduced to 2,000 between 1670 and 1680. The situation was not helped by overcrowding, often numbers of families having to share the same dwelling to pay the rent; hygiene and fresh air were hard to come by. Plague also hit the other two of the Three Cities – Bormla (Cospicua) and L-Isla (Senglea) – though to a lesser extent. It was assumed that it had arrived with a cargo boat, and Valletta, with water between it and them, had time to take some precautions, though destitute prostitutes, presumably migrating from the Three Cities, became more apparent there. Mdina hardly suffered from the plague, but Attard was hard hit.

In 1693, a strong earthquake struck. Although the epicentre was in Sicily, where hundreds were killed in Syracuse and Catania, many of the churches, such as that built by Girolama Ciantar at Fawwara and, indeed, the Mdina Cathedral, and St Agatha Chapel were partly destroyed. The church of the Annunciation at Fawwara was rebuilt in 1708 by **Maria Xeberras**, presumably because it, too, was badly damaged. This tragedy coincided with drought, exacerbated by how much it affected Sicily from where grain came at a time of shortage.

For all the increasing prosperity of the first 170 years of the Knights' rule, for all the piety of many of its women, the seventeenth century ended badly for Malta with drought, bad harvests, plague and earthquake all coming together.

7 – Women of the Eighteenth Century

Women at Work

'In the eighteenth century we come across a very enterprising widow, **Maria Caruana** from Luqa,' writes Paul Cassar in his 'Vignette', running on from his description of the women who helped build Valletta in the late sixteenth century. And he tells how,

> after the death of her husband [she] took over and managed his business of quarrying stone slabs for export. She thus can claim to be the earliest woman industrialist or manageress known to us so far. She was active in 1737 when she had seventeen men in her employment besides a number of children and slaves engaged in carrying fire-wood for the furnace of her limekiln.

Maria was on to a good thing because as husband and wife writing team Robert Attard and Romina Azzopardi note in *Daily Life in Eighteenth Century Malta* (2011), 'It would appear that the quarrying industry was important. The Maltese exported stone to Sicily, the Levant and Smyrna.' And later, 'Streets must have been very dusty because of the booming construction industry.'

It would seem that widows, of all levels of society, had more freedom and, indeed, a different status from married or single women. Caterina Vitale and Caterina Scappi were good examples in the previous century. **Vincenza Matilde Testaferrata** (née Perdicomati-Bologna) is another. Her mother was **Giovanna Fortunata Testaferrata Bologna**, her father Pietro Gaetano Perdicomati Bologna (Count of Catena). She married her cousin 3rd Baron Paulo Testaferrata in 1752. When he died in 1760, leaving her pregnant with their son, she continued in his office of *Despositario* within the Inquisition.

This office was hereditary, particularly through the Testaferrata family – Vincenza's son, Pietro Paulo, was to be the fourteenth appointed. Nevertheless, it does not appear to have been only a title or sinecure, and her accession to it has been deemed important enough to be noted in the internet 'Timelines of Maltese History'. Simon Mercieca in 'How was Judicial Power Balanced in Malta in Early Modern Times?' (2011) describes how

> The [Inquisitor's] Tribunal had the support of a full administrative staff. At the head was the *Depositario* whose position was equivalent to the present day Director of the Courts. He was the Accountant of the Tribunal. He took care of all the payments, including the Inquisitor's salary.

In 1662, Vincenza decided to give up the administration, the Inquisitor having tried to persuade her late husband's uncle, an aged canon, to take on the role. Seeing that if he did so, it would jeopardise Pietro Paulo's succession to the post, he accepted on the understanding that Vincenza remain her son's procurator. The Inquisitor rejected this arrangement, so she continued until 1778, retiring only when Pietro Paulo was seventeen. The last Inquisitor before Napoleon abolished the Inquisition in 1798 described Vincenza as 'The prototype of a titled Maltese Lady'. The suggestion that Vincenza should be 'procurator' to her son is worth noting, as this was traditionally the role of male to female.

In *Daily Life in the Eighteenth Century*, **Maria Rovignano** of Cospicua is shown to have sold cheesecakes with her husband, and **Liberata**, wife of Giovanni **Rissiott**, ran a coffee shop there. That large format, nicely illustrated book, with its irreverent tone and often racy detail, though based on careful research in the archives, covers food, clothes, jewellery, home decoration, living conditions, work and lifestyle of women and men, including the Knights. But its women, on the whole, either are subject to restrictions and limitations on their legal and social rights, or were temptresses, for the lewd society discussed in the last chapter did not dissipate with the turn of the century.

For a serious, in-depth exploration of the life of women of the period, however, you cannot do better than the publications of Yosanne Vella, a Maltese woman historian and educationalist concerned about how the young people of Malta learn history and, in particular, the place of women. She therefore decided, in the first instance, to devote herself to the primary sources and explore the history of eighteenth-century women from several angles in at least four articles: as workers, as trouble makers, as victims of crime and as participants in religion and magic. She starts 'Women and work in eighteenth century Malta' (1999), by protesting that

> Working Maltese women, especially married working women, are considered a 'startlingly' new phenomenon in Maltese society. The human image evoked by the word 'worker' remains stereotypically masculine, despite the fact that Maltese women's work has always existed and extended far beyond that of a housewife and was very real indeed ... I believe their contribution in various ways to the growth and development of their society should not be overlooked or undervalued.

She notes that the population of Malta rose from 20,000 at the time of the Order's arrival in 1530 to 100,000 by the end of the eighteenth century, that towns expanded and that the women she mentions in her paper mainly come from this urban environment. But she starts with agriculture where, naturally, wives and daughters might be employed on the family farms; but she has also found an enlightening register of labourers employed at Marsa to work on fields owned by the Order between 31 August 1771 and 7 May 1774. At the end is a heading 'women', listing a quarter of all the names. Some of them coincide with men's names above, suggesting relationships, even that a married couple was employed, but it also confirms that married women worked outside the home, admittedly earning less than the men; she supposes they may only have been carrying buckets – farm work 'identified as women's work in many parts of Europe'.

While crops included cumin and wheat, the main one was cotton, which was grown over much of the two main islands and increased in importance, providing a living to workers, and a benefit to the economy, from growing to harvesting, to spinning, weaving and exporting. And women played a crucial part because 'the raw cotton was spun at home as a cottage industry by women and children'. This was nothing new, of course, as women had been similarly involved, as previous chapters show, from the earliest times, but it was more industrialised. A telling example of women's involvement comes from the story of two women in 1786 contained in the Palace archives:

> **Maria Lafortuna** quarrelled with **Grazia Micallef** 'who lived near the staircase upon the bastions of Marsamxett' over the 'Payment for cotton'. Maria Lafortuna had apparently given Grazia 'two rotolos [bundles] of cotton' to work for her and she gave her 'fourteen tari' in advance.
> Grazia must have been a spinner and this shows that even in Valletta … women must have engaged in spinning on behalf of other people. It is also interesting to note that Grazia was in the employment of another woman, unlike some European women textile workers, who 'worked not for themselves or for each other, but for a male entrepreneur for whom they did piecework'.

Whatever the rewards of working with cotton, it does seem often to have caused friction, violence even, between women, as Yosanne Vella tells in 'Earthly Madonnas? Women Troublemakers in 18th Century Malta' (1998):

> **Maddalena**, wife of Joseph gave **Giovanna Bellini** of Senglea a rotolo of cotton to be worked for her, plus two tari. Later Maddalena angrily insisted that a quarter was missing from the rotolo she had given Giovanna. She then attacked Giovanna with her hands. Maddalena also injured Giovanna's daughter **Rosaria Saladina** on the head with a stone which she produced from the pocket of her dress.

Times must have been hard, women's wages low, and work not always easy to come by, for **Maria Vella** in 1794 was sometimes a porter (*caddeia*), or a cotton spinner, or a servant. Domestic service was a common occupation, as was laundry work. **Angela d'Anna** was washerwoman to Grand Master Perellos. In 1749, according to Elizabeth Schermerhorn, there were 4,000 slaves in Malta, but is unclear how many of these were women who would also be occupied in domestic work.

A part-time job for older women noted by Romina Azzopardi and Robert Attard was as a professional matchmaker (*huttaba*), like **Teresa Grech** of Luqa who 'charged fees calculated with reference to dowries'. They also note how

Class consciousness was so deeply rooted that class distinctions were mirrored in the quality of bread. The wealthy ate *pane di palazzo* but soldiers and slaves ate rye bread ... **Vincenza Crespi** confessed to the inquisition that the only reason why she became a nun and agreed to remain a nun was that her parents threatened her that 'if she left the convent they would lock her in a cellar, give her black bread and water, and marry her to one of their slaves'.

Qormi was the centre of breadmaking and women worked as both millers and breadmakers. Yosanne Vella notes that 'The woman baker **Margarita**, wife of Francesco **ta' Labiat**, was brought before the Inquisitor in 1744, while in 1748, **Maria Piscopo** from Senglea, who lived with Maria Azzopardi the baker woman, was accused of stealing flour.

In her article about women workers, Yosanne Vella links the woman shop owner with those in 'Women Victims of Crime in Eighteenth Century Malta' (2003) when she describes how **Maria Camilleri** declared in 1796 that 'I have a grocer's shop', reporting that it had been 'robbed'. And **Theresa Barbara** reported in 1793 that a 'filigree jewel' had been stolen from her daughter Anna who 'owned a shop in Senglea'. **Maria Caruana** not only owned a shop in 1797, 'but gold was actually worked in it'. She, too, was a victim of crime when one of her male employees made off with 'one thousand scudi in gold jewellery and in unworked silver'.

Yosanne Vella has also analysed the register issued by the Authorities for the keeping of shops between 1788 and 1796: of the 829 permits, women were directly involved in 199 (24 per cent) of the cases:

the highest number of male/female partnerships is to be found in permits to operate a haberdashery, followed by permits for delicatessen dealers, taverns and cotton production. Women as sole permit holders predominate in cases of cotton production, haberdashery, delicatessen dealing and coffee shops.

One occupation not examined by Yosanne Vella is teaching. In 1734, Grand Master Vilhena set up the *Conservatorio* in Floriana to house pauper girls and teach them various useful crafts. Presumably, they were women's crafts and, therefore, taught by women. Frans Ciappara in his short but scholarly book, full of graphs and tables, *Marriage in Malta in the Late Eighteenth Century: 1750–1800* (1988) notes that 'Both **Rosa Bazati** of Vittoriosa and **Modesta Provedini** of Valletta held classes for girls.' I suspect this would have been at one of the two Schools for Women set up in 1790 by Grand Master de Rohan and Bishop Labini, one in Valletta, the other in Cospicua, as described by Robert Attard in *Malta: A Collection of Tales and Narratives* (2003).

These schools were exclusively for girls, and some of the teachers were women. Robert Attard suggests that 'The focus of education in the two schools was, predictably, catechism, although it appears that other subjects were taught as well.' There were some well-educated young women, but they tended to be upper class, as the cases of Maria Teresa Grech Bologna and Maria Teresa Navarra will show in due course, though it was usually through male tutors.

But some women reached even higher. Charles Savona-Ventura records, in *Knight Hospitaller Medicine in Malta (1530–1798)*, that there were women who served as barber-surgeons. In 1728 there were several of them serving the *Ospedale* and, in 1772, against all the odds, a young woman was sent to study surgery in Florence, paid for by the Order. I wonder what became of her? Women did not start to qualify as doctors in Malta until 1925 (see Chapter 13).

Work as a seamstress at home, but also commercially, was more obvious, but it increased with the increase in consumerism and fashion, described in *Daily Life in Eighteenth Century Malta*, where the intricacies of dress and fashion of both women and men are detailed. But Yosanne Vella tells us of the women who made the clothes: **Domenica Zammit** from Vittoriosa made stockings in 1744; **Gratiulla Aquilina** of Żebbuġ made lace in 1734; **Caterina Bolmetti** and her sister **Maria Maddalena** made silk mantles and may not have always been honest about it, as a case brought against them by **Anna deta ta'Scerri** from Qormi shows. Yosanne Vella surmises,

> The Bolmetti must have had quite a clientele and apparently they were quite skilled too, for silk mantles were not everyday clothes. Before women could do such work they probably required some form of apprenticeship which their parents are likely to have paid for.

The Manoel Theatre had been opened in 1732, and women were early involved in tragic and comic operas; the theatre, its history and its women players are described in the Chapter 17 itinerary that includes Old Theatre Street.

The case of the Bolmetti sisters suggests that the conduct of women entrepreneurs was not always above board. The case of **Margarita Manueli** refers us back to Malta's lower life – which actually extended from the highest to the lowest in the land. Margarita faced an accusation that she

> kept a wine tavern which was frequented continually by women 'worthy of her company' and 'men of the same type'. Obviously this was a brothel, and Margarita Manueli known as La Mugraba is referred to as a 'public prostitute'.

Prostitutes, Courtesans, Wives and Victims

Prostitution and concubinage continued to be rife with the same two causes: the most obvious, perhaps, was economic necessity, but also the attitudes of men, ranging from Knights, through clergy and notables to the lower classes, particularly in the urban centres. Most commentators note the sexual proclivities of the supposedly celibate Knights, but none so succinctly as Paul Cassar in his 'Vignette', drawing on his own earlier work:

> It has been said that 'every respectable family had some knight for their patron as a matter of course and to him the honour of a sister or a daughter was sacrificed equally as a matter of course and that in nine instances out of ten this patron was the common paramour of every female in the family'. While peasant women escaped this influence, towns-women, including married ones, did not.

Was it only advancement, or financial gain, such as land titles, that persuaded husbands and fathers to allow this – assuming it is true – or was it intimidation? The Knights were trained fighters for whom corsairing, and the riches and adventure involved, were as important as protecting Malta. And the Grand Master himself, in spite of all regulations against consorting with women, set the tone. De Valette's and de Paule's mistresses appear in the previous chapter. In the eighteenth century the Spaniard Ramon Perellos y Roccaful was Grand Master between 1697 and 1720. His 'carnal friend', whom he described as an 'old friend', was said to be **Madame Mutett**. She was the Dama Florinda mentioned by a Venetian traveller. When, as Robert Attard and Romina Azzopardi tell us, he gave lands and titles to her relatives, the bishop – with whom, together with the Inquisitor, there was always tension – reported the scandal to the Pope, Perellos ignored the order to resign, continuing to flaunt his relationship in public. When a Knight molested Mme Mutett, Perellos had him 'arrested, tortured and exiled'. As so often, the Maltese language was enriched by an episode in its history: 'The Maltese still use the word *mutetti* to describe a flirty and coquettish behaviour.'

Portuguese Manoel Pinto de Fonesco was Grand Master between 1741 and 1773. His 'whoring and pimping were the talk of the town'; he also held orgies at his palace. But his *maitresse en titre* was Valletta-born **Rosenda** or Monaca **Paulichi** (d.1771) daughter of **Patronilla Ramuzetta** and Alberigo Paulichi. She is said to have had a son by him named Jose Antonio Pinto da Fonseca e Vilhena. Those details come from the Wikipedia entry for the Grand Master and are repeated in another internet source. But a more detailed account is told by Christine Muscat in the section of her book on the Maddalena entitled 'The Grand Master's companion'.

Pinto became a Knight aged 24 in 1705. 'Shortly after his investiture, his companion, the young Rosenda Paulucci [Paulichi] chose to enter the cloister of her own free will, while others claim that *Frà* Pinto placed her in the monastery in order to conceal their relationship.' Rosenda became Sister Melania Paulucci; Pinto became Grand Master in 1741. He continued to support her and she would go to the Manoel Theatre with him. She remained in the Maddalena for about 66 years and, in 1755, was elected Abbess. When she died in 1771, Pinto organised her funeral and wrote her epitaph. If the son was theirs, he was born in the nunnery which, as the case of Flaminia Valenti has shown, was not unusual.

Carmel Testa's *The Life and Times of Grand Master Pinto 1741–1773* (1989) adds to the story:

> The death on 26 February 1771 of an old cloistered nun must surely have brought to his mind happy memories of his long-past youth. A contemporary diarist, who must have known both personages quite well, recorded in this enigmatic matter the event: [translated from the Italian] 'At the Magdalene monastery died the nun Paulicci, a friend of Grand Master Pinto during his youth; whom he assisted with great munificence throughout his reign and paid for all her expenses.' The *amica Paulicci* might, after all, have been the hidden reason why Pinto had delayed taking his vow of celibacy to the very last moment. Most probably it was then that Paulucci took the veil to shut herself completely from the outside world and the bitter-sweet memories of the past.

It was the women associated with the Knights that prompted me into realising that there was a book to be written about women in Malta, but one can have enough of descriptions of debauchery. And what of the women themselves? Were they able to make choices? Or, how did they feel about the lives visited upon them?

One woman, at least, appears to have been able to rise above the tide of the times, at least not ending up in a nunnery of the *Repentite* – whether voluntarily or by command. She was not, however, without trials, tribulations and probably heartache too – but they came through her marriage. **Elisabetta Dorell** (1741–1829), daughter of **Orsola D'Amico Inguanez** and Pietro Paolo Dorell, married Doctor of Laws Diego Moscati Xiberras in 1760, aged 19. She is more commonly known as Bettina Dorell, or simply the Lady Bettina; her husband became 2nd Marquis of Xrobb-il-Ghagin.

The marriage may well have been one of convenience because when Bettina's daughter was born in 1764, Angelo Durani, Inquisitor since 1759, not only stood as godfather – which raised eyebrows – but also held the christening in the chapel of his palace (see Chapter 18 itinerary); what is more, none of Diego Moscati's family attended, though they had been summoned by the Inquisitor to do so. This led to a further summoning before him at which he delivered a diatribe which was recorded for posterity and is relayed in full in Carmel Testa's biography of Grand Master Pinto who had to deal with the fall-out. No one, recently at least, seems to have picked up the fact that Bettina's daughter, ostensibly also her husband's, was called Angela.

Bettina's husband had already taken up with **Rosalea Mompalao** (1743–1785) who came from a family of mistresses to the nobility of Europe: her mother, **Diane de Beauclerk-Lennox** (1727–1764) having by this means had children in England and Paris, had arrived in Malta the year of Rosalea's birth, sung at the Manoel Theatre before the Grand Master, and taken up with Alessandro Mompalao, Barone di Frigenuini. Rosalea's daughter was to continue in the tradition, as introduced in an internet article, 'A Professional Family of Mistresses', by Charles Said-Vassello. The first of Rosalea and Diego Moscati's children, **Saveria Moscati, Baroness di Frigenuini** (1760–1797) was born the year of Bettina and Diego's marriage – which probably did not bode well for the marriage. And when Bettina did not produce a son, but Rosalea did – two of them – Diego sought to divorce his wife and marry his mistress whom he had set up in a house in Valletta, but his family put its foot down.

Sides were taken and the Inquisitor was reported to the Pope for his liaison with Bettina. The Pope

> Instantly flew into a rage when he read the serious accusations levelled against the Inquisitor, such as going arm-in-arm with Bettina at all times of the day and night both in his town and country residence, lunching with her and even taking her with him to Gozo when he visited that island on 17 August.
>
> The Pope ordered Pinto to throw Bettina straight away into a nunnery and send the Inquisitor to Rome after divesting him of the *mantelletta* (official clerical robe denoting his rank).

Durani protested that he was an 'old friend' of the family; that he was never alone with Bettina – 'amongst the first ladies of Malta' – that he was in the habit of admonishing her husband, 'an unprincipled youth'; and that when her husband abandoned her 'in penury' he had helped her financially at the request of her parents.

Whatever Bettina's financial problems, in 1770 she had built a grand palace in Gudja – known as Palazzo Bettina – on which she lavished large sums of money, and where she created a beautiful Palladian garden, inspiring Italian composers who visited to dedicate music to her (see Chapter 22 itinerary). She also paid, just before her death, to have the roof of the nearby Church of Santa Marija ta' Miftuh repaired. She had a mansion in George Street, Birgu (where she was born), also known as the Palazzo Bettina, and later as the Cardinal's House because her nephew (Cardinal Fabrizio Xeberras Testaferrata, the first Maltese) was to own it. Birgu was obviously close to her heart because she donated three paintings by Michele Busuttil to the Church of St Lawrence, and she was buried there in the family vault (see Chapter 18 itinerary). According to Nicholas de Piro's introduction to *Costume in Malta*, Bettina had a reputation as a 'lady of fashion', which would require expenditure out of the ordinary.

In 1766, Durani was packed off to Warsaw as Papal Legate, but that is by no means the end of the saga. Bettina and Diego now started to fight over their only child, **Angela Moscati Xeberras** (1764–1834). When she was 12, Bettina placed her in the nunnery of St Scholastica, Birgu, to be educated (see Chapter 18 itinerary). Diego, recently created a count and with influential friends, obtained an injunction from Grand Master de Rohan in 1776 to

9. Marchesa Elisabetta (Bettina) Moscati Dorell, courtesy of
Baron of San Marciano

place his daughter in the St Catherine nunnery, Valletta, 'away from her mother's influence' (see Chapter 17 itinerary). But Angela was quite a catch: 'It was widely rumoured that eventually she would have an annual income of some 12,000 scudi in her own right.' Her father's family had their eye on an eligible *parti*; Bettina had already made arrangements that she would marry Pietro Paulo, son of the widowed *Depositario* of the Inquisition, Baroness Vincenza Testaferrata.

Diego hurried back from Rome; Bettina filed a lawsuit in the Bishop's Curia for separation from her husband. Angela was taken by her father from St Catherine's and put in St Ursola's (see Chapter 17 itinerary), there to await the arrival of Baron Pietro Paulo Testaferrata and his own choice for her husband, for a decision to be reached. There Carmel Testa finishes the story, but I know from a genealogical table that Angela married twice – to neither of her parents' choices – and outlived both husbands.

Bettina, one assumes, continued to flourish as a grand dame of wealth and property, but when was she lady-in-waiting to Queen Caroline of Naples and the two Sicilies as the sources suggest? And was she at Gudja when the British made her palace their headquarters during the French blockade that started in 1798? However much people might gossip about her family's affairs, she was untouchable; but how happy and fulfilled was she?

Bettina seems to have held her own in the sexualised world of the eighteenth century. But describing women as victims of crime, Yosanne Vella includes different kinds of sexual exploitation of women; she tells of the case of **Maria Mizzi** who, in 1715, accused Albimo Vasallo of

> repeatedly taking men to her house for sexual favours. What prompted Maria to bring a case against Vassallo was the fact she could not refuse anyone, for Albimo forced her every time even against her wishes. When answering the charge, the accused pleaded, 'but Maria is a public prostitute!' To him this justified everything he had done.

This same case is used in the article about women troublemakers and that last sentence is so telling.

Yosanne Vella starts the next paragraph concerning women as victims, 'Women were physically abused by men who felt they could do what they liked because they owned their women.' Severe wife-beating was endemic, as she illustrates with several cases, and the murder of a wife was not unprecedented, as the case of **Teresa Lavi** shows. Her husband Gerolamo forced her to take her pills in which he had mixed poison. Frans Ciapparo pithily explains, 'The relationship between husbands and wives was a poor one. Men believed they were "masters over their spouses", whom they even beat if they refused to comply to their wishes.'

Men believed, too, that they could sexually harass women with impunity, as a case in Yosanne Vella's 'Women Troublemakers' shows, though they could not always get away with it:

> Juliano said that they were all fooling about and having fun when he went over to **Rosa [Bugeja]** and started joking with her by touching her face and hands. Rosa became very angry when he did this and suddenly taking out a knife she gave him a blow. She was detained in prison for twenty days.

In a society where to be a 'fallen woman' had very negative social implications, the fact that some women felt able to report rape suggests that this too was rather more widespread than the cases brought would suggest. One of the most difficult to report must have been by **Maria de Balzan** when, in 1722, her four-year-old daughter **Annucia** was sexually assaulted on her way home from school where she had been learning how to make socks.

It was not unusual for women to grant sexual favours on the promise of marriage. Frans Ciappara explains: 'Sex outside marriage was both illicit and illegal; but this ill-conformed to the practices of the day. Our ancestors tested their women's fecundity before they joined them in wedlock.' Of course this could work out badly both ways: a young woman could trap a man into marriage, as easily as a man could abandon his fiancée, as happened to **Caterina Frendo**. Illegitimate children continued to be a common feature: as many as 7,887 were born in the period 1750–1800, though some may later have been legitimised by marriage.

In all four of her articles about women in eighteenth-century Malta, Yosanne Vella is determined to show the strength and determination of women. Of those victims of crime whose cases were reported, she concludes:

> If one can perhaps make a positive observation from these cases, it would have to be that very often it was the women who took their aggressors to court. ... While it certainly took courage for women like **Felicita Zammit** and **Catherina Bonare** to accuse their husbands or in **Rosa Pierri**'s case, her lover, of beating them, and one especially appreciates the risk Maria Mizzi, a prostitute, took when she started a court case against such a dangerous man as Albimo Vassallo, a man who solicits clients for sex. It was also brave of the several raped women who reported their attackers and one cannot not admire the audacity of **Gratia Psaila** who refused the option of marrying her assailant. These women showed that they were definitely not passive victims; on the contrary they were willing to risk social stigma, to face their aggressors and seek justice.

And even of the troublemakers:

> Women like Rosa show that some Maltese women did not shirk from using weapons or violence if annoyed. These women together with the thieves, con-artists, drunks etc drift away from the stereotyped image of women which the majority of people have. Far from being timid and passive they show that they were real flesh and blood characters who definitely knew how to take care of and protect themselves.

She writes separately of women accused of magic in 'Women, Religion and Magic in 18th Century Malta' (2004), using it as often vengefully as to woo, and notes that of 50 cases she studied of women appearing before the Inquisition, 'more than two-thirds of the women were in trouble precisely because of magic.' And there she concludes:

> It is clear that in fact these women were not rejecting religion in favour of magic, but rather that folk beliefs and superstitions were incorporated into religious beliefs and rituals. Like two faces of the same coin, both religion and magic appealed to women because they could offer an alternative to the limited mother/wife role imposed on them by their society.

Women of the lower orders were sometimes duped into sexual relations through promises of marriage; for women of the upper classes, it was more money that their suitors were after. This seems to have been the case for **Anna Muscati** (d.1797). In 1760, she married penniless Cavalier Don Domenico Parisio of Reggio Calabria, bringing with her a dowry of 80,000 scudi. She lived in Calabria until her health failed, returning to Malta in 1774 and settling with her youngest child, Paulo, at the Villa Parisio, Naxxar. And there Anna might have become lost to history, except that the Villa Parisio, and the Palazzo Parisio in Valletta, continue to be part of Malta's heritage over 200 years later, for much of that time inhabited by Anna's descendants (see Chapter 17 and Chapter 19 itineraries).

Upper-Class Women of Spirit

Suitors after a handsome dowry used every means of entry to a rich family; if a title went with it so much the better – or at least that may be the conclusion to be drawn from one version of the story of **Maria Teresa Navarra**. Maltese titles, as opposed to Sicilian, had been given by the Grand Master, on behalf of the sovereign, for the first time in 1710 – the first, Barone di Gomerino, jointly to Paulo Testaferrata and his wife **Beatrice Cassia** (9th Baroness of Castel Cicciano, a Neapolitan title), and it was inheritable by females. The first grantee of the Count of Bahria was Ignazio Moscati-Falsoni-Navarra in 1743. He had married **Teodora Bonici** in 1732 and the next holder was to be their elder daughter Maria Teresa.

The first of three versions of the story comes from an internet article, another is a *Times of Malta* appreciation of a play intended as the libretto of an opera which has so far proved elusive – *The Heiress of Bahria* by John Cilia La Corte – though I need to take some salient facts from the account in Carmel Testa's biography of Grand Master Pinto. In the internet version, the Conventual Chaplain, Father Zoccolante Samuele, head of the Grand Master's pages, gained entry to the family via friendship with Maria Teresa's father. She was 22 years old and Carmel Testa tells us that she was already

> well versed in literature, she could read and write fluently Italian, Spanish, French and Latin, sang like a nightingale, played to perfection several musical instruments, was addicted to philosophy and to cap the happiness of her doting father had recently turned her attention to mathematics.

Thus Fr Samuele was hired to be her tutor in mathematics and came to the house every day. The play has it that Maria Teresa's interest stemmed from that of her dead 'lover', killed by the Ottomans. In October 1754, tutor and student eloped. They took with them from the Palazzo Falzon in Mdina (see Chapter 20 itinerary) valuables estimated to be worth 30,000 scudi, embarking on a privateer for the Levant. They settled in the house of the French consul in Corfu and at some stage may have been married by papal dispensation. Informed of the robbery by the count, the Governor of Corfu had the couple arrested and sent to Venice for trial. There 'long-haired' Samuele is said to have died. Maria Teresa was placed in a convent but eventually made her way to Syracuse where she married Antonio Stagno, 3rd Count of Casandola and had a son, though he may have been Fr Samuele's. He became 3rd Count Stagno-Navarra.

Carmel Testa's version is rather different, and I sketch the two versions to show the difficulties of being sure of the truth of any historical details, let alone those concerning a young woman of Malta trailing clouds of romance. In this second version there does not necessarily seem to have been a romance between Fr Samuele Sarsano and Maria Teresa: '[He] had left a note to his friend, a knight, avowing that he had not seduced her but had merely acquiesced to her pleas to accompany her on her travels'. And later in another letter: 'Far from enticing the countess to flee with him, she had tormented him with her importunities till he had finally agreed to escort her on her voyages.' They were accompanied by her servant 'the elderly Benigno' and she left a note saying that the valuables taken represented less than half of her dowry. The play, too, suggests that the urge to travel, as Antonio had planned, was a factor that inspired Maria Teresa, and that her tutor wished not only to help her, but also to benefit himself.

In the Carmel Testa version, The French *pinque* on which they travelled was driven to take refuge on Corfu because of the weather. There, to cut a long story short, they were betrayed, and taken while strolling on the beach – 'Maria Teresa putting up a stiff resistance against the rough handling of her captors'. Samuele was thrown into jail, Maria Teresa taken to lodge with the governor's wife. From there she was taken to Venice and put in a convent in Treviso. Samuele remained in prison for 14 years. As for the young countess:

The restless Maria Theresa soon decided that a cloistered life in a nunnery was not to her taste. Some months later her uncle … went to Venice and with the permission of that Republic's Senate took his errant niece with him to Syracuse. On 14 February 1757 she married Count Antonio Stagno from Palermo.

Given the date of that marriage, it is impossible for Fr Samuele to have been the father of Maria Teresa's son.

The affair had caused much gossip in Malta, and humiliation for Maria Teresa's father, *depositario* of the Valletta *Università*; nevertheless, she visited the islands in 1759 and was given an 'ostentatious salute' from the Captain General of the Galleys. Whatever else is true, Maria Teresa Navarra obviously did not lack spirit or enterprise. She may be an example of noblewomen frustrated by the constraints of their society.

Another example, which manifested itself in lashing out, is that of **Pulcra** (Pulcheria) **Testaferrata** (b. *c*.1700), daughter of Marquis Mario Testaferrata, senior Valletta jurat, and his second wife **Elizabeth Castelletti** whom he married in 1697. Pulcra, who was Baroness Castel Cicciano in her own right, was married to Pietro Paulo Testaferrata, but widowed in 1730. In 1738, as John Attard Montalto's internet article 'Testaferrata Petitions the King' recounts, Pulcra was 'involved in a brawl inside the Franciscan church in Valletta'. The reason is never given but the other protagonist was **Francesca Portughes**, wife since 1736 of Giovanni Francesco Bertis, and, perhaps more pertinent, sister of the Bishop's Secretary of State. 'Harsh words were exchanged and Pulcra slapped Francesca several times.'

The two women were restrained by other worshippers of St Mary of Jesus (Ta' Gesu) in St John Street, which housed the family tomb of the Portughes family (see Chapter 17 itinerary). Afterwards, Francesca received a warning, but Pulcra was

> arrested and taken to the public prisons. The next day, as a result of her parents' persistence and the Grand Master's acquiescence, she was transferred to Fort St Elmo. She was detained for several weeks but was released provided she did not venture out of Birgu. In the meantime, Marquis Mario Testaferrata, on behalf of his daughter petitioned the [relevant] Sicilian tribunal. The reaction from Palermo was not only immediate but also favourable.

Prudence then prevailed and 'the issue was allowed to die down'. But that was not the end of Pulcra's untoward behaviour. Following the death of her first husband, she had married Pietro Cassar who, between 1730 and 1740 was Captain of Cospicua in the Three Cities, and was also 'one of the Inquisitor's favourite patentees and "pertained to a conspicuous family which was considered one of the oldest and most noble"'.

Pulcra was not deterred by her previous experience. In January 1751, when she must have been 50 or so, she was served with a summons in a civil lawsuit by a constable (*sbirro*) of the Grand Master (Pinto). And here it is worth remembering that the Grand Master, the Inquisitor and the Bishop of Malta, whoever held the offices, lived in a constant state of tension. The background to the lawsuit is not vouchsafed but:

> The Baroness politely informed the officer that the writ should be served on her lawyer, or her procurator. The sbirro insisted on presenting the summons to the Baroness and would not accept her suggestion that on this occasion she would allow her page to receive the summons. The sbirro became more imprudent, tempers flared and he jostled her page. Throwing the writ on the ground he immediately left the scene. The sbirro got a worse reception when he came again to present a second writ. Pulcra ordered him out of her house and warned him that if he wanted to present the writ she had already indicated her nominees. The sbirro was apparently enjoying himself and provoked the situation with a wide smile. ... A slave who was accompanying the Baroness offered, but to no avail, to receive the writ. Enough was enough. Such impertinent manners were resented by a screaming Baroness who suddenly confronted the sbirro with a swinging broom. After receiving two or three blows, he was thrown downstairs and was lucky enough 'with the grace of God' to escape through the front door.

Undeterred, the Grand Master, having punished his own people, then ordered his public prosecutor to request the Inquisition officials to accompany him to arrest Pulcra, a step for which there was no precedent. The Inquisitor 'secretly sent a warning to his patent holder to take sanctuary so as not to expose her to further violence'.

He then dispatched his captain to accompany the public prosecutor to Pulcra's residence. On arrival, they found the house of the Baroness completely surrounded by a squadron of soldiers and constables as if Pulcra was some 'escaped galley rower, a vile slave, or a public woman'. The only reason for such actions was to give maximum publicity to the whole incident. The house was searched but to no avail. The Baroness had already taken sanctuary in the collegiate church of St Paul in Valletta. The Grand Master, having failed to achieve his initial aim, sent one of his knights to the Baroness, promising her immediate release if she agreed to give herself up. Convinced of Pinto's goodwill, Pulcra complied and she came out of the church. She was abducted and imprisoned in Fort St Elmo. As soon as Pinto was assured of Pulcra's detention he ordered all his trumpeters to summon the people of Valetta while a proclamation was read: 'Whoever is a true and faithful subject of our prince is in duty bound to capture Pulcra Testaferrata wherever she may be and conduct her to the High Court.'

With one fell swoop, John Attard Montalto suggests, the Grand Master had achieved his aim of both exposing the vulnerability of the Inquistor's patent-holders, and ridiculing the privileges and prerogatives of the Holy Office. The Inquisitor bewailed the fact that it was the patent-holders 'who are from the prime and most select nobility of the country' who were attacked, but there was little he could do. Not so Pulcra's family; as far as they were concerned, the matter could not rest. Her husband, remembering how her father had dealt with the previous affair, went to the Inquisitor and informed him that unless Pulcra was released he was going to appeal to the Kingdom of Sicily, 'notwithstanding the consequences'. Reluctantly, therefore, 'Pinto released Pulcra so as to avert any possible interference from the Sicilian Monarchy in the state of affairs in his principality.'

The politics of the two incidents involving Pulcra are, of course, interesting, but it is Pulcra herself who is my main concern, and her resort to physical violence, abuse and screaming when thwarted – behaviour which suggests her only method of asserting herself in a society organised to constrain her.

Not all upper-class women felt the need to break free in some way, and marriage for money was not all one way, as is shown by that of **Maria Teresa Grech** in 1745 to Nicola Perdicomati Bologna, brother of *Depositario* Vincenza Matilde, though there would be something to gain by both sides. The Bologna family's Maltese title was brand new, granted to Nicola's father that year, but the family already had large assets – houses, shops, lands and fields – on both Malta and Gozo. Maria Teresa was not married off for money – her father was the *nouveau riche* legal adviser (*uditore*) to Grand Master Pinto, and as such seen as one of the most powerful men in Malta. Although to the Bolognas it was seen as a misalliance – Grech being merely an upstart lawyer – he did provide access to power, and his daughter's dowry would always be useful. For Grech, the title of an established family was attractive, and to prove his daughter's suitability, to demonstrate his wealth and position, he built the couple the Villa Bologna in Attard, as a wedding present and part of his daughter's dowry (see Chapter 20 itinerary).

Whatever the circumstances of the marriage, it seems to have been a happy one, if an unsigned letter found in the de Piro archives is anything to go by. It is dated 23 December 1753 and scholar of France, Noel Caruana Dingli, deduces from the internal evidence that it was written by Maria Teresa Bologna to her husband Nicola. He was known by the courtesy title of Comte de Boulogne at the French Court where he was staying for a while, having probably travelled to France on family business.

The letter is written in fluent French, leading its interpreter to suggest not only that Maria Teresa was an educated woman but that the Bologna and Grech families were Francophile, and that a French lifestyle was fashionable in certain Maltese circles of the time. It is also full of affection from wife to husband, sprinkled with 'mon cher', 'mon très cher', 'mon cher coeur' and she reveals to him that she gave birth to their second daughter, **Maria Giuseppa Antonia Vincenza**, on 16 November. She reassures him concerning the welfare of members of his family.

In a previous letter, Nicola had asked Maria Teresa to send him her measurements and that of 'La Petite' so that he could buy them both some French shoes. She assures him that she could 'easily find good-quality shoes for herself in Malta'. She is concerned about his health, and ends with the declaration, 'Je ne puis être heureuse sans vous.' Thus, from one piece of paper, Maria Teresa Bologna becomes a real person, and we learn that marriage in Malta could be happy.

There was to be a strange occurrence three years later concerning Maria Teresa's mother-in-law, Giovanna Fortunata Testaferrata, and her own father, told in an internet article by Charles Said-Vassallo ('Polemics Between Maltese Dynasts' (2010)). Nicola's father died in 1756, then,

> During the night of December 17, 1756 the Vice Chancellor of the Order went to the house of the late Count Bologna. Accompanied by 18 soldiers, he ordered the Countess to vacate her house and informed her that he was following the direct instructions of Grand Master Pinto. The Countess was bewildered as she had no idea why she was being treated in such a way. The issue was not subject to discussion. Hastily she collected some clothes and the moment she was out of her palazzo the door was barred.
>
> The Vice Chancellor of the Order, however, notwithstanding the harsh order of the Prince of Malta [the Grand Master], offered Countess Bologna the use of his sedan chair and she was taken to the house of her brother, Mgr Testaferrata. The reason why the recently widowed countess

was evicted is obscure. Some light is shed on the matter in a confidential memorandum dated August 20, 1756, forwarded to the Holy Office in Rome by Inquisitor Salviati. The whole episode appears to have been instigated by none other than Fabrizio Grech, the Grand Master's lawyer, in relation to a dispute between two of the most prominent families on the Island, the Bolognas and the Testaferratas. The lawyer was the father in law of Count Nicola and was not in the least bothered to use his ends to justify his means.

What happened next is left hanging, and Nicola remained in favour, but Maria Teresa, when widowed, appears to have continued one of the family feuds, this time with Nicola's nephew, *Depositario* Vincenza's son, by then Baron Pietro Paulo Testaferrata. The two of them 'disturbed Grand Master de Rohan to such an extent that he decided to impose perpetual silence between the warring parties on 30 June 1783'. Pietro Paulo was to marry for the second time in 1783; the fate of that wife will have to await the French occupation of Valletta in Chapter 8.

The lives of members of the Order and the Maltese touched at certain points. The most obvious regarding women were the sexual relations between Maltese of all ranks and the Knights. But it was very much *de haut en bas*, even to the Maltese nobility created by the Grand Master. A vignette of where they occasionally touched socially is in Raphael J Camilleri Parlato's 'The Ceremonial Entry into Mdina of Grand Master Emmanuel Pinto de Fonseca on the 29th Day of October 1741' in de Piro's *Costume in Malta*. He starts with the procession leaving Valletta:

The Streets of Valletta were decorated and adorned as never before – tapestries and laudatory inscriptions in Latin and Italian hung from the balconies and windows of the Palaces of Strada San Giorgio [Republic Street]. The streets were thronged with cheering subjects, who included the professional and business classes, the men in their wigs and tailed tunics worn over cotton waistcoats, and the women wearing black faldettas over full French style dresses and veils on their heads. Many workers and peasants were to be found in the crowd, the men in their cotton waistcoats and sandals and the women wearing coloured faldettas, head scarves and aprons over their full cotton skirts. The windows and balconies of the palaces of the gentry and nobility were also thronged with curious people waiting to see their new Prince, but in this case the ladies did not wear their faldettas but their brocaded finery, delicate lace veils on their heads and ornate jewellery.

The scene then shifted to Mdina:

The wives of the Mdina officials, and some of the Nobility had moved to their Mdina palaces a few days before to attend the religious functions there on this auspicious occasion, and watch the main part of the festivities from their family seats.

The women had a limited part to play: 'Many members of the families of the Mdina gentry all but filled the cathedral'; and afterwards the Grand Master left on foot to visit the nuns of St Benedict opposite the Palazzo Inguanez: 'These nuns, who came from the most distinguished families of the island, intoned a *Te Deum* and before his departure the prioress [**Melania Platamone**] presented him with a bouquet of gold and silver flowers.' Pinto's biographer adds a telling sentence to his description of the occasion, 'Before leaving, Pinto thanked the abbess and her nuns for their prayers and gifts through the iron grille near the main altar' (see Chapter 20 itinerary).

These two events were a small part of the grand ceremonial and, as far as I can see, women did not attend the banquet that evening, though their husbands, if of significance, did, nor the later reception given by the *Capitano della Verga*.

The main purpose of the new Grand Master's visit to Mdina, as far as the nobles there were concerned, was 'to confirm an oath that the privileges, exemptions, rights and prerogatives enjoyed by that city would be honoured and safeguarded'. The edge behind the apparent warmth of the welcome, and a reason for the presence of noblewomen being limited, is suggested by an opinion expressed in Attard and Azzopardi, *Daily Life in Eighteenth Century Malta*:

> Maltese nobles whose titles had been conferred upon them by the rulers of Sicily considered the knights to be a band of autocratic usurpers who had despoiled them of ancient privileges bestowed upon them by the kings of Spain. Members of the ancient nobility of Mdina lived secluded and tended to keep their women outside the reach of the knights.

But how far did that apply to noblewomen in Valletta where the Order was centred? Was it the men of the family who maintained a separation, or was it the Knights themselves with their formal life of ritual, ceremony and exclusiveness?

How far even noblewomen were excluded from the more respectable part of the Knights' public life is suggested by *Maria Felice Colonna: Il Diario*, edited, in Italian, by Francesca Latini and Joseph Eynaud for publication in 2007. If you thought you would learn anything about the women of Malta from this travel diary, you would be sorely disappointed.

Maria Felice Colonna (1731–1771) was born into the famous Roman Colonna family: her father was Fabrizio Colonna, her mother **Caterina Maria Zeffirina Salviati Rospigliosi**. In 1752, aged 21, she married the Sicilian Giuseppe Letterio Alliata, Prince of Bucheri and Villafranca, who was only a year older, and in September that year they set off on a honeymoon trip to Sicily and Malta – except that it was not a honeymoon that we would recognise. They travelled in the entourage of Felice's not-yet-married older brother, Lorenzo Colonna, Prince of Palliano and Castiglione which included Duke Benedetti and many others, but not, apparently, any other noblewomen though, presumably, Maria Felice had a lady's maid.

On 14 September they reached Malta where Lorenzo was on a two-week diplomatic mission to the Knights. So that is what Maria Felice writes about. She is included in some, but not all, of the ceremonies and engagements, and records details of those events where she appears to have been absent; rarely does she use the pronouns *io* (I), or *noi* (we). So far as she relates, no Maltese women were present.

As an account of politics and diplomacy of the time and place, it is an interesting document; as an insight into how the women of Malta lived, it is barren. You have to wonder what Maria Felice did with herself when she was not included in the party – perhaps she was meeting interesting women – but it was not done to record events outside the mission. Just on one occasion a party goes to the ballet, presumably at the Manoel Theatre; the ballerina was said to be from Holland: a two-word glimpse of a woman, but I'm not sure that Maria Felice was there. If the diary reveals anything feminine it is that she was obviously an educated woman, an adept recorder of a mission important to the men in her life, and illuminating about the Knights of Malta.

Anxious about my interpretation, I contacted one of the editors, Joseph Eynaud, head of the Department of Translation, Terminology and Interpreting Studies at the University of Malta, who replied most enlighteningly: 'Francesca and myself think that the diary is an "idiografo" not written by Maria Felice but dictated by her and annotated by someone in charge of keeping records of her trip. That is why I and We are conspicuously absent.'

What is so extraordinary is that in 1798 everything to do with the Knights was to be swept away, leaving only architectural traces. They were to return in a very limited way, and on sufferance, two centuries later.

8 – The French Revolution in Malta and its Aftermath 1798–1814

Arrival of the French

Revolution was in the air, even in Malta, in the last quarter of the eighteenth century. There had been intimations of uprisings against the Knights but, in 1775, a conspiracy was more serious. The ringleaders were imprisoned or executed; the same happened in 1797. Meanwhile, a successful revolution against the *Ancien Régime* had taken place in France in 1789.

A majority of the Knights in Malta were French; much benefit to the economy had come from France, but the leaders of the French Revolution did not regard the Order favourably; by 1792 the Order in Malta had ceased to be economically viable, particularly as its possessions in France had been appropriated. The new French Republic did, however, appreciate Malta's strategic position. They were not the only ones: so did Britain and Russia.

The First Coalition against Revolutionary France was formed in 1793, and was defeated by forces under Napoleon Bonaparte. The Second Coalition, which included Great Britain, Austria, the Kingdom of Naples (Malta's overlord), Portugal and Russia, was formed in 1798. In late spring that year, Napoleon set off for Egypt, as part of his military campaign. Malta was on the way, and he needed to replenish supplies, particularly of water.

The fleet carrying his forces arrived off Malta on 9 June. The Order refused its request, so French troops were disembarked on the 10th and were soon in control of the countryside. What with pro-French Knights, a vacillating Grand Master, the German Ferdinand de Hompesch, and uncertain Maltese resistance, the Order did not even retire within its fortifications. The prospect of a siege would probably have deterred Napoleon who was anxious to be on his way. On the 11th, Hompesch sought an armistice; it was granted, but the terms were harsh: the Order was to give up the Islands and its property there in exchange for estates and pensions in France. After two and a half centuries of imposing the Order's seemingly indelible stamp on Malta, of transforming it beyond recognition, all was swept away overnight. Tsar Paul of Russia was elected Grand Master in Hompesch's place, and thereafter took a paternal, as well as strategic, interest in Malta.

The story of the next two years or so is magnificently told in Carmel Testa's mammoth *The French in Malta 1798–1800* (1997). The broad sweep is there, but also the detail of how individuals were affected.

On Sunday 10 June, the day before the armistice was sought, a shocking incident occurred down near the waterfront, in the lee of Our Lady of Liesse church. In a warehouse that was also a residence, No. 34 New Street, a narrow street sloping away from today's Victoria Gate, lived the family of a French merchant and ships' chandler called, in brief accounts, Etienne Eynaud (see Chapter 17 itinerary). His full name, though, when in 1771 he married Maltese **Paula Saveria Gonzi** (1756–1833) in St Dominic's Church, Valletta, was Giacinto Stefano Eynaud (as told in a family account by Andy Welsh). Eynaud's Huguenot family, named Agnau, came from Brest; his father was Hyacinth Etienne Agnau. Saveria was the daughter of Notary Pietro Paulo Gonzi and **Anna Gonzi** (née Magri). The couple had ten children, three girls, seven boys.

Carmel Testa describes how families in the area feared French bombardment. The Eynauds' house was considered safe so, that day, **Margerita Magri** was also there with her ten children – her husband was on board Napoleon's ship. Two other French families were also sheltered there: the Patots and François **Damas** from Marseilles with his wife **Elizabeth** (née Lombardi) and their two children. Thirty women, children and men were crowded into the house.

It was not surprising, therefore, that after lunch the children went to play on the open balcony above the main door. Their squeals and shouts in French caught the attention of Maltese soldiers guarding a nearby fortification, their nerves on edge, easily provoked. The soldiers scolded the children; they responded with cheek. The soldiers ran to the Eynauds' house and broke down the door to get at 'armed traitors'. Eynaud and Damas tried to reason with them but, instead, they were set about with musket butts and swords. Damas was decapitated and his corpse thrown into the harbour, Eynaud was mortally wounded and died in the *Sacra Infermeria* the following day.

So much else was happening in the days, weeks and months that followed that it is easy to skim past the agony of those French families – wives brutally widowed before their eyes, children left fatherless and probably later aware that they had innocently caused the tragedy.

On 22 June, as a footnote details, Saveria Eynaud appeared before the newly formed Commission of Government to seek retribution and financial assistance. She was paid 250 francs, a quarter of the annual pension granted her. She also asked to be allowed to live rent free in her house. It is not clear from Carmel Testa's perusal of later documents that her request was granted. Elizabeth Damas was granted an annual pension of 600 francs, but received assistance only for a short time.

Meanwhile, the French were taking over control of the Islands. Napoleon stayed there for six days. At least one source says that he occupied Bettina Dorell's Gudja palazzo. I've even heard it said that she had a one night stand with him. My informant must have had his tongue in his cheek. It is certainly true that Bettina was in Malta then. Carmel Testa notes that she left for Naples and safety in August. A ship on which she was a passenger arrived there with a cargo of cotton on the 23rd. It may be from then that she became lady in waiting to Queen Maria Carolina.

And it is certainly true that Bettina's brother, Baron Giovanni Francesco Dorell, was sympathetic towards the French Revolution and was one of those who signed the petition on Napoleon's behalf calling on the Order to capitulate. But it is clear that Napoleon stayed at the palazzo of Baron Paulo Parisio next to the Auberge of Castille in Merchant Street. There is a plaque to commemorate his stay on the wall of what is now the Ministry for Foreign Affairs (see Chapter 17 itinerary).

Napoleon left Malta under the command of General Claude-Henri Belgrand Vaubois and 3,000 French soldiers. The French administration set up a Commission of Government and established municipalities on which Maltese served. Everything was changed, from weights and measures, to money, to education. Sixty young Maltese men were ordered to France to study. Among those who managed to get their son's name removed from the list was the wealthy widow Giovanna Fontani who was, a few months later, to cause Vaubois considerable embarrassment. Even in the short term, she caused discomfiture.

During its session of 12 July, the Commission of Government approved the payment of 72 scudi to Giovanna 'the price of a silver candlestick which she had been forced to lend to the West Municipality for the use of Napoleon during his stay in Malta. The candlestick was never returned to her.' They got more back than they had paid in compensation because in June the following year the rich were ordered to provide loans to the government; among them was Giovanna Fontani of Merchant Street who loaned 1,500 scudi.

There were many other changes, not just street names – Strada Reale, for example, becoming Rue Nationale (today's Republic Street). And the French authorities found that they were suddenly responsible for numerous charitable institutions – hospitals, and asylums of one sort or another (*conservatorii*) – most of them founded and funded by the Order. A report was commissioned and a list drawn up. The names on it relevant to women and girls consisted of, for example, the *conservatorio* at Floriana built by Grand Master de Vilhena in 1734 and now housing 131 girls looked after by 8 women; and the Maddalena, with its annual income of 400 scudi. They, and the other five on the list, needed 7,631 scudi to be properly run.

Then there were the hospitals – 8 of them, including the *Casetta* which had at least 160 patients; that needed 15,000 scudi per annum. Its income was 2,460 scudi, 1,500 of which came from Caterina Scappi's foundation. The Order had been wont to make up the 12,000 scudi needed. De Vilhena had also founded a hospice at Floriana in 1732 for invalid elderly people or poor females, particularly spinsters. It had 280 inmates of both sexes and required 11,700 scudi per annum. The females wove cotton goods which were sold, half the proceeds going to them, the other half to the hospice. Then there were the alms that had been distributed, and the loaves of bread to beggars and poor novices and the measures of flour to the poor. No wonder the following year loans were demanded from the rich such as Giovanna Fontani.

Everything was to be reorganised. The nuns at Maddalena, for example, were 'decloistered' and they and the women inmates were to join the nuns at St Catherine's nunnery. Many nuns chose, instead, to leave and live with relatives, which was considered something of a scandal. Laws were introduced to restrict the influence of the church. Christine Muscat describes the events in detail.

The French administration had bedded down so quickly that they decided to hold a grand occasion in Palace Square – renamed Place de la Liberté – on 14 July to celebrate their glorious revolution round a Tree and Altar of Liberty set up in the middle. On 6 July, the Commission of Government issued an order 'that during the 14 July festivities all the nobles were to burn their patents and other titles of nobility … "following a request to that effect by many citizens"'. At the same time, all slaves were to be freed.

Another feature of the day was that four orphan girls on whom the government was to settle dowries were to be married. The Gozitans felt left out, so a poor orphan girl from there was to be given a dowry and married that day at the Gozo Matrice in the presence of the Gozo Municipality.

Thus, on the 14th, at 8 am, dressed all in white, came **Victoria Volflomier** – who had been housed and taught a craft at the Floriana *Conservatorio* for seven years – to marry Blaise Marthe, a Frenchman; **Marthe Consolata Arrighi**, the betrothed of Francesco Calderoni; and **Clara Decelis** to marry Giuseppe Cutajar. A girl called Elizabetta was also there, but her fiancé was absent through illness. A great fiesta took place under a sweltering sun before Vaubois led the procession to St John's for the marriage ceremony.

Back in the square, the spectators 'witnessed the local nobles coming forward one after another to throw their titles and other documents of nobility in the fire burning near the Tree of Liberty' while various republican songs were sung. At least they did not lose their heads as aristocrats in France had done. And the day ended with a sumptuous dinner and ball given by Vaubois at the Palace.

But did the marriages of the couples turn out happily? As Carmel Testa explains in a footnote to the wedding, a few months later Giuseppe Cutajar initiated court proceedings against his wife Clara Decelis for having abandoned him, taking all their gold with her. 'Clara, on her part, brought many witnesses to prove that during the time they were living together her husband used to prostitute her with French officers for money.' One witness often saw Cutajar 'bringing his wife to Vaubois's room, at the palace, and then await outside to take the money she had been given'. And so the witnesses on Clara's behalf came and went with their lurid testimonies of Cutajar's prostitution of his wife to French officers.

Such slips could perhaps be glossed over by the public but the French, with their revolutionary anti-clerical stance, had completely misjudged the temper of the Maltese – the strength of the small communities, adherence to their religion and pride in their churches. The removal of the Knights may not have hurt, but the closing of the monasteries and nunneries did. On top of that, the French troops started looting the churches to pay for the expedition to Egypt. When news reached Malta of the defeat on 1 August 1798 of Napoleon and his fleet by Britain's Admiral Nelson at the Battle of Aboukir Bay in Egypt, French invincibility was seen as a chimera.

On 2 September, during an auction of church property in Mdina, Maltese anger erupted into armed insurrection against the French; French soldiers were attacked and killed. Within days, the French garrison had been driven behind the fortifications of Valletta and the Three Cities, surrounded by 10,000 irregular Maltese soldiers. The Mdina *Università* was transformed into a National Assembly which sent an emissary to seek help from King Ferdinand of the Two Sicilies.

On 12 October, British ships, dispatched by Nelson, arrived under Captain Alexander Ball, joining a Portuguese squadron that had arrived a few days earlier, and a blockade of the French began. Vaubois withdrew the last of his forces into Valletta, joined by 100 Maltese citizens. Nelson offered Vaubois terms of surrender, but they were rejected. The blockade was to last until 5 September 1800.

The French garrison on Gozo surrendered to Ball on 28 October, transferring the island to the British, as well as some armaments and 32,000 sacks of flour which was distributed to the 16,000 inhabitants.

To begin with, the French in Valletta and the city's inhabitants managed to survive well enough, though anyone with anti-French sympathies, true or false, was evicted and packed off to the countryside. 'Maltese peasants who were suddenly faced with destitute crowds coming out of the besieged cities (about 1,200 from Cospicua and 400 from Valletta) were further inflamed against the French.'

It is easy enough to picture mothers with babies and children, bewildered, frightened, weighed down with what they could carry with them, not always being well received in the countryside. Some genuine French sympathisers had also been evicted through false information. If they were recognised in the countryside as pro-French they might be killed. **Maria Theresa Bruno** (née Maurin) from Cospicua was left widowed in that way. Her brother was the first President of the Eastern Municipality and, therefore, probably pro-French. She had been married to the lawyer Dr Giovanni Spiridon Bruno for nine years.

At first the free bread rations distributed to needy families in Valletta had worked well enough, but then there were complaints about the system so, on 22 October, the Commission put in charge **Theresa Borg** who had already supervised distribution of the pittance under the Order. When it proved too big a job for her, **Frances Belli** was appointed to do the same in Vittoriosa, **Diana Bruno** in Cospicua and **Mary Borg** in Senglea. But Theresa and Diana did not get on, and on 8 May 1799 the Commission of Government wrote to the Eastern Municipality:

The lack of understanding between Theresa Borg and Diana Bruno in charge of bread distribution at Cospicua has forced us to ask for an explanation to enable us to reach a final decision on a matter of great importance since it concerns the poor. We expect you to tell us not only the exact truth on this matter but also to watch carefully on the distribution of such alms with that care and attention which one ought to exercise to help that section of the population which is most in need. And since now wheat is being given instead of loaves of bread once every ten days, it appears to us to be more opportune for you to be present during the distribution in order to help. In this way the poor will be better served and there will be a final end to the continuous squabbles between these two women.

Theresa Borg may have been a bit of an operator; a footnote details her attempt to get a house rent free on the Rue Nationale.

On 9 October 1798, the Commission had to address the issue of unemployment caused by the insurrection, and it asked the Eastern Municipality for a list of their weaving machines, together with the names and addresses of their owners, and another list of women and men employed in the weaving industry. In December, it began to force those who could not support themselves to leave the blockaded French area in order to conserve supplies of food. This was said to include prostitutes, in reality knitters, spinners, laundresses and dressmakers. The civilian population of 45,000 in 1799 had dropped to 9,000 by 1800.

In January 1799, a plan was hatched within the ranks of the Maltese rebels to seize Valletta and the Three Cities on the night of 11th/12th. It failed and 40 of those taking part were shot in Place de la Liberté, beginning on the 14th. Among them was 61-year-old Father Mikiel Xerri (Scerri) of Żebbuġ, regarded as the hero of the attempt; a plaque was later to be affixed to his house in West Street below the Carmelite Church, and a few feet away from a statue of the leaders of the conspiracy. Less well known is the part played in the enterprise by **Francesca**, the Maltese wife of Neapolitan sea captain Aurelio **Cafiero**. They lived in Senglea but, as Paul Cassar recounts in his 'Vignette', Aurelio, though a foreigner, 'had thrown in his lot with the Maltese insurgents'. He undertook, with the help of his sailors, to attack fort S Angelo at the same time as his co-conspirators entered Valletta. As for Francesca:

> His wife had secretly gone to the Fort held by the French to give him the flag of the King of the Two Sicilies that had been handed to her by Dun Mikiel Scerri ... to be raised on the Fort. The rising of the Maltese failed and her husband was taken prisoner though he subsequently escaped. His wife eluded capture by the French but in spite of her courageous conduct she has remained a very shadowy figure; indeed not even her name was known until very recently and all we know about her, after this episode, is that she later fell ill but was still alive on the 28th May 1800. After that date she disappears from the stage of history.

The executed men were given the opportunity to draw up their wills before their death, and Carmel Testa reproduces some of them and the aftermath, showing how the women in their lives were affected. For example, **Colomba Coivi**, a young girl **Anna Rebuel**, 'and a negress ex-slave' who had resided at the house of Guiliermo Lorenzi were taken to the hospice for the poor in Floriana. Father Xerri's will shows that he left to

Colomba, daughter of Paul **Zammit** of Rabat, all his belongings, furniture, jewellery and everything in his residence in Valletta, which shall be taken by her after his death with the obligation to give to his heirs here under mentioned, his clothes, priestly or lay, as well as his bed and its linen and the writing desk of the testator. ...

The testator imposes on his heirs the obligation of paying to Colomba and her mother **Sapienza** a monthly allowance of five scudi to each one of them, to be paid every quarter, and on the death of either one of them her share would go to increase the allowance of the survivor for the remainder of her life.

Matthew **Pulis**, fumigator at the quarantine department, left a widow, **Maria Teresa** (née Zerafa) who, on 5 April 1799 filed an application before the Justice of the Peace to be appointed legal representative of their six children; and then a second application regarding his assets. He left only 632 scudi. In due course Maria Teresa was given permission to leave Valletta and went as a refugee to Qormi.

Throughout 1799, the situation both inside Valletta and the Three Cities, and in the rest of the country, deteriorated – 'Conditions of the besiegers were', as Charles Savona-Ventura suggests in 'Human Suffering During the Maltese Insurrection of 1798' (1998), 'little better than those of the besieged'. Some '2,000 perished through sickness and hunger, while direct war casualties amount to just 300 men killed and wounded.' But there were women killed too.

It is not quite clear when **Laudonia Moroni** was mortally wounded. Her death does not seem to have been reported until 15 December 1799, but Charles Said-Vassallo suggests in 'Reassessment of Favray's portrait of an elderly lady with infant' (2011) that it was 'during the Maltese insurrection against the French'.

Laudonia was the 'gentle and spiritual' daughter of a Roman senator, Count Annibale Moroni, and in August 1786 she became the second wife of Baron Pietro Paulo Testaferrata, son and heir of the *depositario* Vincenza Matilde Perdicomati Testaferrata. His first wife, the Maltese noblewoman **Maria Anna Manduca**, had died childless; Laudonia had four children. Pietro Paulo appears to have been absent at the time of her death.

Charles Said-Vassallo gives an account of it, untranslated from the Italian report emanating from Rome, in another internet article, 'The Italian wives of Baron Testaferrata'. Laudonia, anxious about the impending upheaval in Italy as Napoleon pursued his Italian campaign, had sought 'tranquillity and security' in Malta, in a mansion at 56 St John Street, Valletta (see Chapter 17 itinerary). It was not to be because, during a bombardment, a cannon ball crashed into the wall of the room where she was lying because of ill health, followed by two bombs, one under a window, the other into the room itself severely injuring Laudonia. She was taken to the countryside but died a few months later.

Where were these armaments fired from, and by whom? The Roman article does not speculate, but an article, to which Charles Said-Vassallo has referred me, suggests that Laudonia's children particularly suffered their great loss because it was caused by 'their own compatriots'. In February 1799, Vincenzo Borg from Birkirkara, one of the Maltese leaders, was behind the erection of two batteries close to Forts Manoel and Tigné, and when General Graham, the new British commander, arrived another battery for mortar pieces and three heavy guns was erected at Sliema under his command. Manoel Island is opposite where Laudonia lived at the end of St John Street, towards the water's edge of Marsmaxett Harbour. Or was it from the French firing back and their shots falling short? Whoever was responsible, four children were left motherless. Pietro Paulo married again four years later and fathered four more children.

Giovanna Fontani, a Rich Widow

The death of another woman that year, mostly told by Carmel Testa, had a different cause but this time, though the outcome was as tragic, the result created a scandal within the French authority. The rich widow **Giovanna Fontani** (*c*.1763–1799), whose candlestick Napoleon had borrowed and not returned, died not from mortar fire, but in childbirth. Except that by then she was no longer a widow.

Giovanna Fontani was the daughter of **Madalena Bouchet** and Antonio Crespi and she had first married Lorenzo Fontani, member of a Florentine banking family, who, there is evidence to suggest, was the natural son of Grand Master de Rohan. They married in Naples in 1783 and, once they were in Malta, Lorenzo was employed in the Grand Master's palace. In 1776, de Rohan made him a 'cofrater of the Order' and later appointed him custodian of his palace. This meant that he had to reside there, and there he died, in 1788.

Giovanna was, indeed, left a rich widow. Her dowry from her parents was 2,000 scudi, a house and garden at Balzan, land and farm houses, and other immovable property. Lorenzo promised his bride a dowry of 20,000 scudi and several houses, their residence at 1–3 Frederick Street (see Chapter 17 itinerary), and a small palace in Castille Square which was let. Following Lorenzo's death, their elder son, Vincenzo, became a favourite of de Rohan, was made Captain of Cavalry when he was five and allowed to live in the palace. In December 1792, aged eight, he was made a Knight of Devotion and, in 1797, de Rohan made the lad Count of Senia. The family was at the top of the social tree.

Then the French invaded and it seems that a French officer, Antoine Gastinel (Castinel), may have been billeted on the rich widow of Frederick Street (re-named Rue de Brutus). However they met, they were secretly married before Vaubois in the palace in June 1799. It appears that Giovanna was already pregnant and it was inappropriate for her, as the widow of Lorenzo Fontani, to be seen in that condition in public, the father a Frenchman. Six months later, in December, aged 36, she died giving birth to a daughter – **Giacobina Fontani-Gastinel**.

The evening of her death, Giovanna had been about to give a dinner party for 20 guests, so that the best silver was on display. To paraphrase the long account given by Carmel Testa, much of the silver disappeared, and a safe full of jewellery and gold articles, valued at 50,000 scudi, was forced open and emptied. Gastinel, left with the responsibility of four step-children and a newborn baby, as well as a rich mansion, was accused of the robbery. But in hauling him before the criminal court, and then transferring the case to the military council, Vaubois incurred the wrath of Gastinel's loyal brother officers who turned on the commander and insulted him roundly. The jewellery mysteriously re-appeared and Gastinel conceded that he had been responsible, but only to save Giovanna's possessions from being taken by the military authorities to pay the garrison.

Gastinel was put on a ship back to France to be tried, together with all the relevant documentation about the case for the minister of justice, but the ship was intercepted by the British. Gastinel was wounded in its capture and taken prisoner of war. The documents went missing, indefinitely. The four children, and baby Giacobina, settled with their grandmother Madalena Crespi at Balzan. Young Vincenzo's career went from strength to strength.

Emma Hamilton

While all this was going on in Malta, events in Naples and Sicily had been dramatic enough, and they affected the islands under that crown's ultimate suzerainty. When Mdina's newly created National Assembly sent a plea for help to King Ferdinand, they could not be aware that, in fact, his Austrian wife, **Queen Maria Carolina** (1752–1814) was in charge, and had been since she was admitted to the Privy Council in 1775.

The Queen's best friend was **Emma Hamilton** (*c*.1765–1815), wife of Britain's Ambassador Sir William Hamilton. She, in turn, since Nelson's return from Egypt to his naval base in Naples, had been getting closer to and more influential over the British admiral.

Emma Hamilton was a bit of a siren. Daughter of a blacksmith, brought up uneducated, she had made the best of her beauty, style and allure to advance her position in the *demi-monde* of London. Aged 18, she arrived in Naples in 1783, taken under the care of the 52-year-old ambassador as the discarded mistress of the Hon. Charles Francis Greville, Hamilton's nephew. When it was clear that the rupture with Greville was complete, she became Hamilton's mistress and, in 1791, his wife. She was 26, he was 60. In London, where they were married, Emma, because of her reputation, was not received at Court, but in Paris she was, and **Queen Marie Antoinette** (1755–1793) was Queen Maria Carolina's sister, so she was in Naples too. There she was described by **Elizabeth Wynne Fremantle** (1778–1857), an Englishwoman whose wedding she organised at the ambassadorial residence in 1797, as 'a charming woman, beautiful and exceedingly good humoured and amiable'.

In the rather unfriendly 'How Lady Hamilton Changed the History of Malta' (2000), Giovanni Bonello suggests that Emma and Maria Carolina – who had borne her husband 18 children – were lovers, to Malta's detriment; I can't see it. He quotes an Italian historian: 'The influence of Emma (Hamilton) on Queen Mary Caroline drove the Two Sicilies to ruin and misery and caused the loss of Malta to the Kingdom.' The queen was also said to be the lover of her French-born, English favourite Sir John Acton, and to be totally dissolute. You can tell she was not popular, and not without cause.

Encouraged by Nelson's victory over the French at Aboukir Bay, egged on by his queen, and encouraged by British diplomacy, King Ferdinand declared war on France. His troops marched on French-occupied Rome in November 1798 but were thrown back, and the French general counter-attacked and took Naples. The Royal Family, the Court, including the Hamiltons, and the government fled to Palermo, Sicily, where they installed themselves, and Nelson, who had ferried the royal party, including the Hamiltons, established his new naval base. Naples was recaptured, with the help of British ships, in June 1799, and they all moved back.

While the Court was still in Palermo, it is said that, because Emma was there, Nelson lingered and neglected the siege of Malta. In early 1800 Lord Keith, Nelson's commander-in-chief, reprimanded him for withdrawing two ships from the blockade for Queen Maria Carolina's use. Keith wrote to Nelson, 'Lady Hamilton has ruled the fleet long enough.' By late March, their relationship was an open secret.

Nelson's visits to Malta had been rare, but in the spring of 1800, he resolved to go and see how the British and Maltese were getting on with the blockade of the French, Vaubois having refused yet again to surrender, in spite of the increasing shortage of food and the ill health of his troops. Although it was a tour of inspection, Nelson was accompanied by Emma and William Hamilton, two unnamed English friends, and a fan of his, 42-year-old Miss **Cornelia Knight** (1757–1837), a poet and artist who had been living in Naples with her mother until her death, and was now under the wing of the Hamiltons. She was known as Nelson's poet laureate, but her panegyrics make rather painful reading.

Cornelia's journal, which originally accompanied her watercolours and sketches, is missing, but she wrote briefly of the plans for the trip in *Personal Reminiscences* (1887):

Lord Nelson's presence being much needed at Malta, to direct the operations of the blockading squadron, Sir William and Lady Hamilton decided to accompany him. At first I declined being one of the party, but when I heard it was the admiral's intention to visit Syracuse, and perhaps other parts of the island [of Sicily on the way], I could not resist the temptation, nor was I disappointed in my expectations.

If she were being honest, she was also keen to follow up her acquaintance with one of Nelson's officers then off Malta. She was to be disappointed in her hopes that the relationship might progress.

The party spent a few days in Syracuse and Cornelia painted a watercolour of the rest of the party in a rowing boat, captioned 'River Anapius with the ruins of the temple of Olympiche Jupiter'. The importance of this image is that seated in the stern is a thin figure in naval dress and prominent gold epaulettes, wearing a large tricorn hat in the style affected by Nelson; he holds a parasol over a woman seated on his left. Small and indistinct though it is, it is the only known, contemporary image of Nelson and Emma Hamilton together.

Cornelia's description of the Maltese trip is also brief:

> Late in the evening of the 3rd [of May] we joined the blockading squadron off Malta, on which island we remained until the 20th, occasionally dining at the governor's Captain Sir Alexander Ball's, and sometimes at the quarters of General Graham, afterwards Lord Lynedoch.

Ball was based at the Villa San Anton, Attard, and Cornelia's sketch is in the Chapter 20 itinerary. General Graham's headquarters were in Bettina Dorell's Gudja palace, though she was probably still in Naples. The party obviously also visited Birkirkara because a sketch of St Helen's church there is included in Cornelia's portfolio (see itinerary).

The *Foudroyant* had sailed first into St Paul's Bay where, as one of Emma's biographers, Kate Williams, tells us, 'The blockading ships fired off spectacular welcoming salutes, and villages across Malta were illuminated.' They stayed there a week.

William Hamilton, with his antiquarian interests, spent the two weeks or so of the visit roaming the island. As Paul Xuereb relates in 'William Hamilton's Account of his First Visit to Malta' (1972), he had been there once before, in 1758, when he was accompanied by his first wife **Catherine** (née Barlow) (1738–1782). He wrote of that earlier visit:

> On our passage from Palermo to Girgenti we were forced by strong contrary winds to put into the Port of Malta, where we were most graciously received by the Grand Master and most hospitably treated by him and the principal Officers of the Order during the ten days that we were kept in their Port. ... He was pleas'd to order all his officers to shew every mark of Attention to Mrs Hamilton ... and me during our stay at Malta ...

In spite of the Grand Master's attention to Catherine Hamilton, the rest of her husband's description of their visit suggests that he alone was shown around 'every fortification', and brought up to date on the military, and the Islands' produce.

Nelson and Emma meanwhile were enjoying something of a honeymoon. Not only was Nelson to describe the trip as 'days of ease and nights of pleasure', but it is clear that their daughter, and her twin who seems to have died, were conceived either in Malta waters on Nelson's flag ship or on the island. Horatia was born at the end of January 1801.

There were moments of danger: the *Foudroyant* sailed too close to the Grand Harbour when after a week it moved from St Paul's Bay to Valletta, and came under fire from the French batteries; Nelson was furious that Emma had been taken into danger, though they were not hit, his anger exacerbated by Emma's refusal to retire from the quarterdeck during the brief exchange. From there the *Foudroyant* sailed to join the southern blockade at Marsa Sirocca (Marsaxlokk) Bay, and it is probably from there that the party went to Gudja, Birkirkara and San Anton.

According to Carmel Testa, the *Foudroyant* 'brought to Malta 8,000 scudi sent by Italansky as Russia's financial contribution to Malta'. This adds to, or clarifies, a confusion caused by the story that Emma Hamilton donated a large amount of money to Malta's cause. Her more recent *ODNB* entry does not mention it. The earlier version reads:

> Her statement that she had brought corn to the value of £5,000 for the relief of the Maltese is ... false; she had no such sum of money at her disposal. She may have been able to influence the dispatch of provisions for the starving Maltese, and it was presumably on some such grounds that Nelson applied to the emperor of Russia, as grand master of the knights of Malta, to grant her the cross of the order. The emperor sent her the cross, naming her at the same time 'Dame Petite Croix de l'Ordre de St Jean de Jérusalem', 21 Dec. 1799.

Giovanni Bonello writes:

> Lady Hamilton's contribution to the Maltese cause during the siege became a subject of debate. When Nelson died and financial difficulties overcame her, she petitioned the British authorities for relief, alleging valuable political services she had rendered to the nation. Prominent among others she listed a donation of £5,000 out of her own personal purse for the purchase of corn for the starving Maltese. This is branded as an outright falsehood by British historians. But Palumbo, never kind on the fatal woman he considered a blight on the affairs of Naples, acknowledges a donation of 500 ounces (of silver) made by her for the relief of the Maltese.

Another of Emma's biographers, Julie Peakman, puts a different slant on the matter:

At Nelson's request, Emma was awarded the Maltese Cross by Tsar Paul of Russia for her services in assisting the starving Maltese, the only time it had ever been awarded to an English woman. Emma wrote to Greville 'I have rendered some service to the poor Maltese. I got them ten thousand pounds and sent them corn when they were in distress.'

Emma does not claim to Greville that it was her money; she may have been responsible, in a roundabout way, for the Russian money – she was very charming and influential – or it could have been money she persuaded Ferdinand and Maria Carolina to donate.

An Italian Wikipedia entry notes that on 21 December 1799 Emma 'received the prestigious honour of Queen of Devotion of the Order of Malta, with a letter signed in person by Tsar Paul I, a decoration rarely given to a woman, especially if not of noble birth'.

Whatever the truth of the story, the portrait that Nelson had painted of Emma in Dresden shows her wearing the Maltese cross and ribbon pinned to her breast. He carried the portrait with him until his death at the Battle of Trafalgar in 1805, calling her 'Santa Emma'.

10.   Emma Hamilton, courtesy of National Maritime Museum,
Greenwich, London

By the summer of 1800, Nelson had been ordered home, William Hamilton's time in Naples had come to an end, and Queen Maria Carolina wanted to go to Austria for a family visit. The party travelled overland together.

In Malta, by the early summer, the situation of the French was desperate. By the beginning of September, members of Vaubois' garrison were dying of starvation and disease at the rate of 100 a day. On 4 September, after holding a council of his officers the day before, Vaubois surrendered to the British under Major-General Henry Pigot. The Maltese were excluded from the negotiations, as was the overlord in Naples represented in Malta by Captain Alexander Ball who had taken over the leadership of the Maltese insurgents. Queen Maria Carolina wrote from Austria to Emma Hamilton in London on 17 October 1800,

… You see Malta is taken, and the French driven out. That is well, but the King and all of us are much mortified that in the capitulation there was no representative of ours there, although we had troops, ammunition, artillery, and positive rights in the Island. The only flag flying was the English – our being so completely duped is the subject of laughter here, and the injury is so much the more painful coming from a friend, otherwise it would be nothing. We are so much the friends of England that we are pleased that such a friendly power should hold a post overlooking Sicily, but the neglect of the forms, and the slights shown to us after so much care, confidence, cordiality, assistance, and the enormous expenses we have been put to, are very painful to think of, that is the truth. Oh! How often have I thought if my friends had been there, this would not have happened.

Aftermath

On 18 May 1802, under article 10 of the Treaty of Amiens between the Coalition and the French, Malta was to be returned to the Order, in spite of representation having been made by a Maltese delegation against it. It was also to be an independent state under the guarantee of the Coalition countries. The treaty was superseded by a return to war against the French. The British continued to administer Malta under Sir Alexander Ball who had been joined by his wife, **Mary Ball** (née Smith Wilson, d.1832). He was Civil Commissioner, de facto Governor, and the couple entertained as such; Mary Ball held receptions at San Anton every Wednesday

There is a brief glimpse of Lady Ball's style in the diary entry of 1 September 1809 of Lord Byron – whose visit will be further discussed in the next chapter. He dined at 'St Antonio the Governor's country seat' and continued, 'Dined at four p.m. with him and my lady Ball (rather stiff). Dinner all one course, with lectures on temperance and commendation of our abstinence.' Perhaps Mary Ball's stiffness had something to do with her husband's health, for he died at San Anton on 25 October, aged only 53. He was buried in Fort S Elmo, and a statue was erected in the Lower Barraca Gardens.

In *The General: The Travel Memoirs of General Sir George Whitmore* edited by Joan Johnson (1987), George Whitmore, responsible for Ball's statue, noted that Mary Ball 'received a pension of £300 per annum for [Ball's] services. ...'. A hero to begin with, Ball was seen as high-handed in his 'rule'.

He was followed by unmarried Sir Hildebrand Oakes. He was already in Malta, having been appointed to command the troops there in 1808; indeed he had served as brigadier-general there between 1802 and 1804. In May 1810, he was made Civil and Military Commissioner of the Islands. On 28 March 1813, a Maltese Brig, the *San Nicola*, sailing under the British flag, arrived at Marsamxett Harbour from Alexandria. There were signs of plague on board and the crew and passengers were confined to the Lazaretto on Manoel Island. But those guarding the sealed ship, as Giovanni Bonello tells the story in 'Mementoes of the 1813 Plague' (2003), boarded it and stole part of the cargo, including linen. The goods were sold on to the cobbler Salvatore Borg of 227 St Paul Street, said to be a receiver of stolen goods. Borg's daughter was the first to show signs of the plague, on 14 April, and by the 16th she and her mother were dead; Borg followed, and later his father and son.

On 6 May, midwife **Maria Agius**, who had attended the wife of Salvatore Borg, was found dead in her house at Strada St Ursola. **Grazia Pisani**, a young girl who had slept in the house of the midwife, also fell ill. On 16 May, the son and daughter of the baker Stellini died at 92 Strada San Christoforo. But these early deaths were not declared pestilential, allowing the plague to spread.

Thieves tended to steal the clothes of plague victims, so that by one route or another, such as refugees from Valletta fleeing to the countryside, the plague spread to the villages, to Mdina, Birkirkara, Qormi and Żebbuġ. S. Sciberras, in his online 'Maltese History' suggests other means:

A family of five children took refuge at the plague hospital where the mother gave birth to a baby. Both mother and baby died of plague some days later. A priest from Zurrieq, who had assisted the mother on her death, became infected. Unaware of the symptoms, he returned to his village where he died of plague on 28th June. A few days before he went to a barber who also died of plague a few days after the priest. Then hundreds more at Zurrieq fell victims of the plague.

S. Sciberras lists other means of infection: 'A foreigner attempted to rape a woman at the plague hospital; a young woman from Valletta took care of two infected orphans until all three died of the plague; a man, who was living with a woman, married her when she was already infected and both died of plague a few days later.'

Hildebrand Oakes was in charge of introducing stringent measures for halting the spread of infection, including the death penalty; and when he retired, ill and exhausted, he was replaced by Sir Thomas Maitland who arrived as Malta's first official British governor on 13 October 1813 and took up the reins of fighting the epidemic, such as closing Qormi from the rest of the island. But in January 1814, the plague arrived in Gozo, starting with the death of a man and his daughter who had been visited by a relative from Qormi, and killing some 200 people.

It was by no means only the poor who died: as Giovanni Bonello writes: 'Baron Testaferrata (actually Testaferrata Desain Cassar) died in the arms of his beautiful wife, "although adorned with the flower of youth, the prestige of birth, the fresh crowns of marriage"'.

By September 1814, following the death of 4,500 of its inhabitants, Maitland declared that Malta had been free of plague for six months. That same year, under the Treaty of Paris, as ratified by the Congress of Vienna, Malta passed under British jurisdiction. By the time Maitland died in Malta in 1824, it had been a British colony for 10 years.

The bitterness felt at Britain's behaviour in 1800 was to linger to such an extent that Carmel Testa writes of the aftermath,

Such arrogance was a presage of things to come for Malta and its inhabitants who were soon to bear a stifling colonial rule where the needs of the English garrison were of paramount importance; this, in turn, forged the local population into a national unity fighting a peaceful but continuous struggle sometimes with a momentary success, often with failure, to safeguard the few rights they had acquired in the past.

In the chapters that follow, the influence of the British, the influx of its citizens and, in particular, material about their presence, even that of its women, is to predominate over that of the Maltese much more than that of Malta's previous overlords ever did.

9 – The Arrival of British Women 1803–1838

'The Maltese are intelligent, hardworking, clever and can surely succeed in all fields of work,' wrote Frenchman Frédéric M Lacroix in *Malte et le Goze* in 1840, adding 'But the English Government looks at the occupation of Malta solely and entirely as an important fortress and is indifferent towards the interests of its inhabitants'. The French and English were not then entirely friendly towards each other, as Carmel Cassar notes in 'Everyday Life in Malta in the Nineteenth and Twentieth Century', the most useful chapter for me in Victor Mallia-Milanes's *The British Colonial Experience 1800–1964: The Impact on Maltese Society* (1988). But there appears to have been some truth in the observation, and there were times when between 25,000 and 30,000 British soldiers were stationed in what, in 1813, had become a British Crown Colony.

What is more, Carmel Cassar himself then suggests, 'The Maltese maintained a cool relationship with the British, mixing very little, at least until the 1930s'. For this reason, and because there is so much more material about and by British women in Malta in the nineteenth century, it is upon them that this chapter concentrates.

Some of the women were passing through – Malta was a common stop between Britain and the Near East and Egypt; often they and their descriptions of places are used in the relevant itinerary rather than in this history section. Others, from 1803, spent time in the islands, attached to the army or government service – where British men replaced Maltese – or in trade, including hotels; those last appear in Chapter 10.

Elena Dodsworth

British women had lived in Malta earlier: the Quaker women proselytisers imprisoned by the Inquisition; more than one generation of Mrs Watts, wives of the British consuls. There is more evidence of the female family of a later British consul, John Dodsworth.

In 'English Privateers at Malta and a British Consul's Misfortunes in the XVIII Century' (1964), Joseph Galea describes how Dodsworth, born in Leghorn (Livorno) to a father in commerce, arrived in Malta as a clerk and sub-pilot of a merchant ship 'flying the colours of England'. He was 'introduced' into the house of the British consul Alexander Young and, within a few weeks, had landed a job at the consulate. Young had an only daughter, Elena, and in due course she and Dodsworth were married. On Young's death in 1743, Dodsworth was appointed consul. Such an appointment was quite specific: it was by the Grand Master, not the British government, and it was to constitute part of the tribunal of *Consolato del Mare* responsible for deciding commercial disputes under the code that governed merchant shipping; and it was an appointment so badly paid that the consul had to involve himself in private enterprise.

Grand Master Pinto's biographer, Carmel Testa, nearly led me astray by suggesting that **Mrs Dodsworth** (née Young) was Maltese. But Roderic Cavaliero, in 'John Dodsworth, a Consul in Malta' (1957), explains the system, which also accounts for the earlier Watts consuls of three generations. Young was the son-in-law of an earlier British consul and such families, settled in Malta, either were, or had to become in order to qualify as consul, Roman Catholic; thus Elena Young would be 'accounted a Maltese as she was a subject of the Grand Master'.

Those three sources detail Dodsworth's chequered career in Malta – one which seems to have been difficult for his wife to cope with, for he was constantly trying to buck the system. One reason was that he felt that French shipping, including privateers, had preferential treatment. The French had a majority among the Knights (three out of the eight *Auberges* were French), and Britain and France were at war between 1754 and 1763. He also had to make money, not always honestly. He rented warehouses on the Marina which he packed with all types of goods, even stolen goods, from English privateers. He had done so well that the family – his wife, mother-in-law (**Mrs Young**), two daughters and three sons – lived in the Villa Bichi (later Villa Bighi) on the promontory that juts into the Grand Harbour between Rinella Bay and Kalkara Creek (see Chapter 18 itinerary). But by 1762, heavily in debt, he had tried the Grand Master's patience too far, and it is now easiest to draw primarily on Christine Muscat's short and simple version of the story in her history of the Maddalena nunnery.

Towards the end of that year, an English privateer, sailing under a Prussian flag, had captured an Austrian ship in Maltese waters. Dodsworth stowed booty from it in his stores. He was ordered to draw up an inventory of his goods and to give up the spoils. But he demurred, claiming diplomatic immunity, putting up the British coat of arms, and barricading the villa. The Grand Master secured permission from Britain to exercise the Maltese courts' jurisdiction. On 7 February 1763, magisterial soldiers surrounded the villa. Dodsworth and his two younger sons were taken to Fort S Elmo and the eldest son sought sanctuary in the Carmelite monastery, moving later to S Roque's. As for Mrs Dodsworth, her mother and two daughters, Pinto had them sent to the Maddalena nunnery, and their woman servant to the *Conservatorio* in Floriana. The family's goods were expropriated and sold at public auction in order to pay off Dodsworth's debts.

John Dodsworth, at least, seems to have left for Spain in 1766 but, commenting on the court case Dodsworth had to face for debt before departing, Roderic Cavaliero writes, 'It was … not until July that Dodsworth at last prepared his case, worn down by fatigue, penury, the desertion of his wife and a little applied starvation.' And later he adds,

Even when he was arrested, the guards were out in double strength to prevent any disorders, or any insult to the arms of His Brittanic Majesty;

the event was orderly enough and the only voice raised was that of Dodsworth's wife, cursing the symbol of all that had brought so much trouble to her and her family.

The story gets increasingly difficult to disentangle as a result of Christine Muscat's further research, part of which appears in 'The Magdalene Church, Valletta' (2014). While the Royal Malta Archives have, as Joseph Galea makes clear, Alexander Young dying in 1743, other archival records have him, in 1767, undersigning a repayment made by his daughter Elena Dodsworth of a loan made to John Dodsworth (*soscritto da mio padre*). The loan was made by **Sister Innocenza Felice Romana**, a wealthy Magdalene nun, probably to pay for the stay in the Maddalena of Mrs Young, Elena Dodsworth and the two Dodsworth daughters. And the repayment was one which the incarcerated Dodsworth himself had failed to make. What happened thereafter remains unclear.

The British families who followed the Dodsworths after 1800 may not have caused as much trouble to the authorities but, as in so many colonial societies, life in Malta was more lively than in the home country. It is worth remembering that Queen Victoria, whose family life and views ushered in an era of so-called Victorian morality, did not come to the throne until 1837.

Lady Hester Stanhope

The first British woman to make, and leave, her mark in the British era, on paper at least, was the well-known traveller and eccentric, 34-year-old Hester Stanhope, whose ship from Gibraltar docked in Malta on 21 April 1810. Thomas MacGill, who arrived with his wife in 1806 and was involved thereafter in all sorts of enterprises, wrote of that time in *A Handbook or Guide for Strangers Visiting Malta* (1839): 'Some Thirty years ago, there were neither a decent inn, or lodging house, in the city of Valletta; at that period, strangers arriving on the island, were forced to depend on the hospitality of the English residents for a dinner.' Hester Stanhope and her entourage were, therefore, lucky.

Lady Hester Stanhope (1776–1839) was the daughter of the third Earl Stanhope and Lady Hester Pitt, daughter of the first Earl of Chatham, and the favourite niece of Prime Minister William Pitt the Younger. She had stayed with him when he was out of office, and was his hostess when he was once again Prime Minister in 1804, until his death in 1806; in his will he left her £1,200 a year. The numerous sources for her colourful life, including her time in Malta, are in the bibliography; as so often, facts are not always consistent, and have to be negotiated. What is more, her entourage is such that there is a danger there, too, of confusion.

Her entourage, her household, apart from her physician Dr Charles Meryon, consisted of women also associated with Pitt. Her companion and secretary, **Elizabeth Williams** (1785–1828) was his ward following the death of her mother when she was 12, and then his 'servant' with whom he had an 'affinity'. Her brother looked after his horses, as his father had done, and Pitt arranged for Elizabeth and her sister, Louisa, to have three years of education. After Pitt's death, when Hester set up her own household, Elizabeth, aged 20, joined her there. The story of the Williams family is told in HD Richards' *Maid of Honour* (2004).

Hester's housekeeper was **Ann Fry** (b.1780). She was four years younger than Hester, and they had been playmates. We know this from a letter Hester wrote to a friend in 1800: 'I want to ask for your advice about an unfortunate woman who was my playfellow.' Ann was 'unfortunate' to have had a daughter out of wedlock that year, and thereafter called herself Mrs Fry. The father of her child may have been Hester's brother who was to commit suicide in 1825; Ann benefited under his will.

Elizabeth Williams' sister, Louisa, had, in the meantime, entered the household of Hester's sister. But in 1807 she had been escorted to Malta by a Williams relative to marry John David, perhaps also related. He had arrived there with the British blockading force in 1799 and returned in about 1801. She became **Louisa Jane David** (1787–1854) the year of her arrival, when her husband was a storekeeper and later Deputy Assistant Commissary General, Purveyor of Civil Hospitals, Gozo.

Hester had been invited by the Governor, Hildebrand Oakes, to stay at the palace, but she wanted to be 'most quiet and at her ease' so, instead, Hester, Elizabeth, Ann and Dr Meryon descended on the household of **Sarah Fernandes** (Fernandez) (née Langford) and her husband of 10 or so years Alexander (Alessandro) of the Commissariat Service since 1798. By 1805 he was Deputy General in Charge of Administration in Valletta. Several sources suggest that Sarah Fernandes was Elizabeth Williams' sister, but that is not so: she was a close friend of Louisa David. John David was by then in charge of the King's bakery, and Fernandes was his superior. The Fernandes house was formerly the French *Auberge*, on the corner of Old Bakery Street and South Street (see Chapter 17 itinerary).

Hester, with her shoulder-length hair – 'cropt' – and independent lifestyle and provocative views, was not an easy person. According to the somewhat jaundiced account of Dr Meryon, after a week in Malta she had contrived 'to affront almost all the women in the place ... She has the most thorough contempt for her sex, at least that part of it who converse on nothing but visits, capes and bonnets and such frivolous subjects.' An exception was Sarah Fernandes who was soon to decamp with her son to manage the farm on land her husband rented on the nearby island of Lampadusa. On 4 June, King George III's birthday, Meryon wrote:

Mrs Fernandez wore a dress given her by Lady Hester that cost £30. I told her she looked like a corpse in a coffin, for it was covered with gold spangles like coffin nails, but certainly was surprisingly handsome, as the ladies' envious looks too plainly testified.

Hester had been prevented from landing in Sicily, as she had planned, because of Napoleon's influence there. Now Emperor of France, he had recently married Marie Louise of Austria and had, therefore, become related to Queen Maria Carolina of Sicily. Hester fretted to leave Malta but was restored to humour by the arrival of Michael Bruce whom she had met in Gibraltar and who was soon not only an admirer but also her lover. (Another source has Bruce travelling from Gibraltar with Hester). She began to move more in Society. One of Bruce's Cambridge friends, John Cam Hobhouse, wrote,

I met Mr Bruce and Lady Hester Stanhope, a masculine woman, who says she would as soon live with packhorses as with women. I met her again the next day at dinner. She seemed to me a violent, peremptory person ... we went together to the opera.

Michael Bruce, 12 years younger than Hester, wrote to his father in May:

Lady H Stanhope who is now my compagnon de voyage is a woman of very extraordinary talent. She inherits all the great and splendid qualities of her illustrious grandfather. For the last five years she has been in a most unsettled state of health and is still very unwell. I hope however that change of scene and change of climate will restore health to her body and tranquillity to her mind.

As the heat of summer began to build up, Hester was increasingly inclined to accept the Governor's invitation to move to his country residence of San Anton at Attard (see Chapter 20 itinerary). On 1 June, therefore, she and her party moved in. She and her lover could now enjoy each other's company in beautiful surroundings away from prying eyes. Dr Meryon could still write of Bruce on 15 June:

... although his age, his person, his known gallantry would be enough to make the tongue of scandal wag against any other woman who, unmarried and in her prime, should trust herself with a single man in a large house, and in the country, yet Lady Hester contrives to do anything that others could not, without incurring the same blame that they would. Besides, she is mended in her health considerably of late, and really begins to look rather winning.

But he also wrote, as a result of the developing relationship between Hester and Bruce, 'I don't like Mr Bruce, he seems desirous of excluding me from the great nobilities with which he is intimate, and of inducing Hester not to bring me forward so much as her accustomed goodness prompted her to do.'

By the end of July, Hester was anxious to leave Malta and move eastwards – her health, and that of Bruce, was suffering – and her ambition knew no bounds, if Meryon is to be believed:

She intends at Constantinople, to make friends with the French ambassador, and through his means to obtain a passport to travel [to] France. Protected by this, she will set off from Turkey, proceed through Hungary, Germany, and arrive at Paris. When there she intends to get into Buonaparte's good graces, study his character, and then set sail for England to plot schemes for the subversion of his plans. Her wonderful mind is equal to the accomplishment of all this, if she can but overcome the first difficulty of entering a hostile country. What she, Lady Hester, will do, time will show, but if Heaven give her health I do not despair the rest.

A reduced party left Malta on 2 August, Elizabeth Williams apparently remaining behind with her sister to pursue a love affair. Hester was either sympathetic or put out, depending on your source. If the former, Hester wished her every happiness and gave her a generous £100 marriage portion; Meryon says that Elizabeth was 'dismissed' with a £100 marriage portion. In Hester's will of 1809, before leaving England, she had left Elizabeth £500 – a very large sum.

Whatever the truth, Elizabeth was to rejoin Hester in Lebanon, where she had settled – Elizabeth's prospective marriage having, apparently, come to nothing – in 1816 and, indeed, to die there, of yellow fever in 1827. Michael Bruce returned to England in 1813, ostensibly because of his father's ill health, and did not return. Dr Meryon left in 1831, and Ann Fry possibly left then, too. Hester indulged in many adventures before dying in poverty in Lebanon in 1839.

But, before all that, the party leaving Malta stopped, among other places, in Athens, and there they met Lord Byron who is to take the Malta story forward. The young man, who was still to become famous, though already a character and budding poet, agreed with his travelling companion, Hobhouse, about Lady Hester Stanhope. He wrote to Hobhouse on 4 October 1810 expatiating on his friend's run-in with Hester in Malta,

I saw the Lady Hester Stanhope at Athens, and do not admire that dangerous thing – a female wit! She told me (take her own words) that she had given you a good set-down at Malta in some disputation about the Navy; from this, of course, I readily inferred the contrary, or in the words of an acquaintance of ours, 'that you had the best of it.'

She evinced a similar disposition to argufy with me, which I avoided either by laughing or yielding. I despise the sex too much to squabble with them, and I rather wonder you should allow a woman to draw you into a contest, in which, however, I am sure you had the advantage; she abuses you so bitterly.

I have seen too little of the lady to form any decisive opinion, but I have discovered nothing different from other she-things, except a great disregard of received notions in her conversation as well as conduct. I don't know whether this will recommend her to our sex, but I am sure it won't to her own.

Constance Spencer-Smith, Susan Fraser and Lord Byron

It is interesting to read there Byron's general opinion of women, because that is not how he had acted in Malta the previous year. He and Hobhouse arrived there on 31 August 1809, as recounted in Ian Strathcarron's *Joy Unconfined: Lord Byron's Grand Tour, re-toured* (2010). Byron was not impressed: he was not given a proper welcome, partly because they came at a politically inopportune moment – war against Napoleon was still in full swing – and the steep streets and steps of Valletta did not help his congenital lameness. They planned to leave as soon as possible.

But then, at the theatre, Byron was introduced to 25-year-old Mrs Spencer-Smith – a beautiful and talented woman with a fascinating past. **Constance Spencer-Smith** (née Herbert, 1785–1829) was one of the daughters of Baron Herbert, Austrian ambassador at Constantinople where she met John Spencer-Smith, British chargé d'affaires there. He was the brother of the better-known Sir Sydney Smith, a naval hero of the American and French revolutionary wars. This family, too, was connected to the Pitts. Constance and John were married in 1798, when he was secretary of legation, and his diplomatic career further developed before he entered Parliament.

Spencer-Smith seems to have been in England when, in 1805, Constance was taking the waters for her health near Vicenza. The war intruding on Northern Italy, she sought refuge, together with her two children, with her sister, the Countess Attems, at Venice. In 1806, perhaps because of her connections by marriage, she was arrested and imprisoned by Napoleon's governor of the city. But her beauty had made its mark on the 20-year-old Sicilian nobleman, the Marquis de Salvo, who, in his *Travels in the Year 1806 from Italy to England* (1807), tells how he rescued her, providing her with boys' clothes and a ladder as she was being taken from Venice as a state prisoner to Valenciennes. Eventually, they reached Gratz and the roof of another sister, the Countess Strassoldo.

This was an obvious story to tantalise the Romantic poet grumbling in Malta. Constance was also accomplished, apparently speaking seven languages and familiar with their literature, and an excellent musician. Then there was her beauty. The Duchess of Abrantes, who also tells her adventures in *Memoirs*, describes:

A young woman, whose delicately-formed and elegant figure, her skin pale and diaphanous, blonde-haired, her movements flowing, all of it an impression impossible to describe, except to say that she was of all creatures, the most graceful, all of which gave her the aspect of an apparition appearing in a happy dream.

What Constance was doing in Malta is nowhere revealed, though there is a suggestion that her marriage was unhappy. Perhaps she had come after her adventures to take refuge with her friend **Susan Fraser**, wife of Captain Percy Fraser, resident commissioner of His Majesty's naval dockyard at

11.   Constance Spencer-Smith, courtesy of Woodsen Research
Center, Fondren Library, Rice University

Malta. Susan, whom Byron also wooed, was a poet herself and had that
year published *Camilla de Florian and Other Poems* (by an Officer's Wife),
a copy of which she gave to him. History does not relate whether or not he
read it, nor what he thought of it, and it has to be said that Susan does not
feature in *Women Romantic Poets 1785–1832: an Anthology* (ed. Jennifer
Breen, 1995). The rather long title poem is, as far as I can make out, about
Knights fighting the Turks, and our heroine later confined in a convent and
receiving her swain there. It starts, and continues

Bright o'er St Elmo's walls, Vallette's tow'rs,
The rising day a flood of glory pours;
From Florian's palace fair Camilla came
And sought, with pensive steps, the sacred fane;

...

'Is't no misfortune, then,' the mourner said,
'That hostile bands our happy isle invade?
'A Despot brings dishonour to our gate;

'And Malta's Knights, unarm'd, his mandates wait.
'Where are the race, that, in Valette's days,
'Won, from a wond'ring world the meed of praise?

What Byron, four or five years her junior, really felt about Constance is open to debate, but she beguiled him enough during that first period together to extract from him his yellow diamond ring. He wrote to his mother about her,

> Since my arrival here, I have had scarcely any other companion. I have found her very pretty, very accomplished, and extremely eccentric. Buonaparte is even now so incensed against her, that her life would be in some danger if she were taken prisoner a second time.

Hobhouse wrote in his diary, 'Lord Byron gallanting at Mrs Fraser's', according to Ian Strathcarron, Constance's 'safe house'. And on 9 September, 'Called on pretty Mrs Commissioner Fraser and Mrs Spencer Smith.' But a later entry reads, 'Went to Mrs Fraser's – unpleasant evening – *rixae feminae* [women's quarrels] – Mrs Spencer Smith being there.' On the 11th, Hobhouse went to the theatre, 'Lord Byron gallanting at Mrs Fraser's.' On the 18th: 'Dined at Mr Fraser's in the evening. Lord Byron tells me at eleven that he is going to fight Captain CC Cary, having through a friend accepted the challenge for next morning at six.'

Though there is an implication that the duel was over Constance, this is not deemed to have been the case. Byron later wrote, 'At Malta I fell in love with a married woman and challenged an aide de camp of General Oakes (a rude fellow who grinned at something, I never rightly knew what) but he explained and apologised, and the lady embarked for Cadiz and so I escaped murder and adultery.' It is assumed that the woman in question was Constance, but if you look through Susan Fraser's book of poems, there are several about Spain, and I have found no connection between Constance and Spain, though her husband did eventually settle in Normandy. Alan Massie, in *Byron's Travels* (1988), writes, instead, that Byron, writing three years later to Lady Melbourne, 'was quite ready to accompany [Constance] to Friuli, where she was supposed to rejoin her husband'. He adds that the plan was thwarted by the treaty after the battle of Wagram which ceded Friuli to the French.

Constance was certainly in Malta in 1810, because she wrote to Byron in September, 'In case your thoughts are still what they were on the 16th September, then set out for Malta at the very first opportunity.' Byron did, indeed, return to Malta, in 1811, but everything had changed: he had a young man with him 'for whom', as Peter Vassallo says in 'Romantic Writers in Malta: Literary and historical perspectives' (1991), 'he had developed a strong Romantic affection.' Neither his health nor his humour was improved by quarantine in the Lazaretto, because he had come from the East, and his ardour for Constance had cooled. His farewell to her was embarrassing and his poem of 26 May that year, 'Farewell to Malta', was handed to Captain Fraser because it praised his wife. It was supposed to be private but got into the public domain and did not go down well in Malta. These are some of the lines:

Adieu, ye females fraught with graces!
Adieu, red coats, and redder faces!
Adieu, the supercilious air
Of all that strut 'en militaire'!
...
And now I've got to Mrs Fraser
Perhaps you think I mean to praise her
And were I vain enough to think
My praise was worth a drop of ink,
A line-or two-were no hard matter
As here, indeed, I need not flatter.
But she must be content to shine
In better praises than in mine.
With lively air, and open heart,
And fashion's ease, without its art,
Her hours can gaily glide along,
Nor ask the aid of idle song.

However badly things ended with Constance, and we know nothing of her side of Byron's second visit, he immortalised her in his poetry. Stanzas 29 and 30 of *Childe Harold's Pilgrimage*, II (1812), specifically connect the Calypso of Homer's *The Odyssey* to the woman 'Florence', actually Constance. In 1812, he wrote to Lady Melbourne of Constance, 'She is now, I am told, writing her memoirs in Vienna, in which I shall cut a very indifferent figure.' Nothing seems to have come of her memoirs, and she died in Vienna in 1829, aged 44. And, in a journal entry of 1821, he noted, writing of German literature, 'I like, however, their women (I was once so *desperately* in love with a German woman, Constance).'

Government Circles

It is not difficult to imagine the gossip surrounding Hester Stanhope, Constance Spencer-Smith and Susan Fraser's time in Malta; indeed, information about the life of British women of a certain class during this period depends on gossip and its recording.

The Whitmore family arrived in Malta in 1811 and were there, on and off, until 1829. The governance of Malta was combined with that of Corfu and officials sometimes moved from one island to the other during their tour of duty. The Whitmores' time in Malta, and that of their contemporaries, is well caught in *The General: The Travel Memoirs of General Sir George Whitmore* (ed. Joan Johnson, 1987). George Whitmore was Colonel Commandant of the Royal Engineers detachment in Malta, responsible for pioneering public works and infrastructure. Whitmore himself was in charge of re-designing the Manoel Theatre and constructing half a dozen other buildings, as well as being much involved during the plague epidemic of 1813 described in the previous chapter. He was also an artist with an observant eye in pen and paint and some of his watercolours and sketches of Malta illustrate his memoirs.

12.   Cordelia Whitmore, from Johnson, *The General*

In 1798 George Whitmore had met and married Cordelia Ainslie in Gibraltar where her father was a Battalion surgeon, and **Cordelia Whitmore** (1780–1757) features in more than one contemporary account, including the marriages of her daughter and sons in Malta to the children of those in their circle. It was, not surprisingly, an incestuous British community, and the story of its women, though usually not dramatic, gives a picture of British life in the Malta which the British found themselves governing.

Cordelia's involvement started early on, hardly had they arrived in Malta after an eventful voyage from Gibraltar; her husband wrote:

Captain Hamilton kept his wife and family in some sort under our care at the Pieta in Malta – we occupied contiguous houses, and Mrs H was brought to bed of an infant whose health was so delicate that my wife was employed day and night about it and, as the family declared, was the instrument by which its life was spared.

While their life was often governed by such domestic ties, the British community was also one many of whose women differed markedly from their Maltese contemporaries of a similar class, and not only in religion and culture. Those married into the Services, and professions and trades attached to them, had often lived abroad in sometimes exotic places far from home. Cordelia, for example, accompanied her husband to the Caribbean in 1800, starting in Martinique and proceeding to Antigua and Dominique where tropical diseases were prevalent among the poor, and a mother had to be ever alert to protect and nurse her family. Cordelia was breast feeding her first son when they arrived there, and had another in Antigua.

Another distinguishing feature in Malta was the change at the top: Knights had been supposedly celibate and, at least, they were unmarried. They dominated an essentially male world. As previous chapters have shown, even upper-class Maltese women were excluded from the Order's celebrations and rituals. By contrast, wives married into the upper echelons of the British colonial establishment played a prominent role in all such public functions. Nicholas de Piro's *Costume in Malta* does, however, make it clear that Maltese women had plenty of opportunity to dress in fine clothes, lace and jewellery. British women had their homes and children, but their role in the Society of the Government and the Services was equally important. George Whitmore wrote of an event during the time of the Marquess of Hastings' governorship:

My family was one of the four whom his Lordship condescended to visit. We got up a fete for him at our house called the Palazzo Leoni on the night of the Festival of St Venera whose church stood at the termination of the long straight walk which ran through our gardens. These gardens laid out in a foreign fashion with walks at right angles, and fountains at their intersections (being in fact groves of orange trees) were peculiarly adapted for such purposes – on this occasion they were profusely lighted, jets and all – with coloured lamps. We had a military band, fireworks and a supper for which an extra temporary room had been constructed. The Royal Family professed themselves pleased and left us early.

Palazzo Leone in Santa Venera (see Chapter 20 itinerary) was the Whitmores' country residence; all such British families decamped to the country at the end of June for several months. In Valletta, the Whitmores had moved to Piazza Celsi (now Independence Square; see Chapter 17 itinerary) and, when the Duke of Buckingham was in town for three weeks in 1828, as Donald Sultana writes in 'The First Duke of Buckingham and Chandos in Malta and Gozo in 1828' (2005),

The performances in the theatre were supplemented by private concerts, sometimes with the participation of Italian opera singers from Naples and Sicily, like the good-looking prima donna whom the Duke heard singing at a dinner party organised by Mrs Whitmore, a gracious hostess, with musical talent and wide interests like her husband.

Mention of 'The Royal Family' at the party at Palazzo Leone was a dig at the Hastings who did tend to act like royalty. Francis Rawdon, 1st Marquess of Hastings (and 2nd Earl of Moira) arrived as Governor and Commander-in-Chief of the Mediterranean on the death of Sir Thomas Maitland in 1824 after a career of highs and lows, including financial difficulties caused by extravagance. He had come from being Governor General in India which he had left somewhat in disgrace. In 1804, he married **Flora Mure-Campbell** (1780–1840), daughter of the 5th Earl of Loudoun, and **Countess of Loudoun** in her own right. They had six children, five of whom accompanied them to Malta – hence 'The Royal Family'. As George Whitmore put it,

On his arrival he was greeted as all rising suns are – his rank, his manners, the courteous reserve, almost regal, dignity he and his family affected seemed to recall to the Maltese the sovereignty of the Order and contrasted in their opinion favourably with the brusque uncourtly habits of Sir Thomas; he was always in full regimentals, wearing the Garter even over the white pantaloons of summer. The formality of his dinner receptions was very striking to us who had been accustomed to general conversation and absence of restraint; we assembled in the drawing room, and formal bow was our greeting – presently those opposite the enfilade of apartments which face the Parade might see a suite of 7 or 8 doors thrown open and advancing slowly through them the Marchioness first, the daughters following two by two and the procession brought up by Miss Rainsford, the daughter of the General who held a temporary command in Gibraltar during the early portion of my residence in that fortress. Her Ladyship and daughters courtesied on entering, we were told off to our respective ladies with the most scrupulous attention to rank and accompanied them to the dining room where a table covered by the dessert greeted us after the Russian fashion, but now adopted by the Marquis because he had no other article of plate than what he borrowed from Hookham Frere; scarce a word was uttered during the meal and we separated early to expatiate on the dullness of the day.

Arabella Stuart (b.1803) was more easily impressed, according to *Arabella's Letters: Together with the Contents of her Small Diary 1823–1828* (1927). Her writings, filled as they are with details of entertainments, give an interesting overview of the life of British women of a certain *milieu* at this stage of British presence. If any judgement is to be made on the frivolity of the life she, and they, led, it is worth remembering to whom she wrote.

Arabella was a member of the branch of a Scottish family settled in Quebec where her widowed mother and some siblings remained, and it is to them that she recounted the sort of detail she knew would interest them. Her brother, James, had earlier arrived in Malta attached to the governorship of Sir Thomas Maitland. When James's wife, **Elizabeth Stuart** (née Seymour), planned to join her husband there, with their children, Arabella was invited to accompany them. They arrived at the beginning of March 1824, and were there for the arrival of the Hastings family. Arabella wrote home:

It is now a fortnight since the Marquis and Marchioness of Hastings, with their family arrived here. The family consists of four daughters and a son (Lord Rawdon, a fine young man of eighteen), and a Miss Rainsford, a friend of the Marchioness. Only one daughter, Lady Flora, is introduced. The Maltese have been enthusiastic in their attentions to them. ... The Marquis is a tall, erect, fine looking man upwards of seventy years of age, most accomplished, and elegant manners which we may naturally expect, as he has long been a personal and intimate friend of his present Majesty. The Marchioness is a fine looking person, about forty years of age, and possesses very pleasing and dignified manners. They will no doubt add much to the Society here, as a Lady Governess was much wanted.

The Marquis, has begun to give dinner parties and James dines with him to-morrow at half past three o'clock, the summer dinner hour at Malta. The Marchioness intends giving evening parties twice a week at the Palace of St. Antonio, about five miles from town, where the gardens for an evening Promenade are very beautiful.

On 1 September 1824 Arabella wrote to her mother:

Last evening we were at a splendid entertainment given to the Marchioness of Hastings by the Merchants. The decorations were under the immediate direction of M. Bong, the French Consul, who displayed great taste. The supper, which was sumptuous, was laid out in a large hall converted into a *Temple of Flora*, and illuminated in a most brilliant manner with Chinese coloured lanterns, suspended from the top by festoons of flowers. The roof was supported by transparent fluted columns, which had a great effect, and on each side of the Hall were allegorical devices, and the arms emblazoned of the families of Hastings and Loudoun. ... We had plenty of dancing, notwithstanding there were about five hundred persons, and everyone looked happy. ...

... The Marchioness of Hastings continues her Conversaziones, or Evenings at home every Thursday – this makes it pleasant and brings the society together. We generally go once a fortnight, make our courtesies to her Ladyship, and walk through the rooms and chat with our acquaintance. Tea and ice creams are handed round, and a variety of other refreshments arranged on tables in one of the rooms. To these the Maltese do great justice, and you would suppose to look at them that they had fasted for two or three days before!

It is clear from Arabella's account that the British and Maltese did mix, at least the women, at least at events at which the Governor's wife was the host. But it is not the only time that Arabella comments on the behaviour of Maltese women towards the refreshments on offer, and the further comments are more overtly critical. It is not clear who the Maltese women were, but her attitude and remarks do suggest a cultural gap. There is also a possible reason for the Maltese women homing in on the food tables: they were divided by language from the British women; and even if they did speak English, or the British women did speak Italian, they had little in common to talk about. To be fair to Arabella and Elizabeth, they were taking Italian lessons three times a week. The question of language – English versus Italian – was to haunt relations and, indeed, to become politically toxic until independence. As for religious differences, the colonial government trod a very careful path not to cross the Roman Catholic Church which played such an integral part in Maltese life.

It would appear from the foregoing accounts that the Marchioness of Hastings did nothing but entertain regally. But there is another view of her by Thomas MacGill in his *Handbook*. He did not move in her circle but had lived in Malta for 20 years when she arrived and knew his way around. He wrote about three of her more useful and probably more fulfilling contributions; for example:

> The stone of Malta, from its softness, and fine grain, works beautifully under the chisel of the sculptor. The Marchioness of Hastings, took great pains in bringing forward this branch of art; and from her fine taste, and the beautiful designs she furnished the leading workmen; their vases, figures and other fancy work, have risen to a pitch of elegance, they never before were capable of producing; they are now exported into all parts of Europe and America.

Describing a place in Floriana, he continues:

> Opposite to this is the house of industry, planned by the humane Marchioness of Hastings; – the original plan of her ladyship, was, that this house should be an asylum for poor children, where they could get a little education, and be brought up to useful domestic arts, fitting them to gain their living as servants, or, in the humble walks of life.

This took place in 1824 and apparently replaced the 1734 *Conservatorio*. More than 300 poor girls were maintained there, according to Walter Bonnici's article on the reforms of the charitable institutions of Malta (2000). They were taught to sew, weave, make cigars and shoes, and plait straw baskets, but were not allowed to go out.

The third view of Lady Hastings is best introduced by George Whitmore's comment on her husband's extravagance:

> The magnificence of his ideas did not, however, diminish in consequence of his poverty. He began by decorating the Palace and I was architect and upholsterer; he next set me to work on St Antonio – a new wing was added for strangers – additions were made and land purchased to add to the gardens, and a chapel intended for domestic use was built after my design.

Thomas MacGill sees the work at San Anton from a different angle:

> The palace of St Antonio, can boast no architectural beauty; it is extensive, and at present commodious. After the arrival of the Marquiss of Hastings, the palace of St Antonio was put into complete repair, under the direction and exquisite taste, of the noble Marchioness, who also enriched the gardens, with many fine shrubs and exotics.

The Duke of Buckingham reported that many of the plants had been brought from India. As for the chapel, which was added by the Marquess himself, it is worth remembering that there was, as yet, no formal Protestant place of worship in Malta; that was to await the arrival of Queen Adelaide in 1839 and is given space in Chapter 11. There was, however, another chapel, in the Governor's Palace in Valletta. The Duke describes being godfather to the daughter of his old friend Colonel Pitt and his wife in 'the government chapel'. Cordelia Whitmore was one of the godmothers.

Thomas MacGill may have noted the innovations of Lady Hastings from long experience of Malta, but I like the woman's view, even if the writer and traveller **Emma Roberts** (1791–1840) was only passing through in 1839. She wrote in *Notes of an Overland Journey through France and Egypt to Bombay* (1841):

> The softness of the stone renders it easily cut, and the Dowager Marchioness of Hastings (who has left imperishable marks of her desire to benefit those who came under her observation), in supplying the best designs, has filled the shops of Malta with a tasteful species of *bijouterie*, which is eagerly sought after by all the visitors.

Party-goer Arabella Stuart also introduces us to the Hastings daughters. First to the eldest, **Lady Flora Hastings** (1806–1839), the only one old enough to have come out into Society in England. She also introduces us to a novel dance. The Stuarts attended a ball in April 1825 and Arabella wrote, 'The Ball was opened by Lady Flora Hastings and Lieutenant Colonel Sir Dudley Hill, 95th, with a vulgar kitchen hop.' Flora was to be involved in a scandal in 1839 when she had become Lady of the Bedchamber to the Duchess of Kent to provide companionship for the future Queen Victoria.

But to Malta she left 'The Maltese Evening Song' which was performed as recently as April 2013 at the Villa Bologna (see Chapter 20 itinerary). The song was published in *Poems by the Lady Flora Hastings* (1841), which her sister Sophia, by then the Marchioness of Bute, edited after Flora's death from cancer in 1839. Written in four stanzas, it was adapted to the Maltese national air sung by peasants when returning at evening from the fields; the first stanza reads:

> When the day and all its labours,
> All its hopes and fears, are o'er –
> Dearest land!
> Then I think upon the waters
> Dashing on the ragged shore
> Ah! The rocks those waves encircle
> I may never gaze on more –
> Dearest land! Dearest land!
>   Fare-thee-well!

The other daughters appear a few days later:

> Yesterday His Majesty's birthday was kept. There was a Levee at the Palace at eleven o'clock and at twelve a salute was fired from the Forts. At five James, with eighty other persons, dined with the Marquis, and at … half past eight I went with Elizabeth to a Ball given by the Marchioness. I cannot tell you much more about it than that I spent a most delightful evening. I had the honour of dancing the first Quadrille with the four Ladies Hastings and Lord Rawdon, and had a Cousin of the Marchioness for a partner – he belongs to the 95th Regiment.

The only other daughter to have left her mark in Malta is **Lady Selina Hastings** (1810–1867). In 1838 she married Captain Charles Henry, who appears to have been a naval officer, and there are two reasons to suppose that she stayed in Malta, or returned. A portrait of her has a Maltese scene in the background. And there is a grave in the Addolorata Cemetery with the inscription: 'A loving tribute for 20 years of faithful service from the daughters of Lady Selina C Henry and Captain Charles J Henry, formerly residents of Malta.' The inscription was to **Elizabeth Bonomo** (*c.*1825–1888) who was, in 1851, working as a nursery maid in the Henrys' household in Kent.

The Hastings governorship was short-lived: in 1826 he had to return to England to face Parliament over his financial affairs in India. Back in Malta he was a broken man. A riding accident exacerbated underlying ill health. Taken to Naples on a Royal Navy ship to recover, he died on board in the harbour. His body was returned to Malta for burial in what is now Hastings Gardens (see Chapter 17 itinerary). His will stipulated that his right hand should be cut off to be put eventually in his wife's coffin.

It is clear that George Whitmore and the Marchioness did not get on, for he wrote of their interchange following her husband's death:

> The Maltese to whom the Marquis was endeared for his urbane [manner] and charities scattered garlands of everlasting flowers on the grave, a copy or two of verses were written on the occasion and an offer was made by his particular friends to subscribe for a monument. I communicated with Lady Hastings on this subject and furnished (as usual) a design but the Marchioness with a somewhat ungracious expression declined the offer, saying that *it was her business* to erect a memorial – which has never been done.

But Arabella Stuart retained her admiration; she wrote, on 18 November 1826, as the governor's family accompanied him to Naples:

> The Marchioness and the Ladies Hastings all go. They will be a sad loss to Malta – not only that they are amiable and agreeable, but the society here is one that requires a head, and the Marchioness, tho' kind and condescending, was a person that all looked up to, not only on account of her rank, but she has a great deal of dignity in her appearance and commands respect. They have been most gracious to me and in March last, when the family returned from England, the Lady Flora Hastings brought me as a gift a book entitled *Tales of the Crusaders*; all agree the author is Sir Walter Scott, a brother of our old friend – and I have been bid more than once to join their family circle, and honoured by their desiring me to sing my Scottish songs.

This entry from Arabella is particularly apposite, because Walter Scott and his daughter, Anne, were to arrive in Malta three years after her departure in 1827. Scott had come for his health, as well as to research what was to prove his last novel, so it is useful to know what sort of British elite he was to encounter.

The Marquess of Hastings was succeeded in 1827 by Major General Sir Frederick Cavendish Ponsonby who was to stay in Malta until 1836. In Donald Sultana's *Benjamin Disraeli: in Spain, Malta and Albania 1830–32* (1976), the Ponsonbys are introduced rather delightfully by both the author of the book and the novelist and future prime minister. The entry also adds some useful gossip about other *gente per bene* of the time:

> The Governor of Malta, Disraeli explained to his father, 'is reputed a very nonchalant personage, and exceedingly exclusive in his conduct to his subjects'. He was Sir Frederick Cavendish-Ponsonby, a general, famous for a cavalry charge at Waterloo, and brother of Lady Caroline Lamb. ... Sir Frederick, as was common in those days, had several children by Lady Emily Bathurst, a daughter of a former colonial Minister, Lord Bathurst. He and Lady Emily – for so she was commonly called as a titled lady

in her own right – lived in the former palace of the Grand Master of the Order of St John, a building much grander than that occupied by Sir George Don at Gibraltar.

... Disraeli reported ... that he had received 'great attention from everybody,' including the Governor, 'who is a most charming fellow, and has been most courteous to me.' His wife 'is very plain and not very popular, being grand, but I rather like her', presumably in response to his dinner with her, on which, however, he did not enlarge before adding ... that he had dined with Sir Frederick and Lady Emily again when Meredith had been presented to the Governor by Sir John Stoddart, the Chief Justice of Malta. At table he had sat next to the wife of Sir Frederick Hankey, 'whom they make much of, but who is rather an old fashioned affair'. On the other hand, Lady Emily's sister, called Mrs Seymour-Bathurst, a leading hostess, first in Malta and later in London, was 'an interesting woman'. Her husband, Colonel Bathurst, was the military secretary, and their house – another splendid palazzo of the Knights – lay a few doors from Beverley's Hotel.

The Duke of Buckingham considered the Ponsonbys to be 'better lodged than most sovereigns in Europe'. Donald Sultana is rather ambiguous about the status of **Lady Emily Bathurst** (1798–1877): she had, in fact married Sir Frederick Ponsonby in 1825, aged 27, and she was, indeed, known as Lady Emily, rather than Lady Ponsonby. The couple had three sons and three daughters, four of the children born in Malta.

Julia Seymour-Bathurst (née Hankey, *c.*1798–1877) had married Lady Emily's brother – Lieutenant Colonel, the Hon. Thomas Seymour-Bathurst – in 1829; his father, the 3rd Earl of Bathurst, had secured the position for him in Corfu, leading to one in Malta, following a time in Parliament. Julia was rated highly enough on the London scene to have had her portrait painted by Sir Thomas Lawrence the year before her marriage, and her son was to become the 6th Earl of Bathurst. To complete the marriage circle, she was the niece of Sir Frederick Hankey.

Frederick Hankey, Chief Secretary of Malta, had met his second wife **Catherine Hankey** (Catterina, née Varlamo, d.1835) when he was posted to Corfu. She was Greek and their son was born in Corfu. Catherine Hankey probably had a rough time in Malta because the family were close neighbours of the Stoddarts in Celsi Square – the Hankeys living in the *Auberge d'Aragon* facing the Stoddarts in the *Auberge d'Allemagne*, and the Chief Secretary and the Chief Justice were at daggers drawn. Catherine's English may have been limited and she did not last long in Malta, dying in 1835 after a long and severe illness; she was initially buried in the Greek Orthodox Cemetery but, when a hotel was built on the site, her remains were re-interred in the Msida Bastion Cemetery (see Chapter 19 itinerary).

Isabella Stoddart (née Moncreiff, 1774–1846), daughter of Sir Henry Moncreiff, 8th Baronet and Church of Scotland Minister, had married Dr John Stoddart, lawyer and journalist, in 1803, against her parents' wishes

– Donald Sultana says 'on grounds of class'. Stoddart then moved in politically advanced literary circles in London. The same year, accompanied by Stoddart's sister **Sarah Stoddart** (1774–1840), they arrived in Malta for Stoddart to take up his post as Admiralty advocate. Sarah was to correspond from there with her close friend, the writer Mary Lamb, but unfortunately only Mary's letters seem to have survived (available online). Sarah has, though, been described in an online chapter about her future husband's life and writings, as 'a well-read, elegant, and well-educated lady, one of the best letter writers of her time'. From Mary's letters one has hints of family tension; she writes of Sarah's brother in 1805:

I mean, is he very happy with Mrs Stoddart. This was a question I could not ask while you were there, and perhaps is not a fair one now; but I want to know how you all went on – and, in short, twenty little foolish questions that one ought, perhaps, rather to ask when we meet, than to write about. But do make me a little acquainted with the inside of the good Doctor's house, and what passes therein.

And in another, Mary writes,

All I can gather from your clear and, I have no doubt, faithful history of Maltese politics is that the good Doctor ... is a *moody* brother, and that your sister in law is pretty much like what all sisters in law have been since the first happy invention of the happy marriage state; ... and that you, my dear Sarah, have proved yourself just as unfit to flourish in a little, proud Garrison Town, as I did shrewdly suspect you were before you went there.

The family returned to England in 1808. Sarah, discovering she was pregnant, married the essayist William Hazlitt. Her brother kept a tight hold on her husband's finances in order to protect her property and, Stoddart, as leader writer then on *The Times*, criticised Hazlitt. The Hazlitts were divorced in 1822.

In 1826, Stoddart was appointed Chief Justice of Malta and Justice of the Vice-Admiralty Court, and knighted. This rise in their fortunes or, at least, status, may account for the Duke of Buckingham's opinion of Isabella Stoddart, as described by Donald Sultana: 'The person in the English establishment who, the Duke of Buckingham gathered[,] suffered from self-deluding fancies like those of the Italian singers was Lady Stoddart.'

Isabella had, during her earlier stay in Malta, impressed her husband's friend the poet Samuel Coleridge who was for a time private secretary to Governor Alexander Ball, but that was more than twenty years earlier. Now the Duke, who had known John Stoddart in his earlier manifestation in England, opined that 'his lady had apparently undergone a transformation, precisely in "manners and countenance", for [he] recorded about her that 'there are many laughable stories about Lady Stoddart, a great, fat, full-blown, scolding woman, who governs Sir John, and fancies she can do the like with the rest of the island.'

It occurs to me that Isabella Stoddart, only too conscious that her husband was a friend of such literary luminaries as Wordsworth and Coleridge, was constantly trying to prove herself a person in her own right. Between 1819 and 1850, she published several volumes, most, but not all, of Scottish stories for children under the pen-name Martha Blackford, and was probably not given any credit by her husband, nor anyone else, for her endeavours. I have only skimmed a couple, but they are perfectly competent, and she did not patronise the children for whom she wrote.

Isabella and John Stoddart's daughter, **Isabella Maxwell Stoddart,** was to marry Cordelia and George Whitmore's son Captain George Whitmore in 1827, best described in Arabella Stuart's most gossipy tone:

> Marriages are now quite the rage here. Last week an *old* Gentleman of the name of Nugent, aged fifty-six, led to the Altar the eldest daughter of Colonel Whitmore of the Engineers, aged twenty six. It is not thought a bad match for her as he has plenty of money and she looks about ten years older than she is, and was not likely to meet with another to land at her feet. Her husband is two years older than her father. Next week her eldest brother of thirty, a Lieutenant of the Engineers, is to be married to Miss Stoddard – daughter of Sir John Stoddard, the President of this Island. This match has been made up in a hurry, as the lady has not been in Malta more than four months. She is a very nice girl and I think they will make a happy couple, tho' she does *look down* on him, as she is about my height and he is not so tall. You will think me very particular in my descriptions and I am afraid scandalous, but I must try some means or other to fill this blank sheet. The second Miss Whitmore is only waiting the arrival of her intended to change her name to Stopford; he is a Captain in the Navy and has been about two years. He is an Honourable and a younger son of Lord Courtoun, who disapproves of the match as she has no money, and hoped that absence might change his mind; but her family say that he is determined to run all risques for his *dear Winny*.

George Whitmore, père, is rather more prosaic:

> The marriages of three of my children followed rapidly after one another – my elder daughter married M Nugent, Collector of Land Revenue to the Island – my second daughter married the Hon. Montagu Stopford and my eldest son to the daughter of Sir John Stoddart.

One should note the dig in Arabella's letter at John Stoddart as 'President of the island', and I get the feeling that her rather snide description of the marriages may have had something to do with the fact that she remained unmarried during her nearly four years in Malta, though she did have to live through an incident at a ball which she described as an officer's 'hateful embrace and his odious kisses' when it became public and, therefore, a scandal.

The snobbery that has been obviously expressed, and the emphasis on class and good form, is given full expression in an account of 4 June 1828 by the Duke of Buckingham:

> Lady Emily Ponsonby gave a dance at the palace. It was very cheerful, and very gay ... In the ball-room was an Englishman, a Mr Hayes, in Turkish dress, and aping Turkish manners. He brought a Greek slave, whom he has just married, and whom he brought to the ball. She was specially ugly, and had neither form nor features to recommend her. If he did choose to buy a wife in open market, he might as well have bought a pretty one. They are going immediately to England; and I am inclined to think that, if his face did not belie him, he will soon recall to this wretched woman that he bought her to be his slave.

Buckingham could be as cutting about women of his own class. This time it was Lady Codrington, wife of the Admiral, who was in his sights. Sir Edward Codrington arrived to take up his appointment as Commander-in-Chief of the Mediterranean in 1827. Very soon, urged on by the British Ambassador at Constantinople, he left with his fleet to tackle piracy in the Eastern Mediterranean. There he eventually engaged with the Turkish fleet, which he defeated at the bloody battle of Navarino – a controversial engagement which led to his recall in 1828. He had married in 1802 Jane Well of Jamaica and it is this **Jane Codrington** (d.1838) about whom Buckingham writes in the year the family was to return to England. He had been dining with her, Lady Emily and Mrs Pitt; the Admiral had been off on a short naval sortie and was imminently due back. 'Lady Codrington and family,' he writes, 'all retired to the verandah, fanning themselves out of the heat of expectation.' When the admiral appeared, he continues,

> The astonished Admiral, who had expected to have gone quietly to his wife and dish of tea, found himself produced in a room full of lights and hot people. Lady C hung on one arm in ecstasy, the daughter on the other with streaming eyes, as if he had come from another battle of Navarino instead of a peaceful cruise of not above fourteen days ... Whilst we performed the Ko Tow, [he] took the hint and became the hero at once, soothing the sympathies of his fat wife and long daughter.

The Duke topped off his attack on poor Jane Codrington with the observation that 'Lady Codrington is not popular here'.

The Codringtons were to be enmeshed in a scandal a generation later, involving their third son, Henry, who had been wounded at the battle of Navarino, as Buckingham also tells us. In 1849, aged 41, he married 21-year-old **Helen Jane Webb Smith** (1828–1875) in Florence. She was a lively lass, brought up in Italy and not well versed in what was expected of her by

English society. In 1857, Codrington was appointed admiral superintendent to Malta where he served until 1863. Helen and their children accompanied him, living at Admiralty House, later the National Museum of Fine Arts (see Chapter 17 itinerary). The year after their return they were involved in a much-publicised divorce. The main co-respondent was a colonel also stationed in Malta but, during the divorce, Helen was accused of having too close a relationship with the publisher and women's activist **Emily Faithful** (1835–1895) who had earlier stayed with them in London. Servants at Admiralty House, including the cook **Mrs Sarah Nichols** who had travelled out to Malta with them, were witnesses and gave lurid accounts of the comings and goings. Helen lost her reputation and her children.

The case is discussed in detail in 'Lesbian Perversity in Victorian Marriage: The 1864 Codrington Divorce Trial' (1997) by feminist Martha Vicinus. A footnote in that article led me to the novel *The Heavenly Twins* (1893) by Frances Bellenden Clarke who rebranded herself as **Sarah Grand** (1864–1943) for its publication, and that is how she became known in her subsequent career. Her writing revolved around the 'New Woman' ideal. One of her two heroines, Evadne, follows her husband, Colonel Colquhoun, an army doctor, to Malta in twists to the plot which it would be a pity to reveal.

It is clear that Sarah Grand drew on her own experience of both marriage and travel in her writing. Aged 16, she had married widowed 39-year-old army surgeon David Chambers McFall, and travelled the world, mostly the Far East, with him during his postings. In 1879, they moved to Malta where she began writing her first novel, *Ideala, a Study from Life* which includes an interlude in China. Malta occupies a fair part of the long and engrossing *The Heavenly Twins*. It is well worth reading, quite apart from its description of a social life in Malta that differs little from what has gone before in this chapter, including the moral double standards of the time. I read it as an e-book, often an advantage with a heavy Victorian novel. Sarah and her husband were no longer together by the time of publication.

Villa Frere

The only woman who does not appear to have attracted criticism was **Elizabeth Frere, Dowager Countess of Erroll** (née Blake, c.1770–1831), wife of John Hookham Frere whose 'plate' Lord Hastings had to borrow for his first grand reception. It is all the more surprising that no scandal trailed behind her to Malta because her first husband, the 16th Earl of Erroll, had committed suicide in 1798 over a matter of honour, and she and John Hookham Frere, diplomat and writer, had been together since at least 1804 (and perhaps 1799) when they married in 1816. In those days she was known as a 'startling Irish beauty' on whose father's country seat in Ireland Maria Edgeworth had modelled that in her best-known work, *Castle Rackrent* (1801).

In 1818, Elizabeth became too ill to remain in England. It is said that she caught a serious cold visiting the British Museum for the opening of the room to house the Greek marbles newly purchased from the Earl of Elgin, and there are also suggestions that her first husband's suicide permanently affected her health. When she failed to rally, Frere, leaving behind a London literary scene of which he was very much a part, hired a brig and took her to Malta in the hopes of recovery. In the summer months, and later permanently, they lived in a grand house with famous gardens in Pietà – Villa Frere (see Chapter 19 itinerary) – a magnet for all his literary friends in Britain and Malta, together with John's sister, **Susannah Frere** (*c.*1777–1839), and Elizabeth's niece, **Honoria Blake** (1800–1878) who served as her companion from 1821. She is better known by her married name, Lady Hamilton Chichester, for her later involvement in the resurrection of Malta's lace industry which features in Chapter 10.

Also part of the household was a Greek orphan – **Statira Livadostro** – who had survived a Turkish massacre in 1822, her surname being after the place from where she had been rescued. She lived, and was educated, as a child of the house; indeed, Elizabeth had adopted her, and left her an 'independence'; Frere gave her away when she married Captain Hope of the Fusiliers.

The Duke of Buckingham had known Frere in England where they were Privy Councillors together, so he called on the family twice and dined with them. He writes in pity rather than criticism of Elizabeth, for he had

Never felt more melancholy in all my life. She remembers too well all that has passed; and in the state of ruin in which she is – kept drunk by opium – she talks of nothing but of times gone by, and persons with whom we passed our early gay days. She was very wild – sometimes laughing, sometimes crying. In short, I was most rejoiced when I escaped.

Elizabeth died in Malta three years later, in January 1831. According to Paul Cassar's 'John Hookham Frere in Malta (1821–1846): A Link with our Social and Cultural Past' (1984) 6,000 'indigent' Maltese went to the Msida Bastion Cemetery after her private funeral 'as a mark of respect' (see Chapter 19 itinerary). He continues,

Several thousands of these needy men and women received alms on this occasion either in the form of bread or of money 'in accordance with the charitable disposition evinced' by her in her lifetime. In fact she was as much distinguished for her benevolence as her husband.

Susannah Frere also died in Malta and is buried in the same cemetery. Paul Cassar writes, 'On the day of her funeral two thousand loaves of bread were distributed to the indigent families that during her lifetime had been the recipients of her bounty.' To help ease the situation of the poor, a Ladies' Malta Charitable Society was set up by **Mrs Samuel Sheridan Wilson** (née Walden, b.*c.*1800) of the London Missionary Society in 1822; the names of both Susannah and John Frere appear in the list of subscribers. Susannah was also a member of The Ladies of the Committee of the Soup Charity which provided the poor with free meals. Honoria stayed on to look after John, and inherited Villa Frere on his death in 1846.

Anne Scott, Mary Davy and Sir Walter Scott

It is into the world created by the Freres, the Hastings, Lady Emily, Lady Stoddart, Arabella Stuart et al. that **Anne Scott** (1803–1833), her brother Captain Walter Scott, and their father, Sir Walter Scott, arrived in late November 1831 on the British man-of-war on which the distinguished man of letters had been granted free passage to seek tranquillity and recovered health; he had recently had a series of strokes.

The Scott party – which included two unnamed servants – started off in quarantine because there had recently been a cholera epidemic in England. But in due course they moved to Beverley's Hotel (see Chapter 17 itinerary) opposite which lived Dr John Davy; he was to be called upon to care for Scott during his three-week stay. It is to Davy's wife that we owe details of it because Scott's son-in-law, John Gibson Lockhart, in writing his *Life of Walter Scott* (1839) drew on her diary. She wrote, as an introduction, 'Before the end of November, a great sensation was produced in Malta, as well it might, by the arrival of Sir Walter Scott.'

Margaret Davy (née Fletcher, 1789–1869) is described by Lt Cdr Dairmid Gunn in a lecture he gave to the Edinburgh Sir Walter Scott Club (2013) as an 'erudite and gifted lady, the daughter of a Scottish Advocate [Archibald Fletcher] and an intellectual blue stocking mother [Eliza Dawson] [who] had been a neighbour of Scott's when [he] was living in North Castle Street, Edinburgh.' Margaret's mother corresponded on equal terms with several of Scott's literary friends, and Margaret was widely read; she would have been able to hold her own in the literary conversations with Scott that she records. Her husband had been in Malta since 1828, travelling back to Scotland to marry her in 1830, and bringing her out when he took up his new position as Assistant Inspector of Hospitals. She had probably just had her first child, **Grace Davy** (b.1831) when the Scotts arrived, was to have another daughter in Malta in 1832, and a son in 1834. The Davy family left in 1835.

Once the Scotts had arrived Margaret wrote:

> … instead of driving Sir Walter to the ordinary lazaretto, some good apartments were prepared at Fort Manoel for him and his family to occupy for the appointed time, I believe nine days. He there held a daily levee to receive the numerous visitors who waited on him.

She was among the first of those, accompanying Lady Emily's brother, Colonel Seymour-Bathurst who, in the absence of the Ponsonbys, was acting Governor, and Julia Seymour-Bathurst, and Margaret described

... how the sombre landing-place of Marsa Muscet (the quarantine harbour), under the heavy bastion that shelters it on the Valetta side, gave even then tokens of an illustrious arrival, in the unusual number of boats and bustle of parties setting forth to, or returning from Fort Manoel, on the great business of the day. But even in the case of one whom all 'delighted to honour', a quarantine visit is a notably uncomfortable thing; and when our little procession had marched up several broad flights of steps, and we found ourselves on a land-place having a wide door-way opposite to us, in which sat Sir Walter – his daughter, Major Scott, and Mrs Dawson standing behind and a stout bar placed across some feet in front of them, to keep us at the legal distance – I could not but repent having gone to take part in a ceremony so formal and wearisome to all concerned. ... we left Mr Frere with him at the bar on our departure. He came daily to see his friend, and passed more of his quarantine-time with him than anyone else.

Mrs Dawson may have been Margaret's relative by marriage, though she doesn't say so; she was **Euphemia Dawson** (née Erskine), eldest daughter of Scott's friend Lord Kinneder, and she had arrived in Malta at much the same time as the Scotts to join her husband, since 1829, Captain George Dawson of the 73rd Regiment; he was in charge of the Lazaretto.

Another old friend and visitor was Chief Justice John Stoddart who, as Donald Sultana quotes in *The Journey of Walter Scott to Malta* (1986), told Scott that his wife, about whom everyone was so rude, would, 'as an old Scotch woman', know, 'how to prepare for you the comforts to which you have been used,' if he was to take up residence with them.

Margaret continues her account:

Sir Walter did not accept the house provided for him by the Governor's order, nor any of the various private houses which to Miss Scott's great amusement, were urgently proffered for his use by their owners – but established himself, during his stay, at Beverley's Hotel, in Strada Ponente. Our house was immediately opposite to this one, divided by a very narrow street; and I well remember, when watching his arrival on the day he took Pratique [release from quarantine] ... nobody was at hand at the moment for me to show him to but an English maid, who, not having my Scotch interest in the matter, only said, when I tried to enlighten her as to the event of his arrival – 'Poor old gentleman, how ill he looks.'

Margaret gives a glimpse there of Anne Scott who was amused by the celebrity-hunters. Since her mother's death, she had, as Dairmid Gunn puts it, 'filled the gap in the domestic scene'. She was, thus, placed in Malta in the unenviable position of being a bit of a nanny, as her father accepted invitations he should have declined, and otherwise over-taxed himself. She wrote to her sister, Sophia, from their quarantine,

What I dread is his going out to dinner. His arrival has caused such a sensation here, and we have so many visitors; I thought we had seen, and 'heard' every lady in Malta through the quarantine barrier, and there is such a lot of people we must still see.

Once they were out, Susannah Frere wrote home of Scott's visit to them, 'He had the good nature to stay three hours, and leave a general persuasion that he was very much amused.' But there was more to it: Margaret Davy wrote, 'He seemed resolutely prudent as to keeping early hours; though he was unfortunately careless as to what he ate or drank, especially the latter – and, I fear, obstinate when his daughter attempted to regulate his diet.' But Anne was obviously a woman of some character, as Dairmid Gunn told his audience in his introduction to the family:

Her father was, at times, critical of her lack of accountancy skills and her irrepressible penchant for satire. The varied nature of Scott's many admirers and friends gave her plenty of opportunities to exercise this form of wit – so disliked by Scott.

13.   Anne Scott, from the internet

Anne, praised for her looks by Susannah Frere, particularly her 'good dark eyes' inherited from her French mother, was also an accomplished musician. And she was quite right to attempt to hold her father back, for Margaret wrote:

> On Monday the 6th he dined at the Chief-Justice, Sir John Stoddart, when I believe he partook too freely of porter and champagne for one in his invalid state. … about 11 o'clock [the following morning] Miss Scott came over to me, looking much frightened, saying that she feared he was about to have another paralytic attack. He had, she said, been rather confused in mind the day before, and the dinner-party had been too much for him. She had observed that on trying to answer a note from the Admiral that morning, he had not been able to form a letter on the paper, and she thought he was now sitting in a sort of stupor. She begged that Dr Davy would visit him as soon as possible, and that I would accompany him, so that he might not suppose it a medical visit, for to all such he had an utter objection. I sent for Dr D instantly, and the moment he returned we went together to the hotel. We found Sir Walter sitting near a fire, dressed … in a large silk dressing-gown, his face a good deal flushed, and his eyes heavy. He rose, however, as I went up to him, and, addressing me by my mother's name, 'Mrs Fletcher', asked kindly whether I was quite recovered from a little illness I had complained of the day before.

By the next morning, the patient was raring to resume his gadding about, proposing a drive in the country to visit San Anton; Margaret was, not surprisingly, anxious:

> It was not without fear and trembling I undertook this little drive – not on account of the greatness of my companion, for assuredly he was the most humane of lions, but I feared he might have some new seizure of illness, and that I should be very helpless to him in such a case. I proposed that Dr D should go instead; but, like most men when they are ill or unhappy, he preferred having *womankind* about him, – said he would like *Mrs* Davy better, so I went.

Margaret saw Scott for the last time on 13 December, the day of the family's departure, when she called to take leave of Anne. He died in September the following year, not without almost finishing the novel he had been researching in Malta, and which he had started to write, *The Siege of Malta*, about the events of 1565. His publisher did not believe it would enhance his reputation, and it was not published in full until 2008. Anne Scott, herself, died the year after her father, aged thirty. She had a weak constitution and, having already nursed her mother through her last illness, her father's death seems to have proved too much for her.

Sarah Austin

Of the distinguished British women associated with Malta, among the most
deserving of the adjective is **Sarah Austin** (née Taylor, 1793–1867). She was,
as her *ODNB* entry states, born into a family that was 'a prominent and
prosperous part of the Unitarian community in Norwich'. Her political father
was active in promoting civil liberties for dissenters and sympathising with
the French Revolution. Her education at home was overseen by her mother
Susanna (née Cook) who encouraged her to read widely and she became
conversant in Latin, French, Italian and German. In 1819, she married the
'brilliant but flawed' John Austin, lawyer, scholar and depressive. Although
they lived impecuniously – Sarah writing and translating European literature
to great acclaim to make ends meet – they moved in rarefied circles: Sarah
was admired by the utilitarian philosophers Jeremy Bentham and the young
John Stuart Mill, the latter regarding her as a substitute mother.

Having resigned the chair of jurisprudence and the law of nations at the
new University of London, and his membership of a subsequent commission,
John Austin was appointed, in 1836, to head a commission to recommend
changes in the constitutional arrangements and legal system of Malta (where
he had earlier served in the army). This initiative followed the change of
government in Britain from Conservative to Whig (Liberal) and the passing
of the Great Reform Act of 1832. At the same time, a liberal movement
agitating for political rights was formed in Malta and sent a new petition to
the British Government.

Sarah went with John to Malta. They were to remain there for 20 months,
and the ups and downs of his work, including disagreements with Chief
Justice John Stoddart and Chief Secretary Frederick Hankey, are detailed
in *Troubled Lives: John and Sarah Austin* (*c*.1985) by Lotte and Joseph
Hamburger. 'The enmity between the Commissioners and Stoddart', they
write, 'arose partly from personal differences but above all from disagreements
about legal matters.' Stoddart was to pull every string to scupper the
Commission's work and, to some extent, succeeded. But there was more to
it than Stoddart: as they also say, 'Opposition to the commissioners among
the English community was inevitable', for the commissioners were accused
of 'encouraging Maltese radicalism'.

The Austins' time in Malta started well: their reception was enthusiastic.
Sarah wrote in a letter from the Lazaretto to her sister contained in *Three
Generations of Englishwomen* (ed. Janet Ross, 1893):

> Imagine these walls and bastions, this Barracca, and every balcony
> overlooking the harbour crowded with people, whose cheers as we entered
> the harbour rang across the waves and re-echoed from side to side, with
> an effect that to me, who expected nothing, was quite over-powering. Till
> this moment I had hardly been conscious of the awful task committed to
> my husband; I felt those cheers, eager and vehement as they were, as the
> voice of suffering calling for help and Justice.

A friend told her later,

> Your reception ... was just what it ought to be everywhere, for I have no doubt that all the Vivats were intended for you, and not for the Philosophers. Doubtless the two disciples of Bentham thought that the Maltese were hailing Liberal Principles ... whereas it was their joy at seeing Donna Amabile Inglese.'

14.   Sarah Austin, courtesy of National Portrait Gallery, London

The couple lived comfortably in Sliema, a village consisting mostly of summer houses. John was regarded as the third ranking man in Malta, after the governor and the archbishop, and as the governor, Lieutenant-General Bouverie, was recently widowed, Sarah took precedence among the women, and sometimes acted as hostess. But she did much more than that, for she immediately loved Malta:

> It was said that she was responsible for the commissioners' recommendation to increase expenditure for elementary education, and she arranged for the establishment of ten new village schools. She 'consider[ed] herself an equal member of the Commission,' and, as she put it, she regarded her

time 'the property of the public.' Sarah recognized that Malta was a mine of valuable and unrecognized works of art and craftsmanship, and she arranged for the sale of gloves and lace in Valletta and in England.

That reference to lace is relevant to the work, too, of Honoria Chichester Hamilton to be given space in Chapter 10. Sarah also did what she could during the cholera epidemic of 1837. She wrote, 'From the first I have endeavoured to make my large house and fine situation useful to convalescents.' By October that year, 4,253 had died from cholera.

In spite of her contribution, Sarah was caught up in the opprobrium heaped upon the Commission – mocked in one publication as 'The Lady Commissioner'. In response, she 'complained about the lack of intelligent society and want of breeding'. And she 'suspected that much of the discontent arose from English insolence and prejudice'. As early as 4 November she was writing again to her sister that

> The result is that the noble Maltese families, poor and proud, depressed and insulted, have retired from the society of the English, and the most complete hatred and *éloignement* prevail. Such are the elements out of which I have to make my society.

And she wrote to Lord Lansdowne,

> Your Lordship doesn't know what it is to be a reformer. When you meet the man whose sinecure you have abolished every day, when you have to encounter every disappointed claimant and every dejected jobber in every ride and walk, you will pity us. But we are harder than the nether millstone.

The other commissioner, George Cornwall Lewis, thought 'The scum of England is poured into the colonies'. Austin himself was 'severely critical of English treatment of the Maltese'.

Sarah had known from the beginning what dangers she ran when she

> ostentatiously befriended the Maltese – like Lewis, she spoke Italian – and she tried to overcome the conventional barriers between the two communities, but she knew her conduct would provoke criticism and during her first fortnight in Malta asked, 'How will the English ladies bear this – so strong a censure, though a tacit one, on their conduct?' Later she wrote to Mill, 'If I escape poisoning you may rejoice. I think I have … reason to have a taster … I am sorry to be an object of hostility to any body, but civility to the Maltese is an inexplicable offence in the eyes of the English ladies.'

Lewis wrote of Sarah during that difficult time that she was glad her daughter Lucie was not with them, to be surrounded and flattered by a whole fleet and garrison, abused by all the English women and girls, worshipped by the poor despised Maltese (whose part she would be sure to take with more zeal than discretion) – spoiled in every way.

The Hamburgers describe the intricacies of the proposed constitutional reforms, and what happened to them, including the British politics involved. The result of the Commission's work was personally double-edged:

The Malta experience was a personal debacle for Austin, despite his and Lewis' considerable achievements. Most of their recommendations were adopted: liberty of the press; reform of all administrative departments, some of which were entirely remodelled; reform of the tariff office, and custom duties, and abolition of the grain system; reform of the government charities; improvements in the university and the lyceum, and the establishment of elementary schools (in which Sarah played a large part); the formation of an efficient civil police; and the simplification of the appellate jurisdiction and the abolition of the offices of chief justice and attorney-general.

But the only praise was private: Sarah was told, 'All that I hear of your joint proceedings is admirable. I believe commissions to be the best instrument of government and yours to be the best of commissions.' It was not enough: the work of the Commission did not lead to any further government appointments for John Austin. Sarah despaired; she wrote in 1839, 'I have my daughter, a handsome and talented girl; but I dare not think of the future'.

Sarah Austin had been intimately involved in the Commission's work which led to changes in the way Malta was governed under the British. There were to be many attempts to introduce further constitutional changes, particularly by the Maltese, during the nineteenth and early twentieth centuries, and gradually more Maltese men played a part. But since women, neither Maltese nor British, were involved, these efforts do not have a place here. To follow them, the general histories of Malta by Carmel Cassar and Brian Blouet are useful. It is ironic, though, that under the new Council of Government of 1887, as Carmel Cassar notes, 'To be eligible to stand for election a candidate had to be registered as a voter and was to possess, either in his name or that of his wife, immovable property in Malta valued at least at £100 ...'. Women's involvement in politics in their own right finally finds its place in Chapter 16.

Malta was to leave its stamp on Sarah Austin; years later she was to say,

In Malta I was first awakened to the detestable state of mind and manners of the large majority of English men (and women) towards all whom it has pleased God to bring into the world under circumstances less favourable than [their own].

As for Sarah's stamp on Malta, the *Malta Government Gazette* of 20 June 1838 observed that by her

> active exertions ... to ameliorate the social system, and to promote every object which might be conducive to the happiness of any class of the people ... By her perseverance the national industry has been excited, and resources have been brought to notice which formerly languished in obscurity.

It is that 'national industry', the craft of women, that is to feature in the following chapter.

It seems a pity to end with a pouring of cold water on the results of the Austin/Lewis commission, and Emma Roberts' view is only that of someone passing through, but she was a well-travelled intellectual, with good connections, and her observations on Malta are among the more thoughtful of those put forward by travellers. Of course, it does depend on whom she talked to in 1839, the year after the Austins left, and she does seem to confirm the problems Sarah Austin faced when she writes,

> I did not hear very flattering accounts of the state of society at Malta, which, like that of all other confined places, is split into factions, and where there seems to be a perpetual struggle, by the least fortunate classes, to assert equality with those whose rank is acknowledged, thus every person attached to the government assumes eligibility for the *entré* into the best circles, while the magnates of the place are by no means inclined to admit them to these privileges. It appeared that the endeavours of the Commissioner to produce a greater degree of cordiality between the Maltese inhabitants and the English residents, so far from succeeding, had tended to widen the distance between them, and that the Maltese were by no means grateful for the efforts made for their improvement. However, though the fruits may not at present appear, the seed having been sown, we may entertain a strong hope that they will show themselves in time.

10 – Women and Work 1803–1900

'The economy of the Maltese Islands under Britain took the form of an artificial cycle determined not by the vicissitudes of the market, but by the exigencies of military security,' writes Salvino Busuttil in 'Malta's Economy in the Nineteenth Century' (1965). And he goes on to describe the economic patterns of that century. But the market and its vicissitudes were more specific where women were concerned.

In the eighteenth century, Maltese women, supposedly confined to home and family, had many paid occupations in the outside world. And paid work in the home meant that they contributed financially as well as gaining satisfaction from more than household chores and childrearing. By the nineteenth century, the picture had begun to change, partly as a result of the fall-off in the demand for Maltese cotton and the goods made from it.

Cotton, Silk and Lace

In *The Story of Malta*, Brian Blouet describes how it had been:

In the villages the manufacture of textiles increased during the Order's rule. Cotton was grown by farmers and spun by wives and offspring. A middleman then purchased the spun cotton and exported it or placed it with a family that specialised in weaving. In country districts the processing of cotton was an important source of income. The industry depended upon exports and when these broke down the countryside suffered.

He goes on to explain the result of the French Revolutionary and Napoleonic Wars that lasted from 1792 until 1815:

The Cotton industry was already in decline. The local industry had lost markets for spun cotton in the Napoleonic Wars and post-war, and American and Egyptian growers dominated the markets. The local cottage spinning and weaving industry could not compete with machine-made products as textile factories became an important element in European industrialisation.

AP Vella explains the process of change in 'The Cotton Textile Industry in Malta' (1966). He quotes E Blanquiere who wrote, following an 1812 visit to Malta,

The staple commodity of the island, and for which it has been celebrated from the remotest antiquity, is cotton: of this there are two qualities, white and coloured; both are still cultivated to a certain extent, although greatly depreciated in value by the introduction of British and foreign manufacturers. There are several private looms employed all over the island, at Città Vechia [Mdina] a very extensive establishment is formed, and gives constant employment to several hundred indigent females, so that every encouragement should be given to the only charitable institution outside the walls of Valletta.

Cotton not only provided employment in charitable institutions: women prisoners were also 'put to spinning cotton'. In the rather specialised article 'Historical criminology and the imprisonment of women in 19th century Malta' (2010), Sandra Scicluna and Paul Knepper detail the nine women in the Great Prison who in 1825 were given this task; they range from **Maddelena Mallia** serving an eight-day sentence for assault to **Ursola Tabone** with a life sentence for 'attempt to poison'.

In 1764, the Spinning Jenny, which helped revolutionise the production of textiles, had been introduced in Britain and, inevitably, the technology travelled. Then, as Andrew Vella writes, 'on the 18th November, 1822, a government proclamation allowed every kind of linen and cloth to be imported into our islands. On the 3rd November, 1837, every tax on imported cotton was removed.'

But it falls to Sarah Austin to show only too clearly and personally the effect on women of this decline in an industry that had sustained Maltese country families since at least the eighteenth century when most agricultural land had been given over to growing cotton. She wrote in a letter home of January 1837, when she had been in Malta for some months:

No country can stand in greater need of enlightenment than this where marriage is so criminally and disgustingly early and so dreadfully prolific. I have seen a husband of fifteen; mothers under twenty with four or five children are not rare; and the recklessness seems to increase with the misery. One cause seems to me that domestic servants are almost all men; in our house, five out of six are men, and I cannot help it. As the cotton spinning and weaving has so greatly declined, there is no employment for girls, and mothers strive to marry their daughters at all events.
... the failure of cotton manufacture – partly caused by the exclusion of Malta cotton from Spain, partly by the introduction of English [cotton?] here – has taken from the people of the Cazals their only means of living, save agriculture; and how insufficient that must be, you may guess.

In the recreation of women's history there is always a difference in perception between that of the resident, like Sarah Austin, who has made a careful study, or keenly observed over time, and the impressions of the traveller spending a few days; and the first is obviously the more valid. Nevertheless, it is worth noting how **Lucinda Darby Griffith** (née Dimsdale, 1822–1893) saw the situation when she passed through with her husband seven years later, in 1844, and recorded it in *A Journey Across the Desert from Ceylon to Marseilles: Comprising Sketches of Aden, the Red Sea, Lower Egypt, Malta, Sicily and Italy* (1845). He sketched the scenes that illustrate the book; she wrote the text in the lively style of an alert 22-year-old (and it is available as a big fat well-scanned volume).

A cousin had arranged rooms for them in the Strada Reale; and to look after them they engaged not a man servant but a maid, **Vicenza**: 'I engaged a Maltese lady's maid today; she speaks English very well and is an excellent woman.' A few days later she wrote: 'I like my Maltese maid very much; she is exceedingly useful and intelligent, and has told me a great many facts relative to the manners and customs of the people, which very likely I might otherwise have remained ignorant of.'

Lucinda is more amused than shocked at early marriage and she elaborates on the House of Industry set up by Lady Hastings in 1824, described in Chapter 9:

> I was much amused when Vicenza, talking of her children, the two biggest of whom are in the Casa Industria, said she thought that the eldest girl, who is just thirteen years old, would be married in a year or two, for now they were allowed to come out of the school for three days every six months, and during that time very likely some young man might see and admire her. I laughed at the idea of such a short acquaintance, but she told me that at the last holidays, sixty girls were married, and the rule had been made on purpose to give them an opportunity, for, during the rest of the year they are never allowed to leave the walls;

And Lucinda, seeing Malta afresh and fleetingly, also notes cotton growing, and women spinning, as they travel towards Crendi (Qrendi):

> The road we followed ran directly inland, towards the centre of the island, and was on the ascent nearly the whole way. Every spot of ground, in any degree capable of being so, was highly cultivated. Large tracts were covered with crops of the cotton plant, just now in full bloom. The flower is generally deep yellow or orange, and contrasts beautifully with the bright green leaves. The plants are about a foot and a half in height. ...
> At the doors of the houses groups of women are generally to be seen spinning, and, with distaff in hand, added to their picturesque costume, would form admirable studies for a painter.

Sarah Austin, with her connection to the Commission, was looking at women's employment, or lack of it, from a different point of view, and she was not a woman to see a problem and not seek to solve it, as the last chapter has shown. She continues the letter of 1837:

> I ventured to send through my sister a petition to Mrs Senior on behalf of some of the poor girls who make lace. I hope by another packet to send her a little specimen of their embroidery, the beauty and cheapness of which may recommend it. It is chiefly done by daughters of decayed families.

The working of lace (*bizzilla*) was becoming a real fillip in the employment and financial security of women and their families. Lacemaking in Malta has, indeed, become a topic for the teaching of Malta's history. On the internet is a University of Malta History of Lace II question: 'Who were Lady Sarah Austin and Lady Hamilton Chichester? Discuss their role in the development of Maltese Lace.'

A couple of tweaks are needed here: first, Sarah Austin did not have a title; second, while she was obviously involved in the promoting of Maltese lace, particularly abroad, it was Lady Hamilton Chichester who should be given most credit. More amusing is an internet article about lace that gives Honoria Hamilton Chichester the dubious honour of being the 'consort of Lord Nelson' – a slip which I hope Chapter 8 dispels. Honoria is fated to be mis-known: Gabrielle Festing, in *John Hookham Frere and his Friends* (1899) calls her Lady Cadogan. There was a much-painted Lady Honoria Cadogan, but not in Malta.

Honoria Blake, the late Lady Erroll's niece, living in the Frere family house at Pietà, did not marry Lord Hamilton Francis Chichester until 1837. But it was in 1833, and three years before Sarah Austin arrived in Malta, that 33-year-old Honoria saw the need to do something about Maltese lace and women's unemployment.

How she came to realise the need probably stemmed from the aura of compassion around Villa Frere (see Chapter 19 itinerary), was touched upon in the last chapter. Paul Cassar introduced the funerals of Lady Erroll and Susannah Frere by the observation:

A crowd of lame, old and blind persons used to gather in the evening at the door of the Villa for alms which were never refused. In fact it has been said that [Frere's] benevolence was imposed upon by all who got near him. The able-bodied also joined the crowd to ask for his help to get employment.

Lacemaking was by no means new in Malta: you only need to look at three wonderful, heavily illustrated books edited by Nicholas de Piro – *The International Dictionary of Artists Who Painted Malta* (1988), *Costume in Malta* (1998), and *Ladies of Malta: in Extravagant and Spectacular Maltese Lace* (2013) – to appreciate that. They contain numerous portraits of much earlier Maltese women and, indeed, Knights of the Order, arrayed in it. What is more, we know the name of the woman who provided lace to the Grand Master in January 1705. In *The Sovereign Palaces of Malta* (2001), another of Nicholas de Piro's richly illustrated volumes, he describes how **Madame La Fontaine** brought 4 metres of lace to the Palace and spent a day sewing it onto something that escapes efforts to determine. The payment of 5 scudi a metre was 'six times more than a sedan carrier [earned] for a day's work'.

From the sixteenth century, lace was made in the Venetian style using needles, which was very time consuming and painstaking; the art was declining, together with the economy. By the early nineteenth century lace tended to be made only for the local market. Honoria Blake introduced the Genoese bobbin style of lacemaking placed over a pillow instead:

A pattern is pinned to the pillow and the thread is twisted or braided and held in place at its intersections by the pins to create the design. The thread is wound onto pairs of bobbins, short spindles made of wood. Sometimes the bobbins are shaped or 'spangled' to help identify the pairs.

15.   The Lacemaker by Dinah Hardiment, from de Piro,
The International Dictionary of Artists Who Painted Malta

The women and girls working with bobbins used the old needle lace patterns with honey-coloured or black Spanish silk thread. The Genoese leaf work was retained but Maltese flourishes such as the eight-pointed cross and wheat-eared motifs were introduced. In Gozo, lacemaking using bobbins was revived by two priests.

Accounts of Honoria Hamilton Chichester's introduction of a new and more economically viable way of making lace imply that it had an immediate impact on female unemployment; but it may have taken a while to change to bobbin from needle lace and to lead to widespread improvement and financial well-being. Salvino Busuttil appears to be writing of 1838 with his less sanguine observations drawn from the Austin/Lewis Commission report:

> Cotton prices had gone down considerably. Many of the farmers were in debt, and no credit was available. Crops were sold at a price varying between one-half and one-third their cost. When bankruptcy overtook him, the farmer would employ himself as a labourer earning from 6d to 8d per day during the harvest; in winter the average farmer's wage was 1d a day, and all his family had to work to avoid starvation.
>
> We are told that the farmer wife's wages would amount to 3d a day in the crop season, while children received an average of 1¼d a day. If one assumes that the farmer had three children working, besides his wife, it would mean that their combined wages were just ten pounds annually, or two pounds per capita. ...
>
> People who followed the traditional employment of lace-making were also in some straits. The average woman spinner worked for something like seventeen hours a day, earning 10 grains (i.e. less than one penny), while a cotton weaver earned 2 taris, or 3.3/10d per day, working thirteen hours. Several children helped in the work, receiving small fractions of one penny daily.

Yet Sarah Austin wrote to England in March that year, not long before she left Malta after her 20-month stay:

> Dear Mrs Senior,
> My commissions for silk and mittens are so numerous and business so thriving that I need not encumber you with anything more unless you wish it. The Queen's commission for eight dozen pairs long and eight dozen pairs short mits, is more than I can get executed with the perfection I wish while I am here. Lady Lansdowne and others are always writing for them. As to the turban, Lady L admires hers so much that she has written to order a dress for Lady Louisa. That, with a scarf for the Queen, will keep my best hands occupied.

Thomas MacGill, publishing his *Handbook* in 1839, after 30 years in Malta, writes, presumably of the period leading up to 1839:

> The spinning and weaving of native cotton, has always been considered the most extensive branch of native industry; though it has ceased to be very profitable, yet many thousands continue to gain a livelihood by it, however miserable. The cotton sail cloth of Malta, is still held in great repute by the levantine navigators, and there is rarely a Greek ship which comes to the Island, that does not extract a supply.
>
> The table covers, bed mats and glass doylies made here, (the manufactory of which was introduced some years ago by the present Bishop) are very

pretty; cloth made from the nankeen cotton of the island was much in vogue some years ago, and is still worn ...

Embroidery on cotton and silk is done to perfection, by the females of the Island, and sent out to adorn those less industrious in the neighbouring states; they make also excellent lace; the lace mitts and gloves wrought by Malta girls, are bought by all ladies coming to the island; orders from England are often sent for them, on account of their beauty and cheapness.

There had been an attempt to introduce the production of Maltese silk, with the planting of mulberry trees for the silkworms in the grounds of the Verdala Palace – 'la Buschetta' (see Chapter 22 itinerary). In 1828, the Duke of Buckingham, Mrs Pitt, and a party from the Duke's yacht went, after a trip to Mdina, to see the cotton and silk factories which 'afforded some occupation to the poor, who are very wretched, and ought, therefore, to be encouraged'.

The silk production venture was largely funded by the financier and philanthropist Moses Montefiore who, with his wife **Judith Montefiore** (née Cohen,1784–1862), visited Malta in 1827 and 1839 on their way to and from Palestine. Judith travelled extensively with her husband to save and protect endangered Jews around the world. The earlier call had been made two months before Buckingham's visit and he noted that the couple 'had entertained a very large number of the factory's employees with their wives and children to a sumptuous dinner in the Hall of St Michael and St George in the lieutenant-governor's palace' (Girgenti, see Chapter 22 itinerary).

Although only passing through in 1839, the observant Emma Roberts interested herself in the relationship between the production of cotton and silk:

The growth of cotton, lately introduced into Egypt, has been injurious to the trade and manufactures of Malta, and the attempt to supply its place with silk failed. In the opinion of some persons, the experiment made had not a fair trial. The mulberry trees flourished, and the silk produced was of an excellent quality; but the worms did not thrive, and in consequence the design was abandoned. Inquiry has shown, that the leaves from old trees are essential to the existence of the silk-worm, and that, had the projectors of the scheme been aware of a fact so necessary to be known, they would have awaited the result of a few more years, which seems all that was necessary for the success of the undertaking.

The newly revived lace industry continued apace, however. A rather informal internet account, 'Lace in Malta' – the one that confuses Honoria and Emma – suggests that 'Queen Vic' only discovered Maltese lace in 1881 when it was shown at the Exhibition of Industries in London. But she clearly knew of it as early as 1838 when she had just come to the throne, and the statue of Queen Victoria, in the square in front of the National Library in Valletta, has a shawl of black Gozitan lace covering her lap (see Chapter

17 itinerary); it is possibly the one mentioned by Sarah Austin. Certainly exposure in London did nothing to harm the lace industry and the other crafts of Maltese women. Maltese lace even travelled as far as Australia. The *Evening News* of Sydney reported on 9 July 1892 that

> The Woollahra private Assembly held its second ball this season on Friday evening, the 1st instant, at Nithsdale, Hyde Park ... About 100 guests were present, and the majority of dresses worn were indeed very handsome and effective. Mrs Chamier wore a trained gown of cream moiré, trimmed profusely with beautiful Maltese lace, the front of the dress being of rich black velvet.

A Captain Frederick Chamier visited Malta in his naval vessel when Sir Thomas Maitland was governor and it may well be he who was responsible for a later Mrs Chamier's beautifully trimmed dress.

In the diary that the Duke of Cornwall's assistant private secretary kept during a tour the Duke and Duchess made of the empire in 1901, Donald Mackenzie noted after a visit to an industrial exhibition in Malta:

> But the section which attracts most attention is that of lace-making, for which the islands of Malta and Gozo have long been famous and which is now being systematically developed. Some specimens which we see being made by young girls seated round a big table seem to prove that the nimble fingers of the female inhabitants have by no means lost their cunning.

Meanwhile, missionaries were taking the Maltese lace technique to the Far East from where, eventually, lace was imported into Malta.

As for Honoria Blake Hamilton Chichester, she inherited Villa Frere when her late aunt's husband, John Hookham Frere, died in 1846. By 1847 she appears to have had grace and favour accommodation at Hampton Court, though she still seems to have spent time in Malta: Florence Nightingale described Lord and Lady Hamilton Chichester on the boat from Marseilles to Malta in 1849 as 'harmless people'. Honoria was widowed in 1854, and died in 1878, aged 78.

The lace industry was given another boost a century later, in 1934 by Cecilia de Trafford, one of the Strickland daughters (see Chapter 14). A further revival at the end of the twentieth century was provided by **Consiglia Azzopardi** of Gozo who also gives courses in Maltese lacemaking in Australia. There are several lacemaking courses available in Malta, including at the University on both islands.

There is a general piece about the history of European lacemaking by Pat Earnshaw in *Costume in Malta*; but most fascinating and informative is the one that follows by Consiglia Azzopardi, 'Lacemaking at the Centre of Gozitan Daily Life'. I would like to quote it all, but this is just a taste:

Elderly Gozitan lacemakers often recount how in their childhood or youth, they would sit at their lace pillow (called 'trajbu') in time for the early morning mass at 'Pater Noster' – about four o'clock in the morning. After mass they returned home, had their usual breakfast consisting mainly of a bowl of small chunks of bread dipped into coffee and milk. Every person in the family then set out to work, either in the fields or in the house, washing, cooking or making lace.

A fine piece of lace was often created as a family project with each member working on his or her section. The various pieces were then sewn together to make a whole collar, tablecloth or whatever had been ordered. The pattern was followed scrupulously as it was generally felt that taking short cuts and curtailing the pattern was not a conscientious way to proceed. Sometimes, members of the family took turns at the lace pillow so that the work never ceased. A mother would cradle her baby while she sat at her lace pillow. And so they would work until dark, and in the case of stringent deadlines, all the lacemakers would proceed by the light of one lamp. During the long winter evenings the family would usually gather in one room, the men helping with the winding of the spools and bobbins.

Women's employment in the cotton industry was to revive briefly during the American Civil War of 1861–65 which stopped the supply of cotton to Europe; as Salvino Busuttil notes, 'While Lancashire suffered, Malta prospered. Cotton production was greatly increased and workers in the industry received good wages.' This no doubt accounts for Carmel Cassar writing in 'Everyday Life in Malta':

In the early part of the nineteenth century, many rural women worked as spinners and weavers in their homes, or as beaters and dyers of cotton at home or in small manufacturing factories. Often they even gave a helping hand in fields or on the farm. In 1861, out of 9,000 workers described as spinners and weavers, together with some other 200 beaters and dyers, 96 per cent were women, whose labour was generally used in the final stages of cloth preparation.

The revival was short-lived and in 1865 Malta suffered another cholera epidemic, resulting in 1,873 deaths. The following year there was a drought.

Another occupation introduced for country families not long before the revival in lacemaking is also mentioned, using idiosyncratic spelling, by Thomas MacGill:

The making of cigars, has become a most important branch of trade here, and gives employment to many thousands of poor families; cigars made here from Havana tobacco, are nearly equal to those imported, and cost less than half the price. From hence cigars are shipped to all parts within the pillars of Herculus, and the home consumption must be immence; they are to be seen in mouths, from the half naked pauper, to the best-dressed gentlemen of society; who, to gratify an undiscribable sensation make themselves disagreeable in delicate female society.

It is well known that Cuban cigars are rolled on the thighs of the women who make them, which creates a nice mid-nineteenth-century Maltese image inside a rude country dwelling. In Chapter 9 it was mentioned in passing that the young women in the House of Industry made cigars, among other crafts, which gives some sort of a date for the introduction of this craft. Carmel Cassar's history notes that by 1856 cigar making provided work for 1,500 people, and cigars were exported to all parts of the Mediterranean but, by the end of the nineteenth century, 'the industry was doing very badly'.

Chapter 7, about women in the eighteenth century, mentioned that women worked as both millers and breadmakers. The British government census of 1861 showed that in Qormi, of the 486 kneaders, the majority were women and, of the 33 bakers, 14 were women.

Education

Sarah Austin's involvement with lacemaking and its selling was a private venture on her part; more public, because it formed part of the Commission's work, was the introduction of primary schools. As a result, too, a department of education was set up and a curriculum began to take form.

When Sarah arrived in Malta, there were, according to Salvino Busuttil, three schools on the islands: one in Valletta, another in Senglea, and a third on Gozo. Government expenditure on all three 'amounted to an annual £400'. Through her prodding, 'the Commissioners recommended that the education vote be raised from £1,725 to £4,000 a year'. Paul Cassar in his 'Vignette' notes that of the two on Malta, one catered for 450 boys, the other 278 girls. These were government-supported schools for a population of some 100,000.

But there were also fee-paying private schools. Albert Ganado, in his 2004 article about nineteenth-century guide books to Malta, notes that 'In 1825 a Young Ladies School was housed at 10 Strada San Cristoforo, Valletta, under the direction of Mrs Naudi and Miss Rosina Nuzzo'. Mrs Naudi could have been **Marguerite Naudi** (née Zammit) who a year earlier had married Giuseppe Naudi. He had trained as a teacher in England and ran a Methodist-financed school in Malta. In 1839, he opened an infant school where girls could stay on after the age of nine. It is fair to deduce that he was G. Naudi who, in 1839, published *Piano di Educazione ed Insegnamento per Scuole Infantile*.

Although biographical details for **Rosina Nuzzo** are lacking, a later teacher at the Young Ladies School was **Maria Teresa Nuzzo** (1851–1923), said by Albert Abela, in his chapter 'Some Notable Maltese Women of the Past' (1997), to be intensely interested in education from an early age 'and by 1867 already in charge of the Nuzzo school in Valletta which was run by her family'. When she was 16, Maria Teresa became responsible for a school run by her aunt, 'who had become blind and died on 4 March 1867'. This aunt may well have been Rosina. Maria Teresa was later the founder of the Congregation of the Daughters of the Sacred Heart (see Chapter 11).

Lorraine Portelli, in 'The Socioeconomic Factors in the Teaching of Needlework in 19th Century Malta' (2009), adds that, in 1825, the girls at that school 'studied reading in English and Italian, arithmetic, writing, embroidery, sewing and cutting-out (dressmaking). It appears from the timetable that needlework took half of the time spent at school.'

There were also private schools run by foreign women. Lorraine Portelli tells us, drawing on the *Malta Government Gazette*, that in 1833 Englishwoman Mrs Vere opened a preparatory School for Girls and taught dressmaking, English, writing, and arithmetic. In 1834, with the help of 'able masters', Italian, needlework and dancing were added. Mrs Vere, it transpires, was **Jane Agnes Vere** (née Bowman), from Morpeth, Northumberland, the widow of Joseph Harrison. In 1824, she had married Charles Vere. He obtained a licence to open a school in 1831; Jane's was a separate one at 5 Strada Stretta, Valletta.

The *Government Gazette* says that in August 1835 Mrs Weisbech opened a 'seminary' in Valletta for a few chosen girls who were taught academic subjects. Plain and ornamental needlework were offered on request. The *Gazette* seems to have misspelt the name which was more likely Weisbeker; her country of origin is unclear. In 1836, she was, instead or as well, giving 'piano lessons at her residence, or at the client's home. Terms moderate'.

Then, in 1838, Mrs Lewis opened a day school for young ladies in Valletta. The curriculum included English, French and Italian, geography, history, writing and arithmetic, music and plain and fancy needlework. The fees were 10 shillings a month. George Cassar has further details of Mrs Lewis in 'A Glimpse of Private Education in Malta 1800–1919' (2000). It seems that French and Italian were an extra 5 shillings a month, and music an extra 10s. She was assisted by what she termed 'able teachers'.

The only Mrs Lewis I can find who might fit the bill is Susan or **Susannah Lewis**, the wife of William Lewis who, in 1833, was first clerk in the Grain Department, and lived at 198 Strada Forni (Old Bakery Street), rent free as authorised by the local government in 1825. The Lewises had eight children in Malta between 1822 and 1840; he died in 1845 as a civil servant. Susannah had a large family to cope with, could she have run a school as well? But an eight-year-old son died in 1836, and a daughter, **Georgina Lewis**, died in 1837, aged eight months, which would have turned her world upside down. And a hint of a teaching family comes when her daughter **Louisa Lewis** (b. 1829, or 1836) became a schoolteacher in 1883.

It is easy to presume that all this education, including, or particularly, the sewing skills, were to make young women qualified to earn money for their families at a time of economic uncertainty, but as the private schools charged fees, they were not accessible to the poor; they were, therefore, preparing girls not so much for economic employment in the home, but to be good housewives and mothers. And who were the pupils? Were they better-off

Maltese children, or British, or a mixture of all the various nationalities then living in Malta?

As far as government schools were concerned, presumably following the 1838 Commission report, Paul Cassar tells us that by 1839 three girls schools were opened in Mdina, Żejtun and Lija 'which were also meant to cater for the girls of neighbouring villages'. And by 1859 'There were at least twenty school mistresses teaching in Government Elementary Schools. The school teacher was thus the first professional woman to appear in our island.'

This seems to be something of an advance, both for schooling and for women as teachers, but in 'Some Working Conditions of Maltese Teachers During the Nineteenth Century and up to World War I' (2010), George Cassar suggests the disadvantages under which teachers, particularly women, laboured; and I have stitched several points together:

> Practically all the members of the Maltese teacher corps came from humble origins and, to some extent, viewed a teaching career as a means to upward social mobility. ... such personal circumstances also made them accept much of what the authorities imposed on them without protest or debate. ... In the public schools, the teacher corps was made up of both males and females. However, females predominated in numbers and this tallied with what was current at the same time in other countries ... at Malta, women did not figure at all in the upper professions while in the lower professions (though this may not be the right nomenclature when referring to teachers along the 1800–1919 period), women made up a much larger proportion. ... The shortage of efficient training and academic background impinged on teachers' standing to a large extent.

George Cassar goes on to quote the author of the Royal Commission of 1878 who queries 'how these poor teachers contrive to clothe themselves as respectable as their official position demands of them, to find themselves with the proper nourishment – bread being said to be dearer in Malta than in London'. One named teacher is then briefly described: Mrs Bonavia 'who in the 1840s served as head teacher of the new school at Cospicua'. The identity of Mrs Bonavia is another that eludes me; it is a mere guess that she could have been **Teresa Bonavia** (née Simiara) who, in 1802 in Cospicua, married Giovanni Bonavia. We do, however, know the conditions under which Mrs Bonavia tried to teach, and her pupils to learn: the school buildings

> were neither spacious enough to accommodate the considerable number of applicants nor suitable for effective teaching and learning. As early as 1843, the elementary school of the harbour town of Cospicua exposed such shortages. ... In 1855 the Valletta Girls' Elementary School was set up within the Valletta Orphanage complex, using one room in which about 300 girls were accommodated. ... The rented girls' schoolhouse at Senglea was not much better. It was crowded to excess, with many students forced to remain standing for lack of space.'

The government did close the Senglea one down and rented a new building, but the situation did not markedly improve over the years. Added to that were the settings of some schools which as late as 1890, were

located in areas where prostitution and gambling were rife. The Model Schools of Valletta were situated on the way to a Government Medical Officer's examination clinic that monitored prostitutes thrice monthly as stipulated by law. These 'common women of Valletta and Floriana' took the shortest way to the clinic and passed by the Valletta schools. While waiting their turn, these women gathered in the wine shops facing the schools 'and the disorder they create, together with the abominal [*sic*] language they make use of, is a most serious annoyance.' The Director, A.A. Caruana, argued that this was scandalous to both the pupils and the female assistant teachers who assembled from all parts of Malta for their Saturday morning training lessons.

How effective were the changes made in education as far as learning was concerned? Carmel Cassar, in his 'Everyday Life' chapter, paints a gloomy picture:

Education was described by the 1838 Royal Commission as 'small in quantity and bad in quality'. Illiteracy was widespread. The *skola tan-nuna* (nursery school) taught children folktales, nursery rhymes, and prayers, but hardly anything else. A Government department for primary schools was set up in 1840, but progress was so slow that by 1861, out of a population of 134,055, less than 8,000 males could read Italian and less than 4,000 could read English.

The low standard of living discouraged parents from sending their boys to school. Boys were made to work at a very early age in order to earn some money. The higher the cost of living, the more this was liable to happen. Girls fared even worse. The 1891 census reported that while 80 per cent of males between the ages of 45 and 50 could not read, 85 per cent of females in the same age-group were illiterate. By the turn of the century, about 30 elementary schools had been set up in Malta and Gozo, together with some 40 infant schools, a few night schools, and one Sunday school.

This is given added weight by the Keenan Commission report of 1879 quoted by Lorraine Portelli:

In nearly all the girls' schools the various branches of Needlework are admirably taught. In their general literacy and professional qualifications the schoolmistresses exhibit many and serious defects, but in nearly every case they display zeal and ability in teaching of Needlework. If they fail to teach the girls how to read or to count, they certainly succeed in teaching them how to sew; whether it is plain or ornamental needlework, or the making of flowers, or the national lace-making, the excellence of the results is equally uniform. ... The universal teaching of Needlework in girls' schools is in perfect consonance with the pursuits and wants of the female population. There is no anomaly in it.

In her conclusion, Lorraine Portelli conveys the dual purpose of teaching girls needlework when she writes,

The consolidation of needlework as a school subject for girls proved a breakthrough in view of the introduction of other domestic subjects, which, like needlework, were considered beneficial for the needs of the population. For many decades, the teaching of needlework was instrumental as a means to answer the social and economic needs of the population. It provided families with girls and housewives who had the capability to contribute toward their well-being by being thrifty and in some cases also earning money for the family. Needlework fitted neatly into the Maltese economic context at the time, providing both income and precious life skills for needy local families, and it continued to do so even in later years.

And, adapting from L Pullicino's 1864 report, she adds a most informative table of 'Occupations of Girls Upon Leaving School During 1863'; it starts with 'Domestic occupations – 242', and thereafter, 'Needlework – 29; School of lace-making – 25; Agriculturalists – 13; Lace makers – 13; Servants – 11; Assistants in schools – 5; Private School mistresses – 1'.

What would Sarah Austin have made of the outcome of her hopes for education in Malta? But Carmel Cassar does go on to end, 'The situation was not much different in most other European countries, including Britain.'

In Malta, there were schools for older children, too, but 'The University, which catered almost exclusively for the well-to-do', had only 86 male students. 'Women did not begin to follow university courses until the 1920s.' One of the problems for education was the perennial one of English versus Italian; Maltese was not yet an educational factor. Emma Roberts, who had lived in, and written about, India, knew which side she was on:

While an undertaking so gigantic as the diffusion of the English language throughout India has been attempted, it seems rather extraordinary that the efforts of the committee should not have been directed to the same result in Malta, and that the progress of education should not have been conducted in the language that promised to prove the most useful to subjects of the British crown; but it appears that the committee decided otherwise, and complaints are making [*sic*], that the instruction now supplied at the schools is of the most superficial nature, and by no means calculated to produce the desired end.

Employment, silk and literacy come together optimistically in what the lady's maid Vicenza told Lucinda Darby Griffith in 1844: 'The Casa Industria is a sort of charity-school, where children are taught some useful trade, and to read and write. The girls make the pretty silk gloves and mittens for which Malta is celebrated.'

And Paul Cassar has unearthed one woman schoolteacher with a name and a teaching history that does not seem unhappy; he writes:

Among these women pioneers there was **Miss Emanuela Azzopardi** (1831–71) from Floriana who after being educated in the private Protestant School of Mr Watson, joined the staff of the Government Primary Schools in 1851 and six years later was promoted to Head Teacher of the Valletta Primary School. She enjoyed such an excellent reputation as teacher and organiser that on her death the Director of Education felt it his duty to perpetuate her memory by the publication of an extensive appreciation of her work and personality.

Mention of Mr Watson's school emphasises the new kind of British resident suggested by Mrs Vere and Mrs Lewis: those not connected with the top of the colonial administration, the armed services, or others of the same class. British merchants and tradespeople early on saw opportunities in Malta; there were a host of incentives, including tax exemption and political stability.

There were two Watson families, with no obvious connection. William Watson was director of the Malta Infant School at 9 Strada Scozzese in 1847; he was still on the electoral list at that address in 1852, but it is likely that the school was opened in about 1839 because, according to George Cassar, although it ended up partly Government funded, it was set up 'through an idea' of Dowager Queen Adelaide who visited Malta for her health in 1838–39 and whose funding of the Anglican St Paul's Church, Valletta is treated in Chapter 11. George Cassar adds,

This establishment was under her patronage and had the sanction of the government of Malta. ... It was to have the same system of education as that in use in Britain. The aim of the school was 'philanthropic, and conducive to the great interest of the country' and it accepted children from two to eight years of age, each child paying a penny a week.

The fee and the school became controversial partly on religious grounds, as it was assumed that it was a Protestant school. But Mr Watson was revealed in 1851 as one of the examiners of the School of the Augustinian Convent, Valletta, and the Infant School's 100 pupils were mostly Roman Catholic. In addition, it had four Jewish pupils.

The Reverend Moses Margoliouth, on his way to the Holy Land in 1847, stopped in Malta and wrote of the Infant School to a relative, that the mistress was 'an expert young woman and not a little conceited; she brings on the children remarkably well'. Who she was we are not told, but I like to think it was William Watson's wife. His first wife, **Margaret Watson** (1820–1843), died of consumption in 1843, aged just 22. It looks as if he re-married in 1844, his second wife being **Caroline Sampson**. How she arrived in Malta is not known; quite often British men returned home to marry, then brought their wives back to Malta. And Watson may well have married a schoolteacher.

But where did Emanuela Azzopardi fit in? She would have been eight in 1839 when the school seems to have been set up, too old to become a pupil. But George Cassar writes,

A final comment regarding the Malta Infant School concerns teacher training. In 1850 the number of young men and women 'the latter in particular, for the purpose of acquiring the art of teaching children, which is by no means easy,' was lacking. Complaining of the scarcity of a sufficient number of good infant schools in Valletta, *The Malta Mail* reported that it had information that the director of the Infant School, Mr Watson, 'would gladly take charge of a class of pupil teachers.' The ages required would be between 15 and 20 years.

So perhaps Emanuela started her teaching career there.

The mention of four Jewish children at the Watson school is a useful reminder that the Jewish community was once again flourishing in Malta. The paternal great great grandfather of Aline P'Nina Tayar arrived there from Tripoli in 1846, and by the time his great grandson, her father, was at school later in the nineteenth century there were 100 or so Jews living in Valletta. She tells the story of her extended family from that first arrival, and not only in Malta, in wonderful detail in *How Shall We Sing? A Mediterranean Journey Through a Jewish Family* (2000); not only that, the first glimpse we get of her great grandmother, **Corinna Tayar** (née Coen), shows Malta as home to interesting and educated immigrants:

The Italian spoken in my father's home and the cause of so much teasing by other children was the legacy of his grandmother, Corinna, and not the affectation of a political statement against British rule of the Maltese islands. Nonna Corinna lived on St Christopher Street. Before her marriage, Corinna Coen had run a Dame's school for Jewish girls in Florence ... [among her possessions] Corinna had also brought an education with her. She had decreed that all her children and grandchildren were to learn reams of Dante by heart because the Divine Poet was her speciality. Maltese scholars sometimes came to her to ask for explications of obscure passages, but they never acknowledged her contribution in their dissertations.

Shops and Hotels

Rather more is known of the second Watson family in Valletta at this time. Elizabeth Watson (née Pilkington, 1778–1836) ran a bookshop at 277 (or 241) Strada Reale, known as EM Watson's bookshop. Paul Cassar, in an article about reading rooms (1992), assumes that EM was a man. He writes,

> Watson was a stationer and Bookseller who appears to have catered for readers of French books of which he imported no less than three hundred in November 1837 and who promoted the sale of a one volume edition of Lord Byron's works …

But Mariana Starke, in the 1836 edition of *Travels in Europe*, makes it clear that the Strada Reale bookseller was 'Mrs Watson', and the initial E is indicative. Elizabeth had married John Watson in Preston, Lancashire in 1802 and, by 1806, they were in Malta, bringing with them two sons. She was to die back in England in 1836 but, before then, she had five more sons, and a daughter, Josephine Mary Watson (1820–1870) in Malta. John Watson was described as a cotton manufacturer when they married and was to try his hand at many ventures during the 42 years he lived in Malta. Some of them flourished. But Thomas MacGill's account of him, in his 1839 *Handbook*, confirms that cotton remained an abiding concern:

> St Julians, being a favourite place, had, within but a few years, become an extensive straggling village, where several English families have villas; we shall take leave to mention the fine house and gardens of Bel-Vedere, the residence of John Watson Esq. who is rendering himself a benefactor to the natives, by his assiduity and exertions in the introduction of the Brazil cotton plant; an uphill task, with people so bigoted to their ancient cotton and customs; – Mr Watson labours both by precept and example, to show them their interest in this.

Thomas MacGill had also arrived in Malta in 1806, and was to live there for 38 years, at least some of the time at 27 Strada Stretta. He was already well travelled and was to continue doing so, publishing a book on his travels between 1803 and 1806 in Turkey, Italy and Russia. He became Greek Consul in Malta but, in the 1820s, he was also involved in the Malta Tanning Company with John Watson and Henry Cowper. At the same time, he interested himself in Malta's education as a member of the *Società delle Scuole Normali della Valletta*, and must have had good Italian and, possibly, Maltese. His wife was Margaret MacGill (née Dempster, *c*.1775–1844) who died two months after him. Both were buried in the Msida Bastion Cemetery, as was their daughter Margaret Wilhelmina MacGill, in 1836, aged 23; another daughter, Ann MacGill Mackenzie (1799–1818), who married in Malta in 1817, died in Naples the following year. As Ann was born in Glasgow in 1799, it may well be that Margaret and Thomas travelled together before they arrived in Malta (see Chapter 19 itinerary).

It looks as if John Watson took over his wife's bookshop when she died, because Thomas MacGill's Malta *Handbook* was said to be available through him at 277 Strada Reale in 1839, but also at Mrs Kilburn's bookshop. **Anna Kilburn** (née Troughton, 1766–1847) had kept a fashion shop at 271 Strada Reale from at least 1816; perhaps she sold books there, too, or turned it into a bookshop later, or had two shops. Her bookshop 'was well frequented by the British community'. Born in Birmingham, she had married John Kilburn in Leghorn (Livorno) in 1793, and their first child, Elizabeth, was born there. They seem to have arrived in Malta in 1803, so may have done so from Italy and, therefore, spoken Italian. Anna was probably pregnant. Three Kilburn children were born in Malta: **Harriet Kilburn** (1803–1807) was baptised in the Anglican chapel in the Governor's Palace, as was **Ann Kilburn** (b.1805) and John Thomas in 1807. Anna's father, Joseph, was in Malta, too, and died there.

Anna died in Malta, aged 79, having lived there for 44 years. She left two daughters and several grandchildren, though her daughter **Elizabeth Gingell** (1793–1841) pre-deceased her. Elizabeth had ten children in Malta with her husband, Edward, seven girls, three boys; four of them died under the age of 21. It is worth noting the children of these various families, not just to give them their place in history, but also to show that not only Maltese families tended to be large; and there would have been many British children also requiring education. The extensive list of graves in the Msida Cemetery, and the youthfulness of some of the deceased, also show a high mortality rate.

According to Mariana Starke in 1836, Madame Le Grand's Milliners and Dressmakers opposite St John's church was 'among the best shops' in Valletta. Could this be the same **Mrs Le Grand** mentioned by naval surgeon Edward Cree in *The Cree Journals* (edited, 1981, Michael Lieven). Cree was stationed for two brief periods in Malta in 1837 and 1839. He wrote in his marvellously chatty diary on 31 August 1837:

> Le Grand, Assistant surgeon at the Hospital, goes on leave to Sicily in the *Hind* and I remain to do duty in his absence. Mrs Le Grand is a very pretty little woman, daughter of the Chaplain of the Embassy at Constantinople. Le Grand was Assistant Surgeon of the *Thalia* and married her there. … We often have a little music and dancing of an evening in Le Grand's or Whitmarsh's rooms, which overlook the harbour, and sit out on the balconies in the quiet warm evenings listening to the songs and music in the Maltese boats, or the military bands from the opposite side, and watch the lights in Valetta reflected in the dark still water, with the boats leaving lines of phosphorescent light in their trail.

And on 4 September he added, 'The days pass away pleasantly enough; evening songs with Mrs Le Grand, who has a pretty Grecian face, accompanied on the guitar by Miss Silver.'

Included in Mariana Starke's 'best shops' is that of 'Mrs Smith who sells hosiery and childbed linen'. From the shops that would be of interest to the visitor to Malta, Mariana goes on to recommend hotels and boarding houses, many of them run by women.

Mariana Starke (1762–1838) started writing about her travels in the Mediterranean in 1824, but she was already a writer, and she had lived in Italy between 1792 and 1798. Following the end of the Napoleonic Wars in 1815, she recognised the growth in the number of Britons travelling abroad, and she saw that many of her readers would now be travelling in family groups and conscious of expense. She therefore included not just advice on luggage and passports but the cost of food and accommodation. She also devised a system of exclamation marks, the precursor of the stars awarded in some of today's travel guides. Her own books, indeed, provided a template for later travel guides produced by her publisher John Murray.

A contemporary British historian wrote that he 'never paid for the smallest trifle without first looking up its price in the travels of a certain Mrs Starke, a book which ... indicates to the prudent Englishman the cost of a turkey, an apple, a glass of milk and so forth'. And that is how Mariana (who, though often called Mrs Starke, was unmarried) treated Valletta following her research trip there. She started her recommendations about hotels:

The best hotels at Valletta, the capital of Malta, are Madame Gouban's Clarence Hotel in Strada Reale close to the palace, the post-office, and Saint George's Square – this inn contains hot and cold Baths, together with a Table d'Hôte, and a good Cook. ...

Mariana's notes had played her false with the spelling of the proprietor's name. The advertisement for the Clarence Hotel shows her to have been **L Goubau**. I remain frustrated at not being able to determine her first name. She was a French widow and ran a French hotel, Le Grand Hôtel Clarence, at 249 Strada Reale, with wines imported from France. The staff spoke not only French but also English and Italian. Prices were moderate for large or small apartments.

In 1835, Duke Pückler-Muskau – with whom Sarah Austin had earlier had a perhaps indiscreet relationship in Germany – arrived in Malta; happily, he arrived and departed before the Austins' stay. He and his retinue 'proceeded', according to Thomas Freller in *Malta and the Grand Tour* (2009) to the Hôtel Clarence. 'The connoisseur Pückler-Muskau – always on the lookout for beautiful ladies – immediately spotted that the owner – Madam Gouban [*sic*], had two good-looking daughters.'

But not everyone had the best experience. Joseph Cassar Pullicino, in his article '19th Century Hotels in Malta'(1981) writes of, and then quotes, Sir Richard Bourke, former Governor of New South Wales, who stayed at the Clarence in 1845:

16.   Hotel Clarence advertisement, courtesy of Giovanni Bonello

Sir Richard learned that his hostess, Mme Goubau, a French widow, had not put him in the good rooms which Lt. Col. Whitty, to whom he had been recommended by letter from Col. Cator sent from Limerick, had engaged for him. 'She made a sort of excuse and told me they would be again vacant in three days. The present sitting room is good enough, but the bedroom is bad. I pay 4/- a day for the rooms, my servant's bed included – 1/6 for breakfast and 3/- for a very decent dinner and dessert. Wine is extra – good Marsala, a Sicilian wine, is charged at 1/6 a bottle, but French and Spanish wines and Port, paying a higher duty, are nearly as dear as in London. Mme. Goubau keeps a good cook and the house is clean. She presented me with a very pretty nosegay on my arrival …'.

Mariana Starke also recommended Dunsfords at 254 Strada Reale, **Madam Morelli** at number 224, **Miss Atkinson's** at 38 Strada Vescovo and **Madam Calleja** near the entrance to the Upper Barracca. Emma Roberts was more than pleased with Dunsford's, which she misspells, in 1839; she wrote about it three times, starting with her arrival:

… a lady, a friend of mine, who had left London a few days before me, was now in Malta, and would proceed to India in the vessel appointed to take the mails. She was staying at Durnsford's Hotel, a place to which I had been strongly recommended. …

... The appearance of our hotel was prepossessing. We entered through a wide gateway into a hall opening upon a small court, in the centre of which stood a large vase, very well sculptured, from the stone of the island, and filled with flowers. A wide handsome staircase, also of stone, with richly-carved balustrades, and adorned with statues and vases, conducted us to a gallery, two sides of which were open, and the other two closed, running round the court-yard, and affording entrance to very good apartments. Everything was perfectly clean; the bedsteads of iron, furnished with mosquito-curtains; and we were supplied immediately with every article that we required. ...

... I can strongly recommend Durnsford's Hotel as a place of residence, the accommodation being excellent and the terms moderate. In remaining any time, arrangement may be made for apartments and board, by which means the rate of living is much cheaper, while the style is equally good.

Emma intended to stay at Dunsford's on her return trip; unfortunately, she was taken ill in India the following year, and died, aged only 49.

Perhaps in 1845 Madame Goubau was already planning to pull out of the Clarence because on 2 October 1846 **Grace Dunsford** took it over and closed it for 'alterations and repairs'. By 1847, she had renamed it Dunsford's Hotel at 249 and 254 Strada Reale and advertised that it combined 'privacy with the domestic comforts of an English establishment. She trusts that by her continued attention to clean apartments, good cuisine, and moderate charges to ensure a continuance of that patronage she has so long enjoyed.'

It looks, therefore, as if Grace merged the two hotels. Her husband, Joseph, had died in Malta in 1841, aged only 37. In 1847 she married Thomas Blair Hood of Ayr, Scotland. But the hotel was still called Dunsford's as late as 1880. In 1853, **Catherine Tobin** stayed there with her husband since 1835, Thomas, during a nine months' tour of Egypt, Palestine, Syria, Turkey and Greece. Her husband was the acknowledged antiquarian but a commentator described her as 'a far more considerable cultural figure'. In *Shadows of the East* (1855) she wrote of the hotel, 'Where we took tea, we bought some specimens of Maltese jewellery, mittens and lace'. Emma Roberts had also admired the mittens:

... the ingenuity of the inhabitants is displayed in several manufactures; the black lace mittens, now so fashionable, being particularly well made. Table-linen, also of superior quality, may be purchased, wrought in elegant patterns, and, if bespoken, with the coat-or-arms or crest worked into the centre or the corners.

A photograph of the Strada Reale taken in 1870 shows a sign which reads 'Dunsford's Clarence Hotel'; its location features in the Chapter 17 itinerary.

As for Madame Goubau, she seems to have reduced her ambitions, because in 1847 she ran a lodging house at 213 Strada San Paolo. The explanation is lost for why she left the Grand Clarence in the main street where everyone who was anyone stayed and, instead, looked after lodgers further away from the action. And what happened to her two lovely daughters?

Beverley's Hotel, where Anne Scott and her father, Sir Walter, stayed in 1831, as described in the previous chapter, had been run by the Beverley family since at least 1826 because **Anne Katherine Elwood** (née Curteis, 1796–1873) stayed there that year. Anne, traveller and writer, was the daughter of a scholar and Member of Parliament and, in 1824, married Major Charles Elwood of the East India Company. The following year she set out with him for India overland – quite an adventure then. She published her letters, written over the next three years as *Narrative of a Journey Overland from England to India* (1830); it was illustrated by them both.

Overland included Malta where, after 'roughing it' from Naples the Elwoods intended to stay a few days, but did so for three months at the 'very excellent' Beverley's Hotel (see Chapter 17 itinerary). Anne expressed 'how positively delightful to the poor weather-beaten wanderers appeared the clean apartments, the neatness and tidiness of everything around Malta'.

In 1827, released from quarantine, Sir Moses and Lady Montefiore stayed there, too, as did **Sarah Lushington** (née Gascoyne, 1790–1839). She had married Charles Lushington in 1805, and he, too, was of the East India Company; indeed, in 1828, the Lushingtons did the journey in the opposite direction from the Elwoods, Sarah writing *Narrative of a Journey from Calcutta to Europe by Way of Egypt in the years 1827 and 1828* (1829). You have to wonder if the two women communicated about their journeys; perhaps they were even vying with each other; even their titles reflected collusion. And Anne Elwood surely recommended Beverley's Hotel to the Lushingtons. Released from quarantine, having travelled from the east, Sarah noted, 'We repaired to Beverley's hotel, the superior accommodation of which, after the Bedouin life we had been leading for months past, and the confinement of the Lazaretto, was highly acceptable.' Glimpses of Mrs Beverley are rare but, while the Montefiores were in the Lazaretto, they were, as Thomas Freller tells us, 'showered with gifts and food, amongst them with "a box of books for our amusement sent by Lady Stoddart, a chest of oranges by Mr Mac Gill, and a plate of cakes by Mrs Beverly"'.

Lucinda Darby Griffith and her husband, as noted earlier in this chapter, chose another place to stay,

> at Madame Morelle's in the Strada Reale, where Captain Maxwell had engaged apartments for us. They were exceedingly comfortable, we had two bed-rooms and a handsome sitting-room, very nicely furnished, with three windows looking to the street, and an enclosed wooden veranda, furnished with windows, which might be shut or opened at pleasure.

Not everyone was so lucky with accommodation in Valletta, nor with their landlady. In 1834, as Thomas Freller quotes, George Waring had this experience:

We have changed our abode several times since we left the lazaret. We first went to the hotel from which we had been supplied with provisions, and then took lodgings for a week, engaging our quarantine servant to wait on us. Finding, however, that both he and our landlady were dishonest, we left our lodgings, and are now at another hotel, where we are very comfortably entertained; but we intend to move into the country shortly.

Who was the dishonest landlady? We should be told.

Finally, there was Mclelland's Hotel situated at 278 Strada Reale and originally called Bentley's Hotel, kept by **Mrs Bentley**. She was the wife of John Bentley, but when he died in 1845, his sister, **Mrs Mclelland**, took it over and, by 1847, it bore her name.

It is striking that so many of Valletta's hotels in the mid-nineteenth century were owned and run by women. Competition between them must have been fierce, and the responsibility and the work involved considerable, given a clientele who were used to comfort, and expected it when they travelled to somewhere like Malta. The hinted-at fate of Madame Goubau suggests how tough it was. An English maid greeted the Scotts when they arrived at Beverley's Hotel, and Lucinda Darby Griffith hired a lady's maid, Vicenza, at Madame Morelle's. But whether or not it was common for women, Maltese or British, to be employed in the hotels is unclear.

Opera singers as working women, of which there were several in the nineteenth century, will appear in the Chapter 17 itinerary (Manoel Theatre).

Perhaps the woman who best sums up a marriage of travel, education, work and the louchness of the pre-Victorian era, as well as adding a touch of glamour, is Miss Hamilton, a friend of the Whitmores who featured in the last chapter. George Whitmore creates a wonderful image of her, though without, unfortunately, background details such as a first name. She must have flourished before 1829 when the Whitmores left Malta. He wrote:

Miss H was of that age which permitted her to follow her inclination for foreign travel without scandal or impediment. She joined our Malta circle with a young black-eyed Sicilian boy, whom she meant to instruct alleging in excuse for such a freak that it was more rational to make a pet of a human creature than of a dog, parrot or cat. She therefore procured masters for her protégé and held him in a sort of intermediate state between page and dependent relative. She was of course very much quizzed for this proceeding but bore it without flinching. For some time the adopted was sufficiently docile and pliant, but his parents, instigated by the priests, began to trouble Miss Hamilton with insinuations that her aim was to convert the boy to Protestantism, while the youth himself – as he grew in age – instead of responding gratefully to her solicitude threw off restraint, disclaimed a female government and became too mannish for a pet, so that his patroness judged it best to transfer him to his natural protectors and packed him off to Sicily.

Miss Hamilton was a clever strong-minded woman possessing of fortune's gifts a sufficiency to enable her to follow her bent and think little of the singularity and isolation of her position; after moving about for a year or two she again established herself in Malta and by way of amusement undertook the management of a dairy, the produce of which she sold.

11 – Women and Good Works 1819–1933

Religious Institutions

Women with few other outlets could find opportunities to raise their status and even express themselves in giving to the Church. While the Church guided most Maltese women at home looking after their families, or who had to earn their living, and religion was no doubt a solace in time of poverty, family upheaval, ill health and death, some women took their faith a step further. They looked at the troubles of others and were inspired to act. In earlier centuries, religious communities had been set up by male clerics or the Knights. By the nineteenth century, women took the initiative. At the same time, and as in earlier years, some women with money used it philanthropically. Not all the women in this chapter are Maltese, but the religious institutions they founded, or of which they were an important part, became part of Malta's fabric.

Madalena Cornelio (d.1814) was the daughter of **Diana Cornelio** (*c*.1719–1799) who, as a widow aged over 80, had been caught up in the bombardment of Senglea in April 1799, during the French occupation. Taking refuge, with many other women, in a nearby church, she had an apoplectic fit and died. In 1794 Madalena and her husband Nicolà Dingli – a rich, childless couple – drew up a will leaving their large house on the water's edge in Senglea, which Madalena had inherited from her parents, to be converted, on their deaths, into a home for six aged relatives who had no one to care for them. They also set up a trust that would pay for the conversion and the running costs. Madalena, by then widowed, died in 1814 and, by 1817, when the *Ospizio* Sant'Anna was inaugurated, it was a home for six aged or disabled women from Senglea or Siġġiewi more generally. Built within it was the chapel of Sant' Anna.

For over 80 years, from 1880, the *Ospizio* was run by the tertiary Franciscan Sisters of the Sacred Heart. In 1980, it was demolished. The new Dar Sant'Anna on Cornelio Dingli Street was inaugurated in 1987. It now looks after 30 local women and men pensioners.

Maria Teresa Pisani (later Sister Maria Adeodata, 1806–1855) could have had an easy life in Malta as the Baronessina di Frigenuini. She was born in Naples to Neapolitan **Vicenza Carrano** and Maltese Benedetto Pisano Mompalao Cuzkeri, Baron of Frigenuini, their only child. Maria Teresa's father took to drink; when his daughter was very young, his wife left him and entrusted her to his mother, **Elizabeth Mamo Mompalao**, who lived in Naples. Elizabeth died when her granddaughter was only ten. She was then sent to a famous boarding school in Naples where the daughters of the *gente per bene* went. There she stayed until she was 17.

In 1821, the Baron was involved in the uprising in Naples and sentenced to death but, as he was a Maltese Baron, he was a British citizen, so his sentence was suspended, and he was deported to Malta. In 1825, his wife and daughter were forced to follow him but, because of his dissolute life in Rabat, they did not live with him. Maria Teresa refused all the proposals of marriage her mother arranged for her, instead attending church and helping the poor she met in the streets. When she felt the calling to become a nun, her parents joined in opposing her, her mother demanding that she wait a year before making a final decision.

On 16 July 1828 Maria Teresa joined the Benedictine community in St Peter's nunnery in Mdina (see Chapter 20 itinerary). She formally became a nun in 1830 and took the name Sister Maria Adeodata. The Notarial Act of Renouncement included the renouncing of her title and the fortune she had inherited from her paternal grandmother, though she first paid off her father's considerable debts, provided for her mother and set up a foundation to enable poor girls to become nuns and to provide charity to several people who sought her help.

17.   Sister Maria Adeodata, from Abela, *Grace and Glory*

Sister Maria Adeodata spent the next 25 years as a cloistered nun at St Peter's performing acts of charity and leading a 'saintly life'. She was elected Abbess in 1851 but had trouble trying to make changes so that the nuns led a life more relevant to their calling, one for which she had for years set an example. It did not make her popular and by 1853 she was no longer Abbess.

Her life at St Peter's – the sacrifices she made, the tasks and functions she willingly performed over the years – is well described in Mario Buhagiar and Stanley Fiorini's *Mdina* (1996).

When the 'holy nun' died in 1855, aged only 49, such pressure came from the community to declare her Venerable that the Church started to investigate her life. In 1898, the Pope declared her Venerable, and she was declared Blessed in 2001. Her feast is celebrated on 25 February, the day of her death, and she is buried in the nunnery's crypt. Maria Adeodata Pisani Maltese stamps were issued in 1991 and 2001.

It was not only in the noble families of Malta that behaviour was somewhat lax. King William IV of England had ten children by the popular actress Dorothea Jordan before he was hauled into line to provide for the succession and, in 1818, before he was even heir presumptive to the throne, married the obscure German princess, **Adelaide of Saxe-Meiningen** (1792–1849). She was 26; he was 27 years older.

Adelaide was a pious woman, perhaps a bit prim for the English court, but she improved William's behaviour: he drank and swore less and became more tactful, though he was to treat their coronation in 1831 as a charade. His queen was much loved by the British people for her modesty, charity and tragic childbirth history. She had at least six attempts to produce an heir – two children died soon after birth, twins were stillborn, and she had two miscarriages. As a result, Queen Victoria came to the throne when Adelaide's husband died in 1837.

Adelaide, too, was desperately ill that year so, late in 1838, in the hopes of regaining her health, the Queen Dowager travelled to Malta and stayed there from 1 December to 1 April 1839. She was the first member of the British Royal Family to visit; many were to do so in the years that followed, some living there for a while, as the itineraries show.

The Chief Secretary of Malta, Hector Greig, kept a record of her visit, published in 1963 as *An Unpublished Diary of Queen Adelaide's Visit to Malta in 1838* (ed. Joseph Galea). He noted of her arrival, in a scene reminiscent of the Grand Master's entry into Mdina all those centuries ago:

On the morning all was bustle; little or no business was done; everybody was devising the best means, and seeking the most advantageous post, to get a sight of her Majesty as she landed or as she passed; the note of preparation for a general illumination was heard in all quarters; and quickly was erected, by subscription among the Maltese, a triumphal arch across the *Strada Reale*, in a line contiguous with the arcades of the *Piazza della Tesoreria*; while the country people were flocking towards the city in hundreds.

The 77th Regiment, by half past one, had already taken up its ground on the quay below the Calcara Gate, and extended its files up to the gate, whence the road was lined by the Royal Marines, which landed from the ships of war, and the 47th and 59th Regiments up to the *Porta Reale*. The Royal Malta Fencible Regiment was extended along *Strada Reale*, and the

92nd Highlanders formed the guard of honour in the *Piazza San Giorgio* in front of the Palace. ...

... The windows and terraces of every building and every bastion were dense with heads, and anxious expectation was expressed in every countenance; the water covered with boats and the shore with people. ...

... Between two lines of boats from the ships, stationary and extending from ship to shore, a barge in which the Queen and the ladies of her suite sat, with a silken royal standard in the stern. ... was seen to advance majestically.

... The inhabitants of Floriana, placed six young girls within the works at the Calcara Gate to welcome the Queen: they were dressed in white garlands of flowers.

Her Majesty was graciously pleased to stop her carriage upon seeing them, and condescended to receive a bouquet and a basket of flowers, as a simple and kind manner.

The charity the Queen practised in her adopted country extended to Malta: Chapter 10 mentioned the setting up of the Watsons' Infant School; Chapter 9 noted that there was no Anglican church in the islands where there were some 2,000 British civilians. Adelaide immediately resolved to do something about it. In *Queen Adelaide's Church, Valletta* (2000) Alan Keighley quotes a letter from her to her niece Queen Victoria as early as 13 December 1838 asking her to put her mind to the matter, and talk it over with her Ministers. On 9 January 1839, Hector Greig noted:

The Governor has announced to Her Majesty's Government the gracious intention of the Queen Dowager to erect, at her sole expense, a church for the use of the Protestant population of this island.

By the express desire of the Queen, the church is with great appropriateness, to be dedicated to Saint Paul from whom was first derived to this island the light of gospel-truth.

This proposal was not mere words: on 20 March Greig noted,

At 2 o'clock Her Majesty the Queen Dowager lays the foundation stone of the Protestant Church. The site was at *Strada Ponente*, Valletta, on the grounds formerly occupied by the *Auberge d'Allemagne*. The Queen, accompanied by the Governor and the Admiral, proceeded to the excavation, the Protestant clergy and the members of the committee leading the way.

St Paul's Anglican Cathedral was consecrated on 1 November 1844 with Queen Adelaide's banner hanging above the choir stalls. The original estimate of its cost was £8,000; in the end it cost £20,000, all of which was met by the Queen, but it did mean that nothing was left in the fund for maintenance. It now dominates Independence Square (see Chapter 17

18.   St Paul's Church by Eliza Gardner, from *A Series of Views in Malta*, courtesy of
Yale Center for British Art Paul Mellon Collection (file no. 2038523-0004)

itinerary). The *Auberge d'Allemagne*, home of Chief Justice John Stoddart, had been demolished to make way for the new cathedral.

It is a wonder that Queen Adelaide had any time to recuperate, as she stayed at the Governor's Palace in the centre of Valletta and was displayed in one way or another nearly every day. Some of her visits to such places as Bormla (Cospicua), opera at the Manoel Theatre, Girgenti (the former Inquisitor's Palace, by then the residence of the Secretary to the Government), and the Union Club (now the Archaeological Museum) appear in the itineraries, as does her day on Gozo just before she left. But she also visited the Manoel Theatre charitably. On 5 February, she went to a recital there, 'a *soiree* given for the benefit of Camilla Darbois, the celebrated soprano' whose time in Malta also appears in the Valletta itinerary (Chapter 17). And the following day,

> At the Theatre at 8 p.m. Morton's much admired comedy 'A Cure for the Heartache' was performed by the 'Gentlemen Amateurs' under the patronage of the Queen, for the benefit of the Ladies' Charitable Society for clothing the poor.

She had already visited the *Ospizio* for 'the maintenance of the aged poor', and the House of Industry at Floriana which Lady Hastings had set up (see Chapter 9).

She wrote to a friend on 12 February:

... I have been in much better health since I have left England & hope to benefit by my spending a winter in a Southern climate, but my cough is still troublesome at times & will I am sure not leave me a pain tho' it may in time be mitigated. We are all much pleased with Malta and like our residence here very much. The weather has been beautiful most of the time we have been absent from home & we have enjoyed it much. I have seen many things which interest me much and shall always remember with pleasure my voyage & sojourn in this pretty little Island full of historical recollection.

After Queen Adelaide's happy visit, British visitors flocked to Malta more than ever which, for an island with economic difficulties, was probably a boon. As for the church which was there for them to attend, it was, on occasion, a bone of contention. Alan Keighley quotes an 1856 newspaper report:

On Thursday last, eleven Maltese of the lower order were brought before the Magistrate, Dr. Ceci for committing a breach of the peace on the previous day. It appears that a marriage took place in Queen Adelaide's Church between an English mechanic, employed in Mr Jackson's new steam bakery, and a Maltese widow who keeps a slop [cheap clothing] shop in Strada San Paolo. The fact of a Roman Catholic being married in a Protestant Church, added to her imitation of English costume, by wearing a bonnet, seemed to excite the ire of the canaille, who accordingly mobbed and insulted the bridal party, by hooting and screeching, as they were quietly proceeding towards their home. The mob consisted of two or three hundred persons of the lowest rabble and the uproar was carried to such a pitch that the interference of a large body of the Police became necessary ... The charge was fully proved against ten of the accused who were fined ten shillings each.

The couple in question were **Maria Carmela Borg** (née Mamo) a widow, and Robert Turner from Kirkside near Leeds, widower.

In 1842, the woman who was to become St Emilie de Vialar was, as St Paul is said to have been nearly two millennia earlier, shipwrecked on Malta. **Emilie de Vialar** (1797–1856) was born into an aristocratic family, the only daughter of three children, in Gaillac, near Toulouse. Her mother, Antoinette, was the daughter of Baron de Portal, a physician raised to the nobility by Louis XVI; her father was Augustine de Vialar. Because of the anti-clerical feeling generated by the French Revolution, Emilie was baptised in secret and taught religion by her pious mother. By the age of seven, she was at the local school but, in 1810, when she was 13, her mother took her to Paris, where her family lived, to be educated. Antoinette, weakened by the birth of her last child, died there that year. Emilie spent two years boarding in a convent in Paris, but then was called home by her widowed father to look after the household. She did so for the next 20 years, refusing to marry, indeed, taking a vow of celibacy, engaged in charitable works, particularly among children neglected by their parents, and arguing with her father about her wish to enter the religious life.

Thirty-five-year-old Emilie's chance to break free came when, in 1832, her maternal grandfather died leaving her and her brothers a considerable fortune. With her share, she bought a large house in Gaillac and moved in with three friends. Eight other women joined a few months later and the local abbé clothed them in religious habits. They made their vows in 1835 and thus was formed the Congregation of the Sisters of St Joseph of the Apparition, with a constitution drawn up by Mother Emilie. They were committed to caring for the sick, at home, in hospital, and in prison, and the education of children.

Meanwhile, Emilie's brother Augustine had moved to Algeria, colonised by the French in 1830, bought properties in Algiers and built a hospital to care for the sick in a country where malaria was prevalent. He begged his sister to come out and help him. Soon after, a cholera epidemic broke out and Emilie and her Sisters proved their full worth. Over the next eight years, Emilie, travelling back and forth to Algeria, set up several Congregations of the Sisters of St Joseph there, as well as one in Tunisia and another in Rome. But she fell out with the Bishop of Algiers who expelled her, causing her great financial loss. It was on this journey from Algiers to France that a storm drove her ship onto Malta.

Most sources leave out Emilie's time in Malta but she is said, with her Sisters, to have stayed in St George's Street, Birgu (Vittoriosa) where they were lent more than one house, one of which may have been Palazzo Bettina (see Chapter 18 itinerary). Bettina had been dead since 1829 but, as the house came to be known as Cardinal's house, it had obviously been left to the son of her sister **Lucretsia Sceberras Testaferrata**, the first and only Maltese Cardinal.

While in Malta, Emilie declared she had received a sign from God to found a congregation there, and opened a school in Birgu; soon after, the Sisters of St Joseph were called to take care of the *Conservatorio* in Cospicua. In the years that followed, the Congregation branched out. In 2006, St Joseph Junior School, Sliema, with its 350 girls, celebrated 150 years since the death of their founder, and the 125th anniversary of the founding of the school, with the performance of a specially written musical that incorporated Emilie's values and virtues entitled *Emilie: Angel of Gaillac*. It encapsulated the altruism of an 'angel' towards the poverty stricken people of her village struggling to survive in the aftermath of the French Revolution. The Congregation also runs schools in Blata-l-Bajda and Paola, an orphanage in Żabbar, the Provincial House in Gżira, and the House for Elderly Nuns and the Retreat House in Rabat.

It is not clear how long Emilie herself stayed in Malta, but while she was there she was approached to found a congregation in Burma. By the time she died, after overcoming many vicissitudes, including bankruptcy, there were 42 of them, not only in Europe and Africa, but also in the Middle East, the Far East and Australia. She died aged 59 in Marseilles; was venerated by the

Pope in 1935, beatified in 1939, and canonised in 1951. The Sister Emilie de Vialar Maltese stamp was issued in 1997.

Adelaide Cini (1839–1885) was the youngest of the 13 children of a rich pasta factory owner of Hamrun; the names of her parents elude me. She is described, in internet sources, as 'thin and weak' when, barely 18 years old, she knocked on the door of St Catherine's nunnery, Strada Reale, Valletta (see Chapter 17 itinerary) and asked Sister Giuseppa Baldachino to accept her as a postulant nun. Although Sister Giuseppa was convinced of Adelaide's religious conviction, she suspected that the initiative had come about as a result of her parents' opposition to a marriage proposal she had received. She advised the unhappy girl to go home and wait to learn what God wanted of her.

Some time later, Adelaide met by chance a young Sicilian prostitute who, the sources say, 'was becoming known for her activities among the more affluent sectors of society'. They became so friendly that Adelaide managed to persuade the young woman to live at the family home. What her parents made of this, history does not reveal but, under Adelaide's guidance, their guest gave up her past life, and the experience alerted Adelaide to where her calling lay.

With the financial backing of Angelica Aspen and her husband John, Adelaide opened the first home for unmarried mothers and, when her father died, she turned the pasta factory into a *Conservatorio* for 'more needy girls' or, less euphemistically, 'women and children who were living off prostitution or who had a criminal record'. Towards the end of the nineteenth century, it was run by the Sisters of Charity of St Jeanne Antide who had been brought to Malta by the civil authorities in 1868 to take over a badly run girls' orphanage in Merchant Street. The Sisters were to run too many institutions in the ensuing years to list, though Sandra Scicluna and Paul Knepper do note in their article on historical criminology that in 1871 they were also 'invited to manage women prisoners'. Their involvement in the *Cini Conservatorio* may have begun after 1885; Adelaide died that year, aged only 46. The Pope declared her venerable in 1910.

In 1939, when war was looming, an emergency maternity hospital was opened in the newly constructed wing of the Adelaide Cini Orphanage, increasing the number of maternity beds from 16 in the Central Hospital to 100 in the Cini. In 1941, it accounted for 14 per cent of Malta's deliveries.

Today, the Dar Qalb ta' Gesu refuge for victims of domestic violence in Santa Venera is better known locally as l-Institut ta' Cini. There, women and children can find shelter in a flatlet for 18 months while they get back on their feet; they are taught skills to enable them to lead an independent life, and encouraged to follow a therapeutic programme to help them get over the abuse and regain self-esteem.

What is striking about this centre is its ability to involve international firms to support it, and not just financially: staff members give up their time, for example, to redecorate the accommodation; another firm has established a digital library so that the children can learn, and their mothers with them.

I particularly like the photograph of an ambassador handing over a sofa 'for the comfort of the residents'. An example of traditional fundraising was the Domestic Violence Theatre Project's *Pretty Lisa*, held at the Manoel Theatre in 2013. An Adelaide Cini stamp was issued in 2007.

The Anglicans were not the only Protestant community to lack their own satisfactory place of worship in Malta. The Presbyterians were without a Church of Scotland. In 1854, a couple arrived who were not only to put that right but also to celebrate their golden wedding anniversary in Malta in 1905.

Jessie Tod Wisely (née Millar, 1827–1910) was a member of the Tod family, active in Scottish temperance; another member was Isabella Tod, campaigner for women's rights. Jessie was also the sister of Dr Millar, Wesleyan Minister at Leghorn (Livorno). There, in 1854, she married the recently ordained George Wisely who had worked in very poor areas of Glasgow and Edinburgh and had teetotal shipping connections. They travelled that year to Malta where George took up his post as Minister of the Free Church of Scotland. Their Scottish connections, and the fact that the Governor was Scottish, facilitated the securing of a site and fundraising from such quarters as the Scottish Temperance League. The new church, built according to their specifications, was completed by 1857, and it is clear that it was a joint husband and wife venture, for her name is with his on the plaque still on the outside of the church in South Street (see Chapter 17 itinerary).

George was an evangelical who expended considerable energy in attempting to convert not only Roman Catholics, but also Muslims and Jews. In 'British Temperance Reformers and the Island of Malta 1815–1914' (1987), ND Denny notes that he had 'several well-educated and under-employed expatriate ladies who translated tract material into both Italian and Maltese'. It is unlikely that they included Jessie, though she seems to have spoken Italian if an incident that suggests her independence and spirit is anything to go by.

In 1864, Giuseppe Garibaldi, hero of the Italian *Risorgimento*, arrived for a very brief visit at the end of April, staying at 184 Strada Santa Lucia, the Imperial Hotel (later St James's Hotel, destroyed by enemy action in the Second World War). The address of welcome, with 190 signatures, was presented by **Baroness Angelica Testaferrata Abela**, daughter of **Elizabeth Mifsud** and Giacinto Tagliaferro and, since 1850, wife of Baron Augusto Testaferrata Abela. Angelica's espousal so publicly of Garibaldi's cause can be considered as the first political involvement by a Maltese woman. Jessie Wisely was among those who called upon Garibaldi. At least six other British women did so, not all of them accompanying their husbands, and three Maltese or Italian women.

An article in *The Tablet* of 23 April, from their Rome correspondent, gives an idea of how brave, or foolhardy, Angelica, Jessie and the other women were, as well as suggesting the complications of Italian politics and how they related to the Maltese, and British residents in Malta:

19. Baroness Angelica Testaferrata Abela,
from de Piro, *Costume in Malta*

Our island [Malta] has been this year dishonoured during the sacred days of Holy Week, by the presence of the great enemy of the Church and the Papacy, the prime instrument of the Italian Revolution, and the chief of that band of adventurers who, in these latter times, have exhausted every description of crime, Giuseppe Garibaldi. ...

...

... There was no lack of hisses and howls, when at a certain hour visitors arrived at the Hotel. These, for the most part, were composed of English residents, a few soldiers and sailors, the Italian Committee, and a few Maltese. ...

... About half a dozen Maltese ladies were also conducted by their husbands and the Times has been indiscreet enough to gibbet their names. ...

...

... The Garibaldians, encouraged by the support of the English in the hotel, without which they would not have dared attempt it, sought to get up a demonstration to their hero.

The report suggests that no one would hire Garibaldi a carriage for his departure so 'finally, an English family lent their private carriage for the purpose'. This is said to have been that of Admiral Superintendent of the Dockyard Horatio Austin, former arctic explorer, who had only been in Malta since the previous year, and his wife, since 1831, **Eliza Rawlinson Austin** (née Hawkins) and their daughter.

Among those publications that reported Garibaldi's visit was *Il Portafoglio Maltese*, an Italian-language weekly. Its political slant varied over the years but in 1861 it was bought by Salvatore Debono. Its relevance is that when he died, his wife Vincenza Debono took over the running of the paper. As Henry Frendo notes in *Mic-Censura ghal-Plurizmu: Il-Gurnalizmu f'Malta 1798–2002* (2003), it would be nearly a century before another woman was in that position in Malta (Chapter 14).

The Wiselys' other contributions to Malta drew on their commitment to temperance; their work took them particularly among soldiers and sailors. Very soon after their arrival they set up a Soldiers and Sailors Home, 'the first outside the United Kingdom'. And in 1860 they established a special Soldiers' Institute and Temperance Hall 'as a counterattraction to Malta's cheap wines and spirits ...'. Their hospital for merchant seamen is now the Boffa Cancer Hospital. They also set up several schools for poor children. George retired as Minister in 1896, but continued to live in Malta until 1914; Jessie died there in 1910 and is buried in the Ta' Braxia Cemetery (see Chapter 19 itinerary). Their two sons, both born in Malta, were killed in the First World War.

Anna Bugeja (Anetta, née Darbois, later Marquesa Bugeja, c.1829–1916) was the daughter of the French opera singer Camilla Darbois to whose benefit *soirée* Queen Adelaide gave her patronage in 1839. Anna seems to have been born the year of her mother's Maltese debut a decade earlier, the year of her father Filippo Darbois' death. In 1835, Camilla was to sing the role of Lodoviska in the opera of the same name by the Maltese composer Vincenzo Bugeja, not to be confused with her future son-in-law.

Anna married Vincenzo Bugeja, known as the philanthropist, in 1851. Although only 31, he was very rich, his wealth mostly gained from gambling in Monte Carlo; indeed, he built the Casino Maltese in the Strada Reale as a gambling Casino. In 1876 he was made a Commander of the Distinguished Order of St Michael and St George (CMG) when the Prince of Wales, later Edward VII, passed through Malta and, in 1887, the Pope created him Marchese Bugeja. But he and Anna had already turned to philanthropy. In 1867, during the cholera epidemic, they had given over their country house at Naxxar as a hospital for hundreds of victims and, in 1880, they built the *Conservatorio* Vincenzo Bugeja in Hamrun. It was to provide a home for at least 50 girls between the ages of five and ten, preferably from 'good families' who had fallen on hard times. The aim was to turn them into good wives and mothers, and it was another of the institutions to be run under the wing of the Sisters of Charity of St Jeanne Antide.

Although the *Conservatorio*, or Institute as it is now called, had some financial difficulties over the years and today is supported and run under the auspices of the Department of Social and Family Welfare, it has considerably widened its scope and ideology, providing residential care for 20 adolescent girls aged between 13 and 18, with psychological, emotional, behavioural and/or social difficulties. They are helped under two therapeutic programmes, Dar Jeanne Antide and Dar Frejda, run by trained social workers, female carers and a psychologist. Their academic education is not neglected and those who are about to marry are provided with a dowry.

Vicenzo died in 1890 and the widowed Marchesa Anna continued their good works. Down the road from the Institute named after her husband is the Bugeja Technical Institute for boys which she opened in 1903. At the same time she noted that St Paul's Bay lacked a church big enough for the needs of the residents, so she asked the Holy See to build one. On 28 September 1904, a deed of donation was signed by Anna, and a new church dedicated to Our Lady of Sorrows was given to the Franciscan Conventuals.

Anna and Vincenzo's tombs are in the Institute's chapel, the foundations for which were laid in 1876, and their portraits hang in one of the boardrooms. You cannot miss the grand building on your right as you drive through Santa Venera from Valletta to Attard or Mdina (see Chapter 20 itinerary).

The poor girls from good families may have been educated to be good wives and mothers at the *Conservatorio* Vincenzo Bugeja, but **Carolina Cauchi** (1824–1907), was an only child born into a family that did not lack means, and she had other ideas. Her mother, **Teresa Gallea Cauchi**, was from Senglea, her father, Nicolo Cauchi, was a Gozitan notary. Although Carolina was born in Senglea, because her father's work took him so often to Gozo, he transferred his family to Rabat (later Victoria) there, to the area of San Gorg tal-Hagar, and Carolina was baptised in its parish church. She was sent to school, though it is not clear if this was on Gozo and, if it was, which school it might have been. When the Austin/Lewis Commission arrived in 1836, there was only one school on Gozo. In any case, Carolina learnt Italian and was conversant with Latin.

As she grew up, it became increasingly clear to Carolina that she wished to devote her life to God. She attempted, unsuccessfully, to join the contemplative Dominican Order in Italy. It was not until 1889, when she was 65, that, together with nine other women, she founded her own contemplative Dominican Congregation on Gozo, where she funded the building of its first nunnery on her own property adjoining the Church of Our Lady of Pompei. She did not live there but often visited. She had a holiday house at Xlendi and, during the summer, she invited the nuns there. They could swim in private in what is now called Caroline's Cave. The Cauchi funds also built the chapel dedicated to Our Lady of Mount Carmel on the Xlendi Road, as well as setting up a bursary for poor seminarians (see Chapter 23 itinerary).

Carolina died in 1907, aged 83. On the centenary of her death, a bronze bust of her was unveiled in the Pompei Sanctuary. Today there are around 150 nuns belonging to the Congregation she founded scattered in various houses in Gozo, Malta, Italy, England, Pakistan, Australia and Sri Lanka.

Maria Teresa Nuzzo was introduced in Chapter 10 where, aged 16 in 1867, she took over the family school when her aunt became blind. She had other family commitments, particularly an aging, ailing father so, although she felt the desire to embrace religious life, she postponed it. When she was 21, she considered taking private vows of poverty, chastity and obedience as a lay person; she did so in 1874. Two years later, when she was 25, her father died. Once again, she felt the urge to enter a nunnery. In 1880, her spiritual director told her, according to her Wikipedia entry, 'You are not suited for the cloister'. With this advice, she continued to run the school and undertake after-hours pastoral care of children in the parishes round about.

Her mother, **Louisa Morrochi Nuzzo**, died in 1881; her elder brother had died earlier in a cholera outbreak. Maria Teresa was now more ambitious: she began to hope she might set up a religious congregation dedicated to education and social work. Although she did not have the necessary financial means, her cousin Enrico Nuzzo had similar dreams: to use his money to help educate the poor, particularly girls. In 1902, building started on a plot with a house near Tas-Samra, Hamrun. Maria Teresa moved into the Nuzzo Institute in 1903, aged 53; the same year she obtained official sanction from the Archbishop to set up the Congregation of the Daughters of the Sacred Heart. In 1907, another house was opened at Żejtun and, through the generosity of the Marchesa Anna Bugeja, the Congregation acquired another at Marsa.

Following Mother Maria Teresa's death in 1923, at the age of 71, houses were set up in Żurrieq, Mellieħa and Rabat. Outside Malta, the Congregation spread to India, Italy, Kenya and Libya. Today, it has two kindergartens, in Hamrun and Żejtun, a primary school at Marsa, a children's home in Żurrieq, and day centres for children at Żejtun and Mellieħa. The Nuzzo Institute still operates in Hamrun.

Because I was brought up in Kenya, I noted particularly a group of five Maltese student volunteers about to set out for the village of Ruiru, near Nairobi, to spend three weeks helping in the Congregation's mission school there, as well as at the local orphanage; the school compound is also a feeding centre 'for people of the streets'.

Even in the second half of the nineteenth century, a family of means, particularly if they were culturally Italian, educated their children in Italy. What may have been a little rarer was the decision of **Fortunata Pace Mifsud** (d.1881) and her husband Dr Pasquale Mifsud of Mdina to send four of their daughters away to school there. They had at least six daughters, **Censina, Nina, Giorgina, Teresa, Elena** and **Maria**, and five sons. The school the couple chose was St Orofrio in Rome, set up by the Sisters of St Dorothy, a congregation founded in Rome by Genoa-born **Paula Frassinetti** (later St Paula, 1809–1882).

In 1877, one of the Mifsud daughters, Maria, fell ill at school. Dr Pasquale hastened to Rome and prepared to take Maria back to Malta, but she was so distressed at leaving the care of the Dorothean Sisters that two of them accompanied her home and looked after her until her death a month later.

When the revolution in Portugal occurred in 1910, the Sisters of St Dorothy had to leave there. Fortunata and Pasquale's son, Mgr Alfredo Mifsud, arranged for some of them to move to Malta and, in 1911, three of them did so. On his death, he bequeathed Casa Mifsud to them as their final nunnery, and there they have flourished and branched out, establishing several schools in Malta.

In 1911, the Zammit Clapp Hospital was opened on the border of Sliema and St Julians, overlooking the Marsamxett Habour. **Emilia Zammit Clapp**

(1842–1917) and her sister **Maria Zammit** were the daughters of **Carmela Zammit** (née Livori) and Emmanuele Zammit. In 1907, Emilia's husband, American businessman Henry Lyman Clapp, died. In his memory, the sisters realised the family's dream of endowing a hospital, initially for the care of seamen. Though their deed of donation was in favour of the government, it was on condition that the hospital was run exclusively, and in perpetuity, by the Nursing Sisters of the Little Company of Mary, traditionally known as the Blue Sisters.

The Blue Sisters had been founded in England by **Mary Potter** (1847–1913) in 1877, and members arrived in Malta in 1894. Preparation for their arrival had been made by the benefactor **Agnese Schembri** (1841–1918) who organised various fund-raising events and was secretary of the committee for the establishment of the Order in Malta. She was also a supporter of the *Conservatorio* Cini. Another member of the preparatory committee was **Ursola Agius Caruana De Piro** (1848–1937) whose son's ventures close this chapter.

Mons Guzeppi De Piro: Founder of the Missionary Society of St Paul (1988), by Alexander Bonnici, translated by Monica de Piro, niece of the subject, shows how good intentions can go wrong. In a way it is related to the story of **Giuseppina Curmi** (1844–1931). She was the daughter of the mayor of Żejtun, Paolo Curmi, member of a family long established in the area. In 1930, at a time of international financial depression, she established the Congregation of the Little Sisters of Jesus of Nazareth, which ran an orphanage which was to house as many as 200 orphans in the difficult years that followed the Second World War. On Maria Giuseppina's death in 1930, her work was continued by Mgr De Piro, priest and missionary, who had acted as her spiritual adviser and trusted friend for many years.

Mgr Joseph De Piro is best known for his founding of the Society of St Paul, but he was involved in many other religious and philanthropical projects to do with the poor in Malta and abroad, sometimes assisted by his mother Ursola De Piro. One of his particular concerns was the needs of poor, unemployed girls so, in 1928, he opened the Laboratory for Needy Girls in rented rooms in St Dominic's and St Christopher Streets, Valletta, and 'placed his endeavours under the protection of the Sacred Heart of Jesus'. Alexander Bonnici quotes what de Piro hoped to achieve:

> The purpose of the Laboratory is to offer help to unemployed girls, especially those who, on leaving the shelter of the various charitable Institutes entrusted to me, will thus be able to find a suitable means of livelihood.

Maria Assunta Borg (née Fabri), a woman of means separated from her husband, offered not only financial support but also to work in the Laboratory, and to live in.

Things started well enough: 'Mgr De Piro was in charge of the Administration and Director of the Laboratory and Maria Assunta generously offered a sum of money and accepted to teach the girls.' From 1928 to 1930, the girls not only learnt useful skills, such as dressmaking, but also received 'moral assistance'. But then Maria Assunta wanted to 'take in girls who had been abused and who had a shady reputation'. That was not De Piro's aim. Maria Assunta lived in, she felt in charge. In November 1930, De Piro suggested she leave and take up residence in Hamrun. Three months later, she confronted him. In all his years directing five institutes he had never faced such a situation; 'he told Borg that if she did not feel she could carry on collaborating peacefully, he was prepared to replace her'.

In March, Maria Assunta went to the Archbishop, who said he would talk to De Piro. His reaction was an attempt to dismiss her. The saga rumbled on; 'There was one opening left to her according to the Bishop's advice, she might start another charitable organisation under the direction of another responsible person.' De Piro closed down the Laboratory; Maria Assunta 'did not start anything on her own initiative, but offered to help the Sisters who were dedicated to social services'. Was it a simple clash of personalities, or was Mgr De Piro, who was so used to running several organisations, unable to cope with a woman of independent ideas who stood up to him and for herself? Or did Maria Assunta assume that because she held the purse strings, she could call the shots? Perhaps a bit of both.

It was at this stage, on the death of Maria Giuseppina Curmi in 1931, that De Piro took over her work. But he died in September 1933, so neither he nor Giuseppina lived to see the day of her Congregation's formal approval by the Church in October. Today, her Congregation is able to be eminently flexible. Part of the Jesus of Nazareth nunnery, as reported in the *Malta Independent* in 2010, was being converted to accommodate eight independent elderly women. This was to give them the chance to spend the day in their own home and, at 5.00 pm, to make their way to the shelter where they would have the opportunity to socialise and spend the night. According to the initiator of the idea, Mother Superior, **Sister Helen Delicata,**

It was the wish of their founder, Maria Giuseppina Curmi ... to make it part of their mission to look after the children and the elderly, to help in the societal problems of the time. When the number of orphans they looked after began to decrease ... they assessed the situation to see where their help was most needed.

A positive conclusion seems to emerge from this chapter. Women in earlier centuries may not always have entered nunneries of their own volition and, therefore, may not necessarily have had an interest in their running, nor their aims. But the women who entered the nineteenth-century ones founded by a woman probably felt, and feel still, more engaged and fulfilled.

12 – Women and Medicine 1846–1909

Malta acquired the soubriquet 'Nurse of the Mediterranean' as early as the Crimean War of 1853–56. Lying as it did on the way from Britain and France to the Black Sea, it acted as a staging post for troops, the women who followed them, materiel, provisions and horses and the wounded and sick. Strange, then, that nursing as a respectable and trained profession for women came so late to Malta as, indeed, elsewhere. Even nuns as nurses of men, particularly the Sisters of Charity, postdate that time. But, in November 1846, a woman doctor arrived in Malta as Principal Medical Officer, and it was not her gender that caused trouble, but her personality and demands for reform.

Dr James Barry

Dr James Miranda Barry (c.1795-1865) arrived in Malta as a male doctor, as the only way she could; indeed, she had been James Barry from the time of her training, and her sex was not to be revealed until her death. She was awarded her MD from Edinburgh in 1812, aged 17 – though there is some dispute about the date of her birth which is given variously as 1789, 1792, 1795 and 1799; I have plumped for 1795. She was, therefore, not only extremely precocious but, technically, the first woman in Britain to qualify as a doctor – years ahead of Elizabeth Garret Anderson, the answer usually required in quizzes; but that was not until 1865, the year of Dr Barry's death.

She was probably born Margaret to Mrs Mary Ann Bulkley or Bulkeley, sister of the well-connected artist James Barry. Her paternity has remained in doubt: her mother was married to Bulkley but also intimate with the Venezuelan general Francisco de Miranda, from whom Margaret took her second name, and David Stuart Erskine, 11th Earl of Buchan, friend of the feminist Mary Wollstonecraft. The transformation from Margaret to James, and the part played in that, and her medical training in Edinburgh, by these two men is sympathetically and convincingly captured in Patricia Duncker's novel *James Miranda Barry* (2000). Parts of the novel are in the first person; the James Barry below is her uncle:

> James Barry stared at me. He said nothing, but puffed convulsively at his cigar. His shirt was no longer clean.
> 'Listen, soldier,' said Francisco, 'would you like to study properly? At a University?'
> 'Yes,' I whispered, suddenly feeling sick and shivery.
> 'Well, that is what you're going to do. There's just one thing that you'll have to remember from now on. You never will be a girl. But you won't find that hard. You'll just go on being a tomboy.'
> The light was gathering strength. I could see their faces now. These were men who were getting older, fatter, grey-haired; the adventure of their

lives was already undertaken and achieved, their roads already chosen. Now they were choosing for me.

'From now on you're going to be a boy. And then a man. Your uncle and I are giving you our names. And David's volunteered to be your patron and your guardian.'

David Erskine laughed hoarsely. It was a wonderful idea. A trick, a masquerade. A joke against the world.

'I'll put my money where my mouth is. And gladly. It's about time I did something for you, child. I'm your banker from now on.' David Erskine chuckled wickedly to himself. He loomed over me in the lightening blue.

'Welcome aboard, James Miranda Barry. You'd be wasted as a woman. Join the men.'

Then they all laughed.

20. James Barry, courtesy of
Wellcome Library, London

In 1813, Dr Barry, small and with delicate hands and a squeaky voice, joined the army and was gazetted hospital assistant, the most junior medical commissioned rank. She was promoted surgeon in 1815, and the following year posted to Cape Town as medical inspector for Cape Colony. Thereafter, she had a remarkable career, proving herself both a first-class doctor and a stickler for things, usually of a reforming nature, being done her way; she was never slow to criticise local handling of medical matters, nor to react to personal remarks, including fighting a duel. While in Cape Town, among other innovations, she performed a caesarean section, a notable first, and became the trusted confidant of, and doctor to, the governor. There is some circumstantial evidence that she conceived a child by him, and gave birth in secret in Mauritius. She seemed to go to there without an obvious reason.

Some sources suggest that Dr Barry may have been hermaphrodite, but it is more generally accepted that she was a woman, and **Sophia Bishop**, the servant who laid her out on her death in her rooms in London, said that not only was the body clearly that of 'a perfect female' – when she thought she was going to be dealing with that of a man – but 'farther that there were marks of her having had a child when very young'. Sophia herself had had nine children so 'I ought to know'. The issue of Dr Barry's sex is meticulously and comprehensively explored, documented and discussed by Rachel Holmes in the most recent biography, *Scanty Particulars: The Secret Life of Dr James Barry* (2000).

I have taken basic facts from Dr Barry's *ODNB* and Wikipedia entries, but for her time in Malta, the most useful sources are the earlier biography by June Rose, *The Perfect Gentleman: The Remarkable Life of Dr James Miranda Barry* (1977), Charles Savona-Ventura's article 'Dr James Barry: An Enigmatic Army Medical Doctor' (1996), and Walter Bonnici's website 'British Army Medical Services and the Malta Garrison 1799–1979' (www.maltaramc.com).

Patricia Duncker does not write about Malta by name in her novel but, given that Dr Barry served in Corfu after Malta, the fictional Mediterranean island can be seen as the novelist's imaginings of what she might have experienced and felt on a merging of the two. In response to my emailed query, the professor of contemporary literature explained that she was not writing a biography, a work of fact, but 'a modern novel that addresses the forms and discourses of Victorian fiction'. She does, in fact, know Malta well. So don't be put off; it is the spirit of Dr Barry and the Mediterranean setting that count.

Dr Barry arrived in Malta, aged about 50, having gone from Cape Colony to Jamaica, from there to St Helena, and then back to the Caribbean. She was to serve in Malta for four and a half years, staying first, probably, at the Clarendon Hotel, Strada San Paolo, then living in Sliema. The story of her stay gives an impression not only of her life as a doctor there, but also of the Malta of the day.

Although it was Dr Barry's medical experience and expertise and reforming agenda that were most noteworthy, her temper, argumentativeness and her inability to obey anyone else's rules were often to the fore; and it was an aspect of that which started her career in Malta. In December 1846, the month after her arrival, an Irish Roman Catholic by birth, she turned up for the service at St Paul's Anglican church in full dress uniform, including her usual elevated shoes, and settled herself in the pew reserved for the clergy. One of the resulting newspaper articles fulminated:

We express our unqualified disapprobation that an officer and a gentleman presuming on his position should dare go into the vestry and there behave in so highly indecorous a manner, as Dr Barry is represented to us to have done. If a report has been done by the clergy to the governor, they too are to blame for giving out of their hands the power delegated to them in things spiritual connected with the Church of St Paul. Had Dr Barry been properly punished, Mr Cleugh would have stopped the service till the clerk or the beadle had ordered the intruder out. We fancy that the little great man would have blushed turnips and cauliflowers, and the effects on his sensitive mind would have been even greater than that produced by the governor.

And the controversy rumbled on in the press. But that was incidental to Dr Barry's work in the islands. Cholera was then the great scourge; there had been an epidemic ten years earlier, so when she was asked to visit a sick woman in a marshy, coastal *casal* near Valletta in September 1848, cholera was assumed and feared. Although the causes of cholera were not to be isolated for another 35 years, she had treated it elsewhere, so she disagreed with the diagnosis of the accompanying police physician, and that of the local doctor who diagnosed typhus. For Dr Barry, it was a question of poverty and the lack of good food. Having also visited a sick man in the *casal*, she wrote, 'We were fortunate enough to obtain for him what he needed – sustenance – and he eventually recovered for I saw him afterwards'. She also reported:

A boy about twelve years of age stretched on a handful of straw on the ground in an open yard under stone stairs, affected with well marked and not to be mistaken Typhus Fever; in an adjoining hovel, an old woman quite scantily provided for in the last states of Fever of a very malignant Typhoid Type. The wretched beings were in the most deplorable plight, surrounded by filth and stench intolerable, without sustenance or support. In fact, I feel inadequate to describe the scene and shrunk from it with horror.

She learnt from the local doctor that the *casal* suffered from remittent and typhus fevers annually because of the marshy, badly drained land, as well as 'their being miserably poor and overcrowded'. She also attacked the open sewers around Valletta itself. If she had but realised, cholera was not caused by the miasma given off, as was then believed, but from drinking polluted water from wells near sewers or from contaminated rivers. Remittent Fever was often called Malta Fever which will have its place later in this chapter.

When Dr Barry disagreed with medical colleagues about whether the cholera they diagnosed was Asiatic cholera, or sporadic cholera, the governor insisted that the medical officers present a united front. She tried to explain, but then had to write,

It is proverbial that all professions, whether legal, ecclesiastical or medical differ and seldom arrive at the same conclusion as to the cause and effect of things; in fact the world in general disagrees ... I even presume to contend that such equality of opinion would in no wise add to the credit of the Profession or ensure the safety of the Public.

She deplored the fact that the soldiers were allowed, through the indiscretion of military medical officers, to learn of the threat of cholera: it would create panic and lead to drunkenness which she saw as one of the scourges of the army. She was herself teetotal and vegetarian – the nickname given to her by her Maltese acquaintances was *Haxxixu* (Maltese for vegetarian). Only 16 people died from the outbreak of fever of 1848, the cause of which remained a mystery.

Conditions in the army barracks and military hospitals also claimed her attention, and she had several interviews with the governor on the subject. She was wiser now than she had been in St Helena where, having made the same complaints less temperately, she had been court-martialled and sent home demoted. In Malta, the governor 'not infrequently condescended to approve of measures suggested by me'.

Charles Savona-Ventura continues Dr Barry's Malta career until 1850 when there was, between June and October, a genuine outbreak of cholera; 4,029 cases were reported, and there were 1,736 deaths. 'Again Dr Barry's contribution to the care of the affected troops was substantial ... Barry records in a memorandum that she had received "the thanks of the Duke of Wellington for my services during the period that island was visited by the cholera".'

Dr Barry left Malta for Corfu in 1851 with the rank of deputy inspector-general of hospitals. On her departure the *Malta Times* noted that 'the soldiers and the poor particularly, as well as a numerous acquaintance amongst the first circles in the island will regret their loss'. The same newspaper, learning of her death in 1865, commented that Dr Barry

> was equally distinguished by his skill and by his pugnacious propensities, the latter being so inconveniently developed upon the slightest difference of opinion with him, that at least no notice was allowed to be taken of his fits of temper.

As for Dr Barry's landlord in Sliema, his verdict was *Dan ix-xitan ghandu icun Mara* (this devil has to be a woman).

During her time in Corfu, Dr Barry tried, as usual, to improve sanitary conditions generally, as well as the conditions and diet of the common soldier. When the Crimean War broke out in 1853, she tried to get posted to the front, but was too senior; she therefore looked after the sick and wounded who started to arrive at her hospital in Corfu, and was renowned for her success rate. When she spent three months' leave with the 4th Division before Sevastapol, she somehow fell out with the great but younger Florence Nightingale, comparatively new to the struggle to reform medical services. Florence was, according to Linda Grant De Pauw in *Battle Cries and Lullabies: Women in War from Prehistory to the Present* (1998), instrumental in influencing Queen Victoria against knighting Dr Barry, on whose death she wrote:

> I never had such a blackguard rating in all my life – I who have had more than any woman – than from this Barry sitting on his horse, while I was crossing the Hospital Square with only my cap on in the sun. He kept me standing in the midst of quite a crowd of soldiers, Commissariat, servants, camp followers, etc., etc., every one of whom behaved like a gentleman during the scolding I received while he behaved like a brute ... After he was dead, I was told that (he) was a woman ... I should say that (she) was the most hardened creature I ever met.

Florence Nightingale, the Crimean War and Malta

Florence Nightingale (1820–1910), too, is part of the history of women and medicine in Malta. She made her name, and revolutionised nursing in Britain and, to some extent, in Malta, as a result of her pioneering work during the Crimean War. But she had visited Malta earlier. In 1849, aged 29, she travelled to Egypt with the already well-travelled artist **Selina Bracebridge** (née Mills, 1800–1874), whom she called her 'spiritual mother', and her husband Charles Bracebridge; they stopped only very briefly in Malta. Being Florence, however, a while before she became famous and powerful, she expressed strong views in a letter home that November contained in *The Collected Works of Florence Nightingale* (ed Lynn McDonald, 2001). The governor, Richard More O'Ferrall, whom she attacked, was not only the first civilian governor of Malta, but also the first Roman Catholic, sent there following a career as a Member of Parliament and government minister. His wife, since 1839, was **Matilda O'Ferrall** (d.1882), daughter of the third Viscount Southwell. Florence started with her arrival in Malta, and then warmed to her theme:

> Then began my first initiation into Arab life. Certainly the gay little Valetta, busily piled up on her barren mount, is as great a contrast to the cities of Sicily, lazily stretched out along the shore, the houses as far apart as possible as one could see. The one island with its beautiful soft blue heights, its olive groves from which the breeze came to us laden with all sorts of odours; the other [island] bare and flat and yellow as a gravel walk, with a few miserable vines cultivated in terraces on soil brought from Sicily, without a tree, without a height, nothing which could tempt any race conceivable by the human imagination to settle there, yet busy, gay and clean, its little streets like a scarf of many colours, its houses stuck all over with coloured boxes for balconies, as clean as a Mussulman. It is stepping from the West to the East at a stride.
>
> As to [governor] Morris O'Ferrall, he has completely fallen into the hands of the Jesuits. You see nothing else at the levees but Jesuits, monks, Ignorantius, and he goes to long Maltese sermons of which he does not

understand a word, as if that could impose upon anybody. Better have sent the *cholera morbus* there, said one person to us, for that injures only the body, but his Jesuits injure body and soul.

His excuse for not admitting the refugees [from Italy] was quite preposterous for, with a garrison of three thousand English and our fleet in the harbour, I ask you what mischief could they have done? If he had said the island was too poor to support them, that would have been something like a reason, but the real fact is that his wife's brother is a Jesuit, that he had opened the island to all the Jesuit refugees and none others. But the most melancholy part of the history is still to come: the unfortunate Romans went to Algiers – there they were of course rejected. Thirteen of them died on the passage which was long – they were two months at sea. They returned to Malta in a state of disease so dreadful that Colonel Johns, the deputy governor (Morris O'Ferrall being then in England) received them, visited them and *at his own expense sent down* twelve hundred mattresses to the Lazzaretto for them, food, medicine, clothes and played the Frère de la Charité while the Jesuit was away. I am glad there was someone to redeem our name. Finally the Greek Consul, whom we know, shipped them off to Greece without taking anything from them when a subscription was made for them. ... I rather give the Maltese, who are fanatical Catholics, credit for not being taken in by [O'Ferrall]. He has curried favour with them in vain.

While this saga is somewhat incidental to the story of women and medicine in Malta, it is worth the diversion: Florence is venturing into quite a controversy with her remarks which were, of course, made in a private family letter, but it is interesting that she had picked up her opinion during her few hours in Malta, presumably from Protestant informants, and her impressions perhaps coloured her later dealings with the islands. The trials of the refugees are, also, very pertinent to the Mediterranean of the twenty-first century.

Very briefly, in 1848/49 most of Italy, and much of Europe, was in revolutionary turmoil. In February 1849 Garibaldi and his followers had, following elections to a constituent assembly, proclaimed a Roman Republic; Mazzini became Prime Minister. But after a two-month siege by French forces, Rome capitulated, and Garibaldi, Mazzini and their followers fled into exile. The refugees about whom Florence writes were some of those exiles.

There was much controversy over O'Ferrall's actions, but he had those willing to explain his position. In the British parliament the Whig MP Benjamin Hawes is reported by *Hansard* as saying that

The refugees to whom reference had been made consisted of persons who had left both Sicily and Italy, and were not confined to parties who had quitted Rome. They had arrived, however, in such crowds at Malta that it was absolutely necessary for the Governor, acting on his own responsibility for the preservation of the peace and tranquillity of the island, to limit the numbers frequenting it. This was not done with any inconsiderateness; on the contrary, whenever sickness was given as a reason for landing, the parties were at once allowed to disembark, and they received every care and attention from the Governor himself. Nevertheless, considering the crowds of all characters who flocked to the island, the Governor had stated, and he (Mr Hawes) thought him justified in so doing, that if he were to be responsible for the tranquillity of the place, he must limit the numbers coming there; and, unless the Governor had intimated to the proper authorities not to allow these parties to land to such a great extent, he would probably have been obliged to take other steps which might have appeared more severe.

In *The Story of Malta*, Brian Blouet not only adds to O'Ferrall's reason for his actions, but contradicts Florence's opinion of Maltese reactions to his governorship. He explains:

As in much of Europe in 1848, there was a revolutionary environment in Malta's harbour towns. Political exiles were extolling republican ideas and breaking the rules of asylum by supporting insurrections in Italy.

In volatile times the Governor's polities and his personal qualities were attacked. O'Ferrall persisted and in 1849 introduced the new constitution that gave the Maltese significant representation in the Council of Government.

Meanwhile, it would be interesting to know what part the controversial Dr Barry played vis–à-vis the sick refugees, and what Matilda O'Ferrall had to say and to endure. It is not clear which governor 'condescended' to go along with Dr Barry's reforming measures; Lieutenant General Patrick Stuart was in post when she arrived, but O'Ferrall was governor from 1847 until she left. He was to resign as governor of Malta in 1851 over the introduction in parliament of anti-Catholic legislation. His resignation was 'against the wishes of many elected members of the Council and a large number of Maltese who signed a petition asking him to stay'.

Florence Nightingale arrived in Malta again at the end of October 1855. This time she was on her way to the Crimea on board the *Vectis* which was usually carrying mails from Marseilles to Malta – a vessel quite unsuited for passengers; and it was to take them on to Constantinople. With Florence were Selina and Charles Bracebridge, there to provide support, and the women she had recruited to nurse under her in the conflict: High Church Anglican Sellonite Sisters, **Mother Eldress Emma Langston** in charge, Roman Catholic Sisters of Mercy from the Convent of the Faithful Virgin in Norwood, **Mother Clare** in charge and, as Alan Delgado describes in *As They Saw Her: Florence Nightingale* (1970), with them [were] a selection of ladies carefully chosen from religious establishments[;] there were also about a dozen professional nurses of doubtful character to make up the total of nearly forty ... in charge of the entire party was a Mrs Clarke, an elderly housekeeper employed by Miss Nightingale.

Once arrived in Malta, Florence was so seasick that she kept to her cabin; Malta was not, this time, to benefit from her strong opinions – they were to come later. What happened when her charges disembarked is told in slightly different versions; in '"The Lady with the Lamp" and the Maltese Connection' (1991); Charles Savona-Ventura decided to quote them both, and I shall do so too because they are different enough to add flavour to the occasion:

The rest of the party went sightseeing in the charge of a major of the militia. The party was made up partly of Anglican sisters in black serge habits, partly of Roman Catholic nuns in white habits, and partly of hospital nurses. The hospital nurses were placed in the middle where they would have no chance to misbehave, and the major marched the party from point to point in military formation. The major would shout, 'Forward black sisters', and the Anglican sisters in their black serge habits got into motion, but then the white nuns would straggle, and there came a shout, 'Halt! Those damned white sisters have gone again.' Malta was full of idle troops, and soon the party was followed by a crowd of soldiers. One of the Anglican sisters heard a sergeant remark that he should think 'them ancient Amazons we read about took a deal of drilling.'

At Malta Mr Bracebridge took all who were well enough ashore sight-seeing. Putting his ideas of discipline into force – perhaps he learned them in the Militia said one of the Sisters maliciously – he marched them through the street. Protestant Sisters first, Catholic nuns last, nurses in the middle where they could do no harm. In the Cathedral, Mass was being celebrated, the nuns began to fall out of their ranks and to sink upon their knees; he was much disconcerted and annoyed. The sun was blazing, the streets were insufferably hot, the glare from the sea and sky was blinding and everybody was worn with sickness, on the whole, therefore, the Sisters were relieved when they got back to the ship. The *Malta Times* of the 14th of November wrote: 'The party landed and visited the objects in Valletta most worthy of notice, and in passing through the streets attracted the sympathy and admiration of the inhabitants, many of whom expressed themselves highly gratified with the interesting and cheerful appearance of these persons.'

Accounts of this incident depict the women concerned as figures of fun, but this is to do them an injustice. **Sarah Anne Terrot** (1822–1902), who had joined the Sellonites in 1847, was the daughter of the Bishop of Edinburgh who could have led a comfortable life at home, but had gone against her father's wishes to pursue a career in nursing. She was highly respectable and respected; several others came from similar backgrounds, and all had been carefully picked. As far as Sarah was concerned, it was a major who was their guide. She does also add to the impression of a group of women at the mercy of an environment not previously encountered when she describes how, when they were being transferred from the *Vectis* to a boat to take them ashore, one of the nurses 'plumped into the water ... but scrambled out without injury beyond a wetting'. And then, presumably, in a soaking wet long skirt, she was subjected to the military tour. Sarah's account of their visit to St John's Church is in Chapter 17 itinerary.

Selina Bracebridge, meanwhile, left as her record of that visit a daguerreotype of 'A Mohammedan Family, from Salonica Baptized at Malta in 1853'. How she came upon this posed family group, all but the father in western dress, is not vouchsafed; all the caption tells us is that the father and two of the sons were studying at the Protestant College.

Mary Seacole (née Grant, 1805–1881) also passed through Malta on her way to Constantinople in 1855. The experienced herbal practitioner, born in Kingston, Jamaica, of Creole Scottish descent, had been rejected by the British War Office when she offered her assistance in the Crimea, so she was on her way there to set up independently what she called her 'British Hotel'. There, much appreciated, she was to cater to, and nurture, sick and convalescent officers.

Mary did not think much of Malta, with good reason. She explained why in *Wonderful Adventures of Mrs Seacole in Many Lands* (ed. Ziggi Alexander and Audrey Dewjee, 1984):

> We stopped at Malta also, where, of course, I landed, and stared about me, and submitted to be robbed by the lazy Maltese with all a traveller's resignation. Here, also, I met friends – some medical officers who had known me in Kingston; and one of them, Dr F——, lately arrived from Scutari, gave me, when he heard of my plans, a letter of introduction to Miss Nightingale, then hard at work, evoking order out of confusion, and bravely resisting the despotism of death, at the hospital of Scutari.

Partly because this black heroine of the Crimean War was neglected for around one hundred years, there has been a sad attempt to pit her and her achievements against Florence Nightingale and hers. But Mary wrote that her only meeting with Florence was friendly enough: she was asked by the woman whose workload, as the above remarks show, she already appreciated, 'What do you want, Mrs Seacole? Anything we can do for you? If it lies in my power, I shall be very happy.' Mary explained how she dreaded trying to get back to her vessel that night, so a bed was found for her, and breakfast sent in with a 'kind message from Mrs Bracebridge'.

Helen Rappaport in *No Place for Ladies: The Untold Story of Women in the Crimean War* (2007) puts a negative spin on this hospitality, because Mary was accommodated in the washerwoman's quarters; but Jane Robinson, in her biography, *Mary Seacole* (2006), is more measured, explaining that no one, not even Florence or Selina, was comfortably housed in the hospital where space was at a premium, and that several invalid nurses were in the same quarters as Mary who got on famously with the washerwoman, swapping life stories. A footnote in Mary's memoirs observes that she 'saw much of Miss Nightingale at Balaclava', though no further meeting is mentioned. There is no note of rancour or rejection: each went about her own separate but complementary mission; Mary was a flamboyant eccentric from the Caribbean, already in her fifties, experienced in dealing with soldiers, Florence a hard-pressed, upper middle class Englishwoman resolute in turning the nursing world on its head amid the anguish and grime of war.

Meanwhile, in September 1854, back in Malta, a number of hospital beds were set aside to receive the sick and wounded from Sevastopol – 2,500 beds in all: 1,500 at the Lazaretto; 500 at the Bighi Naval Hospital (formerly the Villa Bichi, see Chapter 18 itinerary); and 500 other beds still to be arranged. In October 60 prisoners, including a Russian general, arrived, and were confined; and in November the wounded started to arrive. On disembarkation 'the people spontaneously carried those unable to walk upon their shoulders, placed them gently upon carriages, and even carried them to hospital'. But it was not female nurses in clean starched uniforms who received them. The nurses in the hospitals were men: 'On 11 June 1855 a Royal Warrant established a Medical Staff Corps to provide trained men for the care of the sick.' Even those responsible for the laundry were 'washermen'. That is why Florence Nightingale's Crimean team of women nurses was such an innovation.

There was, however, no shortage of women arriving in Malta. An entry in 'The British Army Medical Services and the Malta Garrison' from Walter Bonnici's website, also quoted from above, noted that, on 25 April 1855, 547 men, 50 women and 45 children belonging to the East Kent Militia arrived to form part of the Malta garrison. Then there were the women who planned to travel on eastwards. Helen Rappaport writes,

> Nobody knows how many women travelled east with the British expeditionary force in the spring of 1854. It may have been as many as 1,200; it was certainly at least 750. It is likely that a good three-quarters of the army wives never returned. By the end of the war, an additional 250 women had travelled out to Turkey and the Crimea as nurses.

And she elaborates on what the women might experience on their way to Malta, and what they found when they got there:

> The journey out to the Strait of Gibraltar could take anything from four to ten days, depending on the weather and the type of vessel, after which the troopships tracked the rocky North Africa coast en route to Malta ... After five to eight days at sea, encountering the ferocity of the sirocco wind, the weary travellers would find respite in Malta. For five of the 4th

King's Own women, who had become sick on the voyage, the campaign ended here, where they asked to be put on the next boat back to England. Another 24 women from the 33rd and 41st Regiments, already finding the sea voyage too much for them, also opted to return home ... Then there were those who soon found that staying in Malta and soliciting on shore among the thousands of troops crowding the streets of Valetta was a much easier option than continuing a gut-wrenching sea journey who knows where.

In Malta, where the ships stopped to take on coal, supplies and water, many troops spent days if not weeks waiting to embark for the next stage of the journey east. The 4th [King's Own] were disembarked here and camped at Fort Manuel for sixteen days; the Scots Fusilier Guards, with 25 women in train, holed up in the stifling heat and dry sirocco wind for six weeks. Some officers had brought their mothers as well as wives with them thus far. The air of unreality about it all continued: socializing, picnicking and dining carried on among the officers as though they were in a barrack town in England. But the dream days eventually came to an end; the women hung on as long as they could, but 'heavy were the hearts as that day approached when Malta must be left, the troop-steamer declared in readiness and poor women, whether the wives of officers or soldiers, were left with streaming eyes on the Barraco, while the fine ship glided on towards her Eastern point ...'.

Life was, not surprisingly, easier for officers' wives, one of the best known of whom, not only for her independent spirit, but also because she kept a record, was **Fanny Duberly** (née Locke, 1829–1903). Described as 'a splendid rider, witty, ambitious, daring, lively, loquacious and gregarious', she travelled all the way to the Crimea with her husband Captain Henry Duberly, paymaster to the 8th Royal Irish Hussars. The Duberlys had left England in April 1854 and, like nearly everyone else, she was constantly seasick. Her main concern, though, was for her horses. In *Journal kept during the Russian War* (1856, 2008), she tells of the fate that befell her 'own dear horse ... Never was a more perfect creature, with faultless action, faultless mouth, faultless temper'. After several days of sickness,

We were awoke at four o'clock by the sound of a matin bell, and knew by it that we were off Malta. Looking through the stern windows, we found ourselves at anchor in the harbour; the massive fortifications bristling with guns were close on either side of us, as we lay quiet and motionless on the waveless sea. At eight o'clock Henry went on deck, and soon after returning, put his arms round me, and I knew that my darling horse was out of pain!

Henry went ashore with Captain Fraser, and amid the sultry heat, sweltered up the '*Nix mangiare*' stairs, and through the blinding streets of the town. At ten we received orders to put to sea forthwith; but the wind lay ahead of us, and at five we were barely out of the port. Shortly after, when the calm evening was dressed in all the gorgeous colours of a southern sunset, and whilst the military calls were sounding those stirring notes he loved to hear, my good horse was lowered to his rest among the nautili and wondrous seaflowers which floated round the ship.

Henry Duberly's regiment was part of the British light cavalry that took part in the Charge of the Light Brigade; and Fanny stayed with him throughout his time there.

Florence Nightingale returned to England in 1856 in a state of near collapse. But it was by no means the end of her involvement with Malta, for she had learnt a great deal about nursing, nurses, hospitals and public health reform, and had made her name as an expert in such matters. When, therefore, in 1862, there were plans to build a new *Conservatorio* for the aged and infirm to replace the old *Ospizio*, she was the obvious person to consult. Charles Savona-Ventura records her reply: 'The plans are so good (far better than those of any hospital for men and women I have ever seen) that the difficulty was to find fault. I could not discover a single sanitary lapse.' And in another letter: 'It is consolation to know that there will be one good civil hospital in the British Dominions for an example.' He then adds:

She however submitted various suggestions calculated to render the nurse's life in hospital more tolerable insisting that the night nurse should have a quiet room to sleep in by day by herself and that the scullery, if used as a Nurses' Day Room, should be comfortable and large enough. She also advocated the provision of water closets for the sole use of the nurses. Nightingale included a copy of the plans for the hospital in her book Notes on Hospital published in 1863. The new Asylum for the Aged and incurables, later named St Vincent de Paul Hospital in 1940, was opened on 3 October 1892. A ward in the hospital has been named after Florence Nightingale.

Today the establishment is a hybrid between a nursing home and a hospital, with a total of over 1,100 residents. Five Sisters of Charity, then under the protection of St Vincent de Paul, arrived from Italy in 1868, at the request of the authorities, to staff the badly run orphanage for poor girls. By the following year, the Sisters, trained nurses, started filling vacant places in Government Hospitals and institutions. They later nursed under the protection of St Jeanne Aristide, and are mentioned in Chapter 11. Florence Nightingale chose the Maltese Cross as the design for the pin worn by the graduates of her first nursing school.

As Charles Savona-Ventura shows, Florence was not always so complimentary about Malta and the Maltese – though her reservations did not include the group of Maltese doctors who travelled to the Black Sea to work in the hospital:

21.   Florence Nightingale, courtesy of
Wellcome Library, London

Nightingale in Crimea received a large number of contributions collected in England for the troops. It was difficult to keep check of these stores since 'the Maltese, Greek and Turkish labourers who worked round the hospital were dishonest almost without exception'. On another occasion, two Maltese kitchen-workers were discovered to have hidden goods from the Free Gift Store in their rooms. 'The beds of the Maltese were found to be entirely constructed of piles of stolen goods'.

And that was not the end of it. Florence's sister, **Parthenope** (1819–1890) had married Sir Henry Calvert **Verney** Bt; in doing so, she became stepmother to **Emily Verney** (1843–1872). In 1864, Emily travelled to Malta, sources say in the hopes of ameliorating the tuberculosis from which she suffered. In the years following her return to England, her health deteriorated further, though not apparently caused by tuberculosis. In spite of that, during the Franco-Prussian War of 1870, she served tirelessly on the committee of the National Society for Aid to the Sick and Wounded (later the Red Cross), and persuaded Florence to as well. But Emily died in September 1872, it is said from typhus. Florence wrote of her 'Elle était vraimant le genie de l'Oeuvre des Blessés' [she was really inspired when it came to working for the wounded]. But of the cause of her continuing illness, Florence had written to Emily's father in March 1871,

I was extremely distressed by Emily's illness. She has suffered as everyone does who goes to Malta. They have allowed the rock to become a dirty sodden sponge and hence the fevers. But the question now lies solely with the local people. We have advised the home government to give them £30,000 as a contribution to the improvements leaving them to find £50,000. But they prefer crippling their commerce by quarantine and this depraved taste has been no little pandered to by the health authorities here and at Malta.

There is more to be said about Emily's health and, indeed, that of Florence, in due course.

Cholera 1865

In April 1865, the strength of the British garrison in Malta was 6,105 men, 526 women, and 838 children. On 20 June, an eight-year-old girl, daughter of one of the gunners, died within seven hours of feeling sick; the cause of her death was given as Asiatic cholera. Thirty-four married military families occupying the Lazaretto hospital were immediately moved to an encampment on a dry and airy ridge some distance away.

On 29 June, cholera appeared in the civilian population and, on 24 July, it broke out on Gozo. By August, 30–70 people were falling ill every day, half of them then dying. Women and children proved most at risk. The epidemic lasted until 24 October on Gozo, and 9 November on Malta. By then, there had been 2,362 cases on Malta, with 1,479 deaths – 12 per cent of the population; on Gozo 545 cases and 252 deaths – 10 per cent of the population. Among the soldiers and their families, there were 199 cases, and 142 deaths. In all, there were 3,106 cases and 1,873 deaths. Those are the dry facts, culled from the Malta garrison records. But where had the cholera come from, and who were some of the people involved?

Earlier that year a similar epidemic had broken out in the Middle East, attacking hundreds of Muslim pilgrims, both in Mecca and on their way there. On 9 May, a steamer was carrying some 1,500 pilgrims from Jeddah home to North Africa. On board several passengers died. Soon there was cholera in Alexandria. Then a steamer carrying pilgrims from Alexandria to Tunis arrived in Malta; 61 of them disembarked there. A seven-day quarantine was set in train, but it was too late.

So few names of those who died, let alone those who survived, surface, but if you go through the cemetery records (to be found on www.maltafamilyhistory.com), you can see what happened to some families. On 11 August, William George Brock, four-year-old son of Walter and **Kezia Brock**, died from cholera. On the 13th, Kezia herself, aged 33, died and, on the 14th, her daughter **Louisa Brock** died, aged seven years and eleven months. Who this family was, and what had brought it to Malta, or from where, I have been unable to establish.

One expatriate woman, at least, was involved in nursing victims of the epidemic and organising others to do so. **Bertha Leith Adams** (née Grundy, later de Courcy Laffan, 1837–1912) was the daughter of a Manchester solicitor and his wife, Jane Grundy. In 1859, she met and married Scottish army physician Andrew Leith Adams. They travelled almost immediately with the Cheshire Regiment to its posting, arriving in Malta in June 1860. The couple were to remain there for six years, Andrew making his name in the scientific world for the geological and palaeontological work he carried out in the islands; Bertha, using material from her time there in her later life as a well-known novelist. Their son, Francis, who also became well known, in Australia, as a writer, was born in Malta in 1862.

Not surprisingly, when cholera broke out in the army, Andrew Leith Adams was involved, and was to write a detailed and damning report about the islands' sanitary conditions and the pattern and transmission of the previous cholera epidemics. Almost immediately, the couple decided that two-year-old Francis should be sent home to his grandparents in Manchester; Bertha was no doubt both relieved and bereft. It was a wise move, though, as none of the children of the 22nd Regiment who contracted cholera survived. And Bertha knew how to console herself: when the (nameless) school mistress died, her husband took their two daughters home to England, but left their two boys in Bertha's care. What is more, according to her *ODNB* entry, she 'nursed the sick and dying … organising the soldiers' wives to assist'.

That entry is, though, rather misleading when it notes, 'Adams' novels frequently used her varied experiences: the cholera epidemic in *Madelon Lemoine* (1879) …' I assumed that Malta would feature but, no, it is the cholera epidemic that does. During her time as an army wife, Bertha gained a lot of sympathy for ordinary soldiers and their wives; this is particularly obvious from her novel *A Garrison Romance* (1892) which, featuring the fictional 193rd Regiment of the Line, takes place in Malta. A reviewer wrote in the *Athenaeum*:

> It is rash for a lady to undertake a description of military life, for she can necessarily learn nothing about its details except by hearsay. Yet, though some of her characters are a trifle grotesque, Mrs Adams has not presented us with such caricatures as with Mrs Stannard stand for the representations of 'soldier officers'; and some of them are very tolerably presented… the most attractive feature of the book is the writer's delicate appreciation of the private soldier, whose good and kindly qualities ought to earn him more esteem than he generally receives.

Mrs Stannard was **Henrietta Stannard** (née Palmer, 1856–1911), who, under the pseudonym John Strange Winter, also wrote about military life. Meg Tasker, in her biography of the Adams' son – *Struggle and Storm: The Life and Death of Francis Adams* (2001) picks up comments from Bertha herself:

The 'sunshine, orange groves, and military pomp and glitter of life in Malta' were remembered fondly by Bertha in later life, although she would also write about the cholera epidemic which decimated the community and provided her with experiences of 'an intense and exceptional character'. All grist to the mill, for a writer, but she did not start writing until ten years later, back in England.

When life was not so demanding, the regimental chronicle notes that 'Mrs Leith Adams was the mainstay of concerts for the troops and various entertainments for the boys and for married women and children.'

Bertha was widowed in 1882, before most of her novels were written. She then married Robert Laffan, 16 years her junior. As wife of the headmaster of a boarding school in Stratford-on-Avon, she was not such a success; a later comment about her notes:

> The attributes that the 22nd Regiment had valued in Bertha Leith-Adams – her interest in the 'lower orders' and in 'running things', her ability to provide leadership in a time of crisis – clearly had less currency in the more genteel circle occupied by a headmaster's wife. If only she had kept to organising schoolboys, and minded her own business ...

Those remarks may well have had something to do with her zealous campaigning for working class education, and the raising of women's issues in her writing.

In 1882, there were nationalist uprisings in Egypt which led, on 11 June, to the killing of Europeans. Many of those who escaped fled to Malta, eventually some 6,600. The Chief Secretary from 1855 to 1883 was Sir Victor Houlton. Immediately, his wife set to; indeed, that year **Lady Houlton** (née Hyacinthe Wellesley, 1825–1897, m.1860) introduced to Malta the St John Ambulance Association, a child of the Knights of the Order of St John of Jerusalem. It was to be the first formed outside the United Kingdom. The Association was concerned with training the public in first aid; while the St John Ambulance Brigade was to provide first aid care to the public.

Hyacinthe Houlton (not to be confused, as has happened, with Dame Margaret Hulton, Lady Strickland) organised assistance for three months or so, personally working at providing relief to some 1,200 families. Money for the refugees' relief was raised in London through the Lord Mayor's Fund, and clothing was collected in Malta through the Ladies Clothing Fund led by Lady Houlton. At some stage, she became Dame Hyacinthe Houlton, honoured with the DBE in her own right – it may have been for her work in Malta.

On 25 November 1908, the SS *Sardinia* burst into flames outside the Grand Harbour with the loss of 112 lives. The St John Ambulance nurses hastened to the Customs House which was promptly turned into an emergency hospital to care for the survivors.

Malta Fever – Brucellosis

While cholera and typhus (more accurately described today as typhoid) were a perennial problem in Malta, what was often termed Malta Fever both in and outside the islands was endemic, and also played havoc among the troops who passed through Malta during the Crimean War, as well as those who were garrisoned there. Typical of those who contracted it were Captain Andrew Moynihan, who had been awarded the VC during the Crimean War, and his wife **Ellen Anne Moynihan** (née Parkin). He died in 1866, aged 37; she survived and was left with an 18-month-old son born in Malta and two daughters. She left for Leeds with a pension of £1 a week the following year, and obviously made a success of raising her children, the son born in Malta becoming a surgeon and being raised to the peerage. Dr David Vassallo, from his wide knowledge of the literature, queries this diagnosis of Malta Fever which I have taken from the *ODNB* entry for the Moynihans' son. Moynihan may have died of typhoid.

No one knew what caused Malta Fever – what was later also called undulant fever because of its wave-like nature – nor how it was spread. That was soon to change: the causal relationship between organism and disease was to be established, leading Malta Fever to be known eventually as brucellosis.

In 1881, Dr David Bruce's first position after graduation was as assistant to Dr Herbert Stone in Reigate, Surrey. There he met Mary Sisson Steele, six years his senior, daughter of Dr Stone's predecessor in the practice; she became **Mary Bruce** (1849–1931) in 1883. His entry in the *ODNB* then makes the crucial remark: 'They ... began a lifelong partnership in science and travel'. In 1884, David Bruce, having joined the army, was posted as resident medical officer at the Station Hospital in Valletta – what had been the *Sacra Infermeria* under the Knights, and is now the Mediterranean Conference Centre (see Chapter 17 itinerary). It was there that he came across many cases of the obscure Malta Fever, a prolonged and debilitating fever which was occasionally fatal and often caused chronic ill health and disability.

What followed was often to be described in learned lectures, one of them given by Professor John Eyre in his Hunterian lecture of 1936, 'Undulant Fever – a Retrospective':

[On being posted to Malta with his wife] Bruce speedily realised the all-importance of the so-called Malta Fever, that practically decimated the troops under his charge, and stimulated thereto by the importunities of his wife, who was his partner in the truest sense of the word, set out to discover its cause ... Although their finances were limited, the young couple succeeded in procuring a microscope and ... applied the principles of bacteriology, as postulated by the pioneers of this science, to their investigations of the disease.

Bruce ... was indeed fortunate in that his wife, an artist of no mean ability, was keenly interested in research and readily adapting herself to laboratory work, soon became a technician of the very highest order, and a first class microscopist – a fact which the Royal Microscopical Society recognised later [in 1931] by electing her as its first and so far only, Honorary Female Fellow – an election which gave Lady Bruce (as she had then become), the keenest pleasure.

Bacteriology was then in its infancy, having been introduced by Robert Koch in 1880. On 9 July 1887 the Bruces identified the fatal organism. It would later (1920) become known as *Brucella melitensis* – not only perpetuating the Bruce name, but also linking it indelibly to Malta. In 1888, the Bruces left Malta and worked together for three months in Koch's laboratory in Berlin.

What is not so clear is what medical training and knowledge Mary started out with. She was, of course, a doctor's daughter and, being childless, and without responsibilities in Malta, she may simply have immersed herself in her husband's work. The medical dictionary notes that she 'had inherited her father's ability for accurate painting and sketching. This she used to great effect in her laboratory drawings of Trypanosomes [the cause of sleeping sickness] and other organisms.' But her medical knowledge, at least over the years, extended beyond that.

During David Bruce's 1894 posting to Natal, where the governor had been lieutenant-governor in Malta during their time there, '[Bruce] and his wife spent two years in an isolated camp in the bush in Ubombo Zululand' investigating the tsetse-fly parasite that caused sleeping sickness. During the Siege of Ladysmith in 1899, David Bruce had charge of a large military hospital and acted as operating surgeon 'while his wife assisted him as sister in charge of the operating theatre'. His biographical entry sums up Mary's contribution to his life's work:

In all his work Bruce was assisted by his wife, who accompanied him throughout his foreign service, working in the laboratory and taking charge of camp arrangements. Immediately before his own death, four days after his wife's, Bruce expressed the wish that her role in his scientific work should be recognized. She had been honoured with the Royal Red Cross for her work with the wounded in the siege of Ladysmith, and was appointed OBE for her work for the committees on trench fever and tetanus during the First World War.

An added contribution made by Mary was that, of his 172 published papers, she was co-author of 31.

That first stay in Malta was not the end of the Bruce involvement there, nor the story of brucellosis, for no one yet knew the source of the disease or the method of spread; it was assumed that it might be by mosquito or other insect. The next step in cracking this involves (Matthew) Louis

Hughes, responsible for coining the term 'Undulant Fever'. His interest in Malta Fever was not surprising because, when he entered the Army Medical College in 1890, Assistant Professor David Bruce was on the staff.

In 1890 Louis Hughes was posted to Malta. His father, Colonel Emilius Hughes arrived there a few months later, as Assistant Adjutant General, with his second wife, since 1872, **Ada Hughes** (née Grainger, 1847–1904). Louis lived with his father, stepmother and their four musical daughters in the old *Auberge de France* (see Chapter 17 itinerary). Soon after his arrival, he began to work on the bacteriology of Malta Fever about which he started to publish a series of papers. By 1892, he was officer in charge of the Military Analytical Laboratory, Valletta.

The other event that changed his life was his meeting with **Katherine Winifred Simpson** (d.1967), a doctor's daughter, who had come to visit her sister **Hilda Margaret Godfrey** (née Simpson, 1871–1930). Hilda was married to Masters John Godfrey, army officer and plant collector; he collected Maltese plants for the Natural History Museum, and Hilda must have painted the flowers he collected because her 57 watercolours illustrate their joint 1933 publication *Monograph and Iconograph of Native British Orchidaceae.* (By then he was a colonel and she was dead). Earlier, she had received the Gold Medal of the Royal Horticultural Society.

Louis Hughes married Kate Simpson at St Paul's Anglican Church, Valletta, in 1894. They were living at 9 Strada Scozzese (now Vassalli Street) in 1896 when they both contracted what was later to be called brucellosis and went back to England on sick leave. Louis had all the more reason, in 1897, to publish his *Mediterranean, Malta, or Undulant Fever.* In what has been termed a 'classic monograph', he described the signs and symptoms of undulant fever, but ascribed its causation to the local insanitary conditions. He pointed out the term undulant fever described one of the most constant characteristic features of the disease, namely the undulating of the temperature curve. He included a description of his own illness, and eventual recovery.

Meanwhile, he continued his work on tropical diseases, as well as being sanitary officer to the troops at Aldershot. But in 1899, Louis was chosen by Sir Redvers Buller to accompany him as his personal staff surgeon to South Africa where he was taking command at the beginning of the Boer War. On 15 December 1899, Louis, aged 32, was killed while attending casualties at the Battle of Colenso. That same year, Kate gave birth to their son who was, in due course, to go to Malta as a priest and become prominent in academic circles. She was married again, in 1906, to Percy Thomas Fairbrother. There is no evidence that she was involved in Louis' work, as Mary Bruce had been, in spite of the fact that she, too, was a doctor's daughter; but it is hard to believe that he did not take his work home and use her as a sounding board.

Louis Hughes' reputation rested on his monograph, which contained everything known on the subject up to that date and included a complete bibliography. But he died too young to discover the method of infection by undulant fever; how, indeed, he and Kate had contracted it. That was left to

others. But in 1903, as an extract from an August letter written from Port
Said by ET Sprague, Passed Assistant Surgeon, shows, it was still a mystery:

> I have the honour to report that on the 25th instant there was a short stop
> at Valetta, Malta, and that I embraced the opportunity to visit the military
> hospital, which contains over 300 patients, most of whom were afflicted
> with Malta fever. ...The diagnosis can now be made at an early date by
> use of the micrococcus melitensis ... The method of infection is still under
> discussion, but my informant was of the opinion that the specific organism
> is air-borne and that it is inhaled.

The following year, The Mediterranean Fever Commission was established
by the Royal Society at the request of the Secretary for the Colonies. Its
president was Colonel David Bruce and Mary, who tended to be secretary
to the commissions in which he was involved, went with him on his annual
visit to Malta, as this 1905 photograph of the members of the Commission
shows. Among other distinguished services doctors was the only Maltese,
Dr Themistocles Zammit. The progress of the Commission is best described
in Major David Vassallo's article, 'The Corps Disease: Brucellosis and its
Historical Association with the Royal Army Medical Corps' (1992).

22.   Mary Bruce and Committee, courtesy of David Vassallo

It was Dr Zammit who 'successfully incriminated the Maltese goat as the
animal host of *Micrococcus melitensis*', and was knighted as a result. His
colleague, stationed in Malta, Major William Horrocks

Showed that some of the goats in every herd examined were affected by Malta Fever, and confirmed that M. melitensis was exuded in the milk of these infected goats. This discovery was to have worldwide repercussions, as well as having serious financial implications for Maltese goatherds, for the hardy Maltese goat was renowned for its milk-producing qualities, and had been exported throughout the British empire.

This was an extraordinary blow for the Maltese, who depended on goats. Not only would women and men go from door to door with their goats to fill up the pots of the housewife, as the photograph that follows shows, but they were even more embedded in family life, as Thomas MacGill noted in 1839:

But where is there any thing to match the intelligent looking goat of Malta: the assistant nurse to the ladies of the Island. The Malta goat is taught to suckle children, they soon acquire the art, and appear to like it; it is truly astonishing with what intelligence they do their work. They leave their pasture when they think the child requires a suck, bleat at the door until admitted, scamper to the nursery where the little urchin is placed on a pillow on the floor, the goat lies down beside it, a tit is placed in its mouth, and then it sucks its fill, or when Nanny is of the opinion it has had enough, she rises, goes through her gambols, then bounds off to feed; we have known families where the same goat has suckled five or six children; the children become attached to their quadruped nurse, smile at her gambols, and cry when they think she is neglecting them.

The army and the expatriate community as soon as practical took to imported tinned cows' milk. So thoroughly was brucellosis eradicated from among the troops that in March 1909 a ball was held in the Great Ward of the Station Hospital to celebrate the fact that it was bereft of patients 'by the simple measure of banning goats' milk'.

A first-hand account of the continuing prevalence of brucellosis among the Maltese population comes from the 8,000-page journal, available online, covering 51 years, of Lady Layard. Twenty-five-year-old **Enid Layard** (née Guest, 1843–1912) married her 51-year-old cousin, archaeologist and politician Henry Layard, in 1869. Widowed in 1894, she visited Malta from 10 to 30 November 1908, staying at San Anton with the Duke and **Duchess of Connaught** (1860–1917). The Duke, Queen Victoria's third son, was then High Commissioner in Malta and Commander-in-Chief of the Mediterranean; the Duchess was born Princess Louise of Prussia. Enid wrote on 12 November:

The Maltese suffer terribly from fever which it is now found is the result of drinking goats milk. Twice [since?] the troops here have been forbidden to drink it the fever has entirely disappeared & is now only known amongst the natives of this island who cannot be persuaded to give up their goats.

And archaeologist Margaret Murray wrote of the early 1920s:

> When I was in Malta, no Maltese would believe that the goat was the
> carrier of the Malta-fever germ. 'Yes', they would say, 'the goat certainly
> was ill, but she has quite recovered and gives milk freely.' Then they drank
> the milk unboiled and went down with that deadly fever.

23.   Buying goats' milk, from the internet

As David Vassallo makes clear:

> Malta Fever was to remain rife amongst civilians for many years, its
> incidence only beginning to fall when the Government of Malta established
> a Goats' Milk Pasteurisation Centre … in May 1938. It was only when the
> sale of raw milk was banned throughout Malta and milk pasteurisation
> became compulsory in 1957 that the disease was conquered amongst
> the civil population, after which time it became limited to dairy workers
> and to persons eating raw goats' milk cheeselets, 'gbejniet', a popular
> local delicacy.

By 2000, after further eradication methods, Malta was declared officially
free of brucellosis.

Now that everything has been established regarding Malta Fever, at least
in Malta, it is worth looking back at, for example, the mystery fever of
1848 that confronted Dr Barry and wonder if it, too, wasn't brucellosis.
And I suspect that it may well have been what Emily Verney picked up in

Malta in 1864. This occurred to me when reading 'Alice Catherine Evans (1881–1975)' (2001) by John L Parascandola.

Alice Evans was an American school teacher who enrolled in a two-year course at the College of Agriculture of Cornell University in 1905. After continuing her studies, she qualified as a microbiologist but her work tended to be discounted – she was a woman without a PhD and

> The dairy industry particularly objected to her claim that raw milk might be the source of a disease which in its milder forms resembled influenza and ... severe cases were often mistaken for typhoid fever, malaria or other diseases. They resisted recommendations that all milk be pasteurized. ... She refused to back down and in the course of the 1920s her results were confirmed in several laboratories around the world. ... the work of Alice Evans played a pivotal role in the recognition of brucellosis as a significant public health problem and in the acceptance of the need to pasteurize milk.

In 1922, Alice herself had contracted brucellosis:

> For the next twenty years, her health was impaired by the disease, with periods of incapacitation alternating with periods of partial or complete recovery. Since chronic brucellosis was not recognised at the time, Evans at first had to put up with diagnosis suggesting that she was suffering from imaginary or pretended ills. One can only speculate as to whether her gender was a factor in this situation as well. When she was undergoing surgery for another reason in 1928, however, doctors found lesions from which *Brucella* was cultivated, thus supporting the view that Evans was suffering from brucellosis. Her own later research helped to prove a better understanding of the chronic form of the disease.

Alice lived until 1975, dying at the age of 94 after suffering a stroke. With her work, the story of brucellosis comes full circle from that of Mary Bruce. But there is one more twist in the tail which fits in with Alice Evans' chronic brucellosis. It is now generally accepted, by her latest biographer, Mark Bostridge, and by medical historians, that it was probably the cause of Florence Nightingale's 25 years of ill health following her return from the Crimea.

Just as the Crimean War had revolutionised the nursing profession in the British Empire, Chapter 13 will show how the First World War was to bring with it the introduction of women doctors to care for the sick and wounded. Whether their status and treatment was equal, in the early years, to that of men, was another matter. The story of Dr Barry is, therefore, all the more extraordinary.

13 – War, Riots and Refugees 1914–1922

The First World War

There was no apparent reason for Malta to be involved in the European war that started, where Britain was concerned, on 4 August 1914. Indeed, on the outbreak of hostilities, most of the regular officers of the Royal Army Medical Corps (RAMC) were withdrawn for duty elsewhere and replaced by Territorial Force personnel in September. But it did not much affect the garrison, for health among the troops had been much improved since the discovery that goat's milk was the cause of Malta Fever (brucellosis) and the gradual withdrawal from old and unhealthy barracks into modern buildings. As for the 200,000 or so Maltese, goat's milk was so much part of their diet and the countryside economy that cases of the fever continued at the rate of 400 cases a year. But these were dealt with in civilian hospitals as before.

Then, on 24 February 1915, a cable arrived from the General Officer Commanding, Egypt, enquiring what hospital accommodation was available surplus to requirements. Five hundred beds were offered at once. It was a false alarm: by 3 March notice came that they were not needed. Nevertheless, the governor, Field Marshal Lord Methuen, felt it was wiser to extend Malta's hospital capacity to 3,000, together with 500 beds for convalescents at Fort Chambray on Gozo. And, as George Bruce continues in 'Malta Military Hospitals 1915–1917' (nd),

> A notable feature also from the outset was the valuable help rendered by the ladies of Malta and the Joint Committee of the British Red Cross Society and the St John's Ambulance Association. At a suggestion of His Excellency the Governor a ladies' committee had been formed to organise voluntary aid early in March.

On 25 April 1915, Turkey having entered the war on Germany's side, Allied forces invaded its Gallipoli Peninsula through the Dardanelles Strait. Suddenly these precautions were seen as far-sighted, particularly when it became clear that medical facilities for the sick and wounded near the scene of conflict were out of the question, and that casualties would have to be shipped elsewhere; Malta was to be one of the destinations. That disastrous naval and military intervention was abandoned in early January 1916. But Malta also took in casualties from the Salonica (Thessalonika) campaign to assist Serbia in its war against Bulgaria that started on 5 October 1915 and lasted until 30 September 1918 though, as it progressed, cases became fewer and were of a different kind; then, from April 1917, submarine attacks on hospital ships made it unsafe to continue evacuations to Malta.

On 4 May 1915, 600 wounded arrived in Malta from Gallipoli on 'white ships', hospital ships marked with large red crosses; on the 5th, another 400; and on the 6th, 640. Photographs of those travelling on 'black ships', transport ships, show them lying on open decks, exposed to the sun and heat, looking like closely packed sardines; wards on the lower decks were also crowded and, in addition, poorly ventilated. Many of the casualties were Australians or New Zealanders, hence the term ANZAC, and those who accompanied them often Antipodean nurses.

The transports had been lying offshore ready to take on the wounded, subjected to the constant threat of Turkish shelling. In the memoir of her life as a nurse, *In Gray and Scarlet* (1922), **Rosa Kirkcaldie** (1887–1972) was to describe how, when winter weather set in, 'They came straight from the trenches, their muddy, filthy clothing frozen on them. They were famished, gaunt, and weary, and suffering intolerable pain.' Many of their frost-bitten limbs were gangrenous and required immediate amputation, others suffered from loss of blood. The exhausted nurses cleaned, bandaged, warmed and comforted their patients. The movement of the ships made these tasks more difficult, and the nurses suffered from seasickness as much as their patients. Some of them did a nine-month stint on the hospital ships, accompanying the sick and wounded between Gallipoli and hospitals on Imbros, Lemnos, Salonika, Alexandria, Malta and England. The journey to Malta could take four days but those first transports took ten.

Each hospital ship that arrived in Malta was met by 'a band of ladies [who] welcomed every wounded or sick soldier ... and provided him with refreshments; let it be said that their energy never flagged in spite of the broiling heat of the docks in summer or the cold in the winter months'. Then the men were taken down Kingsway (today's Republic Street), initially, until transport was organised, in cars that had been lent to the authorities. Crowds lined the streets and pressed forward as the sad procession passed, raising their hats or waving handkerchiefs.

On arrival at *Sacra Infermeria*, or Valletta Military Hospital as it was now called, to be assessed, 'each soldier received a greatly appreciated "welcome" parcel of tobacco, matches, stationery, etc. A large sewing party eked out the hospital supplies by providing such articles as pyjamas, shirts and socks.' As Saviour Pisani says in 'The Nurse of the Mediterranean' (2010), the Maltese 'opened the doors of their homes and hearts to them'. Malta reprised the title it had earned during the Crimean War.

Also awaiting those first casualties was **Dr Alice Hutchison** (1874–1953) and other members of the hospital unit she had helped to organise. It consisted of four women doctors, eight matrons, 30 fully trained sisters and 20 from the VAD (Voluntary Aid Detachment), as well as ancillary staff. In 1916, many women doctors were to arrive, and the story of how they came to do so will be told later, but Alice Hutchison does require a little background. Laura McKenna has drawn out her story from Monica Krippner's *The Quality of Mercy: Women at War, Serbia 1915–1918* (1980):

Alice was the daughter of missionary parents in India. She followed her father's footsteps to become a doctor, graduating from Edinburgh University at the age of 25. She worked for a time in the Punjab (through a cholera epidemic) before returning to Scotland. Having already served in the 1912 Balkan war, Alice was one of the first to join the Scottish Women's Hospital at the outbreak of WW1. She took a hospital unit to Calais in late 1914, to treat the Belgian wounded and the following year sailed for Serbia with a team of twenty five nurses cooks and orderlies. They were diverted to Malta at the request of the Governor to help with the huge numbers of wounded arriving from the Dardanelles and Gallipoli landings. The unit was assigned to the 15th century hospital of the Knights of Malta at Valetta.

There is also a description of Alice: 'diminutive and pretty with flaming red-gold hair, always gaily and fashionably dressed ... (known for her) ... intrepid courage, and unfailing resourcefulness and ... devotion to work.' But two of the diary entries Alice made during her unit's two and a half weeks in Malta are best taken from Colonel Walter Bonnici's website of the Royal Army Medical Corp (RAMC) archives (www.maltaramc.com) ('Military Hospitals in Malta during the Great War'). Alice wrote on 4 May, the day the first casualties arrived:

This was a day of waiting. The past preparations were made, beds made, dressing tables ready, dressings cut up, the wards bright with flowers and sunshine. At last, at 5 o'clock the bell clanged; the first batch of wounded had arrived. Down the long stone corridor they came. A giant, gaunt and unkempt, led the van, towering over the little Maltese orderlies who supported him, his bandaged foot held stiffly in front of him. Ragged, dirty, hungry looking, some joking and others doggedly dejected, those who could walk trooped in. Quite silently followed the procession of stretchers with their still burdens. Until late in the evening they came; one by one the beds were filled while doctors and nurses dressed wounds many of which had remained untouched since first-aid was given at Gallipoli ten days ago.

On 7 May medical reinforcements reached Malta, doctors, orderlies and 39 nurses. On the 20th, Alice wrote,

Our patients are a cheery lot. Many of them are members of the brave Australian Contingent who did so much to help in the first terrible days of landing at Gallipoli and thrilling tales they tell of the happenings of those historic hours. Up and down the long wards they fling chaff and repartee to their comrades, wounds are a joke, pain a little bit of the day's work making them all the more eager to get back to the fighting line. Many are soon up and about in corridors and courtyard, lightly and comfortably clad in pyjamas and military caps [and] bandaged legs give the opportunity for fine competitions in hopping or the one-legged jump. And what must be the horror of the shades of the Knights when their old grey courts, those decorous courts in which one pictures the ritual of coloured procession and the solemn music of Gregorian chants, echo to the sound of the latest rag-time, the jingle of Tipperary or 'Who's your lady friend?'

The cheerfulness and bravery of the men often belied the frightfulness of their injuries as the diary of **Isobel Watson Shepherd Meiklejohn** (*c.*1879–1957), one of the four orderlies of the unit, makes clear: 'One boy came in terribly wounded by shrapnel; he suffered agonies, and used to stuff his handkerchief into his mouth when the wounds were being dressed, yet he never complained ...'. Isobel, from Shetland, was a Home Office factory inspector in civilian life, with an MA in hygiene; in Malta those four women orderlies were treated as probationers.

By the end of the month, there were more doctors, ancillaries and 219 nurses; and Alice and her unit were permitted to depart for Serbia where life and the practice of medicine was even more unexpected and demanding, indeed, her women fell into the hands of the Austrians and were interned. Alice protected the Union Jack by wearing it as a petticoat. She ended her medical career at London's Great Ormond Street Hospital for Children.

By the end of May, 4,000 sick and wounded were being treated in eight hospitals; by September, 10,000 had arrived; by March 1916, there were 20,000 hospital beds. In all, from 4 May 1915 until the end of the War, over 136,000 casualties (including 481 women nurses), from both the Mediterranean Expeditionary Force, and the Salonica Expeditionary Force, were treated in Malta, which had been turned into 'a giant hospital'. Only four military hospitals had existed before the War; as it progressed, so did the number of beds created. Not only were civilian hospitals called into service, but also military barracks, schools and other institutions were transformed by the Royal Engineers. At one time there were 28 medical facilities in the archipelago, including convalescent camps.

One of those involved in the hospital expansion was the Principal Matron **Anne Beadsmore Smith** (1869–1960), daughter of a gold and silver merchant who, as a Queen Alexandra's Imperial Military Nursing Service Reserve (QAIMNSR) matron had served in France at the beginning of the War. Later, as Dame Anne, she was Matron-in-Chief of the QAIMNSR between 1919 and 1924. (Her name was not Beardmore as at least one military source suggests.)

One of the hospitals to be transformed was that of the Blue Sisters. The Mother Superior and Nursing Sisters of the Little Company of Mary, whose arrival in Malta in 1894 is described in Chapter 11, offered their services and the beds in their hospital – the Zammit Clapp – and their nursing home at the adjoining Casa Leone XIII. These hospitals were up-to-date buildings, and their offer was gratefully accepted. Patients began to arrive there on 6 May. The Sisters of Charity, who had been in Malta since 1868, also tended sick and wounded soldiers.

What became the Hamrun Hospital had been Bugeja Technical Institute, opened by Marchesa Anna Bugeja in 1903, with which Dr Bruce and his co-authors in compiling their report on military hospitals may have been unfamiliar. Of this new hospital they wrote, 'The nursing duties were performed by No. 1 Mediterranean Nursing Unit – a volunteer body of ladies organised by Lady Ian Hamilton. An officer of the RAMC was in charge.' This sentence needs clarifying.

Jean Hamilton (née Muir, 1861–1941), daughter of Sir John Muir, a prosperous tea planter in India, and Lady Muir, was married to Ian Standish Monteith Hamilton. The couple had met in India where she was on holiday and he was serving, and they married there in 1887; she was to use her fortune to further his career in the army. By 1915, he was General Sir Ian Hamilton, appointed on 2 March to command a force of 75,000 men tasked to seize control of the Dardanelles and capture Constantinople. The failure of this campaign – considered risky and inadvisable by many even before it began – led to the end of numerous careers, including Hamilton's and, temporarily, that of its instigator, Winston Churchill. General Hamilton was made the scapegoat – in spite of the enterprise being hopelessly undermanned and having faced formidable logistical difficulties, none of which was his fault – and he was recalled to London on 16 October 1915.

The Hamiltons both knew Malta well before the War because, between 1910 and 1914, he had been Commander-in-Chief of British forces in the Mediterranean, based in the San Anton Palace which the governor, General Sir Henry Rundle, much to his chagrin, was forced to vacate for them. *Jean, Lady Hamilton: A Soldier's Wife* (2001) by Celia Lee makes clear that, following their return to England at the end of Ian Hamilton's 1910–1914 posting to Malta, Jean did not return to the islands during her husband's trials and tribulations of the Dardanelles campaign. What she set up in Malta must, therefore, have been done before she left, before the War, though there is no mention of it in Celia Lee's extensive use of her diary. The couple were back in England by mid-July 1914, but after the 28 June assassinations at Sarajevo and, certainly, war had been a possibility for some years, which may have been the background for Jean's organising of the No. 1 Mediterranean Nursing Unit.

But Jean Hamilton's biographer, in correspondence with me, does not think that she was involved in nursing at all in Malta. This is a bit of a mystery. In any case, the unit seems to have come into its own once war was declared and many more nurses were needed. As president of the women's branch of Queen Alexandra's Field Force Fund, Jean did send bales of comforts and medical supplies to the troops and to the hospitals in Malta, Mudros and Alexandria. They were packed in her London drawing room.

Even between 1910 and 1914, Jean did not spend all her time in Malta – she suffered badly from asthma there – but she did, at least, make three delightful pastel sketches – two of San Anton, and one of a storm-racked harbour – which are included in the biography, and there is an elegant 1896 portrait of her by John Singer Sargent in London's Tate Britain, as well as the one shown here.

With the flow of casualties from the east came increasing numbers of military nurses sent from Britain. Typical of the newcomers was Rosa

24. Lady Hamilton, courtesy of Ian Hamilton

Kirkcaldie. Born in Sydney to a Scottish father and English mother, she gained her nurse's certificate in Sydney in March 1914. With the outbreak of war, she joined a hospital ship accompanying the Australian Naval and Military Expeditionary Force to German New Guinea. Back in Sydney in December, she was impatient to enlist. By May 1915 she was in England and had joined QAIMNSR and, by the middle of the month, she was in Malta working at the Valletta Military Hospital, so she would have briefly coincided with Dr Hutchison and her unit. Casualties started pouring in, many of them Rosa's compatriots. In October she volunteered to join a hospital ship taking the wounded from Malta to England; and it was in November that she arrived in Gallipoli to help evacuate the wounded. She continued to nurse in Europe during the rest of the War and afterwards resumed her nursing career in Australia. Unfortunately, her memoir has proved unobtainable.

Narelle Hobbes (*c*.1879–1918) was a 36-year-old hospital matron in New South Wales in March 1915 when she, too, travelled to London to join the QAIMNSR. Dr Melanie Oppenheimer, who uncovered her story, writes in 'From Gallipoli to Basra – an Australian nurse's perspective of war':

Narelle walked into a medical crisis with the failed allied campaign in Gallipoli inundating existing military hospitals with sick and injured soldiers. She was transferred to a new hospital on the island of Malta within two weeks of arriving in London, to care for the sick and wounded from Gallipoli. ... her letters are an invaluable insight into the rates of sickness and injury within the troops and her daily nursing routines ... The letters also reveal a professional jealousy between Australian and English nurses, a strong sense of parochialism towards Australians, and dislike of British customs and their class system.

The name of the hospital is not given, though that, too, was probably the Valletta Military. Narelle stayed in Malta for six months and was then transferred to Sicily. Taken ill in India in March 1918, she was invalided back to Australia on a hospital ship, but she died on 10 May and was buried at sea. Those Australian women were anxious to serve; the campaign by Australian women against the war and conscription is described in Chapter 13 of my *Tasmania: Women, History, Books and Places*.

A more general account of nurses in Malta in 1915, one which includes a sprinkling of names, though not enough information to follow up biographical details, is in *Malta: The Nurse of the Mediterranean* (1916) by the Reverend Albert G Mackinnon. He spent six months in Malta, together with his wife, as senior Presbyterian chaplain to the forces. We only meet his wife as **Mrs Mackinnon**, and I can find nothing more about her than the few glimpses he gives us of her as she supported his work. His account tends to be rather obviously for wartime-morale-boosting consumption, unlike the few women's writing not publicly available at the time, and he is a man of his time where women were concerned:

In the summer of 1915 the hospitals were staffed by nearly 300 medical officers, and the nursing sisters reached almost 1,000. Over the latter was Miss **Hoadley**. She was assisted by the matrons of the different hospitals. In the strenuous days they were almost swept off their feet with the sudden inrush of nurses. To appoint these to their several stations, and select for promotion those especially qualified for larger responsibilities, required quick judgement of character as well as business-like gifts. ...

The fully qualified nurses had a great strain put upon them when the sudden inrush of wounded came, but they rose to the occasion manfully. The adjective fits the case, for to all the feminine qualities of tenderness and sympathy which are necessary for a nurse there must be added something almost masculine, not merely strength of muscle, but firmness of will, and powers of quick decision. These were manifested in the hospitals of Malta. The matrons especially, exercised a strong influence in their several spheres. In charge of the Valletta Hospital, and also of the largest home for nurses was **Miss Brown**, and she discharged the duties of her dual office with thoroughness and industry. **Miss McFarlane** who left St Patrick's Camp, for St Andrew's Hospital, and then for the Front, was the subject of many letters of gratitude in the local press from her patients, and the sorrow at her departure was one of the finest testimonies to the power and influence of a good and clever woman in a position of authority. In another chapter I refer to **Miss McDougall**, who has since been promoted from Ghain Tuffieha Camp to Cottonera Hospital. The blend of gentleness and firmness, the happy knack of putting patients and nurses at their ease in her presence, is not the only characteristic of her, but of the other matrons in Malta, whose success has depended so much on mixing in right proportions the official and human elements in their nature.

Miss McDougall is one of his special favourites because she was Scottish and he writes later 'one feels proud of one's country on being introduced to [her]'. And after some more panegyrics about her, he introduces another Scottish matron, **Miss M'Gregor** who shows the world 'the true charm of noble womanhood'. Because Miss Hoadley's name is uncommon, I may have run her down as being Canadian, attached to the Royal Regiment of Canada, with the initial J.

Albert McKinnon also introduces us to the VAD when he writes,

About one-half of the nursing sisters were V.A.D's, or only partly trained nurses; but without their self-sacrificing labours the sick and wounded could not have been properly looked after and nursed. It is only right to say that these so-called partly trained ladies did superb work on many critical occasions, and that many of them were highly educated, and had made big sacrifices in relinquishing home and comforts at the call of duty to nurse the British soldier.

In 1909, the War Office had set up both female and male Voluntary Aid Detachments to fill certain gaps in the territorial medical services; they were organised by their local Red Cross. The scheme proved popular, particularly with women and, immediately prior to the outbreak of war, 1,823 female and 551 male detachments had registered.

A description of the VADS reads:

The women who joined Detachments were a mixture, being a wide range of ages and with different sorts of life skills. As a group they were very much defined by being middle or upper middle-class – in the main they were the daughters of local gentry, landowners, army officers, clergy, and professional men, and also included a good sprinkling of women with an aristocratic background. The majority were young women who had never had any paid employment, and of those who eventually went on to wartime service more than three-quarters had either never worked outside the home, or had done work which qualified them for payment of a minor nature ... In the spring of 1915 the War Office agreed that VADs could be employed in the large military hospitals at home to augment the trained staff, and by early summer of that year in general hospitals overseas as well.

The women who had previously led a comfortable life were soon knocked into shape by their training in British hospitals, and then by the exigencies and, often, horrors, of their wartime work. One of the best known VADs was **Vera Brittain** (1893–1970), brought up in the fashionable spa resort of Buxton, Derbyshire, daughter of a paper manufacturer with middle-class, Edwardian ideas of the place of women. She describes how she became a VAD and the time she spent in Malta, from October 1916 to May 1917, in the wonderful *Testament of Youth* (1933; 1978).

After family battles, she had taken up her place at Somerville College, Oxford University, in October 1914, just after war broke out. But, with her fiancé, Roland, and adored brother, Edward, serving in the army, she decided after her first year to abandon her academic career to serve her country and experience, at least a little, what they were going through. She was devastated in December 1915 to learn that Roland had been killed by a sniper. He was the first of the four young men close to her whom the War destroyed. Malta was, at least, a temporary balm. She opens the chapter 'Tawny Island' devoted to it:

The memory of my sunlit months in the Mediterranean during the War's worst period of miserable stagnation still causes a strange nostalgia to descend upon my spirit. For me, as for the world, the War was a tragedy and a vast stupidity, a waste of youth and of time; it betrayed my faith, mocked my love, and irremediably spoilt my career – yet Malta remains in my recollection as an interval of heaven, a short year of glamorous beauty and delight, in which, for the time being, I came to life again after Roland's death.

Vera's posting to Malta did not start well, for she arrived ill, something she and 15 other VADs picked up on the terrible transport on the last leg there. Her first meeting on arrival was, I deduce, with Anne Beadsmore Smith, though she doesn't name her when she writes:

When the *Galeka* at last docked in the Grand Harbour at Valletta on October 7th, I awoke to find the Principal Matron of Malta standing by my side, looking down at me. A handsome woman of classic proportions, she seemed somehow to restore their lost heroic quality to our vicissitudes, and I grinned apologetically at her from my lowly cot.

'This one can smile, at any rate!' I heard her remark in a singularly gracious voice to the Matron of the *Galeka*.

In the afternoon I was carried off the boat on a stretcher, and pushed into one of the ambulances which were taking the convoy of sick nurses to the Imtarfa Hospital …

It was almost the end of October before Vera was able to convalesce. In due course, she was passed fit for duty and posted to St George's Hospital 'on a lovely peninsula of grey rock and red sand almost encircled by the sea'. She describes both the hospital and the work of the VAD:

The hospital, like Imtarfa, was an ex-barracks built entirely of stone, with marquees for extra beds, and the nursing staff was posted not to wards but to 'blocks' which were long, narrow, two-storied buildings, with open verandahs above and below. Half a dozen or more small wards, each containing from ten to twenty beds, opened off each verandah. In nearly all the blocks the V.A.D was left on duty alone – a responsibility never permitted her at the 1st London General – for either the afternoon or the evening, and was often in charge of over a hundred patients.

25.   Vera Brittain, Malta, courtesy of the William Ready Division
of Archives and Research Collections, McMaster University

But the chapter is by no means full of such practical details: that first paragraph is more indicative of her stay – the changeable weather, the landscapes, burgeoning spring flowers, the freedom to think, time to heal, to write poetry, even to have fun in the middle of the War and her grief, of which there was more to come. I wish I could quote the whole chapter, for nothing evokes more poignantly Malta during the First World War and the life of those women who served in the Mediterranean; typical of the ambiguity and reality of that life is this passage:

> In the third week of November, three hospital ships were sunk almost simultaneously. … we learnt that the *Britannic* had gone down in the Aegean. The news of her loss galvanised the island like an electric shock. A week later, the rescued members of her staff came on to Malta after spending some days in nursing their own sick and wounded at the Russian hospital in Athens, and were distributed among the various hospitals. As the clothing stores in Valletta were now temporarily depleted, we supplied the refugees with our own pyjamas and undergarments and hot-water bottles until they could return to England and re-equip. Boy-Scouts hats from the Serbian Relief Fund picturesquely crowned the miscellaneous garments in which they were arrayed.
>
> Among the sick was a young, cheerful Sister who had made friends with Betty and myself on the voyage to Mudros. We went to see her at the Floriana Hospital, in Valletta, and found her completely changed – nervous, distressed and all the time on the verge of crying. But to talk of the disaster seemed to bring her relief, and from her conversation we learnt the story of the ship's last hours.

That extract is closer to home than it appears out of its full context: the *Britannic* had conveyed Vera and her cohort on that same passage from Mudros to Malta the previous year. Another extract shows what happened as winter turned to the spring of 1917 and fewer patients arrived:

> In Malta the nursing was now very light; most of our patients were convalescent, and off-duty time was plentiful, Many of the V.A.D.s and the younger Sisters, whose work on the blocks no longer exhausted their vitality, began to find scope for superfluous energy in circumventing the Army regulations which, even in the atmosphere of comparative reasonableness that prevailed on the island, forbade the nursing and medical staffs to mix except after elaborate permission had been obtained, and chaperonage, which was hopefully supposed to be effective, provided. Whispered conversations and outbursts of giggling all over the Sisters' quarters proclaimed the existence of numerous minor intrigues. At many of these I could guess, but I did not join them, for my one experience, so far, of mixed parties had not tempted me to desire a repetition.

What follows is the description of a mad visit to *Madame Butterfly* at the Manoel Theatre. Towards the end of her stay,

Rumours that we should all be sent to Salonika because the submarine campaign was making Malta impracticable as a hospital base buzzed continually round the island. Unsettled and restless, we waited impatiently for something to happen.

And happen it did: in May 1917, she received a letter from her brother that another close friend, Geoffrey, from within their close circle had been killed, and that yet another, Victor, had been blinded. She wrote:

That night – quiet as all nights were now that so few sick and wounded were coming from Salonika – I tried to keep my mind from thoughts and my eyes from tears by assiduously pasting photographs of Malta into a cardboard album. The scent of a vase of sweet-peas on the ward table reminded me of Roland's study on Speech Day, centuries ago. Although I had been up for a day and two nights, I felt no inclination to sleep.

She resolves to return to England and take care of Victor. She has to wait nearly a month before permission comes through, and then is told that her party will have to travel overland from Sicily because of the threat of submarines and torpedoes. Finally:

We were taken by transport to the Grand Harbour, and after waiting on docks for about an hour, put on the *Isonzo*. Lady Methuen and party were on board and we had a Japanese destroyer 'Q' as an escort. It was a rough, wet and stormy day, and as there were no chairs we had to sit on deck on our piled-up luggage. Then began about the worst five hours I have ever experienced. Outside the harbour the seas were terrible; I have never known anything so rough, not even in the Bay of Biscay.

Following her time in Malta, Vera nursed in France; there she experienced the War at first hand.

Victor died, releasing her from the obligation she had imposed on herself. She was looking after her parents in their flat in Kensington when the telegram arrived to say that her brother had been killed in Italy on 15 June 1918. The four men who had been so important to her young womanhood were no more. After the War, Vera gradually picked herself up, returned to her studies at Somerville, and became a well-known writer, political activist, pacifist, feminist and mother of her equally well-regarded daughter, Shirley Williams. *Testament of Youth* not only captures Malta during the War, but it is also among the very best of First World War literature – if not the best.

Another VAD about whom a few details are known was the New Zealand artist, **Katherine** (Kitty) **Airini Vane** (née Mair, 1891–1965). Her mother, **Eleanor Sperrey** (EK Mair), was also an established artist. Kitty/Airini travelled to London in 1912 to pursue her artistic career, studying at the Slade. In 1914, she joined the Red Cross as a VAD and was sent to Malta where she met Captain the Hon. Ralph Vane, whom she married there in 1917, giving some indication of the love affairs of the medical women during the War in Malta. In the 1920s and 1930s, during extensive travels, she re-visited Malta. I know of at least four watercolours of Malta – a pair of 'Views of Valletta Harbour', 'Musta' and 'Kalkara'.

In a letter to her brother at the beginning of her time in Malta, Vera Brittain gives us a marvellous introduction to the women doctors who started to arrive in 1916; at the time she was lying on her bed of sickness in the Imtarfa Hospital:

> Everyone here is trying to trace the origin of our disease. We have had quite twelve doctors in here, sometimes five at once. Three of them are lady doctors, all very charming, too, in khaki tussore coats and skirts, dark blue ties and solar topees.

She elaborates on women doctors when she is working at St George's Hospital:

> In Malta we often envied the women doctors, whose complete freedom to associate with their male colleagues appeared to result mainly in the most determined chastity. At St George's the staff included quite a number of medical women, since the War Office, having at last decided to employ them, evidently regarded Malta – where there was now so little serious illness – as a suitable place for such a desperate experiment.
>
> One of these women, an elderly spinster whom everyone called 'Auntie', showed her determination to make herself felt by putting her patients on so many medicines that the V.A.D. who carried the medicine-basket round the block had a back-breaking half-hour after every meal. Another, a small brunette known to the nursing staff as 'Kitty', cultivated a flirtatious femininity, and appeared on her round as orderly officer in frilly evening dresses reminiscent of a four-year-old at a juvenile party. But most of them apparently belonged to the coat-and-skirt species, with an official manner and the traditional belief – which is fast being abandoned by more recently qualified women – that their wisest course was to model themselves upon their male predecessors, thus tending to repeat some of men's oldest mistakes and to reproduce their lop-sided values.

That is very much a VAD describing her seemingly privileged superiors, and slightly unsisterly. Not surprisingly, Vera only half realised what women doctors had to go through to get to practising, even in Malta.

Leah Leneman's 'Medical Women in the First World War – Ranking Nowhere' (1993) shows that it was not easy; she explains how 'when war broke out in 1914 officialdom saw no role for medical women. On attempting to volunteer Dr Elsie Inglis was told by a War Office administrator, "My good lady, go home and sit still".'

Dr Inglis did not do as she was told: together with the National Union of Women's Suffrage Societies, she formed the Scottish Women's Hospitals for Foreign Service. Its doctors first distinguished themselves in France and Serbia. The War Office still refused offers of all-women units for other theatres of war. Leah Leneman continues,

> However, more doctors were required abroad, and in April 1916 the War Office began to recruit women. They were not to be sent to France but to Malta, far from the fighting. (British troops in Salonica needing hospitalisation – primarily because of malaria – went there). And they were not given rank, grading, uniforms, or even the ration and billeting allowance that every male doctor had of right.
>
> So eager were medical women to serve that in spite of these unsatisfactory conditions the appeal for 40 women doctors in April 1916 resulted in 85 sailing to Malta in July.

When they travelled, they were not treated as medical officers, but as soldiers' wives. One of the sources the War Office approached for women doctors was **Louisa Aldrich-Blake** (1865–1925), surgeon at the Elizabeth Garret Anderson hospital, and one of the first women to enter medicine. As Dean of the London School of Medicine for Women she approached all the women on the medical register.

On 1 September **Dr Edith Guest** (b.1873), who had qualified in 1904, was among those sailing for Malta as part of the Women's Medical Unit, RAMC, to augment the 48 who had been sent out in August. It is not clear which hospital she was based at, but it is what she wrote from Egypt when she left Malta to serve there in December 1917 that is of particular interest regarding the status of women doctors:

> Although we are senior in service to many of the men here, yet they all, however young and inexperienced, rank above us, and any youngster will take precedence of us even if we serve ten years. The longer one serves, the more galling this becomes … Our C.O. here is with us heart and soul, but he says nothing will be done except as the result of pressure brought to bear by our representatives at home, and I'm sure he is right.

The 'Lady Doctors' Federation' formed a subcommittee to fight the injustice, and solicited the views and experience of women doctors in the field. One reply came from **Dr Constance Astley-Mayer** (b.1878) in Sinai:

> We certainly think the Federation should press during the war, through the British Medical Association, for proper rank and commissions for the women doctors serving with the RAMC. All right minded colonels in whose hospitals we have worked agree with this.

As she served in Egypt between December 1917 and May 1919, one of the sympathetic colonels was, no doubt, Edith Guest's. But Constance, who had qualified in Edinburgh in 1902, was probably also one of the three women doctors who tended to Vera Brittain wearing their rough silk suits and solar topees. Having embarked for Malta in the first batch of women doctors of August 1916, she served at the Mtarfa Military hospital (see Chapter 20 itinerary).

Dr Gertrude Dobrashian (1887–1975) was a Registrar at the Mtarfa. She, and several of her eight siblings, had been born in Constantinople; her surgeon father, Dr Gabriel Dobrashian, of Armenian descent, came from there. Gertrude registered with the General Medical Council in Edinburgh in 1911 and embarked for Malta in that first August batch. She was eminently qualified to ponder over Vera's mysterious illness because, while in Malta, she undertook an investigation into Bacillary Dysentery from the troops in the Salonica area. She returned to England in January 1917.

The third of the three Mtarfa women doctors mentioned by Vera was probably **Dr Barbara Martin Cunningham** (b.1877). She graduated from Edinburgh with distinction in 1901 and, until August 1916, was medical officer in munitions factories; the Ministry of Munitions had been aware of 20 cases of toxic jaundice in male munitions workers and in 42 female workers. Six men and 12 women had died of liver problems. On 12 August, *The Lancet* published an article of Barbara's, on the symptoms and complications caused by TNT dust in workers, written with **Dr Agnes Livingstone-Learmonth** (née Hamilton, 1877–1936). They both embarked for Malta in the August batch, and both started out at St Patrick's Hospital, but Barbara seems to have transferred to the Mtarfa. She left to serve in Salonica in July 1917 – though her actual departure was delayed by the escort vessels striking mines just outside the harbour. The adventures that followed are another story, but she was mentioned in dispatches and was awarded an OBE in 1918.

It is not possible to mention all the women doctors who saw service in Malta, but 80 of them are listed on Walter Bonnici's RAMC archive website, and you can click on each name to obtain what details there are about them. The 'Kitty' mentioned by Vera Brittain is, unfortunately, not obvious. It would be invidious, though, not to mention the case of **Isobel Addy Tate** (1874–1917), for it shows that not all left Malta safely, either serving elsewhere or pursuing their careers, and emphasises the fact that sickness as much as wounds needed attention, particularly in the second stage of Malta's wartime involvement.

In April 1915, together with six other women doctors, Isobel joined the Serbian Relief Unit under **Mabel St Clair Stobbart** (1862–1954). Mabel was the founder, in 1912, of the Women's Sick and Wounded Convoy Corps and, in 1914, the Women's National Service League. She was also an active supporter of women's suffrage, as was not uncommon among women doctors. When war broke out, she set up a field hospital in Belgium. Isobel, who had received her medical education at Queen's College, Belfast, registered with the General Medical Council of Ireland in 1899; by 1916, she was medical inspector of school children for the Shropshire and Lancashire Education Committee. In Serbia, she was in charge of the X-ray unit, in which she had received special training. But she contracted enteric fever and was hospitalised in Belgrade.

Returned to England later that year, Isobel worked in the radiology department of a hospital in Chichester. In the spring of 1916, she answered Louisa Aldrich-Blake's call, and embarked for Malta in August. She started out at St Paul's Military Hospital, which was used almost exclusively for dysentery and enteric cases, and then moved to the Valletta Military Hospital in charge of the Bacteriological Unit. But she died suddenly at her residence, No. 5 Victoria Junction, Sliema. Her death certificate shows her to have died from a congestion of the brain (due to typhoid). She was buried with full military honours at Pietà Military Cemetery (see Chapter 19 itinerary).

Inevitably nursing staff too became infected when caring for the many cases of infectious diseases that arrived, predominantly bacillary dysentery and a mixture of amoebic and bacillary dysentery. Typical was **Helen Bachelor Taylor** (*c*.1873–1915), a VAD from Bedfordshire. She died of dysentery on 15 November 1915, aged 42, and was also buried in the Pietà Cemetery. During the summer and autumn of 1916, many cases of dysentery from Macedonia were admitted to the Fort Tigné Hospital. Two staff nurses, **Frances Brace** and **Mary Clough**, died of it in the autumn, and **Staff Nurse Dorothy Watson** of the Territorial Force Nursing Service died at St John's Hospital in March 1917.

The close friendship possible among the women doctors, and the commitment they brought to their work, are illustrated through **Dr Helen De Rastricke Hanson** (1874–1926). From 1897 she received her medical education at the London School of Medicine for Women. For three years, from 1905, she worked as a medical missionary in India, returning because of ill health but travelling steerage so she could donate the £5 to the Women's Social and Political Union. Back at home, she became involved in the various other suffrage organisations. In 1914, she joined Mabel St Clair Stobbart's unit to Cherbourg and then became one of the seven women doctors travelling with her to Serbia, thus becoming friends with Isobel. They embarked for Malta together as members of the Scottish Women's Hospital Unit, and served together at the Valletta Military Hospital. Finally, she attended Isobel's funeral.

In July 1917, Helen joined Barbara Martin Cunningham on the ill-fated voyage to Salonica. Although she returned home on leave in July 1918, she went back east and did not return until 1920, when she became Assistant Medical Officer at the Public Health Department, London County Council. Aged 52, she was knocked down by a car and killed. The women doctors that went to Malta had such varied medical careers before arriving there, and the same afterwards, but what extraordinary times they had to look back on, and how much they sacrificed for their vocation.

Also important to the sick and wounded troops who passed through Malta were the women who made their recovery and convalescence more comfortable and entertaining, in addition to the several convalescent camps. Presiding over their endeavours was Lady Methuen. The Rev. Albert Mackinnon writes of 1915, in his rather saccharine way,

[The] varied social work found a ready sympathiser and helper in Lady Methuen. Not only did she organise and superintend, but she visited personally the hospitals, and no visitor left a more gracious memory behind her. She cared for all classes. For the officers she established a homely club, where the strongest refreshment was a good cup of tea, and which was much appreciated by those who frequented it. For the soldiers she was constantly planning some new means of helping them. For the nurses, along with His Excellency, she gave up for several months their beautiful palace of St Antonio, that the nurses might have a holiday there. These acts so thoughtful and generous can never be forgotten as long as the story of Malta's hospitals will be told.

Mary Methuen (nèe Sanford, d.1941) was both Lord Methuen's second cousin and, since 1884, his second wife. They had three sons and two daughters. One daughter, the youngest child, (Ellen) **Seymour Methuen** (1893–1985), accompanied them to Malta when Methuen took up his post in February 1915. As Vera Brittain records, Lady Methuen went on leave at the same time as she left, in May 1917, but she did return.

Seymour Methuen also contributed to the entertainment of the troops; Albert Mackinnon writes,

Lord Methuen has shown himself a true believer in the power of music to soothe and charm, and perhaps the best exponent of his theory was the Hon. Seymour Methuen, who is an accomplished violinist. She was ever ready to place her skill at the service of those who were seeking to entertain the wounded.

Seymour was to marry Captain Cyril Barnes in 1924.

St Andrew's church under Mrs Mackinnon established tea rooms in Valletta, but there were similar establishments elsewhere, often involving Maltese women; her husband writes:

Maltese ladies have been eager to help, and many a private party has been given to Tommy which the world may not hear of, but which he will not forget. The services which Mrs Bonavia has rendered have earned the gratitude of all, the special Tea Room at Sliema, run by her and the ladies of the Red Cross, has proved a most popular rendezvous for the convalescent soldier.

The ladies of St Paul's Church have done their part by providing a roof tea every Sunday afternoon for the wounded, and this has been much appreciated by the men.

26. Marie Bonavia, from Abela, *Grace and Glory*

In 1892, Camilla Vassallo had married the Hon. Edgar Bonavia; this is the **Marie Bonavia** whom all extol. Dr Bruce elaborates:

In May, 1915, the Hon. E. and Mrs Bonavia felt that a tea-room to provide rest and refreshment for sick and wounded able to get about was an urgent need in Sliema .... Having received the approval of the Ladies' Committee and some slight financial backing from the British Red Cross Society, Mrs Bonavia, with a band of helpers, opened a tea-room on May 21st in part of the premises of the Sliema Branch of the Union Club, which was generously lent. The site on the Sliema front was excellent, being in the immediate neighbourhood of several hospitals and on the main road to the more distant group of hospitals around St Andrew's and St George's. The tea-rooms proved a great success, being crowded daily, and especially at the orchestral and other concerts which were given twice weekly. During the 29 months of its existence the Hon. E. Bonavia, CMG, estimates that over 50,000 men have been served, a tribute to the popularity of the institution and to the hard work undertaken by the voluntary workers.

Mrs Radcliffe chaired the 'Ladies Committee' at one time, but she is not among the names in a 2014 article by Michael Galea, 'Malta earns the title "nurse of the Mediterranean"', which are as follows: 'The Countess Lucan, Miss Calvocoressi, Mrs Clapp Zammit, Mrs F.P. Denaro, Mrs A.M. Galea, Mrs Lewis Hall, Miss Gatt and Mrs Pringle.' It has proved difficult to track these women down, apart from Mrs Clapp Zammit who, with her sister, set up the Zammit Clapp Hospital (Blue Sisters Hospital) (see Chapter 11), and Marie Denaro (née Agius, b.1880) whose background is detailed in Chapter 14. Her husband, Frank, whom she had married in 1901, was to be gazetted Colonel of the King's Own Malta Regiment in 1919; her charitable activities were to continue through the Second World War (see Chapter 15). Mrs Lewis Hall was, presumably, the wife of Major Lewis-Hall, in charge of the Army Service Corps. Mrs AM Galea was Elizabeth (née Asphar) wife of the businessman, philanthropist and writer Alfons Maria Galea (see Chapter 16). You would think the Countess Lucan might be the easiest to identify, but I have failed. But the names do indicate the cooperation between Maltese and expatriate women. Michael Galea goes on to note, in pleasing detail,

It was a very active committee, organising concerts by local civic bands, variety entertainment and performances, cinema shows (sometimes screening scenes of the war), excursions, tea sessions, talks; promoting donations in kind such as cakes, fruit, flowers, books (a box of books was received in Malta from Queen Mary), magazines, newspapers, games, playing cards, gramophones, cigarettes, cigars and tobacco.

The committee actively supplied caps, mufflers, gloves (these were with a thumb piece but without divisions for the fingers), mittens (with short fingers or at least a knitted hole to cover the palm and were long above the wrist).

[A] novel idea was the setting up of a club for nurses; they used to meet in the Ladies Room at the Union Club.

The Marquesa Scicluna lent her seaside residence, the Dragonara Villa, St Julian's, near St George's Bay (see Chapter 19 itinerary), as a convalescent home for 20 officers, and provided £100 a month for 12 months for its upkeep. Corinna Abela Pulis, Marchesa Scicluna (b. c.1886), daughter of a Naxxar pharmacist, had married the 45-year-old marquis, Giuseppe Scicluna, in 1901, when she was 21. She was widowed in 1907. After the War, she received the OBE for her 'humanitarian work'. The family also owned the Palazzo Parisio in Naxxar which features during the Second World War and in Chapter 19, as does the work of Corinna's daughter-in-law at the Dragonara.

There was another way that Maltese women were affected by the War: hundreds of Maltese service personnel died on foreign soil; their wives, mothers, daughters and sisters were left to grieve and pick up the pieces of their lives as best they could.

The War may have ended with the armistice of 11 November 1918, but another horror had already started: by 1919, the world was engulfed by the Spanish Flu Pandemic in which 50–100 million died, many of them young and healthy adults. Among the dead was the youngest of the three sons of Dr Archibald Garrod and **Laura Garrod** (née Smith, d.1940). Their two elder sons had already been killed during the War. Only their daughter, **Dorothy Garrod** (1892–1968) was left. Archibald Garrod was, before the War, a distinguished physician at St Bartholomew's Hospital, London; in 1886 he had married the daughter of Sir Thomas Smith Bt, a surgeon also at Barts. The Garrods' two elder sons had been medical men too.

In 1915, Archibald Garrod was promoted to the temporary rank of Colonel in the Army Medical Service and posted to Malta, based at the Cottonera Hospital, to be consulting physician to the Mediterranean Forces. It is fair to assume that his wife was with him, and that there they heard of the deaths of their three sons. Dorothy, having graduated from Newnham College, Cambridge, in 1916, then saw war service in France and grieved the death of the man she had hoped to marry. She was demobilised in Germany in 1919 and joined her parents in Malta where her father was now head of war hospitals. There, among the islands' archaeological ruins, she found her goal in life, to be a prehistorian of the palaeolithic, the Old Stone Age. She was to become a famous archaeologist and Disney Professor of Archaeology at Cambridge, one of a line of women who passed through Malta inspired by its previous civilisations. Her time in Malta, which may have lasted until her parents left in 1921, perhaps also acted as balm to her grief.

Dr Edith Guest was to return to Malta with the archaeologist Margaret Murray in 1921, to help in the excavation of Borġ in-Nadur, and appears again in Chapter 21. Even during the War, Elizabeth Douglas Van Buren, as Chapter 2 describes, had been part of the team excavating a Roman villa near Borġ in-Nadur. There is no evidence that Edith Guest, who did not arrive in Malta until September 1916, met her, though she may have known about her work.

Archaeologists, doctors and trained nurses were the first recognised professional women in Malta. The first Maltese woman doctor, **Blanche Huber** (*c.*1902–1942) entered the University of Malta to read medicine in June 1919, together with **Tessie Camilleri** (b.1901) who read English and was the first woman graduate. Blanche was born in Birkirkara, the daughter of the Hon. Joseph Hubert, Government Treasurer, and **Mary Huber** (née Micallef). She graduated in 1925 and married fellow doctor Joseph Caruana, but she died aged only 40 in 1942. There is a Triq Blanche Huber in Sliema.

Although Maltese women, discouraged by church and family, played a smaller part in the War than foreign ones, it did hasten a process whereby the islands' women were beginning to feel their feet in the world outside their home. On the most frivolous level, as a jingle unearthed by Hillary Briffa has it in 'Malta in the First World War: A Tripartite Linguistic Legacy of Reportage' (2015): 'Scantily dressed as fashion dictates,/Skirts up to their knees.' This process was to become more obvious by the late 1930s. The image by artist Gladys Peto, who accompanied her army doctor husband to Malta for six months between 1924 and 1925, captures the scene, though her *Malta and Cyprus* (1928) gives little impression of the existence of Maltese women.

27.   Short skirts at Mdina by Gladys Peto,
from *Malta and Cyprus*

June 1919 – *Sette Giugno*

1919 was a busy year in more ways than one, the month of June particularly significant. Benignly, it signified the end of the Spanish Flu Pandemic, as it affected Malta. It had made its appearance there almost exactly a year earlier and 20,388 civilians were to suffer; 807 of them died. Gozo suffered most, and women more than men, presumably because they tended to be the carers. A further 5,798 cases, with 109 deaths, affected British service personnel – the number of nurses who succumbed does not seem to have been recorded.

There were other factors, too, undermining the well-being of Malta and the Maltese following the cessation of hostilities. The War had had a major economic impact on the islands, the disruption of trade causing food shortages, and a significant rise in the cost of living. The cost of grain had risen sharply and, thus, the price of bread, the mainstay of the Maltese diet; it had trebled from 2½ pence to 7½ pence per *rotolo*. This was largely because Maltese merchants were penalised by the cost of insuring their cargo during the War due to the threat to shipping in the Mediterranean, though the grain importers and flour millers were assumed to be profiteering. The added burden on women trying to feed their families is not mentioned in what happened next, perhaps because they did not take part in the action.

The rising costs would also have affected the women involved in commercial bread-making. Qormi was the centre for that, and a British Government census for 1861 shows that of the 486 kneaders, the majority were women, and of the 33 bakers, 14 were women. The flour merchants pleaded with the colonial authorities to allow a subsidy but were rebuffed.

There was also constitutional upset: with the end of the War and the Treaty of Versailles, Malta had expected to be granted self-government. When that did not come to pass, local politicians convoked a National Assembly to petition for home rule. It met on 25 February to draft a new self-government constitution. When it met again on Saturday 7 June, a crowd gathered to show its support; anti-British feeling ran high. What happened next would become known as the bread riots of *Sette Giugno* – a day celebrated in Palace Square since 1985 and, formally, with a public holiday since 1989. One reason for the riots that ensued was described by a British Government Minister, following a Commission of Enquiry, as 'The incoherent, unreasoning protest of a hungry populace against its sufferings.'

The first target of the crowd, which soon became a mob, was the Union Jack. Up and down Kingsway they made sure that it was removed, and they forced shops to close. They began to break into buildings, ransacking and destroying. Control was slow in coming. Police pay was inadequate and service conditions poor. One of the crowd's *bêtes noires* was Antonio Cassar Torreggiani. He was head of the Cassar Company which owned the St George's Flour Mills at Marsa. He was also a shipowner. The mill owners were an easy target, though Cassar Torreggiani had risked much by managing to bring in a shipload of wheat without having been able to insure ship or cargo. It was his residence, number 191 in the appropriately named Strada Forni (Old Bakery Street) upon which the mob of 2,000 descended (see Chapter 17 itinerary).

Cassar Torreggiani had a wife and family. In 1910, he had married the beautiful **Marguerita (Maggie) Cali** (1887–1923), daughter of the famous Maltese artist Giuseppe Cali, and sister-in-law of **Maria Cali** (née Corleo, 1884–1947), married to Giuseppe's artist son Ramiro, and an artist in her own right, as a gouache of St Paul's Bay in Nicholas de Piro's dictionary of artists shows. By 1919, the Cassar Torreggianis had four children. Happily, the family were staying in the country, at the Villa Torreggiani (now a restaurant), St Julians. But their town house was ransacked, furniture thrown out of the windows, and some fine oil paintings by Maggie's father torn down and trampled upon. Eventually, after a small police force had retreated from Old Bakery Street, the army arrived, shots were fired, though not under orders, and two demonstrators were killed. Another man was killed later in the day. Given the deaths, it is hard, even at this remove, to fully imagine Maggie's feelings when she next saw her home.

28. Maggie Cassar-Torreggiani,
courtesy of Nicholas de Piro

Crowds formed again on Sunday and congregated outside the residence of another mill owner, Colonel John Lewis Francia, opposite the Opera House in Kingsway. He was a Spanish citizen from Gibraltar in the British Army and appears to have been at home, because he called the police; but the whereabouts of his family at the time has eluded me. His wife was **Teresina Francia** (née Buttigieg) and they, too, had four children. Their house, now known as the Palazzo Ferreria, and housing the Ministry for the Family and Social Solidarity (see Chapter 17 itinerary), was wrecked. If Teresina was there, it would have been a terrifying ordeal, particularly if their children were with them. If she, like Maggie Cassar Torreggiani, had to come back to it later, she, too, deserves sympathy. The marines and seamen sent there to clear Kingsway were ordered not to fire, but a rioter told to move refused and was bayoneted. He died in hospital on 16 June, bringing the total of dead to four. These men became Maltese heroes, but I can find nothing about their mothers, wives, sweethearts, sisters, and their grief.

Rioting continued outside Valletta; those ransacking the residence of grain importer and miller Luigi Farrugia and his wife **Contessa Giovanna Ellul-Lanzon** in Hamrun, as well as the nearby Farrugia mill, were mostly from Qormi though, as far as I know, no women breadmakers were involved.

When peace was finally restored, some of the rioters were court-martialled, others tried in the criminal court. A Commission of Enquiry was set up. Police pay was raised. Antonio Cassar Torreggiani was invited to London where he suggested that a form of self-government would help, and that bread should be subsidised, which it was. On 16 May 1921, a new constitution came into force providing Malta with bi-cameral representative and responsible government.

Carmel Cassar gives details of what followed then and over the years in his concise history: the 'party passions' and 'violent views', particularly between the pro-British, English language and the pro-Italian, Italian language parties. This would only affect women in so far as they took the side of their men, leaving the question: how would they relate to other women in such a small community? – perhaps a continuing quandary.

Maggie Cassar Torreggiani was to die in 1923, aged only 32, giving birth at 74 Kingsway (Casa Rocca Piccola) which her husband had bought in 1919. Their daughter **Phyllis Cassar Torreggiani** (Philomena) (1917–2011) was to become chatelaine there when, in 1938, she married Jerome De Piro, heir to the Barony of Budach (see Chapter 17 itinerary). In 1928 **Malvina Beatrice Francia** (d.1964) was to marry Prime Minister Sir Ugo Mifsud. She was especially affected by the intense partisan rivalries of the political parties because in 1942 her husband collapsed during a speech in the Council defending fellow Nationalists, and died shortly afterwards. The family's second daughter, **Lola Francia**, appears in Chapter 14 as, briefly, does Malvina.

While the events of *Sette Giugno* were taking place, the new governor, General Sir Herbert Plumer, was apparently on board ship within sight of Malta waiting to arrive. He did so on 10 June, together with his wife **Lady Plumer** (née Annie Constance Goss, 1858–1941). Her feelings about what awaited them in her husband's new posting – with guns on the streets, and the remains of rioting evident – are not difficult to imagine. It would be easy to ignore her, but for a delightful description from the *Jerusalem Post* because, in 1925, following Malta, her husband became High Commissioner of the British Mandate for Palestine. The newspaper did not think much of Plumer who, during his time in Malta, later in 1919, had become Field Marshal Viscount Plumer, but

Lady Plumer, in contrast to this short solid man in a bowler hat, was tall and thin, always wore huge feathered hats and had a collection of fans. She sounds like a character created by Oscar Wilde, but she was sympathetic to the suffragettes and danced for joy when she heard that Britain had granted the vote to women. Her husband was not impressed and in fact refused to be president of the Palestine scout movement because girls were included. He was a keen cricketer, while his wife played bridge.

The Plumers may have arrived inauspiciously in Malta, but when they left in 1924, as the London *Times* reported,

Both the outgoing Governor and Lady Plumer were greatly moved as they embarked in the Admiral's yacht Bryony and steamed out of the Grand Harbour escorted by flotillas of shore craft past the famous bastions of the

Knights black with cheering crowds, while bands played and guns fired a last salute.

Of course, that passage can be read two ways because, as Carmel Cassar says, 'During the middle years of British rule many Maltese began to regard the imposition of the colonizing country as rather more oppressive than those of the latter phase of the Hospitallers.'

Refugees 1919–1922

One of the reasons for the rise in the cost of wheat and, thus, the price of bread, was the interruption of the Russian grain trade after the outbreak of war and the Russian Revolution that followed in 1917. It was that revolution that led to another event of 1919 – the influx of Russian refugees. Lord and Lady Methuen would undoubtedly have been relieved to leave Malta before the events of *Sette Giugno*, but they were still in place at San Anton to greet the Dowager Empress of Russia earlier that spring.

Maria Feodorovna (née Princess Dagmar of Denmark, 1847–1928), widow of Tsar Alexander II, was no stranger to Malta. In 1909, she had stayed with the Duke and Duchess of Connaught at San Anton, together with her sister Queen Alexandra of England and her husband Edward VII. She wrote then to her son, Nicholas II, 'I liked Malta so much, it is so delightful, above St Antonio, where the Connaughts live, the garden is a little paradise, full of delightful roses and flowers of all kinds. We passed four charming days there.'

When she arrived on 20 April 1919, the circumstances were rather different. She may not have admitted that her son Nicholas and his family were dead, but she knew that her estates and money had been confiscated, and that her adopted country was perhaps lost to her for ever; she knew, too, that she and her two daughters were refugees, though, lest it be forgotten, imperial refugees.

On 7 April, HMS *Marlborough* had docked at Yalta in the Crimea to take on board Maria Feodorovna and what was expected to be her suite of ten or twelve. When it left on the 11th, it contained 44 members of the imperial family, members of the Russian nobility, and a number of governesses, nurses, maids and manservants, as well as several hundred cases of luggage, that is, 200 tons of it. A useful and up-to-date account of the journey from Yalta, and the stay in Malta, marrying the narrative of several protagonists, is that of Francis Welch's *The Russian Court at Sea: the Voyage of HMS Marlborough, April 1919* (2011).

Maria Feodorovna described her arrival in Malta in her diary: 'Lord and Lady Methuen came on board together with the Admiral. Lord Methuen had been wounded in the Boer War and has a stiff leg. They both seem to be charming people.' She had assumed that she would be continuing on to England in the *Marlborough* and was evasive when Lord Methuen told her that San Anton had been prepared to receive her (see Chapter 20 itinerary).

First Lieutenant Pridham noted in his diary regarding the Dowager Empress and her daughter the Grand Duchess **Xenia Alexandrovna** (1875–1960), her family and those who had accompanied them from Yalta:

The Grand Duchess Xenia and the 'boys' went with her, the remainder being distributed between the various hotels in Sliema. I got them all and their 750 pieces of luggage clear by 3.30 and, marvellous to relate, not a single person or piece of luggage went to the wrong place. Even the Russian servants were kept herded in their correct lots.

At San Anton, Maria Feodorovna observed that they were received by Lord and Lady Methuen

who brought us to our rooms upstairs, which she herself had furnished so beautifully. It was very funny when we went to see where the boys would be accommodated as they were small children's beds since they had thought that they were all young, so we all died of laughter when Lord and Lady Methuen suddenly caught sight of all the big boys!

It is pure luck that we arrived here some days before the other poor souls; Lord Methuen thought that only peasants and simple people would be coming, so he had arranged everything for them in barracks and hospitals. He almost fell over backwards when I told him that they were all our friends and acquaintances from society who could not possibly be put up in hospitals.

Pridham's reaction was:

I hear the advent of the Empress has turned Malta upside down and resulted in a great number of short tempers, most of the staff have been employed trying to find sheets and pillows suitable for the use of Her Imperial Majesty. Lady Methuen has been at her wits' end and driven most others the same way.

The family of Prince Serge Dolgorouky, master of the Empress's household and with her at San Anton – his mother, daughter and niece **Princess Sophia Dolgorouky** (Sofka, 1907–1994) – was in a hotel in Sliema; the party included **Miss King** who had been 11-year-old Sofka's English nanny since she was four. She was a singularly unpleasant woman according to accounts of the voyage. In *Red Princess: A Revolutionary Life* (2007), Sofka wrote later, tellingly in more ways than one:

Miss King had a favourite story of how the manager of the hotel screened off part of the dining-room so as not to embarrass the poor refugees, only to find his indigent guests coming down in full, albeit old-fashioned, evening dress and glittering jewels. Even Miss King was wearing my mother's rope of pearls that she had left during her last visit to the Crimea – but underneath her inevitable high-necked blouses …

I enjoyed Malta. There were morning walks with Miss King watching the women come running out of the houses with jugs as the goat-herd's bell resounded. Then pause as jugs were filled straight from the udder and coins passed from hand to hand, before the flock was driven on with incomprehensible cries.

29.   Sofka Zinovieff, from Zinovieff, *Red Princess*

On 25 April the Canadian registered ship SS *Bermudian* arrived carrying 345 women, 220 men and 133 children; they too had to be accommodated, so rooms were found in St George's, St Andrew's and Tigné Barracks, and St Ignatius College that had all so recently been military hospitals. Maria Feodorovna was to leave for England after eight days' stay; one of those new arrivals recorded,

On the eve of Her departure for England, the Empress announced Her wish to visit all the barracks and camps in which we were accommodated in the environs of the city. Our happiness on seeing Her was clouded by inexpressible sorrow at parting from her. The next day, with heavy hearts, we watched as the dreadnought sailed away into the distance, bearing our Mother Empress.

Once a Grand Duchess: Xenia, Sister of Nicholas II (2004), by Coryne Hall and John Van der Kiste, gives Xenia's account of Malta. Her teenage sons turned the place upside down, in spite of the efforts to rein them in of Methuen's young ADC, Robert Ingham. But Xenia and her mother

> quite 'lost their hearts' to Malta and its people. Years later, when Ingham visited her in England, Xenia told him that 'she had asked the King if she and her mother could make Malta their home'. The King replied that he had already made other arrangements. As they left San Antonio on 29 April Xenia picked four ruby and diamond studs from her white silk blouse. Pressing them into Ingham's hand, she said simply, 'for you to remember me by'.

As soon as the Empress had sailed, the Methuens, too, left, at the end of his time as governor.

It is impossible to find space here to detail even a few of the Russian refugees, let alone give a full picture of the time they spent in Malta; they left at various times and to various places. Many of them had names that resonate in Russian history; among them: **Sofya Feodorovna Kolchak**, wife of the Admiral; **Madame Denikin**, with her husband the General; **Mlle Kornilov**; **Princess Irina Alexandrovna Yousoupov** (with her was not only her husband, Felix, Rasputin's assassin, but their child, an English nanny, two maids and three manservants); **Nathalie Brassov**, morganatic wife of murdered Grand Duke Mikhail Alexandrovich, Nicholas II's brother; a family of Tolstoys, and another of Orlovs.

Sources differ about how many refugees – some of them English – passed through Malta, but it was somewhere between 700 and 800. A useful list is to be found on the Malta Family History website and the plight of some of them is discussed in *Malta and Russia: Journey Through the Centuries, Historical Discoveries in Russo-Maltese Relations* compiled and edited by Elizaveta Zolina (*c*.2002). A few of them at the time, or eventually, settled in Malta. Among the most interesting was Princess **Nathalie Putyatin** (Poutiatine) (later Tabone, 1904–1984). Her story bears telling because, as Tanya Bayona informs us in 'Remembering Nathalie Putyatin', a chapter in the Zolina book, she 'introduced Russian classical ballet to Malta'.

Nathalie was the daughter of **Princess Olga Putyatin** (née Olga Pavlovna Zelenoy, d.1967). Her father, Prince Pavel Putyatin, was one-time equerry to Tsar Nicholas II. Nathalie's first encounter with ballet was a visit as a little girl to the Mariinsky Theatre in St Petersburg; her first dancing master was a former dancer of the Imperial Ballet; later she was briefly taught by the Mariinsky's prima ballerina Tamara Karsarvina. But then came the Revolution. The Tsar abdicated; his brother Grand Duke Mikhail renounced his right to the throne in the Putyatin Palace, Olga Putyatina even providing him with lunch. The Putyatins fled to Odessa, by then joined by Pavel's brother, Prince Mikhail Putyatin, and his wife **Princess Katerina** (1876–1934). Fifteen-year-old Nathalie's Estonian governess **Alicia Strautman** (d.1977) accompanied them but not, apparently, Nathalie's father. When the Red Army neared Odessa, the party travelled to Romania, and then to Constantinople. They were part of the company that reached Malta on the *Bermudian*.

The Putyatins stayed in Malta for two years, maintained, with several others, by the British Government, though it tried hard to disperse them elsewhere. During that time, Nathalie had art lessons from the Russian refugee Professor Nikolai Krassov, Imperial Court architect. He had arrived with his wife and daughter, **Vera Krassov** (b. *c*.1897) who was to marry into the Royal Navy in Malta in 1921. In Tanya Bayona's chapter, there is a charming watercolour by Nathalie of St Ignatius College, presumably where the family was housed. It was some time then that Nathalie spotted Maltese Edgar Tabone who was later to become her husband, but they did not meet until the Putyatins joined Prince Pavel in Paris.

In Paris, Nathalie took piano lessons at the *Conservatoire*, and ballet lessons. She also auditioned, successfully, for Anna Pavlova's Company, but bronchitis prevented her from taking up the engagement. Nathalie and Edgar finally met there and, in 1927, they married, either in Paris or Rome, and returned to Malta. There, Nathalie Putyatin Tabone was eventually encouraged to give ballet lessons. In the 1930s, she performed at the Royal Opera House and the Manoel Theatre, often giving performances for Russian refugees and, in 1939, the first professional academy was built to her specification, and incorporating her family residence – *Otrada*. The building was in Sliema and was known as the Princess Nathalie Poutiatine Academy of Ballet. In 1981, Tanya Bayona, who had been a pupil of Nathalie's, merged with her and it became the Tanya Bayona Princess Poutiatine Academy of Ballet. Maltese ballet dancers were trained there until 2004.

Nathalie's widowed mother joined her in Malta and was to die there. Alicia Strautman, who had remained with Nathalie throughout, died in 1977; Nathalie herself, widowed since 1976, died in 1984 to the sound of lessons taking place. All three women are buried near the chapel in the Ta'Braxia Cemetery (see Chapter 19 itinerary). More than any other Russian refugee, Nathalie Putyatin contributed to Malta's cultural variety and well-being.

The refugees from the Russian Revolution were not the only ones to whom Malta gave sanctuary after the First World War. During the War, Greece and Turkey had been on opposite sides, and Turkey, part of the Ottoman Empire that had been in decline during the nineteenth century, was not on that of the victors. Greek troops landed in Smyrna harbour in May 1919, accompanied by a British destroyer.

Between 1920 and 1922, Greece sought to reconstruct the Byzantine Empire with its capital at Constantinople by further encroachment on to the Turkish mainland. It ended in disaster – the sacking of Smyrna (now Izmir), with its large cosmopolitan, predominantly Greek, population. Henry

Frendo sets the scene when he starts 'Maltese Survivors of Smyrna' (2010), 'To the Greeks, Smyrna represents the "Hellenic Genocide", to the Turks, the "National War of Independence".' He writes of how 'The Turkish cavalry rode in ferociously and victoriously on 9 September 1922' and continues:

> As thick clouds of smoke billowed to the heavens, Western European and American ships moored in the Gulf of Smyrna tried frantically, in the ensuing chaos, to take on as many passport holding European Christian refugees as could make it to the boats in the choppy waters and clamber up to safety from incineration. An estimated 100,000 died in the flames or were otherwise slaughtered on that fateful day, but this figure goes up and up for Armenians, Greeks, Assyrians and others.

Henry Frendo concentrates on the Maltese community of between 1,800 and 3,000, many of whom were fourth generation in Smyrna. The city attracted small business people from Malta, and there were some sailors and labourers. Malta was no longer their home, but that was where many of them, having lost everything, petitioned the British consulate to repatriate them.

Typical of those of Maltese origin was 58-year-old **Maria Borg** who arrived in Malta, together with daughters 20-year-old **Pauline Borg** and **Mary Borg**, aged 17; her husband had died during 'the occupation'. The family settled in Paola. But by no means all the refugees who arrived in Malta were lucky enough to have Maltese roots.

The details of September 1922 are highly contentious but Giles Milton's *Paradise Lost: Smyrna 1922, The Destruction of Islam's City of Tolerance* (2008) has been well received. His account follows events chronologically and concentrates mainly on the Levantine community – Europeans who had settled in Smyrna sometimes generations earlier; typical were the Whittalls who had lived in Turkey for 113 years:

> When Gertrude Bell visited the Whittalls of Smyrna in the spring of 1902, she caught a tantalising glimpse of a private world. The Whittall family had amassed a spectacular fortune over the previous five decades. ...'My Whittall friends ... have the bulk of the English trade in their hands,' noted Bell, 'branch offices all down the southern coast, mines and shooting boxes and properties scattered up and down the S.W. coast of Asia Minor and yachts on the sea.'

It was the matriarch, 'mother of the tribe', **Magdalen Whittall**, who welcomed **Gertrude Bell** (1868–1926) to the family home; she had 13 children and 256 great grandchildren. The Whittalls, of British origin, had not thought of leaving Smyrna, even during the First World War. But in 1922 they were forced to flee, and Giles Milton takes the reader through the day-by-day movements of the extended family from their various properties as the horrifying events unfold. Several members land up in Malta and, unfortunately, that is about the only mention of it in this otherwise engrossing book. But, like many of the other refugees in Malta, they did not have it easy:

> [There] they were lodged in a disused military barracks at the Lazaretto. Among this … batch was Herbert Octavius Whittall, along with many members of his extended family. They were accorded no respect by the British government in whose care they now found themselves. The barracks were damp and unsanitary, and the military rations virtually inedible. 'The food is getting worse and worse,' wrote Herbert Octavius. 'Not fit for a dog.'
>
> He, like all the other Levantine refugees in Malta, felt betrayed and abandoned by Britain. The Whittalls were proud of their British roots and throughout their long years in Turkey they had always viewed Britain as the mother country. Now, they discovered that the feeling was not reciprocated.

Herbert Octavius' wife was **Louisa Whittall** (née Maltass, 1858–1942), mother of six, three of them daughters, and aunt to many nieces. That branch of the family was to end up in Tunis.

On 15 September, the overcrowded hospital ship *Maine* entered Grand Harbour carrying 407 refugees from Smyrna, among whom were 81 of Maltese origin. Typical was the extended Stabile family. Salvatore was a railway employee in Smyrna, his 35-year-old Greek wife **Thenotis Stabile**, who taught classical Greek and music at the Jesuit College and spoke fluent French, had given birth to their son Henry on 3 September. Henry was to become a doctor in Malta. Another *Maine* passenger was eight-year-old **Mary Aicolina** (Aquilina) (1915–2005), travelling with her father, Giorgio, and two older brothers; her mother, Crete-born **Anastasia Kalopedi**, had died in Smyrna some time after her birth. Mary's son George Galdies later became British vice-consul in Turkey and a founding member and trustee of the Levantine Heritage Foundation. On 17 September, 290 British refugees arrived on the *Bavarian* and, the following day, 36 on HMS *King George V*. By the end of 1922, the Maltese authorities had housed some 1,300 refugees from Smyrna – even more than the earlier Russians.

Among the other passengers on the *Maine* were the Issigonis family. It is from Gillian Bardsley's *Issigonis: The Official Biography* (2006) and a statement in it from the *Malta Government Gazette*, that we learn better why the Lazaretto Barracks were chosen for the refugees:

> Information having been received that an infectious or contagious disease, dangerous to mankind, to wit plague, exists at Smyrna, it is hereby declared that Smyrna is an infected place within the meaning of article 1 of the Regulations made under the Fourth Sanitary Ordinance, 1908. 24 August 1922.

Constantine Issigonis, a marine engineer resident in Smyrna was of Greek origin, but had British citizenship. The family of his wife, **Hulda Issigonis** (née Prokopp, 1884–1972), came from Bavaria and ran Smyrna's brewery. Their son Alexander (Alec) was 16 when they were forced to flee Smyrna, but their troubles had started earlier. During the First World War, Constantine's nationality was not the issue; it was the factory that was of interest to the Germans. Alec Issigonis was later to recall how

A German officer came to our house one day in the factory compound and with my mother being German father received him but he was a bit stand-offish. He said to my father that he would like to keep our factories open so that we could repair the German submarines when they came into the harbour. And my father said 'not on your bloody life, get out of here'. And the German said 'I'm afraid it's the other way round, you must get out of here.' So we had to leave our house …

The factories were confiscated and the family moved in with Hulda's sister. In due course Alec was to show an interest in engineering and motor cars, but then came September 1922. This is Alec's version of what followed – one that serves for many of the refugees:

The Turkish army were very close and the British navy … came to evacuate the small colony of British people because they felt that by the time the Turkish army arrived, Smyrna would be in a state of war. So, at midnight one night, some marines came to the house and they said to my mother and father: 'just take some blankets, don't take anything else, you must come immediately.' The Greek soldiers were lying, dead tired in the street, I remember this so well, it was a moonlit night. They took us on board a little ship called the *Antioch*. May [Walker] and Donald and all my friends were there. We were given the choice of either going to Malta or going to Cyprus and my father immediately said Malta because it was nearer to England. In fact almost everybody on the ship said Malta.

The *Antioch* became overloaded, so the family was transferred to the *Maine*. In three days they were in Malta. They, too, landed up in the Lazaretto (see Chapter 19 itinerary). But Constantine was ill, so he was transferred straight from the ship to a 'naval hospital near Attard'. Alec remained with other members of their group in the Lazaretto and Hulda had to divide her time between her son and her husband whose health was deteriorating. Eventually, Hulda, who had no experience of travelling, made the decision to take her son to England by train, leave him there and make the difficult journey back to her husband. He died in Malta in June 1923. In due course, Hulda and Alec settled in Oxford where he was to become Sir Alexander Issigonis, designer of the Mini, perhaps one of the most admired and successful cars of the twentieth century.

Given what refugees such as Nathalie Putyatin and Alexander Issigonis went through when too young to have any say in their fate, it is satisfying to look back at what they returned to the countries that gave them sanctuary. As another phenomenon of this period, I like to think that Blanche Huber was inspired to become a doctor by the women she saw contributing so effectively during the War. In the years to come, other women in Malta were to enter the professions and make similar substantial contributions.

14 – Prelude to War 1930–1940

Women of 1930s Malta

Not surprisingly, the Maltese had mixed feelings about being a British crown colony in the 1930s. They were torn several ways: politically, economically, socially and morally. Malta, with its population of nearly 250,000, was economically dependent on being Britain's Mediterranean naval base; from the 1890s, the crews of the Royal Navy ships based in the Grand Harbour numbered at least 10,000. In 1931, the number of service personnel had increased to more than 16,000: 14,080 with the Royal Navy, 2,066 with the Army, and 421 with the Royal Air Force.

Yet those who swarmed in the back streets of Valletta at night, spending money in bar rooms and music halls, also encouraged prostitution and, thus, the spread of sexually transmitted disease; the Church and God-fearing Roman Catholic citizens were outraged. Those in the political echelons wishing to be less dependent on the spending power of the Royal Navy – which also provided all sorts of employment in the docks – dreamed of encouraging a nice class of tourism, particularly in the winter months. Tourism would stimulate the building industry through the need for hotels, diversify employment, and increase trade for shops and merchants.

Paul Knepper usefully explores the ambiguity of these conflicting factors in 'The "White Slave Trade" and the Music Hall Affair in 1930s Malta' (2009). He describes how

In December 1932, allegations surrounding music halls ignited a furore in Malta. Two London newspapers, the *Daily Herald* and the *News of the World*, printed stories about conditions endured by English women lured to Malta by agents for music halls and cabarets. According to the articles, women were trapped in 'filthy lodgings' and forced to survive on inferior meals in restaurants owned by their employers. They were not given the salary they had expected to receive, nor given respect as performing artistes, but were made to drink with sailors and to give performances in private 'dancing rooms'. The lodging houses were little more than brothels, and when walking in public, the Maltese hissed and booed them, or pelted them with vegetables. In Malta, the music hall industry was little more than a front for 'white slavery'.

An enquiry was carried out among 78 English artistes who denied all allegations. What was uncovered, however, was the corrosive effect on Malta of women from elsewhere in Europe, and on Maltese women from the goings-on at night. A great deal of exploitation existed: women caught up in the sex trade were stripped of their earnings by *souteneurs* or 'white slave traffickers', charged excessive rents for miserable rooms in brothels by 'greedy agents', and exploited by *matrones*, a class of women who made a living by lending jewellery, clothing and money to prostitutes. Ending these exploitative relationships was difficult, owing to the reluctance of women to assist in prosecution of those who mistreated them. Seldom would women give evidence 'against the man that was living on their earnings and who was torturing them physically and morally at the same time'.

The Maltese press were incensed by the slurs on their islands; it was because Malta was 'a small British Colony to be kicked and whipped as the mighty see fit'.

David Niven, who was to become a famous film star, spent two years in the army as a young man, part of it in Malta, where he arrived in 1930. In one paragraph he sums up Malta's social life under the British:

The Marsa Polo Club was the smart place to be – smart in the most colonial sense of the word; it was mounted suburbia. It was parasols and frightfully refained voices. It was 'Boy, bring me a stingar', and naval wives who announced with a smirk – 'We're going to have our bottom scrubbed next week,' ... Girls there were in plenty. Apart from the resident ones, daughters of senior officers and officials, there were also for several months a year hundreds of young and lonely naval officers' wives. There were in addition the 'Fishing Fleet', a motley collection of passedover debs and pink-cheeked country cousins who annually timed their arrival to coincide with the return, after months at sea, of several thousand sex-starved mariners. Finally there were the whores, and Valletta was full of professionals busily catering to the needs of all ranks of the biggest fleet in the world. Many were-mid-European or Russians, refugees of impeccable lineage with sisters plying the same desperate trade in Singapore and fathers driving taxis in Paris.

One of those resident daughters of senior officers was **Rosamund Fisher** (1905–1984), daughter of Admiral Sir William Fisher and **Cecilia Fisher** (née Warre-Cornish, 1886–1965). She gave an example of a different sort of British colonial officer when Joan Alexander interviewed her, by then the Dowager Lady Coleridge, for her biography *Mabel Strickland* (1996):

At one time the Maltese were only allowed to go to the opera on Thursdays, so my father, when C-in-C in Admiralty House, Valletta, broke with tradition and only went on Thursday nights. This suited me because, as I had been to the Convent [of the Sacred Heart] when young, I knew all my age group of Maltese girls and therefore enjoyed seeing them again in their grown-up party frocks. Whereas, on an ordinary night of stuffy and elderly British, I would have known hardly anyone.

In the same interview, Rosamund also told the story of fearful snobbery at the Sliema Club when a Royal Navy lieutenant, Arthur Pitt, insisted, against orders, on marrying her friend **Tania Mifsud** (1920–2001), half-Russian (she was the daughter of a Russian refugee of 1919, **Vera Valentina Mifsud** (née Yarmonkina, 1903–1964)), half-Maltese and a niece of Sir Ugo Mifsud. Their wedding reception was relegated to the roof of the club where they would be out of sight. Rosamund ends by saying,

> This was in 1937 and then in 1938 everything began to change. The war clouds were gathering, and then all the officers got a signal from Admiral Sir Dudley Pound saying that we were to do our utmost to make friends with the Maltese – it was confidential, and we all had to sign it – and we were told we were not to use expressions like 'Malts' in their hearing, because we now needed them as allies!

That Sliema was a hot-bed of snobbery is confirmed by **Christina Ratcliffe** (1914–1988) in *Women of Malta: True Wartime Stories of Christina Ratcliffe and Tamara Marks* (2006, ed. Frederick Galea). Christina sums up her dancing past most succinctly herself:

> When I grew up I was to dance my way from Dukinfield, my birthplace in Cheshire, to the capitals of Europe. I was to trip the light fantastic toe across North Africa and down to Dakar. To waltz in and out of the Spanish Civil War and, finally to take a last curtain call in the battle and siege of Malta.

Desperate for work, she and her friend **Sheila** had accepted a three-month engagement – against the advice of dancer friends – in the music hall Morning Star on St Nicholas Street, Valletta. On the boat from Marseilles to Malta, in March 1937, they were pestered for friendship by a chattering woman whom they sought to evade but, as they were about to disembark, she espied them, and handed them her visiting card with an address in Sliema:

> 'And where are you two going to live?' the little woman asked.
> It was then that it dawned. I didn't know. According to our contracts accommodation was to be provided by the management of the music hall but where it was and what it would be like I had no idea.
> Explaining the situation, I noticed a complete change of attitude in the woman. Her face hardened and she seemed to grow inches taller.
> 'Oh, so you are artistes.' We might have been something the cat had brought in. 'And where, might I ask, are you going to work?'
> Delving into my handbag I produced the contract. I pointed to the address printed on it.
> 'There'
> For a moment I thought we were going to have a fainting case on our hands. But the little woman rallied and took another look at the address

as if to make sure her eyes had not deceived her. Then, apparently fearing contamination, she edged as far away from us as she could. Finally she disappeared from view. Not, unfortunately, overboard.

'Seems she doesn't like artistes,' Sheila remarked.

In 'Crime and Policing: A Few Detectives Would be Very Useful: Crime, Immorality, and Policing in Valletta, 1881–1914' (2009), Paul Knepper explains, without any spin, Valletta's music halls, which had been encouraged to address the problem of drunkenness:

The music halls promoted in Valletta did not resemble the large halls, but the 'free halls' of the Midlands and North of England. In these smaller concert halls and pub concert halls, eating and drinking continued during the performance. Drink remained a mainstay of the music hall economy; often the admission ticket could be exchanged for a drink.

More colour is given in glimpses of Valletta's pre-war night life in *Strada Stretta: 'The Gut' Which for Many Years Lit up Valletta* (2013). To compile it, George Cini interviewed aging denizens of Strait Street and nearby streets for their memories, of pre- and post-war, of their childhoods and families, many of whom lived above the establishments the family ran (see Chapter 17 itinerary). St Nicholas Street was part of the Strait Street scene and Christina Ratcliffe tells of her impression of arriving at the Morning Star:

The name 'music-hall' was somewhat misleading but I suppose it was as suitable a one as any. After all there was music and there was a hall. The music was loud and lively, the hall long and narrow with mirrored walls and a tiled floor packed with dancing couples. The dancers were mainly sailors partnered by dark-haired, heavily made-up girls and sailors partnered by sailors. Those of the clientele who were not dancing were seated on benches and stools around old-fashioned marble-topped tables, smoking and drinking.

Through a haze of blue smoke, I could see at the far end of the hall a set of orange and purple curtains, covering what was presumably the stage; immediately beneath, in the orchestra pit, sat the band – a pianist and a drummer.

'Nice place, eh, girls?' Gianni said, fairly bristling with pride.

At the sight of the two young women, good-looking and obviously rather classier than the usual artistes, the place erupted. It did not take them long to bring matters under control and dictate how they should be received in future. Of the Gut itself, Christina wrote:

To capture its mood, to see the place as it really was, the Gut had to be visited by night. During the hours of daylight it put up its shutters and slept off a hangover in an atmosphere of peace and sobriety, a drab dusty

30.   Christina Ratcliffe,
from Galea, *Women of Malta*

and sunless alley where curiously enough Dirty Dick's had the cleanest look of the lot. In the evenings the Gut leaped to life and opened its doors and its heart to teeming masses of servicemen on the look out for an hour or so of vice and pleasure. Noise was the overriding feature of this alleyway and the later the evening, the louder the racket, as the wine went in and the worst came out – raucous singing, yells, foul language, brawls in plenty. And above it all the din of the scores of jazz bands beating and sawing out their melodies on the rostrums of pocket-sized dance halls. At almost every door sat small groups of heavily made-up women, some young and pretty, others distinctly *passé* but all adorned with gold earrings and bangles and all cajoling the passers-by to sample the delights of their particular establishment.

At the Morning Star, Christina and Sheila were soon joined by **Vera** and **Rosa** who had been among those who warned them against the Malta engagement. Then, as Christina says, 'Putting on what amounted to almost a small revue, well dressed, well presented with talented English girls, the Morning Star very soon became a byword throughout the British Mediterranean Fleet.' She settled down so well, both at work and in her home life in Floriana with her fellow dancers, that she stayed for six months. Then she left to work elsewhere, but she arrived back in 1940 for another engagement; that is a later story.

Officers and other ranks did not mix, and Suzanne Layton would not have visited Strait Street, even for fun, though she and Christina were to work in the same place during the War.

Suzanne Layton (1921–2014) arrived in Malta in 1937. Her mother was **Eleanor Layton** (née Langley), her father, Admiral Geoffrey Layton, second in command of the Mediterranean Fleet – a tyrant, at least towards her, according to *The Same Wife in Every Port* (1998), the autobiography she wrote as Suzanne Kyrle-Pope, the name of her second husband. The information in her book is supplemented by the interview, available to download on the internet, she gave to James Holland for *Fortress Malta: An Island Under Siege 1940–1943* (2003). In his book James Holland weaves a tapestry of chronological events and accounts including, unusually in such books about the War, those of women such as Suzanne.

She was the last child of her parents and, as she starts her book, 'I was supposed to have been a boy. I was to be called Timothy, and my future was mapped out even to the exact date that I would be entered for Dartmouth, and a naval career in my father's footsteps.' Her father's disappointment, which he took out on her at every opportunity, meant that, as an 18-year-old in late 1930s Malta, she at first lacked confidence and had not yet blossomed intellectually. Her life, in a large house in Guardamangia (Gwardamanġa), and that of her sister – **Diana Layton**, aged 25 – were controlled by their father; she writes, making clear, too, the extent of the Royal Navy in Malta,

The Mediterranean fleet was huge in those pre-Second World War days. The Grand Harbour would be full of battleships and cruisers when the fleet was in, and round St Elmo point in Sliema harbour and Lazaretto creek would lie the destroyer and submarine flotillas, MTBs and sloops. There would be parties every night, not only on board ships, but at Army barracks and RAF stations round the island too, and so another fleet would gather, the 'fishing fleet' of hopeful husband-hunting girls, the nieces, cousins, and friends of officers in the command. Diana and I did not count ourselves part of it, as we reckoned that as Father was based in Malta we were there on legitimate grounds.

Girls of the fishing-fleet could, and often did, become blasé and spoilt and Father made a firm rule that Diana and I were only permitted three late nights each a week. A 'late night' was one on which we returned home after 11.00 pm. ...

'I am absolutely not having ... your heads turned from too much attention [he said]. You will do as I say, and that's that!'

In spite of this control, Suzanne details a fairly mindless life of balls, the Sliema Club, tennis parties – which she loathed because of her father's humiliation of her on the court – horse races at Marsa and ships' dances, which were

> very romantic occasions, to which we, as admiral's daughters, were generally invited. The host-ship would be 'dressed overall' for the party, with bunting and coloured lights stretched from bow to stern across the tops of the masts. The quarter-deck would be enclosed with tarpaulins, and decorated with more bunting, flags and lights, and there the ship's band would play for dancing. Guests would go out to the ship either in hired *dghaisers*, the beautiful gondola-like Maltese boats, gaily painted, with high prow and stern, and with large eyes painted each side of the bow, to keep the devil away, or collected at the Customs House jetty by ship's boats. One would cross the harbour, the water alive with dancing reflected lights from all the ships lying at anchor, and then, lifting one's long skirt, would climb the ship's gangway; sometimes, if the sea was a bit rough, one had to jump from the boat, but there would be gallant midshipmen and sailors to ensure one arrived safely on deck. Refreshments and supper would be served below in the wardroom during the evening. Diana and I could have gone to such parties every night and some girls attended two or three on the same evening, but Father's inflexible rule forbade this.

It is difficult for an Englishwoman of the twenty-first century trying to recreate Malta of the 1930s under the British to know how such women were regarded by the Maltese. There is a hint, at least, of how upper-class Maltese felt, if one gives credence to a conversation in *The Brass Dolphin* (1997) by the English novelist Joanna Trollope, writing under the pen-name Caroline Harvey. The novel tells the story, starting in 1938, and continuing through the War, of a young Englishwoman, Lila Cunningham, who comes to Malta with her feckless artist father, to look after the dilapidated Villa Zonda at Santa Venera. She has been given a letter of introduction to a noble family in Mdina by the English owners of the Villa who befriended her in England. The Cunninghams are penniless and, though proud and educated, unconnected to the Laytons and their world. The baroness sister of the noble historian to whom Lila has just become secretary is dressed in immaculate silk and hostile as they sit at impeccable lunch; the baroness deigns to address Lila:

> The Union Club in Valletta', the Baroness said, 'has seven thousand members at present. Almost all of them British servicemen.'
> Lila waited politely.
> 'The social life of the British in Malta since the last war has been perfectly phenomenal. But I imagine I need not inform you of that, Miss Cunningham. I imagine you are entirely familiar with dances and picnics and film shows given on the quarterdeck by your – *hospitable* navy.'

'No,' said Lila, 'no, I'm afraid not. We've only been here a month, and I've met nobody, we've – well, we've been very private.' ...

... 'You mustn't, my dear sister, allow your views of young Englishwomen to be coloured by reports of behaviour at these naval parties Miss Cunningham has the misfortune not to attend.' [Count Julius] glanced at Lila. His eyes were twinkling again. 'There is a young officer's wife, I'm told, who in view of the brilliance of her chevelure and the exuberance of her spirits, is known in Valetta as the Southsea Bubble.'

Suzanne Layton was later to write, 'It was an extraordinary life which ended when war began, and was never resumed in post-war days.'

There were rather more serious women living in and visiting Malta at the time. The reason for Dr Letitia Fairfield's 1938 visit is connected to the area of Valletta in which Christina Ratcliffe worked, where the night life inevitably gave rise to prostitution, and thus to sexually transmitted diseases.

(Josephine) **Letitia Fairfield** (1885–1978) was a public health physician and campaigner for social reform, born in Melbourne, Australia. But the family moved to Britain when she was three. Letitia was the eldest of three sisters, one of whom, Cecilia Fairfield, chose as her *nom de plume* **Rebecca West** (1892–1983). Rebecca and Letitia did not get on, particularly in later life; indeed, Rebecca was to manifest her dislike in the character of Cordelia in her best-selling, loosely autobiographical novel, *The Fountain Overflows* (1957; 1984). This description of Cordelia, contradictorily, says more about the writer than her object:

> We got out at the head of Meadow Walk, and as we went down it we saw the dark blocks of the Infirmary among the reddening trees. We knew a woman medical student who talked of it with awe, as a cathedral of healing. Cordelia sometimes wanted to be a nurse and train there, and when she thought of that her face grew noble and stupid, but stupid in a nicer way than it was when she played the violin. Cordelia would mind leaving Edinburgh more than any of us. All her teachers admired her, they did at every school she went to, they made plans for her, they told her she had only to go on in a straight line and she would be where they wanted her to be, which was where she, with her intense desire for approval, would want to be.

In fact, Letitia became a doctor, awarded her MD degree from the University of Edinburgh in 1911. As a medical student and young doctor she campaigned for women's suffrage, addressing public meetings. After qualification, she began her work in public health for the London County Council (LCC) which was to continue, apart from wartime interruptions, until 1948; she was to become the first woman senior medical officer at the LCC. She was also to be called to the Bar at the Middle Temple, London, in 1923.

On the outbreak of the First World War, she was among those women doctors rebuffed for offering their services, but in 1917 she became a medical officer to the new Women's Army Auxiliary Corps; she was also active in the internal battle that medical women in the armed services waged with the War Office to be appointed on comparable terms to men and, in 1919, she was created CBE in recognition of her war service.

In 1922, Letitia became a Roman Catholic and, during the 1920s, she was a prominent opponent of birth control though, as her *ODNB* entry suggests, 'She later modified her views following a visit to Malta, where problems ensuing from a high birth-rate and poverty were all too apparent.' In 1922, she was sent by the LCC on a mission to the West Indies to advise on how to deal with venereal disease in women; and it was on a similar mission that she was sent to Malta in 1938.

Although there are documents about that visit in the Wellcome Library in London, even the menu for a lunch given by the BMA (Malta Branch), and they would be essential reading for anyone writing in detail about her life, there is a more accessible picture of her Malta visit in *The Bonham-Carter Diaries 1936–1940* (2004, ed. John Manduca). The governor, who never holds back from writing exactly what he thinks, writes first of Letitia on 18 April:

Dr Letitia Fairfield ... came to see me on Wednesday. She is a sister of Rebecca West I believe. She is clearly an interesting and cultivated woman – rather plain to look at, a round face on the plump side, but with eyes wide apart and an attractive smile. She showed herself to be fully aware of the pitfalls in her dealings with the Church authorities here when dealing with social hygiene and venereal disease. She is a Catholic.

And when he got to know her better, he elaborated on 8 May:

We have had staying here since the 3rd Dr Drummond Sheils and Dr Letitia Fairfield, who had been here as delegation from the Social Hygiene Council to advise us on the position in Malta ... I was somewhat nervous about their arrival, because to deal with sexual questions in Malta is a pretty tricky business.

However, Sheils is tactful and Dr Fairfield a perfect marvel at dealing with the church. In fact, I believe that during her last interview with the Archbishop, which took place on Thursday evening, she was able to be comparatively outspoken and teach the old man a thing or two. He is surprisingly ignorant about what happens in Malta, and his attitude is not very different from that of a large number of his clergy ... that if you keep women sufficiently suppressed and ignorant, then evil will not arise.

She surprised the Archbishop by pointing out to him that such things as films and lovemaking in films leaves children and young people comparatively cold and untouched; that a girl learns more about sex on

31. Letitia Fairfield, courtesy of Wellcome Library, London

the first occasion a man put his hand on her arm than she does by any amount of looking at films!

Dr Letitia Fairfield, besides being a woman of outstanding ability, is very feminine. She has a quiet attractive voice, great charm of manner and a lively sense of humour. Both she and Sheils have, of course, very sound judgement. Both lean towards the left, but are full of the saving grace of charity. As I shall receive later on a full report from them, I will record only a few points which have arisen during my conversations with them.

He proceeds to record quite a few of these points, but I will just pick out one strand particularly relevant to what I have written about Valletta's night-life:

Dr Fairfield classed the girls in the following way:

(a) Foreigners employed at the highest class dancing halls are all professional prostitutes.
(b) English girls employed to play cabaret turns are not.
(c) Other foreigners, Germans and Swiss chiefly, are not necessarily prostitutes, but most are.

(d) The Maltese girls employed in bars are usually professional but not invariably so.

It is possible for a girl to keep straight.

The governor's full précis of what he learnt from the visitors, prior to receiving their report, would also be useful to anyone researching sexual health and prostitution of the period.

Following her Malta visit, Letitia was appointed a member of the Ministry of Health's Advisory Committee on the welfare of mothers and young children and, in 1943, she was appointed to the Colonial Office Committee set up to consider the treatment of venereal diseases in women and children. Before and after the War, she helped refugees fleeing from Nazi Germany settle in England. Perhaps it was not surprising that Rebecca was jealous of Letitia, in spite of her own fame; at the same time, it is noticeable that Letitia's famous sibling tends to be mentioned in order to put the well-regarded doctor into context.

There was always the fear that when the time came for orphans to leave their place of relative safety, they would be led astray so, in 1936, not long after his arrival as governor, and before he had the benefit of talking to Letitia Fairfield about prostitution, Charles Bonham-Carter spotted the problem and recorded,

I had a meeting on the 20th with Miss Lola Francia, **Lena Salomone, Mona de Piro d'Amico,** and Casolini (M.O. of the Royal Malta Artillery) and started them as a Committee to run a 'big brother and sister' organisation to look after the children in the orphanage. They seemed keen so I hope they will do well.

But on 8 January 1937, he had occasion to note, in his usual frank manner:

Last year I tried to establish a committee under Miss Lola Francia to undertake to visit the girls in the Orphanage, to look after them while in the Orphanage, taking them out and giving them a little knowledge of the world, and keeping in touch with them after leaving to help them in their difficulties. Lola Francia was not strong enough, however, and though something was done at the beginning, helpers dropped off, and the work became less and less effective. When I returned from leave, therefore, I decided to make another effort and to ask Daisy Agius to undertake the organisation of the work on a much larger scale. She undertook the job at once, and I got an undertaking from the Archbishop that her committee should be allowed to work in the orphanages under his care as well as in the Government institutions. Lola Francia was glad to work under Daisy Agius. She found the responsibility of running a committee herself too much, I think. Daisy Agius (sister of Mrs Denaro) was educated in England, I think. She is short, stout, has a heavy moustache, is remarkably plain, and is a good sort with a heart of gold. And better still she has personality and determination. I hope that in future the girl orphans will have a better chance with her looking after them.

Lola Francia was the sister of Lady Mifsud. Their family home, you may remember, was ransacked on the second day of the *Sette Giugno* riots (Chapter 13). Malvina Francia Mifsud now merited a Bonham-Carter frank appraisal following a dinner party attended by the Mifsuds: 'His wife was a Miss Francia, able, pushing, politically minded, but quite a good sort, I thought.'

Daisy Agius was Marguerite Eugenie Evangeline Agius (1882–1971), and her sister was Marie Denaro whom we met pulling her weight during the First World War and will be seen to continue doing good work during the forthcoming war (Chapter 15). There is a neat connection, too, with a major character in Chapter 16, their niece Josephine Burns Debono. Daisy and Marie were two of the 15 children of Edward Tancred Agius and **Concetta Agius** (née Muscat). A third daughter was Laura, Josephine's mother.

In the mid-nineteenth century, the Agius paterfamilias had moved from Alexandria back to Malta where he made a fortune supplying grain to the Allies during the Crimean War. By 1872, Edward Tancred Agius, of the next generation, was settled in London, increasing the family fortune by transporting coal by rail and sea from the North. Marie, Daisy and Laura were born in England, brought up in Hampstead, and received an English education. Marie married her Maltese husband Frank Denaro in England in 1901. By 1914, several of the girls had made Maltese marriages and were settled there. Five brothers served at the Front during the First World War.

Daisy herself, remaining unmarried, came to Malta relatively late but, with her background, soon established herself, thus coming to the governor's attention. From time to time, in her new role, she reported back to him; in May 1938, he wrote, 'Daisy Agius came to report progress on Saturday. She is getting on with her after-care association slowly but surely, she says. Some of the Mothers Superior are very difficult.' And in November,

Daisy Agius came to see me on the 9th November about her after-care association. She would like to establish a hostel to receive girls in their last year before reaching the age when they leave institutions and give them proper training in domestic work. She asks for a grant (recurrent, I suppose) of £500. It is, of course, an admirable idea and would do valuable work. It would take the girls away from the confinement of an institution for a year before they were thrown out in the world unprotected. It would give them proper training so they would be much less likely to make a mess of the first situation, and perhaps they would be able to regard the male creature as not too god-like. Of course, the committee would keep in touch with the girls after they had left the hostel, and the hostel would act as a home of refuge if needed when they were out of work. The snag, of course, is the £500, but I shall try to find it.

On 15 December there was a further report; this time the association has capital letters:

Yesterday, the 14th, I had a meeting in the morning of the After-Care Association which I got Daisy Agius to start for me last year. They have rendered a most interesting report which shows they have made far more progress than I thought possible in the time. They have met with a good many difficulties and opposition. I can't think why the Church should be frightened of them, because all the workers are Maltese ladies and all, naturally, R.C. The need for the Association has been very fully proved to them all, and they have been able to persuade the Archbishop that they are doing a valuable work. The conditions they found in some of the institutions have been really horrible, and to my mind the cynical and heartless outlooks of some of the Mothers Superior who let the girls leave them quite unprotected and without a knowledge of the world and have no idea what is happening to them, although they have only left a month ago, is quite terrible.

That is the last entry in the diaries about Daisy Agius and her association; she was, like her sister, to be active during the forthcoming war.

Daisy was not the only woman with ambitions to help others of her sex from an interesting angle, and another pair of sisters was to leave even more of a mark on Malta. **Cecilia Strickland** (later de Trafford, 1897–1982) was the second of six daughters, **Mabel Strickland** (1899–1988) the third. Their mother was **Edeline Strickland** (née Sackville, 1870–1918), their father, Gerald Strickland, was born in Malta and was both Lord Strickland of Sizergh Castle since 1928, because of his political activities in England, and 6th Count Catena, since 1875, on account of his mother, **Maria Aloysia Bonici Mompalao** (Luisa) (née Scebberas Bologna, 1833–1907) being the niece and heiress of Nicholas Sceberras Bologna, 5th Count della Catena. Maria was also the wife of Cdr Walter Strickland RN. She was the first of two Strickland women to be involved in Malta's archaeology when she helped the archaeologist Albert Mayr (see Chapter 1).

The Strickland story is usefully told in Joan Alexander's *Mabel Strickland*, though some details are disputed by at least one member of the family. Cecilia and Mabel, in spite of their Anglo-Maltese background, were partly brought up away from either country. Their barrister father was much involved in Maltese politics from 1886 but, in 1902, to stop him causing any further trouble, he was appointed to a series of governorships on behalf of the British Government. The family returned to Malta in 1917, but Edeline Strickland, whose health had been deteriorating for some time, died in 1918.

In 1926, Gerald Strickland remarried; his new wife, **Margaret Strickland** (née Hulton, 1867–1949) came from a wealthy newspaper-owning family which not only played its part in the career of her step-daughter Mabel, but also enabled Margaret to be a philanthropist in her own right. In 1929, she founded St Edward's College for Roman Catholic boys on the lines of an English public school, as well as funding its building, adapted from the Cottonera Hospital in Cospicua (see Chapter 18 itinerary). She helped in the development of the nursing profession in Malta, with the establishment of the Malta Memorial District Nursing Association. This was funded through an annual payment from the Lady Strickland Trust. Her involvement with the building of the Phoenicia Hotel is touched upon in the Chapter 17 itinerary.

In his diaries, Charles Bonham-Carter was to express his appreciation of Margaret in her later years, at the same time bemoaning the continuing political intransigence of her husband. A good example is his entry for 1 January 1937: 'Madge and I have kept friendly with Lord Strickland, but it is impossible to say how long that will last. I hope we shall remain permanently friends with Lady Strickland and Mabel Strickland.' Margaret was created DBE in 1937, perhaps on the recommendation of Bonham-Carter, and was also dame of the grace of St John of Jerusalem.

Cecilia, who had been helping her father with his parliamentary work – he was both leader of the opposition in Malta (1921–1927) then Prime Minister (1927–1932) and, before 1928, a Member of Parliament in England – married Hubert de Trafford in 1927. She had first set eyes on him when her father was governor of Tasmania; his father was a family friend. The couple settled in Malta and, by 1931, they already had two children. It was in that year that she founded the Malta Industries Association, a charitable institution the aim of which was to sell Maltese handcrafts to passengers from the P & O liners calling at Valletta and the large number of service

32.   Cecilia Strickland de Trafford,
courtesy of the family

personnel in Malta. Its larger aim, as her son Anthony de Trafford outlined for me, was to promote the growth of Malta and Gozo industries, arts, crafts and products, to encourage those already existing, introduce new ones and, especially, establish an up-to-date standard in all local articles.

Cecilia opened a shop near the Customs House in Valletta and set about putting together the best products she could find, mainly from a few weavers, lacemaker and filigree workers. Unable to obtain the quality and variety of goods from the few existing weavers, she set about developing that craft as well. She soon realised that she would have to change the association into a limited company, and this she did in 1936.

Apart from the lace workers, women in those days had little scope for employment other than as domestics. Establishing her own weaving factory enabled Cecilia to achieve her objective of providing women with work outside the home, using numerous outbuildings at Villa Trafford in Rabat. Charles Bonham-Carter notes in his diary for 1939 that the introduction of the Minimum Wage Ordinance for Factories impacted on Cecilia's work. Further details on the development of her enterprises are given in the Chapter 20 itinerary that includes the Villa Bologna. In later life, as Chapter 16 shows, Cecilia and Mabel were to take different political paths which caused a certain amount of family friction.

Mabel's career took off in 1935. Her father already published a successful evening paper but, that year, she suggested the need for an English-language daily paper. Gerald Strickland had the political nous, Margaret the money, Mabel the ambition. When asked who would edit it, she replied, I will. After

33.   Mabel Strickland, Editor, from Alexander, *Mabel Strickland*

consulting leading British newspaper owners, Strickland decided to go ahead and handed responsibility of the *Times of Malta* to his daughter.

Mabel was to gather round her a crew of competent women, the first of whom was **Winifred Cutajar Beck**, who had come to Mabel's attention when she addressed envelopes for a party. Winifred was determined to become a journalist and fought her family to enable her to do so. As Mabel's right-hand woman she was to be paid more than her doctor brother, a further bone of contention. She could grasp a situation at a glance and write an article at speed. She spell-checked Mabel; in simple language, she explained the accounts to her which were then sent to Margaret Strickland. She became a stringer in Malta for Reuters and, in 1935, when Mabel visited England, she held the fort. In due course, when the paper was up and running, she was promoted to news editor.

In England Mabel hired **Kay Crowe** with a month till the August launch of the paper. Fifty years later, Kay wrote of those hectic days:

> I was getting my hand in, sub-editing for the weekly, writing up reports, children's articles, and the odd leader, setting up the picture page and book reviewing in preparation for the great day. We were more concerned with mounting a campaign against goats in Valletta than with the distant rumblings coming out of Italy. We all worked frantically as a team until well into the night of August 6th and at 2a.m. on August 7th our first daily newspaper came off the press. We were elated with it even though it left much to be desired, but we were determined that it would grow and flourish in the months to come.

After describing the social life of the period, Joan Alexander tells of another woman's involvement in the paper:

> A spirit of competitiveness among the ladies over their evening dresses gave the dressmakers a flourishing trade, and every young woman aimed at having the beauty of her outfit reported in the 'Times of Malta' in the column 'Gertie Gadfly'. The pretty Rosamund Fisher, daughter of Admiral Sir William Fisher, took a job on the 'Times of Malta' at 3/6 a paragraph, unknown to her friends, or to Mabel. She was able to supply titbits of gossip overheard at parties, and 'puffed-up' the column with descriptions of clothes and social comments. To hide her identity she sometimes put herself in, saying such things as 'Miss Fisher looked simple in sequins'.

Preparations for War

Kay Crowe had ended her piece about the days leading up to the August 1936 launch of the paper, 'Little did we know that in two months Italy would declare war on Abyssinia.' Kathleen Norman's first chapter of *For Gallantry: Malta's Story by a Naval Wife* (1956) is full of the insouciance of 1930s Valletta. She describes 'the world's greatest fleet' lying in Malta's

harbours, and the wonderful parties on board ship that were also enjoyed by
Suzanne Layton. But she starts Chapter II, 'Uneasy Prelude': 'The first heavy
cloud to loom over Malta was when Italy attacked Abyssinia [Ethiopia].'

I have been unable to establish the identity of **Kathleen Norman**. According
to naval records, there were two Royal Navy officers with the surname
Norman on the Malta station during the war, but the wife of neither was
called Kathleen. She was to be in Malta for what followed and to describe it
in detail; perhaps she used a penname out of discretion.

The powers that be had been expecting war; and the following year was
to see the dress rehearsal of the Spanish Civil War, but now Malta, so close
to Italy geographically and, in many respects, culturally, had to make some
preparation for what might come. Kathleen Norman brings the governor's
wife into the story:

Lady Bonham-Carter was quick to realise the terrible shortage of nurses
in the island and threw herself heart and soul into the training of more
women and the betterment of the very poor condition in the civil hospitals.
She raised V.A. detachments and arranged with the military hospital to
give a month's training to the volunteers so that they might have at least
some practical experience.

Many of us took that month's training and very kind Imtarfa was to us,
for our inexperience must have been a sore trial to sisters and orderlies.
We were very grateful for that little bit of training in the years to follow.

Gabrielle Bonham-Carter (née Fisher, 1886–1962) was the second wife,
from 1911, of Malta's governor from 1936 to 1940, and she spent much
time with him there, though she was often unwell and came and returned
to England from time to time. In his diaries he often uses her second name,
Madge. And it is as Madge Bonham-Carter that she was known in England
as a watercolourist and sculptor, exhibiting at the Royal Academy from
1927. In Malta, both the Chief Justice and Stewart Perowne, an official in
the Lieutenant Governor's office, praised her artistic talent and sensibility.
But she was also assiduous in her responsibilities as governor's wife. Her
husband wrote of her, for example, on 1 January 1937:

In regard to work, Madge has proved to be a very live chairman of the
Ladies' Hospital Committee and they are doing very helpful and important
work. She has put new energy into the Girl Guides and she has made a real
start in the redecoration of the palaces.

While many of the VADs were British, as many in those pre-war years
were Maltese. Among them was **Meme Cortis** (1921–) whose *Malta VAD*
(nd) under her married name, Meme Turner, gives a nice description of her
time, starting in 1939, and that of other Maltese VADs, at Mtarfa. She, too,
wrote of Lady Bonham-Carter:

One day on the first week we had a visit from the Governor's wife and after we came off the ward we went to the mess to meet her. She said, 'You are doing wonderful work' and gave us the rest of the day off. I felt like a schoolgirl. It was a change now as I was earning money, 15 shillings a week. I 'phoned home requesting they saved me dinner. My brother answered the 'phone with 'Giving it up already! Are you homesick?' My answer was, 'Far from it! I love it am longing to tell you all about this marvellous place.

34.   Meme Cortis, from Turner, *Malta V.A.D.*

Meme was the eighth of nine children. Her mother died when she was seven, so she was brought up by her eldest sister. Her father was a stationer and newsagent. She was well educated and sportive, and just 18 when she began her VAD training at Mtarfa. She had already done a first aid course and home nursing with the St John Ambulance Brigade, as well as nurse's training at the Blue Sisters Zammit Clapp Hospital. Meme lists the nine Maltese women who started their VAD training with her, as well as those ahead of them, in total 21, and includes group photographs. Eventually, 80 Maltese VADs would have served at Mtarfa; and nurses also arrived from England.

Prime Minister Neville Chamberlain flew to Munich on 16 September 1938 for, as Charles Bonham-Carter has it, 'a personal interview with Hitler'. There were sighs of relief, but they did not last long.

On 24 September, the Governor noted that Madge arrived back from a trip to England and continued:

Her arrival had a very good effect on people, who were grateful that she should have come to share their anxieties. She decided to start a Women's Auxiliary Reserve and has got some ladies to help her to organise it – herself, Lady Pound, Mrs Hunter, Lady Mercieca, Lady Pullicino, Mrs Gatt, Mrs Vella, Mrs Micallef, Baroness Inguanez, etc. I propose to keep the register now being made as a permanency.

Lady Pound (née Betty Whitehead) was the wife, since 1908, of Admiral Sir Dudley Pound, Naval Commander-in-Chief; **Mrs Hunter** was the wife of John Adams Hunter, Lieutenant Governor; **Lady Mercieca** (née Giuseppina (Josephine) Tabone) had been married since 1909 to Professor Sir Arturo Mercieca, Chief Justice; **Lady Pullicino** was the wife of Treasury Counsel, Sir Phillip Pullicino; **Mrs Gatt** was married to Lt-Colonel AJ Gatt, Commanding Officer, Royal Malta Artillery; **Mrs Vella** was the wife of Lt-Colonel EJ Vella, The King's Own Malta Regiment; there were two Micallefs in the government, making it impossible to identify **Mrs Micallef**. But Baroness Inguanez – **Maria Scebberas D'Amico Inguanez, Baroness of Djar-il-Bniet and Buqana** (1865–1947) – was very much there in her own right as the formidable Doyenne of the Maltese Nobility; she was, incidentally, married to Colonel AC McKean. She appears in more detail in the Chapter 20 itinerary.

In *Malta: Blitzed But Not Beaten* (1985), Philip Vella elaborates:

The willingness of Maltese women to play their part was manifest as far back as September 1938 when 3,000 volunteers enrolled in the Women's Auxiliary Reserve set up by Lady Bonham-Carter ... They trained several hundred Air Raid Wardens and Decontaminators; did sewing and knitting for the Forces and refugees; and when war broke out supplied the Three Services, the Civil Government and the Dockyard with trained personnel, thus releasing many men for active service.

Kathleen Norman gives a vivid sketch of that period leading up to September 1939 and introduces us to another woman stalwart involved in preparing women for the coming need for medical training:

I have often thought it was providential that we were trained gradually to the realisation of war. Had anything so shattering as the Siege of Malta broken on us without warning we might not have had the mentality to cope with it.

The summer of 1939 was very tense ... Malta was still gay and social but with a difference. Men snatched an hour or two here and there for a dinner party or a tennis match. Women met to discuss what war work they would do if the storm should break. They filled in forms offering their services in various directions or flocked to First Aid lectures.

The ballroom of the Sliema club, the Regent Dance Hall, the red brocade drawing-room of the Governor's Palace, became the lecture rooms of St John Ambulance.

Our sitting-rooms, where before we had sipped cool drinks and nibbled salted almonds, were filled with earnest ladies, solemnly swathing one another in yards of bandages and asking each other questions about bones and circulations. Army and civilian doctors gave hours of their precious time to training classes.

We all have very tender memories of the charming, white-haired English lady who realised the grave shortage of nurses in the island and gave up her whole time to training volunteers.

She was Miss Yabsley. She had founded and run the English school here for many years, and when she retired she gave up her life to St. John Ambulance and Girl Guides. She must have been seventy but she had the energy and aliveness of a schoolgirl. She was a type of elderly lady in which England seems to specialise – kind, gracious, every whit a woman but with the heart and guts of a general.

Ethel Yabsley (*c*.1870–1942) was very much a settled character in Malta. In 1905 she had founded, with **Madeleine Sceberras**, Chiswick House School, 'an establishment for Protestant young ladies' – this meant mostly the daughters of British families. As for Madeleine, she was known as Miss Shebby and had caused consternation in her family when she became a Protestant. On 14 February 1938, Bonham-Carter made a diary entry that gives a rather different picture of Miss Yabsley from that of Kathleen Norman, and adds a dimension to that of his wife:

I have not yet recorded the result of Madge's effort to put the organisation of the Girl Guides on a proper footing. There was a meeting of the committee at which were present the two Divisional Commissioners, Mrs [Marie] Denaro and Miss Yabsley, the Island Commissioner, Lady Strickland, and other supporters. At the meeting, Gabrielle [Madge] criticised severely the arrangement by which English and Maltese companies and groups were completely separate and there was no mixing of races in companies. The opposition to any change centred in Miss Yabsley and Gabrielle felt that none could be successfully carried out if she remained in her post of joint Divisional Commissioner with Mrs Denaro. She therefore asked Miss Yabsley to come and see her and told her very frankly that the separation in the Girl Guides of the two races was doing infinite harm, that she considered the present organisation was wrong, and suggested to her that she might find it very difficult to carry out new ways loyally and successfully, and that it would be better for her to resign. This was a great shock to the old lady who both stormed and wept. For a time Gabrielle heard nothing more though Miss Yabsley undertook to write. She became a good deal troubled, feeling that she had been brutal. She got hold of Teddy Price [Commissioner Boy Scouts] who undertook to see both Miss

Yabsley and Mrs Denaro and to try to get a working arrangement. He was completely successful and the arrangement is that Mrs Denaro should be Island Commissioner, ... that Miss Yabsley should be one of three Divisional Commissioners under her, and that Lady Strickland, who was Island Commissioner, should become Honorary. Madge is going to get this arrangement confirmed by Guide Headquarters when she is at home. I don't think that it could have been made if Gabrielle had not given Miss Yabsley a pretty good jerk to start with.

The Guides did, indeed, merge in 1938. The war was to bring about changes for both Miss Yabsley and Marie Denaro.

35. Caroline Vernon, courtesy of the family

Even before war was declared by Britain on Germany on 3 September 1939, there was a 'general recall' of service personnel in Malta; this affected, among others, the Vernon family and it is through Caroline Vernon's *Our Name Wasn't Written: A Malta Memoir* (1990) that we get a rare woman's glimpse of class difference among the British service personnel there, and a hint, too, of the different ways of relating to the Maltese. **Caroline Vernon** (née Clark, 1908–1988, m.1931) came from a working class family: her mother, Emma Clark, worked as a jam-maker in Keiller's Factory, London; her father was a winch driver at the Royal Docks.

John Vernon arrived in Malta as a Royal Naval rating, a writer, or clerk, working in the Navy headquarters at S Angelo, the fortress built by the Knights jutting out into the Grand Harbour (see Chapter 17 itinerary). Almost immediately, he telegraphed Caroline suggesting that she and their two children follow; which she did, pregnant as she travelled. She gave birth to their second son in Malta that October.

At first, Caroline is a wife and mother creating a home, shopping in the local shops and markets round Sliema where she is soon well known. She writes, 'I found the shops were very good and the shopkeepers so helpful, especially if one asked for help and did not demand it. They were even more helpful if one did as I did, and bothered to learn a little of their language.'

On 25 August 1939, Caroline received a notice to report to S Angelo the following day and found a dozen or so other wives there too. They were given tuition in cyphering and soon their roster of work. She writes, though:

> I have never seen any remarks about Vice-Admiral Ford's cypher staff. I don't think anyone knew we existed outside the island, but he received many compliments on the quality of our work. One of the younger members, who joined the staff long after us, received the OBE. (I think she was an 'officer's delight' type). It should have gone, instead, to one of the senior members such as **Mrs Tucker** or **Mrs Black**, serious, hardworking, and in from the start.

Caroline took to the work both because she loved it, and because she had 'a very retentive memory'. But things changed when war was declared. Previously women cypher clerks had been volunteers, now they were to be paid, and Caroline notes caustically,

> Once we were on the payroll, officers' wives tried to step in and quite a few ratings' wives were given a chit that their services were no longer required. For about three months I was the only rating's wife on the staff and, as I was so good at the job, I would have requested to see the Vice-Admiral if I had a received a chit. For quite a time my partner was the only one to speak to me. However, quite a few of the Cypher staff were ordered to return to the UK on the *Oronsay*, so the authorities had to train others.

As the months rolled by, Caroline recounts how her work changed, how she was promoted, but there were often the sort of personality clashes, sometimes class-based, that tend to be left out of other accounts.

When war was declared that September, it was a bit of an anti-climax for ordinary people in Malta: nothing happened, though Suzanne Layton noted, 'The Navy began to deploy the ships from the Mediterranean fleet to where they would be most useful in the fight against Germany.' Her father was posted elsewhere, much to her relief. She and her mother stayed but, 'By this time all the fishing-fleet, and many naval wives and families had also begun to move home as and when they could …'. She had met an army officer, John

Parlby, that summer and became engaged to him in October. Her father was amazed that anyone should want to marry her, but disgusted that she was marrying into the army; for Suzanne, anyone who took her away from her father's sphere was good enough.

Suzanne's life during this hiatus period was to revolve around her parts in the productions of the Malta Amateur Dramatic Club, or the MADC, as it was generally known. It had long been a feature of the social scene, and Suzanne captures it well, particularly the women who ran it:

> [It] had a reputation throughout the Mediterranean for its frequent and excellent productions, under the direction of the two famous sisters, **Kay** and **Ella** Warren. They were a legendary pair, Kay being the stronger personality of the two. She was strong-featured, with a stoutish upright figure, a commanding voice, and a keen sense of humour. Ella was the same build as her sister, but a softer version than Kay. They had lived together with their mother for many years in Malta, and were much respected and loved on the island.

The production in rehearsal when war was declared fell through as several of the actors were in the Navy; Suzanne continues,

> Instead, the Warrens planned to organise ... concert-parties, to go round the island, giving shows to the beleaguered garrison troops at their posts, from which the men could hardly ever get away. This was enormous fun, and the roving players drove in Army lorries and whatever transport could be laid on, through darkened roads, lane and tracks, to perform in goat-sheds, barns or wherever sufficient space could be found. Stages were built of planks resting on kerosene drums, green-rooms were little alcoves screened with tarpaulins; we used whatever was to hand, took with us our own costumes, musical instruments and scenery, if any.
>
> We sang, danced and acted sketches and scenes from Noel Coward plays and others. The troops loved it all and so did we.

Suzanne was to marry John Parlby in April 1940, but when Michael Kyle-Pope's submarine was in port, life looked up. He was to be her second husband. The intricacies of her love life, which resolved themselves back in England after the War, are best left to her autobiography.

The month before Suzanne's wedding, the governor was to have one of his last shots at putting Malta right; he wrote on 14 March,

> There has been serious trouble in the Blue Sisters' Hospital. A difficult thing to deal with because the only part of it in which one has any standing is the War Memorial Wards. Since Christmas three nurses have died and one sister and two more nurses are ill with typhoid. I have seen Bernard, Victor Micallef and Mrs Frank [Marie] Denaro. Bernard agrees with what Madge told me, that the nurses are not properly trained as to cleanliness

and he has taken steps to get them instructed, but he is very depending on old Critien [chief government medical officer]. I rather doubt the efficiency of the result. The other two were talking chiefly about the War Memorial Wards. The unsatisfactory way it is being now run, the emptiness of the beds, and so on. I have arranged to see the Mother Superior, a new one, as soon as possible.

It must all have been too much of a strain because in April Bonham-Carter had a heart attack, and it was deemed wise for him to leave his posting a year early. He was replaced by General William Dobbie. On 6 May, Bonham-Carter's last eye-opening diary entry appropriate to this chapter gives a view of the new governor's wife revealed nowhere else, and soon over-ridden by events which gave her more to think about:

> Mrs Dobbie frightened me a bit to start with. She said she would always be polite to foreigners, but could not imagine herself making friends with them. I did not think that very hopeful for a successor to Gabrielle. However, Gabrielle says that the more she sees of her the better she likes her. Mrs Dobbie told her that she had sent her daughter to come at once because she herself was tactless and her daughter was a great help.

Sybil Dobbie (née Orde-Browne, d.1962), married Lieutenant Dobbie in 1904. On marriage, the Dobbies, both members of the Protestant Plymouth Brethren, agreed to dedicate a tenth of their income to 'the Lord's work'. The Roman Catholic Maltese were, perhaps surprisingly, to take to their new governor, appreciating the way he introduced God into the encouraging homilies with which he regularly addressed them. And Mrs Dobbie was to find her feet in war-torn Malta, supported by her daughter, also **Sybil Dobbie** (c.1908–1973), who arrived from Malaya, her father's previous posting, after a demanding journey, in September 1940. The last leg was from Alexandria in a convoy of four merchant ships escorted by six warships. Her account of their war-time stay in Malta, *Grace Under Malta* (1944), is full of interest.

On 10 May 1939, the German army invaded Holland and Belgium. And on the 14th it attacked the French lines, and advanced into France. Mussolini's attitude became increasingly threatening. Bonham-Carter, still in Malta, noted how his successor continued to prepare the islands for what was to come. When Dobbie heard that German personnel were in Italy, he ordered the wives and families into St Andrew's barracks, and the wives and officers of men in the Fleet at sea to be evacuated. The Bonham-Carters left on 24 May 1940. He wrote on the 28th, 'Gabrielle was working up to the very morning on which we left. She handed over all her work in perfect order and I am confident that it will continue.'

Between 27 May and 4 June, British and French troops were evacuated from mainland Europe, known as both the dark and the courageous days of Dunkirk, encouraging both Germany and Italy. In Malta preparations continued, such as those noted by Kathleen Norman:

The hospitals were made ready for casualties. V.A.D.s mostly Maltese girls from sheltered luxurious homes, who had signed on for full time service for the duration, were posted to the military hospital to increase the nursing staff.

Mrs German, an English retired sister, who had worked unceasingly with Miss Yabsley in training voluntary nurses, became matron of a large hospital in the harbour area which she staffed almost entirely with St John Ambulance girls whom she herself had trained. Her hospital did wonderful work throughout the war and especially in the heavy blitzes.

VAD Meme Cortis did not come from a 'sheltered luxurious home', but several of those who trained with her did. Sybil Dobbie was to add to the subject of Maltese 'girls' when she arrived and started seeing what work needed to be done:

I found that it was considered very unusual for the Governor's daughter to do any definite and regular job. Educated Maltese women did not work in ordinary circumstances, and it had been a great innovation for the war when a number of girls from leading families had become V.A.D.s and were working at the military hospital.

By early March 1940, cabaret artiste Christina Ratcliffe was back in Malta; she writes:

The first few weeks of my second Malta tour went by at funeral pace. I spent a lot of time wishing I had stayed at home and a good deal more longing for the expiry of the contract whereby I had bound myself to work for three months in Gianni's gin palace. The situation was vastly different from that of 1937 when, with the other girls, I had stood at the beginning of a road to adventure – when there had been a purpose to our performance in what, after all was nothing more than a low dive. Now with Morocco definitely off, my work seemed aimless and I was conscious, as I had not been before, of the almost sordid atmosphere of my surroundings.

Mercifully, the wild unruly crowds I had met with during my previous visit had departed from the scene and walking home unescorted at night was not the ordeal it used to be. The 'Hi Blondie's' were not that loud and frequent as of yore, the wolf-whistle scarcely audible. Although it would never have done to let Gianni know I was heartily glad that of all of the ships of His Majesty's Navy, only three were now in harbour.

Somehow the time passed, and then everything changed overnight, that of 10 June 1940.

15 – Women at War, Again 1940–1943

Christina Ratcliffe's contract had seven more days to run on 10 June 1940. That evening she was in the almost empty Morning Star, talking to Charlie who was teaching her Maltese; the few people there were listening to Mussolini ranting on the radio when she heard the words, 'as from midnight Italy was at war with Britain and her allies'.

> 'Charlie, have I understood properly?' I asked when the voice had gone off the air. 'Is it really war – for Malta?'
>
> 'I'm afraid so,' he replied. 'Italy's come into it now, against Britain and her allies. And that means against us as well.'

At 6.30 the following morning, the Italian air force started bombing Malta. We know how several women and girls were to experience 11 June. For 25-year-old **Nina Farrugia** and her two sons Joe (4) and Ninu (8) living in Pietà it meant death, and for three-year-old **Josephine Mangion**. In Gzira, between Sliema and Msida, **Mary Doublet** (46), **Lilian Doublet** (7) and **Rosina Vassallo** (3) were killed, as was five-month-old **Doris Galea** in Cospicua. At least their names and ages are recorded, but is there anything else known about them? Did Nina Farrugia and Mary Doublet have husbands, or other children? Did they have nowhere to take shelter when the bombs started to fall? Or perhaps they did not appreciate the significance of the confusing noise – bombs from above and anti-aircraft fire from two British warships in the harbour, and neighbours shouting and screaming. In all, 23 civilians were killed that day. It was only the beginning.

The dockyards were the prime target, as Navy wife Kathleen Norman was only too well aware. Navy families, among them Kathleen with her children and nanny, had been moved into St George's barracks in May, and had spent a week trying to clean their filthy quarters. She does not linger on her experience of the morning of 11 June; instead, she tells how there was help around: in the first air raid Miss Yabsley 'was in the worst districts tending the wounded. She was bombed out of two homes and moved serenely and cheerfully into a third, her St John papers still in order.' Ethel Yabsley was not the only one; Kathleen also writes:

> Into the unknown terror of the first air-raid stepped four English women from their homes and billets near the deadly target. They walked serenely and quietly down the hill, in at the gate and across the whole Dockyard, while the fire bombs and splinters fell around them. They reported for duty at the Casualty Dressing Station....
>
> A few days before Italy declared war the medical officer sent an SOS asking for women volunteers, living within walking distance of the yard, to come to his help in emergency.

Those four women who walked so calmly through the first rain of shrapnel were the nucleus of a nursing service which carried on through all the worst that Malta could offer in two years of bombardment. They were the pioneers of the little band of Naval voluntary nurses, two of whom were on duty in the dressing stations without failure every working day until the Great Blitz was over in the spring of 1942. ...

Mrs Woodland, Mrs Munday and **Mrs Roberts,** wives of civilian dockyard officers, and **Mrs Kent,** the wife of a chief petty officer RN, were the first of the 'Dockyard Team.' All were unpaid, all married women with husbands and homes to care for. Only one was a fully trained nurse.

Within days, 100,000 inhabitants of the docklands, with their goods piled on carts, had taken to the roads, moving inland to stay with family and friends, leaving dogs, cats and chickens roaming the streets, soon starving and forlorn. Many of the little shops moved too. But it was not easy to find sanctuary for everyone. Kathleen Norman also writes of how

A Commander's wife, who lived in the village of Lija found a family of three thousand five hundred refugees on her hands. They were the poorest of the poor from near the harbours. She fed them from a soup kitchen. The village schoolroom became a maternity ward.

As a result of the air raids pro-Italian sentiment, which had previously and naturally been common, quickly dissipated. But what were the feelings of Giuseppina Mercieca, deemed suitable, as wife of the chief justice, to be on Lady Bonham-Carter's Women's Auxilliary Committee in September 1938? On 11 June, her husband was compelled to resign his post because of his pro-Italian sympathies. At the same time, the governor issued detention orders for him and other like-minded men, under the terms of the Malta Defence Regulations. He was interned and then, in 1942, deported with Giuseppina and their daughter **Lilian Mercieca** (1930–1996) and 60 other Maltese, to East Africa. That exile lasted until early 1945.

Inland, at the Mtarfa Military Hospital, VAD Meme Cortis writes of the morning of 11 June:

At dawn ... we heard the first air raid siren warning. This was real, not practice. I had just got up and was getting ready for duty. I dashed to the bedroom window where we could see almost the whole of the island, including the Grand Harbour. We were on top of the Ta' Qali airfield. I could not believe it, as there actually were 'planes coming over, but after the All Clear it was quiet enough.

The airfield was, of course, significant, though in those early days, in spite of the fact that it was known four fighter squadrons would be needed for the defence of Malta, there were only three aircraft there. Nevertheless, there was a Royal Air Force presence and it is now that **Tamara Marks** enters the story; in *Women of Malta*, Frederick Galea alternates her story with that of Christina Ratcliffe. Yugoslav-born Tamara was married to Squadron Leader Ronnie Marks who was stationed at Kalafrana airfield, the base for flying boats; they lived a mile away at Birżebbuġa (see Chapter 21 itinerary). Tamara spoke not only English and French, but at least four other languages as well.

Ronnie Marks had already reported to the airfield that night; Tamara was alone in the house and did not know how long he would be away; she went to sleep at 1 am. She starts her account of what happened next:

> I woke up with a start. Was that someone knocking at the door? Surely not, why, it was only seven o'clock. No one would ever dream of knocking at my door at this unearthly hour and the maid always let herself in quietly; and then another crash. It sounded like guns going off. I jumped out of bed to the tune of all bedlam let loose, put my corduroy trousers on and a pullover. I had to find out what the commotion was about. Were they testing the guns? I hoped it could not possibly be anything else. There was a disquieting roar of aircraft but it seemed unlikely that it could be the Italians. They were too well-known for their *dolce far niente*; they could not possibly start a war so early in the morning when they had the whole day to do it in. I looked out of the window. Flashes of fire and great sheets of smoke were coming from the direction of Kalafrana. The noise was terrific; the doors and windows were rattling as if they would jump off their hinges. I ran in the street. There was no one to be seen, not a soul. I wondered where every one had got to. If only the guns would stop a minute, I could collect my wits and do something. Another sickening thud … That was near. I had heard that under the table was the safest place.

At 9 o'clock Tamara's husband arrived home:

> 'Pack up, dear, you are being evacuated. Quickly, there might be another raid any minute.'
> 'Where are we going? Do you know?'
> 'Not "we", women and children only. Just take your personal things. No household effects at all; you will be able to return.'
> I hurriedly started packing. At the moment an ARP (Air Raid Precautions) woman arrived …
> 'Ah! packing already, that's good. *Rendez-vous* outside the Police Station at ten o'clock sharp.'
> 'Where are we going?'
> 'Naxxar.'

For the next few weeks, RAF families camped in the Scicluna Palazzo Parisio in Naxxar. Life was to be somewhat bizarre (see also Chapter 19 itinerary):

Three calls to order failed to produce any result whatsoever. A wooden mallet was handed to the group captain's wife who looked very natty in a grey travelling suit. She was to be commander-in-chief. Some sort of order was obtained. The roll was called. We were all present. It had been arranged that each group of ten or so would be under the charge of one officer's wife. Many a woman wore her husband's stripes that day – and subsequently. ...

... We settled in. I was amazed and agreeably surprised at the friendliness and adaptability of English women. My three years experience in England had not been very successful and, at Birzebbugia, contacts were superficial. Seeing them at close quarters, I liked them. They were clever at makeshifts, polite and kind to each other. It was like being back at boarding school again. We played pranks, made apple-pie beds, sewed pyjama sleeve ends and legs together and had mock-battles with flit-guns.

Christina Ratcliffe's neighbours in Floriana knocked on her door early that morning and urged her to hurry down to the basement. She prevaricated, sitting at her dressing table undoing her hair curlers:

Then it happened. Without further warning there was a deafening crash and the building rocked and shook as if it were about to collapse. Another crash ... the roar of aircraft ... the drawn out whine of a bomb followed by an ear-splitting explosion ... a loud salvo of gunfire. On reaching the stairs I grabbed hold of the banister and raced down them. One of my slippers fell off. Cinderella-style but I didn't let that bother me – I got rid of the other and continued the descent barefooted. More crashes and roars. I never realised before that it was such a long way down to the cellar and I began to feel that I would never get there alive. But I made it. ...

... 'Billie, where's Billie?' demanded the Roches when they saw I was alone. Their concern for her safety was unnecessary. Before I could reply she came bounding down the last flight of stairs at breakneck speed, a vision of loveliness clad only in a flimsy pair of chiffon cami-knickers, which left nothing at all to the imagination. Like me she had been caught napping.

Newly married Suzanne Layton Parlby was living in St Andrew's barracks as an army wife, sharing the quarter master's house with his wife **Midge Labbet** and her two sons, and **Elizabeth Young**, another captain's wife. Their husbands were on garrison duty. Suzanne's experience of the morning of 11 June was less dramatic than some, and I suspect that she never quite realised how it had been for others:

Italian bombing, such as it was, began quite soon, but it was all their air force could do to hit the island, let alone any specific target, and we were much amused to hear Italian radio news bulletins claiming they had hit 'the main railway station in Malta' (there was no rail system on the island), or had sunk 'HMS *St Angelo* in Valletta harbour (HMS *Angelo* being the naval headquarters, a mediaeval stone fortress on the western side of the harbour entrance). However, we had been ordered to take cover during the periods between the warnings and All Clear sirens, and spent many hours in the slit trench just outside the house, having made it comfortable with deck chairs, rugs and cushions, a tin of biscuits, bottles of water, torches and insect repellent against the sandflies which lived in the rock, ...

Suzanne's experiences were, however, not always to be so anodyne and, in spite of her relaxed attitude, she did help dishing out meals to other ranks' families and she and Elizabeth were VADs. In later months she also took on other duties.

Mabel Strickland, too, had a less unhappy experience that morning, as Joan Alexander tells us:

A few minutes before seven o'clock in the morning, Mabel was being driven home after an exciting night in the office. She had been on the telephone ever since midnight when war had been declared. It was a far too momentous occasion for her to sleep, since there were a great many people to inform, and an equal number of people from whom to glean information. She also had to watch over the editorials at this historic moment. The declaration of war was almost a relief to her after the tedious waiting, and her adrenalin was working overtime. As she reached the Portes des Bombes she peered through the car window and saw a flight of aircraft in the sky. 'Sammy Maynard has manned the Gladiators', she thought to herself. Then she watched as the planes began to drop their bombs, and she heard the wailing of the air raid sirens, and she knew she was looking at Italian planes, and that this was the moment of truth. The waiting was over and war had come to Malta.

There were to be eight air raids that day, 30 in the first week, and many more in the weeks, months, years, to come. And, while the Italians came to be less feared by some, the German bombers were a different matter. And bombing did not only kill and wound people, and flatten buildings, it stopped supplies of essentials, food and fuel, arriving in Malta. Already in July 1940 petrol rationing was introduced and no private cars or hire cars, other than taxis, were allowed on the road.

The women's writing, from which I have quoted in introducing the Second World War as it affected Malta, takes us through the whole war and includes that of Sybil Dobbie who missed the first weeks. They all experienced the war in their own way, and used their particular talents to help themselves and Malta get through it. Their first task and, indeed, that of everyone in Malta, was to seek safety from the air raids. Every possible shelter was used and more tunnels and caves dug into the soft rock of cliff faces. Christina Ratcliffe watched hundreds of people burdened with belongings headed towards her shelter and wrote, 'the tunnel was one vast communal dormitory with rows of mattresses and deckchairs stretching the whole length of the floor. All along the walls were pictures of the Holy Virgin and the Sacred Heart of Jesus.'

She was now jobless, but not for long: soon a party of like-minded artistes in the same straits got together and started rehearsing, giving their first performance on 13 July 1940. Tamara Marks, released from the Palazzo Parisio, noted that

> The great events of the season were the concert parties give by the Whizz-Bangs who maybe were not a first rate group of artists and had a rather limited repertory but they had an unlimited supply of *joie de vivre* and the knack of 'putting it over'. Subsequently I was to know some of the party quite well. ... I must admit we all enjoyed the performance very much. There were scenes and jokes at which no lady should have laughed and yet, although there is not a more prim and proper person than the serviceman's wife, we all laughed uproariously and slyly remembered some of them for future airing.

Tamara and Christina became firm friends and eventually lived in flats near each other. Meanwhile, Tamara was taking a two-month First Aid and Home Nursing course, after which she was appointed to the Floriana Medical Inspection Room as a VAD. She writes,

> Our patients were mostly Maltese labourers working on the camp as cooks, stone masons or shelter excavators but we had soldiers in as well. Most of them suffered from big ugly boils, which it was our duty to prepare for lancing. Later we were allowed to lance them ourselves. We dispensed medicine, syringed ears and bandaged limbs with enthusiasm.

This new Siege of Malta was to be marked by several stages, fuel becoming scarcer, not so much for civilian transport, but for troops and, particularly the aircraft which began to arrive at the end of 1940 to save Malta from falling; food becoming rationed, rations becoming smaller, the fear of starvation looming as convoys failed to reach the island.

By the beginning of 1941, the Germans had taken over the bombing. Sybil Dobbie writes of how 'an old lady, crouching in a shelter during a bad German raid, was once heard fervently praying 'Oh Holy Mother, send over the Italians.'

Then there were the events that everyone remembered. Christina Ratcliffe writes,

> It was on the afternoon of 16th January [1941] that the war really began in earnest for all of us in Malta. Tamara Marks was with me in the apartment when the sirens sounded shortly after lunch. Like many other people we had lost the habit of running to the shelter each time the sirens

went. We had come to accept the *Sinjal ta l-Attakki mill-Ajru* as part of the daily round. Much of our confidence was based on the fact that not all the threatened raids materialised. Very often the Italian aircrews kept well away from the coastline, preferring to drop their bombs in the sea rather than meet the steadily increasing fierceness of our anti-aircraft fire.

But on this occasion there was something sinister in the wail of the siren, a deep note of foreboding reminded me instantly of my promise to [a friend]. With HMS *Illustrious* now berthed in Grand Harbour the names of many of us might well be written on the bombs that were almost certainly to be showered on and around that sitting target. Tamara and I went below.

The aircraft carrier HMS *Illustrious* was bringing vital reinforcements, and arrived already crippled by aerial bombardment. Sybil Dobbie gives the government house version:

We made hurried preparations to receive her. A berth was got ready for her in the harbour, but above all we made ready for her wounded. We heard that she had had very bad casualties, and as she limped into the haven of Malta, and under the protecting shadow of Malta's defences, lines of ambulances were waiting beside the quay, and doctors, nurses, V.A.D.s and orderlies were standing by in the Service hospitals.

They were needed. Numbers and numbers of men, mostly horribly burnt, were hurried in, and all that night and most of the next day the fight for their lives went on. Few of the hospital staffs went off duty that night as one terrible burn after another was dressed. Of course, it was inevitable that a number of the casualties should die but Malta's medical services did wonders and very many recovered. My mother went round the hospitals to see all the *Illustrious* casualties almost at once, and they were a heart-rending sight.

And Meme Cortis describes it from the Mtarfa Military Hospital:

One day on coming back from my night's leave I found an additional hut built in the barracks was open for the biggest number of casualties we had yet seen, from H.M.S. Illustrious. ... Most of the crew were suffering from burns and these cases were immediately transferred to hospital ... This hut alone had 60 badly burnt cases. Some did not survive and some only just about made it. Those that lived struggled hard, for some of them could not move. They were like mummies being covered all over in dressings.

Every one of the nursing staff seemed to be on that ward, dashing around so very busy, and each bed had some sort of transfusion equipment there. ... Every doctor, sister and nurse that was available came to help, with hardly any taking time off except to snatch a drink or a snack. This went on for a few days until the work gradually slowed down.

36.   Dobbie Family, from Dobbie, *Grace Under Malta*

Kathleen Norman puts herself in the shoes of young women like Meme, who was not yet 20, when she writes,

The young Maltese V.A.D.s from their sheltered, luxurious homes, had never seen such sights as these. The men were terribly burned and grievously injured. As the girls saw for the first time the inspired courage of the wounded men their own nerves were steeled to meet their grim tasks. They never flinched or failed.

Kathleen also feels for those stationed near the *Illustrious*:

With a sickening dread, I thought of two women … who were in that turmoil on my responsibility. They were the two dockyard V.A.D.s of the day and I knew they would be in a place of grave danger. 'A' Dressing station, where casualties were taken, was nothing but an ancient sail-loft, with a wide, arched and unsupported roof. The yard was sadly battered that day, and was left full of horror and weariness, but the main target had not been hit. Thanks to her own magnificent shooting and to the good work of the dockyard batteries, *Illustrious* had escaped further harm.

Kathleen also visits *Illustrious*, and describes, ever empathetic, what she saw through the eyes of her companion:

It was the first time I had ever been on board a wounded ship. When I saw *Illustrious*' great torn decks, the aching chasm that reached into her bowels, the little sick-bay that had known such horror, I felt almost as near tears as when I talked with her tired seamen.

The woman who stood beside me had known another war. On her white overall she wore the ribbons of 1914-1918 and of the Royal Red Cross for gallantry in the front line dressing stations of France.

She was **Dorothy Hamilton**, who for a year had devoted all her leisure to training amateur nurses for just such scenes as these. She had been in charge of an Army dressing station outside Valetta and often joined the dockyard staff as well. There was a catch in her voice as she said:

'I haven't seen anything quite like this since I climbed to the top of Menin Ridge twenty-five years ago.'

Illustrious may have held the German bombers at bay, but Senglea took the full brunt of the determined air raids intended for the aircraft carrier. Christina Ratcliffe and Tamara Marks went over during a lull and Tamara wrote:

The destruction that greeted our eyes was appalling, boulders everywhere blocking our path, half-hanging balconies at dangerous angles. It was a problem how to get from one street to another. Mountains of rock slabs had to be climbed with danger to life and limb. One street of about fifty houses had been razed to the ground. Pitiful remnants of frocks, shoes, hats and other oddments were mixed with the rubble. A string of washing flapped dismally against the only remaining wall of a three-storied house. Dead goats seemed to be everywhere. The order forbidding itinerant goats' milk vendors had not come into force in Senglea, it seemed.

Winifred (Winnie) Cutajar Beck of the *Times of Malta*, quoted in Joan Alexander's biography of Mabel Strickland, best describes how one felt during the bombing raids, and how Maltese women were involved in attempting to repel the attackers, reminiscent of the Great Siege of 1565:

The noise! The noise! Sometimes we used to go on a balcony to watch the bombers coming in. The Terror! There was nowhere to go! Nowhere to go! Everything was firing! All the different Sounds! The rumble of the planes' engines – the high pitched screaming of the falling bombs – the barking of the ack-ack guns, the sharp report of the Bofors, the guns booming away from *Terror*, *Aphis* and *Lady Bird* moored in the harbour. It was an inferno, hell on earth! One felt not, if only the bombing would stop, but if only the noise would stop! The gunners were given plugs for their ears. The noise was terrible! Terrible! The women and girls used to go and help the men handle the shells – because the men were growing tired! So they helped the men feed the guns! They had no tin hats – no special shoes – nothing! The women had nothing – but they went to help their menfolk. We had scarcely any protection, and so it was the only thing to do – to help the menfolk handle the shells! Malta fought as a family – the children played with the empty shells of the bombs – that was their game! Children adapt themselves – they adapt to anything! Playing chicken with bombs! Later on I saw a soldier give a little girl twopence and her mother asked her what she was going to do with it, and the little girl said she would spend it on bread – she could think of nothing more important than that!

Mabel, whose father had died in August 1940, leaving her in charge of all the family's print interests, made sure that the *Times* came out every day throughout the War, whatever the destruction of its offices and shortages of essentials. In February 1941, she hired a secretary, 20-year-old **May Agius** (b.1920). Joan Alexander describes May's interview for the job and, in doing so, gives an indelible character sketch of Mabel:

She was tiny, and Mabel looked like a giant beside her. But May was wiry, resilient and sharp-witted. If she appeared humble it was a false impression. When Mabel had finished her test dictation, she looked at May for several minutes, and then asked, 'Are you frightened of me?' Genuinely surprised, May exclaimed, 'No! Why? Should I be?' and was greeted with guffaws of laughter. Everyone was frightened of her, Mabel thought, except Winnie and this extraordinary girl.

May was one of six surviving children of a dispensing chemist with a shop in Valletta. By this time, her brother John, an RAF civilian clerk, was head of the household of adult siblings in the family home in Sliema. May was to stay with Mabel for thirty years, putting up with, in Joan Alexander's words, not May's, 'Mabel's tantrums'.

Another day to remember was 7 April 1941, when German bombers destroyed the Opera House and many other buildings in Kingsway. It was Meme Cortis' day off and she and a friend were in town on their way to catch a bus back to Mtarfa. They heard the siren go and dashed to the nearby shelter, feeling the blast of a bomb, shaken and covered in dust; then:

When we came out of the shelter, our first sight was of the ruined Royal Opera House, a lovely theatre, of which we were so proud, considering it our small Covent Garden. Now it was just a heap of rubble. Not one wall standing ... all flat to the ground with only a few arches left in the basement.

At the same time, May Agius was at the *Times* office; as James Holland, who interviewed John Agius for *Fortress Malta*, tells the story,

[Mabel] was usually quite blasé about taking cover, but on this instance had a strange hunch and insisted May and she go down to the shelter underneath the newspaper offices. Safely underground, they heard the bombs start falling. For some reason, May had an uncontrollable feeling of impending doom. Closing her eyes tight, she hoped her fear would not get the better of her. Then she suddenly remembered the following day was her birthday; she would be 21; she hardly dared believe she would still be alive. Moments later, the building was hit and a choking column of dust filled the cave, accompanied by the now familiar stench of cordite. Panic-stricken, the children in there with them began crying.

May's coat and handbag had been destroyed, but she managed to get the bus to Sliema, seeing bomb damage all the way. Friends tried to hold her back as she approached her street, at least they reassured her that the family, who had been at supper when the siren went, had taken shelter. But the family home was no more. 'I was hurt beyond healing', said May. 'In my home I had lost a companion of my school days and all the sweet surroundings of childhood.' On the third day of rummaging through the ruins, they pulled out their cat, alive.

Different women had different stratagems for when the bombers and fighters were overhead. For Mabel Strickland, the adrenalin usually flowed and she often stayed put. It was much the same for **Queenie Lee**, wife of a Royal Navy officer who had lived in Malta for some years teaching at the Royal Navy Dockyard School, initially a school for the children of Maltese dockworkers, latterly for those of Royal Navy personnel as well. In *Malta: the Last Great Siege* (2003), David Wragg quotes from her otherwise seemingly inaccessible 'Life in Malta' (1943):

Only dire necessity forced us to take to the shelters. Attacks were far too exciting to miss. We groaned when our Hurricanes couldn't overtake the Messerschmitt 109; we cheered ourselves hoarse when gunners or fighters found their target, and blazing machines hurtled to earth followed by swaying parachutists.'

With the dockyards increasingly bombed, and the buildings and houses round about destroyed, remnants of the school moved to St George's barracks where many of the naval families were now housed. Caroline Vernon wrote, 'The Dockyard School finally closed down early in 1942 when the naval schoolteachers were recalled and other naval jobs allotted to them.'

It was particularly difficult for old and infirm refugees from the increasingly devastated Three Cities to find refuge in the countryside; many, therefore, were settled in St George's Government School, Qormi, which consisted of separate girls' and boys' schools in a large complex. In May 1941, the girls' school also served as a home and hospital; the medical superintendent was 42-year-old **Dr Irene Condachi** (1899–1970).

To find Irene Condachi active as a doctor during the War is to begin to answer a question that bothered me throughout the research for this chapter. During the First World War, as Chapter 13 shows, there were dozens of women doctors practising in Malta, admittedly foreign, mostly British. But Maltese Blanche Huber had set an example when she qualified in 1925. Patricia Camilleri, in 'The Rise and Rise of Female Graduates: Some Milestones in Tertiary Education for Women in Malta' (2006), shows that few followed her. **Dr Cettina Bajona** qualified in 1935; **Dr Marcelle Galanopoulo** in 1940 and **Dr Maria Grech Marguerat** in 1943. As for Irene Condachi, whose Greek merchant father had brought his family to Malta, though she started her studies at the University there in 1916, she qualified in Naples in 1926, followed two years later by a special degree in paediatrics from the University of Pavia.

But May 1941 found her back in Malta running a clinic in the school in Qormi – where the nurses were 21 displaced nuns from four different orders, assisted by 'maids, charwomen and washerwomen' – on a day when the Luftwaffe decided to bomb the school. It housed not only 160 elderly refugees, but also 120 boys and girls having lessons that afternoon, alternating with the 120 who had been there in the morning.

Because it was difficult to hear the air raid siren, the drill was that the caretaker would be telephoned and he would sound the alarm to alert everyone to decamp to the shelters that had been dug beneath the school. At 2 pm, the bell rang and headteacher **Riccarda Farrugia** blew her whistle. At 2.15 a lone Junkers-88 fighter bomber dropped its load on the school. Much damage was done, some received minor injuries, but all was well enough, except that the caretaker had not rung the bell. Sixty-seven years later, as the *Times of Malta* related on 18 January 2015, in 'The Qormi school that was saved by the bell', **Lucy Camilleri** (née Formosa) confessed, in an address to senior citizens, that, aged seven, she had always itched to ring the bell and that afternoon she had been unable to resist the temptation. More details are known about Dr Condachi, including of her post-War work. Unfortunately, I have been unable to use them.

That period of German bombing was most severe from January to April 1941. Two events happened in Christina Ratcliffe's life later that year. That with the most long-lasting effect was her meeting with Adrian Warburton (known as Warby), Malta's much-decorated 'ace reconnaissance pilot'. She was to continue loving him even after his mysterious disappearance, and probably until she died in Malta in 1988 (see Chapters 17 and 22 itineraries). In *Warburton's War* (2003), Tony Spooner captures their public image with two quotations from interviews he conducted: 'They were a very glamorous couple'; and 'We shall always remember our Christina', to which he adds, 'With their personalities, zest and determination they were to become living symbols of the island's unconquerable spirit.' Their relationship was, indeed, to become legendary and later to lead to a film and a documentary.

On 15 June, Christina became a civilian plotter in the RAF Operation Room at Lascaris (see Chapter 17 itinerary). She writes,

By this time petrol rationing had been enforced and transport difficulties had arisen for the Whizz-Bangs. We had been reduced to giving three shows a week. With time on our hands, when Cecil Roche (who had now obtained a commission) told **Marigold [Fletcher]** and me that the RAF required twenty Englishwomen to be trained for plotting duties such as were carried out by the Women's Royal Air Force in the UK, we applied for the job. We were chosen from some fifty-nine other applicants and whether Cecil or Marigold's RAF boyfriend, who also worked at Lascaris, had anything to do with the choice is a moot point. But as the saying goes: 'All's fair in love and war,' and this was certainly war.

To visit the Lascaris War Rooms, as the itinerary suggests, is to see Christina and her fellow-plotters so clearly in what was known as 'the Hole' – a rabbit warren of tunnels and rooms blasted out of the rock in the cliff above the Customs House jetty. Tony Spooner notes that Christina was later appointed Captain of D Watch and, finally rose to become assistant to the Controller.

Suzanne Layton Parlby was doing similarly essential work, but for the Army; this is how she describes it:

I started to work in Military intelligence when I moved into Valletta to live. It was only ten minutes walk from the St James Hotel to the Auberge de Castille where I worked in the cipher office, encoding and decoding messages. At first these came through in groups of numbers, which required the relevant books to de- or en-code: the keys changed daily. Then Typex machines arrived, which automatically encoded messages typed in clear, or decoded when the groups of numbers or letters were typed. These also had keys which changed daily, and if the correct key was not typed in at the beginning of the message, then only gobbledy-gook emerged from the machines. The machines made a loud metallic clatter, with which we lived throughout our eight hour shifts.

When the *Auberge de Castille* was bombed, her office was shifted to the Lascaris War Rooms, though neither she nor Christina mention knowing each other. What is more, the St James Hotel, where Suzanne was then living, was hit by a land-mine, which the Germans had started dropping, and collapsed. She and 40 hotel guests were in the shelter underneath it and were terrifyingly entombed by rubble blocking the entrance until they were rescued a few hours later. Her parents had been friends of the Dobbies so she was invited to stay at San Anton until she could find somewhere else to live and writes, 'They were extremely hospitable, and offered accommodation to many who were homeless or recovering from injuries, and to exhausted fighter pilots and submariners, for a few days rest and peace in the country.'

Suzanne moved to a flat in a house in Gwardamaṅga (see Chapter 19 itinerary), and had another scare when she ignored the plea of her maid **Nina** to hurry to the shelter when the siren went. Nina herself did so. The bomb outside the front door blasted Suzanne under the dining room table where she was found by friends 'gulping brandy from a tablespoon!' She became unwell and so was evacuated home to England early in 1942 together with her friend Elizabeth Young who was pregnant. Back in England, Suzanne lived in Oxford and did war work involving reconnaissance maps, based in the Bodleian Library.

At the time of the bombing of Senglea, when it became the Germans' target in the place of the crippled but well-defended *Illustrious*, there was another wave of refugees. Sybil Dobbie describes how she and her father used to

Pass flat carts wending their way outward, bearing pathetic little loads of household goods, cooking pots and bird-cages and mirrors and sacred pictures, all that had been rescued from bombed houses near the harbour, whose owners were trying to find some place to store them in the already crowded inland villages. We gave over some lofts and part of a disused chapel in San Anton Palace to store furniture for refugees, but there was little we could do to mitigate the terrible loss and suffering.

There were women, however, who devoted themselves to those bombed out, through the Help the Homeless Organisation. One of those was Marie Agius Denaro who had started her charitable work during the First World War, and who Charles Bonham-Carter writes about as Island Commissioner of the Girl Guides. Marie was to find herself in Kenya in June 1943 representing Malta's Girl Guides. She told her audience of Kenya's Girl Guides how in Malta they, and the Brownies, 'had distributed gas masks, made treasure bags for the troops, [and] learnt English carols to sing in hospitals'. While staying with family in Kenya, she learnt that her son had been killed. Her story was added to, edited and published by a later generation as *Daughter of an Empire: A Family History* (2003). Marie's sister, Daisy Agius, earlier in charge of Bonham-Carter's After Care Association, was also involved in Help the Homeless and many other charitable organisations.

Sliema-born **Inez Galea** (née Pace, 1892–1976, m.1931), wife of the attorney general, was an equally committed member of the organisation. Albert Abela (in his *Grace and Glory*) quotes praise of her by 'The Pimpernel' on 7 June 1942:

Every day, bombs or no bombs, she goes to help in the Homeless Depot in Valletta or to visit the hospital. She laughs at her bomb-dodging experiences. Watch her at the Depot, sympathising, advising, listening to some tale of tragedy all too common these days. Not for a moment does her interest flag, nor her kindness tire. Quick and efficient, she possesses all the humanity that robs mere efficiency of its coldness.

During the four years of the organisation's existence, about one million garments, shoes etc. were distributed to 36,800 families (over 119,000 individuals).

Also working for the homeless was **Audrey Jackson,** wife of the lieutenant governor, Sir Edward Jackson. She, too, had been a woman relied on by Charles Bonham-Carter; he consulted her, for example, about petrol supplies on 8 September 1939. In March 1940, she was a member of the War Charities Committee chaired by Gabrielle Bonham-Carter and, when the Bonham-Carters had to leave unexpectedly in May, he wrote, 'Gabrielle has arranged to hand over the Service things to Mrs Dobbie and the work connected with the Maltese to Audrey Jackson – the best possible arrangement.' Kathleen Norman, useful chronicler of women's part in the war effort, writes of late 1942, when Audrey's husband had collapsed in August,

Sir Edward Jackson had been invalided home, after a very long term of office. His wife left with him. A woman of great attraction and charm, she had worked unceasingly throughout the war, in collecting and distributing all the clothing for families who had lost their houses. She had been responsible for the apportioning of all the women volunteers in the island to various branches of war service.

Kathleen was just as unstinting in her praise of Sybil Dobbie senior, showing that Bonham-Carter's distribution of labour between her and Audrey Jackson was well judged:

She entered heart and soul into every woman's movement in the island and never spared herself. As Governor's wife she became automatically the controller of the nursing services. She could have been just the figurehead, leaving to others the work and the nursing. She was not that sort of woman. Between her myriad duties she found time to take the courses of lectures, the coaching classes in bandaging and lifting and ward work which were attended by the humblest VADs and she won high marks in the St John Ambulance examinations.

I do wonder, though, how the two women got on for, as will become apparent, Audrey was to play a part in the replacement of William Dobbie as governor.

As for young Sybil Dobbie, she had found the work she could most usefully do: her father's office in the Grand Palace, Valletta, (see Chapter 17 itinerary) was short of staff:

The work was piling up. Could I possibly come into the office for a day or two and help tide things over? As I was doing nothing I was very glad to help, and, as it was only to be temporary, no one made any objections, especially as it was a long time before most people realised what I was doing. But somehow the time lengthened out, and, having gone in for a few days, I remained there for the rest of my time in Malta. My father liked to have me there to handle certain secret papers and to act as confidential secretary both to him and the Military Secretary. ... When 'business was slack' or there was nothing particularly confidential on hand, I used to deal with the many petitions that came in from all over the island, and I also helped the Command Welfare Officer and occasionally the A.D.C. In fact, I became a sort of 'odd-job man' to my father and his staff.

It took Tamara Marks a long time to find a job that contributed to the war effort, and she describes her various attempts, one of them amusingly when she answered an advertisement from a man wanting French lessons, not realising what it might mean. In the end, she was hired to write letters to the families of those service personnel who had been killed, and to sort out their effects. She describes how she felt:

In the beginning I could not open a new file without tears springing to my eyes or write to a mother or wife without feeling miserable all day but I got used to it. Luckily casualties were not as high as one would have expected – on average about two a day. But sorting out belongings and winding up estates was a lengthy job, especially in the case of officers.

The Luftwaffe and their determined bombing returned in December 1941, and it was to last until August 1942. Those months were not good. That winter was particularly cold, and the casualties from bombing raids, including named women, started as early as February 1942.

Ethel Yabsley, now 72, was still going strong. But, as the record for 5 February has it,

At 10.40 during Matins a fearful barrage broke out over Sliema. The whole district rocked, the Church trembled, the crashing of buildings and of broken glass. The noise died down and a few moments later there was a whisper at the church door and Reverend Hugh Farrie fetched his surplice. He had been sent for to see Miss Yabsley who had been badly injured and was lying at the Blue Sisters Hospital. He took her the Blessed Sacrament, and she died within an hour. Her house had a direct hit and she was not in her shelter.

Kathleen Norman wrote, 'She was beloved by English and Maltese alike ... the whole island, and above all the nursing services, mourned her very deeply.' She is buried in the Ta' Braxia Cemetery, Pietà (see Chapter 19 itinerary).

On Sunday afternoon, 15 February, the Regent Cinema in Kingsway was showing *The North-West Mounted Police*, starring Madeleine Carroll, Paulette Goddard and Gary Cooper. At 5.45, a single JU 88 bomber turned inland over Fort S Elmo and aimed a stick of four 250kg bombs along Kingsway. One hit the Casino Maltese, killing at least eight people, the next struck the Grand Palace and the third smashed into the Regent Cinema. Twenty six civilians were killed, 25 servicemen, mostly of the Cheshire Regiment; many were injured, some had a miraculous escape. Tamara

Marks had already seen the film, her friend **Aida Kelly** (*c*.1916–1942) had considered going that day, but in the end didn't. So there may well have been women there. Records do not say. But female relatives would have been affected, and sweethearts home in Cheshire waiting for letters.

Twenty-six-year-old Aida was rather careless about air raids: she liked to go to Hastings Gardens (see Chapter 17 itinerary) and watch what was happening, causing Tamara great anxiety, especially when she was persuaded to join her. 'I've seen a terrific raid!' Aida would announce on her return to the office in nearby Scots (Scozzese) Street (now Vassalli Street). On 24 April she was to meet Tamara at St Andrew's Church in South Street (see Chapter 17 itinerary). But there was a big attack that afternoon and she did not turn up. She would never do so again. Some of her belongings, a shoe, a handbag, were eventually found nearby. Tamara had had enough, and she flew out on 30 May, seen off by her husband and Christina Ratcliffe.

37.   Tamara Marks and Aida Kelly, from Galea, *Women of Malta*

The Luftwaffe were expected to bomb dockyards, airfields and convoys unloading in the harbour, even the tightly packed streets of Valletta and Senglea, but on 25 April they attacked the secluded camp of St George's harbouring naval women and children; nearby were well-marked military hospitals. At 7 am that Saturday, the Stukas flew over the camp dropping bombs as they did so. All the members of the Vernon family – mother, father, three children – wrote their memories of how everyone made a mad scramble for whatever cover was nearer. All found protection except one woman, who was killed. The Vernons, in their editing of Caroline's manuscript, thought it might have been Mrs Midlane, but 41-year-old **Rosa Midlane** was killed on 2 April at Paola. Coincidentally, there was, according to the same records, an earlier bomb attack on St George's. On that occasion, bomb and mine disposal officer, Lieutenant Commander William Hiscock DSC (RN retired) and his wife, **Alice Beatrice Hiscock**, were killed when a bomb fell directly onto their quarters. That April, 6,700 tons of bombs were dropped on Malta.

The Sisters of Charity ran the Hospital for Mental Diseases in Attard. During an air raid, the nuns would shepherd their patients into the cellars, and that happened on 9 May. But two female patients were missing, so 31-year-old **Sister Alexandra Borda** (*c.*1911–1942) from Kalkara, and nurses **Carmela Muscat** and **Teresa Sammut** immediately began a search of the wards. Guns were firing, bombs started to fall; finally the patients were found but at that moment a high explosive bomb hit the hospital and it collapsed. When the dust cleared, doctors and nurses rushed to find them, but the three nurses were dead, the patients severely injured.

On 6 June, VAD Meme Cortis was injured by shrapnel when, in spite of the big red cross painted on the roof of the Mtarfa Military Hospital, it was hit; she wrote: 'They were aiming for Ta' Qali, the home of the Spitfires, and the clock tower on D block made a good landmark'. She went straight to theatre where the shrapnel was removed under local anaesthetic. She was lucky, but undoubtedly shaken, which might account for the few details she thought to give when the hospital area was hit again; she wrote, 'A sad event was the direct hit on the colonel's house and his wife was taken into hospital with multiple injuries, but succumbed shortly afterwards and was buried in the military cemetery just down the hill from our mess in the valley of Mdina.'

But who was the colonel's wife? She deserves a name. As I was writing this chapter I rang Meme, now 93, and apologised for expecting her to remember the colonel's name. 'Hamilton', she replied immediately. With that I was able to find William Hamilton's army records and, in a box on the side: '**Florence May** devoted and courageous wife of Lt Col **Hamilton** died of wounds received during an air raid on 13 July 1942 (Mtarfa Military Cemetery).' The couple had been in Malta since January 1939; by 1940, Hamilton was in charge of Medical Division 90 of the hospital.

Death, injury and the loss of homes were obvious disasters. According to the Malta Family History website, from 11 June 1940 until December 1943, 1,190 civilians were killed outright; 296 died of their wounds; 54 were missing presumed dead; 1,846 were seriously injured, and 1,932 slightly injured. Of the 1,540 dead, 433 were women, 404, children and 703, men. By April 1942, the number of houses destroyed or damaged was estimated at 85 per cent in Floriana, 80 per cent in Senglea, 75 per cent in Kirkop, 75 per cent in Valletta, 70 per cent in Luqa, 70 per cent in Cospicua, 70 per cent in Kalkara, 65 per cent in Vittoriosa (Birgu) and 60 per cent in Gzira. If you scroll down the website, it gives you names, taken from memorials, of those killed, starting with Attard where the nurses in the Hospital for Mental Diseases died – there were 21 deaths there in all, from 18 July 1941 to 22 July 1942, ranging in age from one year to 55. It is worth pausing for a moment to imagine the grief, sense of loss and displacement, particularly for women for whom home was usually their world, who were the carers of the injured, who were attempting to create new homes under very trying circumstances, and to find enough food for their children.

The Luftwaffe bombs of those months meant that the Allied convoys could not get through to bring essential supplies of food and fuel to Malta. Food became increasingly scarce, so much so that on 3 January 1942, the first Victory Kitchen appeared in Lija and on 5 May the rationing of bread – Malta's staple food – came into effect. In April, pasta, rice, tomato paste and tinned milk were rationed; reductions were made in the rations of sugar, oil, coffee, soap and kerosene. By June there were 42 Victory Kitchens. In January 1943, more than 175,536 people were receiving cooked meals from them. Those who registered with a Victory Kitchen had to give up their family ration of preserved meat and tinned fish and, in return, collected a meal, either at noon or 5 pm, to take 'home'.

Philip Vella describes the problems of staffing the Victory Kitchens. Many competent women were already engaged in other essential war work, but inexperienced young women were rounded up, and the Archbishop was approached to allow nuns, too, to become involved. One of the young women was 19-year-old Agatha Barbara who also worked as an air raid warden. She will have a more prominent role in Chapter 16.

The meals served, were, not surprisingly, easy to complain about, and some did. Philip Vella quotes several letters that make unappetising reading. But at least some fun was obtained from singing. One song, translated into English, tune unknown, runs:

Baked Pasta in trays and people in array
At the Victory Kitchens
Minestra and sardines, pasta and beans
At the Victory Kitchens
What a treat on New Years Day! They made us eat sardines
At the Victory Kitchens
Their legs are so fat, they eat so much grub
The girls at the Victory Kitchens
Their hair set all wavy to flirt with the boys in the Navy
The girls at the Victory Kitchens
The kitchen staff were not slow to retaliate
By saying we served you goats meat that you had to eat
From the Victory Kitchens

Christina Ratcliffe summed up the situation:

At first the Victory Kitchens did not meet with much support but as the siege continued and the prospects of relief from outside grew more remote, the kitchens came into their own. It was not long before they were catering for almost the entire civil population. Indeed, it was due to these VKs, as they were dubbed, that the people owed their survival through those grim days of hunger. The black market was rife on the island and had there been no control of what supplies there were, no meting out of a fair share to all, however meagre, Malta might not have been able to claim that there were no deaths from starvation.

There were some who sought a scapegoat for the deteriorating situation. For Mabel Strickland it was Governor Dobbie. She was quite clear that he had it in mind to surrender Malta and, with her contacts in the British Government and with Lord Mountbatten who had been stationed in Malta in the Royal Navy in the 1930s, she started, as early as 1941, agitating for his removal. She was supported by Audrey Jackson who, as wife of the lieutenant governor, had access to internal government gossip. In that spring Audrey had, as Joan Alexander tells it, appealed to Mabel to break censorship: 'Everybody knows you know how to do it! If you don't we will all be prisoners of war in six days – he's preparing to surrender.' And she stood over Mabel as she re-wrote cables until they were deemed satisfactory.

By April 1942, the campaign began to bear fruit. On 7 May, Viscount Gort arrived to replace Dobbie; indeed, the Dobbie family left on the flying boat that had brought him from Gibraltar where he was governor. Sybil Dobbie says nothing about the agitation against her father, but did write of the summer of 1941:

I found, incidentally, at this time that my main function, apart from any work I might do in the office, was to be a public indication of the gravity or otherwise of the situation. I understood that the thought in many people's minds was, 'Well, as long as His Excellency keeps his daughter here, and his wife, he can't think things are too bad.' He mentioned in the broadcast that we were staying. It was a very passive role, but one was glad to feel that one could even be passively useful.

Sybil writes only of their distress that they were not allowed to let anyone know that they were leaving; they could not even say goodbye to close friends and staff. There is no doubt, though, that the war years had worn the governor down – he was taken into hospital a week after his return to England – and Gort did bring fresh impetus to Malta's will and ability to survive, as well as the George Cross to be presented to its people, the ceremony of which took place at a less fraught time. Gort's title was Supreme Commander of the Fighting Services and Civil Administration. What is more, there was agitation in the British Parliament to make sure that Malta was given the wherewithal to hold out. Joan Alexander quotes extracts from a letter that Mabel's sister **Mary Hornyold Strickland** (1896–1970) wrote to her from England, one of which reads:

Dame Irene Ward put a question in the House of Commons as to whether it was Churchill's intention to hold Malta or not. When she did not get a satisfactory answer she threatened to move the adjournment of the House so that the subject could be debated. She refused to be silenced.

The next event to catch people's attention, beyond the daily grind of surviving, took place on 25 July 1942. During the night, an Axis parent ship and a naval auxiliary carrying eight explosive motor boats (EMBs) left Augusta harbour in Sicily with the intention of attacking Malta's Grand Harbour, once the defences had been breached. Two torpedo boats towed a two-man 'pig' – otherwise described as 'one-man submarines', 'in reality human torpedoes'. While one was to blast the defences, the other was to target the submarines at Fort Manoel, which played such havoc with Axis shipping; an air raid was to cover any noise. But, in addition to the harbour's many defences – chains, spikes, nets – the auxiliary ship was picked up on radar and that was the beginning of the plan's unravelling, witnessed from the shore. In *Siege: Malta 1940–1943* (1985), Ernle Bradford describes how

> The people of Valletta were on their roofs and in the streets. The families sleeping outside and on the vantage points of the Upper and Lower Barracca were witnesses to that astonishing display; fire and light, parabolas of tracer, and a sea exploding in flames. With the dawn the Hurricanes were overhead and a battle took place with the escort of Macchi fighters that had been promised the attacking team for first light.

In *The Siege Within the Walls: Malta 1940–1943* (1970), Stewart Perowne quotes a long version of the event, and the lead-up to it that night, that he obtained from Ella Warren, one of the amateur dramatic impresario sisters, then engaged on plotting duties for the Royal Navy; this is part of what she related:

> Woken by the din, throngs of people ran along the front, puzzled at the criss-cross fire and the low searchlights just after an 'all clear'. How they cheered the guns, as they crowded on to the Barraccas! K[ay] saw it from home and couldn't make out what was occurring, tracers, lights and noise giving the effect of a firework display!
>   As the E-boats swept in they were lit up by the faint dawn; they raced through low mist, coloured by the rising sun. The guns of the harbour forts snapped and cracked. There was one explosion. An E-boat blew up against the defences. Three minutes from the start – and it was over! Like another mad charge of the light brigade – and only one derelict boat remained.

Caroline and John Vernon also had a front row view, and she adds to the story:

> The children were, as usual, bedded down in the slit trench and, at about 5am on this beautiful morning, the siren gave its awful wail. John and I

wandered down to the slit trench and suddenly Fort Madliena naval guns opened up and also the Spinola guns, but they were firing out to sea. We saw the first couple of boats explode and wondered what the hell was up. We heard later that they were trying to get into the Grand Harbour. None was successful, and later, a Hurricane pilot, forced to bale out, spotted one of the boats and paddled over in his dinghy. He found the crew dead, and the boat was later taken in tow and brought into harbour and later re-named HMS *Xmas*.

Ella adds a tailpiece to that:

Among the things salved from the boat was a little mascot white furry dog, with a red bow; what girl gave it to what boy? We named him 'Bruno-Bianco' and he swung on a cord above my typewriter and his little black eyes gave nothing away.

Caroline Vernon worked with Ella; and the Vernon family, researching the background for the publication of their mother's memoirs after her death (various editions of the book are now available), wrote,

After the disclosure of the Ultra secret in 1974, many accounts of the war have had to be revised. We ourselves wonder whether Ella Warren, one of our mother's colleagues, who received the MBE, was knowingly working for Ultra when she worked with Lieutenant Commander Carnes, Head of the Watch. Etty Black remembers that Ella often stayed back at the end of a watch typing. Could she have been doing secret work for Ultra or was she just working privately for the Malta Amateur Dramatic Society in her spare time?

Ultra was the codename for the vital dissemination of cryptographic intelligence to Allied commanders. After the War, the Warren sisters were to revive their theatrical company, though Caroline Vernon tells us that eventually Ella went blind.

Such excitements did little to fill empty bellies. When the end of the Siege of Malta was in sight, Mabel Strickland left for England for a well-earned rest and recuperation. In September 1943 she gave an interview on the BBC which Stewart Perowne quotes in full. Asked 'What were the effects of hunger and other shortages?', she replied,

Well, lassitude, frayed tempers, and dirt and scabies. Everything takes twice or three times the time to do ... Standards went down. Our bombed office was swarming with fleas; there was no broom or soap or hot water for cleaning. It was only when life came back that the extent of the human deterioration began to horrify those who had lived it. While the hunger lasted, small things assumed enormous proportions. Likes and dislikes were unaccountable and continuous. ... Everyone lost weight from two to three stone and Malta became like one vast convalescent home in which everyone existed but was slipping backwards until the siege was raised. Everyone lived in hope of good news from the outside world.

On 15 August 1942, some help did at last reach Malta from the outside world and, because it happened on the feast of Santa Marija, it became known as the Santa Marija Convoy – a gift from the Virgin Mary. More formally, the convoy that set out from Gibraltar was called Operation Pedestal.

In Malta, the sound of gunfire on 12 August warned people that a convoy was approaching. The following day, the bastions started to fill with people of all kinds, anyone who had the energy to get there. Three ships dribbled in, their decks shattered, but cargo intact. Somehow, the crowd managed to cheer wildly. But Lord Gort scanned the horizon anxiously for the American tanker *Ohio*. Food was not enough; without fuel, Malta could not survive. That evening another ship limped in. The *Ohio* was still 200 miles away. It had been torpedoed, hit five times by bombs, and then set ablaze by Stukas. Lashed to one of its escorts, towed by another, it edged forward, pointing towards Malta. The Italian navy was in pursuit, but a British submarine, whose captain was in the area against orders, was onto them, allowing the *Ohio* slowly and determinedly to inch its way forward, until it hove into view.

Ten-year-old Cub Michael Vernon wrote later,

I remember the *Ohio*, tied to two ships, coming into the harbour – the ships were below us as we drove down and there were men and bodies on the deck of the *Ohio* – and the barraccas were crowded with people watching this unforgettable sight.

Coming off duty that day, Mabel Strickland heard children chorusing, '*Ohio*, we love you! Oh, *Ohio* we love you so!' And 'Mussolini, are you blind? Or can you see the navy? The navy? The navy?'

From the convoy that had set out, nine merchant ships, two cruisers, one destroyer, and one aircraft carrier had been sunk; two cruisers, one destroyer, and an aircraft carrier had been damaged. But after that, on 13 September, the ceremony of presenting the George Cross to the people of Malta took place in Palace Square. The people realised, however, that they could not afford to splurge; as the governor told them on 29 August, rationing must continue, for who knew how long those supplies would have to last. Without the arrival of the convoy, it had been known in the top echelons of government that Malta would have had to surrender – the document had already been drawn up.

It was in August that Caroline Vernon, suspecting that she was once more pregnant, realised that she and the children must leave; it was not easy to get permission and to arrange, but they flew out to Egypt in October, and then travelled by ship round the Cape to England. Christina Ratcliffe was to end her account, 'Tamara often wrote urging me to join her but I felt that my place was in Malta. I did not want to be a ratcliffe deserting a sinking ship and besides having gone so far I wanted to stay and see things through.'

The worst was soon to be over, and some things started to improve. Mabel's cousin, Teresa (Terry) Strickland, who appeared in Chapter 1 as an archaeologist with Margaret Murray, was, by now, living in New York with her husband Harris Dunscombe Colt. In October 1942, as Nicholas Vella tells it in '"I have a story to tell you": Teresa Strickland Colt and the Malta War Relief Fund' (2000), she started to work tirelessly to increase awareness of the plight of the Maltese islands during the war and to increase the fund's drive to raise money. She liaised with the British War Relief Society, and used first-hand information about Malta. When she asked Governor Gort what specifically was needed, he replied that clothing and shoes were the greatest need, 'as there are still approximately 30,000 people who are short of all forms of clothing.' And, in a subsequent letter, he was even more specific, 'Women's skirts and underclothes, men's coats and trousers and children's clothing of all sorts.' As a result, a clothing drive was launched and 3,000 lbs of used clothes were collected and shipped to Malta, while groups of women also made layettes which could be sent as conditions improved. Later, vitamins were added, and then kitchen utensils. Meanwhile, Terry travelled the country giving talks about the situation in Malta, raising awareness and money.

By November 1942, the Axis had lost the Second Battle of El Alamein and the Allies had landed forces in Vichy French Morocco and Algeria under Operation Torch. The Axis diverted their forces to the Battle of Tunisia, and attacks on Malta were rapidly reduced. The Siege of Malta effectively ended in November 1942.

In Tunis, 33-year-old **Ella Caze de Caumont** (*c*.1909–2003) was in prison when, on 13 November, the RAF started bombing. She had been born Ella Zammit Cutajar; indeed, Charles Bonham-Carter notes meeting her with her family at their place on Comino, but she had married a French nobleman and lived with him in Tunis since 1931. But, as Frederick Galea tells her story in 'Wartime "Cloak and Dagger" Operations from Malta' (nd), 'after the fall of France, when Vichy power took control of Tunis, she felt tremendous sympathy for the RAF pilots who had baled out over Tunisia and had been sent to a concentration camp at Le Clef. She therefore became part of 201 Alouette, a Tunis secret organisation made up of voluntary patriots collaborating with the British Services.'

Three months of planning followed Ella's induction within the communications cum sabotage cell. 201 Alouette had set up contacts with the Inter-Service Liaison Office (ISLO) in Malta, enabling them to meet Malta-based British submarines near Sfax. In 1940, prior to the fall of France, Ella sent information to Malta by radio on troop movements and ships entering and leaving Tunis. By 1941, she planned to return to Malta but, before the plan could be carried out, she was arrested.

That night of British bombing, the prison governor ordered her to hurry up and pack. In the confusion, she managed to escape with three others. In Algiers, suffering from anaemia and scurvy, Ella requested the British to contact ISLO in Malta to acknowledge her. At the American Intelligence Office, General Dwight D Eisenhower 'offered me a Coke and a Camel cigarette.' Two days later, Governor Gort welcomed her to Malta and, in April 1943, he invested her with an MBE. From Malta she made her way to London and was involved in preparations for the Normandy landings. Charles de Gaulle decorated her with the *Croix de la Résistance*.

Malta-born **Henrietta** (Chetta) **Chevalier** (née Scerri, 1901–1973) had married Thomas Chevalier in 1920 in Sliema. But they settled in Rome where Thomas was a representative of Thomas Cook. He died in 1939, leaving Chetta a widow in a country that was going to be at war with her own. Chetta is another of Malta's heroines whom Frederick Galea has made sure is not forgotten; he sent me a short piece 'The Henrietta Chevalier Memorial Garden at the Aviation Museum' to alert me to her. He explains:

One of her sons was imprisoned as Italy entered the war due to being a British subject while her other son, Paul was a clerical officer with the Swiss legation therefore his diplomatic papers ensured his freedom. The youngest daughter had been sent to a convent, while Henrietta, her elderly mother and her five other daughters lived in a small third floor apartment in *Via Dell'Imperio* just outside the Vatican.

Using this apartment, Chetta, known as 'Mrs M', played an important role in an organisation set up by an Irish priest, Monsignor Hugh O'Flaherty, helping Allied soldiers and Jews to escape. Among the boltholes was Chetta's apartment.

At one point ... she had four British soldiers staying with her and when asked by the Major about the risks her comment was 'Absolutely grand, these boys. They are just like my own children. It is all so marvellous'. O'Flaherty warned everyone lodging with her that in the event of any danger, her safety and that of her family had to come first.

Chetta's apartment was also used as a depot for food and supplies, an added danger because the movement of black bags could easily arouse suspicion. When the Gestapo moved into Italy, the Chevalier household was watched round the clock and a number of raids were conducted; each time her lodgers managed to escape, following tip-offs. Chetta's daughter **Gemma Chevalier** had a narrow escape while buying supplies, though she didn't tell her mother.

There is a delightful picture of the household in Brian Fleming's *The Vatican Pimpernel: the Wartime Exploits of Monsignor Hugh O'Flaherty*

(2009). Three members of the priest's organisation call on Chetta on 11 December 1943 and record:

'I expected you,' Mrs Chevalier smiled as we introduced ourselves. Two young girls who had been screaming at each other, fell silent. 'My daughters, Gemma and Mary' ... two other girls appeared and inspected us. Matilda, younger than Gemma was slim, serious and shy. The other, about twelve, was an imp ... 'Come and meet Grandma, the seventh female in the house.' We followed Mrs M into a large kitchen, where a bright fire burned in a wide grate. A basket of vegetables and fruit stood on the floor and large chunks of red meat lay on the table. In the corner by the window an old woman sat in a low chair peeling potatoes. Mrs M's mother, as she looked up, smiled faintly and resumed peeling. 'Some family,' I said, confused. 'Oh that is not all.' She led us to another door in the corridor and pushed it open. Four men lay in one huge bed, their faces turned to us. 'Good morning,' said the four in unison. As Mrs M introduced us to her four private escapers, they climbed out of bed fully dressed. 'They hop into bed every time someone comes to the door,' she explained.

Chetta did more than give shelter: because she had some nursing experience she used to venture out to provide medical assistance to various escapees around the city.

Eventually it was felt that Chetta and her family should be evacuated and one by one they left the apartment and were taken to a farm on the outskirts of the city. She was to spend the rest of her days in Malta and is buried in the Santa Maria Addolorata Cemetery in Paola (see Chapter 22 itinerary). She is remembered by the memorial garden that bears her name at the Aviation Museum, Ta' Qali (see Chapter 20 itinerary). At some stage Gemma met an English soldier, Kenneth Sands, and at the end of the war they were married by Monsignor O'Flaherty.

Victory in Europe was not to be until 8 May 1945, but in Malta the last air raid was on 23 July 1943. Close to home, Italy's army and air force, which had virtually disintegrated, announced an armistice on 8 September 1943. Its navy still contained 206 ships and the Allies coveted them. On the 9th, therefore, Italian ships started to steam towards Malta, attacked by German bombers; one ship was sunk with the loss of many lives. Even so, many started to arrive and drop anchor in St Paul's Bay, Marsaxlokk and outside the Grand Harbour. On the 11th, Admiral Sir Andrew Cunningham sent this signal to London: 'Be pleased to inform their Lordships that the Italian battle fleet now lies at anchor under the guns of fortress Malta.'

Cunningham needed an interpreter, and family history, as related to me by Nicholas de Piro, has it that his aunt Cecilia (Cissie), since 1924 **Marchesa Zimmerman Barbaro** (1904–1990), was chosen. 'I thought it was going to be sad,' she said. But as the admiral's barge approached the Italians, they not only started waving and cheering but also calling out, 'Bella! Bella!'

8 September 1565 had marked the end of the Great Siege by the Turks; it is also celebrated in Senglea as the feast day of the Nativity of Our Lady (see Chapter 18 itinerary) – in 1943 it became a day of triple rejoicing there. Celebrations throughout the islands climaxed on 12 September when the whole population seemed to throng the streets of Valletta. Civilians and soldiers were joined by sailors who had accompanied the Italian warships, the crowds inching their way up beflagged and decorated, but rubble strewn, Kingsway, in a triumphant march to Palace Square.

16 – Women Enter Politics in the Twentieth Century

'There are no finer women in the world than some of the Maltese,' wrote English literature lecturer Eric Shepherd in *Malta and Me* in 1926, 'and I would undertake to form a Senate and Legislative Assembly entirely of Maltese women which would run the Island quietly, prudently and successfully and have plenty of time left over for the care of children and house-hold affairs ...'. Of course, in 1926, women did not even have the vote, let alone access to legislative assemblies. How they achieved both makes a fitting end to this historical sketch.

Some Maltese men of that stratum of society, whose opinions were recorded, did not think too highly of their countrywomen. In his 'Vignette', Paul Cassar, under the sub-heading 'The Anti-feminist Attitude', records some almost laughable prejudices, starting in 1872; they do not deserve the oxygen of repetition here. But we know that, reinforced by the Council of Trent (1545–1563), discussed in Chapter 6, a woman's place was deemed to be in the home and obeying her husband. Some women ignored the constraints, by force of circumstance, privilege or character. But as late as 1938, Charles Bonham-Carter's diary entry about Dr Letitia Fairfield's visit records of the Archbishop: 'He is surprisingly ignorant about what happens in Malta, and his attitude is not very different from that of a large number of his clergy ... that if you keep women sufficiently suppressed and ignorant, then evil will not arise.'

Education was the key to women's advancement and it is noticeable that, while there were schools in nineteenth-century Malta, and girls attended them, the subjects were, on the whole, domestic. The first woman doctor qualified, as we have seen, in 1925, the first lawyer in 1940. It was not only views from the top that were against educating women. Joanna Trollope suggests, in her novel *The Brass Dolphin*, how such attitudes also permeated the lower classes. At the Villa Zonda, Lila Cunningham and her father find the property occupied by the extended family of the late caretaker. Among them is the only one who speaks a few words of English, young Carmela. She and Lila take to each other and, during the War, Carmela is encouraged to read and browbeaten into working on her arithmetic. Eventually she travels to the Dockyard School where Lila teaches. Carmela's mother expresses her views:

'School!' Doris said scornfully. She almost spat. 'School is the troublemaker. Ever since you came, all this talk of school. School is not a woman's life!'

But change had been in the air since the beginning of the twentieth century. In 1907, the writer and philanthropist, Alfons Maria Galea, husband of Elizabeth Asphar Galea, a member of the Ladies' Committee during the First

World War, appealed to women to assert themselves through the cultivation of their intellectual and moral talents. In 1908–9, **Lucia Levanzin** (née Inglott) and her husband Agostino Levanzin sought, through his periodical *In-naħla*, to stir women to upgrade their educational and social status. Lucia was as good as their exhortations: in 1918, she gained her diploma in midwifery from the University of Malta.

Upper- and middle-class women were not expected to work outside the home but, as earlier chapters have shown, plenty of women had to work to provide for themselves or their families. The working-class revolutionary Manwel Dimech had married **Virginia Agius** (1872–1939) in 1900. By 1911, after vicissitudes which have no place here, he was not only politicising the dockyard workers, but also emboldening women workers to fight for their rights through an organisation resembling a trade union – *Ix-Xirka ta' l-Imdawlin* (The League of the Enlightenment); much would be done through education via the Maltese language. As Paul Cassar explains, the women of Malta were

> to break their chains and insist for their rights and for the attainment of equality with men, to demand equal pay for the same kind of work and not to allow themselves any longer to be exploited by their men-folk.

Dimech was excommunicated and then, the British authorities having been convinced that he was a German spy, they exiled him, his wife and children remaining in Malta. Sources available to me do not reveal what became of his call to women, though the events of *Sette Giugno* (see Chapter 13) are said to have contained remnants of his influence. Virginia had lost three children by the time of her husband's exile, and had three still to look after.

It was not until 1928 that **Rosaria Fenech** (née Borg), mother of 11 children, five of them daughters, proposed that women should be given the vote. That same year, **Vincenza Flores** and **Liza Fenech** added to the call for women's enfranchisement, while **Carmela Grima** appealed to Maltese women to take an active part in local political affairs. Liza was, in fact, the first woman to be active in the local politics of the Labour Party, formed following the new Constitution of 1921. In *il-Cotra*, in December 1928, she urged women to participate actively in the future of their country.

In the campaign for the vote that was to end in success, three women predominated: Mabel Strickland, **Josephine Burns Debono** (1908–1996) and **Hélène** (Lily) **Buhagiar** (1888–1975). The first two knew each other well. Mabel had arrived back in Malta in 1917, aged 18, when her father's career as a British governor in foreign fields came to an end. Josephine was only 10 then, and not yet living in Malta, so the undated passage quoted by Joan Alexander in her biography must refer to a few years later, perhaps 1924, when Josephine was 16 and Mabel 25:

> I met Mabel when I left school. I think Lord Strickland's idea was that I should be a companion to Mabel. We were both very strong-minded.

I used to go over to Villa Bologna by train in those days, and arrived about nine o'clock to find everyone still in bed, so I used to go round the garden and chat up anyone I could see. I ended up by doing most of Lord Strickland's correspondence, he really taught me how to write a letter – he never missed a comma, and sometimes I had to do a letter 14 times over. ... My step-father was a de Piro, Gerald Strickland's first cousin through his mother. Working for him I saw the Constitutional Party being concocted. I used to go to all the political meetings – when we had self-government – with Mabel, and to this day I suffer from bruises from bricks and stones the Nationalists threw at us – the usual thing! I think we were pretty brave. It was tough, but it was great fun. We were like two young men – we were both fairly masculine in those days.

Josephine's mother, **Laura Agius** (1876–1969), sister of Marie Agius Denaro and Daisy Agius who appeared in Chapters 13, 14 and 15, was living in London when she met Irishman Hugh Burns and married him in 1903. She was widowed when Josephine was little, though, and moved back to the Agius family in Hampstead. When Josephine was in her mid-teens, Laura settled with children in Malta where she married Charles Mompalao de Piro. Gerald Strickland's mother had married Peter Paul Bonici Mompalao. Josephine and her sister attended the Sacred Heart Convent, Sliema. It is at the end of that schooling that she and Mabel became friends.

It is not clear at what stage Mabel and Josephine started discussing women's issues, but Lord Strickland learnt early on, as he involved himself in Maltese politics, setting up a political party – the Constitutional Party which merged with the Anglo-Maltese Party – that Mabel was a political animal. His daughter Cecilia and Josephine Burns may have helped him with his Maltese and English political correspondence, but with Mabel he could discuss political ideas and, whatever her social inadequacies, and lack of proficiency in the Maltese language, depend on her judgement.

The year Josephine Burns was born was the year that Hélène Buhagiar started to engage with the politics of the art world: she was among the first committee members of the Malta Art Amateur Association founded in 1908.

Hélène was the daughter of **Virginia de Felice** and Nicola Buhagiar. She was not only generally well educated, but she showed an early artistic talent and, according to Lisa Baldacchino's 'Hélène Buhagiar (1888–1975)' (2006), 'perhaps ... attended the painting classes provided by the same Association, which were first given by Ramiro Cali, then by Robert Caruana Dingli. However, she might also have had some type of private tuition with Edward Caruana Dingli himself ...'. Cali was the husband of the artist Maria Corleo Cali (see Chapter 13); and more than one portrait of Hélène is ascribed to Edward Caruana Dingli, as well as a certain similarity in style. Later she undertook 'some form of artistic training with Giuseppe Cali' (Maria's more famous father-in-law). The first exhibition of the Association was held in 1908, and 20-year-old Hélène 'received a positive mention for her exhibited work'. The following year, both she and Maria exhibited.

38.   Hélène Buhagiar, from Abela, *Grace and Glory*

In 1916, Hélène became honorary secretary of what was later the Malta Art Association and subsequently she was treasurer as well. After 1925, however, her name 'becomes synonymous only with the organisation of the exhibitions, not as a participating artist'. It is her committee and administrative work that prepared her for a role in public, for her later association with Mabel Strickland and Josephine Burns Debono in the campaign for women's franchise.

Before the campaign gathered the necessary momentum, Mabel had the opportunity to raise the issue in 1931 before the Royal Commission on Maltese Affairs. The year before, the 1921 Constitution had been suspended because Gerald Strickland, as Prime Minister (1927–1932), was more than usually enmeshed in controversy and hostility with the Church in Malta and, thus, with the Vatican. In an attempt to resolve the impasse, Mabel, on her father's behalf, was, as Joan Alexander explains, taken in London to see 'Lord Asquith, chairman of the Royal Commission formed in April 1931 to assess the pros and cons of Sir Gerald's case against the Maltese clergy'. She was there in her capacity as Assistant Secretary of the Constitutional Party.

The best, perhaps the only, account of what happened there is given by Lillian Sciberras in 'Women and Maltese Politics' (1975), drawing on the Royal Commission's minutes. It is worth quoting Mabel's reply in full to a question about electoral rights because the question of women's franchise is treated at some length from a privileged position: she concentrates on women of property and was talking in her personal capacity. She starts with the position of men, and there are some insertions in what follows of explanation by, I assume, Lillian Sciberras, as well as her omissions; the war in question here, is, of course, that of 1914–1918:

> Miss Strickland: ... I also beg leave to submit that men should enjoy universal suffrage in Malta. The property qualification in their case should be abolished. Women owning property in their own right should be given a vote as a first step towards the political emancipation of the women in Malta. ... (Referring to the then existing hostility of the Church towards the supporters of the Constitutional and Labour parties, she states): There is a further point as to what is happening in Malta to-day, and that is the persecution to which women have been subjected. To my mind this in itself has earned them the right to have a limited franchise by which they can protest ... I am now back to the point of women's franchise on other lines. There are in Malta several ladies who are actively engaged in commerce and in looking after their own property. ...There are others who have been V.A.D.s in the war, and there are also women in the Civil Service ... school teachers. There are also, I understand, 24 women on the district committees of the Labour Party; and although the Labour Party have not put forward this, I understand that it has their support to a very large extent. As regards our own party it has also not been put forward, but it has a fairly good support in a section of our executive committee. ...

Although Mabel was speaking personally, she had also brought with her a petition signed by 428 Maltese women. Frustratingly, I can find nothing about those women – no names, no indication of who collected the names. But it is a significant number, given the public activities of the Maltese women who have appeared in chapters that cover the pre-1931 history of women in Malta. The most useful clauses of the petition read:

> 2. We feel that the time has undoubtedly come for the recognition of the right of women in Malta to take part in the deliberations of the Parliament of the Island, in view of their already active interest in public life, and we petition that their claims as citizens should receive full attention in the event of the Constitution being amended or placed on a permanent and improved basis.

> 3. We sincerely believe that women's influence and increased participation in the public life of Malta will be conducive to the better government of these Islands and will strengthen the sentiments of heartfelt loyalty to Our Gracious Sovereign and the bonds that unite Malta to His Majesty's other Dominions.

But nothing came of either Mabel's representation or the petition. The Royal Commission's report, published a year later, suggested:

> The question of votes for women was referred to but did not appear to have support from any political party. A petition, signed by women, asking for the recognition of votes for women was sent to us but the suggestion was not pressed and we had no other evidence that the extension would be acceptable. It has nothing to do with the present situation in the Island ... In view of the conditions prevailing in Malta we are unable at the present time to propose that women should be admitted to the franchise. If any desire is evinced in that direction, the movement should come from Malta itself and an alteration should not be imposed from outside.

Since the urging of Maltese women was dismissed so comprehensively, the implication is that pressure should come from Maltese men. It is worth bearing in mind what British women had had to go through to obtain the vote, only secured for all women three years before that Maltese petition, indeed the year 1928, when several Maltese women first raised the issue. British men were still not used to women voting, and it is clear that it was not at the top of the agenda of the Maltese male political class, so busy with infighting among themselves. The Constitution was restored in 1932 under the Nationalist prime minister Ugo Mifsud, only to be withdrawn again the following year, and revised in 1936.

The next mention I can find of the enfranchisement of Maltese women comes from a diary entry from Charles Bonham-Carter of 25 May 1938 about various matters concerning the Legislative Council: 'We did not recommend a change in the franchise, except that in a private letter to the Secretary of State [for Colonial Affairs] (my first to Malcolm Macdonald), I told him of my wish to make a start with women's franchise.' The governor had much more to do with Macdonald about constitutional affairs subsequently and, on 10 August 1938, during a brief visit Macdonald made to Malta, even took Mabel Strickland to have tea with him probably in her capacity as influential editor of *The Times of Malta* as well as representing her difficult father on constitutional matters; but no mention is made of women's franchise. Subsequently the governor had both official and private meetings in London with Macdonald, but does not record any conversation on the subject. Then came preparations for war, and the governor's heart attack and replacement.

There is one entry in Bonham-Carter's diary, on 1 March 1939, the interpretation of which so far eludes me and would not be of interest if it did not concern a later active player in the securing of votes for women:

> On Sunday afternoon, I also saw Mrs Joseph Debono at Verdala and discussed with her means by which I could make known the objects for which I am working and to explain them to her. She will write when she has an opportunity. She asked [me?] to see her brother, Mr H.E.P. Burns,

who has been working with Anthony Bartolo for the *Malta Daily News*, which they started together when they left the *Daily Chronicle* and which has just come to an end; and also her husband. Of these a further account will be added later.

The meeting may have had nothing to do with women's affairs but with internal press quarrels about which Josephine was trying to mediate, but the entry, with perhaps a crucial word missing, is certainly ambiguous. Josephine herself had been a journalist in England in the 1920s where she appears to have moved, too, in Fabian Society and socialist circles. She was back in Malta by 1931 when she married Dr Joseph Debono MD, as his second wife. They had four children and she spent most of her life thereafter in Malta.

Before any further action could be contemplated, war was declared and, as Chapter 15 shows, everyone had more immediate problems on which to concentrate. Mabel Strickland's wartime role is described in that chapter. Josephine's husband helped to devise the stringent rationing system that had to be put in place, and she seems to have been involved in the committee that allocated ration coupons. In 1942, Joseph was appointed consultant physician to the Lazaretto Isolation Hospital during the polio epidemic that was another wartime burden.

The Debono family had been evacuated from their home at Ta' Xbiex, on the waterfront between Sliema and Valletta, to Laura Agius' already overflowing home in Rabat. But Josephine describes bomb-destroyed Valletta with feeling in her submission to the short story competition run by the *Observer* in 1951. The competition was won by Muriel Spark but 20 other authors, of the 6,700 entries, were runners-up and were published in *The Observer Prize Stories: The Seraph and the Zambezi* (1952), among them Josephine's 'Christmas, Malta 1942'. She dedicated the story to 'the Countess Mountbatten of Burma'.

Edwina Mountbatten (née Ashley, 1901–1960) accompanied her husband on his Royal Navy tours of duty to Malta both before and after the War, and was to play a part, with her husband, in post-war politics (see also Chapters 17, 19 and 20 itineraries).

Well before the war in Europe was over, but when Malta's worst trials were at an end, politics began to stir again. In July 1943, the colonial secretary made clear that responsible government would be restored on lines similar to the 1921 Constitution and that the Maltese would be consulted on the introduction of a new one. A National Assembly was established in 1944 to discuss Malta's post-war political future, and that same year the Women of Malta Association was founded in order to lobby for female suffrage.

In Ruth Farrugia's chapter 'Female Suffrage in Malta' (2012), she suggests that Josephine 'was the motivator behind this association, as she felt strongly that women deserved to be recompensed for their invaluable contribution during the war'. The link between Josephine and Mabel has been established, but how did Hélène Buhagiar come to be so closely involved? There is a clue in Lisa Baldacchino's article, for it appears that the Malta Arts Association

had been invited to send a delegate(s) to the National Assembly. Prof Sciortino, together with other artist members of the Association, proposed Buhagiar for such a position, but her nomination was severely opposed by other members of the Association on the grounds that it had not yet been decided whether women could form part of the National Assembly. Following this incident, Hélène Buhagiar handed in her resignation after 36 years of dedication to the M.A.A. Following her resignation, Buhagiar got herself involved in the political scene.

It is fair to assume that Hélène's name would not have been proposed if she had not indicated that she wished to be involved; and to do that, she must have already been in close touch with the other women; her consciousness was already well raised.

Joan Alexander has a nice note about the opinion of Mabel held by her cousin Roger Strickland who had, without much enthusiasm, but in deference to the memory of his uncle, taken over the Constitutional Party as leader and chair:

Roger had no opinion of Mabel as a politician, and wrote to [a] friend … that the Maltese people would never put up with her, a mere woman, after the war, and since he did not wish to continue in politics what would become of the Constitutional Party?

In a footnote, Ruth Farrugia, with access to *Ghadma min Ghadmi: grajjet il-mara u jeddijietha* (1992), unfortunately closed to those, like me, without Maltese, suggests that 'Angela Callus … questions whether such a movement for suffrage ever existed and argues that the association was but a group of educated women trying to benefit from proposed reforms'. Nevertheless, 80 women joined the association and a letter went from it to the congress which would convene the National Assembly, asking that the association be allowed to send delegates.

The Constitutional and Nationalist parties were ambivalent about the request, but did not need to express their views because the Church presented such strong opposition to women's inclusion, 'on the grounds that they did not represent anyone but a few women whose heads were filled with these blessed "equal rights"'. Josephine received advice from the secretary general of the General Workers Union and registered the Women of Malta Association as a trade union for women. Eventually, after heated exchanges within the National Assembly, Josephine and Hélène, acting as president and secretary of the association, were allowed in as delegates. Mabel was included to represent the *Times of Malta*, the largest national daily newspaper.

The team of three women must have made quite an impression when they first appeared in the Assembly, held in the St Michael and St George Hall of the Palace. Mabel was nearly six foot, always imposing, intimidating to many. Josephine's exceptional height for a woman came from her Irish forebears, and description of her fearless participation with Mabel at public meetings in their earlier years has already been quoted. As for Hélène, she has been described by another delegate as 'perhaps the tallest woman in Malta and certainly the most cultured'. Women were formally accepted among the 320 or so delegates to the National Assembly on 16 March 1945. What followed is told in detail by Ruth Farrugia; a concise version by Sonia Attard, 'Women voting for the first time: Equality at last!' is accessible on the internet.

On 20 July, Dr Paul Boffa of the Labour Front presented a motion in the National Assembly proposing that all men and women over the age of 18 be given the right to vote. He had married **Genoveffa Cecy** in 1921 and I suspect that she may have influenced him in taking this stand, and that she was a member of the Women of Malta Association, given her later political involvement. That they were a progressive family is suggested not only by his political views, but by the fact that one of their daughters, **Hilda Boffa**, became a doctor. His proposal generated the expected heated exchanges. Ruth Farrugia notes that:

> Some elements within the Nationalist Party were against women being 'burdened' with this responsibility and said that they were not prepared for it. A number of members of the clergy objected on the grounds that such a step would impact negatively on the role of the traditional Maltese woman and have a harmful bearing on her sheltered way of life. Helen Buhagiar took an active part in the debate, promoting the vote for women; an eye-witness account of the session describes her impassioned speech based on the principle that if women were expected to pay taxes like men, then they should be accorded the right to vote in the same way.

Josephine's brother-in-law, the surgeon Peter Paul Debono, also spoke in favour of women's enfranchisement. In due course, Paul Boffa saw the advantage of amending the voting age from 18 to 21. The vote was close, 145 for, 137 against, but it was won: universal suffrage for women and men aged 21 and over.

Later that year, the National Assembly debated women's right to stand for election, following a motion put forward by Josephine and Hélène. The Nationalist Party opposed it, and tried to postpone discussion because it thought 'it was not advisable to impose upon the large female masses an onus and responsibility which the majority would not, perhaps, be prepared to assume'. But that motion, too, was passed, influenced by what women had been prepared to contribute during the War – they filled posts traditionally occupied by men.

A Constitutional Commissioner, Sir Harold MacMichael, arrived in Malta in May 1946. On 5 September 1947, the MacMichael Constitution came into being, and elections were called for six weeks later, 25, 26 and 27 October. Lillian Sciberras quotes clause 11 of a 1947 British Colonial Office document:

> It will be noted with interest that the National Assembly have recommended the extension of the suffrage to women. The Constitution will leave the question of suffrage to be dealt with by law of the Maltese Legislature, but His Majesty's Government takes this opportunity of expressing their approval of this recommendation.

There was anxiety in the male political classes about the inexperienced female vote, at a time, just post-war, when unemployment and the cost of living were rising, but they consoled themselves, as Ruth Farrugia quotes from Joseph Pirotta's *Fortress Colony*:

> Most Maltese women left politics to the men, and therefore it was very probable that the majority of women would vote according to the way their menfolk did. The various parties were unsure as to women's inclination to vote or otherwise, but the campaign's bread-and-butter issues ensured a strong female participation.

Party politics from 1947 onwards were to be as turbulent as ever, so it would be invidious for me, as a post-colonial Englishwoman, to attempt to unravel their intricacies, even about women's involvement. Once the franchise is obtained, once women can stand for election, this story seeks to avoid the passions and controversies and simply to provide a sketch of female events and personalities leading to the appointment of the first woman president of Malta in 1982. The detailed and up-to-date story concerning women's involvement in politics is for Maltese women to tell, as, indeed, scholars such as Angela Callus (1992) and JosAnn Cutajar ('Women and Political Participation in Malta', November 2014) are doing.

Two women stood in the 1947 elections for the 40-seat Legislative Assembly – Hélène Buhagiar, by then 59, for the Democratic Action party (DAP), and 24-year-old teacher Agatha Barbara. Josephine Burns Debono decided not to stand. As for Mabel Strickland, Joan Alexander quotes a Colonial Office explanation:

> She is not standing as a candidate in order that she may deal faithfully and impartially with political matters in her papers. A more cogent reason may be that she fears defeat. She had a very hostile reception in Kingsway on the date of the Proclamation of the Constitution.

Joan Alexander does not elaborate on that incident, but she does add, 'When did Mabel fear anything? The writer can have had no knowledge of her character.'

In spite of letters in the press extolling her virtues, all showing clearly that the women who wrote them understood the importance of their new right, Hélène lost, though she obtained a relatively large number of votes in her district. She did not stand again in subsequent elections. Indeed, after 1947, she seems to drop from view. But the year had been a demanding one for her, perhaps too much so.

Ruth Farrugia suggests that the Women of Malta Association ceased to function in 1946, following its lobbying success. But Lisa Baldacchino describes an exhibition held under its auspices in July 1947, and curated by Hélène. The *Times of Malta* reported a rather ambiguous remark by Josephine two days after the opening:

> Mrs Burns Debono paid tribute to the inspiration, devotion and self-sacrifice of the Honorary Secretary of the Women of Malta Association, Miss Helen Buhagiar, who had initiated the project and had taken full responsibility throughout.

Was the 'project' the exhibition, or was it the Women of Malta Association? If the latter, Josephine is giving the credit to Hélène which has been given to herself. Hélène had certainly attended weekly meetings at the Debono home during their campaigning days.

Agatha Barbara (1923–2002) won her seat; indeed, she was to win in the next ten elections that she fought. She was the daughter of a tug-master, a skilled pilot, but unlettered, a drawback which determined his pay level. Her mother, **Antonia Barbara**, struggled to feed nine children. Her parents somehow managed to pay for her schooling, but her college education was cut short by the War; Chapter 15 mentions her war work. After the War, she became a teacher, but was also becoming politicised. In a 2001 interview (obtained on the internet) the year before her death, she gives some clues:

> After the war, we had many people unemployed – former soldiers, the Drydocks workers – and no Constitution in place. The people governing us were not bothered about how these people were going to live. At the time, there was no social justice at all, I wanted to help put things right. I wanted to help people. That's why I accepted people's encouragement to enter politics.

She was asked if she felt daunted by the fact that she was young and female, and replied:

> I remember the conversation drifted round to a proposal made by the Labour movement at that time to give every citizen over 21 the right to vote. The Church was against the idea of women having the vote and

our colleague, who was an intelligent priest, supported this standpoint of relegating women to the kitchen.

When he was talking, I eventually blew up and told him not to air these views in my presence again. It made me realise that even intelligent and educated priests had this philosophy of the female role, which spurred me on further to show what women could do.

Ruth Farrugia notes that out of a total of 76,745 women registered to vote in 1947, 54,565 women actually voted, 54.4 per cent of the electorate. Sonia Attard gives an idea of the proportion of women voters in various districts. It was the Labour Party that gained the most seats, but there were elections again in 1950, 1951, 1953 and 1955. In 1950, seven women stood, three won; in 1951, six stood and four won.

In 1950, sisters Cecilia and Mabel Strickland resolved to revive their father's old Constitutional Party to counter what they saw as the extreme policies of Labour's Dom Mintoff who had split the Labour Party. As Joan Alexander has it of 1936 and 1944–47:

> In those early days before the war, Mabel looked upon him as a future leader, and was strongly supported in these views by Lord and Lady Mountbatten, and Josephine de Bono. Though the Mountbattens and Josephine de Bono remained staunch supporters, Mabel was soon disenchanted, and from being Dom Mintoff's strongest supporter she became his toughest opponent.

Cecilia and Mabel decided, too, to contest the election that year. Cecilia, under the name Cecilia de Trafford Strickland, went for Gozo where she hoped to pick up votes from among the lace workers and producers of wool and cotton she obtained from there for the enterprise she had set up in 1931 (see Chapter 14). Mabel stood for Sliema, having reluctantly retired for the purpose as editor of the *Times of Malta*, and become, instead, a director of Allied Malta Newspapers. She felt that in that constituency she could count on the votes of her social class, 'though canvassing was torture' and she was not a good speaker.

Neither sister spoke Maltese but, as the text that Cecilia's son sent me notes, she took the trouble to have her speeches translated into Maltese and read them out. 'Despite the smiles she got because of her sometimes-dodgy pronunciation, the voters respected her for her endeavours.' Both women were elected, a result which was to cause problems for Mabel's right-hand woman:

> When Mabel began to attend the Legislative Assembly, May Agius discovered that she had to play an extremely difficult role. With all the other members speaking Maltese, she was expected to translate instantaneously on paper and hand it to Mabel so that she could reply if she desired.

In spite of her language disability, Mabel was, not surprisingly, an active member. Another woman who fought the 1950 election was Genoveffa Boffa, for the Boffa Labour Group, by then separate from the Malta Labour Party. She was unsuccessful.

There had to be new elections in 1951 and, once again, Cecilia and Mabel were elected. But a rift had begun to develop between the two rather different personalities, partly political, partly familial. Their stepmother Margaret had died in 1950 and Cecilia, who had been close to her, had moved with her family into the Strickland home, the Villa Bologna in Attard (see Chapter 20 itinerary), and made considerable changes, including flats and a pottery. Mabel, who had not got on with Margaret, had felt out on a limb for some time and eventually bought the Villa Parisio in Lija (see Chapter 20 itinerary; not to be confused with the Palazzo Parisio in Naxxar, or that in Valletta). She was to remain there for the rest of her life

Then, in 1952, Mabel caused disarray within the Constitutional Party, resigned and created a new one, the Progressive Constitutional Party (PLP). But she was unseated in 1953 by her erstwhile colleagues who retaliated by pointing out that the Progress Press, part of the umbrella organisation of which she was a shareholder, 'had received a government [printing] contract, and challenging her right to a seat in the Legislative Assembly'.

Cecilia, with firm views about equality, decided to support the Labour Party within the legislature. In the 1953 election, when Cecilia stood in Rabat, rather than Gozo, both women lost. Cecilia's life thereafter centred on her family and philanthropic enterprises. In 1956 she established a restaurant in Rabat where, in 1936, she had set up weaving looms. Mabel did not win an election again until 1962, but that did not mean that she was not heavily involved in politics. It was noticeable, though, that Edwina Mountbatten and her husband now turned more to Josephine Burns Debono for what was going on when they visited Malta; 'Mabel slowly but surely became enlightened as far as her friends were concerned, realising to her alarm that she and they were fighting on opposite sides.' Josephine and Edwina introduced the Save the Children Fund to Malta.

Meanwhile, Agatha Barbara continued to win at each election and, when in 1955 Dom Mintoff became Labour Prime Minister, he made her Minister for Education within the Cabinet, the first woman in Malta to hold a ministerial post for some years to come. During the next three years, she saw to it that full-time schooling was made compulsory for all children under 14; that teachers were trained through a teachers' training college and schools built.

Prime Minister Mintoff had round him a group of women advisers in that first administration: Agatha Barbara, Josephine Burns Debono, Cecilia de Trafford, his wife **Moyra Mintoff** (née de Vere Bentinck, 1917–1997), daughter of an admiral whom the young working class man had met in Oxford when he was there as a Rhodes Scholar; and newcomer **Dolores (Dodo) Selby Bennett** (née Lees, 1920–1991), a well-connected Catholic, wartime heroine and Labour candidate in England who had decided to follow her Royal Navy husband to his postings abroad. In *Dodo* (1993) which she wrote under the name Dodo Lees, and which was published after her death, she describes her introduction to Malta:

Mabel ran the *Times of Malta* and was the founder and king pin of the Progressive Constitutional Party and much opposed to the Prime Minister, Dom Mintoff, whose Labour Party had just come into power. Cecilia de Trafford was terrifically pro-Labour. Both of them invited me to lunch, but it was Cecilia and I who fell for one another and she and her children became *very* great friends of mine ...

... A few days later, Cecilia de Trafford invited me to lunch at the Villa Bologna. She said, 'Look, I've been talking about you to Moyra Mintoff ... She's very impressed and she wants you to meet Dom with a view to starting Tourism here in a big way.' So I went and had lunch with Dom, Moyra and Cecilia, and Dom asked me if I thought I was capable of taking charge of Tourism. I said, 'Well, I'm certain I'd be more capable than the people you've got at the moment!' And I certainly was. I mean, I'd been in Fleet Street and I'd spent several years in *Presse et Information* at the American Desk in the Quai d'Orsay, and I could write to my great friend, Jamie's Godfather, Etienne de Crouy-Chanel, for all the gen on how the *Syndicats d'Initiative* ran Tourism in France. So Dom decided to appoint me Tourist Advisory Expert to the Maltese Government.

39.   Dodo Lees Selby Bennett, courtesy of the family

That is Dodo's style, and her book describes her regular visits and work promoting tourism. She bought a house in Gozo and in later years spent summer months there (see Chapter 23 itinerary). She also waged a campaign to allow Catholic women to go to any film they chose.

Of those women, though, it was Agatha Barbara who stayed the course in Maltese politics. In 1958, during the imposition of direct rule, and a bitter general strike in Malta, she was arrested and charged with intimidation; she was sentenced to 43 days of hard labour. Direct rule lasted until 1962, and Malta became independent in 1964, and a republic in 1974 with all executive authority resting in the president who was appointed by the House of Representatives and could also appoint the prime minister. Agatha later served as Minister for Labour, Culture and Welfare, implementing reforms such as an equal pay law and paid maternity leave. At various stages she also served as deputy prime minister and acting prime minister. Then, in 1982, she was elected to a five-year term as President of Malta, another first for her and for women, retiring to her home town of Żabbar in 1987 (see Chapter 18 itinerary). There was not to be another woman president until 2014.

Exactly 20 years after the foundation of the Women of Malta Association, Josephine Debono found herself on the executive committee of another women's organisation, but this time she was not the driving force. That role was taken by **Jane Spiteri** (1922–2008), teacher and social worker, and the organisation was the National Council of Women of which she started as Honorary General Secretary. It, too, was set up to lobby on behalf of women, this time campaigning to ensure that the Independence Constitution included the fundamental principles of equality between women and men, and for the right of equal pay for equal work, the gradual implementation of which began in 1967. The government of 1988 saw the setting up of the Department for the Equal Status of Women, and the Commission for the Advancement of Women. By the time Jane died, aged 86 and honorary president of the Council, she was known as the Grande Dame of women's issues.

There has been some disappointment over the years, and it continues, among those concerned with gender equality in Malta where, in spite of much effort, and definite advances, women's involvement in politics has not been as fast as hoped. But there is similar frustration in many other countries and, in Malta, in 2015, four out of six Euro MPs are women.

My purpose has not been to intervene in the heart-searching into that project but to give some idea of how the history of women in Malta has influenced the present. Some of this recreation of women's history may even be new; I believe it has, anyway, been previously uncoordinated. Having intruded an English perspective this far perhaps allows an English novelist, Joanna Trollope in *The Brass Dolphin*, the last word.

Young Carmela's mother, Doris, is now housekeeper to the historian count in his Mdina palazzo. Sometimes, when she is not at school, Carmela does odd jobs in the count's library:

While she did these things, Count Julius would talk to her. He talked a lot of history, which Carmela disapproved of because there seemed to be so few women in Maltese history.

Women's Places
(Itineraries)

Introduction

I have carefully called this section 'Women's Places', as well as 'Itineraries'. There are places connected with women that a reader visiting Malta, or living there, may want to visit, particularly after reading 'Women's History'. But I see what follows as a record – hitherto non-existent – as much as a number of itineraries. And, as you will see, often the 'itinerary' is impractical to follow. You will want to pick out what interests you – say the life of a particular woman – and what is accessible or manageable. You are likely to be as often an armchair traveller as a darter from place to place (as I have often been). What follow in this introduction are some tips about how best to visit the places you decide upon.

The compactness of the city of Valletta, and its traffic restrictions, determine that you explore it on foot, though cars can drive round its outer ring, and into some fringe streets, and little electric vehicles can, within limits, help the exhausted, overladen or hobbling.

Outside Valletta it is not so simple. There are several ways of doing it; where you stay is a determining factor and whether or not you have or hire a car. On the island of Malta, I did a combination of Hop-On Hop-Off sightseeing bus, with its two distinct routes – north and south; local bus, better when you have begun to know your way about; and hiring the hotel car and driver. In addition, a photographer friend with a car, who knows Malta well, Caroline Bayly Scallon, filled in some essential gaps for me. The itineraries will take those different methods into account. Gozo has a tour of its own (Chapter 23).

Although I am not in the business of promotion, we always stay at the same hotel for my research trips – the Phoenicia; I inevitably drew on the benefits of that in my own explorations and that has probably affected the itineraries, too. It is not only just outside the City walls, but also on the sightseeing bus routes and close to the local bus terminus.

There are two sightseeing bus companies; I've only used 'Malta Sightseeing'. In plumping for this method of getting about, you are not on an organised tour: you decide what you want to see, where you want to get on and off. Apart from a set route and a machine narration on the bus, you are on your own. Take into account that the nature of each long route means that the final bus back is earlier than you might expect. The Gozo tour we took was organised and a bit frustrating as a result.

Because of the different ways of getting about, as well as the nature of the islands' history, I have been slightly eccentric in devising two of the itineraries. One is archaeological. These sites, while in different places on Malta, are all in the same itinerary (Chapter 21). You will not want to, or be able to, do them all on the same day, but they form a definite whole in conjunction with the history section of the book. For the same reason, I have put the Valletta Archaeological Museum there too. For Gozo, the main site and the archaeological museum are part of the itinerary.

There are also places that are not on obvious routes; they, too, have their own itinerary, 'Round and About' (Chapter 22), with as much guidance as practical. Some of the other itineraries are rather long; you would not consider doing them in one go, but they make a neat narrative whole, often connected with particular women or families. The Valletta itinerary is divided into four separate 'part-itineraries', each of which can be treated as a self-contained itinerary.

This is not intended primarily as a guide book. As well as this book, you will undoubtedly need a general guide book, with its detailed maps and practical information, such as opening days and times. Although I have several on my shelves, I have referred most often to the text and maps of Juliet Rix, author of *Malta and Gozo* (Bradt Guide, 2nd edition, 2013; a 3rd edition is in preparation). It is worth going on the internet for the most up-to-date information. If you are staying in a hotel, they should have current sightseeing bus details and a map of the local bus routes. The tourist office was at the southern end of Merchant Street, though I understand it is going to move. Cross-reference to the history section, using the chapter numbers in brackets, is necessary to get the best out of the itineraries.

In case you find this book too heavy to carry around, each itinerary is available separately to print out from www.holobooks.co.uk; click on 'updates and work in progress'. I hope the whole book will also be available in due course as an e-book.

17 – Valletta

Republic Street

The most obvious place to start exploring Valletta is the City Gate, which opens into Republic Street (Triq ir-Repubblika), referred to historically as Strada San Giorgio, Rue de la Republique, Strada Reale and Kingsway. Today, this pedestrian thoroughfare seems redolent of history, in spite of some new buildings. But when the 26-year-old American novelist Edith Wharton visited Malta in 1888 as part of a Mediterranean cruise, her expectations were somewhat dashed, as her record in *The Cruise of the Vanadis* (2003) suggests:

> The Strada Reale ... with its Opera house, its hotels and photograph shops, is provokingly British and modern; one has to wander into the side streets for picturesque effects.
>
> The people are dressed in everyday European clothes, and in fact the reign of the prosaic has settled down upon Malta. As to the Street of the Knights, it filled me with an unreasonable disappointment. I had forgotten that the famous Auberges were probably not built until the end of the 16th or the beginning of the 17th century, and was needlessly aggrieved by their florid, late Renaissance façades, without beauty of detail or dignity of general effect.

See what you think over a century later.

Immediately on your right is the new **Parliament House** the significance of which appears in Chapter 16. Next to it is the quirky new **Royal Piazza Theatre** reconstructed from the 1866 Royal Opera House destroyed during the Second World War. Twenty-four-year-old Canadian-born **Emma Albani** (1847–1930) sang there for the 1870–71 season in *Lucia di Lammermoor* and *Il Barbiere di Siviglia*. Her next stop was a five-year contract at London's Covent Garden. In 1931, **Marion Fawcett** (1877–1957), actor and theatre director, produced there. How the Maltese felt about the destruction of their opera house is well expressed by VAD Meme Cortis in Chapter 15. Other opera singers are introduced in the Marsamxett itinerary that includes the Manoel Theatre (later in this chapter).

Opposite the new open-air theatre, on the left of the street, is the Ministry of Social Policy, Health, the Elderly and Community Care. It was formerly the **Palazzo Francia**, or Buttigieg-Francia, on the site of the Knights' foundry, hence also Palazzo Ferreria. Look out for its typically Maltese enclosed green wooden balconies. It was built in the late nineteenth century by the wealthy parents of Teresina Francia (née Buttigieg) and the coat of arms of **Giovanna Camilleri** and Giuseppe Buttigieg still decorate the façade. In June 1919, Teresina lived there with her husband, mill owner Colonel John Francia, and their four children, including daughters Malvina and Lola (Chapter 14).

But, on Sunday 8 June 1919 the Palazzo was attacked and vandalised by the *Sette Giugno* demonstrators (Chapter 13). Second only in size to the Grand Palace, it was lived in by the family, with an in-house staff of about 25, until 1947. Thereafter, they still kept the best bit as an apartment. It was sold to the government in 1979 to settle death duties.

Also on the left is the **Archaeological Museum**, what was the *Auberge de Provence* under the Knights and the Union Club under the British. As I explained in the Introduction to Women's Places (Itineraries), details of its contents come at the end of the archaeological sites itinerary in Chapter 21.

One of the most obvious places to visit is **St John's Co-Cathedral**, the entrance to which for non-worshippers, and the queue for the ticket office, is on the right. Most visitors go to see the Caravaggio, the vaulted ceiling painted by Mattia Preti, and the general gilded exuberance of the place. I have other reasons to suggest. Maria de Dominici, whose life and work as a painter and sculptor are introduced in Chapter 6, helped Preti paint the ceiling, particularly the female figures. The twice I have gone to admire her work, I have found the crowds and the need to crane one's neck upwards too demanding. There is a suggestion, too, that she painted the figure of Saint Sebastian in the Auvergne Chapel, but that is not borne out by the plaque. I have also searched in vain for the fresco of 'Religion', with its connection with the Virgin Mary, mentioned by Elizabeth Schermerhorn in my Chapter 5, describing the end of the 1565 siege. I cannot think that a guided tour, as presently devised, would be helpful. But one could always ask.

40.   Church of St Giovanni (St John's) by Eliza Gardner, from *A Series of Views in Malta*, courtesy of Yale Center for British Art Paul Mellon Collection (file no. 2038523-0003)

Should you feel frustrated by the crowds, think of Florence Nightingale's nurses and their visit there in 1855 (Chapter 12). Sarah Anne Terrot wrote, in *Reminiscences of Scutari Hospitals* (1898), that it looked

> Very beautiful and gorgeous, but I was too tired to admire it much, and felt annoyed at being guilty of irreverence in walking about and gazing while mass was being celebrated ... We were weary with sleepless nights, and though so early, the sun was dazzling and oppressive, and there seemed a white blaze from bare rocks, and a great want of shade.

Florence Nightingale herself wrote of her 1849 visit: 'We went to St John's, which is beautiful: a row of chapels on either side, each belonging to one of the "lingue" auberges of the Knights, most of them exceedingly rich, in blue and brown and gold, very Arabian colouring.'

There is hardly a woman traveller who does not mention visiting the cathedral, often describing it in more detail than anywhere else in Valletta. Typical are Emma Roberts, who has already appeared in Chapter 10, there in 1841, **Ida Pfeiffer** (1797–1858), who was there a year later, and Lady Layard, who appeared in Chapter 12, there in 1908. Even Edith Wharton admired it in 1888, declaring that it was 'worth the voyage to Malta'. Not everyone felt the same. **Lady Elizabeth Grosvenor, Marchioness of Westminster** (née Lady Elizabeth Leveson-Gower, 1797–1891) visited Malta with her husband in their yacht in 1840/41; she was not to be overwhelmed by anything; she wrote in *Narrative of a Yacht Voyage in the Mediterranean During the Years 1840, 41* (1842):

> But on the whole the building, which had not pleased us on a previous visit, did not improve upon further acquaintance. The pavement is very elaborate, and is entirely composed of the tombs of the Knights, and their squires; each forming one compartment of Pietro-dura workmanship. All, however, being different in detail, though of the same character, the whole is too much like a large piece of marble patchwork, without either grandeur or variety of effect.

There may be one woman buried in St John's, **Mademoiselle de Mignie.** Her mother was said to be the **Countess Mignie Rohan**, as George Whitmore, a contemporary, says, '*Widow* of the *Cardinal* de Rohan'. She may, though, have been a masquerading Englishwoman – Whitmore tells the elaborate tale in his memoirs, *The General* (1987). Whatever the truth, her daughter apparently died during their stay in Malta some time between 1811 and 1813 and, as 'a descendant of the Princes de Rohan, one of whom had been Grand Master ... [the corpse] was carried with great pomp to St John's church exhibited in a chapelle ardente and consigned by the bishop to the vaults of the Grand Master'. In the same crypt Sulpitia de Lango attempted to practise witchcraft in 1617 (Chapter 6).

The clearly signed but apparently insignificant **Regency House** further up on your left, is deceptive. That site has been occupied by several women. In 1644, the building there was a palazzo owned by the merchant Ignazio Ribera and his family. Sultana Basseba, captured by Corsair Knights that year, was taken there to stay (Chapter 5). There, too, three of the women captured with her were taken, perhaps after her death, while they waited to be ransomed from Constantinople.

Fast forward two centuries and the Hotel Clarence, owned by Madame Goubau, was on this site; indeed there were several hotels and lodging houses in the Strada Reale, as related in Chapter 10. Grace Dunsford took over the Clarence in 1846, renaming it Dunsford's. The current building is reconstructed from damage done during the Second World War.

A bit further up on your right is the National Library in front of which, almost obscured by the two outdoor cafés, is the 1891 statue of Queen Victoria, also mentioned in Chapter 10. You cannot help but enjoy American Elizabeth Schermerhorn's description of 'a painfully white statue of Queen Victoria, looking very small and complacent in her voluminous veil of Maltese lace as she sits in the dusty square beside the Grand Master's palace'. I suspect that she researched her history of the Knights in the library behind.

Complacent Victoria may have been but, as this extraordinary photograph shows, she was still sitting there when the Grand Palace to her right, the square in front of her, and the building opposite were bombed on Sunday 15 February 1942, and rubble strewn at her feet (Chapter 15). The long-established Caffe Cordina is a good place for people-watching and for the less nimble to settle with a book and a mini bottle of prosecco.

41.   Queen Victoria statue, from Manduca,
The Bonham-Carter Diaries

The Grand Palace is full of grand paintings of Knights and Grand Masters, scenes of battle and siege, splendid tapestries and hundreds of arms and suits of armour. But there are also odd sightings of women. There are also several accounts of visits by women travellers: once again, Emma Roberts, Ida Pfeiffer, Elizabeth Grosvenor and Enid Layard.

A newcomer's account is contained in Nicholas de Piro's *Sovereign Palaces of Malta* (2001). Major General Sir Henry Bouverie arrived as governor in October 1836. In June that year, his wife, whom he had married in 1826 as a widow, **Julia Bouverie** (née Montolieu, 1785–1836), had died. He was accompanied in his posting by their two children, her four children by her previous marriage and a governess. It is that nameless governess whose account includes a rather poignant passage as she arrives at the palace to look around:

> We ascended a winding stairs of 98 steps which sounds a formidable ascent, but, not long after we reached the summit we found Sir Henry and his children, awaiting our arrival. The latter sprang forward to embrace their sisters, but, all our hearts were too full for utterance at the first moment! ... and Sir Henry showed he felt the vacancy in our party as much as we did.

I wonder if, in fact, the writer wasn't a close relative of Julia's, as she compares her grief to his.

Two paintings concerning women are worth noting: in the minstrels' gallery of the Supreme Council, Adam and Eve, in *The Fall of Man*, are tempted by the head and torso of a woman emerging from the tail of a snake. In the Ambassador's Hall, as Lyudmila Markina tells the story in Elizaveta Zolina, *Malta and Russia* (2002), is a large 1787 portrait of Catherine the Great of Russia as Minerva which was presented in 1790 to Grand Master De Rohan as a gesture of friendship between Russia and the Order.

During the French occupation, 1798–1800, when General Claude-Henri Vaubois had his headquarters at the palace, a young Maltese woman, Clara Decelis, was brought as a 'prostitute' to Vaubois' rooms. She had earlier, as part of the grand occasion in the Place de la Liberté (Palace Square), been married in St John's (Chapter 8). And it is in the palace, perhaps in the chapel, that Vaubois held the secret marriage ceremony of pregnant rich widow Giovanna Fontani to a French officer (Chapter 8).

For more recent women, there is Sybil Dobbie's account of her wartime work in her father's office there, and my favourite image connected with the palace: of the extra-tall threesome – Josephine Debono, Hélène Buhagiar and Mabel Strickland – striding into the 1947 National Assembly meeting held in the Hall of St Michael and St George, also known as the Throne Room (Chapter 16). Until the completion of the new Parliament building, the palace contained the House of Representatives.

Through **Palace Square**, Republic Street narrows and slopes down towards Fort S Elmo. On the left you come to **St Catherine's Nunnery** (Monasteru Santa Katerina on the large plaque outside), founded in 1575 as a home to protect orphan girls from the perils of the world. In 1776, Angela Moscati Xeberras, daughter of Bettina Dorell and Diego Moscati Xeberras, became involved in the tug of war between her parents, as Chapter 7 describes. First her mother placed her in the St Scholastica Nunnery in Birgu, then her father placed her in St Catherine's, then her mother placed her in St Ursola's. Nunneries were a useful depository for families, during disputes, or otherwise.

In 1798, St Catherine's took in nuns hounded out of the Maddalena by the French (Chapter 8). In 1851, it became affiliated with the Augustine Order, so is not open to the public. Nevertheless, if you have strings to pull, as I did, or perhaps even by writing to the Abbess, it is possible to be taken down to the crypt, where generations of nuns have been interred, to see the lavishly decorated statue of the Virgin Mary by Maria de Dominici (Chapter 6).

A little further down on the left, I tried to fathom **Mrs Watson's bookshop** at No. 241 (Chapter 10). It seems to have been overtaken by the Teachers' Union.

Cross over now to the **Casa Rocca Piccola** (74 Republic Street), the only private palazzo open to the public, and home to historian Nicholas de Piro and his wife, Frances de Piro. In his other life he is Nicholas de Piro d'Amico Inguanez, 9th Baron of Budach and 9th Marquis de Piro, and she is the Marchesa. There is a nice story of the occasion when the couple were introduced by a flustered host as 'The most noble Marquis and Mrs de Piro'. And, although he usually eschews the title, he was once told, 'We call you Marquis because it's cool.' That is today's Malta.

To visit the Casa Rocca Piccola is to open a treasure trove of both upper-class Maltese and family history. The palazzo dates back over 400 years to the time of the Knights and contains records and artefacts from then, as well as de Piro family heirlooms and archives. It was acquired, as Chapter 13 tells the story, by Antonio and Marguerita (Maggie) Cassar Torreggiani in 1919, and she died in childbirth there in 1923. Their daughter, Phyllis, inherited the property and married Jerome de Piro.

Two halves of the palazzo were joined together in the 1990s, and the whole opened to the public in 2000. There are tours between 10 and 4 every day except Sunday and public holidays by specialised guides but, if you are lucky, you may be shown round by a family member and experience that extra intimacy. Among antique furniture, china, silver, glass and paintings displayed in many of the 50 rooms, are some items particularly connected with women.

There is a large collection of costumes from the eighteenth to the twentieth century, though because of their delicacy they are only ever on temporary display. The same applies to a fine collection of lace. The history of Maltese lacemaking is told in Chapter 10, and the glory and wide variety of Maltese lace can be well viewed in Nicholas de Piro's *Ladies of Malta* (2013). Part of the de Piro lace collection was accumulated over the years by Cecilia (Aunt Cissie) de Piro who interpreted at the surrender of the Italian Navy in 1943 (Chapter 15).

Among the papers dating from the time of the Knights is the letter Maria Teresa Bologna wrote to her husband in 1753 (Chapter 7).

In the Green Room, the portrait of **Antonia Moscati Gatto Xara**, 3rd Baroness of Benwarrad (1783–1856), by Charles Allingham hangs below that of her second husband, Sir Giuseppe (Joseph) Maria de Piro GCMG, 4th Baron of Budach. It is not surprising that the portrait shows her wearing Maltese lace. They lived in the Palazzo Parisio in Merchant Street which features in due course. Although the Casa Rocca Piccola did not come into the de Piro family until the nineteenth century, it exudes timeless Maltese nobility.

42. Baroness Antonia Moscati Gatto Xara, by Charles Allingham, courtesy of Casa Rocca Piccola Trust

More down to earth is La Giara, a little restaurant, also in the palazzo precincts, serving Sicilian cuisine. Anna Mammino is front of house, her husband the chef.

Walk on down now to **Fort S Elmo** though, since it is a large edifice sprawling over the end of the Sciberras Peninsula, you might view it more rewardingly from the little electric train that you pick up in St John Square and which trundles round the outer walls of the city. But it was in the fortress that Pulcheria (Pulcra) Testaferrata, Baroness Castel Cicciano, was detained when, in 1738, she slapped Francesca Portughues (Chapter 7 and later part-itinerary in this). In 1751, she was detained there again, this time as a result of political manoeuvring by the Grand Master and the Inquisitor. The fort now houses the Military Museum. Among the displays is Christina Ratcliffe's British Empire Medal (Chapter 15, and following itineraries in this chapter as well as Chapter 22 itinerary).

From Republic Street to Marsamxett Habour

It is not easy to decide how to explore Valletta, based as it is on a grid system. I have devised four part-itineraries to cover it, but so much depends on your inclination – they easily merge or mix and match.

If you start at the City Gate, as the Republic Street part-itinerary does, do you forge straight ahead, or do you best use time and energy by almost immediately turning left into Ordnance Street, and then up the incline on your left to the **Hastings Gardens**? From there you have a fine view over Marsamxett Harbour to Manoel Island and the whole area stretching to Sliema. There, too, as you turn right, is the elaborate monument erected in 1827 by the Marchioness of Hastings over her husband's grave, for which she was criticised by George Whitmore who usually dealt with such matters (Chapter 9). There, too, 26-year-old Aida Kelly used to go and watch the bombardment of Valletta by the Luftwaffe before, on 24 February 1942, she was killed nearby after one of those ill-advised sorties (Chapter 15).

Now turn right into the end of Strait Street to reach South Street or, having avoided Hastings Gardens, turn second left off Republic Street into South Street. On your right is **St Andrew's Church** erected in 1857 by both Scottish Jessie Tod Wisely and her husband, George, as the bold plaque on the outside clearly indicates (Chapter 11). For six months during the First World War, the Reverend Albert Mackinnon was senior Presbyterian Chaplain to the forces based there; Chapter 13 describes Mrs Mackinnon's activities. Aida Kelly was due to meet Tamara Marks outside the church on that fateful day.

Down on your right, on the corner of Strait Street, is, as I write, the **National Museum of Fine Arts**, established in 1974 (though I understand that it is to move). It is a bit disappointing as far as women artists are concerned: whatever they have in the vaults was not on display when I visited. You may be lucky and find a special exhibition. The palazzo was first re-built in the 1760s but, after the arrival of the British, it became **Admiralty House** where the Commander-in-Chief of the Mediterranean fleet and his family lived. The behaviour there of both Lady Codrington in 1828 and, between 1857 and 1863, her daughter-in-law is criticised in Chapter 9.

From 1952 to 1954, Lord and Lady Mountbatten lived there when he was Commander-in-Chief. They had lived in Malta for periods before the War (see Chapter 19 itinerary), and were involved in its politics afterwards (Chapter 16). Edwina complained to Prime Minister Nehru of India, recorded in Janet Morgan's biography *Edwina Mountbatten* (1991), that it was not a patch on the Villa Guardamangia (Gwardamanġa): 'Absolutely no view at all, not an inch of garden and the racket day and night is deafening – endless clanging peals of church bells and hooting cars and heavy lorries changing gear, chattering and screaming voices, wirelesses.' An empty bombsite opposite her bedroom window was used by workmen to chisel stone. The house had large rooms for entertaining but in summer they were 'utterly *airless*, only two ceiling fans and no air conditioning'.

The husband of **Juliet Bingley** (née Vick, 1925–2005), Admiral Sir Alexander Bingley, was Commander-in-Chief from 1959, and they, too, lived in Admiralty House. Her *ODNB* entry records that she was closely involved in reform of aspects of the Maltese health and social care system for which she was awarded the Maltese Companion of Honour in 1976. She was another of those women, described in Chapter 16, who was part of a circle round Dom Mintoff and, when he was at odds with the British government, she became an unofficial envoy and messenger between them – a role which continued after she left Malta. She was also a poet, and some of the poems, for example 'Gift from a Queen', contained in *What it Was and What it Was Not* (2002) allude to Malta: 'For her I gave/Antiques from Malta,/Silver buttons/Bent and bruised,/Worn for two hundred years.'

On the corner of South Street and Old Bakery Street stands the **Workers' Memorial Building**, with its plaque commemorating the war workers who were killed there when the building was destroyed in an air raid on 8 April 1942. Today it houses the General Workers Union. In the time of the Knights it was the French *Auberge* but, in 1810, when Lady Hester Stanhope and her entourage moved in, it was the home of Sarah Fernandes and her family (Chapter 9).

In 1891, as Chapter 12 recounts, the newly arrived Hughes family moved into the old *auberge* and, when Dr Louis Hughes married Katherine Simpson in 1894, the reception was held there after what the *Malta Chronicle* called the 'Fashionable wedding at St Paul's' and listed all the presents. By 1896, when they both contracted brucellosis, about which he was to write an important monograph, Katherine and Louis were living at 9 Strada Scozzese (now Vassalli Street) which cuts across South Street, and which had earlier been William Watson's Malta Infant School under the patronage of Queen Adelaide (Chapter 10).

You can now turn into Strait Street, or Old Bakery Street. Let's assume it is the former. Don't go far, because there will be occasion to turn down there later from Republic Street. Just get an impression: it is called **Strait Street** (Strada Stretta) because it is so narrow. It is said that the Knights fought duels here – it was just wide enough for two wielded swords – and it may well have been over women. But in British times Margaret MacGill and her family lived at No. 27, perhaps as early as 1806 (Chapter 10). Probably in the 1830s, Jane Vere ran a school there (Chapter 10).

From Strait Street or Old Bakery Street turn left down **Melita Street** (formerly Britannia Street) and stop on the corner of it and Mint Street in front of a green door, or *remissa*, the sort of portal through which you could drive a cart, next to a smart law firm and opposite another. After the Second World War, artiste Christina Ratcliffe (Chapters 14 and 15) stayed on in Malta. As Frederick Galea discovered for a postscript to *Women of*

Malta that contains what She wrote about Malta, she was a civilian secretary to successive RAF station commanders at Luqa. On the side, she ran an intimate bar – **Café Christina**. And it was here. No one but Christina could have devised this enticing advertisement.

FALL IN. DOWN KINGSWAY TO BLACKLEY'S — MARCH.
HALT. LEFT TURN. 250 PACES DOWN THE SIDE STREET
— QUICK MARCH. YOU'RE THERE! WHERE?

THE CAFE CHRISTINA

66a, Britannia Street, Valletta.

AN ENGLISH BAR WITH A CONTINENTAL
ATMOSPHERE

SOFT LIGHTS — SWEET MUSIC — PALM TREES.

43.   Christina's Café advertisement, courtesy of Frederick Galea

Christina never found anyone to match the mysteriously missing wartime ace Adrian Warburton and became something of a recluse, particularly where journalists were concerned, though she did write part of her story and provided material for the film *Malta Story*, shot in Malta in 1952. She died alone in her Floriana apartment in 1988 and her grave is in the Addolorata Cemetery at Paola (see Chapter 22 itinerary). Warburton's remains were found at a crash site in Bavaria after her death and interred with military honours. The Lascaris War Rooms where Christina worked during the War feature in a later part-itinerary in this chapter.

Walk up now to **Old Bakery Street** (Strada Forni) and along towards St John Street where, on your left, is St Augustine's Church. Walk a little way beyond and, on your right, is clearly marked **No. 191**, with its green door and balconies. Here the Cassar Torreggiani house was attacked and ransacked on the first day of the *Sette Giugno* riots of 1919, as described in Chapter 13.

Go back now to St John Street and go down it towards Marsamxett Harbour. Laudonia Moroni was fatally injured in 1799 during the insurrection against French occupation at No. 56. The house no longer appears to exist and I deduce that it has been subsumed into the social housing in Mattia Preti Square.

Reverse a little way up St John Street and turn left into West Street (formerly Strada Ponente), and walk towards Independence Square. Just before you get to St Paul's Anglican Church, and on your left overlooking the harbour, is what was Palazzo Britto and then, under the British, **Beverley's Hotel**, where Mrs Beverley played a prominent part. Many British visitors stayed there (Chapter 10), including Anne Scott and her father; indeed, there is a plaque commemorating Sir Walter Scott's stay in 1831. Across the street was the house of his doctor, John Davy, and his wife Margaret whose diary recorded the Scott's visit, described in Chapter 9.

Then you are upon **St Paul's Church**, the entrance to which is in West Street, though it fronts on to Independence Square (formerly Piazza Celsi). As Chapter 11 recounts, the church was funded by Queen Adelaide who laid the foundation stone during her stay in 1839. Its construction meant the demolition of the *Auberge d'Allemagne*, pretty much over the head of Chief Justice Sir John Stoddart and Lady Stoddart who used to glower across the square at Chief Secretary Sir Frederick Hankey and his wife in the *Auberge d'Aragon*, now a government ministry (Chapter 9). Two governors' wives died in Malta within a year of each other, which I think is odd. In the church, on the wall on your right, are plaques commemorating the lives of **Maye Fremantle** (née Hall, d.1898) and (Evelyn) **Emily Mary Grenfell** (née Wood, d.1899). A little more is known about Maye: Charles Savona-Ventura notes in *The History of Midwifery Education in the Maltese Islands* (2009):

> Prof Guiseppe Batta Schembri, following the endeavours of Lady Sym Fremantle, in 1896 initiated the Military Midwives Classes held for English speaking women to provide ... midwives for the women of the military personnel stationed in Malta.

Go back a little way along West Street and turn up **Old Theatre Street**. On your left, unmistakably, is the domed **Carmelite Church**. It was severely damaged during the Second World War and re-built to compete successfully with its nearby Anglican rival. Fortunately, much of the contents of the 1570 original survived. These include Maria de Dominici's late 1670s *Beato Franco*, high up in the middle on your left, and hardly discernible because of the infiltration of light and, possibly, neglect.

Here, too, are the graves of Caterina Scappi and Caterina Vitale (Chapter 6), commemorated in both cases by large, ornate plaques, or tomb slabs – Caterina Vitale's, a little hidden but immediately to your right, low down on the wall as you enter; Caterina Scappi's, more obvious, almost opposite on the left wall.

Further up the street, on the same side, is the bijou **Manoel Theatre**, opened in 1732. Previous to that, entertainments had been performed in the various *auberges* but, following a disturbance during the Carnival of 1639, women were debarred from attending them. By at least 1752, opera and ballet were performed at the Manoel. Italian visitor, Princess Maria Felice Colonna, describes ballet there with a Dutch ballerina (Chapter 7).

The oddest line quoted in the many copycat internet histories of the Manoel is that between 1768 and 1770, the impresario 'was a woman, a certain **Natala Farrugia**'. But nowhere can I find any more about this rather advanced woman.

Women opera singers were not uncommon. Saveria Moscati, natural daughter of Bettina Dorell's husband (Chapter 7), had borne a son by 1774 to the Marquis de Piro but, some time between then and 1780 when she

44.   *Strada Teatro* by Mary Baillie-Hamilton, from *Twelve Views of the Mediterranean*, courtesy of The National Trust

temporarily left Malta for Naples, she continued to perform 'at the famous Maltese opera'.

The best known diva was Marseilles-born **Camilla Darbois** (1804–1878). Having studied at the Paris *Conservatoire*, she married merchant Filippo Darbois in 1820, but was widowed by 1829 with three children, including Anetta who became philanthropist the Marquesa Bugeja (Chapter 11). That same year, Camilla made her debut at the Manoel in Donizetti's *L'Esule di Roma*. Her contract was renewed for 12 years which meant that she was still there to perform twice before Queen Adelaide in 1839 (Chapter 11), and retired in 1841.

Italian mezzo **Adelaide Borghi-Mamo** (1826–1901) sang during the Manoel's 1848–50 seasons and married an Italian tenor in Malta in 1849. Scottish-born **Euphrosyne Parepa-Rosa** (née Parepa de Boyesku, 1836–1874), made her debut at the Manoel, aged 19, as Amina in *La Sonnambula*. During a tour of the United States in 1866, she met and married Carl Rosa and, with him, formed the Parepa-Rosa English Opera Company. She died in childbirth aged 37 and is buried in Highgate Cemetery, London.

The Royal Opera House in the Strada Reale opened in 1866, bringing about the demise of the Manoel as the premier opera house until 1960; indeed, thereafter, it had a rather chequered career. However, Lady Layard who was staying at San Anton with the Duke and Duchess of Connaught (Chapter 12), went there twice to the opera in 1908. She wrote in her journal on 11 November:

In the eveng we went to the theatre at Valletta & saw the opera 'Andre Chenier' by Giordano in the Manoel theatre. It was well given & the prima donna has a very fresh if untrained voice [Giuseppina] Ravaglia is her name. The theatre is the oldest one existing in the world, never having been burned down or rebuilt. It is small & clean looking – elliptical in shape – & the stage is so small that the scenery has to be brought in from the street & nailed into place between the acts. The house was not very full – there being another opera going on at the Theatre Royal – & Malta is too small a place to make them both pay.

She says that the Manoel is the oldest theatre; other sources say the second or third oldest. She wrote less happily on 28 November:

After dinner we went off to Valletta to the Manoel Theatre to see the opera 'Siberia' which was very badly sung & a very dismal subject. The music also was unpleasing & full of discords & minor keys. It was a short opera and we got back to San Antonio soon after 11. Had hot soup wh was ready prepared for us in the Duchess' sitting room & then to bed.

You can find details of Giordano's *Siberia*, premiered at La Scala, Milan in 1903, on the internet. The Russian refugee ballerina, Nathalie Poutiatine, danced at the Manoel in the 1930s.

Malta has produced several home-grown women opera singers: Sliema-born Antoinette Miggiani (b.1937) sang first at Covent Garden but made her Manoel debut as Leonora in *La Forza del Destino* in 1963. Among her pupils was Lydia Caruana who made her Manoel debut as Musetta in *La Bohème* in 1995. The soprano Hilda Mallia Tabone appears in the Floriana itinerary in Chapter 19.

If you are treating yourself to a performance at the Manoel, you will also want a good place to eat. One of our favourite restaurants is the Palazzo Preca which, neatly, takes the itinerary back to Strait Street. We usually approach it via Republic Street, turning down St Lucia Street by the Law Courts towards Marsamxett Harbour. You could, just as well, do it via Old Theatre Street. But in St Lucia Street you pass, on your right, the Embassy Cinema. On that site, in 1864, was the Imperial Hotel, at No. 184. There Baroness Angelica Testaferrata Abela and Jessie Tod Wisely called upon Garibaldi (Chapter 11). His stay is marked by a plaque. Suzanne Layton Parlby was staying there when, as St James's Hotel, it was bombed in 1941.

Turn right where St Lucia Street meets Strait Street and you will find Palazzo Preca at No. 54 of what is hardly more than an alley. It was started by the Preca sisters, Ramona, executive chef, and Roberta, who had learned their craft in a family restaurant. It has a womanly feel about it and serves first-rate Maltese food.

The palazzo itself dates from the sixteenth century but is in a thoroughfare which, in the twentieth century, known as the Gut by British service personnel, had its own particular reputation. Its place in Valletta's history is best introduced by artiste Christina Ratcliffe in Chapter 14. Today, butter wouldn't melt in its mouth.

Archbishop and Merchant Streets

Both streets contain strong whiffs of both Caterina Scappi and Caterina Vitale, and Merchant Street is second to Republic Street as a main Valletta thoroughfare. But this part-itinerary could start towards the end of **Old Bakery Street**, just before it meets Archbishop Street, because Caterina Scappi owned **No. 74**; it was her house but it also appears to be one of the first sites for the *Casetta* – hospital for incurable women – which she set up in 1625 (Chapter 6). Next to the post office, when I reconnoitred it, it was the Johann Strauss School of Music. But Giovanni Bonello's 'Memories of Caterina Scappi' (awaiting publication) has 'until recently'.

Turn into Archbishop Street which has been in its day Strada del Popolo, Strada dei Greci and Strada Vescovo, though there is nothing womanly to note yet, so you could approach the street from Palace Square. Walk until you hit **Frederick Street** on your left. On the corner, as I write, is the D'Office Bistro. That whole block into the narrow Frederick Street, full of atmosphere, was rich widow Giovanna Fontani's house (Nos 1 and 2), at the time of French occupation (Chapter 8). There she spent her short married life with her new French husband, and there she died in childbirth.

Back on Archbishop Street, on the other side of Frederick Street, at No. 132A, is **Our Lady of Damascus** Greek Orthodox Church with its association with Greek-born Caterina Vitale (Chapter 6). She both worshipped there and donated to it. Displayed on a lectern at the front of this bijou church is the precious icon Our Lady of Damascus, brought by the Order of St John when they arrived in 1530 (Chapter 5). There is a pleasing link with this icon and Maltese-born Rosanne Dingli's *According to St Luke* which I mentioned in Chapter 2. It is a tautly written art history thriller connected with the Roman Catholic hierarchy over the centuries and will get you thinking. Its main protagonist, the Australian art-restorer Jana Hayes working in Italy, is a determined and skilled woman whose adventures lead her from Italy to Malta and Damascus. There is another icon of the Virgin with the crucified Christ in her arms on a pillar as you enter. Although the church was badly bombed on 24 March 1942, it was faithfully reconstructed.

No. 135, one to the right of the Bistro Angelica, was owned by Caterina Vitale and bequeathed to her niece Annica Faienza. **No. 138** was also owned by Caterina and bequeathed in 1618 to the *Monte di Redenzione degli Schiavi*. This is to the right of the Ambrosia Restaurant at 137 – another pleasing place to eat run by a wife and husband team. Nos 135–138 are really one building destroyed during the war and reconstructed. No. 138 is now Agius Leli Funeral Service. All these current landmarks may of course change over time.

Cross over Merchant Street and St Paul's Street, with a church on your left, and continue down Archbishop Street. No. 143 is marked but of **No. 144** only an old, bleached *remissa* indicates the property Caterina Scappi purchased from **Cecilia Xiblia** of Syracuse and bequeathed to the *Casetta*.

Return now to Merchant Street and turn right until you almost reach the Fort S Elmo end, then start back up. Almost immediately on your left is a road, apparently nameless, running down towards the Grand Harbour. On your left, fenced in, marked by the sign The Chapel of Bones (Ta'Nibbia), are the remains of the **Annunciation Church** and crypt of the *Casetta*. It, too, was destroyed during the War and only some rubble is left.

Opposite, reconstructed from its bombed predecessor, is the **Mediterranean Conference Centre**, what used to be the Order's 1574 *Sacra Infermeria*, and then the British Station Hospital. There Dr David Bruce and his wife Mary did the work that identified the organism that caused Malta Fever, Brucellosis (Chapter 12). During the First World War, it was the Valletta Military Hospital where the wounded from Gallipoli arrived in 1915, where doctors such as Alice Hutchison treated them (Chapter 13).

Go back to Merchant Street. Where there is now an undistinguished modern building with wide steps was the *Casetta* itself. No sign of it remains. Almost opposite is an unmarked church, until recently in sad repair. This was the 1609 **Church of Mary Magdalene**, and the modern school building beside it the **Maddalena Nunnery** (Chapter 6). Caterina Vitale's daughter, Isabella, spent time here (Chapter 6), and Caterina left one-fifth of her property to it, though not voluntarily. Caterina Scappi also left it a bequest. Rosenda Paulichi entered in 1705 (Chapter 7) and Flaminia Valenti in 1636 (Chapter 6), both one-time mistresses of Grand Masters. Elena Dodsworth, her two daughters and her mother-in-law were sent here in 1763 (Chapter 9). This is the place to make full use of Christine Muscat's wonderful *Magdalene Nuns and Penitent Prostitutes*, with its architectural drawings, photographs, paintings, determined women characters and intricate detail of processes. It is supplemented by her article 'The Magdalene Church, Valletta'.

You need to stand here and cast your mind back not just to the women but also to this complex as it was, including the *Sacra Infermeria*, with the longest ward ever built, where patients, but, at one time, no women, ate off silver served by the knights who nursed them, and the Annunciation Church. It must have been truly grand. Some of Valletta is still grand, but not here.

Continue up Merchant Street, weaving your way through the market stalls in the middle of the road until you almost reach the eating-out places, also in the middle. Opposite the Ministry of Economy, Investment and Small Business on your right is **No. 46** on your left. It is now the Inland

Revenue offices, in spite of the faded signage for the Office of the Census for Goldsmiths and Silversmiths. In Caterina Vitale's day it was the *Monte di Pietà e Redenzione degli Schiavi* to which, as described in Chapter 6, she bequeathed much of her fortune.

I found more to it than tax offices when I ventured up steps that probably date back centuries. As I waited to talk to someone who could confirm that I had found the right historical place, I examined the notice board and was delighted to see a notice reading 'Gender Mainstreaming in Practice', and to be told that it is taken seriously. What it means in detail, as I found on the internet, is laid out in 'Gender Mainstreaming in the Malta Public Service: A Manual for Action' (2000), prepared by Angela Callus and Miriam Camilleri, and issued by the Commission for the Advancement of Women. This ties in with what I have briefly noted in my Preface and Chapter 16. It is instructive to link it to Caterina Vitale and her life, times and determination.

If it is Maltese silver filigree jewellery you are after, you will want to turn right into St Lucia Street. There are dizzying displays to choose from. And in this street full of jewellery shops the family of the mysterious and erratic Tiana have theirs in Rosanne Dingli's *The Hidden Auditorium* (2013), another art history thriller that starts in Italy and chases through Malta. But what is the connection between Grixti's jewellers, a wonderful nineteenth-century pendant hidden in a book and the composer Wagner? It is worth finding out.

Further on up Merchant Street on the left, on the corner of St John Street, is the building that was the *Castellania* (the Grand Master's Law Courts), where the portrait of Caterina Scappi shown in Chapter 6 is located but inaccessible. Through the *Castellania* Caterina Vitale regained possession of her dowry and her late husband's property. What is more, in spite of the men-only nature of the *Sacra Infermeria*, she also took over Ettore Vitale's pharmacy providing the Order's hospital with medicines. In due course, her daughter was also to take her case against Caterina there.

A court continued here under the French and the British until 1853, the building later becoming a girls' secondary school. Today it houses various offices under the Ministry of Health. Allegorical female statues of Justice and Truth still stand either side of the central concave bay.

Towards the top of Merchant Street, on the left, is the solid block of the Ministry for Foreign Affairs, what was the Palazzo Parisio, the last site in this part-itinerary. Napoleon stayed here for a few days in 1798 on his way to Egypt, at the beginning of French occupation. The palazzo is connected with that of the same name in Naxxar once owned by Anna Muscati Parisio (Chapter 7). She died the year before the French arrived, but her son Paolo Parisio joined the Maltese people's army at the head of the Naxxar battalion which fought against the French and was knighted by the British. Following his death in 1841, his widow Antonia Moscati Gatto Xara, whom he had married when she was 14, inherited the palazzo – they had no children. She then married Sir Giuseppe Maria de Piro and you may already have seen the couple's portraits in the Casa Rocca Piccola. He donated the Majmuna stone to the nation (Chapter 2 and Chapter 23 itinerary) and, when he died in 1870, his unmarried sister, **Francesca de Piro** (d.1877) became the 5th Baroness of Budach. Antonia may have owned the Villa Bighi on the Kalkara Peninsula, but the description of 'Baroness Zara's' villa contained in Thomas Freller's *Malta and the Grand Tour* was from 1797 when Antonia was only 14. It may, therefore, refer to her mother, though Antonia was married then.

From Merchant Street to the Grand Harbour

You could start this part-itinerary from the Palazzo Parisio end of Merchant Street. But historically it is going to start at the other end, where Archbishop Street crosses over Merchant Street, and over St Paul Street to St Ursula Street. Immediately on your left, on the corner, is **St Ursula Church** with a plaque saying that it is part of the **St Ursula Nunnery** next door. Here the nuns of the Order of Malta – the Ursulines – had their being from 1595 (Chapter 6). And it was to here that poor Angela Moscati Xeberras, moved from nunnery to nunnery by her warring parents, was dispatched by Bettina Dorell from St Catherine's. In the church is a painting by Preti depicting the **Martyrdom of St Ursula**. I have nowhere seen it suggested that Maria de Dominici was involved, given her superior depiction of women; it was painted between 1680 and 1685; she left Malta in 1682.

Continue down St Ursula Street and up a short flight of steps in the street. On the corner of St Ursula and at the bottom of a long flight of St John steps, on the right is the Franciscan church of **St Mary of Jesus**, known as the **Ta' Giesu**. Here Pulcra Testaferrata and Francesca Portughes had their fracas in 1738 (Chapter 7 and Fort S Elmo – see Republic Street part-itinerary earlier in this chapter). Because the door was closed as I arrived at noon on a Sunday I could not determine where the Portughes tombs are.

In 1846, a rather worse incident took place, as Albert Abela describes in *A Nation's Praise, Malta: People, Places and Events* (1994) – a book more accessible than his other collection of articles with the same sub-title, *Grace and Glory* (1997). It was the custom for poor boys to be sent to the Franciscans to keep them out of the confusion on the streets during the last days of Carnival. They were given bread and fruit at a time, under the British, of great poverty. But that Monday 10 February, as the boys trooped to get their food within the church complex, the wrong door was locked; pushing started on the unlit stone steps; pressure built up and boys started to tumble onto each other. One hundred and ten boys were smothered or trampled to death. A British soldier was an eyewitness and wrote home:

When the place was cleared and the doors were opened, the dead and dying were brought out into the streets ... for thirty yards each side of the door [was] strewn with children, some dead, others dying, and others showing symptoms of recovering. Women running up and down, mad with despair seeing their little ones, and to add to the misery of the scene it was dark ...

When a woman would examine her supposed child she would find it was not her own, it was then laid on the ground and the poor disconsolate mother would rush again amongst the little unfortunates to seek her own. I shall never forget this night, cries of despair were uttered by thousands and [were] heard distinctly at Fort Ricasoli and Cottonera.

Now cross back over St Ursula Street and work your way down, via steps towards the Grand Harbour, to the **Victoria Gate**, in an earlier form, the Marina Gate (also *Porta del Monte*). The other side of the Marina Gate was the market depicted by traveller, artist and writer **Constance Gordon Cumming** (1837–1924) on the cover of this book. She visited Malta twice in 1870 and stayed at the Grand Palace with the governor Sir Patrick Grant and his wife since 1844 **Frances Grant** (née Gough, d.1892). Constance wrote briefly of Malta in *Memories* (1904).

Go through the gate and you are on Liesse Hill, running down to Our Lady of Liesse (opposite the Harbour Club Café). Before you get to the church on your right, turn sharply left into a narrow street clearly marked **Triq il-Gdida**. Here Paula and Etienne Eynaud lived; and it was here in 1798 that tragedy overtook the family, and the other families sheltering with them, as French forces started to occupy Malta (Chapter 8). You could also approach it by turning left a bit earlier after Victoria Gate, descending some wide steps down towards the harbour, and turning right down narrower steps into Triq il-Gdida. This would match the photograph in the late Carmel Testa's *The French in Malta*. The house I decided belonged to the Eynauds has the typical green *remissa* door.

Go back now through Victoria Gate and up the steps you descended until you see signs for the **Lascaris War Rooms**. You are searching there, in this maze of tunnels dug into the cliff as bombs started to fall during the Second World War, for where Christina Ratcliffe worked from June 1941 (Chapter 15). If the War in general interests you, take the full tour; beware, though, it is long, hot and airless, as I found to my cost. If you are just after the women civilian plotters, particularly Christina, nip in with earphones to the RAF Operations Room. Looking down, it is an impressive sight and you really can imagine them moving the planes across the vast map. There is also a room full of photographs, some of them showing Christina.

The Lascaris War Rooms can also be reached by turning left just before you reach the **Upper Barracca Gardens**. These are full of monuments to men, though no doubt women went there to catch the air and admire the stupendous view across the Grand Harbour to the Three Cities. On the far right of the Gardens is the lift that will take you down to the water's edge from where you can get a boat over to start the next itinerary – see Chapter 18.

18 – The Three Cities

The Three Cities are Vittoriosa/Birgu, Cospicua/Bormla and Senglea/L'Isla. Most of the Three Cities was badly bombed, much of its three parts destroyed, during the Second World War. Some inkling of what the area went through is contained in Chapter 15. Much earlier, it had been bombarded during the Great Siege of 1565, as described in Chapter 5, which also tells how Birgu grew from a village to the vibrant city of the Order of the Knights of St John following their arrival in 1530. You cannot travel to the other side of the Grand Harbour without bearing those events in mind. And yet, almost miraculously, the Three Cities have been given a new lease of life, partly due to European Union funding. You would really be missing out not to go. Most of the sites concerning women are in Vittoriosa/Birgu.

From the Upper Barracca Gardens of Valletta you get a marvellous view of the Three Cities, and I think the nicest way to get there is to take the lift down from the corner of the gardens to the waterfront and cross the road to the old Customs House behind which is the landing place for the regular passenger ferry which carries you across the Grand Harbour. Ferries go at a quarter to and a quarter past the hour, and return on the hour and the half hour. That is the way we went. Guide books suggest how you make the journey by car or bus. If you are taking the south tour on the Hop-On Hop-Off bus, you could hop off at the Vittoriosa waterfront (and then hop on a later one). Arriving, as we did, at the St Lawrence Wharf, leading into the Marina Waterfront, also known as the Cottonera Marina, determined the order of this itinerary. We were met off the ferry by our friend Colin Westmarland, denizen of Birgu, whose impeccable guidance proved indispensable.

Vittoriosa/Birgu

Historically, you need to begin with **Fort S Angelo** so from the ferry landing turn left and walk along the waterfront past an unimaginable display of wealth contained in the array of large yachts berthed alongside. Eventually you reach steps leading upwards to the walkway that overlooks the moat separating the fort from the peninsula. At the time of devising this itinerary, September 2014, the whole fort was closed for renovation, due to be completed in 2016 in time for Valletta becoming European Capital City of Culture in 2018. Until it becomes accessible, you can let your imagination rip – S Angelo is so full of Malta's history. And when it is accessible, hunt down the evidence of the following people and events.

As Chapter 2 mentions, there was first a Phoenician temple dedicated to the goddess Astarte which, in Roman times, became that to Juno. Some sources suggest it was at Tas-Silġ; I have nowhere seen this contradiction resolved. In the Middle Ages, 1000–1500, the fortress was the residence of the Counts of Malta and of the *Castellans* and their families. As Chapter 3 relates, Ricca Cafor in 1275 and Constanza Monroy in 1426 were confined there when their husbands were in trouble with the powers-that-be.

Upon her release Constanza handed over the contents of the fortress to the representative of Guterra de Nava and, from 1430, the Sicilian Aragonese de Navas provided its governors for centuries to come, one of the de Nava governors also providing the resident ghost – the Grey Lady. She was his mistress who turned up inopportunely to see him when his wife had arrived from Sicily. He hurriedly ordered the guards to relieve him of this embarrassment, which they did by disposing of the young woman in a way that he had apparently not intended. Thereafter, she haunted the fortress. She was seen, for example, in 1940, when she saved the lives of four British soldiers who followed her away from where they had been sleeping during a bombing raid.

The united arms of the Inguanez-Gatto families on the façade are personified by Imperia Gatto Inguanez c.1402–c.1457 who appears in Chapter 3 and Chapter 20 itinerary.

With the arrival of the Order in 1530, S Angelo was extended, becoming the headquarters of the Master. It is here, particularly, that you can imagine what the women who lived in Birgu, or sought refuge there, went through when the Turks attacked in 1565; this whole area bore the brunt. Following this event, Birgu was renamed Vittoriosa. The names are interchangeable, Birgu perhaps predominating.

The Knights moved over to the newly built city of Valletta in 1571 then, in 1583, S Angelo became the nunnery of the 15 nuns of the Order of St Ursula, until they moved in 1595 to their current location in St Ursula Street, Valletta (Chapter 6 and the last Chapter 17 part-itinerary).

On 25 August 1939, Caroline Vernon, as Chapter 14 relates, received notice to report the following day to the Royal Naval Headquarters, renamed HMS S Angelo, to begin training as a cipher clerk in preparation for the coming war.

You started this itinerary facing Senglea/L'Isla across the Dockyard Creek. Now, passing round the headland at the rear of Fort S Angelo, you are facing the Kalkara Peninsula across the Kalkara Creek. The large building over the water started life as the **Villa Bighi**; by at least the 1760s, it was the home of Elena Dodsworth and her intransigent English Consul husband, John, their children and her mother. There they barricaded themselves in when the soldiers of the Order surrounded the villa (Chapter 9).

Thomas Freller quotes a visitor to the Villa Bighi (Bichi) in 1797 which belonged then to 'Baroness Zara':

Parts of the garden were finely laid out, but it cannot be denied that the orange trees, with fruits in abundance, were the real beauty of the place. We went up to the large palace, and here a *janitor* accompanied us around everywhere, except in the apartments; due to the amount of gold and silver kept there he was not entrusted with the keys. The garden was disorderly and in no good taste, but the large open space around the building surrounded by balustrades, erected in stone to this height, with the wonderful view over the sea and town opposite, was the finest I had seen of this kind.

I discuss the possible identity of the baroness in a Chapter 17 itinerary. The building was converted into a hospital during the plague of 1813 (Chapter 9) and later became a Royal Naval hospital. It came into its own during the First World War (Chapter 13). In 1949 Princess Elizabeth visited it, accompanied by Lady Mountbatten, during one of her stays with her husband serving in Malta in the Royal Navy (Chapter 19 itinerary).

Climbing up steps brings you to St Scholastica Street. The Benedictine **St Scholastica Nunnery** and the Benedictine **Church of St Anne** are obvious. From 1532, the nunnery was the Order's *Sacra Infermeria* until it moved to Valletta (see a Chapter 17 itinerary). With the removal of the Knights, the nuns took it over in 1604. The nunnery continues and, through the open outer door, you can see the grilles through which residents traditionally communicated with the outside world. In the façade is the *ruota* where foundlings were placed. Bettina Dorell placed her daughter Angelica Moscati Xeberras here to be educated during her tug of war with her husband (Chapter 7). The relics of second-century martyr St Veneranda (Venera), said to have been brought from Rome in 1728, are venerated in the church.

At the time of the Great Siege, the nuns from two Benedictine nunneries in Mdina, St Peter and St Scholastica, were moved for safety to Birgu, as Chapter 5 recounts. Not all the nuns were particularly well behaved.

Turn left into Hilda Tabone Street, on some maps called Britannic Street. **Hilda Mallia Tabone** (1932–1978) was born and died in Vittoriosa. Employed as an accountant with Simonds Farsons Cisk, founded by the Marquis Scicluna, she was heard singing at the factory's Christmas party at the Phoenicia Hotel in 1950 by the Marchesa Scicluna. It was the beginning of Hilda's soprano career. Perhaps her most appropriate performance and, indeed, the triumph of her career, was at the première of Carmelo Pace's opera *Caterina Desguanez* at the Manoel in 1965. The plot is based on a historical event that took place during the Great Siege. Hilda had married Carmel Mallia in 1962 and her family regrets that the street's name is Hilda Tabone and not Hilda Mallia Tabone.

Further along on the left of this lovely narrow street, which seems little changed since the time of the Knights, is the original *Auberge de France*. There is an ambiguous sentence in John Manduca's *The Three Cities* (2005) which I left it too late to clarify with him. It comes in his entry for the *Auberge de France*: 'Relations between Malta and France were often close and French spoken by many. The daughters of King Louis XV rented a garden in Malta …'. Was it here? The building is now council offices and open to the public.

What is said to be the original *Auberge d'Angleterre*, though this claim is disputed, is beautifully restored in Mistral (Majjistral) Street, a turning on the right, and is now a public library. When the Knights arrived, the English *Langue* bought the mansion from Catherine Abela. The *Langue* ceased to function after Henry VIII's Dissolution of the Monasteries, the ramifications of which and the queens involved, are discussed in Chapter 5.

The next stop is the **Inquisitor's Palace** in Main Gate Street (Triq il-Mina l-Kbira) which you reach by turning right then left from Mistral Street. The palace was the *Castellania* of the Order until it moved to Valletta then, from 1574, housed the Inquisitor and his court. The palace is being restored and is open to the public as the Museum of Ethnography.

Chapter 6 tells the stories of women appearing before the Inquisitor. Isabetta Caruana of Rabat, Gozo and Betta Caloiro stood trial accused of witchcraft in 1599, Caterina Vitale in 1608 and Sulpitia de Lango in 1617. You can see the room where they were tried. Betta spent eight years of her life imprisoned in the cells and, indeed, died there aged nearly 90. Colin and I searched in vain for where she was buried, and he went back some weeks later hoping to find someone better informed, without success. Let's not give up!

The two English Quakers Sarah Cheevers and Katherine Evans who gave the Inquisition a run for its money were imprisoned here from 1658 to 1662. The day we visited, their cell was being restored, but we were able to look in and a detailed notice about them should be back on the door by now. The workman had a large electric fan on a stand; imagine what it was like for the prisoners!

Two other women fared better in the Inquisitor's Palace. Vincenza Matilde Testaferrata began her 18 years as the Inquisition's *Depositario* in 1760 – an unprecedented position for a woman (Chapter 7). And four years later, Bettina Dorell's daughter Angela, who may have been fathered by the Inquisitor, was baptised in the bijou chapel which today looks much as it must have done then (Chapter 7).

Turn down St George's Street from Triq il-Kardinal Fabrizzio Sciberras and on the corner with Wenzu Dyer Street stands Bettina's Palace. It is sometimes called Cardinal's Palace because Bettina's nephew, who became the first Maltese cardinal, was born there and inherited it. The building has a sadly neglected air and even the dolphin door knocker is missing, but the hole it has left does allow you to peer inside. There is not much to see, but all you need is imagination.

Chapter 11 tells the story of Emilie de Vialar, later St Emilie, founder of the Order of St Joseph of the Apparition, who was shipwrecked on Malta travelling with some of her nuns from her mission in Algeria home to France. It is speculated that in George Street they stayed in Palazzo Bettina. Emilie then set up a Congregation in Malta which still flourishes, before moving on.

Wend your way now back towards the waterfront, but stop at the **Church of St Lawrence**. There may have been a Birgu parish church here of that name as long ago as 1090; this was certainly the first Conventual Church of the Order of St John in 1530. If you want to go inside, you probably need to get there before 11.30 am, so you could do so when you first arrive (you can see it from the waterfront). But this itinerary needs it as a climax, not so much because Grand Master de Vallette's natural daughter Isabella Guasconi was married here (Chapter 6), but because Bettina Dorell was buried in the family vault in the Chapel of the Blessed Sacrament, on the right hand side of the high altar, one-third down that side of the nave. The chapel was built in 1786 on land donated by Baroness **Francesca Viani**. Your purpose in visiting it has, however, been thwarted by wartime bombing. The chapel and vault were reduced to rubble. The chapel has been rebuilt and Bettina's grave may well be underneath. There is no sign either of the three paintings by Maltese artist Michele Busuttil which she donated, and no record of them. If they hung in the chapel, they, too, would have been destroyed.

The *Malta Government Gazette* of 16 September 1829 records (and on the opposite page in Italian):

Died on the 8th Instant the Marchioness Elisabetta Moscati Cassia *nata* Dorel, aged 88. She was Lady of Honour to the late Queen of Naples, with whom she resided many years in that capacity. Her remains were interred on the 10th, in the family vault in the Collegiate Church of St Lorenzo at Vittoriosa, attended by a very numerous retinue of friends, by whom she was much lamented for her private virtues, and a great concourse of people who voluntarily joined in this last act of respect, in testimony of the general and extensive acts of charity, which her abundant means enabled her to dispense.

So before you return to the waterfront, and perhaps lunch, spare a thought for the *grande dame* Bettina Dorell, known to all simply as the Lady Bettina. She may have been well born, rich and privileged, but her life was not without adversity in a period when women's lives were much constrained, yet she rose above it all. There will be further meetings with Bettina in the Chapter 22 itinerary that includes Gudja and the Inquisitor's Summer Palace.

Cospicua/Bormla

You could now take the ferry back to Valletta but you have only done one of the Three Cities. There is much less to see concerning women in the other two, but at least one street in Cospicua/Bormla is a must. So, as if from the ferry, turn right instead of left and make your way up to Pilgrimage Street (Triq il-Pellegrinagg) and the Church of the Immaculate Conception which, miraculously, escaped wartime bombing. The first church on the site dates from 1584, but it was enlarged in 1637. What you have come to see is the wooden statue of the Virgin Mary, carved by Maria de Dominici in about 1680 (Chapter 6), and covered in silver in 1905.

The statue is very important to the people of this city. Festivities begin before December but culminate on the 8th – the Feast of the Immaculate Conception – in a procession, led by the statue carried shoulder high. Even the black and white photograph overleaf shows how she shines. But I also notice that women don't seem to feature in the procession; there are only

45.   Maria de Dominici, sculpture of the Virgin Mary in procession,
Cospicua, courtesy of Caroline Said Lawrence

black-clad figures pressed against the wall. I have not managed to be in
Malta on 8th December but the studio of artist Caroline Said Lawrence is in
the same street, and in two emails she has given me invaluable information
and impressions. Apparently Maria de Dominici 'used a young Jewish
resident of Cospicua as her model, wishing to maintain some authenticity in
the likeness of the Madonna'. And, of the procession itself, Caroline writes:

I'm more a spiritual than a religious person but every year I find this
procession a very moving experience. Particularly on its return journey
to the church when it is being brought up my street and passes under
my balcony. The street is heaving with people and those in front of the
statue walk backwards up the hill so as not to turn their backs on the
statue. The crowd of worshippers sing a beautiful song about Bormla
and the community's passionate devotion to the Madonna and those who
can manage to, raise their arms towards the statues. It is a goosebumps
moment and time and again my eyes involuntarily fill with tears.

It is also well worth visiting Caroline's studio at No. 62. Brought up in Kenya, she trained at St Martin's School of Art, London, and her first exhibition was in 1992 in Bahrain. She settled in Malta in 2002. Her background, and the Malta landscape, combine to stimulate her work of mixed media paintings which include depictions of the 'magical antiquity' of the Three Cities.

Senglea/L-Isla

Come back to the waterfront and walk round the end of the creek to Senglea. The severely damaged aircraft carrier *Illustrious* was docked alongside Senglea in 1941, not only for urgent repairs, but also to disembark the members of the crew badly burnt following the air attacks on the vessel. Its presence resulted in the whole area being bombed to smithereens. Tamara Marks describes the scene in Chapter 15. Although Senglea is coming back to life, particularly where a colony of artists has moved in, and it has a quiet and picturesque charm, there are, I believe, only two sites that have a woman connection, and one is a bit nebulous. But if you are in Malta on 8th September, that is the time to go, to see the celebrations for Victory Day.

The 1743 Senglea parish church, **Our Lady of Victories**, is at the landward end of Victory Street. At the other end is a garden – the *Vedette* – from where you get a fine view across the Grand Harbour to Valletta and across Dockyard Creek to Fort S Angelo.

The church, which was severely damaged during the War and re-constructed after it, also has its statue of the Virgin Mary and its procession. This celebrates not only the Feast of her Nativity but also that of the end of the Great Siege of 1565, a promise made during the plague of 1676, and that when the Italian Navy surrendered to the British off Malta in 1943 (Chapter 15).

The origins of this Madonna are more exotic than those of Cospicua's. It is said that in 1618 the statue – known as Il-Bambina – was found floating among wreckage in the Adriatic by one of the Order's galleys. It is assumed to have been the figurehead of a Christian galleon. Two passengers on the galley from Senglea petitioned the captain to donate it to their parish church, which he did. A solid gold crown studded with precious stones, presented by the people of Senglea, was placed on Il-Bambina's head in 1921.

If you stand in front of the Maritime Museum on the waterfront in Birgu and look across Dockyard Creek to Senglea, you will see the house of marine archaeologist **Honor Frost** (*c*.1928–2010). She is the sort of 'artist' who moved into a revitalising area after the War. As early as the 1950s, she was a pioneer in underwater archaeology. In 1967, she was on her way to the Middle East with a diving team when her work was postponed by the Arab-Israeli War. The National Maritime Museum of Malta promptly took up her services and she began a brief but scientific and fruitful excavation of a Roman shipwreck in Mellieħa Bay, confirming that Malta was very much part of a Roman Mediterranean maritime network. Her work was continued after her departure and still is, thanks to the Honor Frost Foundation. Her drawings and notes are stored in the archives of the National Museum of Archaeology, Valletta. She later returned to set up a second home in Senglea. Where exactly it is, and its status, I do not know. But someone will, and it should be noted.

The last site of this itinerary is a bit of an oddity on the map. The address for **St Edwards College** is Triq il-Kottonera, Birgu, but it is away from the centre, near the Żebbuġ Gate, and probably only fits in if you are travelling by car. It is certainly of some significance in its two separate manifestations which create several historical links. From Cospicua you could leave via Cottonera Road.

Florence Nightingale's involvement in Malta's hospitals, following her return from the Crimea in 1856, is partly described in Chapter 12. Her more general criticism of medical facilities for British troops led to the setting up of a Royal Commission of which a sub-committee looked into those on Malta. This resulted in the building of the Cottonera Hospital in 1873. Florence's strictures were carefully followed, not just for the care of patients, but also for the accommodation of nurses, a role increasingly taken on by women.

'Cottonera Hospital and Malta as the Nurse of the Mediterranean' (2014) by John Mark Portelli and Alfred Cassar Reynaud, on the St Edwards website, makes the link with Dr Louis Hughes who, it suggests, based his classic 1897 work 'on his observations at Cottonera Hospital and Malta more generally'. During the First World War (Chapter 13), Cottonera Hospital played a major role, as this photograph illustrates, and one of the consultants from Britain who worked there, Sir Arthur Garrod, his wife and archaeologist daughter, Dorothy, appear in that chapter.

In 1929, the hospital's role was completely changed when Margaret Strickland, Countess of Catena, funded the setting up of St Edwards College for boys which took over and extended the hospital buildings (Chapter

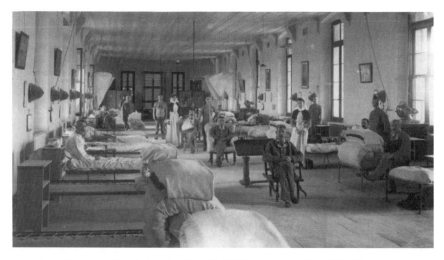

46.   Cottonera Hospital in the First World War, from Manduca, *The Three Cities*

14). Two connections then arose. A young nurse from the hospital, **Violet Briffa**, became matron in the college from 1930 to 1965 – 'a towering personality who left her mark, the result of the realities of World War I and Cottonera on generations of Edwardians'. The second rector of the college was Fr Henry Brackenbury Louis Hughes, son of Dr Hughes and his wife Katherine Hughes.

Żabbar

If you are visiting by car, and if you are interested in Malta's first woman president, Agatha Barbara (Chapter 16), her birthplace, though not one of the Three Cities, can be reached either by going via Cottonera Road from Cospicua, or by driving from St Edward's College. There is a monument to her in Sanctuary Street.

19 – From Floriana to Naxxar via Sliema

When I knew in September 2013 that we were going to stay at the **Phoenicia Hotel**, guide books told me it was in Floriana, so I started googling restaurants there. In fact, the hotel is just outside the City Gate and it is Valletta that draws one in. For this itinerary, however, the hotel fits neatly into Floriana and is a good starting place. But only the first part is walkable.

Unless you are staying in the area that extends from Pietà to St George's Bay via Sliema, you will need a car or public transport, which includes a ferry from Valletta across Marsamxett Harbour to Sliema. And turning inland beyond St George's Bay to Naxxar, for the sake of the story, is definitely a car or bus journey. Some sites may be more suitable for the armchair traveller.

Floriana

The large tablet to the right of the entrance of the hotel reads: 'Hotel Phoenicia, erected at the command of the Lady Strickland DBE, Countess della Catena and happily completed in the year of our Lord MCMXLVII.' It may have been completed in 1947, but Margaret Strickland set the construction of Malta's first luxury hotel in train before the War (Chapter 14). She named the hotel after the Phoenicians who left their mark on Malta (Chapter 2).

The central space was originally a courtyard; roofed over in the 1960s, it is now the Palm Court Lounge. As you enter, your eye is caught by the sculpture of a female nude whose slinky lines suggest it was sculpted in the 1920s or 1930s; in fact it is black painted wood dating from 2007. She presides over afternoon tea, cocktails with the manager or café music played on a grand piano. The career of soprano Hilda Mallia Tabone, who has a street named after her in Birgu, started in the Phoenicia in 1950 when, as the Chapter 18 itinerary relates, she was 'discovered' by the Marchesa Scicluna who will be met at the Palazzo Dragonara towards the end of this one.

Leaving the hotel, turn right down Triq L-Assedju L-Kbir, past the Ministry of Education on the other side of the road, until you reach Hannibal or Hann. Scicluna Street, with the Hotel Excelsior on your right, on the edge of Marsamxett Harbour. Continue along that street, following the sign for Historic Gardens est. 1806, past the public library on your left, until you come, on your right, to that garden, the non-Catholic **Msida Bastion Cemetery**. The first burial took place in 1806; it was consecrated in 1843, and was full by 1856. As it is not mentioned in guide books, note that it is open on Tuesday, Thursday and Saturday, and the first Sunday of the month, 9.30 to midday. The entrance fee in 2013 was 2 Euro.

The cemetery, overlooking the harbour, in the lee of the Msida Bastion, and shaded by trees, is something of a haven, staffed by knowledgeable volunteers based in a little shop at the entrance. It was neglected for years which accounts for many displaced headstones, so you may not find the grave of a long-ago relative, or of Margaret and Thomas MacGill buried there in 1844 (Chapter 10). But the monuments to the most obvious women – introduced in Chapter 9 – are there. You first come across that of Catherine Hankey, Greek wife of Chief Secretary Sir Frederick Hankey. Further along are those of the Freres: Elizabeth (Countess of Erroll), her husband John, and his sister Susannah. They will be met again later in this itinerary at what remains of Villa Frere.

Wend your way back to where you started, but without crossing over to the Phoenicia and, dominating the intersection, is the 1964 bronze **Independence Statue** – a towering, well-built woman on a plinth.

Behind her is the entrance to **Maglio Gardens**, 400 metres long and narrow for the playing of a form of croquet, pallamaglio (pallmall). I would have omitted this site, but for the delightful injunction to his fellow Knights issued by Grand Master Lascaris. If ever we suspected that tales of their less than virtuous lifestyle were exaggerated, this would disabuse us. It has been variously translated from Latin, but my husband prefers his own version:

An end to laziness, to cupid's art!
For you, you Knights, this playground is a gift.
So play! The game here makes you swift
For war; wine, women, dice just sap your heart.

Embedded in the walls are several statues of significant Maltese – none of them women.

Beyond the Maglio Gardens, at the end of Triq Sarria, are the **Argotti Botanic Gardens**. In 1805, medicinal plants and other botanical specimens were collected in the Maglio Gardens. In due course, the Argotti Gardens were established. The first curator was Father Carlo Giacinto and, in 1806, a British woman traveller, perhaps arriving from South Africa, but leaving no record of her name, donated some bulbils (sometimes mistakenly called bulbs) of Cape Sorrel (*Oxalis*; known in Maltese as *Haxixa Ingliza*, English Weed). The low-slung, yellow-flowered *Oxalis* was to spread all over Malta and, indeed, over many parts of Europe. Today's curator, Joseph Buhagiar, when approached, calls it a plant that 'has caused much mischief'. Perhaps it is as well that she remains nameless; still, it would be good to know.

Lady Francis Egerton (née Harriet Catherine Greville, 1800–1866, m.1822) passed through Malta very briefly and recorded in *Journal of a Tour of the Holy Land, in May and June 1840* (1841): 'We also went to the Florian Gardens, a singular place teeming with orange-trees, geraniums, and with other flowers, kept with English neatness.' It is not clear if she refers to the Maglio or Argotti. In 1945, **Beatrice Borg**, wife of Professor John Borg, gave his cactus collection to the Botanic Gardens. Part of them are open to the public from 8.30 am to sunset, and admission is free.

Before you get to the Argotti Gardens, turn right down Vincenzo Bugeja Street and make your way towards La Vittoria Bastion through the Poverista Gate. In the lee of that is the old Floriana *Ospizio*, now used for performances during the Malta Arts Festival. This is the former House of Industry which the Marchioness of Hastings modified in 1824 to teach poor girls useful crafts (Chapter 9) from the Order's *Ospizio* or *Conservatorio* of 1734 which housed elderly women, former women convicts and vulnerable girls (Chapter 7). The complex was severely bombed during the War and the arcade flanking the central courtyard and the imposing entrance with mounted guns on each side were totally destroyed.

Pietà and Gwardamanġa

As the crow flies, you can from Floriana cross over to the **Ta' Braxia Cemetery**, on the left going towards Sliema off Triq Indipendenza. There you will find the graves of the following: governor's wife, Evelyn Emily Grenfell to whom there is a plaque in St Paul's Anglican Church, buried in 1899, Jessie Tod Wisely, joint founder of St Andrew's Church, South Street, in 1910 (Chapter 11), and 72-year-old teacher Ethel Yabsley, killed in a bombing raid on 5 February 1942 (Chapter 15). The graves of two members of the Russian refugee Poutiatine family and their retainer are also there. Princess Olga died in 1967, Alicia Strautman in 1977, and ballet dancer Nathalie Poutiatine in 1984 (Chapter 13).

At the bottom of the Ta' Braxia is a signpost indicating the **Pietà Military Cemetery** at the beginning of Triq id Duluri (Our Lady of Sorrows Street). Dr Isabel Addy Tate, who served in Malta during the First World War (Chapter 13), died there of typhoid in November 1915, when the cemetery was established, and was buried there with full military honours, attended by women colleagues who had served with her. VAD Helen Bachelor Taylor died the same month of dysentery.

Behind and above the cemeteries is Gwardamanġa Hill in the hamlet of Pietà. The first port of call here is **Villa Gwardamanġa** (Guardamangia) in Telgħet Gwardamanġa Street, its name clearly on the wall by the front door. This villa was leased by Lord Louis Mountbatten in about 1929 while he was serving with the Mediterranean Fleet and, from time to time, Edwina joined him there. But, during the War, it was divided into four flats, one of which was rented by Suzanne Layton Parlby and another young wife, when they had been bombed out of St James Hotel (Chapter 15).

In 1948, Mountbatten was appointed Rear Admiral, Commanding the First Cruiser Squadron Mediterranean. By this time, he had bought Villa Gwardamanġa and Janet Morgan describes how Edwina set about trying to make something of it, while they lived at the Hotel Phoenicia from where, as her daughter Pamela relates, 'we were nearly asked to leave' when the family's pet mongoose got loose and created chaos. In December, Edwina told Nehru, 'Villa going backwards'. To cheer herself up, she bought plants for the garden and 'enchanting goldfish with lazy, swishy tails, 18 at 4d each'. They moved in on 29 December 'gassed by paint and cold intense'. By 1949, the family of three employed a staff of 19: a butler, a housekeeper, two housemaids, two charwomen (shared with the ship in harbour), six stewards, three cooks, two Marine drivers, a Marine valet and a coxswain.

At various times between 1949 and 1951, Princess Elizabeth and her Royal Navy husband, Prince Philip, stayed at the villa, and the Queen paid it a nostalgic visit in 1992. In 1952, the Mountbattens moved to Admiralty House, when he was appointed Commander-in-Chief (Chapter 17 itinerary). Then Edwina looked back more kindly on Gwardamanġa. The villa, with its once-grand porch, is now in a rather a sorry state and an aging woman neighbour may remonstrate with you should you stop to gawp.

Off Telgħet Gwardamanġa Street is the slip road leading to St Luke's Hospital. This used to be the main hospital, and in the grounds is the **Karin Grech Rehabilitation Hospital**. The story of **Karin Grech** (1962–1977) is one of great tragedy. In 1977 the Maltese Medical Association was in a long-running dispute with the Labour government, and the doctors at St Luke's were on strike. Dr Edwin Grech, who had been working in England, was asked to come back to head the department of Obstetrics and Gynaecology, which he did, thus being labelled a strike-breaker. Fifteen-year-old Karin was studying in England, but had returned home for Christmas. On 28 December, a large brown envelope containing a small pen-shaped parcel in Christmas wrapping arrived and Karin, in the presence of her brother, opened it. It was a letter-bomb which exploded in her hands. She died half an hour later in St Luke's. The perpetrator was never found. The hospital was built in her memory in 1981 and there is a Karin Grech Gardens in San Gwann containing a sculpture of her.

Maltese-born Aline P'Nina Tayar, who explores her Jewish diaspora roots in her writing, drew on Karin's tragic story for her novel *Island of Dreams* (2012). This time it is a wife who opens the packet intended for her doctor husband. Her murder in 1977 leads to ramifications for three cousins, Ellie, Claire and Vanna, who meet up in Malta from Brussels, Jerusalem and Sydney in 2011. While the murder of the mother of one of them 34 years earlier is the back story, Ellie, the political activist, becomes caught up in the contemporary tragedy of refugees from Africa arriving in Malta, or drowning at sea.

The grounds of St Luke's are also the best, perhaps the only, place to see the remnant of the gardens of Villa Frere which the Frere family built and embellished on land owned by the St Catherine's Nunnery (Chapter 17 itinerary) following their arrival in 1821. Their life in Malta is described in Chapter 9, and the involvement of Lady Erroll's niece, Honoria Blake Hamilton Chichester, in Maltese lace in Chapter 10. If you drive straight through the hospital grounds you cannot mistake the sad remains of the Villa's Greek temple (*tempietto*) on the left of the internal road. The Hookham Frere Primary School is a little way to the right of the *tempietto*, built on what was the Japanese gardens and wilderness. The nursing school was built on the upper reaches of the gardens and, in 1984, a helipad was built, together with a wide parking lot, next to the *tempietto*.

To see Villa Frere itself, make your way down to the main road along the waterfront (I did all this area in a car with a driver; probably not easy on foot unless you are staying nearby). You should then be able easily to spot the three-storeyed mansion, standing between Villa Ciantar and Bezzina House. It is painted half-way up in peeling dark red and has three enclosed green wooden balconies and three green-shuttered French windows leading on to a long, open balcony with a bay centre.

Lady Grosvenor, who did not think much of St John's Cathedral (Chapter 17), knew the Freres and wrote of Villa Frere in 1840, after the deaths of both Elizabeth and Susannah, but while Honoria was still there looking after John:

> We found him in his pretty garden or rather series of gardens on the side of a hill behind his house, which are attained by long flights of steps with terraces and walks, cut out of the rock, ornamented with columns, balustrades and other devices, in the Maltese stone, and extremely pretty.

Following John's death, Honoria and her husband, Lord Hamilton Francis Chichester, lived in the villa. Edward Lear wrote to a friend in 1866 (contained in *Later Letters of Edward Lear*, 1911):

> The chief person here after the Govr. General and top Admiral, is Lady Hamilton Chichester. Mr. Hookham Freer, who married her aunt, Lady Erroll, left her a fine house and gardens and I suppose she is a 'power in the State' as she is now an R.C. and I fancy is influential.

Manoel Island

There are many places from which you can see Manoel Island in Marsamxett Harbour, and forming Sliema and Lazaretto Creeks. It is significant for the **Lazaretto** (quarantine station) set up as early as 1592 as wooden huts to protect Malta from infectious diseases; its permanent structure dates from 1643 (Chapter 6). At times, too, under the British the nearby Fort has been military barracks and the Lazaretto turned into married quarters; indeed, military wives and daughters were buried in its cemetery (Chapter 12).

Nineteenth-century travellers and twentieth-century refugees confined to the Lazaretto, and writing about it and its lack of delights, abound, as Chapters 9, 10 and 13 suggest. Some died there. Typical was **Ann Flynn**, Lady Montefiore's maid, who developed pleurisy returning with the couple from a visit to the Holy Land in July 1839 (Chapter 10). Her employers erected a fulsome tombstone which still stood in 1970 but was destroyed that year when the cemetery was razed to the ground.

It may well be from here that Laudonia Testaferrata was fatally injured by shell fire in her house at the waterfront end of St John Street, Valletta, facing the island (see Chapter 17 itinerary) when Maltese insurgents used it as a base against the French in January 1799 (Chapter 8).

Sir John Franklin, who in later life disappeared trying to discover the Northwest Passage, served in the Mediterranean in the 1830s. His new wife, **Jane Franklin** (née Griffin, 1791–1875) would, as Frances Woodward describes in *Portrait of Jane: A Life of Lady Franklin* (1951), follow him, but also dart off on her own travels. Jane visited Malta several times and writes tellingly of trying to communicate with him at the Lazaretto:

> My first communication with Sir John was by means of a letter brought to me by Commissioner Briggs, which turned me sick and ever continues to do so when I inhale its peculiarly offensive fumigation. Then he came alongside himself with his yellow flag, and his yellow-cuffed guardiano, and then I was put into a boat with *my* yellow flag, and guardiano (and to make the livery more complete I put on my yellow scarf also) and we were both landed on a narrow platform in front of the Lazaretto, and narrowly watched on each side lest we should approach too near, during half an hour's conversation. The next day ... I was landed on a rock with my guardiano and Sir John came off in a boat with his, and we had another conversation. They tell me it was nearly two hours long. However this may be, the fatigue of standing a long while in the heat and speaking at the pitch of my voice to make Sir John hear, united with the blinding effect of the bright water, and the dazzling buildings so overcame me that I was fit for nothing but my wretched berth on my return to the ship.

(Jane's time as governor's wife in Tasmania is covered in depth in my *Tasmania: Women, History, Books and Places.* Her quarantine in Crete is described in the web update to my earlier book in the same series, see www. holobooks.co.uk.)

The Franklins avoided breaking the rules; perhaps they learnt from the experience of poor **Lady Georgina Walpole** (1795–1859, m.1827), daughter of the 2nd Earl of Oxford, wife of traveller and missionary Joseph Wolff. Gabrielle Festing tells of the occasion when he was in the Lazaretto on his return from one of his missions, and she was staying on the island:

> [She] ... went to see him from behind the grille. Delighted at her appearance, he rolled up his handkerchief and flung it at her. The health guards protested against this demonstration of conjugal love for they considered that by coming in contact with the handkerchief Wolff's wife had exposed herself to the possibility of infection. They, therefore, insisted on her following her husband into quarantine – which she had to do.

Some of these historic buildings on Manoel Island are undergoing restoration, so they are probably best viewed from the nearby mainland until completion.

Sliema and Beyond

The neo-classical **The Hotel Palazzo Capua**, adjoining the The Victoria Hotel and the The Palace in Gorg Borg Olivier Street, Sliema, has an intriguing history. The story of Irish **Penelope Caroline Smyth** (1815–1882) and her husband Carlo di Borbone, Prince of Capua, is told in most detail in the chapter 'The Prince of Capua: An Exile in Malta' by Albert Abela in *Nation's Praise: Malta*.

Penelope and Carlo eloped from Naples, which she had been visiting with her sister, to Scotland in April 1836 and married at Gretna Green; thereafter they married more formally more than once. Carlo's brother, King Ferdinand II of The Two Sicilies, refused to recognise the morganatic marriage, one that had taken place without his permission, exiled Carlo and confiscated all his property.

Travelling as Count and Countess Mascali, the couple arrived in Malta in September 1836. Selma Hall, Sliema, later known as Palazzo Capua, was to be their home on at least three occasions over the next 14 years. Their first son was born there in March 1837, and later a daughter. Meanwhile, they were dogged by lack of funds – although Penelope did have an income of her own – Ferdinand's suspicions of conspiracy, and his attempts to cause them diplomatic problems. More than once in Sliema they faced acute financial embarrassment, once even involving the bailiffs. They left Selma Hall and Malta for the last time in 1850. Nine years later, Ferdinand died and his son, Francis II, restored Carlo's property. Later still, after her husband's death in 1862, Penelope was recognised as Princess Capua (Principessa di Capua); she was also known as Princess Carolina Bourbon of Capua.

A century later, in the early 1940s, Palazzo Capua housed the government Capua Orphanage under the Sisters of Charity; it became St Jeanne Antide Home in 1963, and closed in 1978 when the orphans were transferred to the Conservatorio Vincenzo Bugeja (Chapter 11 and Chapter 20 itinerary). By the 1980s the palazzo had fallen into disuse and neglect. Eventually it was meticulously restored and opened as The Palazzo Capua Hotel. The connection with the Capuas is maintained by the Princess Penelope suite and the Prince Charles of Capua suite.

Sliema today is not quite as it was then, though behind the coastal development of hotels and modern shops, as Juliet Rix expresses it in her *Malta and Gozo* guide book, is 'a quietly elegant residential area with some lovely old buildings, colourful *gallariji*, churches and pretty squares'. But, without addresses, imagination is required to conjure up the homes of others who lived there: Sarah Austin (Chapters 9 and 10); Dr James Barry (Chapter 12) and, of course, the ultimate snob who accosted Christina Ratcliffe on the boat from Marseilles (Chapter 14). The bastion of snobbishness, the Sliema Club (Chapter 14), has changed location since its founding in Ghar il-Lembi Street in 1874. The original Union Club in the Strada Reale, in what was the *Auberge de Provence*, and is now the Archaeological Museum, was, of course, men only, not allowing women in until 1907, and then on sufferance with their own side entrance – that is, until 1910 when, under pressure from the Duchess of Connaught, one was opened on the façade of the *Auberge*. Women did not become full members of the Malta Union Club, now in a modern building at 1 Triq Tigné, Sliema, until 1992. Those descendants of the *gente per bene* of the past who enjoy posh shopping are known as *Slimzi*.

The Zammit Clapp Hospital (Blue Sisters Hospital) founded by sisters Emilia Zammit Clapp and Maria Zammit some time after 1907 (Chapter 11) is now the Zammit Clapp Nursing Home for the Elderly in Triq Dun Anton Tabone, St Julians. Nearby, in Sacred Heart Avenue, is the Sacred Heart Convent where admiral's daughter Rosamund Fisher (Chapter 14) and political activist Josephine Debono and her sister (Chapter 16) went to school.

The northern route Hop On Hop Off sightseeing bus, ending (and starting) as it does in Sliema, passes the gates to the **Dragonara Casino and Hotel**, Dragonara Road, St Julians, as does transport to catch the Gozo ferry. But the casino beyond, on Dragonara Point, used to be the Palazzo Dragonara, seaside summer residence of the Scicluna family, built in 1870 by banker and first Marquis, Emanuele Scicluna, and the nearer hotel was built in the gardens.

The widow of Emanuele's nephew, the second Marquesa, Corinna, lent the palazzo to 20 officers as a convalescent home during the First World War (Chapter 13). But it was **Maria Violette Testaferrata Moroni-Viani**, 7th Baroness of Tabria (1897–1955), married to John, 3rd Marquis Scicluna, in 1921, and known affectionately in family stories as Granny Vi, who discovered soprano Hilda Mallia Tabone in the Phoenicia Hotel in 1950.

Marquesa Violette was the daughter of the Baron of Tabria and **Maria Mizzi** (m.1895). Big and tall, she was a strong woman and quite a character. During the Second World War she volunteered rooms at the palace for Malta Relief Fund Committee meetings, for sewing and knitting parties and anything else that needed doing. She also organised concerts in aid of the Fund, the Spitfire Fund and the Sanatorium Fund, and held parties for the forces. She was a brilliant pianist and there were two Bechsteins in the drawing room on which four hands played such pieces as the *Warsaw Concerto* (1941). The philanthropist Sciclunas further embellished the Dragonara, but also used it to house 100 people made homeless by bombing.

Violette took three of her children off to Caracas, Venezuela, following the Berlin airlift of 1948 and opened a pizzeria, only returning when her son got sunstroke. Her daughter, **Corinne Ramsay Scicluna** (1923–2007), did not travel with them as she had married a British naval officer in 1947 and inherited her Tabria title. We shall meet Corinne's daughter and granddaughter shortly.

The whole area the other side of St George's Bay from the former Scicluna residence was a British military base between 1850 and 1979. On the seaward side of the main road returning from the North Tour, or going to and from the ferry to Gozo, you pass the low-slung Pembroke barracks, the only sign left of what is now the residential town of Pembroke. But here was **St George's Hospital** where VAD Vera Brittain nursed during the First World War; Chapter 13 contains her description of the place and her time there.

The naval women and families who remained in Malta during the Second World War, such as Kathleen Norman and Caroline Vernon, were, as Chapter 15 relates, housed in the **St George's Barracks** which were bombed

47.   Marquesa Violette Scicluna, courtesy of Palazzo Parisio

on 25 April; the Vernons all wrote about the event. The barracks have been converted into housing. Two sites further towards the ferry terminal are in Chapter 23 itinerary.

Naxxar

Here the connections with places earlier in this itinerary force me to create a diversion, and take you to Naxxar, a hilltop village overlooking the sea. It will only work if, leaving the Pembroke site, and turning inland, you are doing so by car (or you could catch the 225 bus via San Gwann where there is a statue of Karin Grech). We did not approach Naxxar this way on either visit. The first time, it was after having been driven hither and yon all over the island visiting sites off the straight and narrow. The second time, we went to have lunch at the **Palazzo Parisio** and interview the 10th Baroness of Tabria (née **Marie Christiane Ramsay Scicluna**) whom everyone knows as Muffy, and her daughter **Justine Pergola**; we travelled then by taxi from the Phoenicia and returned by local bus.

The story of Palazzo Parisio starts in 1774 with Anna Muscati Parisio when she moved back to Malta because of ill health and an ill-judged marriage (Chapter 7). It passed to her son and was inherited by his widow Antonia, 3rd Baroness Benwarrad, as was the Palazzo Parisio in Merchant Street, Valletta (see Chapter 17 itinerary). But from her and her second husband it passed to the Jesuits until it came into the possession of the Scicluna family of Dragonara Palace and was extended and beautified from villa to palazzo by Giuseppe Scicluna, 2nd Marquis, and his wife Corinna Abela Pulis (Chapter 13).

During the Second World War, as Chapter 15 and Tamara Marks' account relate, the palazzo became home to the wives and families of Royal Air Force personnel. But there must also have been Maltese families sheltered there from the bombing because in Rosanne Dingli's *Counting Churches* (2011) the story 'The Most Fortunate Children' tells of such a family; introducing the palazzo and its inmates she writes:

> The orchard in the grounds of the palace of the Marquis in Naxxar was sealed off. From the high parapet of the forecourt at Parisio Palace, the children could see the Marquis's men harvest sacks full of oranges.
>
> There were about forty children of different ages, from barely walking toddlers to adolescents of fourteen. And among them, of course, were the four children of Spinola.

The Spinola family probably picks up on the Dragonara Palace/Scicluna connection.

The 2nd Marquis and Marquesa Violette had married in Naxxar Parish Church opposite the palazzo and she donated the unique *pavaljun* (canopy) under which its statue of the Bambina stands.

In due course, the palazzo became the responsibility of Muffy and Justine who, working as a team, turned it into this unmissable stop, which they run. You can either eat or simply visit the rooms furnished and decorated by earlier generations not lacking funds or flair. The Luna Restaurant at Palazzo Parisio is for lunch or tea, the Luna de Sera for dinner, and the Luna Lounge for cocktails, and it leads into beautiful gardens that are available, too, for events such as gala dinners and weddings. We have only had lunch, when the food, wine and ambience were classy. There is also a boutique. Mother and daughter have inherited something of the earlier Scicluna women.

Half a mile's walk from Naxxar, or a bus ride on the No. 35, is San Pawl tat-Targa. Behind St Paul's Church is the creeper-covered Gauci Tower, built in 1548 after Francesco Gauci's wife was kidnapped during a corsair raid. The effect is a little spoilt by electricity cables.

Għargħur

Back at Naxxar, do consider catching the No. 31 local bus just beyond the palazzo back to Valletta. It was pure chance that it took us past Għargħur which had taken my fancy from reading Vera Brittain's description of an outing there from St George's Hospital:

> In Gargar Ravine, a deep valley where the greenest grass in Malta was strewn with grey boulders of incalculable age, scarlet anemones and a dozen varies of vetch – yellow and mauve and cerise and orange and purple – sprang up beneath the old stumpy trees, with their dry, hollow trunks and dark, smooth leaves. The ravine must have been an ancient watercourse, for maidenhair fern grew in the damp crevices of the rocks and between the stones of the steps leading upwards to cultivated fields. The asphodels and oxalis were now over, but heavy masses of magenta clover, four times the size of the English variety, covered the ground, and mauve and pink gladioli held their slender, spiky heads erect in the warm scented air.

Much of inland Malta lacks scenic splendour but the Għargħur gorge, which was part of the British military's nineteenth-century Victoria Lines, and which we came across unexpectedly, is different, almost mysterious. Well worth a visit in the spring. The village of Għargħur itself has a long history; relevant to our story is its vulnerability to raids from the sea. Early houses were built with a secret room in which females would hide during those attacks. Exiles from Celano, described in Chapter 3, settled here in 1223 and built the *casal*'s oldest church, St John's.

When I mentioned Vera Brittain's account to artist Anna Grima, she gave me the lovely ink drawing of a girl tending her goats at Għargħur shown on the back cover.

20 – From Valletta to Mdina

Hamrun, Santa Venera and Birkirkara

For a newcomer, your best bet may be to take the northern tourist route on the Hop-On Hop-Off bus from Valletta. For the initiated, the local bus (51, 52) from the City Gate terminus works well. En route either way, you pass through Hamrun, Santa Venera and Birkirkara which, from the main road, is simply ribbon development from Valletta. There is no hopping on and off here, though you can, of course, from the local bus, but you would need to know where you are going to explore.

If you don't fancy venturing behind the main road, look out, as you pass, for a grand-looking building behind railings with an important gate. This was the **Vincenzo Bugeja Institute**, founded for poor girls in 1880 by the Marquis Bugeja and his wife Anna (Chapter 11). They are both buried in the San Vincenzo chapel in the grounds. The complex is now a ministry.

The institute is also bounded by Triq il-Kbira San Giusepp which contains two other historic sites. The Whitmore family's summer residence was the **Casa Leone Palace** and Gardens (also known as Palazzo Manoel, 1730). Here they entertained the new governor, the Marquis of Hastings, Lady Hastings and their daughters on the night of the Feast of St Venera some time after 1824 (Chapter 9). The gardens, now called Romeo Romano, were opened to the public in 1977. In the same street, Adelaide Cini set up the **Cini Institute**, as Chapter 11 describes, initially for unmarried mothers, some time after 1858. She is buried in the chapel there.

When Harry Luke was lieutenant governor, from 1930 to 1938, he lived in the Casa Leone with his wife **Joyce Luke** (née Fremlin, 1894–1973). She was on the advisory board of Cecilia de Trafford's Malta Industries Association until it became a company (Chapter 14). During the Lukes' occupation of the Casa, the Warren sisters (Chapter 15) put on several Malta Amateur Dramatic Club productions in the garden, including Shakespeare.

In 1903, Maria Teresa Nuzzo, who had earlier been a school teacher (Chapter 10), set up what became the Nuzzo Institute and founded Daughters of the Sacred Heart (Chapter 11). The headquarters and a school are in Triq S Frangisk, Hamrun.

Eighteenth-century baroque **St Helen's Parish Church**, Birkirkara, has no obvious woman connection beyond its name and the sketch overleaf by Cornelia Knight made in 1800 when she visited Malta with Nelson and Lady Hamilton at the time of French occupation (Chapter 8). It is worth seeing because this area looked rather different then. On Wednesdays and Fridays a large market surrounds the church.

Attard

The first major stop from Valletta is Attard where there are two unmissable places. The tourist bus drops you a few yards from the **San Anton Palace**

48.   St Helen's Church, Birkirkara by Cornelia Knight, from *Foudroyant* Sketchbook, courtesy of James Marshall and Marie-Louise Osborn Collection Beinecke Rare Book and Manuscript Library, Yale University

gates; the local bus does so on a parallel road, meaning that you have to rely on the driver telling you where to descend and then trot down a wide road, past the side of the Corinthia Palace Hotel – a useful pit stop – on your left, to the San Anton gates ahead.

After 1800, everyone who was anyone during the British period visited San Anton or stayed there. But it was built in 1623 by Fr Antoine de Paule as a summer retreat shortly before he became Grand Master, and there he entertained his mistress Flaminia Valenti (Chapter 6). You can see the wooden door through which she entered the grounds in the top right hand wall of the private part of the gardens, and if you go out of the back gate into St Anthony Street (Triq Sant'Antnin), and turn right until you reach No. 25, now private property, you will be in front of the villa he built for her. After de Paule's death in 1736, Flaminia entered the Maddalena and San Anton became the country residence of the Grand Masters.

Lady Hamilton and Cornelia Knight visited Captain Sir Alexander Ball there in 1800 when it was the headquarters of Maltese resistance against the French; Cornelia's sketch shows San Anton from a distance and how Attard, too, has changed. After Emma Hamilton, the most noteworthy guest was, in 1810, Lady Hester Stanhope who stayed there with her lover and entourage (Chapter 9). Of those who visited, Lady Grosvenor, in 1840, introduces us to an unexpected guest:

49.   San Anton by Cornelia Knight, from *Foudroyant* Sketchbook, courtesy of
the James Marshall and Marie-Louise Osborn Collection Beinecke Rare Book
and Manuscript Library, Yale University

We stopped, in passing at St Antonio, the governor's country house, the garden of which is pretty, with numbers of pepper trees and geraniums, but quite dried up by the heat, no effectual rain having fallen in Malta for three years. This place was then inhabited by the Emir of the Druses, with his wife and suite, who, having revolted from Mehemet Ali, had abandoned Mount Lebanon, and were about to proceed to Constantinople.

The Emir and his wife are out-of-the-ordinary denizens of San Anton. Their presence is best described by the 'governess' to Governor Bouverie's children quoted in Nicholas de Piro's *The Sovereign Palaces of Malta*. It was Bouverie who lent the Maronite Chief of Lebanon – not a nice man – and his wife the residence after a British man-of-war had brought him, his family and his suite from Sidon to Malta. She was not very impressed by 'Mrs Besheer' (Bechir):

The Emir's wife was said to be about 23 years old although the Emir himself was about 80 and had two pretty children about 6 and 9 years old. – Mrs Emir was a pretty pleasing woman richly dressed in a tunic of green velvet and trousers of white exquisitely embroidered in gold – a cap of red velvet sitting close to her head, and richly studded with jewels and a plait of brown hair crossed over her forehead – This sounds pretty and becoming, and might have been so had a little more neatness prevailed,

396 Women's Places (Itineraries)

but her skin looked unwashed, her hair uncombed, her fingers unfit to wear courtly ornaments and in short, her whole appearance denoted a Slovern who might have slept in her finery.

Lady Montefiore, who knew about these things, having often visited that part of the world, calls the young woman **Princess Báheeyát Eddoonyá** (Beauty of the World).

There were other royal inhabitants. The Connaughts lived there, and Lady Layard describes in her diary her stay with them in 1908. Queen Victoria's son, Alfred, Duke of Edinburgh, and his wife since 1874, **Grand Duchess Maria Alexandrovna of Russia** (1853–1920), lived there from 1886 to 1889 when he was Commander of the Mediterranean Fleet. Their daughter **Princess Marie** (1875–1938), later Queen of Romania, was 11 when they arrived and describes with nostalgia many years later their happy, if privileged, years at San Anton and in Malta in *The Story of My Life* (1934); of their first morning she writes:

Our bedroom opened out on to a wee stone flight of stairs leading into the garden. Half-way down those stairs was a little flat roof on to which you could step. The first look down from that roof into San Antonio gardens belongs to 'ecstasies' I can never forget. ...

After exploring the garden with her sister she continues,

... An enchanted world indeed. ... Fairyland!
Hand in hand Ducky and I stood looking down upon all this, amazed, speechless. It was a revelation, its perfect beauty actually made tears of emotion well up in our eyes.

It might be a bit over-blown, as was much of Marie's life, but the full account of her stay in Malta is nicely done. Ducky, then aged nine, was **Princess Victoria Melita** (1876–1939), born in Malta during their father's earlier Royal Navy posting, as her second name suggests, at San Anton. She was to become Grand Duchess of Hesse and the Rhine and later eloped with Grand Duke Kyril of Russia.

The large public gardens as you enter the main gate are worth visiting, particularly on a hot day, and you can walk through the concourse of the palace to the back gate, but not visit the interior of it, which is now the President's residence. I was particularly keen to see the Russian chapel and did manage, for the sake of this book, and much escorted, to do so.

Albert Abela in 'A Note about the Russian Chapel at San Anton Palace', contained in Elizaveta Zolina's book of essays, suggests that Maria Alexandrovna, Duchess of Edinburgh, a devout Orthodox Christian, worshipped in the chapel. Following their departure, it was known as the Russian Chapel, and was used again with that in mind when Dowager Empress Maria Feodorovna of Russia passed through Malta as a refugee in

50. Daughters of the Duke and Duchess of Edinburgh, San Anton,
1888: *left* Princess Marie; *right* Princess Victoria Melita,
from Van der Kiste, *Princess Victoria Melita*

1919 (Chapter 13). Lord Methuen's ADC, Captain Robert Ingham, noted in his diary that April:

All this week we continued to make everything more perfect in the Palace and fitted up an old Chapel, making it conform as far as possible to a Greek Orthodox Church. We had a simple but beautiful stone altar carved from the local soft stone, which took only a few days ...

In the chapel is an icon of St George presented by the first Russian woman pilot-cosmonaut, **General Valentina Tereshkova** (b.1937) in 1995, prompted by interest in the chapel by the President's wife, **Gemma Mifsud Bonnici** (née Bianco), and the efforts of **Dr Elizaveta Zolina** (d.2004), Director of the Russian Centre for Science and Culture.

Some royal visitors planted a tree to celebrate their stay. Maria Feodorovna, having planted the oak *Quercus Rober*, jabbed at the Kaiser's tree with her parasol and declared, 'Horrid man – why don't you pull it up?'

At the back gate of San Anton, turn left into St Anthony Street, cross over Lord Strickland Street, and continue. On the opposite side of the road, on your right, is the sign for Villa Bologna – the wedding present Fabrizio Grech had built in 1745 for his daughter Maria Teresa when, as recounted in Chapter 7, she married Nicola Perdicomati Bologna, 2nd Count della Catena.

At the beginning of the twentieth century, it was the home of Lord Strickland, 6th Count della Catena, his wife Edeline and their family, including Cecilia and Mabel (Chapter 14). Soon after the family's return from Gerald Strickland's postings abroad in 1918, Edeline died. His new wife, Margaret, came to live at the Villa in 1926. She was a keen gardener, and she was rich, so that the work she initiated, inside and out, was nothing but the best, and there the Stricklands entertained.

Gerald died before Margaret and, when she died in 1949, her step-daughter Cecilia, by then de Trafford, moved into the villa in 1951. Her earlier philanthropical and her political ventures are detailed in Chapters 14 and 16. In 1950 she decided to set up a pottery again and did so first in what had been her father's workshops. It moved to the stables after a few years and expanded.

Following Cecilia's death in 1982, most of her enterprises, already in decline because of local economic and political circumstances, ceased, in spite of her son Anthony's efforts to develop the weaving. But the pottery continued and, in 2009, her grandson Jasper de Trafford returned with his wife from London and took over management of pottery and Villa Bologna. Today, the shop at the villa thrives. **Annie** from Rabat, who was a weaver in Cecilia's Rabat weaving enterprise from 1954, serves in it. The grounds, open to the public, are available for events; Chapter 9 tells how, in 2013, Lady Flora Hastings' 'The Maltese Evening Song', composed some time after the governor and his family arrived in 1824, was performed there.

Lija

When, as a result of the changes at the Villa Bologna, Mabel Strickland had to find a new home, she chose Lija – which is not far by car from Attard. **Villa Parisio**, where she settled for the rest of her life, is in the little square that opens out from narrow Mabel Strickland Street. Given her larger than life nature and political activities, it is not surprising that untoward events occurred there, typified by one described by her biographer, Joan Alexander. The King of Sweden, Princess Alice and the Mountbattens had been invited for lunch,

> The time came to leave, and on these occasions the big double front doors were usually thrown open, but now the doors stuck and would not open. Princess Alice, who was slightly deaf, impatiently nudged Edwina inferring they should leave, not realising what had happened. On the other side of the door where the official cars waited the sailors began pushing, whilst

indoors the smart guests began pulling. This went on for some time until suddenly the doors gave way with a resounding crash sending the sailors flat on their faces and the royal guests flat on their backs. As with so many things connected with Mabel everyone was rolling about with laughter.

Princess Alice was probably Lord Mountbatten's sister, **Princess Andrew of Greece** (1885–1969)

Ta' Qali and the Aviation Museum

Mabel Strickland and Lija may have followed on naturally for the story, but it was a diversion: this itinerary is now back on the tour bus. Hop on outside the Corinthia Palace and hop off at the next stop, Ta'Qali Crafts Village and the Aviation Museum. Apart from any purchases you may wish to make at the former, it is the Museum that I direct you to because there you find the Memorial Garden to wartime heroine Henrietta Chevalier (Chapter 15).

Mosta and the Cumbo Tower

Back on the bus, descend again at Mosta, not to admire the historic dome of the cathedral that resisted wartime bombing but from there to walk for 20 minutes via Triq Kurat Calleja, into Triq I-Torri to the Cumbo Tower. From here, as Chapter 4 relates, the legendary Bride of Mosta, Marianna Cumbo, was kidnapped on her wedding morning in 1526 by Turkish corsairs.

51. Cumbo Tower, photograph by Caroline Bayly Scallon

The tower, attached to its walled villa, is on the outskirts of Mosta, but I approached it by car from another direction, without seeing other buildings, in some ways more atmospheric. It seemed to stand there, unprotected, vulnerable, in the open landscape. It is privately owned. I also arrived at the Gnien L-Gharus public gardens overlooking Mosta in the same way. Though named for the kidnapped bride, it did not catch my imagination.

Mdina and Rabat

Back on the tour bus, as you bowl along towards a walled city on a hill rising out of flat fields, it is time to get ready for medieval Mdina, the Melita of Roman times, Mdina (the Fortress) under the Arabs. Its story starts in Chapter 2.

The first time I saw Mdina, many years ago, was at night and we seemed to be the only people there. Not for nothing has it been known as the 'Silent City'. That is rather as Lady Grosvenor experienced it by day in 1840:

> We continued on our way to Città Vecchia, a small handsome city, six miles from Valetta, placed upon a rising ground near the centre of the island, with houses, like large palaces, of stone, solidly built, and much ornamented in the Vanburgh style; but the appearance of the town reminded me singularly of the city in the Arabian Nights, of which the inhabitants had been changed to stone – so grandly desolate and depopulated it seemed.

That is not how it is today, though it is still a must, even as you dodge tour groups in the main street. I suggest you read Chapters 3, and 5–7 to gain an overall impression of Mdina, its women, of course, its position before the arrival of the Knights in 1530, how it survived attacks by the Turks and how, in the time of the Knights, the Order sucked out its status. But it is still possible to reconstruct its importance through its places.

The Hop-On Hop-Off bus drops you in the gardens a few steps away from the **City Gate**, the local bus a little further away; you need to be alert because the driver may or may not remind you to descend. Once through this impressive entrance, look back up at it. On the right is a statue of patron saint St Agatha, beneath that is the Inguanez coat-of-arms, a family we met in Chapter 3 and are about to meet again.

A step away, bearing left is Villegaignon Street which runs the length of the town. The first place on the right hand side is **St Agatha Chapel**, built in 1417 by Paola Castelli, heiress to the Barony of Buqana, which she inherited from her mother Marguerita Murana, and *Capitano* and *Castellan* Francesco Gatto, 3rd Baron di Djar il Bniet (Chapter 3). It was badly damaged in the earthquake of 1693, but rebuilt.

Next to it is **St Peter's Church**, running through to the **Benedictine Nunnery**, of which it is a part, facing the parallel street, St Paul's. Margarita d'Aragona was responsible for the foundation of this complex (Chapter 3).

Chapter 5 tells how the nuns moved from Mdina to Birgu at the time of the 1565 Great Siege and their not entirely virtuous behaviour there. Chapter 11 introduces Maria Teresa Pisani, later Sister Maria Adeodata, who joined the community here in 1828 and was elected abbess in 1851 – not an easy task, as it turned out. It is still a closed order.

Opposite St Peter's in Villegaignon Street is the **Inguanez Palace**, home of Paola Castelli's daughter Imperia Gatto Inguanez who, when she married Antonio Inguanez in about 1421, united two of Mdina's most powerful families. What you see here is the servants' entrance and where the carriages entered. Walk a little further, turn left into Mesquita Street and you come to the grand front entrance, firmly closed because it is still lived in by the Inguanez family.

If Imperia was an important personage, and probably a strong woman, so was at least one of her descendants. Sir Harry Luke, lieutenant governor from 1930 to 1938 wrote of her and Maltese titles in *An Account and Appreciation of Malta* (1949):

There are twenty-nine of these Maltese peerages, most of them feudal grants by the Grand Masters but one of them going back as far as the year 1350. The holder of this venerable title and the *doyenne* of the Maltese Nobility for the unprecedented period of sixty-seven years before her deeply regretted death in 1947 was the Most Noble Mary Sceberras Trigona D'Amico Inguanez, twentieth Baroness in her own right of Diar-il-Bniet and Bukana and sixteenth Baroness, by a different descent, of Castel Cicciano.

But the Baroness was more than a string of titles: Governor Charles Bonham-Carter, who dealt with her both socially, often, and as a committee member (Chapter 14) records a flesh and blood woman. He introduces her on 26 April 1936:

On Saturday we dined with Luke and met Baroness Inguanez, the head of the Maltese nobility, a perfectly charming and very beautiful old lady who looks about fifty and is I suppose nearly seventy … a very pleasant evening.

She was 71. On 14 June that year he wrote, 'We have dined out twice, first on Friday with Baroness Inguanez – a charming party, beautifully done by a perfect hostess.' But she wasn't always perfectly charming: he had to record on 9 April 1937:

Dinner was a great success and everyone played up, the only contretemps was that Baroness Inguanez cut Baron de Piro d'Amico dead in the morning room. She really is a naughty old woman and I must tackle her about it. If she cannot leave her private enmities behind in my house, she shall not come here again.

52.   Baroness Mary Sceberras Trigona D'Amico
Inguanez, courtesy of Casa Rocca Piccola Trust

What caused the *froideur* one can only guess. They both had d'Amico blood, so it could have been a family feud, or they may have had political differences. He was a nationalist; she was the widow, since 1933, of a former British army officer, Colonel Alexander McKean. They met when he was ADC to the lieutenant governor, and military secretary, married in 1890 and he retired to Malta in 1898 (or 1908), becoming a member of the Maltese senate in 1923. The Inguanez coat-of-arms above the Mdina gate had been removed by the French – along with all titles – in 1798; the British re-installed the titles and, in 1886, when Mary reached her majority, the Inguanez coat-of-arms.

Swivel round and you are in Gatto-Murina Street at the back of what was the **Palazzo Gatto-Murina**. There is an entrance there; you can also go in from Villegaignon Street, but I'm afraid you are in for a bit of a disappointment: the tourist trade has taken it over. There is a café (Palazzo Gatto Murina Mdina Café) and a touristy shop, both empty of customers when I ventured in past a smoking assistant. 'How are the mighty fallen?' comes to mind. Neither Paola nor Imperia, nor even the Baroness, would be impressed.

On your right is St Paul Square and the **Cathedral**; it, too, was badly damaged by the earthquake, and rebuilt. Joan Alexander introduces us to one of the reasons for entering at the beginning of her biography:

Outside St Agatha's Chapel a fine drizzle blurred the mourners' faces, the outline of the coffin, and the edges of the honey coloured buildings of Mdina. Surreptitiously the occasional mourner shook open a black umbrella. A teasing wind slightly raised the mantillas of the women ...

... At an unbalancing but suitably slow pace the cortège moved past the Palazzo Inguanez, past Casa Testaferrata, the Banca Giuratale and Palazzo S. Sofia, until it reached St Paul Square, and crossed to the Cathedral entrance.

It was, of course, the 1998 funeral cortège of one of Malta's greatest *grandes dames*, Mabel Strickland or, as she was better known, 'Miss Mabel'. She is buried under a slab set into the floor immediately to your left as you enter the Cathedral. If you say what you have come for you won't have any fuss.

Back in Villegaignon Street, on the left, on the corner of **Triq San Pietru**, is a large marble Madonna and Child. The church and 'The Old Priory' at No. 3 belong to the Carmelites and are another of Margarita d'Aragona's foundations, though Cosmana Navarra contributed funds for the building of the church and monastery in 1660 (Chapter 6). Part of the priory is a museum and there is a quiet courtyard garden, but monks still live there. A French attempt to ransack the church in 1798 led to the Maltese insurrection against occupation (Chapter 8).

Back in the main street, on the right, is the thirteenth-century **Palazzo Falzon** (also known as the Norman House, though it is medieval), open to the public; but nowhere in its visitors' literature, or in guide books, can I find mention of either women in general or, in particular, Maria Teresa Navarra. But Claude Busuttil, in 'A Double Act for the "Norman House": Palazzo Falzon or Palazzo Cumbo-Navarra?' (1999) details the history of the house, including various women owners over the centuries, and also makes clear that it was from here that Maria Teresa Navarra eloped with Fra Samuele in 1754 (Chapter 7). So, if you do decide to tour the palazzo, at least think of her, though, unfortunately, she may have eloped from the Palazzo in Gudja later owned by Bettina Dorell.

At the end of the street, on the right, is a building of a different architecture called *Beaulieu*. This was the Benedictine St Scholastica nunnery before it moved over to Birgu in 1604 (see Chapter 18 itinerary). The front of the building looks out on to the bastion from which you get a marvellous panoramic view of the island stretching to the sea. I can't help thinking that it was here that the Benedictine nuns processed round Bastion Square in 1551 with their image of St Agatha held aloft and cowed the besieging Turks below into retreating (Chapter 5).

A less fortunate street scene occurred, as Chapter 4 relates, in 1545 when Paula Kibeylet, concubine of a cleric, was 'sentenced to be led on an ass through the public thoroughfares of Mdina and Rabat ... and to be whipped'.

From Bastion Square, too, looking over to the ridge opposite to the left, you can see **Mtarfa** (Imtarfa) **Military Hospital**. VAD Vera Brittain was taken there when, arriving in Malta to nurse in October 1916, she was so ill. She rather pleasingly describes the women doctors who treated her (Chapter 13). During the Second World War, Maltese VAD Meme Cortis nursed there (Chapters 14 and 15), and colonel's wife, Florence May Hamilton, died there of injuries received during a bombing raid. You can get to the Mtarfa itself if you stay on the local bus, No. 51, on which you travelled to Mdina. After a wait of a few minutes it does a turnaround here. Archaeological finds have been excavated on Mtarfa Ridge (Chapter 2).

If after all that you are hungry for lunch, and if you are with someone who needs to sit out the sites while sipping prosecco and waiting for you, we find the **Trattoria AD1530** on the ground floor of the Xara Palace Relais and Chateaux (hotel) in St Paul Street and facing the Museum of Natural History, fits the bill. From the cathedral you turn left. The hotel itself is said to be 'exclusive' with, I believe, a restaurant upstairs to match. Lunch apart, the baroque **Palazzo Xara** was built in 1624 for Baroness Xara, a member of the Moscato Parisio family. The palazzo was converted into a hotel in 1949 by Mabel Strickland, but needed restoration under new ownership in 1995.

After lunch, wiggle round to the right to the nearby main gate or, if you are at Bastion Square, make your way back to the main gate, out into the gardens and, bearing right, you will reach Rabat in a few steps. Go straight through the wide square, with gardens to the right and, at the end, facing you, is the Roman *Casa Domus*. Malta was, as Chapter 2 relates, Roman for seven centuries. *Casa Domus* is your best chance to gain even an inkling of how Roman women, rich ones at least, probably of the mercantile class, lived at some stage, probably 125–75 BC.

In the modern lobby, just through the turnstile, is a large, headless statue of Astarte, indicating continuing Punic influence. The *casa* is noted for its fine mosaics, one of them a satyr being attacked by two women or nymphs. One of the marble heads is probably Antonia the Younger, and a headless statue may be of (Claudia) Antonia. Bone hairpins are also displayed.

Leaving the *Casa Domus*, bear right and turn down St Paul Street. In passing, should you need a pit stop or, indeed, an unexpected place for lunch, don't turn up your nose at the **Rising Sun Bar** on the right of the street. You will see why.

Further down on the right is the **Cosmana Navarra Restaurant** which is where we had expected to lunch but it was overwhelmed with bus tour clientele. This was a pity because, as Chapter 6 suggests, Cosmana, whose house this was, dominates this part of Rabat. She had built the parish church, **St Paul's**, which is in the square upon which the restaurant fronts. From her house she could watch the construction progress of years. She is buried in the side chapel of the church with her coat-of-arms above. This is not totally accessible: it seems to form part of a tour of the St Paul Catacombs beneath, which starts in the Wignacourt Musem. I eschewed the tour but, citing this book, was allowed to race upstairs in the Museum to view the portrait of Cosmana in Chapter 6.

More interesting than the St Paul's Catacombs, famous though they may be, are those of Sicilian-born St Agatha whose time in Malta is described in Chapter 2. From the exit on the left furthest away from the church in Parish Square is St Agatha Street. On the left of that is another entrance to St Paul's Catacombs; opposite that is a locked gate saying St Agatha – ignore it. Further on, on the right, are the **St Agatha Catacombs**, museum and church. Here Agatha took refuge for some months in AD 249. It is just as likely, I suggest, that early seeds of Christianity were sown in Malta by her as by St Paul.

The grotto tour takes about 20 minutes and includes not only frescoes of St Agatha, and other women saints such as St Lucy and St Barbara, but also evidence of a Jewish community in Rabat, in particular an inscription indicating the burial of Eulogia, an elder of the Synagogue in her own right in the fourth or fifth century. It can be hot down there, and a bit claustrophobic. In the museum upstairs there is an alabaster statue of St Agatha, martyred on her return to Sicily. Inside the church is another statue of her, said to have been what was paraded by the Benedictine nuns round Bastion Square when the Turks were besieging the walled city in 1551.

You might assume that the **Lunziata** (Annunciation) **Church**, Rabat, is but a step away. Funded by a bequest in Margarita d'Aragona's will, and attached to her country estate at San Leonardo (Chapter 6), it is not so easy to track down, and is a good mile away. I failed to get there but Caroline Scallon, whose photograph this is, did it for me by car and also advises

53. Annunciation Church, Rabat, photograph by Caroline Bayly Scallon

taking the Rabat-Dingli bus, No. 52, via Barka. People do hike there, as information on the internet suggests, and the rector might open the church for you. Marriages can be held and it is here that a new altar was provided by Marietta Bonello in 1644 (Chapter 6). Margarita's estate became a Carmelite monastery attached to the one in St Peter Street, Mdina; it is now a Carmelite House of Prayer and retreat centre.

You can now catch the 52 bus back to Rabat, Mdina or Valletta or, if you have stayed in Rabat, the 51 or 52 back to Valletta from the garden side of the square; alternatively, if you are on the northern tour you can hop on the bus going in the opposite direction.

21 – Archaeological Sites

Ħal Saflieni Hypogeum and Tarxien Temples

While the Chapter 20 itinerary takes advantage of the 'North Tour' sightseeing bus, supplemented by local buses, this itinerary makes most use of the 'South Tour'. The first archaeological stop is Tarxien where there are two sites: the Ħal Saflieni Hypogeum – or underground burial vault – and the Tarxien Temples, the historical setting for both of which is in Chapter 1. You have to book for a guided tour of the Hypogeum in advance, to limit numbers and thus minimise damage. It is in Burial Street, Paola, which from the Hop-On Hop-Off bus means going back and turning to the left. Get off at the same stop for the Tarxien Temples, but they are a fair walk back – turn to the right and find Neolithic Temples Street. It was not adequately signposted from the main road when we went; press the driver for precise directions and remember how to get back to the stop!

I exhausted my liking for caves in Crete, so have not visited the Hypogeum, but it is said to be special. It is from the Saflieni period, 3300–3000 BC, and the most fascinating archaeological find was the so-called 'Sleeping Lady', given pride of place in the Valletta Archaeological Museum and in literature.

Underground burial sites lend themselves to mystery and myth; the Hypogeum is no exception. One of the stories is more 'concrete' than the other because Harry Luke quotes in full the letter he received in the 1930s from two English women – their names discreetly withheld – passing through Malta on a steamer:

Sir,

Miss ___ and I visited the Hypogeum last Saturday morning at 11 a.m. We were taken down by a guide to join other visitors from our ship (the P. and O. s.s. *Balranald*) and, after finishing the last bit of their tour with them, we were asked by the guide to stay down there while he let them out.

We waited about five minutes, and then, as time was short, began to explore by ourselves. We had gone nearly as far as it is possible to go, and had reached the end of the pathway leading to the 'Holy of Holies,' when the lights were turned out and we heard the entrance door at the top shut and bolted. We called immediately very loud, and when no answer came realised it had been done intentionally and that we were in a pretty serious predicament.

After a very horrible twenty minutes spent groping about in the pitch darkness we found steps leading up to a room, in the farther corner of which was a glimmer of light. Eventually we arrived at the staircase and daylight.

At the top we tried to open the doors with two keys hanging on the wall, but finding them useless we waved them out of the bars of the doors and shouted our hardest to a girl leaning out of the window of a house opposite. She saw us quite soon and came running across. The three of us pulling together forced the doors open, and at the same moment the guide appeared from a door at the side. We took no notice of his gesticulations, but went straight back to the bus and to the ship.

I enclose our entrance tickets and an order for five shillings which we should like given to the girl who came to help us, if she can be found. She was fairly tall, with dark bobbed hair, and was dressed in green. She could not talk any English.

Hoping we are not troubling you unnecessarily, and hoping also that anything of the sort may be prevented happening in the future,
We remain,
Your obedient servants,
[two signatures]

Luke traced the girl in the green dress, and gave her the 5 shillings but, writing his book years later, he could recall no other follow-up. I think I can work out what might have happened, but I leave it to you!

The other story concerned either a Miss Lois Jessup who worked for the British Embassy (there would have been no British Embassy in Malta; perhaps it was that in Rome) or a Mrs Constance Lois Jessop from New York – this in an account from the *National Geographic*. On a first tour to the Hypogeum, Lois saw some ghostly 'tall humanoids' processing in a layer beneath her. She made a second visit after 30 children and their teacher(s) had disappeared in the same passage that she had explored. But a new guide denied all knowledge. She noticed there had been a cave-in. Mothers could hear their children screaming but could not tell where from. It is perfectly safe to visit the Hypogeum today; although archaeologists found buried there the bones of 6,000 or so people from the Ħal Saflieni period, the only ghosts will be in your imagination.

The Tarxien Temples are quite different: their excavated remains are all above ground. The most striking find there was the lower half of a statue of a large figure known as a 'fat lady'. A replica is in place, and a reconstruction of the original is in the Valletta Archaeological Museum. The controversy surrounding the sex of so-called 'fat ladies' is explored in Chapter 1. One of the terracotta figures Sara A Rich allies to midwifery in Neolithic Malta came from a rubbish dump outside the Tarxien Temple complex, and Diana Woolner found the graffiti of ships on a slab in one of the temples.

Tas-Silġ

The next archaeological stop of the bus is Għar Dalam but, as far as this itinerary is concerned, there are two sites before it, both of which I visited by car with a driver. The tour bus narration airily pointed out that 'over there' was once a temple of Juno. It meant Tas-Silġ on a slight incline just north-east of the fishing village of Marsaxlokk.

This site was not open to the public in the autumn of 2013, but a newspaper article suggested that it was only a question of time. In the meantime, you can request entry from Heritage Malta; but I found it possible to see the site without going in. Before you get to it, the little church – Our Lady of Snows (Madonna ta' Tas-Silġ) – is easier to spot. Bettina Dorell's daughter, named on the plaque outside as Angiolina Muscat Cassia Dorell, had it built in 1834, replacing an earlier one (Chapter 7). The text continues, 'The church had a small palace built next to it and the Marchioness left in her will that whoever decided to continue to provide spiritual services in the church would benefit from the property, fields and the palace she left.' Today, the palace is a monastery, but weddings can be held in the church

With the church on your right, don't go straight ahead, which seems the more obvious route, but slightly swivel and turn up to the left and, keeping left, you will find the archaeological site is then on both sides of the road. The Temple of Juno is, as Chapter 2 recounts, that connected with the Roman Verres; but there is a Phoenician layer beneath and a temple to Astarte, as Italian teams, including women archaeologists, have discovered. Other finds include murex shells used for dyeing cloth which links this site to the next on this itinerary. Neolithic finds, mostly pottery shards, have been excavated beneath the Phoenician layer, including a 'fat figure'.

Birżebbuġa, Borġ in-Nadur and Għar Dalam

Of these three places, the Hop-On Hop-Off bus only stops at Għar Dalam. The adventurous could probably hike back to Birżebbuġa; or the local bus from Valletta (82, 85) is an option; mine was again a car.

The earliest Sicilians to arrive, in about 5000 BC, did so in the Birżebbuġa area, and the earliest finds of their presence are linked to Għar Dalam (Cave of Darkness). Chapter 1 tells of the women who lived there in Neolithic times and the women archaeologists, led by Margaret Murray, who excavated, starting in 1920.

The archaeologists stayed first at the Sailors' Hotel in Birżebbuġa. Of their 1923 visit, Gertrude Caton-Thompson, who appears first in the Introduction, writes of them renting a house there:

Only two bedrooms were available (the third we needed for store), so Dr Guest and I made the best of each other. The room by night was largely occupied also by fleas and mosquitos. What struck us as interesting was that all the fleas came to me and the mosquitos to her. We exchanged the position of beds standing in diagonally opposite corners to see what happened. Just the same. We fell to argument. She maintained that biologically we must belong to different blood groups: I maintained entomologically that mosquitos and fleas were as incompatible to each other as black to whites. We never got the answer.

It is revealing that as recently as the 1920s someone who, when older, was to become a leading archaeologist, could make such an unscientific assumption about racial differences. Margaret Murray and Edith Guest excavated the Bronze Age site Borġ in-Nadur, Gertrude at Għar Dalam.

Claudia Sagona drew Birżebbuġa and Borġ in-Nadur and, indeed, Tas-Silġ together in her article about cloth dyeing detailed in Chapter 2. The dyeing pits were on the foreshore at Birżebbuġa and in Borġ in-Nadur, the murex shells were found at Tas-Silġ. It is fair to assume that women were involved in many of the processes of the textile industry.

Earlier than the Murray excavations, Elizabeth Douglas Van Buren excavated a Roman villa near Borġ in-Nadur with Thomas Ashby in 1915 (Chapter 2). Although Ta' Kaccatura is not open to the public, you can watch a satisfying YouTube exploration of it. Elizabeth seems to be the earliest woman archaeologist in Malta, though governor's wife Helen Smyth attended Anetto Caruana's excavations at Ghajn Klieb between 1890 and 1892 (Chapter 2), and Donna Luisa Strickland those of Albert Mayr at Mnajdra in 1901 (Chapter 1).

As you enter Birżebbuġa, there is a sign; take the turning right up a small hill and wiggle round to the left and you come to the fence around Borġ in-Nadur (Fortress on the Nadur Hill). Once again, you could approach Heritage Malta to enter, or you could view from the gate.

Tamara Marks and her husband lived in airforce accommodation in Birżebbuġa at the beginning of the Second World War (Chapter 15).

Għar Dalam and its museum are on the main road, the next Hop-Off stop after Marsaxlokk, and open to the public.

Ħagar Qim and Mnajdra

These sites are said to be in Qrendi, but they are within the boundary of the village and the Hop-Off bus drops you on their doorstep. A church in Qrendi and the nearby Maqluba depression are in Chapter 22 itinerary. If you were travelling by car, it would make sense to do them all together. A local bus is also an option.

Excavation started at Ħagar Qim, which dates from the Tarxien period (3000–2500 BC), in 1839 and it was assumed for some time to be Phoenician; indeed, those travellers who rushed to see this marvel thought that it was. Lady Frances Egerton wrote in 1840:

> One afternoon we devoted to a ride to Crendi where there are some lately discovered and most curious Phoenician remains, wholly unaccounted for and incomprehensible. They have more similarity to Stonehenge than any other place I have seen but they are unlike that.

At much the same time, Lady Grosvenor wrote of finds she had seen in the public library, which predated the Archaeological Museum:

Here ... are placed the wonderful little idols, lately discovered at Crendi, eight miles from Valletta and supposed to be Phoenician; they are about the size and shape of some of the fat Chinese porcelain monsters, but made of stone, about six inches high, and headless. By the appearance of the holes in which the heads were fixed, they must have been of metal. The ruins in which they were found, were only lately discovered, in the middle of a bare plain, and partaking of the Druidic character, are curious and inexplicable.

And **Isabella Romer** (1798–1852), English novelist and travel writer, wrote of the excavations in *A Pilgrimage to the Temples and Tombs of Egypt, Nubia and Palestine in 1845–6* (1846) that they 'brought to light the remains of what is supposed to have formed part of either a Phoenician Temple, or a place of sepulture ...'. And **Eliza Gardner** (1820–1878) called her drawing, seen here, 'Phoenician ruins, Crendi'. She was married to William Bethell Gardner of the Royal Horse Artillery, and they seem to have arrived in Malta in 1847. Their infant son Alexander was buried in the Msida Bastion Cemetery in 1848. Together the couple produced *A Series of Views in Malta* (1852), she the drawings, he the text. The headless 'Venus of Malta', whose sex is definite, was found at Ħagar Qim and several 'fat' figures whose sex is open to discussion (Chapter 1).

Mnajdra is 480 yards due west of Ħagar Qim, down a paved slope towards the sea. Its three structures, the excavation of which started in 1840, are smaller and better preserved – discounting vandalism in 2000 which has been repaired. The upper structure dates from the Ġgantija phase

54. Phoenician Ruins, Crendi (Ħaġar Qim) by Eliza Gardner, from *A Series of Views in Malta*, courtesy of Yale Center for British Art Paul Mellon Collection (file no. 2038523-0002)

(3600–3200 BC). One interpretation, reported by Juliet Rix, is that the plan of one of these temples 'suggests a primeval form with the worshippers entering the womb-like entrance in a rite of fertility'. The second figurine from which Sara Rich drew her conclusions for 'Midwifery and Neolithic Malta' (Chapter 1) was found here.

This is the last archaeological stop on the South Tour route.

Mġarr

The North Tour, which you may have made use of from Valletta to Mdina, has one more archaeological stop, Mġarr. You may need to be quite keen to get off, though this area is important archaeologically and, as Juliet Rix notes, there is a good restaurant in the village.

The Skorba site, excavated in the 1960s, is linked to the Grey Skorba Phase (4400–4300 BC) and the Red (4400–4100 BC). From the Mġarr Phase (3800–3600 BC) evidence of huts and, therefore, a Neolithic village, have been found. From both phases recognisably female figurines have emerged. I suggest how women may have lived then in Chapter 1. Parts of the site are behind wire netting, others are in private, farming, hands. The situation may change, as may archaeological finds. It is worth monitoring these online when planning a visit.

Archaeological Museum, Valletta

This very easy to spot museum in Republic Street is in continual development and, thus, improvement. You may be disappointed if particular figures are at exhibitions abroad, as the 'Sleeping Lady' from the Saflieni Hypogeum was in the autumn of 2013. But she was back the following year and is really very special, lying there in a room of her own. Make sure you peer round and look at her back, and note the traces of red ochre. You can get replicas of her, sometimes in the museum shop, but I decided against in the end. A better representation is contained in the wonderful photographs by Daniel Cilia in Isabelle Vella Gregory's *The Human Form in Neolithic Malta*.

Other finds that should be there include the colossal statue from Tarxien, and the headless 'Venus of Malta' from Ħagar Qim; look at her back, too. There is a headless Ħagar Qim group and Red Skorba figurines. There is a case of Tarxien heads – note the hairstyles and features – and little Tarxien figures pointing to different parts of their anatomy. There are jewellery and ornaments – for example of shells and teeth – from various places, found mainly with burial remains. Since my last visit, the rooms upstairs contain Bronze Age and Phoenician/Carthaginian finds. The museum continually develops what it exhibits.

22 – Round and About

This itinerary comprises places that don't fit into other itineraries and probably require independent travel by local bus or by car. An order of some sort was required; it is determined by a semi-meaningless topographical arc.

Paola – Santa Maria Addolorata Cemetery

If you are visiting the Tarxien Temples and the Ħal-Saflieni Hypogeum independently (Chapter 21 itinerary), you may want to include the Addolorata in your visit. Paola (Pawla) is a seventeenth-century town tacked on to the north edge of Tarxien, and the address of the cemetery is Vjal Santa Lucija, Paola. If you follow the signs to the airport it is clearly visible.

There have been nearly 300,000 burials there so you need to know in advance what you are looking for, either by going online or enquiring at the information office. The first burial was of a 'beggar' from Naxxar, Anna Magro, in 1872. You may want to visit the grave of Christina Ratcliffe if you have been taken with the story of her life in Malta told in Chapters 14 and 15 and Chapter 17 itinerary. Frederick Galea has taken the trouble to provide coordinates for her grave: East Division, Section MA-D, Grave No. 4. Inscribed on the headstone is 'Christina of George Cross Island'. Henrietta Chevalier (Chapters 15 and 20) is also buried here, as is the nurse of the Hastings/Henry family (Chapter 9), Elizabeth Bonomo.

Luqa

The village of Luqa was not always overtaken by an airport and, since the building of the nearby Malta International, it is returning to some semblance of its past though one still talks of Luqa airport, even of the newer one. Chapter 6 tells of the women from Luqa who helped build Valletta following the Great Siege of 1565. Chapter 7 tells of Maria Caruana, widow of Luqa, who inherited her husband's quarry and was successfully managing it in 1737.

Rosanne Dingli's *Death in Malta* (2001) is a mystery set near Luqa and near the limestone quarries. An Australian writer has rented a farmhouse in the hopes of overcoming writer's block. As well as trying to solve the mystery of some large wine jars, he falls in love with a Maltese woman and has to deal with the remnants of his marriage in Australia while maintaining links with his daughter. A good read for coming in to land, or taking off.

Gudja

Gudja is on a slight hill hard by the airport and, indeed, overlooks it. It is not hard to spot Bettina's Palazzo: it stands proudly on the main road between Gudja and Ghaxaq. It is known as Palazzo Dorell or Palazzo or

Villa d'Aurel. Some sources say that Bettina built it in 1770, others date it to before her time. What is clear is that, as Chapter 7 relates, she lavished great care, and money, on her summer place, particularly the gardens.

Bettina does not seem to have been in Malta, in spite of suggestions to the contrary, when the British Army took over her palazzo as their headquarters during the French occupation, 1798–1800. Emma Hamilton and Cornelia Knight visited General Thomas Graham there with Nelson in 1800 – a visit which Cornelia briefly describes (Chapter 8). There is a suggestion that Napoleon stayed there, but that is unlikely: he did stay in the Palazzo Parisio, Merchant Street, Valletta. But the Palazzo does vie with the Palazzo Falzon in Mdina as that from which Maria Teresa Moscati-Falsoni-Navarra eloped in 1754 (Chapter 7), thus contradicting its date of construction.

In 1830, Bettina paid to have the roof of the nearby fifteenth-century church of Santa Marija Ta'Bir Miftuh repaired. A fresco on the north wall of a woman in early sixteenth-century dress holding a lily may be the portrait of a benefactor from the Bonici family whose emblem is a lily. The medieval church is on the Luqa–Gudja road and almost overtaken by the airport.

Qrendi

Consider stopping in Qrendi if you are visiting the nearby archaeological sites of Ħagar Qim and Mnajdra independently. The thirteenth-century chapel **Tal-Hniena** (our Lady of Mercy or Our Lady of Ransom, also known as Chiesa Della Misericordia) on the south-east of the village was rebuilt in 1650. Its attraction for this itinerary is that it contains the painting 'Christ's Crucifixion', attributed to Suor Maria de Dominici (Chapter 6). The chapel was firmly closed, not to say deserted, when I visited. There were, apparently, no mass times available.

A short and easy walk from Qrendi is the **Maqluba Depression** caused, probably in 1343, by a collapse of the underlying limestone strata, either by a violent storm or an earthquake. Not surprisingly, a myth grew up. A group of bad people were living in the new hamlet. God warned them, through a virtuous woman, to mend their ways, but they took no notice. So God made the earth swallow the hamlet and all save the good woman.

Fawwara

Formally in the Siġġiewi area, but right on the Gebel (Garden) Ciantar heights overlooking the sea is **Our Lady of Carmel**, first built in 1616 at a time of severe drought by Girolama Ciantar; a spring then emerged from the rocks. Girolama was introduced in Chapter 6 concerning the setting up of the Ciantar Foundation and the funding of the Maddalena. Nearby is the **Annunciation Church,** rebuilt in 1708 by Maria Xerberras.

Fawwara is, it seems from the internet, the sort of place you hike to in order to explore this area of the island, partly wild cliff tops, partly well-cultivated fields.

Girgenti, Buskett Gardens and Verdala Palace

In the fertile Girgenti valley, close to Siġġiewi, is the Prime Minister's summer residence, known as both the **Inquisitor's Summer Palace** and the Girgenti Palace. Though it is occasionally open to the public, perhaps it is only worth noting if you are passing by. It was built by an Inquisitor in 1625 and became, thereafter, the summer residence of the Inquisitors. It is there, rumour had it, that Inquisitor Angelo Durani regularly took married Bettina Dorell whose daughter, Angela, was christened in his Birgu palace chapel (Chapter 7 and Chapter 18 itinerary).

In 1827, Judith Montefiore and her husband held a dinner party in what was then the lieutenant governor's summer place, to thank the silk-workers (Chapter 10). On 30 January 1839, the account of Queen Adelaide's stay in Malta records that:

> The Queen, accompanied by the greater part of her suite, drove to the Inquisitor's Palace, the country residence of Mr Greig, the Secretary to the Government. ...
>
> Her Majesty was much pleased with the scenery in that neighbourhood, and with the grounds and garden of the *Gran Fontana* which adjoin the house, and the day being one of those fine mild days for which the winter season in Malta is remarkable, with a clear and transparent atmosphere that gives life and vivacity to every object, the Queen had a full opportunity of observing the verdure and beauty which the island presents at this season of the year.
>
> After partaking of luncheon, the Queen and party left the Inquisitor's about 3 p.m.

The whole record of the Queen's Malta visit is said to be the notes of her host at the palace, Sir Hector Grieg. He noticeably wrote that entry from happy experience.

North of the palace are the **Buskett Gardens** (il-Buskett – Boschetto – Little Wood). Where mulberry trees were planted in the nineteenth century for the silk experiment (Chapter 10) is now a public park, continuing the function described by the Duke of Buckingham following his 1828 visit (except that there are now cafés and pizzerias): 'Here on the feast of St John, all the natives of Malta come in picnic parties and the most of them, especially the old people, wear the dresses they were married in which they carefully preserve for this purpose and day.' Today, you can hold your wedding, or other event there. For a simple outing to get away from the heat and enjoy trees, as the Maltese have done for generations, take a local bus, continuing from Rabat.

As you drive up to the Buskett Gardens, you can see the **Verdala Palace**, built in 1586 as a country retreat for the Grand Master. It is now that of the president, and only open to the public for a charity ball in August. Like the Grey Lady ghost at San Angelo, Birgu, Verdala has its Blue Lady, said

55.   Verdala Palace by Eliza Gardner, from *A Series of Views in Malta*, courtesy of Yale Center for British Art Paul Mellon Collection (file no. 2038523-0001)

to have been the niece of Grand Master de Rohan. She rejected the suitor chosen for her so was imprisoned in her room. Trying to escape through the window, she fell to her death. Several people over the centuries have experienced her presence.

Lady Layard, staying with the Duke and Duchess of Connaught at San Anton in 1908, wrote in her journal on 29 November:

At 3.30 the D and Dss drove me in their motor to Verdala to see the Governor's summer palace. We passed thro' Notabile [Mdina]. We found the Govr and Lady Grant waiting to receive the Connaughts. The Palace is a sort of medieval strong tower in a pine wood – built abt 1583 by G. Master Verdala & most picturesque. It is surrounded by a moat now made into a garden – & has terraces going down the side of the hill. The interior consists of one large hall surrounded by rooms on each side & 4 small towers at the 4 corners – The rooms on this floor have all wagon roof ceilings. The 2nd floor was added by Pinto & the ceilings are square. We went by the winding staircase on to the roof wh is flat & made of big slabs of stone. From there the view is magnificent – One can see the sea at intervals all the way round & one realizes that one is on a not very large island.

You may not be able to have the same experience, but there is a pleasing YouTube tour of the palace and Buskett Gardens.

Żebbuġ

My main reason for visiting Żebbuġ was the parish church which contains two paintings by Maria de Dominici (Chapter 6). We went easily by local bus (62; from the stop you wiggle round to your left to St Philip's Square).

Like most churches, **St Philip's** has its hours and we had to hang around until 6 pm. With permission to enter the Sacristy, I found Maria's 'Visitation' easily enough, though not hung to its advantage. The 'St John of the Cross' eluded me, but I have since learnt from the parish priest that it is in store and exhibited during the feast of St Philip that starts on the second Sunday in June.

Further down the main street is the church of **San Rocqe**. As Chapter 6 recounts, in 1592 plague hit Malta. Katerina Vassalo and her husband Tomas vowed that they would build the church if Żebbuġ were spared, which it was, and they did. They also bequeathed a nearby field so that produce could be sold to pay for an annual celebration of Holy Mass on the French saint's feast day. Żebbuġ, meaning Olives, produced them in Roman times, and the town was later famous for sailcloth made from locally grown cotton (Chapter 10). Restoration of the church was completed in 2007. On the outskirts of Żebbuġ is the little church of **Tal-Hlas**, dedicated to mothers in labour.

On her way back from visiting the Inquisitor's Palace, Queen Adelaide 'stopped a short time at *Casal Zebbug* where the clergy of the parish were in waiting to receive her at the church, surrounded by the numerous population of the *Casal*'.

Castello Zammitello

You could catch a bus to Mġarr, then change to one taking you to Gnejna Bay, or you could walk the half mile from Mġarr. It would fit in well if you planned to visit the Skorba archaeological site (Chapters 1 and 21). More than one guide book suggests that this castle was built in the nineteenth century; they are mistaken: it dates from the seventeenth century and its story should be read with that of the Cumbo Tower in Chapters 4 and 20, for it was from here, it is said, that Lucia, only daughter of Baron Bernado Zammit, disappeared from her bedroom on the morning of her wedding to a rich, elderly Sicilian count. The castle is now a wedding venue! Don't forget the Gauci Tower near Naxxar with its Turkish corsair kidnap connection.

56.   Castello Zammitello, photograph by Caroline Bayly Scallon

Selmun Palace

There are three places either to visit or observe from a distance on the way to catch the Gozo ferry. Dominating the landscape – the hill and the Mistral Valley – as you pass St Paul's Bay and drive towards Mellieħa, is the fortified Selmun Palace. In her heyday, it was owned by Caterina Vitale and it and the surrounding lands are what, in 1619, she bequeathed to the *Monte di Redenzione degli Schiavi*. In the nearby chapel, dedicated to Our Lady of Ransom, is the portrait of Caterina by Antoine Favray (Chapter 6). Selmun was at one time a hotel and it would be easy to be misled on the internet that it is still so. Its future is, I gather, yet to be decided. There is a short but useful YouTube look at the outside.

Mellieħa

Mellieħa, also on a hill, is a popular resort town leading down to a beach. But it also contains two chapels, or sanctuaries, dedicated to the Madonna. **Our Lady of the Grotto** (il Madonna Tal-Għar) is an underground chapel where believers pray for intervention for their sick child, and the walls are hung with children's clothes and letters of supplication or thanks. The nearby **Sanctuary of Our Lady of Melleiħa** is the oldest Marian shrine in Malta. The rock painting of the Madonna is attributed to St Luke from when he and St Paul are said to have been shipwrecked nearby. But the style dates somewhere between the twelfth and the fourteenth centuries. The marine archaeologist, Honor Frost, found evidence of Roman shipping in the bay (Chapter 18).

St Agatha's Tower

Further on towards the ferry terminal, this time on the left, on the Marfa Ridge, is St Agatha's Tower, also known as the Red Tower, for obvious reasons. It was built in 1647–48, and dedicated to the martyred saint believed to have saved Mdina in 1551 (Chapters 2, 5 and 20); it had a St Agatha chapel set into an alcove. It has been restored and is open to the public – worth it for the view over Għadira Bay and the wetland and saltland **Wild Life Sanctuary** run by Birdlife Malta, where hunting of the migrating birds is prohibited. It is a bit of a climb up steps to reach the tower from the carpark, but there are those who walk it from Mellieħa Bay.

A little further from the tower, and it is only a 20 minute ferry ride to Gozo – not counting queuing time!

23 – Gozo

Introduction

The only time we went on an organised tour was to Gozo. It was not ideal: we neither visited all the places on their itinerary, nor saw all the places I wanted for mine. Of course, as a tourist, you can go independently. There is now a reasonable local bus service and Juliet Rix, *Malta and Gozo* (2013) provides a map of its routes. The order of places in this itinerary is historical, rather than topographical or tour ordained. The island is small enough – 9 by 4½ miles (14 by 7km) – for that to be practical.

Gozo is said to be rather different from Malta, quieter, more rural, its own island, with its own pockets of history and its own culture. The subtleties of the different cultures within the Maltese archipelago are epitomised by this finding by LH Dudley Buxton from 'Personal and Place Names in Malta' (1921):

> In Malta, if a man marries, his wife adopts the family nickname. For example, if he is called Tal Naxaro, she will become Tal Naxaro also. In Gozo, however, the husband, when he marries, adopts the nickname of his wife's family, in other words the sur-nickname of his mother-in-law.

The difference in tempo is confirmed by the fact that, to get away from it all, many Maltese and several British and other Europeans have holiday homes there. But many visitors go just for the day, and going with a tour group prevents a full appreciation of what Gozo has to offer.

The record of Queen Adelaide's stay in Malta states only: 'Saturday, 30 March 1839. The Queen, accompanied by the Governor, the Lieutenant Governor, Admirals Stopford and Louis, boards the *Firefly* to visit Gozo.'

We would be none the wiser about the details of this visit if it were not for Royal Navy surgeon Edward Cree and, particularly, a delicious watercolour – 'Queen Adelaide and the royal cortège in Gozo' – in both his original journal in the Royal Maritime Museum, Greenwich, and Michael Levien's *The Cree Journal*. But there was more than the image, as Cree's always colourful account suggests:

> We all mustered in full dress to receive her. As soon as her suite of about twenty were on board we started out of harbour with the royal standard at the main. The weather was fine but wind NW and we did not go very fast. I was introduced to Sir David Davies, the Queen's Physician, who asked me to give a dose of quinine to the Countess of Sheffield, one of the Queen's ladies – a beautiful woman.
>
> We got to Gozo about 2 p.m. and landed at Fort Chambray under a royal salute. All the conveyances on the island were only three calashes – one of which the Queen occupied. There were two or three horses and all

the rest of the suite were mounted on donkeys, and off they set, a motley crowd. Smith, Moore and I soon followed on donkeys.

Cree and his mates then hived off on their own, but he continues,

> After a little refreshment we had to return as fast as we could to get to the ship before the Queen and her party. At a turn of the road we fell in with the whole party, and old Smith's donkey, which was a long-legged, bony beast, took it into his head to stop in the middle of the road in front of the royal cortège and bray and commit other unpolite nuisances, which example was followed by the other donkeys. Old Smith whacked and whacked his beast, but it only made him bray the louder and make other unpleasant noises, which caused much confusion and laughter amongst the whole party. Maids of Honour and Ladies-and Lords-in-Waiting and officers of the Household the donkey did not care a curse for, but would just take his own time and complain loudly if they wanted to hurry him.
>
> The Queen was expected to come to Rabbato and when we arrived at the entrance of the town we found the guard turned out and all the inhabitants dressed in their best, who cheered old Smith when he entered on his noble steed, to which he graciously took off his cap and bowed. All the party came helter-skelter down to the landing-place and were all on board by 6 p.m.

When Adelaide visited Malta, Queen Victoria, her husband's successor, had been on the throne for two years; fifty years later, in 1887, to celebrate Victoria's Golden Jubilee, Gozo's capital, Rabat, was renamed Victoria. But Gozitans still tend to use the old name.

Ġgantija and Xagħra Stone Circle

If you pronounce the name of the megalithic temple complex Ġgantija to yourself, it is clear why legend has it that the stones were erected by a broad-bean eating female giant, with her child under one arm and a 20-ton stone slab under the other; or was she the Great Goddess Sansuma, or the Great Earth Mother? Chapter 1 discusses the controversy of goddesses and the figurines found at Malta and Gozo's Neolithic sites.

There are two temples at Ġgantija side by side, the larger south one is older, about 3600 BC and better preserved. The Xagħra Stone Circle was excavated by a team led by Caroline Malone and her husband; there is less female archaeological input into Ġgantija – which is why I latched on to **Nelly Erichsen** (1862–1918) and **Rose Elizabeth Cleveland** (1846–1918).

In *Malta: Phoenician, Punic and Roman*, Anthony Bonanno mentions and illustrates an inscription found on the floor of the south temple. Further investigation reveals that, translated, it says, 'To the love of our Father Jahwe', and that it was found by Nelly and Rose in 1912 at a time when, as visitors to Ħagar Qim believed, these structures were Phoenician (800–480 BC).

Nelly, an English illustrator and painter, and Rose, scholarly sister of the United States President, and often his First Lady, lived together in Italy, at Bagni di Luca. Their life stories are interesting, but nothing seems to be known about their visit to Malta, except the inscription, which they reported to the museum authorities. It seemed to suggest a Jewish presence in Malta dating back to seafaring tribes some one and a half millennia before St Paul's shipwreck, but Anthony Bonanno is satisfied that it is a fake Phoenician one made by a nineteenth-century French engineer and antiquarian. Unfortunately, I learnt of the inscription too late to seek it out.

Since I visited the site, the visitor centre has been rebuilt and a museum created. Some, but not all, of the artefacts from Ġgantija and the Xagħra Stone Circle have been transferred there.

Don't completely ignore the rather touristy stalls, at least those run by women selling hand-knitted jerseys, possibly their own work. They are mostly of artificial fibre and don't wear that well (though I have already enjoyed mine for two winters), but they are very warm, stylish and inexpensive, and provide the makers and sellers such as Frances with a living.

While the Ġgantija site is much visited, the Xagħra Stone Circle (also known as the Brochtorff Circle), 400 or so yards to the west of Ġgantija, related to it, and overlooking it, is only open by appointment. The fragile natural cave, not a built site, was excavated by Caroline Malone and her colleagues, starting in 1987. In spite of its relative inaccessibility, and lack of much to see, this hypogeum/necropolis, from which fragments of 800 or so burials were excavated, has, as Chapter 1 recounts, revealed more about life in Gozo and the Maltese archipelago from 4000 to 2500 BC, than anywhere else, mainly because of modern scientific and scholarly techniques.

One of the finds is the two fat figures sitting on a couch; they are part of the controversy surrounding sex and religion. Professor Caroline Wilkinson reconstructed the skull of a woman who lived here over 5,000 years ago – to be seen at Ġgantija or on the internet – wonderful!

Calypso Cave and Ramla Bay

Just beyond Ġgantija, on Gozo's northern coast above Ramla Bay, is the Calypso Cave where Gozitans and, indeed, the Maltese, believe that the alluring nymph Calypso kept the Greek hero Odysseus in thrall for seven years. This belief was, according to Dodo Selby Bennett Lees' son, fostered by Dodo as part of her tourism project (Chapter 16). The cave itself, set into the cliff, was closed some years ago because of danger, but you can look down at the wild cliff face to where it is, and the view is worth the stop; what is more it is important for tourism, and thus Gozo's economy. The Calypso Boutique sets the scene and we bought two jerseys from Vinny, knitted by her.

Looking down on Ramla Bay beach from the Calypso lookout post, you need to see the 19-room Roman villa, once excavated but now, having given up some secrets, returned for preservation to the sand (Chapter 2).

Rabat's Citadel

The next most useful stop is Gozo's capital, Rabat and, in particular, the Citadel, a bit of a climb up a flight of steps. Immediately facing you is the **Cathedral** which has had several manifestations. When work began after the 1693 earthquake that damaged or destroyed so many buildings in the archipelago, the remains emerged of a Roman temple of Juno and, perhaps, that of the Phoenician goddess Astarte.

In the chapel dedicated to Christ the Saviour there is a bust, taken from the prow of a ship and donated in 1614, of the second- or third-century English martyr St Ursola, a princess of Britannia. She became the patron saint of Gozo, her intercession sought against an invasion of locusts, plague and cholera, as well as earthquakes.

Turn left from the Cathedral (right from the steps leading up to the Citadel) and you come to the **Archaeological Museum**. Some of the finds from Ġgantija and the Xagħra Stone Circle are still here.

Roman finds are on the first floor. Most immediate as you enter is the headless statue of Empress Julia Augusta (also known as Livia) whose story is told in Chapter 2, together with that of the Gozitan priestess Lutatia. The inscription of Lutatia's dedication to the Empress, offered some time between AD 14 and AD 29, is beneath the statue. Another inscription was dedicated in AD 195 to Empress Julia Domna. Although its existence is known, its whereabouts are not. There are also some exhibits from the Ramla Bay villa.

There are some intriguing displays on the ground floor as you enter the exhibits. Beyond the inland village of Kerċem is the coastal Punic temple site of **Ras il-Wardija** from where, as Chapter 2 relates, the graffito that may, or may not, have been the symbol of the goddess Tanit was stolen and then recovered. The graffito is in the Medieval section because, as curator George Azzopardi explains, it may, in fact, be 'a graffito of that period. This is not certain but less certain is the (presumed) Tanit symbolism borne by the graffito'. You may need to establish the accessibility of the archaeological site, with its stunning position, before planning to visit it. Alternatively, it can be viewed on YouTube.

Malta fell to the Arabs in AD 870. From AD 1173/4 comes the touching funerary slab dedicated to the Muslim girl or woman Majmuna. Its authenticity, too, has been questioned, as Chapter 2 describes. A translation of the Kufic text is also in the chapter.

For the final exhibit of womanly interest, we leap to the time of the Knights and the function then of the citadel, for it is redolent of both danger and safety. Until 1637, all Gozitan citizens had, by law, to make their way there every evening during the summer, the corsair season, to spend the night and, thus, be protected from raids by Turkish corsairs. In 1533, as Chapter 5 relates, Michael Danfasio did not take his family to safety so that the women were kidnapped.

It was in 1551, though, that the worst of these raids took place: the citadel fell to the Turks and over 6,000 women, children and men were taken into slavery. A thousand died during the raid, including the De Opuo family because, to spare them from slavery, Don Bernardo De Opuo killed his nameless wife and daughters and was then himself felled in the fighting. A plaque commemorating this was affixed to the site of their house; the original is now here in the same hall as the Tanit and Majmuna artefacts.

The other side of the Cathedral from the Museum of Archaeology is **Triq Bernardo De Opuo**. So momentous was 1551 in Gozo's history, and so brave was De Opuo considered, that the street in which the family's house was situated was named for him. The house built on the site of their original home is opposite the Folklore Museum; the plaque is a replica. With a different surname, the family's end is told in Dorothy Dunnett's *The Disorderly Knights.*

In the **Folklore Museum** artefacts concerning women include a room-sized loom, lacemaking equipment and costumes.

It is not clear within today's citadel where the Castrum (or fortified castle) was in medieval times when, in 1299, Countess of Malta Lukina's mother, Clara de Rocka was impelled by her husband's will to continue living there. The Citadel was much rebuilt by the Knights, particularly following 1551 and 1565. As the Folklore Museum consists of houses of Sicilian-Catalan architecture, this street may be as close as you will get.

The Opera Houses

Visitors go to Gozo for the peace and quiet, the landscape, the churches, the archaeological sites, the museums or the beaches and diving, but there is more. Perhaps the island's most enticing modern cultural event is the opera season. There are two opera houses in Rabat – the Astra and the Aurora – both in Republic Street, the main thoroughfare, both with chandeliers and tiers of boxes. The standard of production and performance is apparently high, often with foreign soloists. Unfortunately, we have not been in Malta late enough in October to benefit. As I write, *La Traviata* and *La Bohème* are going to vie with each other. One year, when neither would back down, they both performed *Aida*.

Rundle Gardens

The countryside may be peaceful, towns filled with tourists rarely are, so if you are seeking an oasis on a hot, tiring day, just past the Aurora Opera House are the Rundle Gardens (Gnien Rundle) where in August an annual agricultural fair is held, as well as occasional concerts and other events. The gardens are apparently named after Sir Leslie Rundle, governor 1909–1915 who, it is said, personally established them. But I suspect that his wife **Eleanor Rundle** (née Campbell, 1856–1934, m.1887) had a hand in it.

I have two reasons, slight, perhaps, for thinking this. One is a story told to Nicholas de Piro by his grandmother, **Nicolina, Baroness of Budach** (née Apap Bologna, b.1875, m.1901) which he then relayed in *The Sovereign Palaces of Malta*. It starts, '... Lady Rundle wandered about the lovely gardens of San Anton as other governors' wives had done before her. She was alert to any improvements worth suggesting ...'. The story continues with her buying a dozen plant pots for the garden and filling them with geraniums, not quite appreciating Maltese ways – they were chamber pots. At least it gave Maltese visitors a laugh.

The second clue is perhaps more telling. In 'Rundle Gardens in Gozo', Albert Abela writes, 'The Rundles' love for gardens was evinced by their great interest in the Malta Horticultural Society ...'. It occurs to me that Eleanor would have had more time than her husband to superintend the establishment of the gardens in Gozo.

The other end of Republic Street leads out to the north-west of the island.

Sanctuary of Ta' Pinu

Though the guided tour takes you to the centre of Rabat, it does not take you round the citadel, which is no bad thing, though it gives you limited time to explore there. You are given plenty of time at the next stop.

On the way to Għarb from Rabat, standing alone on a low flat hill, is a very large modern church. There used to be a small chapel here and in the 1880s **Karmela Grima** would stop to pray there on her way home to Għarb from the fields. One evening, she heard a woman's voice calling her from the

57.   Karmela Grima, from Abela, *Grace and Glory*

chapel and, on entering it, was told to say three Hail Marys. Karmela became ill, but when she recovered, news of it spread and the chapel became a place of pilgrimage and prayers for the sick. In the 1920s, the grander church was built, funded by the local community, on land donated by the De Piro family. Hanging on the walls of the side chapels leading to the old chapel are hundreds of votive offerings, crutches, children's clothes, photographs, letters. There is a statue of Karmela in the front garden.

In the church square in **Għarb** itself, Karmela's house, built in the early eighteenth century, is now a **Folklore Museum** of 28 rooms depicting the past life of Gozo's inhabitants and their crafts, including a weaving room, a bread-making room, a cheese room, and a jam-making mill.

Azure Window

The reason you may lose time, and thus miss sites that were on the programme, is because of overlong enforced stays at sites like the Azure Window on the north-west coast. This natural arch, formed millions of years ago when a limestone cave collapsed, should be a must, but it is spoilt by a dozen tourist stalls and a basic café where we impatiently roosted, while watching divers getting in and out of wet suits. There was a time, almost within living memory, when this place would have been quieter, tempting one to clamber over the rocks and appreciate it. If you were to visit it by sea, or take to the sea, archaeologist Gertrude Caton-Thomson's experience of 1922 might prove useful:

> There was a memorable visit to Gozo in a naval launch organised by a Commander Noel, who brought, besides the Pringles, Mrs Mayo and me, and Sir Edgar and Lady Barnard. We lunched beneath the great megaliths, and on the return journey to Valletta harbour pulled into a well-known 'blue grotto' in the cliffs. It was indeed a limpid, vivid blue; but having got in on a swell, it was only with the greatest difficulty we got out again. The tide had turned, the wind had risen, breakers pounded, soaking us, and the launch refused to back out in spite of its crew of four sailors whose united strength eventually succeeded.

St Lawrence, Kerċem and Xlendi

These villages to the west of Gozo are where mainlanders and foreigners, often artists and writers, have bought houses over the years. In **St Lawrence**, which you drive through to reach the Azure Window, the artist Anna Grima and her husband have a house. Journalist **Ann Monsarrat** (née Griffiths, b.1937/8) and her novelist husband Nicholas lived there from the late 1960s. Their house, and similar ones built to deter Turkish corsairs, is an unassuming, low stone building along worn tracks, with a single door set in the wall.

Ann, as an unwell widow, has had to move to Valletta in recent years, but she has written and been interviewed about her early life in Gozo. In 2005, she told how it had been, and how it had changed:

> There used to be many shabby areas and a general feeling of poverty. In the villages many houses were without electricity and for many families their only supply of water came from the village pump. America was still sending food parcels to the older inhabitants. Kerosene for cooking and light was delivered door to door by donkey cart. Children, especially the boys, left school at a very early age, often at ten or eleven, to help in the home and fields and many women rarely left the house except to go to church. ...
>
> ... It is very different now when so many families have television and there is a sense of real prosperity. There is also more compassion for the disadvantaged and fewer restrictions for the young. At festas when we first arrived, the girls all stood on one side of the square and the boys on the other, eyeing each other from a distance. Only the boys were allowed to follow the procession. However, there are several things I miss from those earlier, simpler days, like the great flocks of sheep and goats which rustled past the house every morning and evening and the donkeys, which pulled the ploughs and were for many the only means of transport. It was a much quieter island then.

Barbara Greene Strachwitz, who trekked with her cousin Graham through Liberia in 1935, and wrote a first-rate account of the journey, *Too Late to Turn Back* (1981; 1991), owned a similar house to the Monsarrats in Kerċem. Her daughter, Ilona, who inherited the house, tells me how a Polish friend of her mother's learnt to come to grips with Gozitan ways. When her swimming pool needed repair and help from the architect failed to come after two months, she offered him a bottle of whiskey and an end to nagging; but if the workmen did not come the following day, he had to give her a bottle. Workmen were there at 7.30.

In *Dodo*, Dodo Lees (Chapter 16) wrote of **Xlendi**:

> In May, '65, Cecilia [de Trafford] wrote to me from Xlendi, the fishing village in Gozo where she had a little house, informing me that, because of all I'd done for Malta, Fidel, a fisherman – he's dead now – was willing to sell me his house for a thousand pounds, the price he would ask from another fisherman. ...
>
> ... Cecilia said, 'You must come out and look at it. I'm sure you'll want it.' So I went out immediately because Xlendi is very, very pretty. It's in a bay which is like a little fjord, and it's down a sort of gorge with rocks on either side and enormous, spectacular cliffs, very high and very steep that go sheer down to the sea.

And she writes engagingly of her life on and off there. In the epilogue to her book, her husband wrote: 'Dodo died on 26th August 1991, a few days after returning from her beloved Gozo.' Her son James replied to my email:

> We still keep her house in Xlendi where she used to entertain Dom Mintoff and Admiral John Templeton Cothill during the negotiations with the British Government. I can well remember them both coming to Sunday lunch several times and seeing the prime minister and the senior British naval officer in the Mediterranean sitting in the hammock and a deck chair reading my 'Beano' comics! We still have the hammock but not the comics. I also remember Dom skiing into Xlendi Bay behind the Admiral's barge.

Dodo's ashes were scattered in that bay.

Like everywhere else, Xlendi, on the south-west coast, has moved on, though our tour missed it out so I cannot tell you first hand exactly what to expect. But remnants of the past are still there, such as **Ta' Carolina**, the secluded bay where the Dominican nuns of the order founded by Carolina Cauchi in 1889 could swim in private when they visited her Xlendi house. So is **Our Lady of Mount Carmel** on the Xlendi Road which she funded (Chapter 11).

Joan Alexander wrote of **Dr Constance Strickland** (1912–1979), Cecilia and Mabel's youngest sister, that, aged 27, 'She had bought herself a tower in Gozo, perhaps to establish her independence, where she escaped from the

58.   Carolina Cauchi, from Abela, *Grace and Glory*

tensions of Villa Bologna generated by her step-mother and Mabel.' In 1956, Constance set in motion the restoration of the **Xlendi Tower**, built originally in 1650, but it was not entirely successful. The tower is on the headland the other side of Xlendi from Ta' Carolina and, until further work is done, is not open to the public.

Dodo Lees' reading of the difference between the people of Gozo and those of the bigger island makes a fitting end to this introduction to the women's places of the archipelago:

Gerald de Trafford, Cecilia's eldest son, lent me a plumber and a drains chap from the Villa Bologna. They would arrive on the first ferry at six and leave on the last ferry at five. They wouldn't sleep in Gozo. They were poles apart in those days, the Maltese and the Gozitans. For a Maltese peasant to go to Gozo, and for a Gozitan peasant to go to Malta, was much more difficult than going to Australia.

Bibliography

Many of the articles and books detailed here can now be read on, or downloaded from, the internet; typical are the articles from *Melita Historica*, the journal of the Malta Historical Society. But I have only put under 'internet' the most obvious, such as Wikipedia, or material which only seems to be available on the internet. As far as internet material is concerned, I have not always given a website because, in my experience, it is often easier simply to type in the name or subject of one's search. And I have not noted all the internet sites from which I gleaned cumulative snippets of information; that would be impracticable. Internet material I have noted often has no date and may have become irretrievable. I have used internet material if it sounds right, and when there is nothing else available, as is often the way with details about women. It is always worth going onto the internet to see if a book or article is digitally available there.

Women's Works (general reader)

Abrantes, Duchess of, *Memoirs of Napoleon, his Court and Family* (London, R Bentley, 1836)

Alexander, Joan, *Mabel Strickland* (Malta, Progress Press, 1996)

Alexander, Ziggi and Dewjee, Audrey eds, *Wonderful Adventures of Mrs Seacole in Many Lands* (Bristol, Falling Wall Press, 1984)

Brittain, Vera, *Testament of Youth* (London, Virago Press, 1978; first published 1933)

Bruce, Ian, *The Nun of Lebanon: The Love Affair of Lady Hester Stanhope and Michael Bruce* (London, Collins, 1951)

Caton-Thompson, Gertrude, *Mixed Memoirs* (Gateshead, Paradigm, c.1983)

Cortis, Meme, see Turner, Meme

Debono, Josephine, 'Christmas, Malta 1942' in *The Observer Prize Stories: The Seraph and the Zambezi* (London, 1952)

Denaro, Marie, *Daughter of an Empire: A Family History* (Malta, David Arrigo, 2003)

De Pauw, Linda Grant, *Battle Cries and Lullabies: Women in War from Prehistory to the Present* (Oklahoma, University of Oklahoma Press, 1998)

Dingli, Rosanne, *Death in Malta* (Bristol, Bewrite Books, 2001)

—— *Counting the Churches* (USA, Createspace, 2011)

—— *According to Luke* (USA, Createspace, 2012)

—— *The Hidden Auditorium* (USA, Createspace, 2013)

Dobbie, Sybil, *Grace Under Malta* (London, Lindsay Drummond, 1944)

Duberly, Frances, *Journal Kept during the Russian War* (London, Longmans, 1856, 2008)

Duncker, Patricia, *James Miranda Barry* (Basingstoke, Picador, 2000)

Dunnett, Dorothy, *The Disorderly Knights* (London, Cassell, 1966)

Edgeworth, Maria, *Castle Rackrent* (Ware, Hertfordshire, Wordsworth Editions, 1994; first published 1801)

Egerton, Lady Francis, *Journal of a Tour in the Holy Land, in May and June 1840* (London, Harrison, 1841)

Ellis, Kirsten, *Star of the Morning: The Extraordinary life of Lady Hester Stanhope* (London, Harper Press, 2008)

Elwood, Anne, *Narrative of a Journey Overland from England ... to India* (London, Colburn and Bentley, 1830)

Fremantle, Anne ed., *The Wynne Diaries: The Adventures of Two Sisters in Napoleonic Europe* (London, Oxford University Press, 1952)

Galea, Frederick R ed., *Women of Malta: True Wartime Stories of Christina Ratcliffe and Tamara Marks* (Malta, Wise Owl Publications, 2006)

Gibb, Lorna, *Lady Hester: Queen of the East* (London, Faber, 2005)

Gordon Cumming, Constance, *Memories* (Edinburgh, William Blackwood, 1904)

Grand, Sarah, *The Heavenly Twins* (London, Hodder & Stoughton, 1893)

Griffith, Lucinda Darby, *A Journey Across the Desert from Ceylon to Marseilles: Comprising Sketches of Aden, the Red Sea, Lower Egypt, Malta, Sicily and Italy* (London, British Library Historical Print Editions, nd, first published 1845)

Grosvenor, Lady Elizabeth, *Narrative of a Yacht Voyage in the Mediterranean during the Years 1840, 41* (London, John Murray, 1842)

Hamburger, Lotte and Hamburger, Joseph, *Troubled Lives: John and Sarah Austin* (Toronto, University of Toronto Press, c.1985)

Hamel, Frank, *Lady Hester Lucy Stanhope* (London, Cassell, 1913)

Harvey, Caroline, see Trollope, Joanna

Hoe, Susanna, *Crete: Women, History, Books and Places* (Oxford, HOLO Books: The Women's History Press, 2005)

—— *Tasmania: Women, History, Books and Places* (Oxford, HOLO Books: The Women's History Press, 2010)

Holmes, Rachel, *Scanty Particulars: The Secret Life of Dr James Barry* (London, Viking, 2000)

Kirkcaldie, Rosa, *In Gray and Scarlet* (Melbourne, Alexander McCubbin, 1922)

Knight, Cornelia, *Personal Reminiscences* (New York, Scribner Armstrong, 1876)

Krippner, Monica, *The Quality of Mercy: Women at War, Serbia 1915–1918* (Newton Abbot, David and Charles, 1980)

Kyrle-Pope, Suzanne, *The Same Wife in Every Port* (County Durham, The Memoir Club, 1998)

Layton, Suzanne, see Kyrle-Pope, Suzanne

Lee, Celia, *Jean, Lady Hamilton: A Soldier's Wife* (Cecilia Lee, 2001)

Lees, Dodo, *Dodo* (Worcester, The Self Publishing Association, 1993)

Leith-Adams, Bertha, *A Garrison Romance* (London, Jarrold & Sons, 1892)

Lushington, Sarah, *Narrative of a Journey from Calcutta to Europe by Way of Egypt in the Years 1827 and 1828* (London, John Murray, 1829)

Manley, Deborah, *Malta: A Traveller's Anthology* (Oxford, Signal Books, 2010)

Marie, Queen of Romania, *The Story of My Life* (London, Cassell, 1934)

Meryon, CL, *Travels of Lady Stanhope* (London, Henry Colburn, 1846)

Montefiore, Judith, *Notes from the Private Journal of a Visit to Egypt and Palestine by Way of Italy and the Mediterranean* (London, Joseph Rickerby, 1844)

Morgan, Janet, *Edwina Mountbatten* (London, Fontana, 1991)

Murray, Margaret, *My First Hundred Years* (London, John Murray, 1963)

Muscat, Christine, *Magdalene Nuns and Penitent Prostitutes* (Malta, BDL Publishing, 2013)

Norman, Kathleen, *For Gallantry: Malta's Story by a Naval Wife* (Ilfracombe, Arthur H Stockwell, 1956)

Peakman, Julia, *Emma Hamilton* (London, Haus, 2005)

Peto, Gladys, *Malta and Cyprus* (Toronto, JM Dent, 1928)

Pfeifer, Ida, *A Visit to the Holy Land, Egypt and Italy* (London, Ingram, Cooke, 1951)

Rappaport, Helen, *No Place for Ladies: The Untold Story of Women in the Crimean War* (London, Aurum, 2007)

Rawdon-Hastings, SFC ed., *Poems Written by the Lady Flora Hastings* (Edinburgh, William Blackwood & Sons, 1841)

Roberts, Emma, *Notes of an Overland Journey through France and Egypt to Bombay* (London, WH Allen, 1841)

Robinson, Jane, *Mary Seacole: The Charismatic Black Nurse Who Became a Heroine of the Crimea* (London, Constable and Robinson, 2006)

Romer, Isabella, *A Pilgrimage to the Temples and Tombs of Egypt, Nubia and Palestine in 1845–6* (London, Richard Bentley, 1846)

Rose, June, *The Perfect Gentleman: The Remarkable Life of Dr James Miranda Barry* (London, Hutchinson, 1977)

Ross, Janet ed., *Three Generations of Englishwomen* (London, T Fisher, 1893)

Seacole, Mary, see Alexander, Ziggi

Sheppard, Kathleen L, *The Life of Margaret Alice Murray: A Woman's Work in Archaeology* (Plymouth, Lexington Books, 2013)

Shindler, Karolyn, *Discovering Dorothea: The Life of the Pioneering Fossil-Hunter Dorothea Bate* (London, HarperCollins, 2005)

Starke, Mariana, *Travels in Europe* (London, John Murray, 1836)

Stuart, Arabella M, *Arabella's Letters: Together with the Contents of her Small Diary 1823–1828* (London, Hodder & Stoughton, 1927)

Tayar, Aline P'Nina, *How Shall We Sing: A Mediterranean Journey Through a Jewish Family* (Sydney, Pan Macmillan, 2000)

—— *Island of Dreams* (Charleston, Ondina Press, 2012)

Terrot, Sarah, *Reminiscences of Scutari Hospitals* (Edinburgh, A Stevenson, 1898)

Tobin, Catherine, *Shadows of the East* (London, Longmans, 1855)

Trollope, Joanna (Caroline Harvey pseud.) *The Brass Dolphin* (London, Corgi Books, 1998)

Turner, Meme, *Malta V.A.D.* (London, Mrs Carmela Turner, nd)

Van der Kiste, Corynne Hall, *Once a Grand Duchess: Xenia, Sister of Nicholas II* (Stroud, Alan Sutton, 2004)

Vernon, Caroline, *Our Name Wasn't Written: A Malta Memoir* (Campbell ACT, Australia, Imagecraft, 1990)

Wedgwood, CV, 'The Conversion of Malta' in *Velvet Studies* (London, Jonathan Cape, 1946)

Wharton, Edith, *The Cruise of the Vanadis* (New York, Rizzoli International Publications, 2003)

Williams, Kate, *England's Mistress* (Bath, Windsor/Paragon, 2009)

Woodward, Frances, *Portrait of Jane: A Life of Lady Franklin* (London, Hodder & Stoughton, 1951)

Zinovieff, Sofka, *Red Princess: A Revolutionary Life* (London, Granta Books, 2007)

Specialist Works by and about Women

Abela, Albert, 'Some Notable Maltese Women of the Past' in his *Grace and Glory, Malta* (*c*.1997)

Anon (an Officer's Wife, Susan Fraser), *Camilla de Florian and Other Poems* (London, printed for the author, 1809)

Azzopardi, Consiglia, 'Lacemaking at the Centre of Gozitan Daily Life' in Nicholas de Piro and Vicki Ann Cremona, *Costume in Malta* (1998)

Baillie-Hamilton, Mary Cospatrick, *Twelve Views of the Mediterranean, Grecian Archipelago, Bosphorus and Black Sea* (London, no publisher, 1857)

Baldacchino, Lisa, 'Hélène Buhagiar 1888–1975' in *Treasures of Malta*, Vol. 37, Christmas 2006

Bayona, Tanya, 'Remembering Nathalie Putyatin' in Elizaveta Zolina, *Malta and Russia* (*c*.2002)

Berry, Francis, *The Bride of Mosta: A Ballad* (Malta, PEG, 2005)

Biaggi, Cristina, 'The Significance of the Nudity, Obesity and Sexuality of the Maltese Goddess Figures' in Anthony Bonanno, *Archaeology and Fertility Cult* (1986)

Bingley, Juliet, *What it Was and What it Was Not* (Ware, Rockingham Press, 2002)

Bonanno, Anthony, 'Women and Society in Prehistoric and Ancient Gozo' in Joseph Grima ed., *60th Anniversary of the Malta Historical Society* (2010)

Bonello, Giovanni, 'New Light on Majmuna's Tombstone' in his *Deceptions and Perceptions* (2000)

—— 'How Lady Hamilton Changed the History of Malta' in his *Deceptions and Perceptions* (2000)

—— 'Law v Fashion: The Maltese Saga' in his *Figments and Fragments* (2001)

—— 'Mementoes of the 1813 Plague' in his *Convictions and Conjectures* (2003)

—— 'But Who Was Caterina Vitale?' in his *Reflections and Rejections* (2004)

—— 'Some Rare Examples of Women Knights of Malta' in his *Closures and Disclosures* (2006)

—— 'Murder in a Hospitaller Monastery' in his *Closures and Disclosures* (2006)

Bostridge, Mark, *Florence Nightingale: The Making of an Icon* (London, Chatto & Windus, 2008)

Breen, Jennifer ed., *Woman Romantic Poets 1785–1832: An Anthology* (London, JM Dent, 1995)

Busuttil, Joseph, 'The Ceres Inscription' in *Journal of Faculty of Arts* (University of Malta, Vol. 5, No. 2 (1972) 155–161

Bute, Marchioness of ed., *Poems by the Lady Flora Hastings* (Edinburgh, William Blackwood & Sons, 1841)

Camiz, Franca Trinchieri, '"*Virgo-non Sterilis*" ... Nuns as Artists in Seventeenth Century Rome' in Geraldine Johnson and Sara F Mathews Grieco eds, *Picturing Women in Renaissance and Baroque Italy* (Cambridge, Cambridge University Press, 1997)

Cassar, Carmel, *Sex, Magic and the Periwinkle: A Trial at the Malta Inquisition Tribunal 1617* (Malta, Pubblikazzjonijiet Indipendenza, 2000)

—— *Witchcraft, Sorcery and the Inquisition* (Malta, Mireva Publications, 1996)

—— *Daughters of Eve: Women, Gender Roles, and the Impact of the Council of Trent in Catholic Malta* (Malta, Mireva Publications, 2002)

—— 'Magic, Heresy and the Broom Riding Midwife Witch – the Inquisition Trial of Isabetta Caruana' (Malta Historical Society, 2003)

—— 'The World of Caterina Vitale: A Sixteenth Century Lady of Greek Parentage in Malta' in *Studi Sull'Oriente Cristiano*, Vol. 13, No. 1 (Rome, Academia Angelica Costaniniana di Lettere Arti e Scienze, 2009)

—— 'The Jewesses of Malta: Slaves and Pedlars, Healers and Diviners' in *Studi Sull'Oriente Cristiano*, Vol. 17 No. 2 (Rome, Academia Angelica Costaniniana di Lettere Arti e Scienze, 2013)

Cassar, Paul, 'Women in Malta: An Historical Vignette' in *Scientia* Vol. 38, 1975–77, 5-25

Cohen, Gatzel M and Joukowsky, Martha Sharp eds, *Breaking Ground: Pioneering Women Archaeologists* (Ann Arbor, University of Michigan Press, 2004)

Cutajar, Josann, 'Women and Political Participation in Malta' (Malta, Office for Democratic Institutions and Human Rights (ODIHR), 2014)

Delgado, Alan, *As They Saw Her: Florence Nightingale* (London, Harrap, 1970)

De Piro, Nicholas, 'Mattia Preti and the Young Maltese Artist Nun' in his *The Temple of the Knights of Malta* (1999)

Ehrenberg, Margaret, *Women in Prehistory* (London, British Museum Press, 1995)

Evans, Katherine and Cheevers, Sarah, *This is a Short Relation of Some of the Cruel Sufferings of Katherine* etc. (London, 1662)

Farrugia, Ruth, 'Female Suffrage in Malta' in Blanca Rodriguez-Ruiz and Ruth Rubio-Marin, *The Struggle for Female Suffrage in Europe* (2012)

Galea, Joseph ed., Hector Greig, *An Unpublished Diary of Queen Adelaide's Visit to Malta in 1838* (Malta, Progress Press, 1963)

Gardner, William and Eliza, *A Series of Views in Malta* (London, Dickinsons Brothers, 1852)

Gill, Catie, 'Evans and Cheevers's *A Short Relation* in Context: Flesh, Spirit, and Authority in Quaker Prison Writings, 1650–1662' in *Huntington Library Quarterly*, Vol. 72, No. 2, June 2009, 257–272

Glaze, Delia, *Dictionary of Women Artists* (London, Fitzroy Dearborn, 1997)

Goodison, Lucy and Morris, Caroline eds, *Ancient Goddesses* (London, British Museum Press, 1998)

Gregory, Isabelle Vella, *The Human Form in Neolithic Malta* (Malta, Midsea Books, 2008)

Greig, Hector, see Galea, Joseph

Johnson, Geraldine A and Mathews Grieco, Sara F, *Picturing Women in Renaissance and Baroque Italy* (Cambridge, Cambridge University Press, 1997)

Jusova, Iveta, *The New Woman and the Empire* (Columbia, Ohio State University Press, *c.*2005)

Keighley, Alan, *Queen Adelaide's Church, Valletta* (Trowbridge, Wilts, A Keighley, 2000)

Knepper, Paul, '"The White Slave Trade" and the Music Hall Affair in 1930s Malta' in *Journal of Contemporary History*, Vol. 44, No. 2, 2009, 205–220

Kraemer, Ross S, 'A New Inscription from Malta and the Question of Women Elders in the Diaspora Jewish Communities' in *Harvard Theological Review*, Vol. 78, Issue 3–4, October 1985, 431–438

Latini, Francesca and Eynaud, Joseph, *Maria Felice Colonna: Il Diario* (Florence, Autore Libri, 2007)

Leneman, Leah, 'Medical Women in the First World War – Ranking Nowhere' in *British Medical Journal*, Vol. 307, December 1933, 18–25

McDonald, Lynn ed., *The Collected Works of Florence Nightingale* (Waterloo, Ont., Wilfrid Laurier University Press, 2001–)

Malone, Caroline, 'God or Goddess: The Temple Art of Ancient Malta' in Lucy Goodison and Caroline Morris, *Ancient Goddesses* (1998)

Markina, Lyudmila, 'Catherine the Great's Portrait at the Valletta Palace' in Elizaveta Zolina, *Malta and Russia* (*c.*2001)

Murray, Margaret, *Excavations in Malta* (London, Bernard Quaritch, 1923–1929)

—— *The Corpus of Bronze-Age Pottery of Malta* (London, Bernard Quaritch, 1934)

Muscat, Christine, 'The Magdalene Church, Valletta' in Georg Peresso, *Il-Mara ta'Dlielh Twil* (Malta, Horizons, 2014)

Parascandola, John L, 'Alice Catherine Evans (1881–1975)' in *Journal of Public Health Policy*, Vol. 22, No. 1, 2001, 105–111

Portelli, Lorraine, 'The Socioeconomic Factors in the Teaching of Needlework in 19th Century Malta' in *Family and Consumer Sciences Research Journal*, Vol. 38, Issue 2, December 2009, 134–141

Rich, Sara A, 'Midwifery and Neolithic Malta: Interpreting and Contextualizing Two Terracotta Figures' in *Journal of Applied Anthropology*, Omerta, 2008, 260–268

Richards, HD, *Maid of Honour* (Caerphilly, Lazy Cat, 2004)

Rodriguez-Ruiz, Blanca and Rubio-Marin, Ruth, *The Struggle For Female Suffrage in Europe: Voting to Become Citizens* (Boston, Brill, 2012)

Rountree, Kathryn, 'Goddess Pilgrims as Tourists', in *Sociology of Religion*, Vol. 63, No. 4, Winter 2002, 475–496

—— 'The Case of the Missing Goddess: Plurality, Power and Prejudice in Reconstructions of Malta's Neolithic Past' in *Journal of Feminist Studies in Religion*, Vol. 19, No. 2, Fall 2003, 25–43

Sagona, Claudia, 'Silo or Vat? Observations on the Ancient Textile Industry in Malta ...' in *Oxford Journal of Archaeology*, Vol.18, Issue 1, February 1999, 23–60

—— *The Archaeology of Punic Malta* (Leuven, Peeters, 2001)

Savona-Ventura, Charles, '"The Lady with the Lamp" and the Maltese Connection' in *The Sunday Times* (Malta), 22 December 1991, p3

—— 'Dr James Barry: an Enigmatic Army Medical Doctor' in *Maltese Medical Journal*, Vol. 8, No. 1, 1996, 41–47

—— *Knights Hospitaller: Medicine of Malta* (Malta, PEG, 2004)

—— *The History of Midwifery Education in the Maltese Islands* (Faculty of Medicine and Surgery, University of Malta, 2009)

Schermerhorn, Elizabeth, *Malta of the Knights* (London, William Heinemann, 1929)

Sciberras, Lillian, 'Women and Maltese Politics' in *The Malta Yearbook* (Malta, 1975, pp372–383)

Sorlini, Giulia Battiti, 'The Megalithic Temples of Malta' in Anthony Bonanno, *Archaeology and Fertility Cult* (1986)

Swinton, John, 'Some Observations Upon an Inedited Greek Coin of Philistis, Queen of Syracuse, Malta, and Gozo, Who Has Been Passed Over in Silence by All the Ancient Writers' in *Philosophical Transactions (1683–1775)*, Vol. 60, 1770, 80–93

Veen, Veronica, *The Goddess of Malta* (Haarlem, Holland, Inanna-Fia Publications, 1992)

Vella, Yosanne, 'Earthly Madonnas? Women Troublemakers in 18th century Malta' in *Storja*, Vol. 98, 1998, Malta University Historical Society

—— 'Women and Work in Eighteenth Century Malta', in *Women's History Notebooks*, Vol. 6, No. 1, Winter 1999, Women's History Network, Sussex

—— 'Women victims of crime in eighteenth century Malta', in *Proceedings of History Week*, 2003, The Malta Historical Society.

—— 'Women, Religion and Magic in 18th century Malta', in *Women's History Network*, Issue 46, Spring 2004, Aberdeen

Vicinus, Martha, 'Lesbian Perversity in Victorian Marriage: The 1864 Codrington Divorce Trial' in *Journal of British Studies*, Vol. 36, Issue 1, January 1997, 70–98

Wettinger, Godfrey, 'Concubinage Among the Clergy of Malta and Gozo ca. 1420–1550', *Journal of the Faculty of Arts* (University of Malta), Vol. VI, No. 4, 1977, 165–188

—— 'Wife versus Concubine in Gozo in 1486' in Joseph Grima ed., *60ᵗʰ Anniversary of the Malta Historical Society* (2010)

Xuereb, Paul, 'Maltese Women through Foreign Eyes' (Malta, 1972)

Zolina, Elizaveta ed., *Malta and Russia: Journey through the Centuries, Historical Discoveries in Russo-Maltese relations* (Malta, E Zolina, *c.*2002)

Melita Historica Articles (The Malta Historical Society)

Bonnici, Walter, 'Joseph Beckett Henry Collings and the Reform of Charitable Institutions of Malta', Vol. 13, No. 1, 2000, 77–94

Buhagiar, Mario, 'Gozo in late Roman, Byzantine and Muslim Times', Vol. 12, No. 2, 1997, 113–129

Busuttil, Claude, 'A Double Act for the "Norman House": Palazzo Falzon or Palazzo Cumbo-Navarra?', Vol. 12, No. 4, 1999, 411–418

Busuttil, Joseph, 'The Maltese Textile Industry in Antiquity', Vol. 4, No. 3, 1966, 215–219

Cassar, George, 'A Glimpse of Private Education in Malta 1800–1919', Vol. 13, No. 1, 2000, 59–75

—— 'Some Working Conditions of Maltese Teachers During the Nineteenth Century and up to World War I', Vol. 15, No. 3, 2010, 279–302

Cassar, Paul, 'Psychological and Medical Aspects of the Siege of 1565', Vol. 1, No. 3, 1954, 129–140

—— 'Female Employees in the Medical Services of the Order of St John in Malta', Vol. 7, No. 3, 1978, 225–233

—— 'John Hookham Frere in Malta (1821–1846): A Link with our Social and Cultural Past', Vol. 9, No. 1, 1984, 49–73

Cassar Pullicino, J, '19th Century Hotels in Malta', Vol. 8, No. 2, 1981, 109–124

Denaro, Victor, 'Houses in Merchants Street, Valletta', Vol. 2, No. 3, 1958, 158–171

—— 'Houses in Kingsway and Old Bakery Street, Valletta', Vol. 2, No. 4, 1959, 201–215

—— 'The Manoel Theatre', Vol. 3, No. 1, 1960, 1–4

—— 'More Houses in Valletta', Vol. 3, No. 2, 1961, 1–8

Denny, ND, 'British Temperance Reformers and the Island of Malta 1815–1914', Vol. 9, No. 4, 1987, 329–345

Fiorini, Stanley, 'The Resettlement of Gozo after 1551', Vol. 9, No. 3, 1986, 203–244

—— 'The De Malta Genoese Count of Malta: c.1192–1320', Vol. 2, No. 4, 1999, 366

—— 'Sibilla d'Aragona and the Foundation of the Saqqajja Benifice on Gozo', Vol. 12, No. 4, 1999, 367–372

Ganado, Albert, 'Bibliographical notes on Melitensia – 2', Vol. 14, No. 1, 2004, 67–94

Luttrell, Anthony, 'Christian Slaves at Malta: 1271', Vol. 9, No. 4, 1987, 381–383

Mallia-Milanes, Victor, 'English Merchants' Initial Contacts with Malta: A Reconsideration', Vol. 6, No. 4, 1975, 342–361

Muscat, Joseph, 'The Tarxien Ship Graffiti Revisited', Vol. 13, No. 1, 2000, 49–57

Said-Zammit, George A, 'The Phoenician and Punic Necropoleis of Rabat, Malta' Vol. 13, No. 2, 2001, 117–146

Scannura, Charles Galea, 'The Office of the Secrezia of Malta Previous to the Coming of the Knights of Malta', Vol. 6, No. 2, 1973, 107–132

Sultana, Donald, 'The First Duke of Buckingham and Chandos in Malta and Gozo in 1828', Vol. 13, No. 3, 2002, 285–311

Vella, AP, 'The Cotton Industry in Malta' Vol. 4, No. 3, 1966, 210–214

Vella, Nicholas, 'I Have a Story to Tell You: Teresa Strickland Colt and the Malta Relief Fund', Vol. 13, No. 1, 2000, 39–48

Wettinger, Godfrey, 'The Pawning of Malta to Monroy', Vol. 7, No. 3, 1978, 265–283

—— 'Honour and Shame in Late Fifteenth Century Malta', Vol. 8, No. 1, 1980, 65–77

—— 'The Young Widow on Gozo Who Remarried Too Soon 1465–68', Vol. 12, No. 2, 1997, 139–150

—— 'Donna Simona Caruana alias Baldes: Twice Married and Twice Divorced', Vol. 13, No. 2, 2001, 147–163

Xuereb, Paul, 'Sir William Hamilton's Account of his First Visit to Malta', Vol. 6, No. 1, 1972, 22–24

General Articles and Chapters

Abela, Albert, 'A Note about the Russian Chapel at San Anton Palace' in Elizavita Zolina, *Malta and Russia* (*c.*2002)

—— 'Rundle Gardens in Gozo' in his *Grace and Glory, Malta* (*c.*1997)

Aloisio, Mark A, 'The Maltese *Corso* in the Fifteenth Century' in *Medieval Encounters*, Vol. 9, Issue 2, 2003, 193–203

Ashby, Thomas, 'Roman Malta' in *The Journal of Roman Studies*, Vol. 5, 1915, 23–80

Bauckham, Richard, 'The Estate of Publius (Acts 28:7)' in Son Sang-Won, *History and Exegesis* (London, T & T Clark, 2006)

Bresc, Henri, 'The "Secrezia" and the Royal Patrimony in Malta 1240–1450' in Anthony Luttrell, *Medieval Malta* (1975)

Buhagiar, Mario, 'The Jewish Catacombs of Roman *Melite*' in *The Antiquaries Journal*, Vol. 91, September 2011, 73–100

Busuttil, Salvino,'Malta's Economy in the Nineteenth Century' in *Journal of Faculty of Arts* Vol. 3, No. 1, 1965, 44–65

Buxton, Leonard Dudley, 'Personal and Place Names in Malta' in *Man*, Vol. 21, October 1921, 146–147 (Royal Anthropological Institute)

—— 'The Ethnology of Malta and Gozo' in *The Journal of the Royal Anthropological Institute*, Vol. 52, July–December 1922, 164–211

Cachia, Stefan, 'Husband-Wife Relations in Late Medieval Malta 1486–1488' in *Storja*, 2001, 5–13

Cassar, Carmel, 'Everyday Life in Malta in the Nineteenth and Twentieth Centuries', in Victor Mallia-Milanes, *The British Colonial Experience* (1988)

Cassar, Charles, 'Concepts of Health and Illness in Early Modern Malta' in *Quaderns de l'Institut Català d'Antropologia*, Vol. 17/18, 2002 (Barcelona, Institut Català d'Antropologia)

Cassar, Paul, 'The *Gabinetto di Lettura* or Reading Rooms in the 19th Century' in *Proceedings of History Week 1986 – Malta* (The Historical Society, 1992, 1–4)

Cavaleiro, R, 'John Dodsworth, a Consul in Malta' in *The Mariner's Mirror*, Vol. 43, Issue 4, 1957

Dalli, Charles, 'Satellite, Sentinel, Stepping Stone: Medieval Malta in Sicily's Orbit' in A Bonanno and P Militello eds, *Malta in the Hybeans* (Palermo, *Progetto Kasa, Officina di Studi Medievali*, 2008) 245–258

Ellul-Micallef, Roger, 'The Development of Malta's Medical Services during the time of the Order' (paper presented to Mediterranean Rehabilitation Conference, Malta, 2000)

Eyre, John, 'Undulant Fever – A Retrospective' (Hunterian lecture, 1936)

Fiorini, Stanley, 'The Three-Year Famine and the *Ambaxata Di Malta*: 1468–69' in Joseph Grima ed., *The 60th Anniversary of the Malta Historical Society*, 117–138 (2010)

Freller, Thomas, 'The Capture of the *Gran Galeone* by the Knights of Malta (28th September 1644) – *Casus Belli*?' in Toni Cortis and Timothy Gambin, *De Triremibus: Festschrift in Honour of Joseph Muscat* (2005)

Frendo, Henry, 'Maltese Survivors of Smyrna' in Joseph Grima ed., *The 60th Anniversary of the Malta Historical Society*, 355–370 (2010)

Galea, Joseph, 'English Privateers at Malta and a British Consul's Misfortunes in the XVIII Century' in *Scientia*, Vol. XXX, No. 3, July–September 1964, 110–127

Gunn, Dairmid, 'Scott and Malta: A Mediterranean Adventure' (talk given to the Edinburgh Sir Walter Scott Club, 11 April 2013)

Knepper, Paul, 'Crime and Policing: A Few Detectives Would be Very Useful: Crime, Immorality and Policing in Valletta, 1881–1914' in *Journal of Social History*, Winter 2009, 385–406

Malta Government Gazette

Mercieca, Simon, 'How was Judicial Power Balanced in Malta in Early Modern Times?' in *Journal of Civil Law Studies*, Vol. 4, Issue 2, December 2011, 449–480 (Malta)

Pisani, Saviour, 'The Nurse of the Mediterranean' in *Malta Medical Journal*, Vol. 22, No. 3, 2010, 27–30

Said, Edward, 'The Picturesque Grounds of the Villa Frere, Pietà' in *Treasures of Malta*, Vol. 75, Summer 2013 (Malta, Fondazzjoni Patrimonju Malti)

Savona-Ventura, Charles, 'Human Suffering During the Maltese Insurrection of 1798' in *Storja*, 1998, 48–65

Vassallo, David, 'The Corps Disease: Brucellosis and its Historical Association with the Royal Army Medical Corps' in *Journal of the Royal Army Medical Corps*, 1992, 138, 140–150

Vassallo, Peter, 'Romantic Writers in Malta: Literary and Historical Perspectives' in Stanley Fiorini and Victor Mallia-Milanes eds, *Malta: A Case Study in International Cross Currents* (1991)

Wettinger, Godfrey, 'The Arabs in Malta' in Mid-Med Bank ed., *Malta: Studies of its Heritage and History* (Malta, Mid-Med Bank, 1986) 87–104

―― 'Aspects of Daily Life in Late-Medieval Malta and Gozo' in Stanley Fiorini and Victor Mallia-Milanes eds, *Malta: A Case Study in International Cross-Currents* (1991)

―― 'Corsairs in Gozo in 1533' in Toni Cortis and Timothy Gambin eds, *De Triremibus: Festschrift in Honour of Joseph Muscat* (2005) 459–488

Woolner, Diana, 'Graffiti of Ships at Tarxien, Malta' in *Antiquity*, Vol. 31, Issue 122, June 1957, 60–67

General Reference

Abela, Albert, *A Nation's Praise, Malta: People, Places and Events* (Malta, Progress Press, 1994)

―― *Grace and Glory, Malta: People, Places & Events: Historical Sketches* (Malta, Progress Press, c.1997)

Attard, Robert, *Malta: A Collection of Tales and Narratives* (Malta, Edward Debono Foundation, 2003)

―― and Azzopardi, Romina, *Daily Life in Eighteenth Century Malta* (Malta, Midsea Books, 2011)

Bardsley, Gillian, *Issigonis: The Official Biography* (Thriplow, Icon, 2008)

Blouet, Brian, *The Story of Malta* (Malta, Allied Publications, 7th edition, 2007)

Bonanno, Anthony, *Archaeology and Fertility Cult in the Ancient Mediterranean* (Amsterdam, Gruner, 1986)

―― *Roman Malta: The Archaeological Heritage of the Maltese Islands* (Rome, Confederazione Mondiale degli Exallievi ed Exallieve di Don Bosco, 1992)

―― *Malta: An Archaeological Paradise* (Malta, MJ Publications, 9th edition, 2003)

―― *Malta: Phoenician, Punic and Roman* (Malta, Midsea Books, 2005)

Bonello, Giovanni, *Deceptions and Perceptions* (Malta, Fondazzjoni Patrimonju Malti, 2000)

―― *Figments and Fragments* (Malta, Fondazzjoni Patrimonju Malti, 2001)

—— *Versions and Diversions* (Malta, Fondazzjoni Patrimonju Malti, 2002)

—— *Convictions and Conjectures* (Malta, Fondazzjoni Patrimonju Malti, 2003)

—— *Reflections and Rejections* (Malta, Fondazzjoni Patrimonju Malti, 2004)

—— *Closures and Disclosures* (Malta, Fondazzjoni Patrimonju Malti, 2006)

Bonham-Carter, Charles, see Manduca, John

Bradford, Ernle (trans) Francisco Balbi Correggio, *The Siege of Malta* (London, Folio Society, 1965)

—— *Siege: Malta: 1940–1943* (Barnsley, Pen & Sword Military Classics, 1985)

Buckingham and Chandos, Duke of, *The Private Diary of* (London, Hurst and Blackett, 1862)

Buhagiar, Mario, *The Christianisation of Malta: Catacombs, Cult Centres and Churches in Malta to 1530* (Oxford, Archaeopress, 2007)

—— and Fiorini, Stanley, *Mdina: The Cathedral City of Malta* (vol. 1, Malta, Central Bank of Malta, 1996)

Byron, Lord, *Childe Harold's Pilgrimage*, II (London, John Murray, 1814)

Cassar, Carmel, *Society, Culture and Identity in Early Modern Malta* (Malta, Mireva Publications, 2000)

—— *A Concise History of Malta* (Malta, Mireva Publications, 2002)

Cassar, Paul, *Medical History of Malta* (London, Wellcome Historical Medical Library, 1965)

Ciappara, Frans, *Marriage in Malta in the Late Eighteenth Century* (Malta, Associated News, 1988)

Cini, George, *'The Gut' which for Many Years Lit up Valletta* (Malta, Allied Publications, 2013)

Correggio, Francisco Balbi, see Bradford, Ernle

Cortis, Toni and Gambin, Timothy, *De Triremibus: Festschrift in Honour of Joseph Muscat* (Malta, Publishers Enterprises Group, 2005)

Cree, Edward, see Levien, Michael

Dalli, Charles, *Malta: The Medieval Millennium* (Malta, Midsea Books, 2006)

De Piro, Nicholas, *The International Dictionary of Artists Who Painted Malta* (Malta, Said International, 1988)

—— *The Temple of the Knights of Malta* (Malta, Miranda Publications, 1999)

—— *The Sovereign Palaces of Malta* (Malta, Miranda Publications, 2001)

—— *Ladies of Malta: in Extravagant and Spectacular Maltese Lace* (Malta, BDL, 2013)

—— and Vicki Ann Cremona eds, *Costume in Malta* (Malta, Patrimonju Publishing, 1998)

De Salvo, Marquis, *Travels in the Year 1806 from Italy to England* (London, Richard Phillips, 1807)

Ellul-Micallef, Roger, *Zammit of Malta* (Malta, BDL, 2013)

Evans, John, *Malta* (London, Thames and Hudson, 1959)

Festing, Gabrielle, *John Hookham Frere and His Friends* (London, J Nesbit, 1899)

Fiorini, Stanley, *Documentary Sources of Maltese History, parts 1, 2 and 3* (Malta, University of Malta, 1996–)

—— and Mallia-Milanes, Victor eds, *Malta: A Case Study in International Cross Currents* (Malta, Malta University Publications, 1991)

Fleming, Brian, *The Vatican Pimpernel: The Wartime Exploits of Monsignor Hugh O'Flaherty* (New York, Skyhorse, 2009)

Freller, Thomas, *Malta and the Grand Tour* (Malta, Midsea Books, 2009)

Frendo, Henry, *Party Politics in a Fortress Colony: The Maltese Experience* (Malta, 3rd edition, Midsea Books, 1913)

Godfrey, Masters John and Godfrey, Hilda, *Monograph and Iconograph of Native British Orchidaceae* (Cambridge, Cambridge University Press, 1933)

Grima, Joseph F ed., *60th Anniversary of the Malta Historical Society: A Commemoration* (Malta, Malta Historical Society, 2010)

Holland, James, *Fortress Malta: An Island Under Siege 1940–1943* (London, Phoenix Paperback, 2003)

Howlett, D ed., *The Dictionary of Medieval Latin: from British Sources* (Oxford, Oxford University Press, 2007)

Hutton, Ronald, *Pagan Britain* (New Haven, Yale University Press, 2013)

Johnson, Joan ed., *The General: The Travel Memoirs of General Sir George Whitmore* (Gloucester, Alan Sutton, 1987)

Lacroix, Frederic, *Malte et Goze* (Paris, Firmin Didot, 1840)

Lear, Edward, *Later Letters of Edward Lear* (London, T Fisher Unwin, 1911)

Levien, Michael ed., *The Cree Journals: The Voyages of Edward H Cree* (Exeter, Webb & Bower, 1981)

Lockhart, John Gibson, *Memoirs of the Life of Sir Walter Scott, Bart,* 7 vols (Edinburgh, Robert Cadell, 1837–38)

Luke, Harry, *An Account and Appreciation of Malta* (London, George G Harrap, 1949)

Luttrell, Anthony, *Medieval Malta: Studies on Malta before the Knights* (London, The British School at Rome, 1975)

—— *The Making of Christian Malta* (Aldershot, Ashgate Variorum, 2002)

MacGill, Thomas, *A Handbook or Guide for Strangers Visiting Malta* (Malta, 1839; Kessinger Legacy Reprints nd)

Mackenzie, Donald, *The Web of Empire: A Diary of the Imperial Tour of the Duke and Duchess of Cornwall in 1901* (London, Macmillan, 1902)

Mackinnon, Albert G, *Malta: The Nurse of the Mediterranean* (London, Hodder & Stoughton, 1916)

Mallia-Milanes, Victor, *The British Colonial Experience 1800–1964: The Impact on Maltese Society* (Malta, Mireva Publications, 1988)

Malone, Caroline and Bonanno, Anthony eds, *Mortuary Customs in Prehistoric Malta: Excavations of the Brocktorff Circle at Xaghra* (Oakville, USA, McDonald Institute for Archaeological Research, 2009)

Malta Government Gazette

Manduca, John ed., *The Bonham-Carter Diaries 1936–1940* (Malta, PEG, 2004)

Massie, Alan, *Byron's Travels* (London, Sidgwick & Jackson, 1988)

Micallef, John, *The Scicluna Saga* (Malta, Farsons Foundation, 2008)

Milton, Giles, *Paradise Lost: Smyrna 1922, The Destruction of Islam's City of Tolerance* (London, Sceptre, 2008)

Perowne, Stuart, *The Siege Within the Walls: Malta 1940–1943* (London, Hodder & Stoughton, 1970)

Said-Zammit, George A, *The Architectural Heritage of the Maltese Islands* (Malta, the Minor Seminary, 2008)

Savona-Ventura, Charles, *Knight Hospitaller Medicine in Malta (1530–1798)* (Malta, Publishers Enterprises Group, 2004)

—— *Ancient and Medieval Medicine in Malta: before 1600AD* (Malta, Publishers Enterprises Group, 2004)

Scott, Walter, *The Siege of Malta* (Edinburgh, Edinburgh University Press, 2008)

Selby Bennett, Chips, *Seahorse!: Between the Sea and the Saddle* (Tiverton, Halsgrove, 2005)

Seltman, Charles, *Women in Antiquity* (London, Pan, 1956)

Shepherd, Eric, *Malta and Me* (London, Selwyn Blount, ?1926)

Skeates, Robin, *An Archaeology of the Senses: Prehistoric Malta* (Oxford, Oxford University Press, 2010)

Spooner, Tony, *Warburton's War* (Wilmslow, Goodall, 2003)

Strathcarron, Ian, *Joy Unconfined: Lord Byron's Grand Tour, Re-Toured* (Oxford, Signal Books, 2010)

Sultana, Donald, *Benjamin Disraeli: in Spain, Malta and Albania 1830–32* (London, Tamesis, 1976)

—— *The Journey of Walter Scott to Malta* (New York, St Martin's Press, 1986)

Tasker, Meg, *Struggle and Storm: The Life and Death of Francis Adams* (Victoria, Australia, Melbourne University Press, 2001)

Testa, Carmel, *The Life and Times of Grand Master Pinto 1741–1773* (Malta, Midsea Books, 1989)

—— *The French in Malta 1798–1800* (Malta, Midsea Books, 1997)

Trump, David, *Malta: An Archaeological Guide* (Malta, Progress Press, 3rd edition, 2000)

Vella, Philip, *Malta: Blitzed But Not Beaten* (Malta, Progress Press, 1985)

Welch, Francis, *The Russian Court at Sea: the Voyage of HMS Marlborough, April 1919* (London, Short Books, 2011)

Wettinger, Godfrey, *Slavery in the Islands of Malta and Gozo ca. 1000–1812* (Malta, PEG, 2002)

Wragg, David, *Malta: The Last Great Siege* (Barnsley, Leo Cooper, 2003)

Zarb-Dimech, A, *Malta during the First World War 1814–1918* (Malta, 2004)

Internet Material

www.archive.rootsweb.ancestry.com

Attard, Sonia, 'Women voting for the first time: Equality at last!' www.aboutmalta.com

Australian Dictionary of Biography

Bonnici, Alexander, *Mons Guzeppi de Piro: Founder of the Missionary Society of St Paul* (1988) www.maltafamilyhistory.com

Bonnici, Walter, 'British Army Medical Services and the Malta Garrison 1799–1979', www.maltaramc.com

Bruce, George, 'Malta Military Hospitals 1915–1917' (nd)

'Lord Byron and his Times: Letters and Journals of Lord Byron'

Callus, Angela and Camilleri, Miriam, 'Gender Mainstreaming in the Malta Public Service: A Manual for Action' (Malta, Commission for the Advancement of Women, November 2000)

Camilleri, Patricia, 'The Rise and Rise of Female Graduates: Some Milestones in Tertiary Education for Women in Malta' (2006) www.timesofmalta.com

Caruana Dingli, Noel, 'Maria Teresa Grech'

Cilia, John La Corte, 'Margarita d'Aragona'

'David Niven in Malta' www.thephora.net

Evening News, Sydney

Galea, Michael, 'Malta earns the title "nurse of the Mediterranean"' (www.timesofmalta.com 2014)

Griscti-Soler, Albert, 'Margarita d'Aragona'

'History of the Ursulines'

Jerusalem Post

'Lace in Malta'

Layard, Lady, 'Journal' (Robert and Elizabeth Barrett Browning, a database, Baylor University) www.leventineheritage.com

Malta Chronicle

www.maltagenealogy.com

Malta Independent

'Maria Teresa Navarro'

Marmarà, Desmond Zammit, '1565 Malta Celebrates the historically important victory of the Great Siege' (*Times of Malta*, 2009)

Montalto, John Attard, 'Testaferrata Petitions the King'

Oppenheimer, Melanie, 'From Gallipoli to Basra – an Australian nurse's perspective of war' (2004)

Oxford Dictionary of National Biography (*ODNB*)

Portelli, John Mark and Reynaud, Wilfred Cassar, 'Cottonera Hospital and Malta as the Nurse of the Mediterranean' (St Edwards Website, 2014)

www.records.ancestry.com.au

Said-Vassallo, Charles, www.saidvassallo.com 'A Professional Family of Mistresses'

—— 'Polemics Between Maltese Dynasts' (2010)

—— 'Reassessment of Favray's portrait of an elderly lady with infant' (2011)

—— 'The Italian wives of Baron Testaferrata'

Scicluna, Sandra and Knepper, Paul, 'Historical criminology and the imprisonment of women in 19th century Malta' (2010) www.tcr.sagepub.com
'Timelines of Maltese History'
The Times (London)
The Times of Malta
University of Malta History of Lace II, 'Who were Lady Sarah Austin and Lady Hamilton Chichester?'
Welsh, Andy, 'Giacinto Stefano Eynaud'
Wettinger, Godfrey, interview with Adel S Bishtawi (2011)
Wikipedia

Guide Books

Blasi, Abigail, *Malta and Gozo* (Lonely Planet Publications, 2013)
Gaul, Simon, *Malta, Gozo and Comino* (London, Cadogan Guides, 2003)
McGregor Eadie, Peter, *Malta and Gozo, Blue Guide* (London, A & C Black, 1995)
Malta (London, Insight Guides, 2012)
Manduca, John, *Malta & Gozo: Sun, Sea & History* (Malta, PEG, 2003)
—— *The Three Cities: Vittoriosa, Senglea and Cospicua* (Malta, PEG, 2005)
Rix, Juliet, *Malta and Gozo* (London, Bradt Guides, 2nd edition, 2013)

Unpublished Material

Bonello, Giovanni, 'Memories of Caterina Scappi' (awaiting publication)
Briffa, Hillary, 'Malta in the First World War: A tripartite linguistic legacy of reportage' (conference presentation, King's College London, 2015)
De Piro, Nicholas, *The National Portrait Gallery of Malta* (awaiting publication)
Galea, Frederick, 'Wartime "Cloak and Dagger" Operations from Malta'
—— 'The Henrietta Chevalier Memorial Garden at the Aviation Museum'
Knight, Cornelia, 'Cornelia Knight's *Foudroyant* Sketchbook' in Beinecke Rare Books and Manuscripts, Yale University
Wettinger, Godfrey, *Daily Life in Medieval Malta* (awaiting publication by University of Malta)

Index

For reasons of length and confusion, it would be impractical to include here all the many women mentioned by name. Included are those who have a substantial or significant entry in the text. The more useful page number for a particular woman is in bold. Husbands, on the whole, are omitted, though if significant to the narrative they may be in brackets after their wives. Some modern male scholars who contribute to recreating women's history are included. Some aspects of women are listed separately, but for many subjects, look under the entry Women, and a sub-entry within it; the same rationale applies to other groups, such as archaeological sites and phases, churches, women travellers, Grand Masters of the Order of St John whose behaviour touched upon the lives of women.

Dunnett, Dorothy 71–2, 424
Durani, Angelo (Inquisitor) 125–6

Edinburgh (see also Universities) 178, 219,
    234, 264, 290
Edinburgh, Duke and Duchess of (and Marie
    and Melita) 396–7
Education (including women school teachers)
    61, 120, 122, 140, 168, 182–3,
    196–204, 209, 217, 221, 223, 242,
    265, 294, 319, 335–6, 345, 347
Egypt (and Egyptology, Egyptians and
    Alexandria) 17, 19, 21–23, 27–9, 82,
    111, 138, 141, 146, 152, 154, 187,
    193, 207, 231, 240, 242, 250–1, 254,
    263–4, 294, 306, 330, 370
Ehrenberg, Margaret 8
Environment (drought and earthquake) 10,
    18, 47, 55, 92, 118, 195, 414
Epidemics and pandemics 47, 55, 94,
    117–18, 152–3, 164, 178, 184, 195,
    217, 221, 229, 240–2, 252, 280, 341,
    375, 379, 417, 423
Eulogia 37–8, 405
Evans, Alice 249
Eynaud family, 138–9, 372

Faenza, Annica (see also Caterina Vitale)
    100, 103–4, 106–7, 368
Fairfield, Dr Letitia 290–3, 335
Feminism 8, 11, 91, 111, 176, 226, 261, 335
Fernandes, Sarah and family 157, 363
Figurines (including Fat Lady, Sleeping Lady,
    Venus of Malta; see also Controversies)
    9–13, 16–17, 407–8, 411–12, 422
Fiorini, Stanley 46–7, 50–1, 56–7, 73–5, 80,
    93, 113, 213
Fisher, Rosamund (later Lady Coleridge; and
    family) 284–5, 298, 389
Floriana (and *Conservatorio* and House of
    Industry) 40–1, 122, 143, 155, 168,
    199, 201, 214–15, 260, 288, 311, 313,
    325, 364, 367, 382–4
Fontani, Giovanna (later Gastinel) 140,
    145–6, 359, 368
Forts (see also Manoel Island)
    S Angelo 31, 44, 55, 70, 94, 143, 304,
    312, 373–4, 379, 415; S Elmo 92, 132
    152, 155, 323, 359, 361, 369, 371
France (the French, language, occupation of
    Malta, Normans, Angevins) 7, 39–40,
    42–3, 45, 65, 68, 75, 85–7, 97–9, 103,
    130–1, 134–5, 138–55, 157–60, 162,
    167, 181–2, 187, 197, 203, 205–6, 211,
    216–17, 221, 226, 232, 245, 253, 261,
    263, 269, 280, 306, 310, 316, 323,
    331, 348, 359–60, 363–4, 368, 370,
    372, 375–6, 386, 393–4, 402–3, 414,
    422
Francia, Teresina Buttigieg (and Colonel
    John and family) 272–3, 293–4, 355
Franklin, Jane (Lady and Sir John) 286–7
Fraser, Susan 160–3
Frendi, Henry 221, 278–9
Frere, Elizabeth Countess of Errol (and John
    Hookham, and family, and Villa; see
    also Blake, Honoria) 166, 176–91, 190,
    194, 383, 385–6
Frost, Honour 379–80

Galea, Frederick 310, 331–2, 363–4, 413
Gallipoli campaign 250–2, 255–6
Gardens (see also San Anton)
    Argotti Botanic (Floriana) 383; Buskett
    415–17; Gnien L-Gharus (Mosta) 400;
    Maglio (Floriana) 383; Romeo Romano
    (Case Leone) 393; Rundle (Rabat, Gozo)
    424–5; San Gwann (Karin Grech) 385,
    390; Ta' Qali Memorial 399
Garibaldi, Giuseppe 219–21, 232, 367
Garrod, Dorothy and family 269, 380
Gatto family 50, 54–6, 65, 68, 72, 374,
    400–2
Gauci family (and Tower) 67, 391, 418
George Cross 330, 327, 413
Germany (and Germans) 22, 37–8, 42, 109,
    138, 163, 186–7, 205, 213, 250, 255,
    281, 292, 303–4, 306, 312–13, 316–17,
    319–21, 323–4, 333, 336, 362
Girl Guides 299, 302, 321
Goddess, Movement 10–11
Goddesses 10–17, 29
    Astarte 25, 28–9, 31, 373, 423; Ceres
    (Demeter) 32; Isis 28–9; Juno (Hera) 29,
    31; Mother Goddess 10–12, 14–15, 20,
    28; Persephone (Proserpina) 32; Sansuna
    (also giant) 10, 421; Tanit 28, 423
Gordon Cumming, Constance 372
Gozo (and Gozitan) xii, 9, 13–15, 19–20,
    23–4, 28–9, 31–4, 39–41, 43, 45–6,
    48–53, 55–7, 59, 61–2, 65, 68–76, 85,
    92, 108, 126, 133, 141–2, 153, 157,
    191, 193–6, 199, 222, 240, 250, 270,
    297, 346–7, 348, 353, 389, 418,
    420–29
Gozo/Malta differences xiii, 420, 429
Grand Harbour 143, 155, 242, 258, 261,
    273–4, 280, 283, 288, 304, 309, 314,

Also from HOLO Books: The Women's History Press

www.holobooks.co.uk

Of Islands and Women 1
Susanna Hoe   MADEIRA: WOMEN, HISTORY, BOOKS AND PLACES
paperback 180pp published 2004 1 map and 25 illustrations ISBN 9780953773084
Madeira – Travel – History (update www.holobooks.co.uk 2005)

In the 19th century, many people visited Madeira in the hopes that the dry, warm winter might help them recover from illness – usually consumption (tuberculosis). Today, travellers still go for the winter sun and for the magnificent walking, tropical and temperate gardens 100 or more years old, glorious wild flowers and trees and unparalleled mountain views. The history of Madeira's women and the writing of women travellers about the island are less well known than they should be. This livret combines a flavour of all these elements for the visitor or the armchair traveller.

Of Islands and Women 2
Susanna Hoe   CRETE: WOMEN, HISTORY, BOOKS AND PLACES
paperback 408pp published 2005 2 maps and 31 illustrations
Crete – Travel – Archaeology – Legend – History ISBN 9780953773077
(updates www.holobooks.co.uk 2007)

Once upon a time, Europa emerged from the waves at Matala on the back of a bull – the god Zeus in disguise. There, too, the author broke her ankle as she followed Europa to nearby Gortyn – whose famous law code has much to say about women. Europa was the mother of Minos, of the Minoans, (and of the concept of 'Europe'). Millennia later, Harriet Boyd was the first woman archaeologist to discover and direct her own dig, at Gournia – a perfect Minoan town. This livret links legend and archaeology by writing and place, but does not neglect the island's other women. Over the centuries they were subject to numerous violent changes of overlord – Mycenean, Roman, Byzantine (twice), Saracen, Venetian, Ottoman – but somehow have emerged as Cretans.

Of Islands and Women 3
Susanna Hoe   TASMANIA
Paperback 436pp published 2010 ISBN 9780954405663

In 1792 Louise Girardin – disguised as a French sailor – was the first white woman to visit Van Diemen's Land (Tasmania). She was followed by Martha Hayes who stepped ashore in 1803 among the first British settlers and convicts; she was the pregnant 16-year-old mistress of their leader. But Aboriginal women had already lived on the island for perhaps 40,000 years. The first to be named in exploration literature is Ouray-Ouray; the best known is Trukanini, erroneously called the last Tasmanian when she died in 1876. In the 1970s, Aboriginal rights became a live issue, often with women in the forefront, as they were, too, in environmentalism. This book gathers together these strands, and that of a vibrant women's literature, linking them to place – an island of still unspoilt beauty and unique flora and fauna.

Susanna Hoe   AT HOME IN PARADISE: A HOUSE AND GARDEN IN PAPUA NEW GUINEA
paperback 208pp published 2003 1 map 215 × 240mm ISBN 9780953773091 – Papua
New Guinea – Travel – Autobiography/Biography

*How would Margaret have written her story if she had been able to? I tried to help her
to learn to read and write but I could never see into her mind – there was too much that
divided us, in spite of all that drew us together. But sometimes, and once in particular, I
felt that she knew I was recording everything she told me.*

This is how the author introduces us to the family's cleaner in her diary of a stay in
Papua New Guinea – home of the bird of paradise. Through the gradual accumulation
of detail, the reader gets to know Margaret, her extended family, her unreliable husbands
and her independent spirit. Then there is Kaman, the outrageous gardener, who has to be
prised away from his creation so that his employers can enjoy planting and tending, as
well as admiring and eating its produce. There is endless scope for misunderstanding and
enlightenment as the tropical seasons come and go and relationships develop.

**Susanna Hoe   TRAVELS IN TANDEM: The Writing of Women and Men Who Travelled
Together**
Paperback 320pp published 2012 10 maps 34 illustrations ISBN 9780954405694

'The book grew out of a habit, early adopted when on her travels ... of writing ... an
unpretending narrative of the previous day's proceedings to be sent home to her father.'
Thus wrote Thomas Brassey of his wife Annie. As for his own account of their travels,
Susanna Hoe describes it as 'full of reports of experts ... and often about exports.'
And she explores the question, are women travel companions' accounts more generally
'unpretending narratives', and men's the opposite? The theme expanded when the author
was asked, 'Do women write with more immediacy, with more colour, more empathy and
more attention to detail?'
    Using extensive quotations, the author pursues those and other questions through
the relations and accounts of couples visiting or living in foreign places, from Liberia to
Siberia, from Vanuatu to Chinese Turkestan, between 1664 and 1973.

CHINA

**Susanna Hoe   WATCHING THE FLAG COME DOWN: An Englishwoman in Hong Kong
1987–1997**
Paperback 224pp published 2007 1 map ISBN 9780954405670
Hong Kong – China – Autobiography – Biography – Travel – Politics – History –
Women's Studies (updates www.holobooks.co.uk 2007)

At midnight on 30 June 1997 Hong Kong reverted to Chinese sovereignty after 150 years
of British rule. The moment when the British flag came down was dramatic enough but
the 10 years leading up to it were full of surprising incident and change. These 'Letters
from Hong Kong', written by an Englishwoman who was involved in those events from
1987, are both an unusual historical record and a heartwarming account of women's
domestic, intellectual and political activity. An epilogue brings Hong Kong up to date ten
years after the Handover.

Susanna Hoe   WOMEN AT THE SIEGE, PEKING 1900
Paperback 430pp published 2000 4 maps 44 illustrations ISBN 9780953773060
China – History – Women's Studies

The Boxer uprising; the siege of the legations; 55 days in Peking; foreign troops looting
China's capital; these are images from books and films over the past 100 years. Now the
story is told from the women's point of view, using their previously neglected writings and
giving a new dimension.

HOLO Books is agent in the United Kingdom for:

Susanna Hoe   CHINESE FOOTPRINTS: EXPLORING WOMEN'S HISTORY IN CHINA, HONG KONG AND MACAU
Roundhouse Publications (Asia) 1996 paperback 351pp 41 illustrations
ISBN 9789627992035
China – Hong Kong – Macau – History – Historiography – Women's Studies – Travel

This book is as much about the author's task of historical re-creation as it is about the lives, loves and struggles of women such as the 1930s civil rights campaigners Shi Liang, Agnes Smedley and Stella Benson; autobiographical writer Xiao Hong; Olympic sportswoman, traveller and writer Ella Maillart; icon of revolutionary China Soong Ching Ling; philanthropist Clara Ho Tung; and Clara Elliot, who lived in Macau at the time of Hong Kong's cession to Britain.

Nan Hodges & Arthur W. Hummel (eds)   LIGHTS AND SHADOWS OF A MACAO LIFE: THE JOURNAL OF HARRIETT LOW, TRAVELLING SPINSTER
Bear Creek Books (USA) published 2002 2 vols paperback 833pp 10 illustrations
(set) ISBN 9780938106296
China – History – Historiography – Women's studies

Lights and Shadows of a Macao Life, the title chosen by Harriett Low for her journal, aptly describes the conflicting emotions of the first American woman to live in China. Making a rude transition from the tranquillity of Salem, Massachusetts into a world of sampans and sedan chairs, women with bound feet and men with queues, the lively young American records a detailed portrait of her life in Macao from 1829–1834. In these diaries, published for the first time as a complete edition, Harriett Low displays wit and courage as she metamorphoses from a socially naive girl into a mature, independent woman. This is an important addition to the historiography of the China Coast.